CFA Institute®
CFA Program

AF886042

ALTERNATIVE INVESTMENTS AND PORTFOLIO MANAGEMENT

CFA® Program Curriculum

2020 • LEVEL I • VOLUME 6

WILEY

ISBN 978-1-946442-81-9 (paper)
ISBN 978-1-950157-05-1 (ebk)

SKY58AA04F9-020C-43A5-9B94-4F96E47A1C8A_091620

Please visit our website at
www.WileyGlobalFinance.com.

WILEY

FSC
www.fsc.org
MIX
Paper from responsible sources
FSC® C084269

CONTENTS

How to Use the CFA Program Curriculum

Congratulations on your decision to enter the Chartered Financial Analyst (CFA®) Program. This exciting and rewarding program of study reflects your desire to become a serious investment professional. You are embarking on a program noted for its high ethical standards and the breadth of knowledge, skills, and abilities (competencies) it develops. Your commitment to the CFA Program should be educationally and professionally rewarding.

The credential you seek is respected around the world as a mark of accomplishment and dedication. Each level of the program represents a distinct achievement in professional development. Successful completion of the program is rewarded with membership in a prestigious global community of investment professionals. CFA charterholders are dedicated to life-long learning and maintaining currency with the ever-changing dynamics of a challenging profession. The CFA Program represents the first step toward a career-long commitment to professional education.

The CFA examination measures your mastery of the core knowledge, skills, and abilities required to succeed as an investment professional. These core competencies are the basis for the Candidate Body of Knowledge (CBOK™). The CBOK consists of four components:

- A broad outline that lists the major topic areas covered in the CFA Program (https://www.cfainstitute.org/programs/cfa/curriculum/cbok);
- Topic area weights that indicate the relative exam weightings of the top-level topic areas (https://www.cfainstitute.org/programs/cfa/curriculum/overview);
- Learning outcome statements (LOS) that advise candidates about the specific knowledge, skills, and abilities they should acquire from readings covering a topic area (LOS are provided in candidate study sessions and at the beginning of each reading); and
- The CFA Program curriculum that candidates receive upon examination registration.

Therefore, the key to your success on the CFA examinations is studying and understanding the CBOK. The following sections provide background on the CBOK, the organization of the curriculum, features of the curriculum, and tips for designing an effective personal study program.

BACKGROUND ON THE CBOK

The CFA Program is grounded in the practice of the investment profession. Beginning with the Global Body of Investment Knowledge (GBIK), CFA Institute performs a continuous practice analysis with investment professionals around the world to determine the competencies that are relevant to the profession. Regional expert panels and targeted surveys are conducted annually to verify and reinforce the continuous feedback about the GBIK. The practice analysis process ultimately defines the CBOK. The

CBOK reflects the competencies that are generally accepted and applied by investment professionals. These competencies are used in practice in a generalist context and are expected to be demonstrated by a recently qualified CFA charterholder.

The CFA Institute staff, in conjunction with the Education Advisory Committee and Curriculum Level Advisors, who consist of practicing CFA charterholders, designs the CFA Program curriculum in order to deliver the CBOK to candidates. The examinations, also written by CFA charterholders, are designed to allow you to demonstrate your mastery of the CBOK as set forth in the CFA Program curriculum. As you structure your personal study program, you should emphasize mastery of the CBOK and the practical application of that knowledge. For more information on the practice analysis, CBOK, and development of the CFA Program curriculum, please visit www.cfainstitute.org.

ORGANIZATION OF THE CURRICULUM

The Level I CFA Program curriculum is organized into 10 topic areas. Each topic area begins with a brief statement of the material and the depth of knowledge expected. It is then divided into one or more study sessions. These study sessions—19 sessions in the Level I curriculum—should form the basic structure of your reading and preparation. Each study session includes a statement of its structure and objective and is further divided into assigned readings. An outline illustrating the organization of these 19 study sessions can be found at the front of each volume of the curriculum.

The readings are commissioned by CFA Institute and written by content experts, including investment professionals and university professors. Each reading includes LOS and the core material to be studied, often a combination of text, exhibits, and in-text examples and questions. A reading typically ends with practice problems followed by solutions to these problems to help you understand and master the material. The LOS indicate what you should be able to accomplish after studying the material. The LOS, the core material, and the practice problems are dependent on each other, with the core material and the practice problems providing context for understanding the scope of the LOS and enabling you to apply a principle or concept in a variety of scenarios.

The entire readings, including the practice problems at the end of the readings, are the basis for all examination questions and are selected or developed specifically to teach the knowledge, skills, and abilities reflected in the CBOK.

You should use the LOS to guide and focus your study because each examination question is based on one or more LOS and the core material and practice problems associated with the LOS. As a candidate, you are responsible for the entirety of the required material in a study session.

We encourage you to review the information about the LOS on our website (www.cfainstitute.org/programs/cfa/curriculum/study-sessions), including the descriptions of LOS "command words" on the candidate resources page at www.cfainstitute.org.

FEATURES OF THE CURRICULUM

OPTIONAL SEGMENT

Required vs. Optional Segments You should read all of an assigned reading. In some cases, though, we have reprinted an entire publication and marked certain parts of the reading as "optional." The CFA examination is based only on the required segments, and the optional segments are included only when it is determined that they might help you to better understand the required segments (by seeing the required material in its full context). When an optional segment begins, you will see an icon and a dashed vertical bar in the outside margin that will continue until the optional segment ends, accompanied by another icon. *Unless the material is specifically marked as optional, you should assume it is required.* You should rely on the required segments and the reading-specific LOS in preparing for the examination.

END OPTIONAL SEGMENT

Practice Problems/Solutions *All practice problems at the end of the readings as well as their solutions are part of the curriculum and are required material for the examination.* In addition to the in-text examples and questions, these practice problems should help demonstrate practical applications and reinforce your understanding of the concepts presented. Some of these practice problems are adapted from past CFA examinations and/or may serve as a basis for examination questions.

Glossary For your convenience, each volume includes a comprehensive glossary. Throughout the curriculum, a **bolded** word in a reading denotes a term defined in the glossary.

Note that the digital curriculum that is included in your examination registration fee is searchable for key words, including glossary terms.

LOS Self-Check We have inserted checkboxes next to each LOS that you can use to track your progress in mastering the concepts in each reading.

Source Material The CFA Institute curriculum cites textbooks, journal articles, and other publications that provide additional context or information about topics covered in the readings. As a candidate, you are not responsible for familiarity with the original source materials cited in the curriculum.

Note that some readings may contain a web address or URL. The referenced sites were live at the time the reading was written or updated but may have been deactivated since then.

Some readings in the curriculum cite articles published in the *Financial Analysts Journal*®, which is the flagship publication of CFA Institute. Since its launch in 1945, the *Financial Analysts Journal* has established itself as the leading practitioner-oriented journal in the investment management community. Over the years, it has advanced the knowledge and understanding of the practice of investment management through the publication of peer-reviewed practitioner-relevant research from leading academics and practitioners. It has also featured thought-provoking opinion pieces that advance the common level of discourse within the investment management profession. Some of the most influential research in the area of investment management has appeared in the pages of the *Financial Analysts Journal*, and several Nobel laureates have contributed articles.

Candidates are not responsible for familiarity with *Financial Analysts Journal* articles that are cited in the curriculum. But, as your time and studies allow, we strongly encourage you to begin supplementing your understanding of key investment management issues by reading this practice-oriented publication. Candidates have full online access to the *Financial Analysts Journal* and associated resources. All you need is to log in on www.cfapubs.org using your candidate credentials.

Errata The curriculum development process is rigorous and includes multiple rounds of reviews by content experts. Despite our efforts to produce a curriculum that is free of errors, there are times when we must make corrections. Curriculum errata are periodically updated and posted on the candidate resources page at www.cfainstitute.org.

DESIGNING YOUR PERSONAL STUDY PROGRAM

Create a Schedule An orderly, systematic approach to examination preparation is critical. You should dedicate a consistent block of time every week to reading and studying. Complete all assigned readings and the associated problems and solutions in each study session. Review the LOS both before and after you study each reading to ensure that you have mastered the applicable content and can demonstrate the knowledge, skills, and abilities described by the LOS and the assigned reading. Use the LOS self-check to track your progress and highlight areas of weakness for later review.

Successful candidates report an average of more than 300 hours preparing for each examination. Your preparation time will vary based on your prior education and experience, and you will probably spend more time on some study sessions than on others. As the Level I curriculum includes 19 study sessions, a good plan is to devote 15–20 hours per week for 19 weeks to studying the material and use the final four to six weeks before the examination to review what you have learned and practice with practice questions and mock examinations. This recommendation, however, may underestimate the hours needed for appropriate examination preparation depending on your individual circumstances, relevant experience, and academic background. You will undoubtedly adjust your study time to conform to your own strengths and weaknesses and to your educational and professional background.

You should allow ample time for both in-depth study of all topic areas and additional concentration on those topic areas for which you feel the least prepared.

As part of the supplemental study tools that are included in your examination registration fee, you have access to a study planner to help you plan your study time. The study planner calculates your study progress and pace based on the time remaining until examination. For more information on the study planner and other supplemental study tools, please visit www.cfainstitute.org.

As you prepare for your examination, we will e-mail you important examination updates, testing policies, and study tips. Be sure to read these carefully.

CFA Institute Practice Questions Your examination registration fee includes digital access to hundreds of practice questions that are additional to the practice problems at the end of the readings. These practice questions are intended to help you assess your mastery of individual topic areas as you progress through your studies. After each practice question, you will be able to receive immediate feedback noting the correct responses and indicating the relevant assigned reading so you can identify areas of weakness for further study. For more information on the practice questions, please visit www.cfainstitute.org.

CFA Institute Mock Examinations Your examination registration fee also includes digital access to three-hour mock examinations that simulate the morning and afternoon sessions of the actual CFA examination. These mock examinations are intended to be taken after you complete your study of the full curriculum and take practice questions so you can test your understanding of the curriculum and your readiness for the examination. You will receive feedback at the end of the mock examination, noting the correct responses and indicating the relevant assigned readings so you can assess areas of weakness for further study during your review period. We recommend that you take mock examinations during the final stages of your preparation for the actual CFA examination. For more information on the mock examinations, please visit www.cfainstitute.org.

Preparatory Providers After you enroll in the CFA Program, you may receive numerous solicitations for preparatory courses and review materials. When considering a preparatory course, make sure the provider belongs to the CFA Institute Approved Prep Provider Program. Approved Prep Providers have committed to follow CFA Institute guidelines and high standards in their offerings and communications with candidates. For more information on the Approved Prep Providers, please visit www.cfainstitute.org/programs/cfa/exam/prep-providers.

Remember, however, that there are no shortcuts to success on the CFA examinations; reading and studying the CFA curriculum *is* the key to success on the examination. The CFA examinations reference only the CFA Institute assigned curriculum—no preparatory course or review course materials are consulted or referenced.

SUMMARY

Every question on the CFA examination is based on the content contained in the required readings and on one or more LOS. Frequently, an examination question is based on a specific example highlighted within a reading or on a specific practice problem and its solution. To make effective use of the CFA Program curriculum, please remember these key points:

1. All pages of the curriculum are required reading for the examination except for occasional sections marked as optional. You may read optional pages as background, but you will not be tested on them.
2. All questions, problems, and their solutions—found at the end of readings—are part of the curriculum and are required study material for the examination.
3. You should make appropriate use of the practice questions and mock examinations as well as other supplemental study tools and candidate resources available at www.cfainstitute.org.
4. Create a schedule and commit sufficient study time to cover the 19 study sessions, using the study planner. You should also plan to review the materials and take practice questions and mock examinations.
5. Some of the concepts in the study sessions may be superseded by updated rulings and/or pronouncements issued after a reading was published. Candidates are expected to be familiar with the overall analytical framework contained in the assigned readings. Candidates are not responsible for changes that occur after the material was written.

FEEDBACK

At CFA Institute, we are committed to delivering a comprehensive and rigorous curriculum for the development of competent, ethically grounded investment professionals. We rely on candidate and investment professional comments and feedback as we work to improve the curriculum, supplemental study tools, and candidate resources.

Please send any comments or feedback to info@cfainstitute.org. You can be assured that we will review your suggestions carefully. Ongoing improvements in the curriculum will help you prepare for success on the upcoming examinations and for a lifetime of learning as a serious investment professional.

Alternative Investments

STUDY SESSION

Study Session 17 Alternative Investments

TOPIC LEVEL LEARNING OUTCOME

The candidate should be able to demonstrate a working knowledge of alternative investments, including hedge funds, private equity, real estate, commodities, and infrastructure. The candidate should be able to describe key attributes and considerations in adding these investments to a portfolio.

Investors often turn to alternative investments for potential diversification benefits and higher returns. As a result, alternative investments now represent meaningful allocations in many institutional and private wealth portfolios. Although the category of "alternative investments" is not always clearly or precisely defined, alternative investments often have a number of characteristics in common. These include lower levels of liquidity, transparency, and disclosure vs. traditional asset classes (equity, fixed income), more complex legal structures, and performance-based compensation arrangements.

ALTERNATIVE INVESTMENTS

STUDY SESSION 17

Alternative Investments

This study session provides an overview of the more widely used alternative investments, including hedge funds, private equity, real estate, commodities, and infrastructure investment. Each is examined with emphasis on their distinguishing characteristics, considerations for valuation, and potential benefits and risks. Similarities and differences with traditional investments (stocks, bonds) are also considered.

READING ASSIGNMENTS

Reading 50	Introduction to Alternative Investments by Terri Duhon, George Spentzos, CFA, FSIP, and Scott D. Stewart, PhD, CFA

READING

50

Introduction to Alternative Investments

by Terri Duhon, George Spentzos, CFA, FSIP, and Scott D. Stewart, PhD, CFA

Terri Duhon is at Said Business School, Oxford University, Morgan Stanley, and Rathbone Brothers (United Kingdom). George Spentzos, CFA, FSIP (United Kingdom). Scott D. Stewart, PhD, CFA, is at Cornell University (USA).

LEARNING OUTCOMES

Mastery	*The candidate should be able to:*
☐	a. compare alternative investments with traditional investments;
☐	b. describe hedge funds, private equity, real estate, commodities, infrastructure, and other alternative investments, including, as applicable, strategies, sub-categories, potential benefits and risks, fee structures, and due diligence;
☐	c. describe potential benefits of alternative investments in the context of portfolio management;
☐	d. describe, calculate, and interpret management and incentive fees and net-of-fees returns to hedge funds;
☐	e. describe issues in valuing and calculating returns on hedge funds, private equity, real estate, commodities, and infrastructure;
☐	f. describe risk management of alternative investments.

INTRODUCTION

1

Assets under management in vehicles classified as alternative investments have grown rapidly since the mid-1990s. This growth has largely occurred because of interest in these investments by institutions, such as endowment and pension funds, as well as by high-net-worth individuals seeking diversification and return opportunities. Alternative investments are perceived to behave differently from traditional investments. Investors may seek either absolute return or relative return.

CFA Institute acknowledges the research assistance of John W. Stewart, CFA, on the data analysis in this reading.

Some investors hope alternative investments will provide positive returns throughout the economic cycle; this goal is an absolute return objective. Alternative investments are not free of risk, however, and their returns may be negative and/or correlated with other investments, including traditional investments, especially in periods of financial crisis. Some investors in alternative investments have a relative return objective. A relative return objective, which is often the objective of traditional investment portfolios, seeks to achieve a return relative to an equity or fixed-income benchmark.

This reading is organized as follows. Section 2 describes alternative investments' basic characteristics and categories, general strategies of alternative investment portfolio managers, the role of alternative investments in a diversified portfolio, and investment structures used to provide access to alternative investments. Sections 3 through 7 describe features of hedge funds, private equity, real estate, commodities, and infrastructure, respectively, along with issues in calculating returns to and valuation of each.[1] Section 8 briefly describes other alternative investments. Section 9 provides an overview of risk management, including due diligence, of alternative investments. A summary and practice problems conclude the reading.

2 ALTERNATIVE INVESTMENTS

"Alternative investments" is a label for a disparate group of investments that are distinguished from long-only, publicly traded investments in stocks, bonds, and cash (often referred to as traditional investments). The terms "traditional" and "alternatives" should not be construed to imply that alternatives are necessarily uncommon or relatively recent additions to the investment universe. Alternative investments include investments in such assets as real estate and commodities, which are arguably two of the oldest investment classes.

Alternative investments also include non-traditional approaches to investing within special vehicles, such as private equity funds, hedge funds, and some exchange-traded funds (ETFs). These funds may give the manager flexibility to use derivatives and leverage, make investments in illiquid assets, and take short positions. The assets in which these vehicles invest can include traditional assets (stocks, bonds, and cash) as well as other assets. Management of alternative investments is typically active. Passive versions of commodity and real estate investments are also available, but hedge funds, private equity, and infrastructure investments are almost always actively managed. Alternative investments often have many of the following characteristics:

- Narrow manager specialization
- Relatively low correlation of returns with those of traditional investments
- Less regulation and less transparency than traditional investments
- Limited and potentially problematic historical risk and return data
- Unique legal and tax considerations
- High fees
- Concentrated portfolios
- Restrictions on redemptions (i.e., "lockups" and "gates")

1 CFA Institute acknowledges the contributions of Michael Underhill of Capital Innovations, LLC, to the section on infrastructure.

Although assets under management (AUM) in alternative investments have grown rapidly, they remain smaller than either fixed-income or equity investable assets, as illustrated in Exhibit 1.

Exhibit 1 Global Assets under Management, December 2014

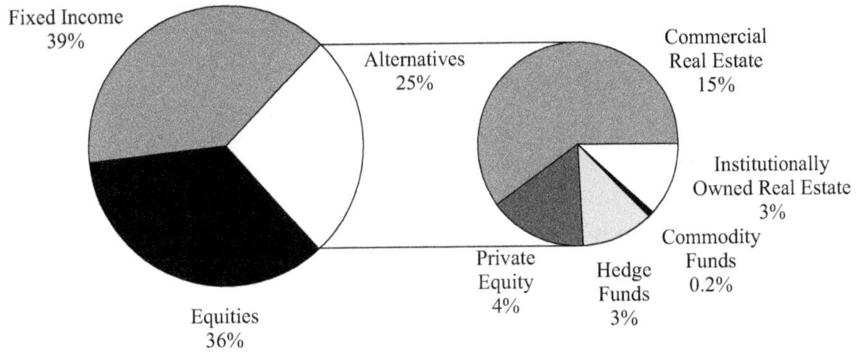

Sources: Based on data from Boston Consulting Group and DTZ Research.

Alternative investments are not free of risk, and their returns may be correlated with those of other investments, especially in periods of financial crisis. During a long historical period, the average correlation of returns from alternative investments with those of traditional investments may be low, but in any particular period, the correlation can differ from the average. During periods of economic crisis, such as late 2008, correlations among many assets (both alternative and traditional) can increase dramatically.

Investors must be careful in evaluating the historical record of alternative investments because reported return data can be problematic. Further, reported returns and standard deviations are averages and may not be representative of sub-periods within the reported period or future periods. Many investments, such as direct real estate and private equity, are often valued using estimated (appraised) values rather than actual market prices for the subject investments. As a result, the volatility of their returns, as well as the correlation of their returns with the returns of traditional asset classes, will tend to be underestimated. Private equity market returns may be estimated using the technique proposed by Woodward and Hall (2004) to address data problems with historical published indexes, which reflect underlying investments held at cost.[2] The record of alternative investment universes, such as hedge fund indexes, may be subject to a variety of biases, including survivorship and backfill biases. "Survivorship bias" relates to the inclusion of only current investment funds in a database. As such, the returns of funds that are no longer available in the marketplace (have been liquidated) are excluded from the database. "Backfill bias" occurs when a new fund enters a database and historical returns of that fund are added (i.e., "backfilled"). These biases can lead to returns that are artificially high—causing the index returns to be biased upward. This phenomenon occurs because "survivorship bias" typically results in poorly performing funds being excluded from the database and backfill bias typically results in high-performing funds being added to the database. In addition, different

2 This technique involves statistical estimation of quarterly market returns using published fund index and security market index returns.

weightings and constituents in index construction can significantly affect the indexes and their results and comparability. For example, commodity indexes can be weighted heavily in one particular sector, such as oil and gas.

Exhibit 2 shows the historical returns to various investment classes, as well as the standard deviations of the returns, based on selected indexes. The indexes were selected for their breadth and data quality but may not be fully representative of returns to the investment class, and there may be issues with the data. For example, the return to the S&P Global REIT Index may not be representative of returns to equity investment in real estate through private markets (direct ownership of real estate). Private equity and venture capital monthly market-based returns are unavailable, so the returns in Exhibit 2 are modeled using the technique proposed by Woodward and Hall (2004). Hedge fund returns are based on managed fund valuations, not underlying securities prices. The average annual returns and standard deviations are shown for three periods: the 25-year period of Q1 1990–Q4 2014, the period Q4 2007–Q4 2009, and the recent 5-year period of Q1 2010–Q4 2014.

Exhibit 2 Alternative Investment Historical Returns and Volatilities

	Q1 1990–Q4 2014		Q4 2007–Q4 2009		Q1 2010–Q4 2014	
Index	**Mean**	**St. Dev.**	**Mean**	**St. Dev.**	**Mean**	**St. Dev.**
Global stocks	6.9%	16.5%	−10.8%	24.2%	10.7%	15.9%
Global bonds	6.3	5.8	6.7	9.0	2.6	4.8
Hedge funds	7.2	6.0	−4.9	8.0	3.4	4.1
Commodities	2.2	21.8	−15.9	32.1	−5.0	18.1
Real estate	10.4	18.1	−17.6	33.8	15.4	17.7
Private equity	15.4	20.3	−10.0	27.8	20.7	19.4
Venture capital	15.0	47.2	−9.5	29.9	33.6	35.3
One-month Libor	3.42	0.70	1.9	0.5	0.2	0.0

Note: Mean and standard deviation are based on annualized US dollar returns.
Sources: Global stocks = MSCI All Country World Index (ACWI); global bonds = Bloomberg Barclays Global Aggregate Index; hedge funds = Hedge Fund Research, Inc. (HFRI) Fund of Funds Composite Index; commodities = S&P GSCI Commodity Index; real estate = S&P Global REIT Index; private equity is modeled using Cambridge Associates and S&P MidCap indexes; and venture capital is modeled using Cambridge Associates and NASDAQ indexes.

During the 25-year period, the mean returns to hedge funds, real estate, private equity, and venture capital exceeded the mean returns to global stocks and bonds. The average standard deviation of all but hedge funds also exceeded the average standard deviation of global stocks and bonds. Hedge funds appear to have had a higher average return and a lower standard deviation than global stocks for the 25-year period, but this result may be caused, at least partially, by hedge fund indexes' reporting biases. Commodities had the lowest mean return for the 25-year period and a higher standard deviation than all but venture capital. The higher mean returns of alternative investments, except for commodities,[3] compared with stocks and bonds may be the result of active managers' exploitation of less efficiently priced assets, illiquidity premiums, and/or account leverage. The higher mean returns may also be the result of tax advantages. For example, real estate investment trusts (REITs) may not be subject to taxes at the fund level if they meet certain conditions.

3 It is important to note that the risk/return profile of "commodities" is heavily influenced by the choice of index. The commonly used S&P GSCI Commodity Index had a high exposure to energy (78.6% in May 2008).

In a poorly performing economy, the use of leverage and investment in illiquid assets may be reasonably expected to lead to poor results. Leveraged investments are more sensitive to market conditions than similar unleveraged investments, and illiquid assets may be difficult to sell and are exposed to high transaction costs during market downturns. From Q4 2007 through Q4 2009, a period categorized as a time of financial crisis, the mean returns to alternative investments other than hedge funds were similar to or even lower than those to global stocks, and the standard deviations exceeded those of global stocks. Alternative investments did not provide the desired protection during the Q4 2007–Q4 2009 period. It is the long-term return potential, however, that attracts many investors, and real estate, private equity, and venture capital performed very well from Q1 2010 through Q4 2014, the five-year period following the financial crisis. During this period, real estate, private equity, and venture capital had average annual returns exceeding the average annual return of global stocks. Also during this period, hedge fund and commodity average annual returns were less than the average annual return of global stocks.

The 2015 annual report for the Yale University Endowment provides one investor's reasoning behind the attractiveness of investing in alternatives:

> The heavy [73%] allocation to nontraditional asset classes stems from their return potential and diversifying power. Today's actual and target portfolios have significantly higher expected returns than the 1985 portfolio with similar volatility. Alternative assets, by their very nature, tend to be less efficiently priced than traditional marketable securities, providing an opportunity to exploit market inefficiencies through active management. The Endowment's long time horizon is well suited to exploit illiquid, less efficient markets such as venture capital, leveraged buyouts, oil and gas, timber, and real estate.[4]

The links between this quote and the expected characteristics of alternative investments are clear: diversifying power (low correlations among returns), higher expected returns (positive absolute return), and illiquid and potentially less efficient markets. These links also highlight the importance of having the ability and willingness to take a long-term perspective. Allocating a portion of an endowment portfolio to alternative investments is not unique to Yale. As of August 2015, INSEAD had allocated 38% of its endowment to alternative investments, including real estate, hedge funds, and private equity and debt. The remaining 62% was invested in traditional financial assets, such as global stocks and bonds.[5] These examples are not meant to imply that every university endowment fund invests in alternative investments, but many do.

High-net-worth investors have also embraced alternative investments. According to the Spectrem Group's 2014 study of American investors, 42% of investors with more than $25 million in assets have invested in hedge funds and 69% of investors with more than $125 million have invested in hedge funds. The study's authors noted that wealthy investors were choosing alternatives for higher returns and improved diversification.[6] The increasing interest in alternative investments by both institutional investors and high-net-worth individuals has resulted in significant growth in each

---

4 https://static1.squarespace.com/static/55db7b87e4b0dca22fba2438/t/58e69e2fd2b857ee1524caa1/1491508800738/Yale_Endowment_15.pdf (p. 7).

5 https://www.insead.edu/sites/default/files/assets/dept/give/docs/INSEAD-Endowment-Report-2014-2015.pdf.

6 http://spectrem.com/Content_Press/december-3-2014-press-release.

category of alternative investments since the beginning of 2000. The following examples illustrate growth in the categories of private equity, real estate, and commodities in the period up to 2016.

- Global private capital fundraising was approximately $551 billion in 2015, compared with $238 billion in 2000.[7]
- Global REITs grew to $1.7 trillion in market value by 2016. In 1990, the market capitalization of global REITs was less than $734 billion.[8]
- The number of institutional investors actively investing with commodity trading advisers (CTAs) grew to 1,067 investors in 2015, up from just 331 in 2008.[9]

The enthusiasm for alternative investments was tested during 2008, when assets under management in alternative investments declined as losses were incurred and investors withdrew funds. However, alternative investments continue to represent a significant proportion of the portfolios of pension funds, endowments, foundations, and high-net-worth individuals. By 2012, a resurgence of interest in alternative investments occurred.

EXAMPLE 1

Characteristics of Alternative Investments

Compared with traditional investments, alternative investments are *most likely* to be characterized by high:

A leverage.

B liquidity.

C regulation.

Solution:

A is correct. Alternative investments are likely to use more leverage than traditional investments. Alternative investments are likely to be more illiquid and subject to less regulation compared with traditional investments.

2.1 Categories of Alternative Investments

Considering the variety of characteristics common to many alternative investments, it is not surprising that no consensus exists on a definitive list of these investments. There is even considerable debate as to what represents a category versus a sub-category of alternative investments. For instance, some listings define distressed securities as a separate category, whereas others consider distressed securities a sub-category of the hedge funds and/or private equity categories, or even a subset of high-yield bond investing. Similarly, managed futures are sometimes defined as a separate category and

7 "2016 Preqin Global Private Equity & Venture Capital Report."

8 www.cohenandsteers.com/insights/education/about-reits and Ernst & Young, "Global Perspectives: 2016 REIT Report" (www.ey.com/Publication/vwLUAssets/global-perspectives-2016-reit-report-ey/$File/ey-global-perspectives-2016-reit-report.pdf).

9 http://docs.preqin.com/reports/Preqin-Special-Report-CTAs-June-2016.pdf.

sometimes as a sub-category of hedge funds. The following list offers one approach to defining broad categories of alternative investments. Each category is described in detail later in this reading.

- **Hedge funds.** Hedge funds are private investment vehicles that manage portfolios of securities and derivative positions using a variety of strategies. They may use long and short positions and may be highly leveraged, and some aim to deliver investment performance that is independent of broad market performance.
- **Private equity.** Investors can invest in private equity either via direct investment (including co-investment) or indirectly via private equity funds. Private equity funds generally invest in companies (either startup or established) that are not listed on a public exchange, or they invest in public companies with the intent to take them private. The majority of private equity activity involves leveraged buyouts of established profitable and cash-generative companies with solid customer bases, proven products, and high-quality management. **Venture capital**, a specialized form of private equity, typically involves investing in or providing financing to startup or early-stage companies with high growth potential and represents a small portion of the private equity market.
- **Real estate.** Real estate investments may be in buildings and/or land, including timberland and farmland, either directly or indirectly. The growing popularity of securitizations broadened the definition of real estate investing. It now includes private commercial real estate equity (e.g., ownership of an office building), private commercial real estate debt (e.g., directly issued loans or mortgages on commercial property), public real estate equity (e.g., REITs), and public real estate debt investments (e.g., mortgage-backed securities).
- **Commodities.** Commodity investments may be in physical commodity products, such as grains, metals, and crude oil, either through owning cash instruments, using derivative products, or investing in businesses engaged in the production of physical commodities. The main vehicles investors use to gain exposure to commodities are commodity futures contracts and funds benchmarked to commodity indexes. Commodity indexes are typically based on various underlying commodity futures.
- **Infrastructure.** Infrastructure assets are capital-intensive, long-lived, real assets, such as roads, dams, and schools, that are intended for public use and provide essential services. Infrastructure assets may be financed, owned, and operated by governments, but increasingly the private sector is investing in infrastructure assets. An increasingly common approach to infrastructure investing is a public–private partnership (PPP) approach in which governments and investors each have a stake. Investors may gain exposure to these assets directly or indirectly. Indirect investment vehicles include shares of companies, ETFs, private equity funds, listed funds, and unlisted funds that invest in infrastructure.
- **Other.** Other alternative investments include tangible assets (such as fine wine, art, antique furniture and automobiles, stamps, coins, and other collectibles) and intangible assets (such as patents and litigation actions).

2.2 Returns to Alternative Investments

Portfolio managers invest in one of two basic ways to achieve returns: passively or actively. Passive investments focus on index or asset class coverage. Some portfolios of real estate, commodity, and infrastructure instruments may be passively managed to provide exposure to these alternative asset classes. However, alternative investments are generally actively managed.

Investors frequently look to alternative investments for diversification and a chance to earn relatively high returns on a risk-adjusted basis. However, there is a naive attraction to alternative investments based on their expected returns without consideration of their non-typical risks. Risks can be considered both on a standalone basis and within the context of a portfolio and may include low liquidity, limited redemption availability and transparency, and the challenge of manager diversification.

A commonly reported risk ratio is the Sharpe ratio, which equals an investment's return, net of a risk-free rate, divided by its return standard deviation. The Sharpe ratio has shortcomings, however. It equally penalizes upside and downside volatility, fails to capture non-symmetric distributions, and may not fully reflect tails in return distributions. The return distributions to alternative investments are typically non-symmetric and skewed, making the Sharpe ratio a less-than-ideal measure. Other risk measures, such as those that emphasize downside risk, are also frequently considered.[10] A popular downside measure is the Sortino ratio, which uses a numerator similar to that of the Sharpe ratio: mean realized return less target return. If the target return is specified as the risk-free rate of return, the Sortino ratio's numerator is the same as the Sharpe ratio's. The Sortino ratio replaces, in the denominator, the standard deviation of returns with a downside deviation that is the standard deviation of the returns that are below the target return.

Sharpe and Sortino ratios for traditional and alternative investments, based on the same information used in Exhibit 2, are shown in Panel A of Exhibit 3. In calculating the Sortino ratio, the target return was assumed to be 0%.

Other downside risk measures, such as the chance of losing a certain amount of money in a given period, are also used in practice. Panel B of Exhibit 3 includes some other measures indicative of downside risk: the frequencies of monthly returns less than –1%, –5%, and –10% from 1990 through 2014 and, in the right-hand column, the worst return reported in a month.

Exhibit 3

Sharpe Ratios, Sortino Ratios, and Downside Risk Measures, Based on 1990–2014 Returns

Panel A Sharpe and Sortino Ratios (using annualized returns)

Index	Sharpe Ratio	Sortino Ratio
Global stocks	0.21	0.43
Global bonds	0.49	1.09
Hedge funds	0.63	0.74
Commodities	–0.06	0.12

10 The Sharpe ratio is discussed in greater detail in the reading "Statistical Concepts and Market Returns." Several other risk measures are used in practice and are discussed throughout the CFA Program curriculum.

Exhibit 3 (Continued)

Index	Sharpe Ratio	Sortino Ratio
Real estate	0.38	0.79
Private equity	0.59	1.19
Venture capital	0.25	0.63

Panel B Downside Frequencies

	Frequency of Monthly Return Less Than . . .			Worst Monthly Return
Index	–1%	–5%	–10%	
Global stocks	32.0%	9.3%	1.7%	–19.8%
Global bonds	14.7	0.0	0.0	–3.8
Hedge funds	12.3	1.0	0.0	–7.5
Commodities	37.7	17.0	5.3	–28.2
Real estate	27.7	7.0	2.3	–30.5
Private equity	29.3	8.7	2.0	–22.3
Venture capital	36.0	23.7	13.7	–40.5

Sharpe ratios (using Libor as a proxy for the risk-free rate) indicate that on the basis of reported data, during the 25-year period from 1990 through 2014, hedge funds offered the best risk–return trade-off and commodities offered the worst. The Sortino ratio, however, using a target return of 0%, indicates that private equity and global bonds offered superior risk–return trade-offs during this period. Global fixed-income investments displayed the most attractive downside risk profile (see Panel B), in part as a result of the bond bull market during this 25-year period. Venture capital had the least attractive downside risk profile, but its higher reported return (see Exhibit 2) resulted in higher Sharpe and Sortino ratios than global stocks and commodities had during the period.

The Sharpe ratio and downside risk measures do not take into account the potentially low level of correlation of alternative investments with traditional investments. A less-than-perfect correlation between investments reduces the standard deviation of a diversified portfolio below the weighted average of the standard deviations of the investments.

2.3 Portfolio Context: Integration of Alternative Investments with Traditional Investments

A key motivation cited for investing in alternative investments is their diversifying potential: Investors perceive an opportunity to improve the risk–return relationship within the portfolio context. Given the historical return, volatility, and correlation profiles of alternative investments, combining a portfolio of alternative investments with a portfolio of traditional investments potentially improves the overall portfolio's risk–return profile. Adding alternative investments to a portfolio of traditional assets can increase the Sharpe ratio of the overall portfolio owing to potentially higher returns to the portfolio and/or less-than-perfect correlation with traditional investments. In identifying the appropriate allocation to alternative investments, however, an investment manager is likely to consider more than just mean return and average standard deviation of returns. When considering potential portfolio combinations, the manager's analysis may include historical downside frequencies, worst return in a month for potential portfolio combinations, liquidity considerations.

The purported diversification benefits and improved risk–return contributions of alternative investments to portfolios explain why institutional investors, such as pension funds, may allocate a portion of their portfolios to alternative investments. There are challenges, however, including obtaining reliable measures of risk and return, identifying the appropriate allocation, and selecting portfolio managers. It is important to note that expected diversification benefits from alternative investments are not always realized, including sometimes when they are most needed. Correlations between risky investments increase during periods of market stress and can approach 1.0 during financial crises, as seen in Exhibit 2.

2.4 Investment Structures

A partnership structure is a common structure for many alternative investments, such as hedge funds, infrastructure funds, and private equity funds. In this approach, the fund manager is the **general partner** (GP) and investors are **limited partners** (LPs). Limited partnerships are restricted to investors who are expected to understand and to be able to assume the risks associated with the investments. These types of fund investments, because they are not offered to the general public, are less regulated than offerings to the general public.[11] The GP runs the business and theoretically bears unlimited liability for anything that might go wrong.

Limited partners own a fractional interest in the partnership based on their investment amount and according to the terms in the partnership documentation. These partnerships are frequently located in tax-efficient locations, which benefit both the GP and the LPs. Funds set up as private investment partnerships typically have a limit on the number of LPs.[12]

Funds are generally structured with a **management fee** based on assets under management (sometimes called the "base fee") plus an **incentive fee** (or **performance fee**) based on realized profits. Sometimes, the fee structure specifies that the incentive fee is earned only after the fund achieves a specified return known as a hurdle rate. Fee calculations also take into account a **high-water mark**, which reflects the highest cumulative return used to calculate an incentive fee. In other words, it is the highest value, net of fees, of the fund investment by the individual LP. Note that not all LPs will have the same high-water mark, because it depends on the timing of their individual investment. The use of high-water marks protects clients from paying twice for the same performance.

---

11 In the United States, the Securities Act of 1933 regulates the process by which investment securities are offered. Most alternative investment funds are structured as "private placements," which are defined within Regulation D of the Securities Act and are sometimes called "Reg D Offerings."

12 Because of the inherent risk involved in alternative investments, investment is typically restricted to a specified number of investors meeting certain criteria. The number and criteria can be specified by regulation or set by the fund.

HEDGE FUNDS

3

In 1949, Alfred Winslow Jones, a sociologist investigating fundamental and technical research to forecast the stock market for *Fortune* magazine, set up an investment fund with himself as GP. The fund followed three key tenets: (1) Always maintain short positions, (2) always use leverage, and (3) charge only an incentive fee of 20% of profits with no fixed fees. Jones called his portfolio a "hedged" fund (eventually shortened to "hedge fund") because he had short positions to offset his long positions in the stock market. Theoretically, the overall portfolio was hedged against major market moves.

Although Jones's original three tenets still have some relevance to the hedge fund industry, not all hedge funds maintain short positions and/or use leverage, and most hedge funds have some non-incentive fees. A contemporary hedge fund may have the following characteristics:

- It is an aggressively managed portfolio of investments across asset classes and regions that is leveraged, takes long and short positions, and/or uses derivatives.
- It has a goal of generating high returns, either in an absolute sense or over a specified market benchmark, and it has few, if any, investment restrictions.
- It is set up as a private investment partnership open to a limited number of investors willing and able to make a large initial investment.
- It imposes restrictions on **redemptions**. Investors may be required to keep their money in the hedge fund for a minimum period (referred to as a **lockup period**) before they are allowed to make withdrawals or redeem shares. Investors may be required to give notice of their intent to redeem; the **notice period** is typically 30–90 days in length. Also, investors may be charged a fee to redeem shares.

Funds of hedge funds are funds that hold a portfolio of hedge funds. They create a diversified portfolio of hedge funds accessible to smaller investors or to those who do not have the resources, time, or expertise to choose among hedge fund managers. Also, funds of hedge funds, commonly shortened to "funds of funds," are assumed to have some expertise in conducting due diligence on hedge funds and may be able to negotiate better redemption terms than individual investors can. Funds of funds invest in numerous hedge funds and may diversify across fund strategies, investment regions, and management styles. The distinction between a single hedge fund and a fund of funds is not necessarily clear-cut because hedge funds can invest in other hedge funds. Each hedge fund into which a fund of funds invests is structured to receive a management fee plus an incentive fee. The fund of funds itself is also structured to receive a management fee and may also receive an incentive fee.

Hedge fund managers are less restricted than traditional investment managers and thus may have the flexibility to invest anywhere they see opportunity. Most hedge funds have broadly stated strategies to allow flexibility. Hedge funds are often given additional latitude to invest a percentage of the AUM, generally less than 20%, without any real limitations. A hedge fund can also be structured as part of one "asset management" business that is "contracted" to manage several different funds in addition to managing money directly (e.g., SuperStar Asset Management might manage SuperStar Credit Fund, SuperStar Commodities Fund, and SuperStar Multi-Strategy Fund).

The growing popularity of hedge funds is illustrated by AUM and net asset flows for the period of 1990 through 2015. Hedge Fund Research, Inc., (HFRI) reports that AUM grew from approximately $39 billion in 1990 to $491 billion in 2000 and to $2.9 trillion in 2015.[13]

13 That is, January 2016.

Exhibit 4 compares the returns and a variety of risk and performance measures of the HFRI Fund of Funds Composite Index, the MSCI ACWI, and the Bloomberg Barclays Global Aggregate Index. The HFRI Fund of Funds Composite Index is an equally weighted performance index of funds of hedge funds included in the HFR Database. Hedge fund indexes suffer from issues related to self-reporting, but the HFRI Fund of Funds Composite Index reflects the actual performance of portfolios of hedge funds. This index may show a lower reported return because of the added layer of fees,[14] but it may represent average hedge fund performance more accurately than HFRI's composite index of individual funds.

As shown in Exhibit 4, over the 25-year period, hedge funds had higher returns than stocks and bonds had and a standard deviation almost identical to that of bonds. As a result, the Sharpe ratio for hedge funds appeared to dominate these and other investments (see Exhibit 3) in both return and risk. Note that the returns and volatilities (standard deviations) represent an average and are not representative of any single year. Hedge funds do not appear as attractive as bonds if returns are adjusted for downside deviation, as reflected in the Sortino measures in Exhibit 4. The "worst drawdown," reflecting the period of largest cumulative negative returns for hedge funds and global equities, occurred during the period that began in 2007 (when each peaked) and ended in 2009.

Exhibit 4 Risk–Return Characteristics of Hedge Funds and Other Investments, 1990–2014

	FOF Hedge	Global Stocks	Global Bonds
Annualized return	7.2%	6.9%	6.3%
Annualized volatility	6.0%	16.5%	5.8%
Sharpe ratio	0.63	0.21	0.49
Sortino ratio	0.74	0.43	1.09
Percentage of positive months	69.3%	61.3%	62.7%
Best month	6.8%	11.9%	6.2%
Worst month	−7.5%	−19.8%	−3.8%
Worst drawdown	−22.2%	−54.6%	−10.1%

Sources: Fund-of-funds (FOF) hedge data are from the HFRI Fund of Funds Composite Index; global stock data are from the MSCI ACWI; global bond data are from the Bloomberg Barclays Global Aggregate Index.

3.1 Hedge Fund Strategies

Hedge funds are typically classified by strategy, although categorizations vary. Many classifying organizations focus on the most common strategies, but others have classification systems based on different criteria, such as the underlying assets in which the funds are invested. Also, classifications change over time as new strategies, often based on new products and opportunities in the market, are introduced. Classifying hedge funds is important so that investors can review aggregate performance data, select strategies to build a portfolio of funds, and select or construct appropriate performance benchmarks. In 2015, HFRI identified four broad categories of strategies:

14 A fund of funds has an extra layer of fees. Each hedge fund in which a fund of funds invests is structured to receive a management fee plus a performance fee, and the fund of funds itself may also be structured to receive a management fee plus a performance fee.

event driven, relative value, macro, and equity hedge.[15] Exhibit 5 shows the approximate percentage of hedge fund AUM by strategy, according to HFRI, for 1990, 2010, and 2015. Based on percentage of hedge fund AUM by strategy, event-driven and relative value strategies have grown in popularity during the last 25 years, while macro and equity hedge funds have declined in popularity.

Exhibit 5 Percentage of AUM by Strategy

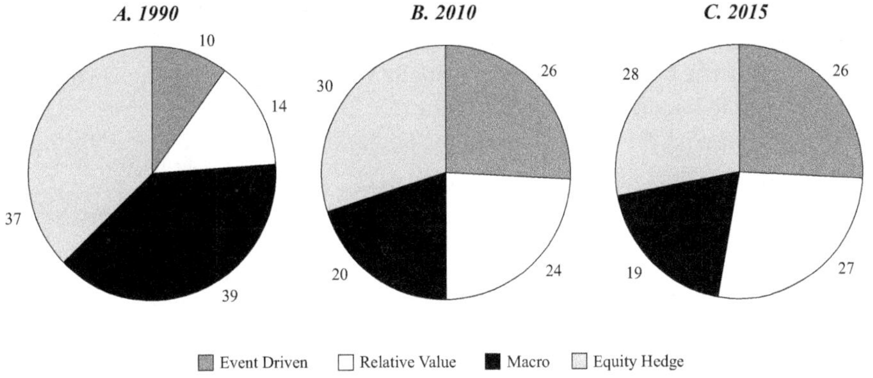

3.1.1 *Equity Hedge Strategies*

Equity hedge strategies can be thought of as the original hedge fund category. They are focused on public equity markets and take long and short positions in equity and equity derivative securities. Some hedge funds, called "equity-only funds," invest exclusively in public equity securities. Equity hedge strategies that are not focused on individual equities are categorized generally as event-driven or macro strategies. Equity hedge strategies use a bottom-up, as opposed to top-down, approach. Other investors that are not structured as hedge funds may use some similar strategies. Examples of equity hedge strategies include the following:

- **Market neutral.** These strategies use quantitative (technical) and/or fundamental analysis to identify under- and overvalued equity securities. The hedge fund takes long positions in securities it has identified as undervalued and short positions in securities it has identified as overvalued. The hedge fund tries to maintain a net position that is neutral with respect to market risk as well as other factors (size, industry, etc.). Ideally, the portfolio should have a beta of approximately zero. The intent is to profit from individual securities' movements while remaining independent from market risk.
- **Fundamental growth.** These strategies use fundamental analysis to identify companies expected to exhibit high growth and capital appreciation. The hedge fund takes long positions in identified companies.
- **Fundamental value.** These strategies use fundamental analysis to identify companies that are undervalued. The hedge fund takes long positions in identified companies. The "deep value" approach takes an extreme, even "distressed," point of view on its investments.

15 The Chartered Alternative Investment Analyst (CAIA) Association classifies hedge funds into four broad categories: corporate restructuring, convergence trading, opportunistic, and market directional. These categories approximately coincide with event driven, relative value, macro, and equity hedge, respectively.

- **Quantitative directional.** These strategies use technical analysis to identify companies that are under- and overvalued and to ascertain relationships between securities. The hedge fund takes long positions in securities identified as undervalued and short positions in securities identified as overvalued. The hedge fund typically varies levels of net long or short exposure depending on the anticipated market direction and stage in the market cycle. Similar long–short approaches that are based on fundamental analysis exist.
- **Short bias.** These strategies use quantitative (technical) and/or fundamental analysis to identify overvalued equity securities. Although many funds will have some shorts but maintain a "net long" position (more long positions than short ones), this is the opposite approach, usually with only short positions (though possibly some long hedges to be "net short"). The fund typically varies its net short exposure on the basis of market expectations, looking to go fully short in declining markets.
- **Sector specific.** These strategies exploit manager or structural expertise in a particular sector and use quantitative (technical) and fundamental analysis to identify opportunities in the sector. Technology, biotech/life sciences, and financial services are common investment sectors for these types of hedge funds.

3.1.2 *Event-Driven Strategies*

Event-driven strategies seek to profit from short-term events, typically involving potential changes in corporate structure, such as an acquisition or restructuring, that are expected to affect individual companies. This strategy is considered "bottom up" (company-level analysis followed by aggregation and analysis of a larger group, such as an industry), as opposed to "top down" (global macro analysis followed by sectoral/regional analysis followed by company analysis). Investments may include long and short positions in common and preferred stocks, as well as debt securities and options. Further subdivisions of this category by HFRI include the following:

- **Merger arbitrage.** Generally, these strategies involve going long (buying) the stock of the company being acquired and going short (selling) the stock of the acquiring company when the merger or acquisition is announced. The manager may expect to profit from the deal spread, which reflects the uncertainty of the deal closing, or may expect the acquirer to ultimately overpay for the acquisition and perhaps suffer from an increased debt load. The primary risk in this strategy is that the announced merger or acquisition does not occur and the hedge fund has not closed its positions on a timely basis.
- **Distressed/restructuring.** These strategies focus on the securities of companies either in bankruptcy or perceived to be near to bankruptcy. Hedge funds attempt to profit from distressed securities in a variety of ways. The hedge fund may simply purchase fixed-income securities trading at a significant discount to par. This transaction takes place in anticipation of the company restructuring and the fund earning a profit from the subsequent sale of the securities. The hedge fund may also use a more complicated approach, for example, buying senior debt and shorting junior debt or buying preferred stock and shorting common stock. These transactions take place in expectation of a profit as the spread between the securities widens. The fund may also short sell the company's stock, but this transaction involves considerable risk given the potential for loss if the company's prospects improve.
- **Activist.** The term "activist" is short for "activist shareholder." These strategies focus on the purchase of sufficient equity in order to influence a company's policies or direction. For example, the activist hedge fund may advocate for

divestitures, restructuring, capital distributions to shareholders, and/or changes in management and company strategy. These hedge funds are distinct from private equity because they operate primarily in the public equity market.

- **Special situations.** These strategies focus on opportunities in the equity of companies that are currently engaged in restructuring activities other than mergers, acquisitions, or bankruptcy. These activities include security issuance or repurchase, special capital distributions, and asset sales/spinoffs.

3.1.3 *Relative Value Strategies*

Relative value funds seek to profit from a pricing discrepancy (an unusual short-term relationship) between related securities. The expectation is that the pricing discrepancy will be resolved over time. Examples of relative value strategies include the following:

- **Fixed-income convertible arbitrage.** These market-neutral (a theoretical zero-beta portfolio) investment strategies seek to exploit a perceived mispricing between a convertible bond and its component parts (the underlying bond and the embedded stock option). The strategy typically involves buying convertible debt securities and simultaneously selling the same issuer's common stock.
- **Fixed-income asset backed.** These strategies focus on the relative value between a variety of asset-backed securities (ABS) and mortgage-backed securities (MBS) and seek to take advantage of mispricing across different ABS.
- **Fixed-income general.** These strategies focus on the relative value within the fixed-income markets. Strategies may incorporate long/short trades between two corporate issuers, between corporate and government issuers, between different parts of the same issuer's capital structure, or between different parts of an issuer's yield curve. Currency dynamics and government yield curve considerations may also come into play when managing these fixed-income instruments.
- **Volatility.** These strategies typically use options to go long or short market volatility either in a specific asset class or across asset classes. Option prices reflect implied volatility, and an increase in market volatility leads to an increase in option prices. Dynamic hedging with the underlying assets or derivatives is used to offset related risks.
- **Multi-strategy.** These strategies trade relative value within and across asset classes or instruments. Rather than focusing on one type of trade (e.g., convertible arbitrage), a single basis for trade (e.g., volatility), or a particular asset class (e.g., fixed income), this strategy looks for investment opportunities wherever they might exist.

3.1.4 *Macro Strategies*

Macro hedge funds emphasize a top-down approach to identify economic trends evolving across the world. Trades are made on the basis of expected movements in economic variables. Generally, these funds trade opportunistically in the fixed-income, equity, currency, and commodity markets. Macro hedge funds use long and/or short positions to potentially profit from a view on overall market direction as influenced by major economic trends and/or events.

Many hedge funds start as a focused operation, specializing in one strategy or asset class, and, if successful, may diversify over time to become multi-strategy funds. Large multi-strategy funds and funds of funds are similar in offering diversification among hedge fund strategies. With funds of funds, the investor is hiring the fund-of-funds manager to select hedge fund strategies among various fund groups. With multi-strategy funds, the strategies are run within one fund group. A multi-strategy hedge fund does not have the extra layer of fees associated with a fund of funds. However, a fund of funds may offer compensating advantages, such as access by smaller investors, a diversified hedge fund portfolio, better redemption terms, and due diligence expertise.

3.2 Hedge Funds and Diversification Benefits

Given the broad range of strategies across hedge funds, general statements about hedge fund diversification benefits are not necessarily meaningful.

However, the commonly observed less-than-perfect correlation of hedge fund returns with stock market returns does imply some level of diversification benefits. The claim is sometimes made by hedge funds that their performance is uncorrelated, not just less than perfectly correlated, with stock market performance, but overall this claim is unsubstantiated. Looking at Exhibit 6, the claims of lack of correlation with the stock market appear to be supported from 2000 through 2001 but not in 2008 or from 2010 through 2014. During financial crisis periods, the correlation between hedge fund performance and stock market performance may increase. However, the losses for hedge funds in this analysis were less than for the equity markets in 2008.

Exhibit 6 Returns for Hedge Funds, Global Stocks, and Bonds, 2000–2014

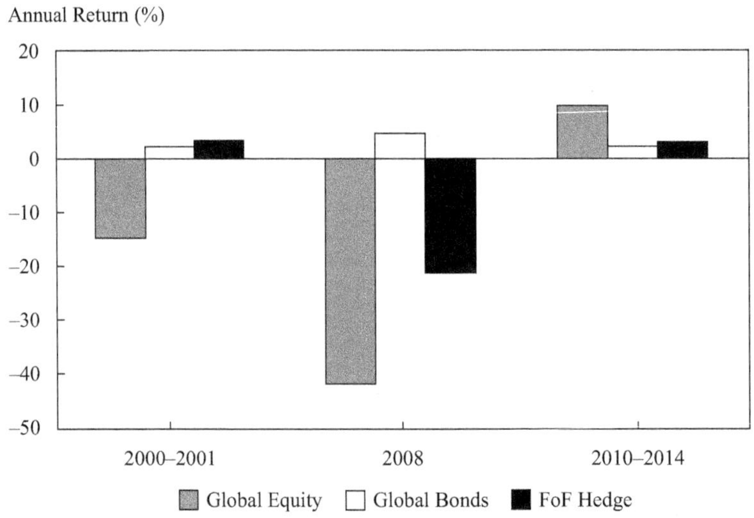

3.3 Hedge Fund Fees and Other Considerations

Hedge fund assets under management grew to $2.9 trillion by the end of 2015 but remain a small percentage of the asset management business overall. Hedge funds, however, earn a significantly higher percentage of fees. For example, according to one estimate for 2013, hedge funds managed less than 3% of total managed funds (hedge funds plus mutual funds) but earned more than 30% of managed fund revenue (fees).[16] Fund revenue depends on fee structure and fund performance.

16 Estimate prepared by Citigroup Inc. and reported by Bloomberg (29 January 2015).

3.3.1 *Fees and Returns*

It is important to consider a hedge fund's fee structure prior to making an investment. This fee structure accounts for the disproportionately high revenues earned relative to mutual funds and affects the returns to investors. A common fee structure in the hedge fund market was once "2 and 20," which reflects a 2% management fee and a 20% incentive fee; both fees are paid by LP investors. The average industry fee is now closer to a 1.6% management fee and 17.75% incentive fee.[17] Additionally, funds of hedge funds may charge investors a 1% management fee and a 10% incentive fee. The incentive fee may be calculated on profits net of management fees or on profits before management fees (in other words, the incentive fee is calculated independent of management fees).

Generally, the fee structure specifies that the incentive fee is earned only after the fund achieves a specified return known as a hurdle rate. The hurdle rate is frequently set on the basis of a risk-free rate proxy (e.g., Libor or a specified Treasury bill rate) plus a premium but may be set as an absolute, nominal, or real return target. The incentive fee can be based on returns in excess of the hurdle rate (hard hurdle rate) or on the entire return (soft hurdle rate).

The fee structure may specify that before an incentive fee is paid following a year in which the fund's value has declined, the fund's value must return to a high-water mark. A high-water mark is the highest value reported by the fund for each of its investors net of fees. In other words, high-water marks reflect the highest cumulative return used to calculate an incentive fee. The hedge fund must recover its past losses and return to its high-water mark before any additional incentive fee is earned. Clients are not charged an incentive fee if the latest cumulative return does not exceed the prior high-water mark. This use of a high-water mark protects clients from paying twice for the same performance. Although poorly performing hedge funds may not receive an incentive fee, the management fee is earned irrespective of returns. Given that different clients invest at different times, it is possible that not all clients will be at their respective high-water marks at the same time: A client who invests on a dip will enjoy the fund's recovery and pay an incentive fee, whereas a client who invested at the top will need to earn back what she had lost before having to pay that incentive fee.

Although "2 and 20" and "1 and 10" represent commonly quoted fee structures for hedge funds and funds of hedge funds, respectively, many fee structure variations exist in the marketplace. Hedge funds charge different rates, and different classes of investors may have different fee structures within the same fund. Hedge funds may be willing to negotiate terms, including fees and notice and lockup periods, with potential investors. A fee structure may differ from 2 and 20 on the basis of the promised length of the investment. In other words, the longer investors agree to keep their money in the hedge fund, the lower the fees. A fee structure may also vary from 2 and 20 on the basis of supply and demand as well as historical performance. Sometimes, rebates or reductions in fees are given to investors or to the placement agent who introduces investors to the hedge fund.

The following example demonstrates fee structures and their effect on the resulting returns to investors.

17 Fees on new funds have declined through the years. HFRI reported in March 2016 that management fees for new funds averaged 1.6% and incentive fees averaged 17.75% in 2015. In 2007, it reported that new fund incentive fees averaged 18.5%.

EXAMPLE 2

Fee and Return Calculations

AWJ Capital is a hedge fund with $100 million of initial investment capital. It charges a 2% management fee based on year-end AUM and a 20% incentive fee. In its first year, AWJ Capital has a 30% return. Assume management fees are calculated using end-of-period valuation.

1 What are the fees earned by AWJ if the incentive and management fees are calculated independently? What is an investor's effective return given this fee structure?

2 What are the fees earned by AWJ assuming that the incentive fee is calculated on the basis of return net of the management fee? What is an investor's net return given this fee structure?

3 If the fee structure specifies a hurdle rate of 5% and the incentive fee is based on returns in excess of the hurdle rate, what are the fees earned by AWJ assuming the performance fee is calculated net of the management fee? What is an investor's net return given this fee structure?

4 In the second year, the fund value declines to $110 million. The fee structure is as specified for Question 1 but also includes the use of a high-water mark (computed net of fees). What are the fees earned by AWJ in the second year? What is an investor's net return for the second year given this fee structure?

5 In the third year, the fund value increases to $128 million. The fee structure is as specified in Questions 1 and 4. What are the fees earned by AWJ in the third year? What is an investor's net return for the third year given this fee structure?

6 What are the arithmetic and geometric mean annual returns for the three-year period based on the fee structure specified in Questions 1, 4, and 5? What is the capital gain to the investor for the three-year period? What are the total fees paid to AWJ for the three-year period?

Solution to 1:

AWJ fees

$130 million × 2% = $2.6 million management fee

($130 million – $100 million) × 20% = $6 million incentive fee

Total fees to AWJ Capital = $8.6 million

Investor return: ($130 million – $100 million – $8.6 million)/$100 million = 21.40%

Solution to 2:

$130 million × 2% = $2.6 million management fee

($130 million – $100 million – $2.6 million) × 20% = $5.48 million incentive fee

Total fees to AWJ Capital = $8.08 million

Investor return: ($130 million – $100 million – $8.08 million)/$100 million = 21.92%

Solution to 3:

$130 million × 2% = $2.6 million management fee

($130 million – $100 million – $5 million – $2.6 million) × 20% = $4.48 million incentive fee

Total fees to AWJ Capital = $7.08 million

Investor return: ($130 million – $100 million – $7.08 million)/$100 million = 22.92%

Solution to 4:

$110 million × 2% = $2.2 million management fee

No incentive fee because the fund has declined in value.

Total fees to AWJ Capital = $2.2 million

Investor return: ($110 million – $2.2 million – $121.4 million)/$121.4 million = –11.20%

The beginning capital position in the second year for the investors is ($130 million – $8.6 million) = $121.4 million. The ending capital position at the end of the second year is ($110 million – $2.2 million) = $107.8 million.

Solution to 5:

$128 million × 2% = $2.56 million management fee

($128 million – $121.4 million) × 20% = $1.32 million incentive fee.

The $121.4 million represents the high-water mark established at the end of Year 1.

Total fees to AWJ Capital = $3.88 million

Investor return: ($128 million – $3.88 million – $107.8 million)/$107.8 million = 15.14%

The ending capital position at the end of Year 3 is $124.12 million. This amount is the new high-water mark.

Solution to 6:

Arithmetic mean annual return = (21.4% – 11.20% + 15.14%)/3 = 8.45%

Geometric mean annual return = [Cube root of (124.12/100)] – 1 = 7.47%

Capital gain to the investor = ($124.12 million – $100 million) = $24.12 million

Total fees = ($8.6 million + $2.2 million + $3.88 million) = $14.68 million

---

As the example illustrates, the return to an LP investor in a fund differs significantly from the return to the fund. Hedge fund indexes generally report performance net of fees. If fee structures vary, however, the net-of-fees returns may vary among investors and from that included in the index. The multilayered fee structure of funds of hedge funds has the effect of further diluting returns to the investor, but this disadvantage can be balanced with several positive features. Funds of hedge funds may provide a diversified portfolio of hedge funds, may provide access to hedge funds that may otherwise be closed to direct investments, and may offer expertise in and conduct due diligence in selecting the individual hedge funds. Fund-of-funds money is considered "fast" money by hedge fund managers because fund-of-funds managers tend to be the first to redeem their money when hedge funds start to perform poorly,[18] and they may also have negotiated redemption terms that are more favorable (for example, a shorter lockup period and/or notice period).

EXAMPLE 3

Comparison of Returns—Investment Directly into a Hedge Fund or through a Fund of Hedge Funds

An investor is contemplating investing €100 million in either ABC Hedge Fund (ABC HF) or XYZ Fund of Funds (XYZ FOF). XYZ FOF has a "1 and 10" fee structure and invests 10% of its AUM in ABC HF. ABC HF has a standard "2 and 20" fee structure with no hurdle rate. Management fees are calculated on an annual basis on AUM at the beginning of the year. For simplicity, assume that management fees and incentive fees are calculated independently. ABC HF has a 20% return for the year before management and incentive fees.

1 Calculate the return to the investor from investing directly in ABC HF.
2 Calculate the return to the investor from investing in XYZ FOF. Assume that the other investments in the XYZ FOF portfolio generate the same return before management fees as ABC HF generates and have the same fee structure as ABC HF has.
3 Why would the investor choose to invest in a fund of funds instead of a hedge fund given the effect of the "double fee" demonstrated in the answers to Questions 1 and 2?

Solution to 1:

ABC HF has a profit before fees on a €100 million investment of €20 million (= €100 million × 20%). The management fee is €2 million (= €100 million × 2%), and the incentive fee is €4 million (= €20 million × 20%). The return to the investor is 14% (= [20 – 2 – 4]/100).

Solution to 2:

XYZ FOF earns a 14% return or €14 million profit after fees on €100 million invested with hedge funds. XYZ FOF charges the investor a management fee of €1 million (= €100 million × 1%) and an incentive fee of €1.4 million (= €14 million × 10%). The return to the investor is 11.6% (= [14 – 1 – 1.4]/100).

Solution to 3:

This scenario assumed that returns were the same for all underlying hedge funds. In practice, this result will not likely be the case, and XYZ FOF may provide due diligence expertise and potentially valuable diversification.

The hedge fund business is attractive to portfolio managers because fees can generate significant revenue if the fund performs well and AUM are significant. Many new hedge funds launched in the late 1990s and early 2000s. However, not all hedge funds remain in business long. One study suggests that more than a quarter of all hedge funds fail within the first three years because of performance problems—failure to generate sufficient revenue to cover the fund's operating costs.[19] This outcome is one

18 Anecdotal evidence suggests that many funds of funds that cater to high-net-worth investors move money faster than funds of funds that serve institutional clients.
19 Brooks and Kat (2002).

of the reasons survivorship bias is a major problem in hedge fund indexes. Because of the survivorship and backfill biases, hedge fund indexes may not reflect actual average hedge fund performance but, rather, reflect only the performance of hedge funds that are performing well and thus "survived" in the market place.

3.3.2 *Other Considerations*

Hedge funds may use leverage to seek higher returns on their investments. Leverage has the effect of magnifying gains or losses because the hedge fund can take a large position relative to the capital committed. Hedge funds leverage their portfolios by borrowing capital from prime brokers and/or using derivatives.

For example, if a hedge fund expects the price of Nestlé SA to increase, it can take a number of actions to benefit from the expected price increase. The fund can buy a thousand shares of Nestlé, buy 10 futures contracts on Nestlé on the NYSE Euronext, buy call options on 1,000 shares of Nestlé, or sell put options on a thousand shares of Nestlé. The profit or loss from holding the futures will be similar to the profit or loss from holding the shares, but the capital requirement for the investment in the futures is far lower. If the hedge fund had bought calls on 1,000 shares of Nestlé, the fund would have paid a relatively small premium and potentially experienced a significant profit if Nestlé had increased in price. The maximum loss to the fund would have been the premium paid. If the hedge fund had sold puts on 1,000 shares of Nestlé in expectation of the price rising and the puts were not exercised, the fund would have a maximum profit equal to the relatively small premium received. If Nestlé had declined in price, however, the potential loss could be extremely large.

Investors, including hedge funds, are required to put up some collateral when using derivatives if they are going to be exposed to potential losses on their positions. This collateral requirement helps protect against default on the position and helps protect the counterparty (or clearinghouse) to the derivative. The amount of collateral depends on the investment's riskiness as well as the creditworthiness of the hedge fund or other investor. Collateral cannot be otherwise invested in a fund's strategy and thus may be a drag on performance.

The borrowing of capital often takes the form of buying on margin. By borrowing, a hedge fund can invest a larger amount than was invested in the fund. Hedge funds normally trade through **prime brokers**, which provide services including custody, administration, lending, short borrowing, and trading. A hedge fund will normally negotiate its margin requirements, interest, and fees with its prime broker(s). The hedge fund deposits cash or other collateral into a margin account with the prime broker, and the prime broker essentially lends the hedge fund the shares, bonds, or derivatives to make additional investments. The margin account represents the hedge fund's net equity in its positions. The minimum margin required depends on the investment's riskiness and the creditworthiness of the hedge fund.

The smaller the margin requirement, the more leverage is available to the hedge fund. Leverage is a large part of the reason that hedge funds make either larger-than-normal returns or significant losses; the leverage magnifies both gains and losses. If the margin account or the hedge fund's equity in a position declines below a certain level, the lender initiates a margin call and requests the hedge fund put up more collateral. Inability to meet margin calls can have the effect of magnifying or "locking in" losses because the hedge fund may have to liquidate (close) the losing position. This liquidation can lead to further losses if the order size is sufficiently large to move the security's market price before the fund can sufficiently eliminate the position.

Another factor that can lock in or magnify losses for hedge funds is investor redemptions. Redemptions frequently occur when a hedge fund is performing poorly. In the hedge fund industry, a **drawdown** is a reduction in net asset value (NAV)[20] to below the high-water mark. When drawdowns occur, investors may decide to exit the fund or redeem a portion of their shares. Redemptions may require the hedge fund manager to liquidate some positions and incur transaction costs. As previously mentioned, the reduction or liquidation of a position may further magnify the losses on the position. Funds sometimes charge redemption fees to discourage redemption and to offset the transaction costs for the remaining investors. Notice periods try to allow the hedge fund manager to liquidate a position in an orderly fashion without magnifying the losses. Lockup periods, where investors cannot withdraw their capital, provide the hedge fund manager the required time to implement and potentially realize a strategy's expected results. If the hedge fund experiences a drawdown shortly after a new investment, the lockup period will force these investors to stay in the fund for a period of time rather than be allowed to immediately withdraw. A hedge fund's ability to demand a long lockup period and still raise a significant amount of investment capital depends a great deal on the reputation of either the firm or the hedge fund manager. Funds of hedge funds may offer more redemption flexibility than afforded by direct investment in hedge funds because of special redemption arrangements with the underlying hedge fund managers, maintenance of a cash fund, or access to temporary financing.

Although hedge funds are not subject to extensive regulation globally, oversight has increased. In the United States, hedge funds larger than $100 million are required to be registered with the Securities and Exchange Commission (SEC). Additional regulation has been established in recent years. Under the Alternative Investment Fund Managers Directive (AIFMD), hedge funds that operate or market themselves in the European Union (EU) must be authorized. The AIFMD was implemented in the EU in 2013, and in the United States, regular submission of the risk disclosure document Form PF to the Financial Stability Oversight Council has been required since 2012. Regulation may not require hedge funds to be transparent to outsiders or proactive in communicating their strategies and reporting their returns.

Offshore jurisdictions (for example, the Cayman Islands) are often the locale for registering hedge funds, whether managed in the United States, Europe, or Asia. However, some hedge funds choose to register domestically. The choice to register in, for example, the United States or the United Kingdom may result from the added credibility of registering with the SEC or the Financial Services Authority, respectively. Sometimes, onshore hedge funds set up complementary offshore funds to attract capital from various investor types and origins.

EXAMPLE 4

Effect of Redemption

A European credit hedge fund has a very short notice period of one week because the fund's managers believe that it invests in highly liquid asset classes and is market neutral. The fund has a small number of holdings that represent a significant portion of the outstanding issues of each holding. The fund's lockup period has expired. Unfortunately, in one particular month, because of the downgrades of two large holdings, the hedge fund has a drawdown (decline in NAV) of more

20 NAV per share is the value of the fund's total assets minus liabilities, divided by the number of shares outstanding.

than 5%. The declines in value of the two holdings result in margin calls from their prime broker, and the drawdown results in requests to redeem 50% of total partnership interests. The combined requests are *most likely* to:

A force the hedge fund to liquidate or unwind 50% of its positions in an orderly fashion throughout the week.

B have little effect on the prices received when liquidating the positions because the hedge fund has one week before the partnership interests are redeemed.

C result in a forced liquidation, which will further drive down prices and result in a bigger drawdown, so that the remaining investors will redeem their partnership interests, leading to fund liquidation and closure.

Solution:

C is correct. One week may not be enough time to unwind such a large portion of the fund's positions in an orderly fashion so that the unwinding does not further drive down prices. A downgrading is not likely to have a temporary effect, so even if other non-losing positions are liquidated to meet the redemption requests, it is unlikely that the two large holdings will return to previous or higher values in short order. Also, the hedge fund may have a week to satisfy the requests for redemptions, but the margin call must be met immediately. Thus, it is common for a large forced liquidation to drive down prices, resulting in further drawdowns and redemption requests, which ultimately risk the fund's existence.

3.4 Hedge Fund Valuation Issues

Valuations are important for calculating performance and meeting redemptions. The frequency with which and how hedge funds are valued vary among funds. Hedge funds are generally valued on a daily, weekly, monthly, or quarterly basis. The valuation may use market or estimated values of underlying positions. When market prices or quotes are used for valuation, funds may differ in which price or quote they use (for example, bid price, ask price, average quote, or median quote). A common practice is to use the average quote: (Bid + Ask)/2. A more conservative and theoretically accurate approach is to use bid prices for longs and ask prices for shorts, because these are more realistic prices at which the positions could be closed.

The underlying positions may be in highly illiquid or non-traded investments, and therefore, it is necessary to estimate values because there are no reliable market values. Estimated values may be computed using statistical models. Any model should be independently tested, benchmarked, and calibrated to industry-accepted standards to ensure consistency of approach. Because of the potential for conflicts of interests affecting estimates of value, hedge funds should develop procedures for in-house valuations, communicate these procedures to clients, and adhere to them.

Liquidity is an important issue for valuation but is particularly so for strategies involving private investments, convertible bonds, collateralized debt obligations, distressed debt, and emerging market securities, which may be relatively illiquid. If a quoted market price is available, the use of liquidity discounts or "haircuts" is actually inconsistent with valuation guidance under most generally accepted accounting standards. Many practitioners, however, believe that liquidity discounts are necessary to reflect fair value. This assumption has resulted in some funds having two NAVs—trading and reporting. The trading NAV incorporates liquidity discounts, based on the size of the position held relative to the total amount outstanding in the issue and its trading volume. The reporting NAV is based on quoted market prices. Again, redemption fees can offset trading costs in illiquid assets for investors that remain in the fund.

EXAMPLE 5

Hedge Fund Valuation

A hedge fund with a market-neutral strategy restricts its investment universe to domestic publicly traded equity securities that are actively traded. In calculating net asset value, the fund is most likely to use which of the following to value underlying positions?

A Average quotes

B Average quotes adjusted for liquidity

C Bid price for shorts and ask price for longs

Solution:

A is correct. The fund is most likely to use average quotes. The securities are actively traded, so no liquidity adjustment is required. If the fund uses bid–ask prices, it will use ask prices for shorts and bid prices for longs; these are the prices at which the positions are closed.

3.5 Due Diligence for Investing in Hedge Funds

When investing in hedge funds, investors must consider many issues. A basic question is whether one wants to rely on the expertise of a manager of a fund of hedge funds to invest in a portfolio of hedge funds or whether one has the expertise to undertake the hedge fund investment selection process. Funds of hedge funds potentially offer the benefits of providing a diversified portfolio of hedge funds, supplying expertise in conducting due diligence, and negotiating favorable redemption terms. These potential benefits come at the cost of an additional layer of fees. Also, although a fund of hedge funds may provide expertise in due diligence, the investor should still conduct due diligence when choosing a fund of hedge funds.

Investors in hedge funds should consider many factors in their decision-making process. This section highlights some of the key due diligence points to consider but does not provide an exhaustive list of factors. Key factors to consider include investment strategy, investment process, competitive advantage, track record, size and longevity, management style, key person risk, reputation, investor relations, plans for growth, and risk management systems.

Investment strategy and process are challenging to fully assess because hedge funds may limit disclosure in order to maintain their competitive advantage and to not give away information that is considered proprietary. It should be possible, however, to identify in which markets the hedge fund invests, the general investment strategy (for example, long–short, relative arbitrage, and so on), the basic process to implement this strategy, and the benchmark against which the fund gauges its performance.

Track record is a commonly viewed consideration because it should be readily available and is often assumed to be an indicator of future performance and risk (perhaps incorrectly, based on studies of performance persistence).[21] Investors should determine how the returns are calculated (e.g., based on estimates of value or market prices) and reported (e.g., before or after fees) and how the returns and risks compare with some benchmark. The investor should inquire about the fee structure because, as demonstrated earlier, this information will affect the return to the investor.

21 For a discussion of institutional investors' record at selecting managers, see Stewart, Heisler, Knittel, and Neumann (2009).

Size and longevity are also common items for review.[22] The older a fund is, the more likely it has not caused significant losses to its investors (otherwise, it is likely to have experienced redemptions, been unable to raise further capital, and thus liquidated). As a result, older funds are likely to have experienced growth in AUM through both capital appreciation and additional investments (capital injections). Many investors require hedge funds to have a minimum track record of two years before they will invest. This requirement makes it particularly difficult for startup funds to raise money because their managers need capital to invest before they can build a track record. In many cases, startup funds receive money from seed investors who want a share of the business for their investment.

A hedge fund's size can be an important consideration for investors because many investors set a minimum size on their investments to justify the time and expense to conduct due diligence, but they also want to ensure that they do not impose business risk by being too large of a percentage of a fund's overall AUM. For example, if one investor represents 50% of the AUM, then the decision of that investor to liquidate his holdings will likely cause a crisis for the hedge fund's existence. Of course, such an investor may be able to negotiate favorable fees or other terms with the manager. Combining these concepts, if an investor's minimum investment size is $10 million and the investor's fund ownership limit is 10%, the minimum hedge fund size the investor can consider is $90 million.

The hedge fund due diligence process also focuses on many qualitative factors, including management style, key person risk, reputation, investor relations, and plans for growth. A thorough due diligence process will also include a review of management procedures, including leverage, brokerage, and diversification policies. The use of leverage and counterparty risk can significantly affect a fund's risk and performance. In addition to gathering information about the fund's prime broker and custody arrangements for securities, the investor should identify the auditor of the hedge fund and ensure that the auditor is independent and known for conducting competent audits.

Risk management of systems is an important consideration for reviewing a hedge fund. Relevant risk management questions to ask are varied and related to the type of securities in which the fund invests. Ultimately, the answers should provide to investors confidence that the fund performs risk management in a rigorous fashion. In many cases, particularly with smaller funds or those that invest in more unusual or illiquid assets, the answers to these questions may indicate either that the systems and processes are simplistic or that the answers themselves are very complex. Commonly, hedge fund managers believe that their strategies, systems, and processes are proprietary, and they are unwilling to provide much information to potential investors. This reluctance can make due diligence very challenging. Regulation of hedge funds is likely to continue to increase in the future, which may further help with the due diligence process.

EXAMPLE 6

Due Diligence

HF 1 and HF 2 invest in the same asset class using a similar investment strategy. A potential investor has gathered the following data from the hedge funds:

22 For a discussion of quantitative factors investors use to select investment managers, see Heisler, Knittel, Neumann, and Stewart (2007).

Characteristic	HF 1	HF 2
Annualized returns	15%	10%
Sharpe ratio	1.3	1.6
Size (US$ millions)	200	500
Fees	1.5 and 15	2 and 20
Track record	2 years	5 years

Based on the information in the table, the investor is *most likely* to:

A invest in HF 2 because of its higher Sharpe ratio.

B question how the annualized returns are calculated for each fund (whether net of fees or gross of fees as well as details on the performance fee calculation) before making a decision.

C invest in HF 1 because of its higher returns and lower fees.

Solution:

B is correct. It is important to know how returns are calculated and whether they are comparable before making any decision. If both returns are reported net of fees, the higher fees on HF 2 may account for most of the difference in returns between the two funds.

4 PRIVATE EQUITY

Private equity refers to investment in privately owned companies or in public companies with the intent to take them private. There are different stages and types of private equity investing. The focus of private equity firms, which may manage many private equity funds, may change over time as business conditions and the availability of financing change. A possible categorization of private equity identifies leveraged buyouts, venture capital, development capital, and distressed investing as primary private equity strategies.

Leveraged buyouts (LBOs) or highly leveraged transactions refer to private equity firms establishing buyout funds (or LBO funds) that acquire public companies or established private companies with a significant percentage of the purchase price financed through debt. The target company's assets typically serve as collateral for the debt, and the target company's cash flows are expected to be sufficient to service the debt. The debt becomes part of the target company's capital structure if the buyout goes through. After the buyout, the target company becomes or remains a privately owned company.

Venture capital entails investing in or providing financing to private companies with high growth potential. Typically, these are startup or young companies, but venture capital can be provided at a variety of stages. In contrast, **development capital** generally refers to minority equity investments in more mature companies that are looking for capital to expand, restructure operations, enter new markets, or finance major acquisitions.

Distressed investing typically entails buying the debt of mature companies experiencing financial difficulty. These companies may be in bankruptcy proceedings, have defaulted on debt, or seem likely to default on debt. Some investors attempt to identify companies with a temporary cash flow problem but a good business plan that will help the company survive and, in the end, flourish. These investors buy the company's debt in expectation of both the company and its debt increasing in value. Turnaround investors buy debt and plan to be more active in the management and direction of the company. They seek distressed companies to restructure and revive.

The level of activity in private equity has grown over time, but it is cyclical. The cyclicality is shown visually in Exhibit 7, which displays committed capital raised by funds between 2004 and 2015. Note that detailed information on private equity activity is not always readily available.

Exhibit 7 Committed Capital Raised for Private Equity Funds, 2004–2015

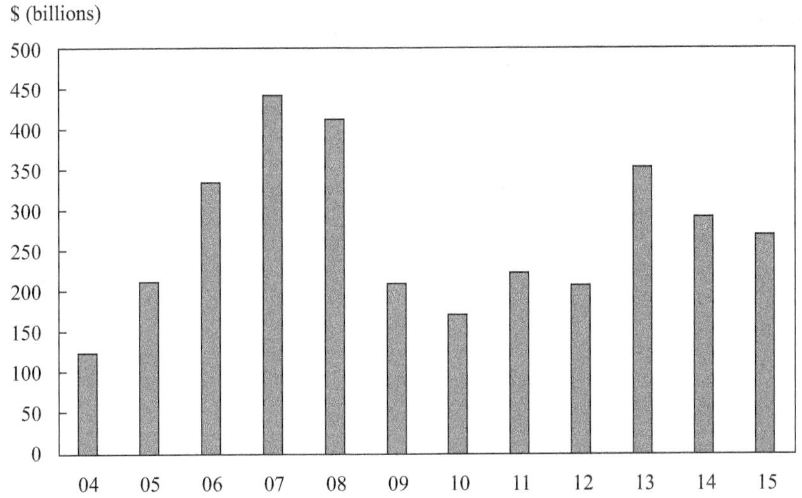

Source: PitchBook, PE Activity, 2014 and 2015.

4.1 Private Equity Structure and Fees

Like hedge funds, private equity funds are typically structured as partnerships in which outside investors are limited partners and the private equity firm, which may manage a number of funds, is the general partner. Most private equity firms charge both a management fee and an incentive fee on a fund basis. The management fees generally range from 1% to 3% of **committed capital**. Committed capital is the amount that the LPs have agreed to provide to the private equity fund. Private equity funds raise committed capital and draw down on those commitments over three to five years when they have a specific investment to make. Until the committed capital is fully drawn down and invested, the management fee is based on committed capital, *not* invested capital. The committed capital basis for management fees is an important distinction from hedge funds, whose management fees are based on AUM. After the committed capital is fully invested, the fees are paid only on the funds remaining in the investment vehicle; as investments are exited, capital is paid back to the investors and investors no longer pay fees on that portion of their investment.

For most private equity funds, the GP does not earn an incentive fee until the LPs have received back their initial investment. The GP typically receives 20% of the total profit, net of any hard hurdle rate, of the private equity fund as an incentive or profit sharing fee.[23] The LPs receive 80% of the total profit of the equity fund plus the return of their initial investment. If distributions are made on the basis of profits earned

23 The incentive fee may also be calculated on a deal-by-deal basis.

over time rather than upon exit from investments of the fund, the distributions may result in receipts by the GP of more than 20% of the total profit. Most private equity partnership agreements include policies that protect the LPs from this contingency. These policies include prohibiting distributions of incentive fees to the GP until the LPs have received back their invested capital, setting up an escrow account for a portion of the incentive fees, and incorporating a **clawback** provision that requires the GP to return any funds distributed as incentive fees until the LPs have received back their initial investment and 80% of the total profit.

In addition to both management and incentive (profit-sharing) fees, LBO firms may generate income from sources other than the fund's management fees and profit sharing. These income sources include a fee paid to the firm for arranging the buyout of a company, compensation if an intended acquisition falls through, and a fee for arranging for divestitures of assets after the buyout is complete. Private equity firms may also charge consulting fees directly to underlying companies.

4.2 Private Equity Strategies

There are many private equity strategies. A common categorization, as indicated earlier, identifies leveraged buyouts, venture capital, development capital, and distressed investing as the primary strategies, but LBOs and venture capital are the dominant strategies.

4.2.1 *Leveraged Buyouts*

LBOs are sometimes referred to as "going private" transactions because, after the acquisition of a publicly traded company, the target company's equity is substantially no longer publicly traded. The LBO may also be of a specific type. In **management buyouts** (MBOs), the current management team is involved in the acquisition, and in **management buy-ins** (MBIs), the current management team is being replaced and the acquiring team will be involved in managing the company. LBO managers seek to add value from improving company operations, growing revenue, and ultimately increasing profits and cash flows. The sources of growth in cash flows in order of contribution include organic revenue growth, cost reduction/restructuring, and acquisitions. The potential returns in this category, however, result to a large extent from the use of leverage. If debt financing is unavailable or costly, LBOs are less likely to occur.

4.2.1.1 LBO Financing Debt is central to the structure and feasibility of buyouts in private equity. Target companies are rarely purchased using only the equity of the buyout company. To potentially increase equity returns and increase the number of transactions a particular fund can make, private equity firms use debt to finance a significant proportion of each deal (in other words, they use leverage). For example, in a buyout deal, a private equity firm may invest equity representing 30% of the purchase price and raise the rest of the purchase price in the debt markets. It may use a combination of bank loans—often called "leveraged loans" because of the amount of the company's capital structure they represent—and high-yield bonds.

To protect investors, leveraged loans often carry covenants that may require or restrict certain actions. For instance, the covenants may require the company to maintain specified financial ratios within certain limits, submit information so that the bank can monitor performance, or operate within certain parameters. The covenants may restrict the company from further borrowing (in other words, no additional bonds can be issued and no additional funds can be borrowed from banks or other sources), or they may impose limits on paying dividends or making operating decisions. Similarly, bond terms may include covenants intended to protect the bondholders. One of the key differences between leveraged loans and high-yield bonds, however, is that leveraged loans are generally senior secured debt whereas the bonds are unsecured in the case of bankruptcy. Even given covenants on the bonds, the bonds issued to finance an LBO are usually high-yield bonds that receive low quality ratings and must offer high coupons to attract investors because of the amount of leverage used.

A typical LBO capital structure includes equity, bank debt (leveraged loans), and high-yield bonds. Leveraged loans often provide a larger amount of capital than either equity or high-yield bonds. As an alternative to high-yield bonds, **mezzanine financing** may also be used.[24] Mezzanine financing refers to debt or preferred shares with a relationship to common equity resulting from a feature such as attached warrants or conversion options. Being subordinate to both senior and high-yield debt, mezzanine financing typically pays a higher coupon rate. In addition to interest or dividends, this type of financing offers a potential return based on increases in the value of common equity.

The variety of available financing choices provides flexibility for a target company to match its repayment schedules with expected inflows, and it also permits higher levels of leverage compared with traditional bank debt. The optimal capital structure takes into account a variety of factors, including the company's projected cash flows, investor willingness to purchase different types of debt and accept different levels of leverage, the availability of equity, and the required rates of return for equity and various types of debt considering leverage. The optimal capital structure will be different for every deal.

4.2.1.2 Characteristics of Attractive Target Companies for LBOs Private equity firms invest in companies across many sectors, although an individual firm may specialize in a certain sector or sectors. Whatever the targeted sector(s), private equity firms look for several characteristics, any one of which may make a company particularly attractive as an LBO target. The characteristics include the following:

- **Undervalued/depressed stock price.** The private equity firm perceives the company's intrinsic value to exceed its market price. Private equity firms are, therefore, willing to pay a premium to the market price to secure shareholder approval. Firms try to buy assets or companies cheaply, and they may focus on companies that are out of favor in the public markets and have stock prices that reflect this perception.
- **Willing management and shareholders.** Existing management is looking for a deal. Management may have identified opportunities but does not have access to the resources to make substantial investments in new processes, personnel, equipment, and so on, to drive long-term growth. Current shareholders may have insufficient access to capital and welcome a private equity partner. Family business owners may want to cash out. Private equity firms can provide management and owners with the time and capital to expand a company or turn it around.
- **Inefficient companies.** Private equity firms seek to generate attractive returns on equity by creating value in the companies they buy. They achieve this goal by identifying companies that are inefficiently managed and that have the potential to perform well if managed better.
- **Strong and sustainable cash flow.** Companies that generate strong cash flow are attractive because in an LBO transaction, the target company will be taking on a significant portion of debt. Cash flow is necessary to make interest payments on the increased debt load.

---

24 This type of loan is referred to as *mezzanine financing* because of its location on the balance sheet and is a *type* of financing.

- **Low leverage.** Private equity firms focus on target companies that currently have no significant debt on their balance sheets. This characteristic makes it easier to use debt to finance a large portion of the purchase price.
- **Assets.** Private equity managers like companies that have a significant amount of unencumbered physical assets. These physical assets can be used as security, and secured debt is cheaper than unsecured debt.

4.2.2 *Venture Capital*

Venture capital (VC) is often categorized by the stage at which the company of interest (the portfolio company) receives it. The company in which a private equity firm is investing is often called the **portfolio company** because it will become part of the fund's portfolio. The VC stages range from inception of an idea for a company to the point when the company is about to make an IPO (initial public offering) or be acquired. The investment return required varies on the basis of the company's stage of development. Investors in early-stage companies will demand higher expected returns relative to later-stage investors, because the earlier the stage of development, the higher the risk. The ultimate returns realized depend on the portfolio company's success in transitioning from a startup to a going and growing concern.

Venture capitalists, like all private equity managers, are not passive investors. They are actively involved with the companies in which they invest. A VC fund typically receives an equity interest in the company in which it is investing. A VC fund may also provide some debt financing.

1 *Formative-stage financing* occurs when the company is still in the process of being formed and encompasses several financing steps, described as follows:
   a *Angel investing* is capital provided at the idea stage. Funds may be used to transform the idea into a business plan and to assess market potential. The amount of financing at this stage is typically small and provided by individuals (often friends and family) rather than by VC funds.
   b *Seed-stage financing* or seed capital generally supports product development and/or marketing efforts, including market research. This point is generally the first stage at which VC funds invest.
   c *Early-stage financing* (early-stage VC) is provided to companies moving toward operation but before commercial production and sales have occurred. Early-stage financing may be provided to initiate commercial production and sales.
2 *Later-stage financing* (expansion VC) is provided after commercial production and sales have begun but before any IPO. Funds may be used for initial expansion of a company already producing and selling a product or for major expansion, such as physical plant expansion, product improvement, or a major marketing campaign.
3 *Mezzanine-stage financing*[25] (mezzanine venture capital) is provided to prepare a company to go public. It represents the bridge financing needed to fund a private firm until it can complete an IPO or be sold.

Formative-stage financing generally is done via ordinary or convertible preferred share sales to the investor(s) (VC fund), and management retains control of the company. Later-stage financing generally involves management selling control of the company to the VC investor; financing is provided through equity and debt (the fund

25 The term "mezzanine-stage financing" is used because this financing is provided at the stage between being a private and a public company. The focus is on *when* the financing occurs.

may also use convertible bonds or convertible preferred shares). The debt financing is not intended for income generation to the VC fund; rather, it is for the recovery and control of assets in a bankruptcy situation. Simply put, debt financing provides more protection to the VC fund than equity does.

To make an investment, a venture capitalist needs to be convinced that the portfolio company's management team is competent and has a solid business plan with strong prospects for growth and development. Because these investments are not in mature businesses with years of operational and financial performance history, the uncertainty involved with VC investing pertains to accurately estimating company valuation based on future prospects. This estimation is more of an unknown than in LBO investing, which targets mature, underperforming public companies. As the portfolio company matures and moves into later-stage financing, the level of certainty around valuation increases but usually remains less than it is with an LBO investment.

4.2.3 *Other Private Equity Strategies*

There are several other specialties for private equity firms. These specialties include development capital, also called "minority equity investing," which earns profits from funding business growth or restructuring. Many times, minority equity investing is initiated and sought by management, which is interested in realizing earnings from selling a portion of its shares before the company can go public. Although this scenario occurs most commonly with private companies, publicly quoted companies sometimes seek private equity capital in opportunities called PIPEs (private investment in public equities).

Other private equity strategies may involve providing specific financing (for example, mezzanine funds) or investing in companies in specific industries. As the financial environment changes and evolves, additional strategies may emerge.

4.2.4 *Exit Strategies*

The ultimate goal for private equity is to improve new or underperforming businesses and exit them at higher valuations. Private equity firms buy and hold companies for an average of five years. The time to exit, however, can range from less than six months to more than 10 years. Before deciding on an exit strategy, private equity managers take into account the dynamics of the industry in which the portfolio company competes, overall economic cycles, interest rates, and company performance.

The following are common exit strategies pursued by private equity portfolio managers:

- **Trade sale.** This strategy refers to the sale of a company to a strategic buyer, such as a competitor. A trade sale can be conducted through an auction process or by private negotiation. Benefits of a trade sale include (a) an immediate cash exit for the private equity fund, (b) potential for high valuation of the asset because strategic buyers may be willing and able to pay more than other potential buyers as a result of anticipated synergies, (c) fast and simple execution, (d) lower transaction costs than an IPO, and (e) lower levels of disclosure and higher confidentiality than an IPO because the private equity firm is generally dealing with only one other party. Disadvantages of trade sales include (a) possible opposition by management, (b) lower attractiveness to employees of the portfolio company than an IPO, (c) a limited number of potential trade buyers, and (d) a possible lower price than in an IPO.
- **IPO.** This approach involves the portfolio company selling its shares, including some or all of those held by the private equity firm, to public investors through an IPO. Advantages for an IPO exit include (a) potential for the highest price; (b) management approval, because management will be retained; (c) publicity for the private equity firm; and (d) potential ability to retain future upside

potential, because the private equity firm may choose to remain a large shareholder. Disadvantages for an IPO exit include (a) high transaction costs paid to investment banks and lawyers; (b) long lead times; (c) risk of stock market volatility; (d) high disclosure requirements; (e) a potential lockup period, which requires the private equity firm to retain an equity position for a specified period after the IPO; and (f) the fact that an IPO is usually appropriate only for larger companies with attractive growth profiles.

- **Recapitalization.** Recapitalization occurs when the private equity firm increases leverage or introduces it to the company and pays itself a dividend. A recapitalization is not a true exit strategy, because the private equity firm typically maintains control; however, it does allow the private equity investor to extract money from the company and pay its investors. A recapitalization may be a prelude to a later exit.
- **Secondary sales.** This approach represents a sale of the company to another private equity firm or another group of investors.
- **Write-off/liquidation.** A write-off occurs when a transaction has not gone well and the private equity firm is updating its value of the investment or liquidating the portfolio company to move on to other projects.

The foregoing exit strategies may be pursued individually, combined together, or used for a partial exit strategy. For example, it is not unusual to see a private equity fund sell a portion of a portfolio company to a competitor via a trade sale and then complete a secondary sale to another private equity firm for the remaining portion. Company shares may also be distributed to fund investors, although such a move is unusual.

4.3 Private Equity: Diversification Benefits, Performance, and Risk

Private equity funds may provide higher return opportunities relative to traditional investments through their ability to invest in private companies, their influence on portfolio companies' management and operations, and their use of leverage. Investments in private equity funds can add diversity to a portfolio composed of publicly traded stocks and bonds because they may have less-than-perfect correlation with those investments.

Exhibit 8 shows the mean annual returns for the Cambridge Associates US Private Equity Index, the NASDAQ and S&P 500 indexes, and the Cambridge Associates mPME (Modified Public Market Equivalent) S&P 500 Index for a variety of periods ending 31 December 2014. Public market equivalent (PME) index returns use internal rate of return (IRR) calculations to simulate investment of private equity cash flows in a market index, such as the S&P 500. The technique involves recording the timing of cash flows for the fund and computing period returns, assuming the flows are invested in a market index instead of the fund. The returns in Exhibit 8 show that US private equity funds, based on the Cambridge Associates' estimates, on average outperformed stocks, based on the NASDAQ and S&P 500 indexes, only in the 10- and 20-year periods ending 31 December 2014. The returns to US private equity underperformed these indexes' returns for the one- and three-year periods and were similar for the five-year period ending 31 December 2014. The mPME index returns were more similar to the S&P 500 returns than to returns on private equity.

Exhibit 8 Comparison of Mean Annual Returns for US Private Equity, US Stocks, and a PME Index

	1 Year	3 Years	5 Years	10 Years	20 Years
US Private Equity[a]	11.3	15.6	15.8	12.9	13.5
NASDAQ	13.4	22.1	15.9	8.1	9.6
S&P 500	13.7	20.4	15.5	7.7	9.9
mPME S&P 500[b]	13.6	20.5	15.5	8.7	8.7

[a] Private equity returns are net of expenses; US stocks and the mPME index are gross.
[b] Cambridge Associates mPME.
Source: US Private Equity Index and selected benchmark statistics, 31 December 2014, Cambridge Associates.

Published private equity indexes may be an unreliable measure of performance, however, because of challenges in measuring the historical performance of private equity investing. As with hedge funds, private equity return indexes rely on self-reporting and are subject to survivorship, backfill, and other biases. These characteristics typically lead to overstatement of published returns. Moreover, prior to 2009, in the absence of a liquidity event, private equity firms did not necessarily mark their investments to market. This failure to mark to market leads to understatement of measures of volatility and correlations with other investments. Thus, data adjustments are required to more reliably measure the benefits of private equity investing.

Exhibit 9 lists annualized standard deviations of published quarterly and annual returns of private equity investments from 1990 through 2014. The volatility calculated using published quarterly returns reflects few liquidity events and results in much lower volatility estimates than using annual returns does. Note that the difference between the two measures (quarterly and annual) using the MSCI World Index is insignificant because the stocks in the index are marked to market regularly. In July 2009, private equity firms began reporting investments at their estimated fair values; these estimates are frequently based on market multiples. This change in valuation methodology is reflected in the new International Private Equity and Venture Capital Valuation Guidelines.[26]

Exhibit 9 Annualized Standard Deviations of Returns to Private Equity Investments, 1990–2014

	Quarterly	Annual
Venture capital*	22.3	54.5
Private equity*	12.8	21.1
MSCI World	17.1	18.4

* Cambridge Associates, LLC, January 1990–December 2014.

According to the historical standard deviations of annual returns shown in Exhibit 9, private equity investments, including venture capital, are riskier than investing in common stocks. Investors should require a higher return from accepting a higher risk, including illiquidity and leverage risks.

26 Interestingly, based on the calculations of author Scott Stewart, data since July 2009 are inconsistent with improvements in marking to market.

Even given its higher risk, private equity, including venture capital investing, may provide benefits to a diversified portfolio. If investors believe they can identify skillful private equity fund managers (managers who can identify attractive portfolio companies and invest in them at reasonable valuations, as well as improve their operations and profitability), they may benefit from superior returns (returns in excess of those expected given the additional leverage, market, and liquidity risks). Kaplan and Schoar (2005) found significant differences in the returns to the top quartile of funds compared with the bottom quartile of funds; the cash flow IRR was 22% a year for the top quartile, compared with 3% a year for the bottom quartile, from 1980 through 2001. Further, Kaplan and Schoar found evidence of performance persistence. Identifying top-performing funds appears to be critical.[27]

4.4 Portfolio Company Valuation

In order to identify and invest in attractive portfolio companies, private equity professionals must be able to value those companies. Three common approaches are used in the private equity industry to value a company: market or comparables, discounted cash flow (DCF), and asset based. Which approaches are favored depend in part on the portfolio company's industry, and it is common for funds to use more than one approach to arrive at a value.

A market or comparables approach values a company or its equity using multiples of different financial measures. For example, an earnings before interest, taxes, depreciation, and amortization (EBITDA) multiple is commonly used in valuing large, mature private companies that are capital intensive and leveraged. The EBITDA multiple may be determined by looking at the market value of equity plus debt (enterprise value) of a similar publicly traded company or the price recently paid for a comparable business, divided by EBITDA. For other types of companies, multiples based on net income or revenue may be more appropriate. Net income and revenue multiples may be based on the multiples from transactions in comparable companies but are frequently based on heuristics.[28]

EXAMPLE 7

Portfolio Company Valuation

A private equity fund is considering purchasing a radio broadcaster that had an EBITDA of $200 million. In the past year, three radio broadcasting companies were sold for 8 × EBITDA, 10 × EBITDA, and 9 × EBITDA. Based on this information, the maximum value the private equity fund is most likely to assign to the broadcaster is:

A $1,600 million.

B $1,800 million.

C $2,000 million.

27 See the CFA Institute Research Foundation's 2013 monograph *Manager Selection* for information on selecting skillful alternative investment managers.

28 Heuristics are mental shortcuts based on experience and knowledge that simplify decision making. They are sometimes called "rules of thumb."

Solution:

C is correct. The maximum value the private equity fund is most likely to assign is that using the highest multiple (10 × \$200 million = \$2,000 million). The minimum value the seller may be willing to accept is that using the lowest multiple. In negotiations, growth prospects, risk, size, current market conditions, and so on, will likely be considered.

A DCF approach values a company or its equity as the present value of the relevant expected future cash flows. Future free cash flow projections may be discounted to compute a present value for the portfolio company or its equity. Free cash flow to the firm discounted at the weighted average cost of capital may be used to estimate the company's value. Free cash flow to equity discounted at the cost of equity may be used to estimate the value of the company's equity. One simple approach takes a measure such as income or cash flow and divides it by a capitalization rate to arrive at a value estimate. This approach is conceptually different but practically similar to using an income- or cash-based multiple. If the value estimated using a DCF approach is higher than the investment's current price, the opportunity may be an attractive one.

An asset-based approach values a company using the values of its underlying assets less the value of any related liabilities. The approach assumes that a company's value equals the sum of the values of the company's assets minus its liabilities. The valuations can be arrived at using market (fair) values or other values, such as liquidation values. Fair values assume an orderly transaction, whereas liquidation values assume a distressed transaction. In a weak economic environment, liquidation values will most likely be far lower than the immediately previous fair values because there will tend to be many assets for sale and fewer potential buyers.

4.5 Private Equity: Investment Considerations and Due Diligence

Current and anticipated economic conditions, including interest rate and capital availability expectations, are critical factors to consider when evaluating an investment in private equity. Refinancing risk must also be evaluated. If refinancing becomes unavailable, a lack of financing can result in default. The extent to which there is undrawn but committed capital can also affect the private equity sector and the returns to investors.

Investing in private equity firms requires patience. Investors who are comfortable with long-term commitment of funds and illiquidity are best suited to considering private equity investing. Private equity typically requires a long-term commitment by an LP because of the long time lag between investments in and exits from portfolio companies. Once a commitment has been made and an investor becomes an LP, the investor has very limited liquidity choices. Because illiquidity can cause cash flow risks for investors, there should be a liquidity risk premium.

Assuming these characteristics are acceptable, the investor must consider the choice of GP. In this regard, many of the due diligence questions for hedge fund selection are relevant for private equity. Some of the important issues to investigate are the GP's experience and knowledge—financial and operating—the valuation methodology used, the alignment of the GP's incentives with the LPs' interests, the plan to draw on committed capital, and the planned exit strategies.

5 REAL ESTATE

Real estate investing is typically thought of as either direct or indirect ownership (equity investing) in real estate property, such as land and buildings. However, it also includes lending (debt investing) against real estate property—for example, providing a mortgage loan or purchasing mortgage-backed securities (MBS), with the property generally serving as collateral.

Key reasons for investing in real estate include the following:

- Potential for competitive long-term total returns driven by both income generation and capital appreciation
- Prospect that multiple-year leases with fixed rents for some property types may lessen cash flow effects from economic shocks
- Likelihood that less-than-perfect correlation with other asset classes may provide diversification benefits
- Potential to provide an inflation hedge if rents can be adjusted quickly for inflation

Real estate property ownership is represented by a title and may reflect access to air rights, mineral rights, and surface rights, in addition to the rights of use of buildings and land. Titles can be purchased, leased, sold, mortgaged, or transferred together or separately, in whole or in part. Much real estate is residential, but if it is owned with the intention to let, lease, or rent it in order to generate income, it is classified as commercial (i.e., income-producing) real estate. In addition to residential real estate classified as commercial, commercial real estate includes other types of real estate properties, such as office and retail properties.

Institutional ownership of commercial property totaled close to \$2.5 trillion as of 2014, as shown in Exhibit 10, up from \$2.1 trillion in 2008.

Exhibit 10 Institutionally Owned Global Real Estate Property AUM, 2014 (US\$ millions)

Europe	922,064
North America	1,244,464
Australasia	102,672
Asia	136,896
Latin America	23,808
Other	50,096
Total	**2,480,000**

Source: Based on data from Property Funds Research.

Real estate property exhibits unique features compared with other investment asset classes. The basic indivisibility, unique characteristics (i.e., no two properties are identical), and fixed location of real estate property have implications for investors. For example, the size of investment may have to be large (indivisible), and the investment may be relatively illiquid. Also, real estate property typically requires operational management. Real estate is often subject to wide-ranging government regulations affecting what can be done to modify the existing land or property and to whom and how ownership can be transferred, in addition to other restrictions. Local or regional markets and real estate property values can be independent of countrywide or global price movements, because local factors may override wider market trends. Cross-border investment in real estate is increasingly common and requires knowledge of country, regional, and local markets.

5.1 Forms of Real Estate Investment

Real estate investing may take a variety of forms. Real estate investments may be classified along two dimensions: (1) debt or equity based and (2) in private or public markets. Equity investments in real estate that occur in the private markets often conclude as direct investments in real estate. The investment capital required to finance real estate property purchases comes from either debt financing or equity financing. A well-known form of debt financing of real estate purchases is mortgages. Private investors—institutional and individual—real estate corporations, and REITs may provide the equity financing for the purchase.

REITs are publicly traded shares of a portfolio of properties. Similarly, mortgages may be packaged and securitized into asset-backed securitized debt obligations (i.e., MBS) that represent rights to receive cash flows from portfolios of mortgage loans. Exhibit 11 shows some examples of the basic forms of real estate investments.

Exhibit 11 Basic Forms of Real Estate Investments and Examples

	Debt	Equity
Private	■ Mortgages ■ Construction lending	■ Direct ownership of real estate: Ownership can be through sole ownership, joint ventures, or real estate limited partnerships. ■ Indirect ownership via real estate funds
Public	■ MBS (residential and commercial) ■ Collateralized mortgage obligations	■ Shares in real estate development corporations ■ Shares of REITs

Within the basic forms, there can be many variations.

- Direct ownership can be free and clear, whereby the title to the property is transferred to the owner unencumbered by any financing lien, such as from a mortgage. Initial purchase costs associated with direct ownership may include legal expenses, survey costs, engineering/environmental studies, and valuation (appraisal) fees. In addition, ongoing maintenance and refurbishment charges are also incurred. The property must be managed, which has related costs. The owner may manage the property or may employ a local managing agent.
- Leveraged ownership occurs when the property title is obtained through an equity purchase combined with debt (mortgage financing). In addition to the initial purchase costs, there are mortgage arrangement fees. A mortgage is secured by the property, and in the event of a breach of lending terms, the creditor can petition for the title. Any appreciation (depreciation) of the property's value plus the net operating income in excess of the debt servicing costs provides investors with a leveraged gain (loss) on their equity.

- Financing provided to leveraged owners is frequently in the form of standalone mortgage loans. These loans represent passive investments in which the lender expects to receive a predefined stream of payments throughout the finite life of the mortgage. The loan may become a form of property ownership if the borrower defaults. Investments may be in the form of "whole" loans based on specific properties (typically, direct investment through private markets) or through participation in a pool of mortgage loans (typically, indirect investment in real estate through publicly traded securities, such as MBS).
- Real estate equity investors may use different types of pooled vehicles arranged by an intermediary. These vehicles include the following:
  - Real estate limited partnerships offer exposure to real estate projects while preserving limited liability (up to the amount of the initial investment) and leaving management and liability to GPs who specialize in real estate management.
  - Publicly traded shares of a pool of properties in a special trust (i.e., REITs): REITs invest in various types of real estate and provide retail investors with access to a diversified real estate property portfolio and professional management. REITs are typically required to distribute most of their taxable income to their shareholders.
- Securitization of residential and commercial mortgages provides institutional investors with access to a diversified portfolio of mortgages and allows the original lenders to alter their portfolio of investments. Mortgages are combined into a pool, which is then divided by investment banks into sections called "tranches." The tranches, having different payment characteristics and credit ratings, are then sold to investors. These securities are generally not considered alternative investments but are held as part of a fixed-income (or credit) portfolio.

REITs and partnerships have fees for managing the assets embedded in their valuations. Fee structures for real estate investment funds can be similar to those for private equity funds, with investment management fees based on either committed capital or invested capital. These fees typically range from 1% to 2% of capital per annum. Funds also charge performance-based fees, similar to a private equity fund.

5.2 Real Estate Investment Categories

The majority of real estate property may be classified as either commercial or residential. In this reading, residential properties are defined narrowly to include only owner-occupied single residences (often referred to as "single-family residential property"). Residential properties owned with the intention to let, lease, or rent them are classified as commercial. Commercial properties also include office, retail, industrial and warehouse, and hospitality (e.g., hotel and motel) properties. Commercial properties may also have mixed uses. Commercial properties generate returns from income (e.g., rent) and capital appreciation. Several factors will affect opportunities for capital appreciation, including development strategies, market conditions, and property-specific features.

5.2.1 *Residential Property*

For many individuals and families, real estate investment takes the form of direct equity investment (i.e., ownership) in a residence with the intent to occupy.[29] In other words, a home is purchased. Given the price of homes, most purchasers cannot pay 100% cash up front and must borrow funds to make the purchase. Any appreciation (depreciation) in the value of the home increases (decreases) the owner's equity in the home and is magnified by any mortgage leverage.

Financial institutions are the main providers (originators) of debt financing (typically, through mortgages) for homeownership. The originators of single-family residential mortgages are making a direct debt investment in the home. Before offering a mortgage, the due diligence process should include the following:

- ensuring that the borrower is making an appropriate equity investment in the home (in other words, paying an adequate proportion of the purchase price),
- conducting a credit review of the borrower,
- establishing that the borrower has sufficient cash flows to make the required payments on the mortgage and to maintain the home,
- appraising (estimating the value of) the home, and
- ensuring that adequate and appropriate insurance is in place on the home and, in some cases, on the borrower.

Home loans may be held on the originator's balance sheet or securitized and offered to the financial markets. Securitization provides indirect debt investment opportunities in residential property via securitized debt products, such as residential mortgage-backed securities (RMBS), to other investors.

5.2.2 *Commercial Real Estate*

Commercial property has traditionally been considered an appropriate direct investment—equity and debt—for institutional funds or high-net-worth individuals with long time horizons and limited liquidity needs. This perception of appropriateness for only certain types of investors was primarily the result of the complexity of the investments, the large investments required, and the relative illiquidity of the investments. Direct equity investing (i.e., ownership) is further complicated because commercial property requires active day-to-day management. The success of the equity investment is a function of a variety of factors, including how well the property is managed, general economic and specific real estate market conditions, and the extent and terms of any debt financing.

In order to provide direct debt financing, the lender (investor) will conduct financial analyses to establish the borrower's creditworthiness, to ensure that the property will generate cash flows sufficient to service the debt, to estimate the value of the property, and to evaluate economic conditions. The estimate of the property value is critical because the relative size of the loan to the property value (loan-to-value ratio) determines the amount of risk that is held by the lender versus the borrower (equity holder). The borrower's equity in the property is an indicator of commitment to the success of the project and provides a cushion to the lender because the property is generally the sole collateral for the loan.

---

29 Residential properties (single or multi-family) are considered commercial property if they are maintained as rental properties.

5.2.3 *REIT Investing*

REITs are listed on stock exchanges in more than 35 countries, and their combined market capitalization exceeded $1.1 trillion in 2016.[30] The risk and return characteristics of REITs depend on the type of investment they make. Mortgage REITs, which invest primarily in mortgages, are similar to fixed-income investments. Equity REITs, which invest primarily in commercial or residential properties and use leverage, are similar to direct equity investments in leveraged real estate.

Gross income from rents represents a relatively predictable income stream and, after servicing the debt, is a source of return to equity REITs. Although the regulations with respect to REITs vary among countries, in general, equity REITs have an obligation to distribute the majority of their income to shareholders to retain their regulatory tax-advantaged status. Often, at least 90% of revenue (including rent and realized capital gains), net of expenses, must be distributed in the form of dividends.

The business strategy for equity REITs is simple: Maximize property occupancy rates and rents in order to maximize income and dividends. Equity REITs, like other public companies, must report earnings per share based on net income as defined by generally accepted accounting principles (GAAP).

5.2.4 *Mortgage-Backed Securities*

The MBS structure is based on the securitization model of buying a pool of assets and assigning the income and principal returns into individual security tranches, as illustrated in Exhibit 12 for commercial mortgage-backed securities (CMBS). On the right-hand side of the exhibit, the ranking of losses indicates the priority of claims against the real estate property. MBS may be issued privately or publicly. These securities are often included in broad fixed-income indexes and in indexes that are used to indicate the performance of real estate investments.

Exhibit 12 CMBS Security Structure

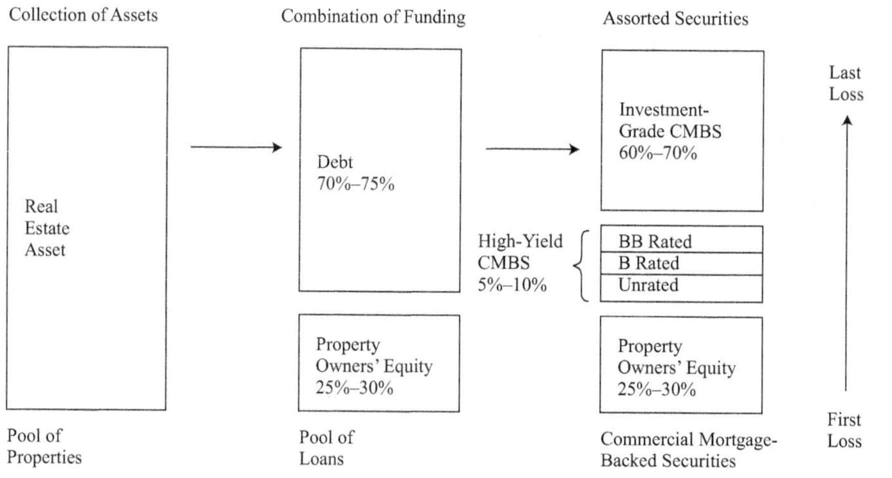

5.2.5 *Timberland and Farmland*

Timberland offers an income stream based on the sale of trees, wood, and other timber products and has been not highly correlated with other asset classes. Timberland can be thought of as both a factory and a warehouse. Timber (trees) can be grown and

30 National Association of Real Estate Investment Trusts, July 2016.

easily stored by simply not harvesting. This feature offers the flexibility of harvesting more trees when timber prices are up and delaying harvests when prices are down. Timberland has three primary return drivers: biological growth, commodity price change of lumber (cut wood), and underlying land price change.

Farmland is often perceived to provide a hedge against inflation. Like timberland, the returns include an income component related to harvest quantities and agricultural commodity prices. Farmland consists of two main property types: row crops that are planted and harvested (i.e., more than one planting and harvesting can occur in a year depending on the crop and the climate) and permanent crops that grow on trees or vines. Unlike with timberland, farm products must be harvested when ripe, so there is little flexibility in production. Farmland may also be used as pastureland for livestock. Similar to timberland, farmland has three primary return drivers: harvest quantities, commodity prices (e.g., the price of corn), and land price change.

5.3 Real Estate Performance and Diversification Benefits

A variety of indexes globally are intended to measure returns to real estate. These indexes vary in the selection and valuation of components and longevity. A real estate index can generally be categorized as an appraisal index, a repeat sales (transaction-based) index, or a REIT index. Appraisal indexes use estimates of value (appraisals) as inputs. These evaluations, conducted by experts, often rely on comparable sales and cash flow analysis techniques and can be quite subjective, especially when there are few comparable properties. The appraisals should be done periodically, often annually, but some appraised values included in an index may be from more than one year earlier. This stale pricing factor—especially since appraisals are strongly influenced by their comparables—may result in indexes that understate volatility.

Repeat sales indexes are constructed using repeat sales of properties. The changes in property prices with repeat sales are measured and used to construct the index. These indexes suffer from a sample selection bias because the properties that sell in each period vary and may not be representative of the larger market. Also, the properties that transact do not represent a random sample and may be biased toward those that have increased or decreased in value, depending on current economic conditions. The higher the number of sales, the more reliable and relevant the index.

REIT indexes are constructed using the prices of publicly traded shares of REITs. The more frequently the shares trade, the more reliable the index. These indexes are not necessarily representative of the properties of interest to the investor because of different geographies, property types (residential, commercial, etc.), and property quality.

Investors will find a variety of indexes to choose from and may find one that is relevant to them. Investors should be aware, however, of how the index is constructed and the inherent limitations resulting from the construction method. Investors should also be aware that the apparent low volatility and low correlation of real estate with other asset classes may result from these limitations.

Exhibit 13 provides a comparison of returns on US real estate based on different indexes. The National Council of Real Estate Investment Fiduciaries (NCREIF) constructs a variety of appraisal-based indexes. The National Association of Real Estate Investment Trusts (NAREIT), together with the FTSE Group and the European Public Real Estate Association, constructs a variety of indexes based on the prices of shares of REITs and listed real estate companies. The NAREIT returns based on publicly traded US REIT share prices are clearly more volatile—displaying a higher standard deviation and a lower worst-calendar-year return—than the NCREIF returns based on appraisals. The NCREIF Farmland index shows the least reported volatility. The lowest annualized return shown is that of commercial property based on appraisals (NCREIF Property index).

Exhibit 13 Historical Returns of US Real Estate Indexes, 1991–2014

	NCREIF Data			NAREIT
	Property*	Timber	Farmland	All REITs
Annualized return	7.8%	10.5%	11.9%	11.9%
Annualized standard deviation	8.6%	9.2%	6.9%	18.9%
Worst calendar year	−16.9%	−5.2%	2.0%	−37.3%

* Commercial real estate property

Exhibit 14 displays global and regional REIT returns. The table shows some disparity among regional returns and supports the importance of knowledge of country, local, and regional markets. A cursory examination, however, indicates a significant degree of correlation among the regional returns. In fact, the correlations between the regional and global returns all exceed 0.9.

Exhibit 14 Historical Returns of Global REITs

	Global	Americas	Asia-Pacific	Europe	Middle East/Africa
3 Years	15.1%	13.8%	15.3%	18.2%	19.1%
5 Years	11.5%	15.5%	7.6%	9.6%	
10 Years	6.7%	7.8%	6.6%	4.1%	
15 Years	9.9%	12.4%	7.4%	9.8%	
Standard deviation (15 years)	23.4%	21.6%	28.1%	30.0%	

Note: Data are as of 31 December 2014.
Source: Based on data from FTSE NAREIT.

From 1990 through 2014, the monthly return correlations of global REITs (S&P Global REIT Index) with global stocks (MSCI ACWI) and global REITs with global bonds (Bloomberg Barclays Global Aggregate Index) were 0.62 and 0.35, respectively. Correlations of global real estate and equity returns are relatively high, and correlations of global real estate and bond returns are lower. The returns from investing in REITs and investing in equities are more highly correlated with each other than with bonds because they are affected similarly by the business cycle (i.e., economic expansion tends to support both equity and property prices).

5.4 Real Estate Valuation

Until a property is actually sold, real estate values can only be estimated. This estimation process is often referred to as appraising the property. A variety of approaches are used to value real estate property. Common techniques for appraising real estate property include comparable sales, income, and cost approaches.

- **Comparable sales approach.** This approach involves determining an approximate value based on recent sales of similar properties. Adjustments are made for differences in key characteristics of the property being appraised and the sold properties identified as similar. Key characteristics include condition, age, location, and size. Adjustments are also made for price changes in the relevant real estate market between dates of sales.

- **Income approach.** Direct capitalization and discounted cash flow approaches are income-based approaches to appraising an income-producing property.
  - The direct capitalization approach estimates the value of an income-producing property based on the level and quality of its net operating income (NOI). Similar to EBITDA, NOI represents the income to the property after deducting operating expenses, including property taxes, insurance, maintenance, utilities, and repairs but before depreciation, financing costs, and income taxes. NOI is a proxy for property-level operating cash flow. The expected annual NOI is divided by a capitalization rate (cap rate) to estimate the property's value. A cap rate is a discount rate less a growth rate. The reciprocal of the cap rate is a multiple that can be applied to NOI. The cap rate is estimated for a given property based on relevant information, including cap rates on sales of comparable properties, general business conditions, property quality, and assessment of management. The analysis might include assessing the strength of tenants, the level of landlord involvement, the extent and adequacy of repairs and improvements, the vacancy rate, management and operating costs, and expected inflation of costs and rent.
  - The discounted cash flow approach discounts future projected cash flows to arrive at a present value for the property. Typically, the analysis involves projections of annual operating cash flows for a finite number of periods and a resale or reversion value at the end of that total period. The projected resale value is often estimated using a direct capitalization approach.
- **Cost approach.** This approach evaluates the property's replacement cost by estimating the market value of the land and the costs of rebuilding using current construction costs and standards. Costs include building materials, labor to build, tenant improvements, and various "soft" costs, including architectural, engineering, and construction supervision costs; legal, insurance, and brokerage fees; and environmental assessment costs. The cost of rebuilding is the replacement cost of the building(s) in new condition and is adjusted to take into account the location and condition of the existing building(s).

A combination and reconciliation of the values from the different approaches is typically performed to increase confidence in the appraisal.

5.4.1 *REIT Valuations*

REITs are composed of a portfolio of real estate properties and/or mortgages, and as a result, a REIT security's valuation depends on the entire pool's characteristics. There are two basic approaches to estimating a REIT's intrinsic value: income based and asset based. The value estimates can be compared with the REIT's observed market price.

Income-based approaches for REITs are typically similar to the direct capitalization approach. A measure of income, which is a cash flow proxy, is capitalized into a value indication by using a cap rate (an alternative calculation could multiply the income measure by the reciprocal of the cap rate). Two common measures used are funds from operations (FFO) and adjusted funds from operations (AFFO). FFO, in its most basic form, equals net income plus depreciation charges on real estate property less gains from sales of real estate property plus losses on sales of real estate property. These adjustments to net income effectively exclude depreciation and the gains and losses from sales of real estate property from FFO. Depreciation is excluded because it represents a non-cash charge and is often unrelated to changes in the value of the property. Gains and losses from sales are excluded because they are assumed to be non-recurring. AFFO adjusts FFO for recurring capital expenditures. It is similar to a free cash flow measure.

The cap rate and its reciprocal multiple are estimated on the basis of a variety of factors, including market cap rates and current market and economic conditions, expectations for growth in the relevant measure, risks associated with the REIT's underlying properties, the financial leverage of the REIT, and multiples of recent transactions.

Asset-based approaches calculate a REIT's net asset value. Generally, a REIT's NAV is calculated as the estimated market value, based on appraisals, of a REIT's total assets minus the value of its total liabilities. REIT shares frequently trade at prices that differ from NAV per share. Both premiums and discounts to the NAV are observed in the day-to-day fluctuations of the REIT's share price.

5.5 Real Estate Investment Risks

Real estate investments, like any investment, may fail to perform in accordance with expectations. Property values are subject to variability based on national and global economic conditions, local real estate conditions, and interest rate levels. Other risks inherent to real estate investment include the ability of fund management to select, finance, and manage real properties, as well as changes in government regulations. Management of the underlying properties includes handling rentals or leasing of the property, controlling expenses, directing maintenance and improvements, and ultimately disposing of the property. Expenses may increase because of circumstances beyond management's control or be covered by insurance. Returns to both debt and equity investors in real estate depend to a large extent on the ability of the owners or their agents to successfully operate the underlying properties.

Investments in distressed properties and property development are subject to greater risks than investments in properties with stable operations and/or in sound financial condition. Property development is subject to special risks, including regulatory issues, construction delays, and cost overruns. Regulatory issues include the failure to receive zoning, occupancy, and other approvals and permits, as well as the effect of environmental regulation. Economic conditions can also change during the development and disposition period, which can be very lengthy. Adverse effects of regulatory issues and changes in economic conditions include increasing construction time or the time until a property is fully leased out, increasing construction costs, and decreasing the level of rents relative to initial expectations. Acquisitions and developments may be financed with lines of credit or other forms of temporary financing rather than long-term debt financing. There is a risk that long-term financing with acceptable terms might not be available when desired. Financing problems with one property may delay or limit further development by the same owner.

It is important to recognize that the vast majority of equity investment real estate funds pursue leverage to potentially increase returns to their investors. Leverage magnifies the effects of both gains and losses, because of operations and changes in property value, on the equity investors. Leverage increases the risk to debt investors as well as to equity investors. Leverage increases the risks that the real estate fund will have insufficient funds to make expected interest payments and that the debt investor will receive less than the entire principal upon repayment. As the loan-to-value ratio increases, the latter risk increases.

6 COMMODITIES

Commodities are physical products that can be standardized on quality, location, and delivery for the purpose of investing. Returns on commodity investments are primarily based on changes in price rather than on income from interest, dividends, or rent. In fact, holding commodities (i.e., the physical products) incurs costs for transportation and storage. Thus, most commodity investors do not trade actual physical commodities but, rather, trade commodity derivatives. The underlying object for the commodity derivative may be a single commodity or an index of commodities.

Trading in physical commodities is primarily limited to a smaller group of entities that are part of the physical supply chain. Some investors that are not part of the supply chain may invest in physical commodities, but the commodities are typically those that are non-perishable, of high value relative to weight and volume, and easily stored at relatively low cost. Because of these logistical issues, most investors invest in commodities using commodity derivatives. Because the prices of commodity derivatives are, to a significant extent, a function of the underlying commodity prices, however, it is important to understand the physical supply chain and general supply–demand dynamics for a commodity. The supply chain consists of entities that actually produce the commodities, users of the commodities, and participants in between. These entities may trade commodity derivatives for hedging purposes. Other investors, sometimes referred to as speculators, trade commodity derivatives in search of profit based largely on changes or expected changes in the price of the underlying commodities. Non-hedging investors include retail and institutional investors, hedge funds, proprietary desks within financial institutions, and trading desks operating within the physical supply chain.

Commodity sectors include precious and base (i.e., industrial) metals, energy products, and agricultural products. Exhibit 15 shows some examples of each type. The relative importance, amount, and price of individual commodities evolve with society's preferences and needs. For example, the increasing industrialization of China, India, and other emerging markets has driven strong global demand for commodities. Developing markets need increasing amounts of oil, steel, and other materials to support the manufacturing, infrastructure development, and consumption demands of their populations. Emerging technologies, such as advanced cellphones and electric vehicles, may create demand for new materials or destroy demand for old resources. Thus, commodities of interest evolve over time.

Exhibit 15 Examples of Commodities

Sector	Sample Commodities
Energy	Oil, natural gas, electricity, coal
Base metals	Copper, aluminum, zinc, lead, tin, nickel
Precious metals	Gold, silver, platinum
Agriculture	Grains, livestock, coffee
Other	Carbon credits, freight, forest products

Commodities may be further classified on the basis of a variety of factors, including physical location and grade or quality. For example, there are many grades and locations of oil. Similarly, there are many grades and locations of wheat. Commodity derivative contracts specify such terms as quantity, quality, maturity date, and delivery location.

Commodity derivatives may be attractive to investors not only for the potential profits but also because of the perceptions that commodities are effective hedges against inflation (i.e., commodity prices historically have been positively correlated with inflation) and that commodities are effective for portfolio diversification (i.e., commodity returns have historically low correlations with returns of other investments). Institutional investors—particularly endowments, foundations, and, increasingly, corporate and public pension funds, as well as sovereign wealth funds—are allocating more of their portfolios to investments in commodities and commodity derivatives. There were $326 billion in commodity investments under management in 2015, compared with less than $20 billion in 2001.[31]

6.1 Commodity Derivatives and Indexes

The majority of commodity investing is implemented through derivatives, and commodity futures are a popular type of derivative.[32] Commodity derivatives include futures, forwards, options, and swaps. These contracts may trade on exchanges or over the counter (OTC). They are described as follows:

- Futures and forward contracts are obligations to buy or sell a specific amount of a given commodity at a fixed price, location, and date in the future. Futures contracts are exchange traded, are marked to market daily, and may or may not be settled with the delivery or receipt of the physical commodity at the end of the contract. Forward contracts trade OTC, and the expectation is that delivery and receipt of the physical commodity will occur. Counterparty risk is held at the exchange and clearing broker levels for futures contracts and between the two counterparties for forward contracts.
- Option contracts for commodities give their holders the right, but not the obligation, to buy or sell a specific amount of a given commodity at a specified price and delivery location on or before a specified date in the future. Options are generally on futures contracts and can be either exchange or OTC traded.
- Swap contracts are agreements to exchange streams of cash flows between two parties based on future commodity or commodity index prices. One party typically makes fixed payments in exchange for payments that depend on changes in a specified commodity or commodity index price.

Commodity indexes typically use the price of futures contracts on the commodities included in them rather than the prices of the commodities themselves in order to make themselves investable and replicable. As a result, the performance of a commodity index can differ from the performance of the underlying commodities. Commodity indexes also vary in the commodities included in them and the weighting methods used. Thus, they vary in their exposures to specific commodities or commodity sectors.

6.2 Other Commodity Investment Vehicles

Commodity exposure can be achieved through means other than direct investment in commodities or commodity derivatives. Alternative means of achieving commodity exposure include the following:

- Exchange-traded products (either funds or notes) may be suitable for investors who can buy only equity shares or who seek the simplicity of trading them through a standard brokerage account. Exchange-traded products (ETPs) may invest in commodities or futures of commodities. For example, the SPDR Gold Shares attempts to track the price of physical gold by holding bullion in vaults in accordance to its NAV. It owned more than $38 billion in gold bullion as of October 2016. ETPs may use leverage and may be long or short (also known as

---

31 Managed futures strategies; source: BarclayHedge (www.barclayhedge.com/research/indices/cta/Money_Under_Management.html).

32 Stoll and Whaley (2009) reported commodities indexing totaling $174 billion as of July 2009.

"inverse"). Similar to mutual funds and unit trusts, ETPs charge fees that are included in their expense ratios, although the ETP expense ratios are generally lower than those of most mutual funds.

- Common stock of companies exposed to a particular commodity—such as Royal Dutch Shell, which is exposed to oil—may be purchased. Investors may consider owning shares in a few commodity-exposed companies in order to have a small exposure to commodities. Due to company hedging policies and other idiosyncratic factors (e.g., interest rates, taxes, geographic exposure), the performance of the stocks may or may not track the performance of the underlying commodities.
- Managed futures funds are actively managed investment funds. Professional money managers invest in the futures market (and sometimes the forward market) on behalf of the funds. These funds historically focused on commodity futures, but today they primarily invest in other futures contracts, such as those based on equities, fixed income, or foreign exchange. Managed futures funds may concentrate on specific commodity sectors or may be broadly diversified. They are similar to hedge funds in that each fund has a GP and fees typically follow a "2 and 20" structure. Some funds operate similarly to mutual funds, with shares that are available to the general public, whereas others operate like hedge funds and restrict sales to high-net-worth and institutional investors. The former may appeal to retail investors because of the professional management, low minimum investment, and relatively high liquidity. Given their broad exposures to non-commodity asset classes, these funds are often more akin to global macro in style.
- Individual managed accounts are similar to managed futures funds but are managed for a single client (e.g., an individual or institution), rather than a fund.
- Funds that specialize in specific commodity sectors exist. For example, private energy partnerships, similar to private equity funds, are a popular way for institutions to gain exposure to the energy sector. Management fees can range from 1% to 3% of committed capital, with a lockup period of 10 years and extensions of 1- and 2-year periods. Publicly available energy mutual funds and unit trusts typically focus on the oil and gas sector and often act as fixed-income investments, paying out dividends from rents or capital gains. They may focus on upstream (drilling), midstream (refineries), or downstream (chemicals). Management fees for these funds are in line with those of other public equity managers and range from 0.4% to 1%.

6.3 Commodity Performance and Diversification Benefits

The arguments for investing in commodities include the potential for returns, portfolio diversification, and inflation protection. Investors may invest in commodities if they believe prices will increase in the short or intermediate terms. If commodity prices determine inflation index levels, then over time, on average, commodities should yield a zero real return but serve as a real hedge against inflation risk. Commodity futures contracts may offer liquidity or other premiums, creating the opportunity for a real return different from zero.

The portfolio diversification argument is based on the observation that commodities historically have behaved differently from stocks and bonds during the business cycle. Exhibit 16 shows the correlation between selected commodity, global equity, and global bond indexes. In the 25-year period from 1990 through 2014, commodities exhibited a low correlation with traditional assets; the correlations of commodities with global stocks and global bonds were 0.247 and 0.183, respectively. The correlations of stocks, bonds, and commodities are expected to be positive because each of the assets has some exposure to the global business cycle. Note that the selected commodity index—the S&P GSCI (Goldman Sachs Commodity Index)—is heavily weighted toward the energy sector and that each commodity may exhibit unique behavior.

Exhibit 16 Monthly Commodity Return Correlations, 1990–2014

	Global Stocks	Global Bonds	Commodities	One-Month Libor	US CPI
Global stocks	1.000	0.307	0.247	−0.054	−0.029
Global bonds		1.000	0.183	0.049	−0.038
Commodities			1.000	0.060	0.315
One-month Libor				1.000	0.166

Sources: Global stocks = MSCI ACWI; global bonds = Bloomberg Barclays Global Aggregate Index; commodities = S&P GSCI.

The argument for commodities as a hedge against inflation is related to the fact that some commodity prices affect inflation calculations. Commodities, especially energy and food, affect consumers' cost of living. The positive correlation of 0.315 between monthly commodity price changes and monthly changes in the US CPI supports this assertion. The monthly return correlations between the US CPI and global stocks and global bonds are close to zero. The volatility of commodity prices, especially energy and food, is much higher than that of reported consumer inflation. Consumer inflation is computed from many products used by consumers, including housing, that change more slowly than commodity prices. Commodity investments, especially when combined with leverage, exhibit high volatility and have led to many well-publicized losses among commodity players. Exhibit 17 provides a sample of these losses.

Exhibit 17 Large Commodity Investor Losses

Affected Company	Loss
Bank of Montreal (2007)	Wrong-way bets on natural gas led to a pre-tax loss of US$663 million.
Amaranth Advisors LLC (2006)	Bad bets on natural gas triggered US$6.6 billion of losses and closure of the US$12 billion hedge fund.
China Aviation Oil (Singapore) Corp. (2004)	Loss of US$550 million on speculative oil futures trades, forcing debt restructuring

Source: "The 20 Biggest Trading Disasters," *Telegraph* (January 2008).

6.4 Commodity Prices and Investments

Commodity spot prices are a function of supply and demand, costs of production and storage, value to users, and global economic conditions. Non-hedging investors with positions in physical commodities may be accumulating or divesting a particular commodity. Supplies of commodities are determined by production and inventory levels as well as the actions of non-hedging investors. Demand for commodities is determined by the needs of end users and the actions of non-hedging investors.

Commodity supplies cannot be altered quickly by producers because extended lead times often exist and affect production levels. For example, agricultural output may be altered by planting more crops and changing farming techniques, but at least one growing cycle is required before the actual output occurs. And for agricultural products, at least one factor that is outside of the producer's control—the weather—will significantly affect output. Increased oil and mining production may require a number of years to build the necessary infrastructure. Weather can also have a significant effect on oil production in parts of the world. For commodities, suppliers' inability to quickly respond to changes in demand levels may result in supply levels that are too low in times of economic growth and too high in times of economic slowing. In addition, despite advancing technology, the cost of new supply may grow over time. For example, the cost of new energy and mineral exploration tends to exceed that of past finds because the easy discoveries tend to be exploited first. If production costs are high, producers are unlikely to produce more than what is needed to meet anticipated demand and are unlikely to maintain more than modest levels of inventory, leading to the risk of shortages and price spikes.

Overall demand levels are influenced by global manufacturing dynamics and economic growth. Manufacturing needs can change in a period of months as orders and inventories vary. Investors seek to anticipate these changes by monitoring economic events, including government policy, inventory levels, and growth forecasts. When demand levels and investors' orders to buy and sell during a given period change quickly, the resulting mismatch of supply and demand may lead to price volatility.

6.4.1 *Pricing of Commodity Futures Contracts*

It is important to understand futures contracts and the sources of return for each commodity futures contract because commodity investments often involve the use of futures contracts. These contracts trade on exchanges. The buyer (i.e., the long side) of a futures contract is obligated to take delivery of the commodity or its cash equivalent based on the spot price at expiration and will pay a settlement price. The settlement price is calculated as specified in the contract based on its standard quantity (e.g., 1,000 barrels for Brent Crude Oil). In other words, the long side is obligated to buy the commodity at the final settlement price and take delivery at one of the locations specified in the contract. The long side of a futures contract increases in value when the underlying commodity increases in value. The seller of a futures contract (i.e., the short side) is obligated to deliver the commodity at the location specified in the contract or its cash equivalent based on the settlement price at expiration.

Parties to a futures contract are required to make an initial margin contribution on the contract (i.e., provide collateral) on their own margin account. Futures contracts and margin accounts are marked to market daily, which means that on a daily basis, the futures exchange calculates price changes in the contract and the values of the margin accounts increase or decrease depending on the price direction and positions. If the value in a margin account declines sufficiently, the investor will receive a margin call and will be required to make an additional payment into the margin account. If the investor is unable or unwilling to do so, her position will be closed by her clearing broker.

Given the characteristics of a commodity, the price of a futures contract (futures price) may be approximated by the following formula:[33]

Futures price ≈ Spot price $(1 + r)$ + Storage costs − Convenience yield

where r is the period's short-term risk-free interest rate. Arbitrage opportunities exist if the futures price differs from the spot price compounded at the risk-free rate. For example, if a commodity's spot price (current price available for immediate physical delivery) is 100, the risk-free rate is 5%, and the one-year futures price is 107 as opposed to 105, an arbitrageur can buy the commodity for 100 and sell a futures

33 Futures pricing is discussed in greater detail in Level II of the CFA Program curriculum.

contract for 107. Assuming no storage costs, when the commodity is delivered for 107, the arbitrageur earns 2 points in excess of that earned investing in the risk-free asset. However, commodities typically incur a storage cost. The buyer of a futures contract, in effect, gains access to the commodity in the future without buying it now and incurring storage costs. The futures price includes an amount for storage costs of the underlying commodity during the life of the contract. The storage and interest costs together are sometimes referred to as the "cost of carry" or the "carry." Finally, the buyer of the futures contract has no immediate access to the commodity but will receive it in the future. The buyer has given up the convenience of having physical possession of the commodity and having it immediately available for use. The futures price is adjusted for the loss of convenience; the convenience yield is subtracted to arrive at the futures price. The value of convenience may vary over time and across users. For example, the convenience yield to having heating oil in January in Canada is higher than the convenience yield to having heating oil in Canada in July or to having heating oil in Australia in January.

Futures prices may be higher or lower than spot prices depending on the convenience yield. When futures prices are higher than the spot price, the commodity forward curve is upward sloping and the prices are referred to as being in contango. *Contango* occurs when there is little or no convenience yield. When futures prices are lower than the spot price, the commodity forward curve is downward sloping and the prices are referred to as being in backwardation. *Backwardation* occurs when the convenience yield is high.

There are three sources of return for each commodity futures contract: the roll yield, the collateral yield, and the change in spot prices for the underlying commodity.

6.4.1.1 Roll Yield The term "roll yield" refers to the difference between a commodity's spot price and the price specified by its futures contract (or the difference between two futures contracts with different expiration dates). The formula shows that with a convenience yield high enough to position the futures price below the spot price, the price of the futures contract generally rolls up to the spot price as the expiry date of the futures contract approaches. This price convergence earns the bearer of the futures contract a positive roll yield. This explanation is called the *theory of storage*. An alternative theory, called the *hedging pressure hypothesis*, suggests the difference between the spot and futures prices is determined by user preferences between producers and consumers and risk premiums.

6.4.1.2 Collateral Yield The collateral yield component of commodity index returns is the interest earned on the collateral posted as a good-faith deposit for the futures contracts (plus invested cash up to the value of the underlying asset). In measuring this return component, index managers typically assume that futures contracts are fully collateralized and that the collateral is invested in risk-free assets. Thus, the returns on a passive investment in commodity futures are expected to equal the return on the collateral plus a risk premium (i.e., the hedging pressure hypothesis) or the convenience yield net of storage costs (i.e., the theory of storage).

6.4.1.3 Change in Spot Prices The primary determinant of spot (or current) prices is the relationship between current supply and demand, as discussed earlier.

INFRASTRUCTURE

7

The assets underlying infrastructure investments are real, capital intensive, and long-lived. These assets are intended for public use and provide essential services. An example is an airport. Most infrastructure assets are financed, owned, and operated by governments, but increasingly, infrastructure assets are being financed privately. The use of public–private partnerships (PPPs) is increasing with local, regional, or national governments partnering with investors. By the end of 2014, infrastructure funds had invested more than $200 billion in infrastructure projects, up from $6 billion in 2004.[34]

The intent of infrastructure investor(s) may be to lease the assets back to the government, to sell newly constructed assets to the government, or to hold and operate the assets. From an investment perspective, if the assets are being held and operated, the relatively inelastic demand for the assets and services is advantageous; regulation and the high costs of the assets create high barriers to entry, which give the provider of the services a strong competitive position. Maintenance and operating costs should also be considered.

Investors expect these assets to generate stable cash flows, which adjust for economic growth and inflation. Investors may also expect capital appreciation depending on the type of investment.

Investing in infrastructure may enable investors to add an income stream, to further diversify their portfolio by adding an asset class with a low correlation with other investments, and to gain some protection against inflation. Infrastructure investments, which are in long-lived assets, may also better match the longer-term liability structure of some investors, such as pension funds and life insurance companies. Allocations to infrastructure investments have increased not only because of renewed interest by investors (demand side) but also because of an increase in investment opportunities provided by governments due to their desire to expand the financing of infrastructure assets and to privatize the provision of services.

7.1 Categories of Infrastructure Investments

Infrastructure investments are frequently categorized on the basis of underlying assets. The broadest categorization is into economic and social infrastructure assets. Economic infrastructure assets are necessary to support economic activity, and they include such assets as transportation and utility assets. Transportation assets include such assets as roads, bridges, tunnels, airports, ports, and railway lines. Utility assets include assets to transmit, store, and distribute gas, water, and electricity; generate power; treat waste; and broadcast and transmit information. The latter assets may be categorized separately as communication assets. Social infrastructure assets are directed toward human activities and include such assets as educational, health care, and correctional facilities.

Infrastructure investments may also be categorized by the underlying asset's stage of development. Investing in existing infrastructure assets may be referred to as "brownfield investment." The assets may be currently owned by a government that wants to privatize the asset, to lease out the asset, or to sell and lease back the asset. Typically, some financial and operating history is available on the asset. Investing in infrastructure assets that are to be constructed may be referred to as "greenfield investment." The intent may be to hold and operate the assets or to lease or sell the assets to the government after construction.

34 Preqin Performance Analyst, 2015.

Infrastructure investments may also be categorized by the geographical location of the underlying assets. Infrastructure investments are available globally. Risks and expected returns may differ on the basis of the underlying asset's category, stage of development, and geographical location. The form of investment also affects risks and expected returns.

7.2 Forms of Infrastructure Investments

Infrastructure investments, similar to real estate investments, may take a variety of forms. The investment form potentially affects the investment's liquidity as well as the cash flows and income streams to the investor. An investor may invest directly in the underlying assets, but most investors invest indirectly. Investing directly in infrastructure provides control over the asset and the opportunity to capture the asset's full value. However, it entails a large investment, resulting in concentration and liquidity risks, and the assets must be managed and operated. Indirect investment vehicles include investment in an infrastructure fund (similar in structure to private equity funds) and infrastructure ETFs, as well as in shares of companies. Investors concerned about liquidity and diversification may choose to invest through publicly traded infrastructure securities and/or master limited partnerships.

Publicly traded infrastructure securities provide the benefit of not only liquidity but also reasonable fees, transparent governance, market prices, and the ability to diversify across underlying assets. Investors should be aware, however, that publicly traded infrastructure securities represent a small segment of the infrastructure investment universe and tend to be clustered in categories of assets. Master limited partnerships (MLPs) trade on exchanges and are pass-through entities similar to REITs. As with REITs, regulations may vary across countries, and income is passed through to the investors for taxation. MLPs generally distribute most free cash flow to their investors. Typically, the GP manages the partnership, receives a fee, and holds a small partnership interest, with LPs owning the remaining majority partnership interest.

7.3 Risk and Return Overview

The lowest-risk infrastructure investments have more-stable cash flows and higher dividend payout ratios but also typically have fewer growth opportunities and lower expected returns compared with higher-risk infrastructure investments. For example, an investment in an MLP with a brownfield investment in an asset that is being leased back to a government, such as a school, or in an asset with a history of steady cash flows, such as certain toll roads, represents a low-risk infrastructure investment. An investment in a fund that is building a new power plant without operating history (a greenfield investment) is riskier.

Risks include revenues being different from expectations, leverage creating financing risk, operational risk, and construction risk. An inherent risk for many infrastructure investments is regulatory risk. Because essential services are often being provided, governments typically regulate many aspects of infrastructure investments, including the sale of the underlying assets; operations of the assets, including service quality; and prices/profit margins. Global infrastructure investing introduces additional risks, such as currency, political, and profit repatriation risks.

Preqin maintains a return series of private funds investing in infrastructure deals. Standard & Poor's, FTSE, and other firms publish indexes of publicly traded infrastructure companies.

OTHER ALTERNATIVE INVESTMENTS

8

Numerous other investments do not fit within the definition of traditional investments (i.e., long-only investments in stocks, bonds, and cash) and may be considered alternative investments. Many of these other investments are categorized as collectibles.

Collectibles are tangible assets such as antiques and fine art, fine wine, rare stamps and coins, jewelry and watches, and sports memorabilia. Collectibles do not provide current income, but they can potentially provide long-term capital appreciation, diversify a portfolio, and be a source of enjoyment while held. There is no guarantee, however, that an investor will realize any of these benefits. Collectibles can fluctuate dramatically in value and be highly illiquid, with potential difficulty in realizing gains. Transactions can occur in a number of ways and settings, including through professional auctioneers; in local flea markets, online auctions, garage sales, and antique stores; or directly with personal collectors. Investors must have a degree of expertise; otherwise, one may be vulnerable to fads, fakes, and fraud. Also, some collectibles must be stored in appropriate conditions to preserve their quality and avoid declines in value because of the asset's deterioration. Wine should be cellared, art should be kept in a humidity- and temperature-controlled environment, and coins and stamps must be handled with care to preserve their value. Although some collectibles (e.g., some great wines; fine art; and rare stamps, coins, and trading cards) have experienced great appreciation, this result is by no means the norm.

The popularity of art as an investment has led to the creation of a number of art price indexes. For example, Artprice provides statistics, econometric data, and indexes to help measure returns on artworks. Another company that develops indexes, Art Market Research, does not restrict itself to art but has more than 500 indexes in three broad categories: Painting; Antiques, Collectibles, Etc.; and Other Markets. These indexes range from very broad (e.g., Painting [General] and Antiques [General]) to more specific (e.g., Chinese Ceramics [General] and Ancient Coins [General]) to very specific (e.g., Wrist-Watches Patek Philippe, Continental Flint-Lock Pistols 1700–1800, and in wine, Château Lafite 1961). Subscribers are even able to specify parameters and create their own indexes. Christie's first published an index of wine auction prices (listed by château) in 1972.

RISK MANAGEMENT OVERVIEW

9

Alternative investments pose unusual challenges for investors seeking to manage risk. They are often characterized by asymmetric risk and return profiles, limited portfolio transparency, and illiquidity. Investors in alternatives may be exposed to a variety of risks, including operational risk, financial risk, counterparty risk, and liquidity risk. The returns to some types of alternatives, such as private equity, may rely to a great extent on manager skill rather than on general asset class performance. For these reasons, traditional risk and return measures (such as mean return, standard deviation of returns, and beta) may not provide an adequate picture of alternative investments' characteristics. Moreover, these measures may be unreliable or not representative of specific investments.

9.1 Investment and Risk Management Process

Investment risk management is not solely the responsibility of either the investor or the manager of an investment portfolio. The investor, possibly in consultation with others, decides on an allocation to alternative investments. The investor then needs to choose the vehicles and managers of the investments as well as the amounts that will be allocated to each alternative investment class and manager. Risk has to be taken into account and due diligence conducted in making these decisions. The investment portfolio manager has to make investment decisions consistent with the portfolio's established investment policies or amend those policies appropriately. Investor due diligence investigates more thoroughly how the portfolio manager effectively manages portfolio risk. Pension consultants, wealth managers, and individual investors all need to recognize that risk management processes can differ substantially between different alternative investment categories.

9.1.1 *Risk Management Issues*

Risks vary among alternative investments. The risks associated with investing in private markets (e.g., private equity funds and real estate ownership) differ from the risks associated with investing in public markets (e.g., commodity futures and REITs). Private equity and direct real estate ownership may involve selecting companies or properties, managing them, and then selling them years later. Private equity and direct real estate funds may have long lockup periods. As a result, investors' capital may be tied up for many years. Periodic valuations can be challenging because of sparse transactions. As a result, any malfeasance or mismanagement may go undetected for years, so investor due diligence and auditing is more critical in these circumstances. The illiquid nature of alternative investments also means that poor manager selection can create a lingering drag on the portfolio. Limited partnership vehicles may limit the visibility of underlying holdings and liquidity because the legal structure stands between investors and their assets.

Portfolios of publicly traded securities are more liquid and have prices that are more timely and observable than those of privately held assets. For investors who seek liquidity, such publicly traded securities as shares of REITs, ETFs, and publicly traded private equity firms may serve as the means for investing in alternatives. Finally, the manager's strategy may be available via a separate account, so holdings are more transparent and valuation issues are more easily settled.

9.1.2 *Risk Issues for Implementation*

For allocation purposes, the investor should recognize that historical returns and the standard deviation of those returns using indexes may not be representative of the returns and volatility of specific alternative investment funds. This often implies that those investments' reported correlations with other investments may vary from the index correlations. As is always the case, even if these are relevant and representative measures of historical performance, past performance is not necessarily representative of future performance. The performance of alternative investments can be highly correlated with the business cycle, especially for commodities and real estate investments, and may be susceptible to bubbles (i.e., much higher prices than are justified by fundamentals) owing to money flow and investor sentiment. Investors should consider market conditions and the manager's skill in those conditions before making allocation changes.

When selecting managers or funds, the investor should recognize that returns and risks may differ significantly among individual managers or funds and the overall investment class. Large institutional investors deal with this challenge by diversifying across managers or funds, but this approach may not be practical for smaller investors. As a result, these smaller investors may be forced to invest in publicly traded securities (e.g., ETFs) or with a limited number of large, diversified funds.

Alternative investment portfolio managers need to be mindful of several risks. In the case of illiquid investments, most notably in private equity or venture capital, there is a real possibility of 100% loss of equity on individual investments. Even liquid investments, such as managed futures, can experience high volatility. As a result, portfolios should be diversified sufficiently to reduce the possibility of this outcome at the portfolio level. Investors commonly require managers to follow diversification concentration guidelines or look for managers that hedge more fully to limit these risks. At the same time, the manager should avoid diluting the opportunity for making substantial returns by arbitrarily identifying a target number of investments and, in the process, selecting inferior investments. Finally, investors and managers should describe in fund guidelines the management of the risk associated with the use of leverage.

Performance fee structures, although high, may encourage alignment of interests between investors and managers. Established portfolio managers, however, may seek to attract large amounts of capital and to profit from the management fees based on AUM or committed capital without seeking superior performance. Performance fees may also encourage hedge fund managers who experience a large loss to liquidate their funds instead of working them back to par. Investors, therefore, should note the impact of fund size and capacity as well as the manager commitment to the clients.

9.1.3 *Due Diligence Issues Regarding Risk*

Due diligence of alternative investment managers necessitates special procedures beyond the process required for a manager of a portfolio of publicly traded securities. Historical performance measures may be unreliable or not representative as a result of intermediate valuation estimates and narrow portfolio diversification. With the limited transparency and long horizons of many alternative investments, the honesty of the company's staff needs to be carefully reviewed.

Hedge funds will have trading desks much like long-only investment firms, but private equity and real estate companies usually make investment decisions via an investment committee of partners. The investment committee may or may not include external non-executive directors or subject matter experts. The committee votes on the rationale, analysis, and suitability of every investment and requires a majority in favor before investor funds are committed. This committee may also oversee and vote on investments' exit strategies, including timing and realization price.

Independent valuation of illiquid underlying assets (an audit) should be performed regularly. Often, this analysis is done in conjunction with a portfolio review explaining the performance of every transaction in detail, its status, and the future strategy for the portfolio. Limits on security type, leverage, sector, geography, and individual positions should be well defined in the offering memorandum, and the positions should be carefully monitored by the manager and regularly reported to clients.

Hedge fund risk is often monitored by a chief risk officer, who should be separated from the investment process. As part of the risk management process, a hedge fund needs to establish and maintain limits on leverage, sector, and individual positions. Investments in physical commodities may be subject to counterparty risks, and public security hedge funds (those in equity, fixed-income, and managed futures strategies) are particularly affected by leverage risks. The exposure to counterparty risk and leverage risk should be regularly monitored and reported. Policies limiting leverage, positions, and sectors as well as counterparty exposures may be adopted.

One issue for investors is that hedge funds and commodity funds might seek to keep their positions and strategies private to extend the life of their alpha process (i.e., their process for adding value through active investing) and preserve their relative expertise. This lack of transparency makes it difficult for the investor to effectively manage diversification across funds and to conduct adequate due diligence.

9.2 Risk–Return Measures

The Sharpe ratio is a risk–return measure frequently reported because of its ease of calculation and understandability. However, the Sharpe ratio is not the appropriate risk–return measure for some alternative investments because measures of return and standard deviation may be irrelevant or unreliable given the assets' illiquid nature. The illiquid nature of these assets means that estimates, rather than observable transaction prices, may have been used for valuation purposes. As a result, returns may be smoothed and/or overstated and the volatility of returns understated. Also, the use of standard deviation to measure risk ignores the diversification effect for a broad portfolio of managers and alternative investments.

Many alternative investments do not exhibit close-to-normal distributions of returns, which is a crucial assumption for standard deviation's validity as a comprehensive risk measure. Alternative investment returns tend to be leptokurtic, or negatively skewed (in other words, they have fat tails characterized by positive average returns and long tails downside characterized by potential extreme losses). For this reason, a measure of downside risk, ideally non-normal, would be useful. Downside risk measures focus on the left side of the return distribution curve, where losses occur. For example, value at risk (VaR) is a measure of the minimum amount of loss expected for a given period at a given level of probability. In other words, this measure can answer such questions as, What is the minimum amount expected to be lost in a year with a 5% probability? This measure, however, if it is calculated using standard deviation, will underestimate the VaR for a negatively skewed distribution. Shortfall or safety-first risk measures the probability that the portfolio value will fall below some minimum acceptable level over a given period. In other words, this measure can answer such questions as, What is the probability of losing 20% of principal in any given year? Shortfall risk also uses standard deviation as the measure of risk. The Sortino ratio, another risk–return measure, uses downside deviation, rather than standard deviation, as a measure of risk. Assuming normal probability distributions when calculating these measures will lead to underestimating downside risk for a negatively skewed distribution.

Understanding and evaluating "tail events"—low-probability, severe instances of stress—is an important yet extraordinarily difficult aspect of the risk management process. Stress testing/scenario analysis is often used as a complement to VaR to develop a better understanding of a portfolio's potential loss under both normal and stressed market conditions. Stress testing involves estimating losses under extremely unfavorable conditions. Quantitative or systematic processes are likely easier to examine than more discretionary investment approaches.

9.3 Due Diligence Overview

Manager selection is a critical factor in portfolio performance. A manager should have a verifiable track record and display a high level of expertise and experience with the asset type. The asset management team should be assigned an appropriate workload and provided sufficient resources. Moreover, it should be rewarded with an effective compensation package to ensure alignment of interest, continuity, motivation, and thoughtful oversight of assets.

Fraud, although infrequent, is always a possibility. The investor should be skeptical of unusually good and overly consistent reported performance. Third-party custody of assets and independent verification of results can help reduce the chance of an investor being defrauded. Diversification among managers is also wise. Finally, separate accounts make theft more difficult because the investor retains custody of the assets and sometimes can select the prime broker or other service providers, binding them to the client's interest.

For an investor considering a new investment, a proper due diligence process should be carried out to ensure that the targeted investment is in compliance with its prospectus and that it will meet his investment strategy, risk and return objectives, and restrictions. Existing investors should monitor results and fund holdings to determine whether a fund has performed in line with expectations and continues to comply with its prospectus.

Exhibit 18 lists key items that should be considered in a typical due diligence process.

Exhibit 18 A Typical Due Diligence Process

Organization	■ Experience and quality of management team, compensation, and staffing ■ Analysis of prior and current funds ■ Track record/alignment of interests ■ Reputation and quality of third-party service providers (e.g., lawyers, auditors, prime brokers)
Portfolio management	■ Investment process ■ Target markets/asset types/strategies ■ Sourcing of investments ■ Role of operating partners ■ Underwriting ■ Environmental and engineering review process ■ Integration of asset management/acquisitions/dispositions ■ Disposition process, including its initiation and execution
Operations and controls	■ Reporting and accounting methodology ■ Audited financial statements and other internal controls ■ Valuations—frequency and approach(es) ■ Insurance and contingency plans
Risk management	■ Fund policies and limits ■ Risk management policy ■ Portfolio risk and key risk factors ■ Leverage and currency—risks/constraints/hedging
Legal review	■ Fund structure ■ Registrations ■ Existing/prior litigation
Fund terms	■ Fees (management and performance) and expenses ■ Contractual terms ■ Investment period and fund term and extensions ■ Carried interest ■ Distributions ■ Conflicts ■ Limited partners' rights ■ "Key person" and/or other termination procedures

Alternative investing may add value to an investor's portfolio. To be effective, however, alternative investing requires thoughtful implementation, including consideration of the amount to allocate to alternative investments and of diversification among alternative investments. Valuation issues, manager selection, and risk management should also be considered.

SUMMARY

This reading has provided an overview of the characteristics, potential benefits, and risks of alternative investments. It also described features of some categories of alternative investments. Including alternative investments in an investor's portfolio may result in a higher Sharpe ratio for the overall portfolio because of diversification benefits. However, these benefits do not come without associated risks. It is important for investors to understand these risks before including alternative investments in their portfolios. Some key points of the reading are summarized as follows:

- Alternative investments are supplemental strategies to traditional long-only positions in stocks, bonds, and cash. Alternative investments include investments in long–short public market strategies and such less common assets as private equity, real estate, infrastructure, and commodities. Often these investments are made via limited partnerships and special purpose vehicles.
- Alternative investment strategies are typically active, return-seeking strategies that often have different risks from those in indexed public markets.
- Characteristics common to many alternative investments, when compared with traditional investments, include the following: lower liquidity, less regulation, lower transparency, higher fees, and limited and potentially problematic historical risk and return data.
- Alternative investments often have complex legal and tax considerations and may be highly leveraged.
- Alternative investments are attractive to investors because of the potential for portfolio diversification (reduced risk) and higher portfolio returns when added to a portfolio of traditional investments.
- The risks associated with alternative investments must be factored into the investment decision-making process.
- Many alternative investments are valued by using estimated values rather than actual market prices. These values are then reported to index providers for performance-reporting purposes. As a result, the volatility of returns and correlation of returns vis-à-vis traditional investments will tend to be underestimated. It is important to identify and understand how alternative investments are valued, particularly owing to illiquidity.
- Indexes for alternative investments may be subject to a variety of biases, including survivorship and backfill biases.
- Many alternative investments, such as hedge and private equity funds, use a partnership structure with a general partner that manages the business and limited partners (investors) who own fractional interests in the partnership.
- The general partner typically receives a management fee based on assets under management or committed capital (the former is common to hedge funds and the latter is common to private equity funds) and an incentive fee based on realized profits.
- Hurdle rates, high-water marks, lockup and notice periods, and clawback provisions are often specified in a partnership agreement.
- The fee structure affects the returns to investors (limited partners) in such alternative investments as hedge and private equity funds.
- Hedge funds are typically classified by strategy. One such classification includes four broad categories of strategies: event driven, relative value, macro, and equity hedge.

- Primary private equity fund strategies include leveraged buyouts, venture capital, development capital, and distressed investing. Leveraged buyouts and venture capital are the dominant strategies.
- Real estate investing includes direct and indirect ownership of real estate property and lending against real estate property.
- Real estate property has some unique features, including basic indivisibility, heterogeneity (no two properties are identical), and fixed location.
- The required amount to directly invest in real estate may be large in order to achieve adequate diversification, and the investment may be relatively illiquid. Various investment forms, such as REITs and mortgage securitizations, partially address these issues.
- Commodity investments may involve investing in actual physical commodities or in producers of commodities, but more typically, these investments are made using commodity derivatives (futures or swaps).
- Returns to commodity investing are based on changes in price and do not include an income stream, such as dividends, interest, or rent (apart from income earned on the collateral).
- Infrastructure assets are capital intensive, long-lived, real assets that are intended for public use and provide essential services. Investors expect these assets to generate stable cash flows, which typically are adjusted upward with economic growth and inflation, and they may also expect capital appreciation of the infrastructure assets.
- Category, stage of development, and geographic location of underlying assets and the form of infrastructure investment affect risks and expected returns of infrastructure investments.
- Managing risks associated with alternative investments can be challenging because these investments are often characterized by asymmetric risk/return profiles, limited portfolio transparency, and illiquidity.
- Traditional risk and return measures (such as mean return, standard deviation of returns, and beta) may provide an inadequate picture of alternative investments' risk and return characteristics. Moreover, these measures may be unreliable or not representative of specific investments.
- Operational, financial, counterparty, and liquidity risks may be key considerations for those investing in alternative investments.
- It is critical to perform due diligence to assess whether or not (a) the manager can effectively pursue the proposed investment strategy; (b) the appropriate organizational structure and policies for managing investments, operations, risk, and compliance are in place; and (c) the fund terms appear reasonable.
- The inclusion of alternative investments in a portfolio, including the amounts to allocate, should be considered in the context of an investor's risk–return objectives, constraints, and preferences.

REFERENCES

Brooks, C., and H. Kat. 2002. "The Statistical Properties of Hedge Fund Index Returns and Their Implications for Investors." *Journal of Alternative Investments* 5 (2): 26–44.

Heisler, J., C. Knittel, J. Neumann, and S. Stewart. 2007. "Why Do Institutional Plan Sponsors Hire and Fire Their Investment Managers?" *Journal of Business and Economic Studies* 13 (1): 88–118.

Kaplan, Steven N., and Antoinette Schoar. 2005. "Private Equity Performance, Returns, Persistence, and Capital Flows." *Journal of Finance* 60 (4): 1791–1823 .

Stewart, S., J. Heisler, C. Knittel, and J. Neumann. 2009. "Absence of Value: An Analysis of Investment Allocation Decisions by Institutional Plan Sponsors." *Financial Analysts Journal* 65 (6): 34–51. .

Stoll, Hans R., and Robert E. Whaley. 2009. "Commodity Index Investing and Commodity Futures Prices." Working paper, Vanderbilt University.

Woodward, Susan, and Robert Hall. 2004. "Benchmarking the Returns to Venture." National Bureau of Economic Research (January).

PRACTICE PROBLEMS

1 Which of the following is *least likely* to be considered an alternative investment?

A Real estate

B Commodities

C Long-only equity funds

2 Private equity funds are *most likely* to use:

A merger arbitrage strategies.

B leveraged buyouts.

C market-neutral strategies.

3 An investor is seeking an investment that can take long and short positions, may use multi-strategies, and historically exhibits low correlation with a traditional investment portfolio. The investor's goals will be *best* satisfied with an investment in:

A real estate.

B a hedge fund.

C a private equity fund.

4 Relative to traditional investments, alternative investments are *least likely* to be characterized by:

A high levels of transparency.

B limited historical return data.

C significant restrictions on redemptions.

5 Alternative investment funds are typically managed:

A actively.

B to generate positive beta return.

C assuming that markets are efficient.

6 Compared with traditional investments, alternative investments are *more likely* to have:

A greater use of leverage.

B long-only positions in liquid assets.

C more transparent and reliable risk and return data.

7 The potential benefits of allocating a portion of a portfolio to alternative investments include:

A ease of manager selection.

B improvement in the portfolio's risk–return relationship.

C accessible and reliable measures of risk and return.

8 An investor may prefer a single hedge fund to a fund of funds if he seeks:

A due diligence expertise.

B better redemption terms.

C a less complex fee structure.

9 Hedge funds are similar to private equity funds in that both:

A are typically structured as partnerships.

B assess management fees based on assets under management.

C do not earn an incentive fee until the initial investment is repaid.

10 An investor seeks a current income stream as a component of total return, and desires an investment that historically has low correlation with other asset classes. The investment *most likely* to achieve the investor's goals is:

A timberland.

B collectibles.

C commodities.

11 Both event-driven and macro hedge fund strategies use:

A long–short positions.

B a top-down approach.

C long-term market cycles.

12 Hedge fund losses are *most likely* to be magnified by a:

A margin call.

B lockup period.

C redemption notice period.

13 The first stage of financing at which a venture capital fund *most likely* invests is the:

A seed stage.

B mezzanine stage.

C angel investing stage.

14 What is the most significant drawback of a repeat sales index to measure returns to real estate?

A Sample selection bias

B Understatement of volatility

C Reliance on subjective appraisals

15 Compared with direct investment in infrastructure, publicly traded infrastructure securities are characterized by:

A higher concentration risk.

B more-transparent governance.

C greater control over the infrastructure assets.

16 An equity hedge fund following a fundamental growth strategy uses fundamental analysis to identify companies that are *most likely* to:

A be undervalued.

B be either undervalued or overvalued.

C experience high growth and capital appreciation.

17 Which of the following is most likely to be available when conducting hedge fund due diligence?

A The benchmark used by the fund

B Information on systems risk management

C Details of investment strategies and processes

18 A private equity fund desiring to realize an immediate and complete cash exit from a portfolio company is *most likely* to pursue a(n):

A IPO.

B trade sale.

C recapitalization.

19 As the loan-to-value ratio increases for a real estate investment, risk *most likely* increases for:

A debt investors only.

B equity investors only.

C both debt and equity investors.

20 Which of the following forms of infrastructure investments is the most liquid?

A An unlisted infrastructure mutual fund

B A direct investment in a greenfield project

C An exchange-traded master limited partnership (MLP)

21 An investor chooses to invest in a brownfield rather than a greenfield infrastructure project. The investor is *most likely* motivated by:

A growth opportunities.

B predictable cash flows.

C higher expected returns.

22 The privatization of an existing hospital is best described as:

A a greenfield investment.

B a brownfield investment.

C an economic infrastructure investment.

23 A hedge fund invests primarily in distressed debt. Quoted market prices are available for the underlying holdings but they trade infrequently. Which of the following will the hedge fund *most likely* use in calculating net asset value for trading purposes?

A Average quotes

B Average quotes adjusted for liquidity

C Bid prices for short positions and ask prices for long positions

24 Angel investing capital is typically provided in which stage of financing?

A Later-stage.

B Formative-stage.

C Mezzanine-stage.

25 If a commodity's forward curve is in contango, the component of a commodities futures return *most likely* to reflect this is:

A spot prices.

B the roll yield.

C the collateral yield.

26 United Capital is a hedge fund with $250 million of initial capital. United charges a 2% management fee based on assets under management at year end, and a 20% incentive fee based on returns in excess of an 8% hurdle rate. In its first year, United appreciates 16%. Assume management fees are calculated using end-of-period valuation. The investor's net return assuming the performance fee is calculated net of the management fee is *closest* to:

A 11.58%.

B 12.54%.

C 12.80%.

27 Capricorn Fund of Funds invests GBP 100 million in each of Alpha Hedge Fund and ABC Hedge Fund. Capricorn FOF has a "1 and 10" fee structure. Management fees and incentive fees are calculated independently at the end of each year. After one year, net of their respective management and incentive fees, the investment in Alpha is valued at GBP80 million and the investment in ABC is valued at GBP140 million. The annual return to an investor in Capricorn, net of fees assessed at the fund of funds level, is *closest* to:

A 7.9%.

B 8.0%.

C 8.1%.

28 The following information applies to Rotunda Advisors, a hedge fund:

- $288 million in assets under management (AUM) as of prior year-end
- 2% management fee (based on year-end AUM)
- 20% incentive fee calculated:
  - net of management fee
  - using a 5% soft hurdle rate
  - using a high-water mark (high-water mark is $357 million)
- Current year fund return is 25%

The total fee earned by Rotunda in the current year is *closest* to:

A $7.20 million.

B $20.16 million.

C $21.60 million.

29 A hedge fund has the following fee structure:

Annual management fee based on year-end AUM	2%
Incentive fee	20%
Hurdle rate before incentive fee collection starts	4%
Current high-water mark	$610 million

The fund has a value of $583.1 million at the beginning of the year. After one year, it has a value of $642 million before fees. The net return to an investor for this year is *closest* to:

A 6.72%.

B 6.80%.

C 7.64%.

30 Ash Lawn Partners, a fund of hedge funds, has the following fee structure:

- 2/20 underlying fund fees with incentive fees calculated independently
- Ash Lawn fees are calculated net of all underlying fund fees
- 1% management fee (based on year-end market value)
- 10% incentive fee calculated net of management fee
- The fund and all underlying funds have no hurdle rate or high-water mark fee conditions

In the latest year, Ash Lawn's fund value increased from $100 million to $133 million before deduction of management and incentive fees of the fund or underlying funds. Based on the information provided, the total fee earned by *all* funds in the aggregate is *closest* to:

A $11.85 million.

B $12.75 million.

C $12.87 million.

31 Risks in infrastructure investing are *most likely* greatest when the project involves:

A construction of infrastructure assets.

B investment in existing infrastructure assets.

C investing in assets that will be leased back to a government.

32 An investor in a private equity fund is concerned that the general partner can receive incentive fees in excess of the agreed-on incentive fees by making distributions over time based on profits earned rather than making distributions only at exit from investments of the fund. Which of the following is most likey to protect the investor from the general partner receiving excess fees?

A A high hurdle rate

B A clawback provision

C A lower capital commitment

33 Until the committed capital is fully drawn down and invested, the management fee for a private equity fund is based on:

A invested capital.

B committed capital.

C assets under management.

34 An analyst wanting to assess the downside risk of an alternative investment is *least likely* to use the investment's:

A Sortino ratio.

B value at risk (VaR).

C standard deviation of returns.

35 An effective risk management process used by alternative investment funds *most likely* includes:

A in-house valuations.

B internal custody of assets.

C segregation of risk and investment process duties.

SOLUTIONS

1 C is correct. Long-only equity funds are typically considered traditional investments and real estate and commodities are typically classified as alternative investments.

2 B is correct. The majority of private equity activity involves leveraged buyouts. Merger arbitrage and market neutral are strategies used by hedge funds.

3 B is correct. Hedge funds may use a variety of strategies (event-driven, relative value, macro and equity hedge), generally have a low correlation with traditional investments, and may take long and short positions.

4 A is correct. Alternative investments are characterized as typically having low levels of transparency.

5 A is correct. There are many approaches to managing alternative investment funds but typically these funds are actively managed.

6 A is correct. Investing in alternative investments is often pursued through such special vehicles as hedge funds and private equity funds, which have flexibility to use leverage. Alternative investments include investments in such assets as real estate, which is an illiquid asset, and investments in such special vehicles as private equity and hedge funds, which may make investments in illiquid assets and take short positions. Obtaining information on strategies used and identifying reliable measures of risk and return are challenges of investing in alternatives.

7 B is correct. Adding alternative investments to a portfolio may provide diversification benefits because of these investments' less than perfect correlation with other assets in the portfolio. As a result, allocating a portion of one's funds to alternatives could potentially result in an improved risk–return relationship. Challenges to allocating a portion of a portfolio to alternative investments include obtaining reliable measures of risk and return as well as selecting portfolio managers for the alternative investments.

8 C is correct. Hedge funds of funds have multi-layered fee structures, while the fee structure for a single hedge fund is less complex. Funds of funds presumably have some expertise in conducting due diligence on hedge funds and may be able to negotiate more favorable redemption terms than could an individual investor in a single hedge fund.

9 A is correct. Private equity funds and hedge funds are typically structured as partnerships where investors are limited partners (LP) and the fund is the general partner (GP). The management fee for private equity funds is based on committed capital whereas for hedge funds the management fees are based on assets under management. For most private equity funds, the general partner does not earn an incentive fee until the limited partners have received their initial investment back.

10 A is correct. Timberland offers an income stream based on the sale of timber products as a component of total return and has historically generated returns not highly correlated with other asset classes.

11 A is correct. Long–short positions are used by both types of hedge funds to potentially profit from anticipated market or security moves. Event-driven strategies use a bottom-up approach and seek to profit from short-term events typically involving a corporate action, such as an acquisition or a restructuring. Macro strategies seek to profit from expected movements in evolving economic variables.

12 A is correct. Margin calls can magnify losses. To meet the margin call, the hedge fund manager may be forced to liquidate a losing position in a security, which, depending on the position size, could exert further price pressure on the security, resulting in further losses. Restrictions on redemptions, such as lockup and notice periods, may allow the manager to close positions in a more orderly manner and minimize forced-sale liquidations of losing positions.

13 A is correct. The seed stage supports market research and product development and is generally the first stage at which venture capital funds invest. The seed stage follows the angel investing stage. In the angel investing stage, funds are typically provided by individuals (often friends or family), rather than a venture capital fund, to assess an idea's potential and to transform the idea into a plan. Mezzanine-stage financing is provided by venture capital funds to prepare the portfolio company for its IPO.

14 A is correct. A repeat sales index uses the changes in price of repeat-sale properties to construct the index. Sample selection bias is a significant drawback because the properties that sell in each period vary and may not be representative of the overall market the index is meant to cover. The properties that transact are not a random sample and may be biased toward properties that changed in value. Understated volatility and reliance on subjective appraisals by experts are drawbacks of an appraisal index.

15 B is correct. Publicly traded infrastructure securities, which include shares of companies, exchange-traded funds, and listed funds that invest in infrastructure, provide the benefits of transparent governance, liquidity, reasonable fees, market prices, and the ability to diversify across underlying assets. Direct investment in infrastructure involves a large capital investment in any single project, resulting in high concentration risks. Direct investment in infrastructure provides control over the assets and the opportunity to capture the assets' full value.

16 C is correct. Fundamental growth strategies take long positions in companies identified, using fundamental analysis, to have high growth and capital appreciation. Fundamental value strategies use fundamental analysis to identify undervalued companies. Market-neutral strategies use quantitative and/or fundamental analysis to identify under- and overvalued companies.

17 A is correct. It should be possible to identify the benchmark against which the fund gauges its performance in the hedge fund due diligence process. It should also be possible to establish the range of markets in which the fund invests as well as the fund's general strategy. Hedge funds consider their strategies, systems, and processes to be proprietary and are unwilling to provide much information to potential investors.

18 B is correct. Private equity funds can realize an immediate cash exit in a trade sale. Using this strategy, the portfolio company is typically sold to a strategic buyer.

19 C is correct. The higher the loan-to-value ratio, the higher leverage is for a real estate investment, which increases the risk to both debt and equity investors.

20 C is correct. A publicly traded infrastructure security, such as an exchange-traded MLP, provides the benefit of liquidity.

21 B is correct. A brownfield investment is an investment in an existing infrastructure asset, which is more likely to have a history of steady cash flows compared with that of a greenfield investment. Growth opportunities and returns are expected to be lower for brownfield investments, which are less risky than greenfield investments.

22 B is correct. Investing in an existing infrastructure asset with the intent to privatize, lease, or sell and lease back the asset is referred to as a brownfield investment. An economic infrastructure asset supports economic activity and includes such assets as transportation and utility assets. Hospitals are social infrastructure assets, which are focused on human activities.

23 B is correct. Many practitioners believe that liquidity discounts are necessary to reflect fair value. This has resulted in some funds having two NAVs - for trading and reporting. The fund may use average quotes for reporting purposes but apply liquidity discounts for trading purposes.

24 B is correct. Formative-stage financing occurs when the company is still in the process of being formed and encompasses several financing steps. Angel investing capital is typically raised in this early stage of financing.

25 B is correct. Roll yield refers to the difference between the spot price of a commodity and the price specified by its futures contract (or the difference between two futures contracts with different expiration dates). When futures prices are higher than the spot price, the commodity forward curve is upward sloping, and the prices are referred to as being in contango. Contango occurs when there is little or no convenience yield.

26 B is correct. The net investor return is 12.54%, calculated as:

End of year capital = \$250 million × 1.16 = \$290 million

Management fee = \$290 million × 2% = \$5.8 million

Hurdle amount = 8% of \$250 million = \$20 million;

Incentive fee = (\$290 – \$250 – \$20 – \$5.8) million × 20% = \$2.84 million

Total fees to United Capital = (\$5.8 + \$2.84) million = \$8.64 million

Investor net return: (\$290 – \$250 – \$8.64) / \$250 = 12.54%

27 A is correct because the net investor return is 7.9%, calculated as:

First, note that "1 and 10" refers to a 1% management fee, and a 10% incentive fee.

End of year capital = GBP140 million + GBP80 million = GBP220 million

Management fee = GBP220 million × 1% = GBP2.2 million

Incentive fee = (GBP220 – GBP200) million × 10% = GBP2 million

Total fees to Capricorn = (GBP2.2 + GBP2) million = GBP4.2 million

Investor net return: (GBP220 – GBP200 – GBP4.2) / GBP200 = 7.9%

28 A is correct. Rotunda earns a management fee of \$7.20 million but does not earn an incentive fee because the year-end fund value net of management fee does not exceed the high-water mark of \$357 million.

Rotunda fees:

End-of-year AUM = Prior year-end AUM × (1 + Fund return) = \$288 million × 1.25 = \$360 million

\$360 million × 2% = \$7.20 million management fee

\$360 million – \$7.2 million = \$352.8 million AUM net of management fee

The year-end AUM net of fees does not exceed the \$357 million high-water mark. Therefore, no incentive fee is earned.

29 C is correct. The management fee for the year is

$\$642 \times 0.02 = \$12.84$ million.

Because the ending value exceeds the high-water mark, the hedge fund can collect an incentive fee. The incentive fee is

$\{\$642 - [\$610 \times (1 + 0.04)]\} \times 0.20 = \$1.52$ million.

The net return to the investor for the year is

$[(\$642 - \$12.84 - \$1.52)/\$583.1] - 1 \approx 0.07638 \approx 7.64\%$.

30 B is correct. Total fees paid to all funds (underlying funds and Ash Lawn) are $12.75 million, consisting of underlying fund fees of $9.26 million and Ash Lawn fees of $3.49 million, calculated as follows:

Underlying fund fees:

Management fee = $133 million × 0.02 = $2.66 million.

Incentive fee = ($133 – $100) million × 0.20 = $6.60 million.

Total underlying fund fees ($2.66 + $6.60) million = $9.26 million.

Ash Lawn fees:

AUM at end of year, net of underlying fund fees = $133 million – $9.26 million = $123.74 million.

Ash Lawn management fee = $123.74 million × 0.01 = $1.24 million (rounded).

AUM net of underlying fund fees and Ash Lawn management fee = ($123.74 – $1.24) million = $122.50 million (rounded).

Ash Lawn incentive fee = ($122.50 – $100) million × 0.10 = $2.25 million (rounded).

Total Ash Lawn fees = ($1.24 + $2.25) million = $3.49 million (rounded).

Total fees of underlying funds and Ash Lawn:

($9.26 + $3.49) million = $12.75 million (rounded).

31 A is correct. Infrastructure projects involving construction have more risk than investments in existing assets with a demonstrated cash flow or investments in assets that are expected to generate regular cash flows because the assets will be leased back to a government.

32 B is correct. A clawback provision requires the general partner in a private equity fund to return any funds distributed (to the general partner) as incentive fees until the limited partners have received back their initial investments and the contracted portion of the total profits. A high hurdle rate will result in distributions occurring only after the fund achieves a specified return. A high hurdle rate decreases the likelihood of, but does not prevent, excess distributions. Management fees, not incentive fees, are based on committed capital.

33 B is correct. Until the committed capital is fully drawn down and invested, the management fee for a private equity fund is based on committed capital, not invested capital.

34 C is correct. Downside risk measures focus on the left side of the return distribution curve where losses occur. The standard deviation of returns assumes that returns are normally distributed. Many alternative investments do not exhibit

close-to-normal distribution of returns, which is a crucial assumption for the validity of a standard deviation as a comprehensive risk measure. Assuming normal probability distributions when calculating these measures will lead to an underestimation of downside risk for a negatively skewed distribution. Both the Sortino ratio and the value-at-risk measure are both measures of downside risk.

35 C is correct. Investment risk should be monitored by a chief risk officer who is separated from the investment process. Risk factors monitored include leverage, sector, and individual position limits as well as counterparty risks. Independent (as opposed to in-house) valuation of underlying positions should be performed and reviewed on a regular basis. Third-party custody of assets can help reduce the chance of fraud.

Portfolio Management

STUDY SESSION

Study Session 18	Portfolio Management (1)
Study Session 19	Portfolio Management (2)

TOPIC LEVEL LEARNING OUTCOME

The candidate should be able to explain and demonstrate the use of fundamentals of portfolio and risk management, including return and risk measurement, and portfolio planning and construction.

PORTFOLIO MANAGEMENT

STUDY SESSION

18

Portfolio Management (1)

This study session introduces the concept of a portfolio approach to investments. The needs of individual and institutional investors are each examined, along with the range of available investment solutions. The three main steps in the portfolio management process (planning, execution, and feedback) are outlined. Common measures of portfolio risk and return and the introduction of modern portfolio theory—a quantitative framework for asset pricing and portfolio selection—then follow.

READING ASSIGNMENTS

Reading 51	Portfolio Management: An Overview by Owen M. Concannon, CFA, Robert M. Conroy, DBA, CFA, Alistair Byrne, PhD, CFA, and Vahan Janjigian, PhD, CFA
Reading 52	Portfolio Risk and Return: Part I by Vijay Singal, PhD, CFA
Reading 53	Portfolio Risk and Return: Part II by Vijay Singal, PhD, CFA

READING

51

Portfolio Management: An Overview

by Owen M. Concannon, CFA, Robert M. Conroy, DBA, CFA, Alistair Byrne, PhD, CFA, and Vahan Janjigian, PhD, CFA

Owen Concannon, CFA, is at Neuberger Berman (USA). Robert M. Conroy, DBA, CFA, is at the Darden School of Business, University of Virginia (USA). Alistair Byrne, PhD, CFA, is at State Street Global Advisors (United Kingdom). Vahan Janjigian, PhD, CFA, is at Greenwich Wealth Management, LLC (USA).

LEARNING OUTCOMES

Mastery	*The candidate should be able to:*
☐	a. describe the portfolio approach to investing;
☐	b. describe the steps in the portfolio management process;
☐	c. describe types of investors and distinctive characteristics and needs of each;
☐	d. describe defined contribution and defined benefit pension plans;
☐	e. describe aspects of the asset management industry;
☐	f. describe mutual funds and compare them with other pooled investment products.

INTRODUCTION

1

This reading provides an overview of portfolio management and the asset management industry, including types of investors and investment plans and products. A portfolio approach is important to investors in achieving their financial objectives. We outline the steps in the portfolio management process in managing a client's investment portfolio. We next compare the financial needs of different types of investors: individual and institutional investors. We then describe both defined contribution and defined benefit pension plans. The asset management[1] industry, which serves as a critical link between providers and seekers of investment capital around the world, is broadly discussed. Finally, we describe mutual funds and other types of pooled investment products offered by asset managers.

1 Note that both "investment management" and "asset management" are commonly used throughout the CFA Program curriculum. The terms are often used interchangeably in practice.

2 A PORTFOLIO APPROACH TO INVESTING

One of the biggest challenges faced by individuals and institutions is to decide how to invest for future needs. For individuals, the goal might be to fund retirement needs. For such institutions as insurance companies, the goal is to fund future liabilities in the form of insurance claims, whereas endowments seek to provide income to meet the ongoing needs of such institutions as universities. Regardless of the ultimate goal, all face the same set of challenges that extend beyond just the choice of what asset classes to invest in. They ultimately center on formulating basic principles that determine how to think about investing. One important question is: Should we invest in individual securities, evaluating each in isolation, or should we take a portfolio approach? By "portfolio approach," we mean evaluating individual securities in relation to their contribution to the investment characteristics of the whole portfolio. In the following section, we illustrate a number of reasons why a diversified portfolio perspective is important.

2.1 Historical Example of Portfolio Diversification: Avoiding Disaster

Portfolio diversification helps investors avoid disastrous investment outcomes. This benefit is most convincingly illustrated by examining what may happen when individuals have *not* diversified.

We are usually not able to observe how individuals manage their personal investments. However, in the case of US 401(k) individual retirement portfolios,[2] it is possible to see the results of individuals' investment decisions. When we examine their retirement portfolios, we find that some individual participants make sub-optimal investment decisions.

During the 1990s, Enron Corporation was one of the most admired corporations in the United States. A position in Enron shares returned over 27 percent per year from 1990 to September 2000, compared to 13 percent for the S&P 500 Index for the same time period.

2 In the United States, 401(k) plans are employer-sponsored individual retirement savings plans. They allow individuals to save a portion of their current income and defer taxation until the time when the savings and earnings are withdrawn. In some cases, the sponsoring firm will also make matching contributions in the form of cash or shares. Individuals within certain limits have control of the invested funds and consequently can express their preferences as to which assets to invest in.

Exhibit 1 Value of US$1 Invested from January 1990 to September 2000 Enron vs. S&P 500 Composite Index (01/01/1990 = US$1.00)

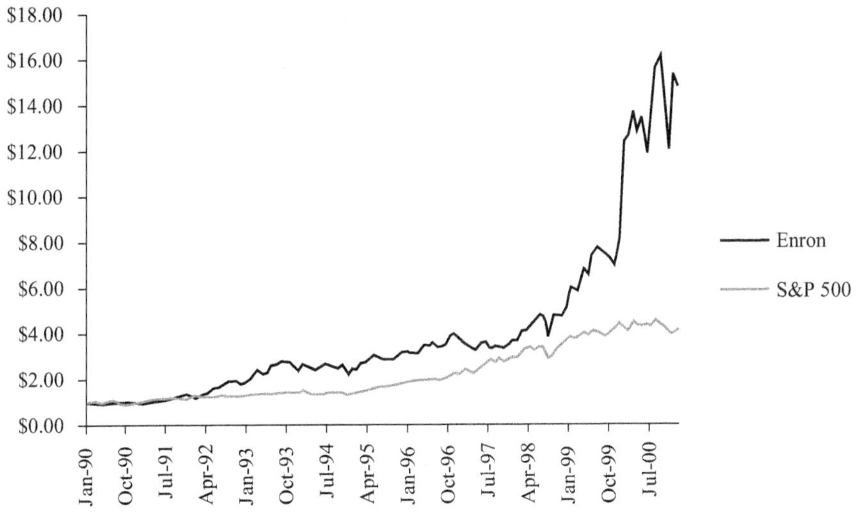

Source: Thomson Reuters Datastream.

During this time period, thousands of Enron employees participated in the company's 401(k) retirement plan. The plan allowed employees to set aside some of their earnings in a tax-deferred account. Enron participated by matching the employees' contributions. Enron made the match by depositing required amounts in the form of Enron shares. Enron restricted the sale of its contributed shares until an employee turned 50 years old. In January 2001, the employees' 401(k) retirement accounts were valued at over US$2 billion, of which US$1.3 billion (or 62 percent) was in Enron shares. Although Enron restricted the sale of shares it contributed, less than US$150 million of the total of US$1.3 billion in shares had this restriction. The implication was that Enron employees continued to hold large amounts of Enron shares even though they were free to sell them and invest the proceeds in other assets.

A typical individual was Roger Bruce,[3] a 67-year-old Enron retiree who held all of his US$2 million in retirement funds in Enron shares. Between January 2001 and January 2002, Enron's share price fell from about US$90 per share to zero.

3 Singletary (2001).

Exhibit 2 Value of US$1 Invested from January 1990 to January 2002 Enron vs. S&P 500 Composite Index (1/1/1990 = US$1.00)

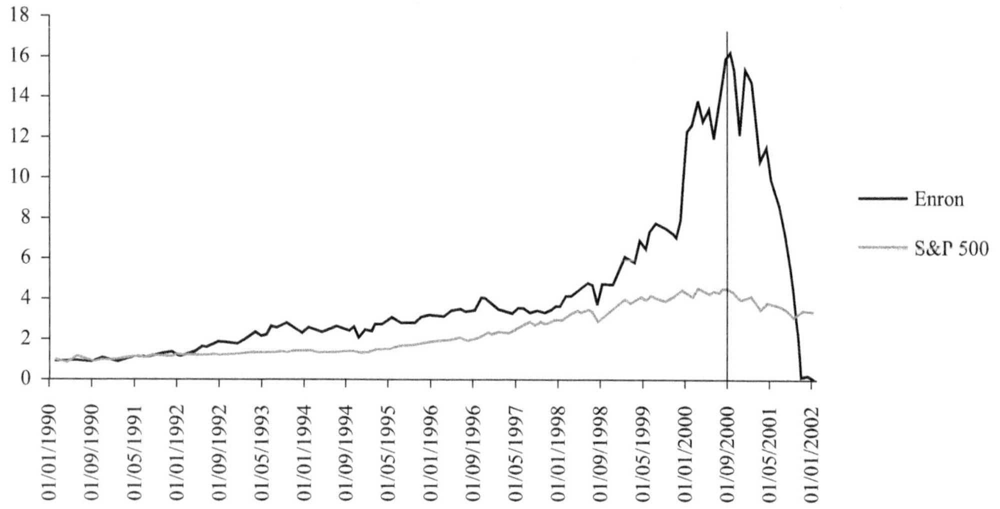

Source: Thomson Reuters Datastream.

Employees and retirees who had invested all or most of their retirement savings in Enron shares, just like Mr. Bruce, experienced financial ruin. The hard lesson that the Enron employees learned from this experience was to "not put all your eggs in one basket."[4] Unfortunately, the typical Enron employee did have most of his or her eggs in one basket. Most employees' wages and financial assets were dependent on Enron's continued viability; hence, any financial distress on Enron would have a material impact on an employee's financial health. The bankruptcy of Enron resulted in the closing of its operations, the dismissal of thousands of employees, and its shares becoming worthless. Hence, the failure of Enron was disastrous to the typical Enron employee.

Enron employees were not the only ones to be victims of over-investment in a single company's shares. In the defined contribution retirement plans at Owens Corning, Northern Telecom, Corning, and ADC Telecommunications, employees all held more than 25 percent of their assets in the company's shares during a time (March 2000 to December 2001) in which the share prices in these companies fell by almost 90 percent. The good news in this story is that the employees participating in employer-matched 401(k) plans since 2001 have significantly reduced their holdings of their employers' shares.

Thus, by taking a diversified portfolio approach, investors can spread away some of the risk. Rational investors are concerned about the risk–return trade-off of their investments. The portfolio approach provides investors with a way to reduce the risk associated with their wealth without necessarily decreasing their expected rate of return.

2.2 Portfolios: Reduce Risk

In addition to avoiding a potential disaster associated with over investing in a single security, portfolios also generally offer equivalent expected returns with lower overall **volatility** of returns—as represented by a measure such as standard deviation. Consider

4 This expression, which most likely originated in England in the 1700s, has a timeless sense of wisdom.

this simple example: Suppose you wish to make an investment in companies listed on the Hong Kong Stock Exchange (HKSE) and you start with a sample of five companies.[5] The cumulative returns for 16 fiscal quarters are shown in Exhibit 3.

Exhibit 3 Cumulative Wealth Index of Sample of Shares Listed on HKSE (initial amount= US$1.00)

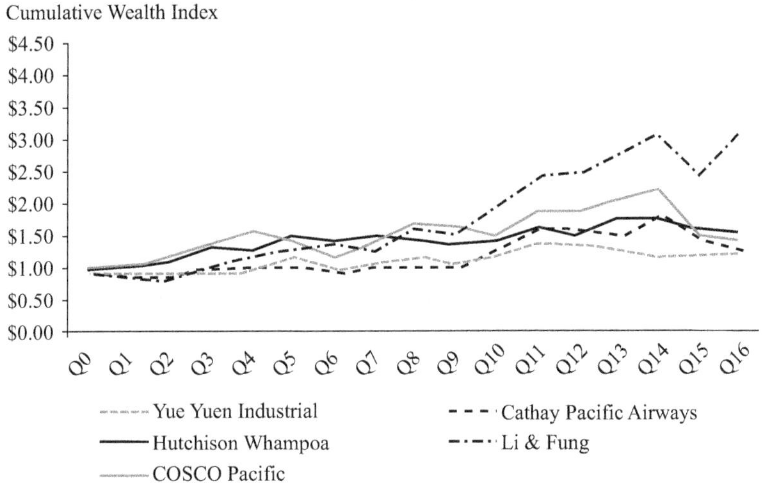

Source: Thomson Reuters Datastream.

The individual quarterly returns for each of the five shares are shown in Exhibit 4. The annualized means and annualized standard deviations for each are also shown.[6]

Exhibit 4 Quarterly Returns (in Percent) for Sample of HKSE Listed Shares over 16 Fiscal Quarters

	Yue Yuen Industrial	Cathay Pacific Airways	Hutchison Whampoa	Li & Fung	COSCO Pacific	Equally Weighted Portfolio
Q1	−11.1%	−2.3%	0.6%	−13.2%	−1.1%	−5.4%
Q2	−0.5	−5.4	10.8	1.7	21.0	5.5
Q3	5.7	6.8	19.1	13.8	15.5	12.2
Q4	5.3	4.6	−2.1	16.9	12.4	7.4
Q5	17.2	2.4	12.6	14.5	−7.9	7.8
Q6	−17.6	−10.4	−0.9	4.4	−16.7	−8.2
Q7	12.6	7.4	4.2	−10.9	15.4	5.7
Q8	7.5	−0.4	−3.6	29.2	21.9	10.9
Q9	−7.9	1.3	−5.1	−2.0	−1.6	−3.1
Q10	8.2	27.5	0.1	26.0	−10.1	10.3
Q11	18.3	24.3	16.5	22.8	25.7	21.5
Q12	0.1	−2.6	−6.7	−0.4	0.3	−1.8

(continued)

5 A sample of five companies from a similar industry group was arbitrarily selected for illustration purposes.
6 Mean quarterly returns are annualized by multiplying the quarterly mean by 4. Quarterly standard deviations are annualized by taking the quarterly standard deviation and multiplying it by 2.

Exhibit 4 (Continued)

	Yue Yuen Industrial	Cathay Pacific Airways	Hutchison Whampoa	Li & Fung	COSCO Pacific	Equally Weighted Portfolio
Q13	−6.2	−4.2	16.7	11.9	11.1	5.8
Q14	−8.0	17.9	−1.8	12.4	8.4	5.8
Q15	3.5	−20.1	−8.5	−20.3	−31.5	−15.4
Q16	2.1	−11.8	−2.6	24.2	−6.1	1.2
Mean annual return	7.3%	8.7%	12.3%	32.8%	14.2%	15.1%
Annual standard deviation	20.2%	25.4%	18.1%	29.5%	31.3%	17.9%
Diversification ratio						71.0%

Source: Thomson Reuters Datastream.

Suppose you want to invest in one of these five securities next year. There is a wide variety of risk–return trade-offs for the five shares selected. If you believe that the future will replicate the past, then choosing Li & Fung would be a good choice. For the prior four years, Li & Fung provided the best trade-off between return and risk. In other words, it provided the most return per unit of risk. However, if there is no reason to believe that the future will replicate the past, it is more likely that the risk and return on the one security selected will be more like selecting one randomly. When we randomly selected one security each quarter, we found an average annualized return of 15.1 percent and an average annualized standard deviation of 24.9 percent, which would now become your expected return and standard deviation, respectively.

Alternatively, you could invest in an equally weighted portfolio of the five shares, which means that you would invest the same dollar amount in each security for each quarter. The quarterly returns on the equally weighted portfolio are just the average of the returns of the individual shares. As reported in Exhibit 4, the equally weighted portfolio has an average return of 15.1 percent and a standard deviation of 17.9 percent. As expected, the equally weighted portfolio's return is the same as the return on the randomly selected security. However, the same does not hold true for the portfolio standard deviation. That is, the standard deviation of an equally weighted portfolio is not simply the average of the standard deviations of the individual shares. In a more advanced reading we will demonstrate in greater mathematical detail how such a portfolio offers a lower standard deviation of return than the average of its individual components due to the correlations or interactions between the individual securities.

Because the mean return is the same, a simple measure of the value of diversification is calculated as the ratio of the standard deviation of the equally weighted portfolio to the standard deviation of the randomly selected security. This ratio may be referred to as the **diversification ratio**. In this case, the equally weighted portfolio's standard deviation is approximately 71 percent of that of a security selected at random. The diversification ratio of the portfolio's standard deviation to the individual asset's standard deviation measures the risk reduction benefits of a simple portfolio construction method, equal weighting. Even though the companies were chosen from a similar industry grouping, we see significant risk reduction. An even greater portfolio effect (i.e., lower diversification ratio) could have been realized if we had chosen companies from completely different industries.

This example illustrates one of the critical ideas about portfolios: Portfolios affect risk more than returns. In the prior section portfolios helped avoid the effects of downside risk associated with investing in a single company's shares. In this section we extended the notion of risk reduction through portfolios to illustrate why individuals and institutions should hold portfolios.

2.3 Portfolios: Composition Matters for the Risk–Return Trade-off

In the previous section we compared an equally weighted portfolio to the selection of a single security. In this section we examine additional combinations of the same set of shares and observe the trade-offs between portfolio volatility of returns and expected return (for short, their risk–return trade-offs). If we select the portfolios with the best combination of risk and return (taking historical statistics as our expectations for the future), we produce the set of portfolios shown in Exhibit 5.

Exhibit 5 Optimal Portfolios for Sample of HKSE Listed Shares

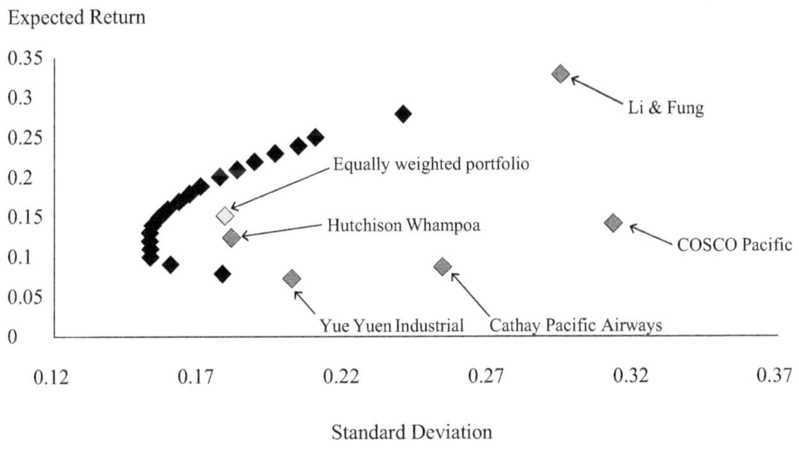

Source: Thomson Reuters Datastream.

In addition to illustrating that the diversified portfolio approach reduces risk, Exhibit 5 also shows that the composition of the portfolio matters. For example, an equally weighted portfolio (20 percent of the portfolio in each security) of the five shares has an expected return of 15.1 percent and a standard deviation of 17.9 percent. Alternatively, a portfolio with 25 percent in Yue Yuen Industrial (Holdings), 3 percent in Cathay Pacific, 52 percent in Hutchison Whampoa, 20 percent in Li & Fung, and 0 percent in COSCO Pacific produces a portfolio with an expected return of 15.1 percent and a standard deviation of 15.6 percent. Compared to a simple equally weighted portfolio, this provides an improved trade-off between risk and return because a lower level of risk was achieved for the same level of return.

2.4 Historical Portfolio Example: Not Necessarily Downside Protection

A major reason that portfolios can effectively reduce risk is that combining securities whose returns do not move together provides diversification. Sometimes a subset of assets will go up in value at the same time that another will go down in value. The fact that these may offset each other creates the potential diversification benefit we attribute to portfolios. However, an important issue is that the co-movement or correlation pattern of the securities' returns in the portfolio can change in a manner unfavorable to the investor. We use historical return data from a set of global indexes to show the impact of changing co-movement patterns.

When we examine the returns of a set of global equity indexes over the last 15 years, we observe a reduction in the diversification benefit due to a change in the pattern of co-movements of returns. Exhibits 6 and 7 show the cumulative returns for a set of five global indexes[7] for two different time periods. Comparing the first time period, from Q4 1993 through Q3 2000 (as shown in Exhibit 6), with the last time period, from Q1 2006 through Q1 2009 (as shown in Exhibit 7), we show that the degree to which these global equity indexes moved together increased over time.

Exhibit 6 Returns to Global Equity Indexes Q4 1993–Q3 2000

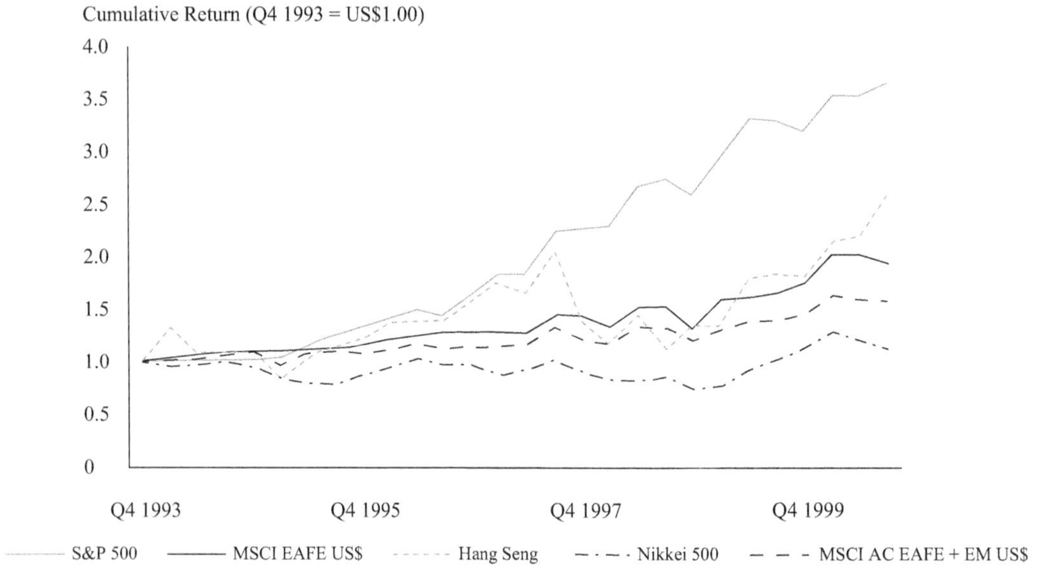

Source: Thomson Reuters Datastream.

7 The S&P 500, Hang Seng, and Nikkei 500 are broad-based composite equity indexes designed to measure the performance of equities in the United States, Hong Kong SAR, and Japan. MSCI stands for Morgan Stanley Capital International. EAFE refers to developed markets in Europe, Australasia, and the Far East. AC indicates all countries, and EM is emerging markets. All index returns are in US dollars.

Exhibit 7 Returns to Global Equity Indexes Q1 2006–Q1 2009

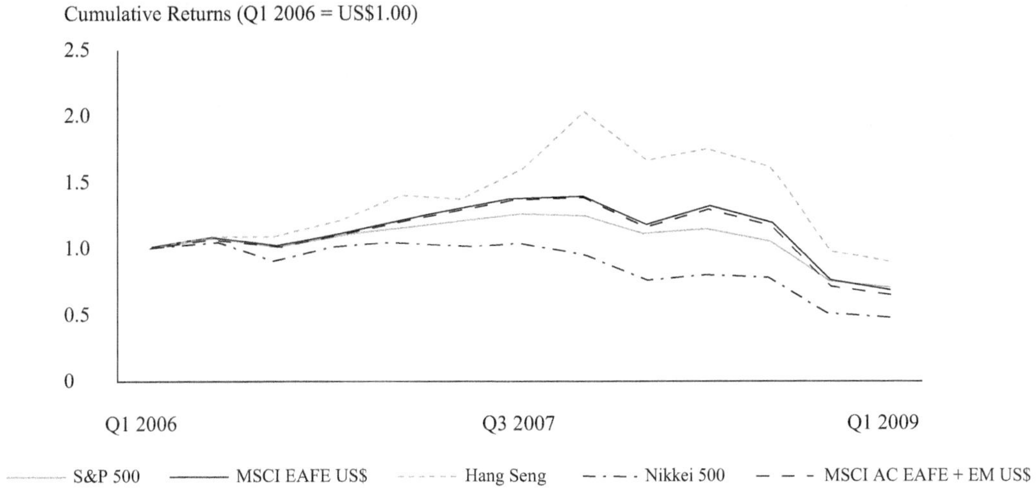

Source: Thomson Reuters Datastream.

The latter part of the second time period, from Q4 2007 to Q1 2009, was a period of dramatic declines in global share prices. Exhibit 8 shows the mean annual returns and standard deviation of returns for this time period.

Exhibit 8 Returns to Global Equity Indexes

	Q4 1993–Q3 2000		Q1 2006–Q1 2009		Q4 2007–Q1 2009	
Global Index	**Mean**	**Stand. Dev.**	**Mean**	**Stand. Dev.**	**Mean**	**Stand. Dev.**
S&P 500	20.5%	13.9%	−6.3%	21.1%	−40.6%	23.6%
MSCI EAFE US$	10.9	14.2	−3.5	29.4	−48.0	35.9
Hang Seng	20.4	35.0	5.1	34.2	−53.8	34.0
Nikkei 500	3.3	18.0	−13.8	27.6	−48.0	30.0
MSCI AC EAFE + EM US$	7.6	13.2	−4.9	30.9	−52.0	37.5
Randomly selected index	12.6%	18.9%	−4.7%	28.6%	−48.5%	32.2%
Equally weighted portfolio	12.6%	14.2%	−4.7%	27.4%	−48.5%	32.0%
Diversification ratio		75.1%		95.8%		99.4%

Source: Thomson Reuters Datastream.

During the period Q4 2007 through Q1 2009, the average return for the equally weighted portfolio, including dividends, was −48.5 percent. Other than reducing the risk of earning the return of the worst performing market, the diversification benefits were small. Exhibit 9 shows the cumulative quarterly returns of each of the five indexes over this time period. All of the indexes declined in unison. The lesson is that although portfolio diversification generally does reduce risk, it does not necessarily provide the same level of risk reduction during times of severe market turmoil as it does when the economy and markets are operating 'normally'. In fact, if the economy or markets fail totally (which has happened numerous times around the world), then diversification is a false promise. In the face of a worldwide contagion, diversification was ineffective, as illustrated at the end of 2008.

Exhibit 9 Return to Global Equity Indexes Q4 2007–Q1 2009

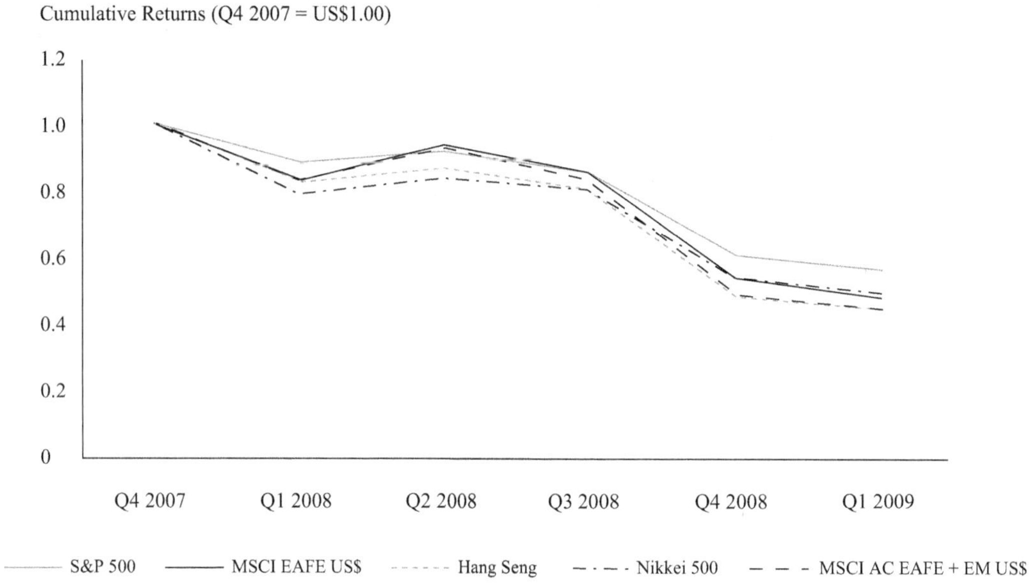

Source: Thomson Reuters Datastream.

Portfolios are *most likely* to provide:

A risk reduction.

B risk elimination.

C downside protection.

Solution:

A is correct. Combining assets into a portfolio should reduce the portfolio's volatility. However, the portfolio approach does not necessarily provide downside protection or eliminate all risk.

2.5 Portfolios: Modern Portfolio Theory

The concept of diversification has been around for a long time and has a great deal of intuitive appeal. However, the actual theory underlying this basic concept and its application to investments only emerged in 1952 with the publication of Harry Markowitz's classic article on portfolio selection.[8] The article provided the foundation for what is now known as **modern portfolio theory** (MPT). The main conclusion of MPT is that investors should not only hold portfolios but should also focus on how individual securities in the portfolios are related to one another. In addition to the

8 Markowitz (1952).

diversification benefits of portfolios to investors, the work of William Sharpe (1964), John Lintner (1965), and Jack Treynor (1961) demonstrated the role that portfolios play in determining the appropriate individual asset risk premium (i.e., the return in excess of the risk-free return expected by investors as compensation for the asset's risk). According to capital market theory, the priced risk of an individual security is affected by holding it in a well-diversified portfolio. The early research provided the insight that an asset's risk should be measured in relation to the remaining systematic or non-diversifiable risk, which should be the only risk that affects the asset's price. This view of risk is the basis of the capital asset pricing model, or CAPM, which is discussed in greater detail in other readings. Although MPT has limitations, the concepts and intuitions illustrated in the theory continue to be the foundation of knowledge for portfolio managers.

STEPS IN THE PORTFOLIO MANAGEMENT PROCESS 3

In the previous section we discussed a portfolio approach to investing. When establishing and managing a client's investment portfolio, certain critical steps are followed in the process. We describe these steps in this section.

- The Planning Step
  - Understanding the client's needs
  - Preparation of an investment policy statement (IPS)
- The Execution Step
  - Asset allocation
  - Security analysis
  - Portfolio construction
- The Feedback Step
  - Portfolio monitoring and rebalancing
  - Performance measurement and reporting

3.1 Step One: The Planning Step

The first step in the investment process is to understand the client's needs (objectives and constraints) and develop an **investment policy statement** (IPS). A portfolio manager is unlikely to achieve appropriate results for a client without a prior understanding of the client's needs. The IPS is a written planning document that describes the client's investment objectives and the constraints that apply to the client's portfolio. The IPS may state a benchmark—such as a particular rate of return or the performance of a particular market index—that can be used in the feedback stage to assess the performance of the investments and whether objectives have been met. The IPS should be reviewed and updated regularly (for example, either every three years or when a major change in a client's objectives, constraints, or circumstances occurs).

3.2 Step Two: The Execution Step

The next step is for the portfolio manager to construct a suitable portfolio based on the IPS of the client. The portfolio execution step consists of first deciding on a target asset allocation, which determines the weighting of asset classes to be included in the portfolio. This step is followed by the analysis, selection, and purchase of individual investment securities.

3.2.1 *Asset Allocation*

The next step in the process is to assess the risk and return characteristics of the available investments. The analyst forms economic and capital market expectations that can be used to form a proposed allocation of asset classes suitable for the client. Decisions that need to be made in the **asset allocation** of the portfolio include the distribution between equities, fixed-income securities, and cash; sub-asset classes, such as corporate and government bonds; and geographical weightings within asset classes. Alternative assets—such as real estate, commodities, hedge funds, and private equity—may also be included.

Economists and market strategists may set the top down view on economic conditions and broad market trends. The returns on various asset classes are likely to be affected by economic conditions; for example, equities may do well when economic growth has been unexpectedly strong whereas bonds may do poorly if inflation increases. The economists and strategists will attempt to forecast these conditions.

Top down—A **top-down analysis** begins with consideration of macroeconomic conditions. Based on the current and forecasted economic environment, analysts evaluate markets and industries with the purpose of investing in those that are expected to perform well. Finally, specific companies within these industries are considered for investment.

Bottom up—Rather than emphasizing economic cycles or industry analysis, a **bottom-up analysis** focuses on company-specific circumstances, such as management quality and business prospects. It is less concerned with broad economic trends than is the case for top-down analysis, but instead focuses on company specifics.

3.2.2 *Security Analysis*

The top-down view can be combined with the bottom-up insights of security analysts who are responsible for identifying attractive investments in particular market sectors. They will use their detailed knowledge of the companies and industries they cover to assess the expected level and risk of the cash flows that each security will produce. This knowledge allows the analysts to assign a valuation to the security and identify preferred investments.

3.2.3 *Portfolio Construction*

The portfolio manager will then construct the portfolio, taking account of the target asset allocation, security analysis, and the client's requirements as set out in the IPS. A key objective will be to achieve the benefits of diversification (i.e., to avoid putting all the eggs in one basket). Decisions need to be taken on asset class weightings, sector weightings within an asset class, and the selection and weighting of individual securities or assets. The relative importance of these decisions on portfolio performance depends at least in part on the investment strategy selected; for example, consider an investor that actively adjusts asset sector weights in relation to forecasts of sector performance and one who does not. Although all decisions have an effect on portfolio performance, the asset allocation decision is commonly viewed as having the greatest impact.

Exhibit 10 shows the broad portfolio weights of the endowment funds of Yale University and the University of Virginia as of June 2017. As you can see, the portfolios have a heavy emphasis on such alternative assets as hedge funds, private equity, and real estate—Yale University particularly so.

Exhibit 10 Endowment Portfolio Weights, June 2017

Asset Class	Yale University Endowment	University of Virginia Endowment
Public equity	19.1%	26.7%
Fixed income	4.6	9.1
Private equity	14.2	15.7
Real assets (e.g., real estate)	18.7	12.1
Absolute return (e.g., hedge funds)	25.1	19.6
Cash	1.2	2.3
Other	17.2	14.5
Portfolio value	US$27.2bn	US$8.6bn

Sources: "2017 Yale Endowment Annual Report" (p. 2): www.yale.edu/investments/Yale_Endowment_17.pdf; "University of Virginia Investment Management Company Annual Report 2017" (p. 26): http://uvm-web.eservices.virginia.edu/public/reports/FinancialStatements_2017.pdf.

Risk management is an important part of the portfolio construction process. The client's risk tolerance will be set out in the IPS, and the portfolio manager must make sure the portfolio is consistent with it. As noted above, the manager will take a diversified portfolio perspective: What is important is not the risk of any single investment, but rather how all the investments perform as a portfolio.

The endowments shown above are relatively risk tolerant investors. Contrast the asset allocation of the endowment funds with the portfolio mix of the insurance companies shown in Exhibit 11. You will notice that the majority of the insurance assets are invested in fixed-income investments, typically of high quality. Note that the Yale University portfolio has less than 5 percent invested in fixed income, with the remainder invested in such growth assets as equity, real estate, and hedge funds. This allocation is in sharp contrast to the Massachusetts Mutual Life Insurance Company (MassMutual) portfolio, which is 80 percent invested in bonds, mortgages, loans, and cash—reflecting the differing risk tolerance and constraints (life insurers face regulatory constraints on their investments).

Exhibit 11 MassMutual Portfolio, December 2017[9]

Asset Classes	Portfolio %
Bonds	56%
Preferred and common shares	9
Mortgages	14
Real estate	1
Policy loans	8
Partnerships	5
Other assets	5
Cash	2

Source: "MassMutual Financial Group 2017 Annual Report" (p. 8): www.massmutual.com/mmfg/docs/annual_report/index.html.

The portfolio construction phase also involves trading. Once the portfolio manager has decided which securities to buy and in what amounts, the securities must be purchased. In many investment firms, the portfolio manager will pass the trades to a buy-side trader—a colleague who specializes in securities trading—who will contact a stockbroker or dealer to have the trades executed.

3.3 Step Three: The Feedback Step

Finally, the feedback step assists the portfolio manager in rebalancing the portfolio due to a change in, for example, market conditions or the circumstances of the client.

3.3.1 *Portfolio Monitoring and Rebalancing*

Once the portfolio has been constructed, it needs to be monitored and reviewed and the composition revised as the security analysis changes because of changes in security prices and changes in fundamental factors. When security and asset weightings have drifted from the intended levels as a result of market movements, some rebalancing may be required. The portfolio may also need to be revised if it becomes apparent that the client's needs or circumstances have changed.

3.3.2 *Performance Evaluation and Reporting*

Finally, the performance of the portfolio must be evaluated, which will include assessing whether the client's objectives have been met. For example, the investor will wish to know whether the return requirement has been achieved and how the portfolio has performed relative to any benchmark that has been set. Analysis of performance may suggest that the client's objectives need to be reviewed and perhaps changes made to the IPS. As we will discuss in the next section, there are numerous investment products that clients can use to meet their investment needs. Many of these products are diversified portfolios that an investor can purchase.

9 Asset class definitions: Bonds—Debt instruments of corporations and governments as well as various types of mortgage- and asset-backed securities; Preferred and Common Shares—Investments in preferred and common equities; Mortgages—Mortgage loans secured by various types of commercial property as well as residential mortgage whole loan pools; Real Estate—Investments in real estate; Policy Loans—Loans by policyholders that are secured by insurance and annuity contracts; Partnerships—Investments in partnerships and limited liability companies; Cash—Cash, short-term investments, receivables for securities, and derivatives. Cash equivalents have short maturities (less than one year) or are highly liquid and able to be readily sold.

TYPES OF INVESTORS

4

The portfolio management process described in the previous section may apply to different types of investment clients. Such clients are broadly divided among individual (or retail) and institutional investors. Each of these segments has distinctive characteristics and needs, as discussed in the following sub-sections.

4.1 Individual Investors

Individual investors have a variety of motives for investing and constructing portfolios. Short-term goals can include providing for children's education, saving for a major purchase (such as a vehicle or a house), or starting a business. The retirement goal—investing to provide for an income in retirement—is a major part of the investment planning of most individuals. Many employees of public and private companies invest for retirement through **defined contribution pension plans** (DC plans). DC plans are retirement plans in the employee's name usually funded by both the employee and the employer. Examples include 401(k) plans in the United States, group personal pension schemes in the United Kingdom, and superannuation plans in Australia. With DC plans, individuals will invest part of their wages while working, expecting to draw on the accumulated funds to provide income during retirement or to transfer some of their wealth to their heirs. The key to a DC plan is that the employee accepts the investment and inflation risk and is responsible for ensuring that there are enough assets in the plan to meet their needs upon retirement.

Some individuals will be investing for growth and will therefore seek assets that have the potential for capital gains. Others, such as retirees, may need to draw an income from their assets and may therefore choose to invest more in fixed-income and dividend-paying shares. The investment needs of individuals will depend in part on their broader financial circumstances, such as their employment prospects and whether or not they own their own residence. They may also need to consider such issues as building up a cash reserve and the purchase of appropriate insurance policies before undertaking longer-term investments.

Asset managers serving individual investors typically distribute their products directly to investors or through intermediaries such as financial advisers and/or retirement plan providers. The distribution network for individual investors varies globally. In the United States, financial advisers are independent or employed by national or regional broker–dealers, banks, and trust companies. Additionally, many asset managers distribute investment strategies to investors through major online brokerage and custodial firms.

In Europe, retail investment product distribution is fragmented and, in turn, varies by country/region. In continental Europe, for example, distribution is primarily driven through financial advisers affiliated with retail and private banks. In the United Kingdom, products are sold through independent advisers as well as through advisers representing a bank or insurance group. Retail distribution in Switzerland and in the Nordic countries is driven mainly through large regional and private banks. In contrast to the United States and Europe, in many Asian markets retail distribution is dominated by large regional retail banks and global banks with private banking divisions.

Globally, many wealth management firms and asset managers target high-net-worth investors. These clients often require more customized investment solutions alongside tax and estate planning services.

4.2 Institutional Investors

Institutional investors primarily include defined benefit pension plans, endowments and foundations, banks, insurance companies, investment companies, and sovereign wealth funds. Each of these has unique goals, asset allocation preferences, and investment strategy needs.

4.2.1 *Defined Benefit Pension Plans*

Pension plans are typically categorized as either defined contribution (DC) or defined benefit (DB). We previously described DC plans, which relate to individual investors. **Defined benefit pension plans** (DB plans) are company-sponsored plans that offer employees a predefined benefit on retirement. The future benefit is defined because the DB plan requires the plan sponsor to specify the obligation stated in terms of the retirement income benefits owed to participants. Generally, employers are responsible for the contributions made to a DB plan and bear the risk associated with adequately funding the benefits offered to employees. Plans are committed to paying pensions to members, and the assets of these plans are there to fund those payments. Plan managers need to ensure that sufficient assets will be available to pay pension benefits as they come due. The plan may have an indefinitely long time horizon if new plan members are being admitted or a finite time horizon if the plan has been closed to new members. In some cases, the plan managers attempt to match the fund's assets to its liabilities by, for example, investing in bonds that will produce cash flows corresponding to expected future pension payments. There may be many different investment philosophies for pension plans, depending on funded status and other variables.

An ongoing trend is that plan sponsors increasingly favor DC plans over DB plans because DC plans typically have lower costs/risk to the company. As a result, DB plans have been losing market share of pension assets to DC plans. Nevertheless, DB plans, both public and private, remain sizable sources of investment funds for asset managers. As Exhibit 12 shows, global pension assets totaled more than US$41 trillion by the end of 2017. The United States, United Kingdom, and Japan represent the three largest pension markets in the world, comprising more than 76% of global pension assets.

Exhibit 12 Global Pension Assets (as of year-end 2017)

Country/Region	Total Assets (US$ billions)
United States	25,411
United Kingdom	3,111
Japan	3,054
Australia	1,924
Canada	1,769
Netherlands	1,598
Switzerland	906
South Korea	725
Germany	472
Brazil	269
South Africa	258
Finland	233
Malaysia	227
Chile	205
Mexico	177

Exhibit 12 (Continued)

Country/Region	Total Assets (US$ billions)
Italy	184
France	167
Chinese mainland	177
Hong Kong SAR	164
Ireland	157
India	120
Spain	44
Total	**41,355**

Note: Column does not sum precisely because of rounding.
Source: Willis Towers Watson.

By geography, the United States and Australia have a higher proportion of pension assets in DC plans, whereas Canada, Japan, the Netherlands, and the United Kingdom remain weighted toward DB plans (see Exhibit 13).

Exhibit 13 Pension Plan Type by Geography

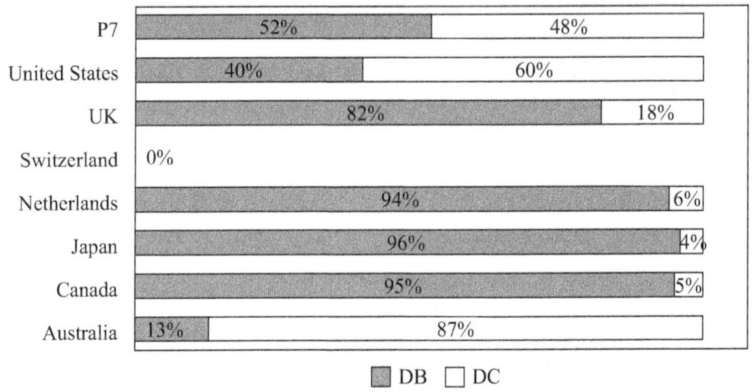

Notes: "P7" represents the combination of the seven countries listed. No data were available for Switzerland for this study.
Sources: Willis Towers Watson and secondary sources.

4.2.2 *Endowments and Foundations*

Endowments are funds of non-profit institutions that help the institutions provide designated services. In contrast, foundations are grant-making entities. Endowments and foundations collectively represent an estimated US$1.6 trillion in assets in the United States, which is the primary market for endowments and foundations.

Endowments and foundations typically allocate a sizable portion of their assets in alternative investments (Exhibit 14). This large allocation to alternative investments primarily reflects the typically long time horizon of endowments and foundations, as well the popularity of endowment-specific asset allocation models developed by Yale University's endowment managers David Swensen and Dean Takahashi.

Exhibit 14 Asset Allocations for US College and University Endowments and Affiliated Foundations (as of 30 June 2017, dollar weighted)

Asset Class	Percentage Allocation
Domestic equity	15
Fixed income	7
Foreign equity	20
Alternatives	54
Cash	4

Source: National Association of College and University Budget Officers and Commonfund Institute.

A typical investment objective of an endowment or a foundation is to maintain the real (inflation-adjusted) capital value of the fund while generating income to fund the objectives of the institution. Most foundations and endowments are established with the intent of having perpetual lives. Exhibit 15 describes the Yale University endowment's approach to balancing short-term spending needs with ensuring that future generations also benefit from the endowment, and it also shows the Wellcome Trust's approach. The investment approach undertaken considers the objectives and constraints of the institution (for example, no tobacco investments for a medical endowment).

Exhibit 15 Spending Rules

The following examples of spending rules are excerpts from the Yale University endowment (in the United States) and from the Wellcome Trust (in the United Kingdom).

Yale University Endowment

> The spending rule is at the heart of fiscal discipline for an endowed institution. Spending policies define an institution's compromise between the conflicting goals of providing substantial support for current operations and preserving purchasing power of Endowment assets. The spending rule must be clearly defined and consistently applied for the concept of budget balance to have meaning.
>
> The Endowment spending policy, which allocates Endowment earnings to operations, balances the competing objectives of providing a stable flow of income to the operating budget and protecting the real value of the Endowment over time. The spending policy manages the trade-of between these two objectives by combining a long-term spending rate target with a smoothing rule, which adjusts spending in any given year gradually in response to changes in Endowment market value.
>
> The target spending rate approved by the Yale Corporation currently stands at 5.25%. According to the smoothing rule, Endowment spending in a given year sums to 80% of the previous year's spending and 20% of the targeted long-term spending rate applied to the fiscal year-end market value two years prior.

Exhibit 15 (Continued)

Source: 2017 Yale Endowment Annual Report (p.18) [http://investments.yale.edu/endowment-update/]

Wellcome Trust

Our overall investment objective is to generate 4.5% percent real return over the long term.

This is to provide for real increases in annual expenditure while reserving the Trust's capital base to balance the needs of current and future beneficiaries.

We use this absolute return strategy because it aligns asset allocation with funding requirements and provides a competitive framework in which to judge individual investments.

Source: Wellcome Trust website (https://wellcome.ac.uk/about-us/investments)

4.2.3 *Banks*

Banks are financial intermediaries that accept deposits and lend money. Banks often have excess reserves that are invested in relatively conservative and very short-duration fixed-income investments, with a goal of earning an excess return above interest obligations due to depositors. Liquidity is a paramount concern for banks that stand ready to meet depositor requests for withdrawals. Many large banks have asset management divisions that offer retail and institutional products to their clients.

4.2.4 *Insurance Companies*

Insurance companies receive premiums for the policies they write, and they need to invest these premiums in a manner that will allow them to pay claims.

Insurance companies can be segmented into two broad types: life insurers and property and casualty (P&C) insurers. Insurance premiums from policyholders comprise an insurance company's general account. To pay claims to policyholders, regulatory guidelines maintain that an insurance company's general account is typically invested conservatively in a diverse allocation of fixed-income securities. General account portfolio allocations differ among life, P&C, and other specialty insurers (e.g., reinsurance) because of both the varying duration of liabilities and the unique liquidity considerations across insurance type.[10] In contrast to the general account, an insurer's surplus account is the difference between its assets and liabilities. An insurer's surplus account typically targets a higher return than the general account and thus often invests in less-conservative asset classes, such as public and private equities, real estate, infrastructure, and hedge funds.

Many insurance companies have in-house portfolio management teams responsible for managing general account assets. Some insurance companies offer portfolio management services and products in addition to their insurance offerings. An increasing trend among insurers (particularly in the United States) is outsourcing some of the

10 For example, life insurers tend to invest in longer-term assets (e.g., 30-year government and corporate bonds) relative to P&C insurers because of the longer-term nature of their liabilities.

portfolio management responsibilities—primarily sophisticated alternative asset classes—to unaffiliated asset managers. Several insurers manage investments for third-party clients, often through separately branded subsidiaries.

4.2.5 *Sovereign Wealth Funds*

Sovereign wealth funds (SWFs) are state-owned investment funds or entities that invest in financial or real assets. SWFs do not typically manage specific liability obligations, such as pensions, and have varying investment horizons and objectives based on funding the government's goals (for example, budget stabilization or future development projects). SWF assets more than doubled from 2007 to March 2018, totaling more than US$7.6 trillion.[11] Exhibit 16 lists the 10 largest SWFs in the world. The largest SWFs tend to be concentrated in Asia and in natural resource-rich places.

Exhibit 16 Largest Sovereign Wealth Funds (as of August 2018, in US$ billions)

Place	Sovereign Wealth Fund (Inception Year)	Assets
Norway	Government Pension Fund—Global (1990)	1,058
Chinese Mainland	China Investment Corporation (2007)	941
UAE – Abu Dhabi	Abu Dhabi Investment Authority (1976)	683
Kuwait	Kuwait Investment Authority (1953)	592
Hong Kong SAR	Hong Kong Monetary Authority Investment Portfolio (1993)	523
Saudi Arabia	SAMA Foreign Holdings (1952)	516
Chinese Mainland	SAFE Investment Company (1997)	441
Singapore	Government of Singapore Investment Authority (1981)	390
Singapore	Temasek Holdings (1974)	375
Saudi Arabia	Public Investment Fund (2008)	360
Total SWF Assets under Management		**8,109**

Source: SWF Institute (www.swfinstitute.org).

Investment needs vary across client groups. With some groups of clients, generalizations are possible. In other groups, needs vary by client. Exhibit 17 summarizes needs within each group.

Exhibit 17 Summary of Investment Needs by Client Type

Client	Time Horizon	Risk Tolerance	Income Needs	Liquidity Needs
Individual investors	Varies by individual	Varies by individual	Varies by individual	Varies by individual
Defined benefit pension plans	Typically long term	Typically quite high	High for mature funds; low for growing funds	Varies by maturity of the plan

11 SWFI, "Sovereign Wealth Fund Rankings" (https://www.swfinstitute.org/sovereign-wealth-fund-rankings/; retrieved October 2018).

Exhibit 17 (Continued)

Client	Time Horizon	Risk Tolerance	Income Needs	Liquidity Needs
Endowments and foundations	Very long term	Typically high	To meet spending commitments	Typically quite low
Banks	Short term	Quite low	To pay interest on deposits and operational expenses	High to meet repayment of deposits
Insurance companies	Short term for property and casualty; long term for life insurance companies	Typically quite low	Typically low	High to meet claims
Investment companies	Varies by fund	Varies by fund	Varies by fund	High to meet redemptions
Sovereign wealth funds	Varies by fund	Varies by fund	Varies by fund	Varies by fund

THE ASSET MANAGEMENT INDUSTRY

5

The portfolio management process and investor types are broad components of the asset management industry, which is an integral component of the global financial services sector. At the end of 2017, the industry managed more than US$79 trillion of assets owned by a broad range of institutional and individual investors (Exhibit 18).[12] Although nearly 80% of the world's professionally managed assets are in North America and Europe, the fastest-growing markets are in Asia and Latin America.

Exhibit 18 Global Assets under Management (AUM) by Region (year-end 2017)

	Market Size (US$ trillions)	Market Share (%)
North America	37.4	47%
Europe	22.2	28
Japan and Australia	6.2	8
Chinese mainland	4.2	5
Asia (excluding Japan, Australia, and Chinese mainland)	3.5	4
Latin America	1.8	2
Middle East and Africa	1.4	2
Total Global AUM	79.2	100%

Notes: Total Global AUM in this exhibit represents assets professionally managed in exchange for a fee. The total of US$79.2 trillion includes certain offshore assets that are not represented in the specific regional categories above.
Source: Boston Consulting Group.

12 http://image-src.bcg.com/Images/BCG-Seizing-the-Analytics-Advantage-June-2018-R-3_tcm9-194512.pdf (accessed on 6 September 2018).

The asset management industry is highly competitive. The universe of firms in the industry is broad, ranging from "pure-play" independent asset managers to diversified commercial banks, insurance companies, and brokerages that offer asset management services in addition to their core business activities. Given the increasingly global nature of the industry, many asset managers have investment research and distribution offices around the world. An asset manager is commonly referred to as a **buy-side firm** given that it uses (buys) the services of sell-side firms. A **sell-side firm** is a broker/dealer that sells securities and provides independent investment research and recommendations to their clients (i.e., buy-side firms).

Asset managers offer a broad range of strategies. Specialist asset managers may focus on a specific asset class (e.g., emerging market equities) or style (e.g., quantitative investing), while "full service" managers typically offer a wide variety of asset classes and styles. Another type of asset manager firm is a "multi-boutique," in which a holding company owns several asset management firms that typically have specialized investment strategies. The multi-boutique structure allows individual asset management firms to retain their own unique investment cultures—and often equity ownership stakes—while also benefiting from the centralized, shared services of the holding company (e.g., technology, sales and marketing, operations, and legal services).

5.1 Active versus Passive Management

Asset managers may offer either active or passive management. As of year-end 2017, active management considerably exceeded passive management in terms of global assets under management and industry revenue (Exhibit 19), although passive management has demonstrated significant growth.

Exhibit 19 Global Asset Management Industry Assets and Revenue (as of year-end 2017)

Category	Assets (US$ trillions)	Revenue (US$ billions)	Market Share by Assets (%)	Market Share by Revenue (%)
Actively Managed	**64**	**258**	**80%**	**94%**
Alternatives	12	117	15	43
Active Specialties	15	55	19	20
Multi Asset Class	11	27	14	10
Core	26	59	33	21
Passively Managed	**16**	**17**	**20%**	**6%**
Total	**80**	**275**	**100%**	**100%**

Note: Some columns may not sum precisely because of rounding.
Source: Boston Consulting Group.

Through fundamental research, quantitative research, or a combination of both, active asset managers generally attempt to outperform either predetermined performance benchmarks, such as the S&P 500, or, for multi-asset class portfolios, a combination of benchmarks. In contrast to active managers, passive managers attempt to replicate the returns of a market index. Despite the rise of passive management in asset share, its share of industry revenue remains small given the low management fees relative to active management. As Exhibit 19 illustrates, passive management represents a fifth of global assets under management but only 6% of industry revenue.

Asset managers are increasingly offering other strategies beyond traditional market-cap-weighted exposures. Some of these other strategies, commonly known as **smart beta**, are based on such factors as size, value, momentum, or dividend characteristics. Smart beta involves the use of simple, transparent, rules-based strategies as a basis for investment decisions. Typically, smart beta strategies feature somewhat higher management fees and higher portfolio turnover relative to passive market-cap weighted strategies.

5.2 Traditional versus Alternative Asset Managers

Asset managers are typically categorized as either "traditional" or "alternative." Traditional managers generally focus on long-only equity, fixed-income, and multi-asset investment strategies, generating most of their revenues from asset-based management fees. Alternative asset managers, however, focus on hedge fund, private equity, and venture capital strategies, among others, while generating revenue from both management and performance fees (or "carried interest"). As Exhibit 19 demonstrates, alternative asset managers have a relatively low proportion of total global assets under management but generate a disproportionately high total of industry revenue.

Increasingly, the line between traditional and alternative managers has blurred. Many traditional managers have introduced higher-margin alternative products to clients. Concurrently, alternative managers seeking to reduce the revenue volatility associated with performance fees have increasingly offered retail versions of their institutional alternative strategies (typically referred to as "liquid alternatives") as well as long-only investment strategies. These liquid alternatives are often offered through highly regulated pooled investment products (e.g., mutual funds) and typically feature less leverage, no performance fees, and more liquid holdings than typical alternative products.

5.3 Ownership Structure

The ownership structure of an asset manager can play an important role in retaining and incentivizing key personnel. Portfolio managers who have personal capital invested in their firms or investment strategies are often viewed favorably by potential investors because of perceived alignment of management and client interests.

The majority of asset management firms are privately owned, typically by individuals who either established their firms or play key roles in their firms' management. Privately owned firms are typically structured as limited liability companies or limited partnerships.

While less common than privately owned managers, publicly traded asset managers have substantial assets under management. A prevalent ownership form in the industry is represented by asset management divisions of large, diversified financial services companies that offer asset management alongside insurance and banking services.

5.4 Asset Management Industry Trends

The asset management industry is evolving and continues to be shaped by socio-economic trends, shifting investor demands, advances in technology, and the expansion of global capital markets. Three key trends that we discuss in this section include the growth of passive investing, "big data" in the investment process, and the emergence of robo-advisers in the wealth management industry.

5.4.1 *Growth of Passive Investing*

As we saw in Exhibit 19, passively managed assets comprised nearly a fifth of global assets under management at the end of 2017. Management of passive assets is concentrated among a reasonably small group of asset managers and tends to be concentrated in equity strategies. As shown in Exhibit 20, the top three managers account for 70% of industry's assets. One key catalyst supporting the growth of passive investing is low cost for investors—management fees for index (or other passive) funds are often a fraction of those for active strategies. Another catalyst is the challenge that many active asset managers face in generating ex ante alpha, especially in somewhat more-efficiently priced markets, such as large-cap US equities.

Exhibit 20 Top Five ETP Managers Globally (as of 30 July 2017)

ETP Provider	Assets (US$ billions)	Market Share (%)
iShares	1,583	37
Vanguard	803	19
State Street Global Advisors	596	14
PowerShares	132	3
Nomura	100	2

Source: ETFGI.

5.4.2 *Use of "Big Data" in the Investment Process*

The prevalence of new data is extraordinary: In 2013, IBM estimated that 90% of the world's entire universe of data was created in the previous two years. The digitization of data and an exponential increase in computing power and data storage capacity have expanded additional information sources for asset managers. Massive amounts of data containing information of potential value to investors are created and captured daily. These data include both structured data—such as order book data and security returns—and data lacking recognizable structure, which is generated by a vast number of activities on the internet and elsewhere (e.g., compiled search information). The term "big data" is used to refer to these massively large datasets and their analysis.

Asset managers are using advanced statistical and machine-learning techniques to help process and analyze these new sources of data. Such techniques are used in both fundamentally driven and quantitatively driven investment processes. For example, computers are used to "read" earnings and economic data releases much faster than humans can and react with short-term trading strategies.

Third-party research vendors are supplying a vast range of relevant new data for asset managers, such as data used for time-series and predictive models. Among the most popular new sources of data are social media data and imagery and sensor data.

- **Social media data**. Real-time media and content outlets, such as Twitter and Facebook, provide meaningful market and company-specific announcements for investors and asset managers. In addition, the aggregation and analysis of social media users can aid key market sentiment indicators (e.g., short-term directional market movements) and indicate potential specific user trends related to products and services.
- **Imagery and sensor data**. Satellite imagery and geolocation devices provide vast real-time data to investment professionals. As the cost of launching and maintaining satellites has decreased, more satellites have been launched to track

sensors and imagery that are relevant to economic considerations (e.g., weather conditions, cargo ship traffic patterns) and company-specific considerations (e.g., retailer parking capacity/usage, tracking of retail customers).

The challenge for asset managers is to discover data with predictive potential and to do so faster than fellow market participants. Many market participants are participating in an "information arms race" that has required substantial investments in specialized human capital (e.g., programmers, data scientists), technology, and information technology infrastructure to effectively convert various forms of structured and unstructured data into alpha-generating portfolio and security-level decisions.

5.4.3 *Robo-Advisers: An Expanding Wealth Management Channel*

Robo-advisers represent technology solutions that use automation and investment algorithms to provide several wealth management services—notably, investment planning, asset allocation, tax loss harvesting, and investment strategy selection. Investment and advice services provided by robo-advisers typically reflect an investor's general investment goals and risk tolerance preferences (often obtained from an investor questionnaire). Robo-adviser platforms range from exclusively digital investment advice platforms to hybrid offerings that offer both digital investment advice and the services of a human financial adviser.

At the end of 2017, robo-advisers managed an estimated US$180 billion in assets,[13] and market participants expect that number to grow considerably over time. This expected rapid growth in robo-advisory assets is based on several industry trends:

- **Growing demand from "mass affluent" and younger investors**: Traditional investment advice has often underserved younger and "mass affluent" investors with lower relative levels of investable assets. Given the efficiencies of robo-advisers and the scalability of technology, customized but standardized investment advice now can be offered to a wide range and size of investors.
- **Lower fees**: The cost of digital investment advice provided by robo-advisers is often a fraction of traditional investment advice channels because of scalability. For example, in the United States, a typical financial adviser may charge a 1% annual advisory fee[14] based on a client's assets, while robo-adviser fees typically average 0.20% annually.[15] Additionally, robo-advisers often rely on lower fee underlying portfolio investment options, such as index funds or ETFs, when constructing portfolios for clients.
- **New entrants**: Reflecting low barriers to entry, large wealth management firms have introduced robo-adviser solutions to service certain customer segments and appeal to a new generation of investors. In addition to these large wealth managers, other less-traditional entrants, such as insurance companies and asset managers, are developing solutions to cross-sell into their existing clients. Many market observers expect that non-financial firms (large technology leaders) will also become key players in the robo-adviser industry as they look to monetize their access to user data.

---

13 S&P Global Market Intelligence.

14 http://www.riainabox.com/blog/2016-ria-industry-study-average-investment-advisory-fee-is-0-99-percent.

15 Deloitte, "Robo-Advisors Capitalizing on a Growing Opportunity" (https://www2.deloitte.com/content/dam/Deloitte/us/Documents/strategy/us-cons-robo-advisors.pdf).

6 MUTUAL FUNDS AND POOLED INVESTMENT PRODUCTS

In the asset management industry, a challenge faced by all investors is to and find the right set of investment products to meet their needs. There is a diverse set of investment products available to investors, ranging from a simple brokerage account in which the individual creates her own portfolio by assembling individual securities, to large institutions that employ individual portfolio managers to meet clients' investment management needs. Among the major investment products offered by asset managers are mutual funds and other pooled investment products, such as separately managed accounts, exchange-traded funds, hedge funds, and private equity/venture capital funds.

6.1 Mutual Funds

Rather than assemble a portfolio on their own, individual investors and institutions can turn over the selection and management of their investment portfolio to a third party. One way of doing this is through a **mutual fund**. This type of fund is a comingled investment pool in which investors in the fund each have a pro-rata claim on the income and value of the fund. The value of a mutual fund is referred to as the "net asset value." It is computed daily based on the closing price of the securities in the portfolio.

Mutual funds represent a primary investment product of individual investors globally. According to the International Investment Funds Association, worldwide regulated open-end fund assets totaled US$50 trillion as of the first quarter of 2018. Exhibit 21 shows the growth of global open-end funds over the past five years by region. Mutual funds provide several advantages, including low investment minimums, diversified portfolios, daily liquidity, and standardized performance and tax reporting.

Exhibit 21 Worldwide Regulated Open-End Funds: Total Net Assets (as of year-end, in US$ trillions)

	2011	2012	2013	2014	2015	2016	Q1 2018
World	**27.9**	**31.9**	**36.3**	**38.0**	**38.2**	**40.4**	**50.0**
Americas	14.6	16.5	18.9	20.0	19.6	21.1	24.9
Europe	10.3	11.9	13.6	13.8	13.7	14.1	18.1
Asia and Pacific	2.9	3.3	3.7	4.1	4.7	5.0	6.8
Africa	0.1	0.1	0.1	0.1	0.1	0.1	0.2

Notes: Components may not add to the total because of rounding. Regulated open-end funds include mutual funds, exchange-traded funds (ETFs), and institutional funds.
Source: International Investment Funds Association (IIFA).

Mutual funds are one of the most important investment vehicles for individuals and institutions. The best way to understand how a mutual fund works is to consider a simple example. Suppose that an investment firm wishes to start a mutual fund with a target amount of US$10 million. It is able to reach this goal through investments from five individuals and two institutions. The investment of each is as follows:

Investor	Amount Invested (US$)	Percent of Total	Number of Shares
Individuals			
A	$1.0 million	10%	10,000
B	1.0	10	10,000
C	0.5	5	5,000
D	2.0	20	20,000
E	0.5	5	5,000
Institutions			
X	2.0	20	20,000
Y	3.0	30	30,000
Totals	**$10.0 million**	**100%**	**100,000**

Based on the US$10 million value (net asset value), the investment firm sets a total of 100,000 shares at an initial value of US$100 per share (US$10 million/100,000 = US$100). The investment firm will appoint a portfolio manager to be responsible for the investment of the US$10 million. Going forward, the total value of the fund or net asset value will depend on the value of the assets in the portfolio.

The fund can be set up as an open-end fund or a closed-end fund. If it is an **open-end fund**, it will accept new investment money and issue additional shares at a value equal to the net asset value of the fund at the time of investment. For example, assume that at a later date the net asset value of the fund increases to US$12 million and the new net asset value per share is US$120. A new investor, F, wishes to invest US$0.96 million in the fund. If the total value of the assets in the fund is now US$12 million or US$120 per share, in order to accommodate the new investment the fund would create 8,000 (US$0.96 million/US$120) new shares. After this investment, the net asset value of the fund would be US$12.96 million and there would be a total of 108,000 shares.

Funds can also be withdrawn at the net asset value per share. Suppose on the same day Investor E wishes to withdraw all her shares in the mutual fund. To accommodate this withdrawal, the fund will have to liquidate US$0.6 million in assets to retire 5,000 shares at a net asset value of US$120 per share (US$0.6 million/US$120). The combination of the inflow and outflow on the same day would be as follows:

Type	Investment (US$)	Shares
Inflow (Investor F buys)	$960,000	8,000
Outflow (Investor E sells)	–$600,000	–5,000
Net	$360,000	3,000

The net of the inflows and outflows on that day would be US$360,000 of new funds to be invested and 3,000 new shares created. However, the number of shares held and the value of the shares of all remaining investors, except Investor E, would remain the same.

An alternative to setting the fund up as an open-end fund would be to create a **closed-end fund** in which no new investment money is accepted into the fund. New investors invest by buying existing shares, and investors in the fund liquidate by selling their shares to other investors. Hence, the number of outstanding shares does not change. One consequence of this fixed share base is that, unlike open-end funds in which new shares are created and sold at the current net asset value per share, closed-end funds can sell for a premium or discount to net asset value depending on the demand for the shares.

There are advantages and disadvantages to each type of fund. The open-end fund structure makes it easy to grow in size but creates pressure on the portfolio manager to manage the cash inflows and outflows. One consequence of this structure is the need to liquidate assets that the portfolio manager might not want to sell at the time to meet redemptions. Conversely, the inflows require finding new assets in which to invest. As such, open-end funds tend not to be fully invested but rather keep some cash for redemptions not covered by new investments. Closed-end funds do not have these problems, but they do have a limited ability to grow. Of the total net asset value of all US mutual funds at the end of 2017 (US$19 trillion), only approximately 1 percent were in the form of closed-end funds.

In addition to open-end or closed-end funds, mutual funds can be classified as load or no-load funds. The primary difference between the two is whether the investor pays a sales charge (a "load") to purchase, hold, or redeem shares in the fund. In the case of the **no-load fund**, there is no fee for investing in the fund or for redemption but there is an annual fee based on a percentage of the fund's net asset value. **Load funds** are funds in which, in addition to the annual fee, a percentage fee is charged to invest in the fund and/or for redemptions from the fund. In addition, load funds are usually sold through retail brokers who receive part of the upfront fee. Overall, the number and importance of load funds has declined over time.

6.2 Types of Mutual Funds

The following section introduces the major types of mutual funds differentiated by the asset type that they invest in: money market funds, bond mutual funds, stock mutual funds, and hybrid or balanced funds.

6.2.1 *Money Market Funds*

Money market funds are mutual funds that invest in short-term money market instruments such as treasury bills, certificates of deposit, and commercial paper. They aim to provide security of principal, high levels of liquidity, and returns in line with money market rates. Many funds operate on a constant net asset value (CNAV) basis where the share price is maintained at $1 (or local currency equivalent). Others operate on a variable net asset value (VNAV) basis where the unit price can vary. In the United States, there are two basic types of money market funds: taxable and tax-free. Taxable money market funds invest in high-quality, short-term corporate debt and federal government debt. Tax-free money market funds invest in short-term state and local government debt. Although money market funds have been a substitute for bank savings accounts since the early 1980s, they are not insured in the same way as bank deposits.

6.2.2 *Bond Mutual Funds*

A bond mutual fund is an investment fund consisting of a portfolio of individual bonds and, occasionally, preferred shares. The net asset value of the fund is the sum of the value of each bond in the portfolio divided by the number of shares. Investors in the mutual fund hold shares, which account for their pro-rata share or interest in the portfolio. The major difference between a bond mutual fund and a money market fund is the maturity of the underlying assets. In a money market fund the maturity is as short as overnight and rarely longer than 90 days. A bond mutual fund, however, holds bonds with maturities as short as one year and as long as 30 years (or more). Exhibit 22 illustrates the general categories of bond mutual funds.[16]

16 In the United States, judicial rulings on federal powers of taxation have created a distinction between (federally) taxable and (federally) tax-exempt bonds and a parallel distinction for US bond mutual funds.

Exhibit 22 Bond Mutual Funds

Type of Bond Mutual Fund	Securities Held
Global	Domestic and non-domestic government, corporate, and securitized debt
Government	Government bonds and other government-affiliated bonds
Corporate	Corporate debt
High yield	Below investment-grade corporate debt
Inflation protected	Inflation-protected government debt
National tax-free bonds	National tax-free bonds (e.g., US municipal bonds)

6.2.3 *Stock Mutual Funds*

Historically, the largest types of mutual funds based on market value of assets under management are stock (equity) funds.

There are two types of stock mutual funds. The first is an actively managed fund in which the portfolio manager seeks outstanding performance through the selection of the appropriate stocks to be included in the portfolio. Passive management is followed by index funds that are very different from actively managed funds. Their goal is to match or track the performance of different indexes. The first index fund was introduced in 1976 by the Vanguard Group.

There are several major differences between actively managed funds and index funds. First, management fees for actively managed funds are higher than for index funds. The higher fees for actively managed funds reflect its goal to outperform an index, whereas the index fund simply aims to match the return on the index. Higher fees are required to pay for the research conducted to actively select securities. A second difference is that the level of trading in an actively managed fund is much higher than in an index fund, which depending on the jurisdiction, has tax implications. Mutual funds are often required to distribute all income and capital gains realized in the portfolio, so the actively managed fund tends to have more opportunity to realize capital gains. This results in higher taxes relative to an index fund, which uses a buy-and-hold strategy. Consequently, there is less buying and selling in an index fund and less likelihood of realizing capital gains distributions.

6.2.4 *Hybrid/Balanced Funds*

Hybrid or balanced funds are mutual funds that invest in both bonds and stocks. These types of funds represent a small fraction of the total investment in US mutual funds but are more common in Europe. These types of funds, however, have gained popularity with the growth of lifecycle funds. Lifecycle or Target Date funds manage the asset mix based on a desired retirement date. For example, if an investor is 40 years old in 2019 and planned to retire at the age of 67, he could invest in a mutual fund with a target date of 2046 and the fund would manage the appropriate asset mix over the next 27 years. In 2019 it might be 90 percent invested in shares and 10 percent in bonds. As time passes, however, the fund would gradually change the mix of shares and bonds to reflect the appropriate mix given the time to retirement.

6.3 Separately Managed Accounts

A fund management service for institutions or individual investors with substantial assets is the **separately managed account** (SMA), which is also commonly referred to as a "managed account," "wrap account," or "individually managed account."

SMAs are managed exclusively for the benefit of a single individual or institution. Unlike a mutual fund, the assets of an SMA are owned directly by the individual or institution. The main disadvantage of an SMA is that the required minimum investment is usually much higher than with a mutual fund.

Large institutional investors are generally the dominant users of SMAs. SMAs enable asset managers to implement an investment strategy that matches an investor's specific objectives, portfolio constraints, and tax considerations, where applicable. For example, a public pension plan investing in an asset manager's large value equity strategy might have a socially responsible investment preference. In this case, the plan sponsor may wish to exclude certain industries, such as tobacco and defense, while also including additional companies that are deemed favorable according to other environmental, social, and governance (ESG) considerations.

6.4 Exchange-Traded Funds

Exchange-traded funds (ETFs) are investment funds that trade on exchanges (similar to individual stocks) and are generally structured as open-end funds. ETFs represent one of the fastest-growing investment products in the asset management industry. According to BlackRock, global ETF assets increased from US$428 billion in 2005 to US$4.9 trillion as of June 2018. Long-term investors—both institutional and retail—use ETFs in building a diversified asset allocation. While ETFs are structured similarly to open-end mutual funds, some key differences exist between the two products. One difference relates to transaction price. Because they are traded on exchanges, ETFs can be transacted (and are priced) intraday. That is, ETF investors buy the shares from other investors just as if they were buying or selling shares of stock. ETF investors can also short shares or purchase the shares on margin. In contrast, mutual funds typically can be purchased or sold only once a day, and short sales or purchasing shares on margin is not allowed. Mutual fund investors buy the fund shares directly from the fund, and all investments are settled at the net asset value. In practice, the market price of the ETF is likely to be close to the net asset value of the underlying investments.

Other key differences between ETFs and mutual funds relate to transaction costs and treatment of dividends and the minimum investment amount. Dividends on ETFs are paid out to the shareholders whereas mutual funds usually reinvest the dividends. Finally, the minimum required investment in ETFs is usually smaller than that of mutual funds.

6.5 Hedge Funds

Hedge funds are private investment vehicles that typically use leverage, derivatives, and long and short investment strategies. The origin of hedge funds can be traced back as far as 1949 to a fund managed by A.W. Jones & Co. It offered a strategy of a non-correlated offset to the "long-only" position typical of most portfolios. Since then, the hedge fund industry has grown considerably, with global hedge fund assets totaling US$3.3 trillion as of May 2017.

Hedge fund investment strategies are diverse and can range from specific niche strategies (e.g., long–short financial services) to global multi-strategy approaches. Consequently, hedge funds are often used by investors for portfolio diversification purposes. In general, hedge funds share a few distinguishing characteristics:

- *Short selling*: Many hedge funds implement short positions directly or synthetically using such derivatives as options, futures, and credit default swaps.
- *Absolute return seeking:* Hedge funds often seek positive returns in all market environments.

- *Leverage:* Many hedge funds use financial leverage (bank borrowing) or implicit leverage (using derivatives). The use and amount of leverage are dependent on the investment strategy being implemented.
- *Low correlation:* Some hedge funds have historically exhibited low return correlations with traditional equity and/or fixed-income asset classes.
- *Fee structures:* Hedge funds typically charge two distinct fees: a traditional asset-based management fee (AUM fee) and an incentive (or performance) fee in which the hedge fund earns a portion of the fund's realized capital gains.[17] Hedge funds have traditionally charged management fees of 2% and incentive fees of up to 20%, although there has been downward pressure on those fees amid increased competition and the availability of competing products.

Hedge funds are not readily available to all investors. They typically require a high minimum investment and often have restricted liquidity by allowing only periodic (e.g., quarterly) withdrawals or having a long fixed-term commitment.

6.6 Private Equity and Venture Capital Funds

Private equity funds and **venture capital funds** are alternative funds that seek to buy, optimize, and ultimately sell portfolio companies to generate profits. As of December 2017, assets under management in the private equity industry totaled US$3.1 trillion, a historical high point.[18] Most private equity and venture capital funds have a lifespan of approximately 7–10 years (but usually subject to contractual extensions). Unlike most traditional asset managers that trade in public securities, private equity and venture firms often take a "hands-on" approach to their portfolio companies through a combination of financial engineering (e.g., realizing expense synergies, changing capital structures), installment of executive management and board members, and significant contributions to the development of a target company's business strategy. The final investment stage, often referred to as the "exit" or "harvesting" stage, occurs when a private equity or venture capital fund divests its portfolio companies through a merger with another company, the acquisition by another company, or an initial public offering (IPO).

As with most alternative funds, the majority of private equity and venture capital funds are structured as limited partnerships. These limited partnership agreements exist between the fund manager, called the general partner (GP), and the fund's investors, called limited partners (LPs). The funds generate revenue through several types of fees:

- *Management fees:* Fees are based on committed capital (or sometimes net asset value or invested capital) and typically range from 1–3% annually. Sometimes these fees step down several years into the investment period of a fund.
- *Transaction fees:* Fees are paid by portfolio companies to the fund for various corporate and structuring services. Typically, a percentage of the transaction fee is shared with the LPs by offsetting the management fee.

---

17 Performance fees are often subject to high-water mark provisions, which preclude a manager from earning a performance fee unless the value of a fund at the end of a predefined measurement period is higher than the value of the fund at the beginning of the measurement period. The unpredictability of future performance leads to uncertainty in performance fee revenue, which is regarded as less reliable than revenue derived from management fees.

18 https://www.pionline.com/article/20180724/ONLINE/180729930/preqin-private-equity-aum-grows-20-in-2017-to-record-306-trillion# (accessed 13 November 2018)

- *Carried interest:* Carried interest is the GP's share of profits (typically 20%) on sales of portfolio companies. Most GPs do not earn the incentive fee until LPs have recovered their initial investment.
- *Investment income.* Investment income includes profits generated on capital contributed to the fund by the GP.

SUMMARY

- A portfolio approach to investing could be preferable to simply investing in individual securities.
- The problem with focusing on individual securities is that this approach may lead to the investor "putting all her eggs in one basket."
- Portfolios provide important diversification benefits, allowing risk to be reduced without necessarily affecting or compromising return.
- Understanding the needs of your client and preparing an investment policy statement represent the first steps of the portfolio management process. Those steps are followed by asset allocation, security analysis, portfolio construction, portfolio monitoring and rebalancing, and performance measurement and reporting.
- Types of investors include individual and institutional investors. Institutional investors include defined benefit pension plans, endowments and foundations, banks, insurance companies, and sovereign wealth funds.
- The asset management industry is an integral component of the global financial services sector. Asset managers offer either active management, passive management, or both. Asset managers are typically categorized as traditional or alternative, although the line between traditional and alternative has blurred.
- Three key trends in the asset management industry include the growth of passive investing, "big data" in the investment process, and robo-advisers in the wealth management industry.
- Investors use different types of investment products in their portfolios. These include mutual funds, separately managed accounts, exchange-traded funds, hedge funds, and private equity and venture capital funds.

REFERENCES

Lintner, John. 1965. "The Valuation of Risk Assets and the Selection of Risky Investments in Stock Portfolios and Capital Budgets." *Review of Economics and Statistics*, vol. 47, no. 1 (February):13–37.

Markowitz, Harry M. 1952. "Portfolio Selection." *Journal of Finance*, vol. 7, no. 1 (March):77–91.

Sharpe, William F. 1964. "Capital Asset Prices: A Theory of Market Equilibrium under Conditions of Risk." *Journal of Finance*, vol. 19, no. 3 (September):425–442.

Singletary, Michelle. 2001. "Cautionary Tale of an Enron Employee Who Went for Broke." Seattlepi.com (10 December): http://www.seattlepi.com/money/49894_singletary10.shtml.

Treynor, J. L. 1961. "Toward a Theory of Market Value of Risky Assets." Unpublished manuscript.

PRACTICE PROBLEMS

1 Investors should use a portfolio approach to:

A reduce risk.

B monitor risk.

C eliminate risk.

2 Which of the following is the *best* reason for an investor to be concerned with the composition of a portfolio?

A Risk reduction.

B Downside risk protection.

C Avoidance of investment disasters.

3 With respect to the formation of portfolios, which of the following statements is *most accurate*?

A Portfolios affect risk less than returns.

B Portfolios affect risk more than returns.

C Portfolios affect risk and returns equally.

4 Which of the following institutions will *on average* have the greatest need for liquidity?

A Banks.

B Investment companies.

C Non-life insurance companies.

5 Which of the following institutional investors will *most likely* have the longest time horizon?

A Defined benefit plan.

B University endowment.

C Life insurance company.

6 A defined benefit plan with a large number of retirees is *likely* to have a high need for

A income.

B liquidity.

C insurance.

7 Which of the following institutional investors is *most likely* to manage investments in mutual funds?

A Insurance companies.

B Investment companies.

C University endowments.

8 With respect to the portfolio management process, the asset allocation is determined in the:

A planning step.

B feedback step.

C execution step.

9 The planning step of the portfolio management process is *least likely* to include an assessment of the client's

A securities.

B constraints.

C risk tolerance.

10 With respect to the portfolio management process, the rebalancing of a portfolio's composition is *most likely* to occur in the:

A planning step.

B feedback step.

C execution step.

11 An analyst gathers the following information for the asset allocations of three portfolios:

Portfolio	Fixed Income (%)	Equity (%)	Alternative Assets (%)
1	25	60	15
2	60	25	15
3	15	60	25

Which of the portfolios is *most likely* appropriate for a client who has a high degree of risk tolerance?

A Portfolio 1.

B Portfolio 2.

C Portfolio 3.

12 Which of the following investment products is *most likely* to trade at their net asset value per share?

A Exchange traded funds.

B Open-end mutual funds.

C Closed-end mutual funds.

13 Which of the following financial products is *least likely* to have a capital gain distribution?

A Exchange traded funds.

B Open-end mutual funds.

C Closed-end mutual funds.

14 Which of the following forms of pooled investments is subject to the *least* amount of regulation?

A Hedge funds.

B Exchange traded funds.

C Closed-end mutual funds.

15 Which of the following pooled investments is *most likely* characterized by a few large investments?

A Hedge funds.

B Buyout funds.

C Venture capital funds.

SOLUTIONS

1 A is correct. Combining assets into a portfolio should reduce the portfolio's volatility. Specifically, "individuals and institutions should hold portfolios to reduce risk." As illustrated in the reading, however, risk reduction may not be as great during a period of dramatic economic change.

2 A is correct. Combining assets into a portfolio should reduce the portfolio's volatility. The portfolio approach does not necessarily provide downside protection or guarantee that the portfolio always will avoid losses.

3 B is correct. As illustrated in the reading, portfolios reduce risk more than they increase returns.

4 A is correct. The excess reserves invested by banks need to be relatively liquid. Although investment companies and non-life insurance companies have high liquidity needs, the liquidity need for banks is on average the greatest.

5 B is correct. Most foundations and endowments are established with the intent of having perpetual lives. Although defined benefit plans and life insurance companies have portfolios with a long time horizon, they are not perpetual.

6 A is correct. Income is necessary to meet the cash flow obligation to retirees. Although defined benefit plans have a need for income, the need for liquidity typically is quite low. A retiree may need life insurance; however, a defined benefit plan does not need insurance.

7 B is correct. Investment companies manage investments in mutual funds. Although endowments and insurance companies may own mutual funds, they do not issue or redeem shares of mutual funds.

8 C is correct. The client's objectives and constraints are established in the investment policy statement and are used to determine the client's target asset allocation, which occurs in the execution step of the portfolio management process.

9 A is correct. Securities are analyzed in the execution step. In the planning step, a client's objectives and constraints are used to develop the investment policy statement.

10 B is correct. Portfolio monitoring and rebalancing occurs in the feedback step of the portfolio management process.

11 C is correct. Portfolio 3 has the same equity exposure as Portfolio 1 and has a higher exposure to alternative assets, which have greater volatility (as discussed in the section of the reading comparing the endowments from Yale University and the University of Virginia).

12 B is correct. Open-end funds trade at their net asset value per share, whereas closed-end funds and exchange traded funds can trade at a premium or a discount.

13 A is correct. Exchange traded funds do not have capital gain distributions. If an investor sells shares of an ETF (or open-end mutual fund or closed-end mutual fund), the investor may have a capital gain or loss on the shares sold; however, the gain (or loss) from the sale is not a distribution.

14 A is correct. Hedge funds are currently exempt from the reporting requirements of a typical public investment company.

15 B is correct. Buyout funds or private equity firms make only a few large investments in private companies with the intent of selling the restructured companies in three to five years. Venture capital funds also have a short time horizon; however, these funds consist of many small investments in companies with the expectation that only a few will have a large payoff (and that most will fail).

READING

52

Portfolio Risk and Return: Part I

by Vijay Singal, PhD, CFA

Vijay Singal, PhD, CFA, is at Virginia Tech (USA).

LEARNING OUTCOMES

Mastery	The candidate should be able to:
☐	a. calculate and interpret major return measures and describe their appropriate uses;
☐	b. compare the money-weighted and time-weighted rates of return and evaluate the performance of portfolios based on these measures
☐	c. describe characteristics of the major asset classes that investors consider in forming portfolios;
☐	d. calculate and interpret the mean, variance, and covariance (or correlation) of asset returns based on historical data;
☐	e. explain risk aversion and its implications for portfolio selection;
☐	f. calculate and interpret portfolio standard deviation;
☐	g. describe the effect on a portfolio's risk of investing in assets that are less than perfectly correlated;
☐	h. describe and interpret the minimum-variance and efficient frontiers of risky assets and the global minimum-variance portfolio;
☐	i. explain the selection of an optimal portfolio, given an investor's utility (or risk aversion) and the capital allocation line.

INTRODUCTION

1

Construction of an optimal portfolio is an important objective for an investor. In this reading, we will explore the process of examining the risk and return characteristics of individual assets, creating all possible portfolios, selecting the most efficient portfolios, and ultimately choosing the optimal portfolio tailored to the individual in question.

During the process of constructing the optimal portfolio, several factors and investment characteristics are considered. The most important of those factors are risk and return of the individual assets under consideration. Correlations among individual assets along with risk and return are important determinants of portfolio risk. Creating a portfolio for an investor requires an understanding of the risk profile of the investor. Although we will not discuss the process of determining risk aversion for individuals or institutional investors, it is necessary to obtain such information for making an informed decision. In this reading, we will explain the broad types of investors and how their risk–return preferences can be formalized to select the optimal portfolio from among the infinite portfolios contained in the investment opportunity set.

The reading is organized as follows: Section 2 discusses the investment characteristics of assets. In particular, we show the various types of returns and risks, their computation and their applicability to the selection of appropriate assets for inclusion in a portfolio. Section 3 discusses risk aversion and how indifference curves, which incorporate individual preferences, can be constructed. The indifference curves are then applied to the selection of an optimal portfolio using two risky assets. Section 4 provides an understanding and computation of portfolio risk. The role of correlation and diversification of portfolio risk are examined in detail. Section 5 begins with the risky assets available to investors and constructs a large number of risky portfolios. It illustrates the process of narrowing the choices to an efficient set of risky portfolios before identifying the optimal risky portfolio. The risky portfolio is combined with investor risk preferences to generate the optimal risky portfolio. A summary concludes this reading.

2 INVESTMENT CHARACTERISTICS OF ASSETS

Financial assets are frequently defined in terms of their risk and return characteristics. Comparison along these two dimensions simplifies the process of building a portfolio from among the multitude of available assets. In this section, we will compute, evaluate, and compare various measures of return and risk.

2.1 Return

Financial assets normally generate two types of return for investors. First, they may provide periodic income through cash dividends or interest payments. Second, the price of a financial asset can increase or decrease, leading to a capital gain or loss.

Some financial assets provide return through only one of these mechanisms. For example, investors in non-dividend-paying stocks obtain their return from price movement only. Similarly, you could also own or have a claim to assets that only generate periodic income. For example, defined benefit pension plans and retirement annuities make income payments as long as you live.

In the following section, we consider the computation and application of various types of returns.

2.1.1 *Holding Period Return*

Returns can be measured over a single period or over multiple periods. Single period returns are straightforward because there is only one way to calculate them. Multiple period returns, however, can be calculated in various ways and it is important to be aware of these differences to avoid confusion.

A **holding period return** is the return earned from holding an asset for a single specified period of time. The period may be 1 day, 1 week, 1 month, 5 years, or any specified period. If the asset (bond, stock, etc.) is bought now, time ($t = 0$), at a price of 100 and sold later, say at time ($t = 1$), at a price of 105 with no dividends or other income, then the holding period return is 5 percent [(105 – 100)/100)]. If the asset also pays an income of 2 units at time ($t = 1$), then the total return is 7 percent. This return can be generalized and shown as a mathematical expression in which P is the price and I is the income:

$$R = \frac{(P_1 - P_0) + I_1}{P_0}$$

The subscript indicates the time of the price or income, ($t = 0$), is the beginning of the period and ($t = 1$) is the end of the period. The following two observations are important.

- We computed a capital gain of 5 percent and a dividend yield of 2 percent in the above example. For ease of illustration, we assumed that the dividend is paid at time $t = 1$. If the dividend was received any time before $t = 1$, our holding period return would have been higher because we would have earned a return by reinvesting the dividend for the remainder of the period.
- Return can be expressed in decimals (0.07), fractions (7/100), or as a percent (7%). They are all equivalent.

The holding period return can be computed for a period longer than one year. For example, you may need to compute a three-year holding period return from three annual returns. In that case, the holding period return is computed by compounding the three annual returns: $R = [(1 + R_1) \times (1 + R_2) \times (1 + R_3)] - 1$, where R_1, R_2, and R_3 are the three annual returns.

2.1.2 *Arithmetic or Mean Return*

When assets have returns for multiple holding periods, it is necessary to aggregate those returns into one overall return for ease of comparison and understanding. Most holding period returns are reported as daily, monthly, or annual returns. When comparing returns across assets, it is important that the returns are computed using a common time period.

There are different methods for aggregating returns across several holding periods. The remainder of this section presents various ways of computing average returns and discusses their applicability.

The simplest way to compute the return is to take a simple arithmetic average of all holding period returns. Thus, three annual returns of –50 percent, 35 percent, and 27 percent will give us an average of 4 percent per year $= \left(\frac{-50\% + 35\% + 27\%}{3}\right)$. The arithmetic average return is easy to compute and has known statistical properties, such as standard deviation. We can calculate its standard deviation to determine how dispersed the observations are around the mean or if the mean return is statistically different from zero.

In general, the arithmetic or mean return is denoted by $\bar{R}_i$ and given by the following equation for asset i, where R_{it} is the return in period t and T is the total number of periods:

$$\bar{R}_i = \frac{R_{i1} + R_{i2} + \dots + R_{i,T-1} + R_{iT}}{T} = \frac{1}{T}\sum_{t=1}^{T} R_{it}$$

2.1.3 *Geometric Mean Return*

The arithmetic mean return assumes that the amount invested at the beginning of each period is the same. In an investment portfolio, however, even if there are no cash flows into or out of the portfolio, the base amount changes each year. (The previous year's earnings must be added to the beginning value of the subsequent year's investment—these earnings will be "compounded" by the returns earned in that subsequent year.) We can use the geometric mean return to account for the compounding of returns.

A geometric mean return provides a more accurate representation of the growth in portfolio value over a given time period than does an arithmetic mean return. In general, the geometric mean return is denoted by $\bar{R}_{Gi}$ and given by the following equation for asset i:

$$\bar{R}_{Gi} = \sqrt[T]{(1 + R_{i1}) \times (1 + R_{i2}) \times \ldots \times (1 + R_{i,T-1}) \times (1 + R_{iT})} - 1$$

where R_{it} is the return in period t and T is the total number of periods.

In the example in Section 2.1.2, we calculated the arithmetic mean to be 4 percent. Exhibit 1 shows the actual return for each year and the balance at the end of each year using actual returns. Beginning with an initial investment of €1.0000, we will have a balance of €0.8573 at the end of the three-year period as shown in the third column. Note that we compounded the returns because, unless otherwise stated, we earn a return on the balance as of the end of the prior year. That is, we will receive a return of 35 percent in the second year on the balance at the end of the first year, which is only €0.5000, not the initial balance of €1.0000. Let us compare the balance at the end of the three-year period computed using geometric returns with the balance we would calculate using the 4 percent annual arithmetic mean return from our earlier example. The ending value using the arithmetic mean return is €1.1249 (=1.0000 × 1.04^3). This is much larger than the actual balance of €0.8573. In general, the arithmetic return is biased upward unless each of the underlying holding period returns are equal. The bias in arithmetic mean returns is particularly severe if holding period returns are a mix of both positive and negative returns, as in the example.

Exhibit 1

	Actual Return for the Year (%)	Year-End Amount	Year-End Amount Using Arithmetic Return of 4%	Year-End Amount Using Geometric Return of –5%
Year 0		€1.0000	€1.0000	€1.0000
Year 1	–50	0.5000	1.0400	0.9500
Year 2	35	0.6750	1.0816	0.9025
Year 3	27	0.8573	1.1249	0.8574

2.1.4 *Money-Weighted Return or Internal Rate of Return*

The arithmetic and geometric return computations do not account for the cash flows into and out of a portfolio If the investor had invested €10,000 in the first year, €1,000 in the second year, and €1,000 in the third year, then the return of –50 percent in the first year significantly hurts her. On the other hand, if she had invested only €100 in the first year, the effect of the –50 percent return is drastically reduced.

The **money-weighted return** accounts for the money invested and provides the investor with information on the return she earns on her actual investment. The money-weighted return and its calculation are similar to the **internal rate of return** and the yield to maturity. Just like the internal rate of return, amounts invested are cash outflows from the investor's perspective and amounts returned or withdrawn by the investor, or the money that remains at the end of an investment cycle, is a cash inflow for the investor.

The money-weighted return can be illustrated most effectively with an example. In this example, we use the returns from the previous example. Assume that the investor invests €100 in a mutual fund at the beginning of the first year, adds another €950 at the beginning of the second year, and withdraws €350 at the end of the second year. The cash flows are shown in Exhibit 2.

Exhibit 2

Year	1	2	3
Balance from previous year	€0	€50	€1,000
New investment by the investor (cash inflow for the mutual fund) at the start of the year	100	950	0
Net balance at the beginning of year	100	1,000	1,000
Investment return for the year	−50%	35%	27%
Investment gain (loss)	−50	350	270
Withdrawal by the investor (cash outflow for the mutual fund) at the end of the year	0	−350	0
Balance at the end of year	€50	€1,000	€1,270

The internal rate of return is the discount rate at which the sum of present values of these cash flows will equal zero. In general, the equation may be expressed as follows, where T is the number of periods, CF_t is the cash flow at time t, and IRR is the internal rate of return or the money-weighted rate of return:

$$\sum_{t=0}^{T}\frac{CF_t}{(1+\text{IRR})^t}=0$$

A cash flow can be positive or negative; a positive cash flow is an inflow where money flows to the investor, whereas a negative cash flow is an outflow where money flows away from the investor. We can compute the internal rate of return by using the above equation. The flows are expressed as follows, where each cash inflow or outflow occurs at the end of each year. Thus, CF_0 refers to the cash flow at the end of Year 0 or beginning of Year 1, and CF_3 refers to the cash flow at end of Year 3 or beginning of Year 4. Because cash flows are being discounted to the present—that is, end of Year 0 or beginning of Year 1—the period of discounting CF_0 is zero.

$$CF_0 = -100$$
$$CF_1 = -950$$
$$CF_2 = +350$$
$$CF_3 = +1{,}270$$

$$\frac{CF_0}{(1+\text{IRR})^0}+\frac{CF_1}{(1+\text{IRR})^1}+\frac{CF_2}{(1+\text{IRR})^2}+\frac{CF_3}{(1+\text{IRR})^3}$$

$$=\frac{-100}{1}+\frac{-950}{(1+\text{IRR})^1}+\frac{+350}{(1+\text{IRR})^2}+\frac{+1270}{(1+\text{IRR})^3}=0$$

$$\text{IRR} = 26.11\%$$

IRR = 26.11% is the internal rate of return, or the money-weighted rate of return, which tells the investor what she earned on the actual euros invested for the entire period. This return is much greater than the arithmetic and geometric mean returns because only a small amount was invested when the mutual fund's return was −50 percent.

Next, we'll illustrate calculating the money-weighted return for a dividend paying stock. Consider an investment that covers a two-year horizon. At time $t = 0$, an investor buys one share at \$200. At time $t = 1$, he purchases an additional share at \$225. At the end of Year 2, $t = 2$, he sells both shares for \$235 each. During both years, the stock pays a per-share dividend of \$5. The $t = 1$ dividend is not reinvested. Exhibit 3 shows the total cash inflows and outflows.

Exhibit 3 Cash Flows

Time	Outflows
0	\$200 to purchase the first share
1	\$225 to purchase the second share

Time	Inflows
1	\$5 dividend received from first share (and not reinvested)
2	\$10 dividend (\$5 per share × 2 shares) received
2	\$470 received from selling two shares at \$235 per share

To solve for the money-weighted return, we use either a financial calculator that allows us to enter cash flows or a spreadsheet with an IRR function.[1] The first step is to group net cash flows by time. For this example, we have −\$200 for the $t = 0$ net cash flow, −\$220 = −\$225 + \$5 for the $t = 1$ net cash flow, and \$480 for the $t = 2$ net cash flow. After entering these cash flows, we use the spreadsheet's or calculator's IRR function to find that the money-weighted rate of return is 9.39 percent.[2]

$$CF_0 = -200$$

$$CF_1 = -220$$

$$CF_2 = +480$$

$$\frac{CF_0}{(1+\text{IRR})^0} + \frac{CF_1}{(1+\text{IRR})^1} + \frac{CF_2}{(1+\text{IRR})^2}$$

$$= \frac{-200}{1} + \frac{-220}{(1+\text{IRR})^1} + \frac{480}{(1+\text{IRR})^2} = 0$$

$$\text{IRR} = 9.39\%$$

Now we take a closer look at what has happened to the portfolio during each of the two years. In the first year, the portfolio generated a one-period holding period return of (\$5 + \$225 − \$200)/\$200 = 15 percent. At the beginning of the second year, the amount invested is \$450, calculated as \$225 (per share price of stock) × 2 shares, because the \$5 dividend was spent rather than reinvested. At the end of the

1 In this particular case we could solve for r by solving the quadratic equation $480x^2 - 220x - 200 = 0$ with $x = 1/(1 + r)$, using standard results from algebra. In general, however, we rely on a calculator or spreadsheet software to compute a money-weighted rate of return.

2 Note that the calculator or spreadsheet will give the IRR as a periodic rate. If the periods are not annual, we annualize the periodic rate.

second year, the proceeds from the liquidation of the portfolio are \$470 (as detailed in Exhibit 3) plus \$10 in dividends (as also detailed in Exhibit 3). So in the second year the portfolio produced a holding period return of (\$10 + \$470 – \$450)/\$450 = 6.67 percent. The mean holding period return was (15% + 6.67%)/2 = 10.84 percent. The money-weighted rate of return, which we calculated as 9.39 percent, puts a greater weight on the second year's relatively poor performance (6.67 percent) than the first year's relatively good performance (15 percent), as more money was invested in the second year than in the first. That is the sense in which returns in this method of calculating performance are "money weighted." Although the money-weighted return is an accurate measure of what the investor actually earned on the money invested, it is limited in its applicability to other situations. For example, it does not allow for return comparison between different individuals or different investment opportunities. Two investors in the *same* mutual fund or with the same portfolio of underlying investments may have different money-weighted returns because they invested different amounts in different years.

EXAMPLE 1

Computation of Returns

Ulli Lohrmann and his wife, Suzanne Lohrmann, are planning for retirement and want to compare the past performance of a few mutual funds they are considering for investment. They believe that a comparison over a five-year period would be appropriate. They are given the following information about the Rhein Valley Superior Fund that they are considering.

Year	Assets Under Management at the Beginning of Year (€)	Net Return (%)
1	30 million	15
2	45 million	–5
3	20 million	10
4	25 million	15
5	35 million	3

The Lohrmanns are interested in aggregating this information for ease of comparison with other funds.

1 Compute the holding period return for the five-year period.
2 Compute the arithmetic mean annual return.
3 Compute the geometric mean annual return. How does it compare with the arithmetic mean annual return?
4 The Lohrmanns want to earn a minimum annual return of 5 percent. Is the money-weighted annual return greater than 5 percent?

Solution to 1:

The holding period return is $R = (1 + R_1)(1 + R_2)(1 + R_3)(1 + R_4)(1 + R_5) - 1 = (1.15)(0.95)(1.10)(1.15)(1.03) - 1 = 0.4235 = 42.35\%$ for the five-year period.

Solution to 2:

The arithmetic mean annual return can be computed as an arithmetic mean of the returns given by this equation:

$$\overline{R}_i = \frac{15\% - 5\% + 10\% + 15\% + 3\%}{5} = 7.60\%$$

Solution to 3:

The geometric mean annual return can be computed using this equation:

$$\begin{aligned}\overline{R}_{Gi} &= \sqrt[T]{(1 + R_{i1}) \times (1 + R_{i2}) \times \ldots \times \left(1 + R_{i,T-1}\right) \times (1 + R_{iT})} - 1 \\ &= \sqrt[5]{1.15 \times 0.95 \times 1.10 \times 1.15 \times 1.03} - 1 \\ &= \sqrt[5]{1.4235} - 1 = 0.0732 = 7.32\%\end{aligned}$$

Thus, the geometric mean annual return is 7.32 percent, slightly less than the arithmetic mean return.

Solution to 4:

To calculate the money-weighted rate of return, tabulate the annual returns and investment amounts to determine the cash flows, as shown in Exhibit 4. All amounts are in millions of euros.

Exhibit 4

Year	1	2	3	4	5
Balance from previous year	0	34.50	42.75	22.00	28.75
New investment by the investor (cash inflow for the Rhein fund)	30.00	10.50	0	3.00	6.25
Withdrawal by the investor (cash outflow for the Rhein fund)	0	0	−22.75	0	0
Net balance at the beginning of year	30.00	45.00	20.00	25.00	35.00
Investment return for the year	15%	−5%	10%	15%	3%
Investment gain (loss)	4.50	−2.25	2.00	3.75	1.05
Balance at the end of year	34.50	42.75	22.00	28.75	36.05

$CF_0 = -30.00$, $CF_1 = -10.50$, $CF_2 = +22.75$, $CF_3 = -3.00$, $CF_4 = -6.25$, $CF_5 = +36.05$.

For clarification, it may be appropriate to explain the notation for cash flows. Each cash inflow or outflow occurs at the end of each year. Thus, CF_0 refers to the cash flow at the end of Year 0 or beginning of Year 1, and CF_5 refers to the cash flow at end of Year 5 or beginning of Year 6. Because cash flows are being discounted to the present—that is, end of Year 0 or beginning of Year 1—the period of discounting CF_0 is zero whereas the period of discounting for CF_5 is 5 years.

To get the exact money-weighted rate of return (IRR), the following equation would be equal to zero. Instead of calculating, however, use the 5 percent return to see whether the value of the expression is positive or not. If it is positive, then the money-weighted rate of return is greater than 5 percent, because a 5 percent discount rate could not reduce the value to zero.

$$\frac{-30.00}{(1.05)^0} + \frac{-10.50}{(1.05)^1} + \frac{22.75}{(1.05)^2} + \frac{-3.00}{(1.05)^3} + \frac{-6.25}{(1.05)^4} + \frac{36.05}{(1.05)^5} = 1.1471$$

Because the value is positive, the money-weighted rate of return is greater than 5 percent. Using a financial calculator, the exact money-weighted rate of return is 5.86 percent.

2.1.5 *Time-Weighted Rate of Return*

An investment measure that is not sensitive to the additions and withdrawals of funds is the time-weighted rate of return. The **time-weighted rate of return** measures the compound rate of growth of $1 initially invested in the portfolio over a stated measurement period. For the evaluation of portfolios of publicly traded securities, the time-weighted rate of return is the preferred performance measure as it neutralizes the effect of cash withdrawals or additions to the portfolio, which are generally outside of the control of the portfolio manager. To compute an exact time-weighted rate of return on a portfolio, take the following three steps:

1. Price the portfolio immediately prior to any significant addition or withdrawal of funds. Break the overall evaluation period into subperiods based on the dates of cash inflows and outflows.
2. Calculate the holding period return on the portfolio for each subperiod.
3. Link or compound holding period returns to obtain an annual rate of return for the year (the time-weighted rate of return for the year). If the investment is for more than one year, take the geometric mean of the annual returns to obtain the time-weighted rate of return over that measurement period.

Let us return to our dividend stock money-weighted example and calculate the time-weighted rate of return for that investor's portfolio. In that example, we computed the holding period returns on the portfolio, Step 2 in the procedure for finding the time-weighted rate of return. Given that the portfolio earned returns of 15 percent during the first year and 6.67 percent during the second year, what is the portfolio's time-weighted rate of return over an evaluation period of two years?

We find this time-weighted return by taking the geometric mean of the two holding period returns, Step 3 in the procedure above. The calculation of the geometric mean exactly mirrors the calculation of a compound growth rate. Here, we take the product of 1 plus the holding period return for each period to find the terminal value at t = 2 of $1 invested at t = 0. We then take the square root of this product and subtract 1 to get the geometric mean. We interpret the result as the annual compound growth rate of $1 invested in the portfolio at t = 0. Thus we have

$$(1 + \text{Time-weighted return})^2 = (1.15)(1.0667)$$

$$\text{Time-weighted return} = \sqrt{(1.15)(1.0667)} - 1 = 10.76\%$$

The time-weighted return on the portfolio was 10.76 percent, compared with the money-weighted return of 9.39 percent, which gave larger weight to the second year's return. We can see why investment managers find time-weighted returns more meaningful. If a client gives an investment manager more funds to invest at an unfavorable time, the manager's money-weighted rate of return will tend to be depressed. If a client adds funds at a favorable time, the money-weighted return will tend to be elevated. The time-weighted rate of return removes these effects.

In defining the steps to calculate an exact time-weighted rate of return, we said that the portfolio should be valued immediately prior to any significant addition or withdrawal of funds. With the amount of cash flow activity in many portfolios, this task can be costly. We can often obtain a reasonable approximation of the time-weighted rate of return by valuing the portfolio at frequent, regular intervals, particularly if additions and withdrawals are unrelated to market movements. The more frequent the valuation, the more accurate the approximation. Daily valuation is commonplace. Suppose that a portfolio is valued daily over the course of a year. To compute the time-weighted return for the year, we first compute each day's holding period return. We compute 365 such daily returns, denoted $r_1, r_2, ..., r_{365}$. We obtain the annual return for the year by linking the daily holding period returns in the following way: $(1 + r_1) \times (1 + r_2) \times ... \times (1 + r_{365}) - 1$. If withdrawals and additions to the portfolio happen only at day's end, this annual return is a precise time-weighted rate of return for the year. Otherwise, it is an approximate time-weighted return for the year.

If we have a number of years of data, we can calculate a time-weighted return for each year individually, as above. If r_i is the time-weighted return for year i, we calculate an annualized time-weighted return as the geometric mean of N annual returns, as follows:

$$r_{TW} = \left[\left(1 + r_1\right) \times \left(1 + r_2\right) \times \ldots \times \left(1 + r_N\right)\right]^{1/N} - 1$$

Example 2 illustrates the calculation of the time-weighted rate of return.

EXAMPLE 2

Time-Weighted Rate of Return

Strubeck Corporation sponsors a pension plan for its employees. It manages part of the equity portfolio in-house and delegates management of the balance to Super Trust Company. As chief investment officer of Strubeck, you want to review the performance of the in-house and Super Trust portfolios over the last four quarters. You have arranged for outflows and inflows to the portfolios to be made at the very beginning of the quarter. Exhibit 5 summarizes the inflows and outflows as well as the two portfolios' valuations. In the table, the ending value is the portfolio's value just prior to the cash inflow or outflow at the beginning of the quarter. The amount invested is the amount each portfolio manager is responsible for investing.

Exhibit 5 Cash Flows for the In-House Strubeck Account and the Super Trust Account

	Quarter			
	1 ($)	2 ($)	3 ($)	4 ($)
In-House Account				
Beginning value	4,000,000	6,000,000	5,775,000	6,720,000
Beginning of period inflow (outflow)	1,000,000	(500,000)	225,000	(600,000)
Amount invested	5,000,000	5,500,000	6,000,000	6,120,000
Ending value	6,000,000	5,775,000	6,720,000	5,508,000
Super Trust Account				
Beginning value	10,000,000	13,200,000	12,240,000	5,659,200

Exhibit 5 (Continued)

	Quarter			
	1 ($)	2 ($)	3 ($)	4 ($)
Beginning of period inflow (outflow)	2,000,000	(1,200,000)	(7,000,000)	(400,000)
Amount invested	12,000,000	12,000,000	5,240,000	5,259,200
Ending value	13,200,000	12,240,000	5,659,200	5,469,568

Based on the information given, address the following.

1 Calculate the time-weighted rate of return for the in-house account.

2 Calculate the time-weighted rate of return for the Super Trust account.

Solution to 1:

To calculate the time-weighted rate of return for the in-house account, we compute the quarterly holding period returns for the account and link them into an annual return. The in-house account's time-weighted rate of return is 27 percent, calculated as follows:

$$\text{1Q HPR: } r_1 = (\$6{,}000{,}000 - \$5{,}000{,}000)/\$5{,}000{,}000 = 0.20$$
$$\text{2Q HPR: } r_2 = (\$5{,}775{,}000 - \$5{,}500{,}000)/\$5{,}500{,}000 = 0.05$$
$$\text{3Q HPR: } r_3 = (\$6{,}720{,}000 - \$6{,}000{,}000)/\$6{,}000{,}000 = 0.12$$
$$\text{4Q HPR: } r_4 = (\$5{,}508{,}000 - \$6{,}120{,}000)/\$6{,}120{,}000 = -0.10$$

$$(1 + r_1)(1 + r_2)(1 + r_3)(1 + r_4) - 1 = (1.20)(1.05)(1.12)(0.90) - 1 = 0.27 \text{ or } 27\%$$

Solution to 2:

The account managed by Super Trust has a time-weighted rate of return of 26 percent, calculated as follows:

$$\text{1Q HPR: } r_1 = (\$13{,}200{,}000 - \$12{,}000{,}000)/\$12{,}000{,}000 = 0.10$$
$$\text{2Q HPR: } r_2 = (\$12{,}240{,}000 - \$12{,}000{,}000)/\$12{,}000{,}000 = 0.02$$
$$\text{3Q HPR: } r_3 = (\$5{,}659{,}200 - \$5{,}240{,}000)/\$5{,}240{,}000 = 0.08$$
$$\text{4Q HPR: } r_4 = (\$5{,}469{,}568 - \$5{,}259{,}200)/\$5{,}259{,}200 = 0.04$$

$$(1 + r_1)(1 + r_2)(1 + r_3)(1 + r_4) - 1 = (1.10)(1.02)(1.08)(1.04) - 1 = 0.26 \text{ or } 26\%$$

The in-house portfolio's time-weighted rate of return is higher than the Super Trust portfolio's by 100 basis points.

Having worked through this exercise, we are ready to look at a more detailed case.

EXAMPLE 3

Time-Weighted and Money-Weighted Rates of Return Side by Side

Your task is to compute the investment performance of the Walbright Fund during 2014. The facts are as follows:

- On 1 January 2014, the Walbright Fund had a market value of $100 million.
- During the period 1 January 2014 to 30 April 2014, the stocks in the fund showed a capital gain of $10 million.
- On 1 May 2014, the stocks in the fund paid a total dividend of $2 million. All dividends were reinvested in additional shares.
- Because the fund's performance had been exceptional, institutions invested an additional $20 million in Walbright on 1 May 2014, raising assets under management to $132 million ($100 + $10 + $2 + $20).
- On 31 December 2014, Walbright received total dividends of $2.64 million. The fund's market value on 31 December 2014, not including the $2.64 million in dividends, was $140 million.
- The fund made no other interim cash payments during 2014.

Based on the information given, address the following.

1 Compute the Walbright Fund's time-weighted rate of return.

2 Compute the Walbright Fund's money-weighted rate of return.

3 Interpret the differences between the time-weighted and money-weighted rates of return.

Solution to 1:

Because interim cash flows were made on 1 May 2014, we must compute two interim total returns and then link them to obtain an annual return. Exhibit 6 lists the relevant market values on 1 January, 1 May, and 31 December as well as the associated interim four-month (1 January to 1 May) and eight-month (1 May to 31 December) holding period returns.

Exhibit 6 Cash Flows for the Walbright Fund

1 January 2014	Beginning portfolio value = $100 million
1 May 2014	Dividends received before additional investment = $2 million
	Ending portfolio value = $110 million
	$\text{Holding period return} = \dfrac{\$2 + \$10}{\$100} = 12\%$
	New investment = $20 million
	Beginning market value for last 2/3 of year = $132 million
31 December 2014	Dividends received = $2.64 million

Exhibit 6 (Continued)

Ending portfolio value = \$140 million

$$\text{Holding period return} = \frac{\$2.64 + \$140 - \$132}{\$132}$$

$$= 8.06\%$$

Now we must geometrically link the four- and eight-month returns to compute an annual return. We compute the time-weighted return as follows:

Time-weighted return = 1.12 × 1.0806 − 1 = 0.2103

In this instance, we compute a time-weighted rate of return of 21.03 percent for one year. The four-month and eight-month intervals combine to equal one year. (Taking the square root of the product 1.12 × 1.0806 would be appropriate only if 1.12 and 1.0806 each applied to one full year.)

Solution to 2:

To calculate the money-weighted return, we find the discount rate that sets the sum of the present value of cash inflows and outflows equal to zero. The initial market value of the fund and all additions to it are treated as cash outflows. (Think of them as expenditures.) Withdrawals, receipts, and the ending market value of the fund are counted as inflows. (The ending market value is the amount investors receive on liquidating the fund.) Because interim cash flows have occurred at four-month intervals, we must solve for the four-month internal rate of return. Exhibit 6 details the cash flows and their timing.

$CF_0 = -100$

$CF_1 = -20$

$CF_2 = 0$

$CF_3 = 142.64$

CF_0 refers to the initial investment of \$100 million made at the beginning of the first four-month interval on 1 January 2014. CF_1 refers to the cash flows made at end of the first four-month interval or the beginning of the second four-month interval on 1 May 2014. Those cash flows include a cash inflow of \$2 million for the dividend received and cash outflows of \$22 million for the dividend reinvested and additional investment respectively. The second four-month interval had no cash flow so CF_2 is equal to zero. CF_3 refers to the cash inflows at the end of the third four-month interval. Those cash inflows include a \$2.64 million dividend received and the fund's terminal market value of \$140 million

Using a spreadsheet or IRR-enabled calculator, we use −100, −20, 0, and \$142.64 for the $t = 0$, $t = 1$, $t = 2$, and $t = 3$ net cash flows, respectively.[3] Using either tool, we get a four-month IRR of 6.28 percent. The quick way to annualize this is to multiply by 3. A more accurate way is $(1.0628)^3 - 1 = 0.20$ or 20 percent.

$$\frac{CF_0}{(1+IRR)^0} + \frac{CF_1}{(1+IRR)^1} + \frac{CF_2}{(1+IRR)^2} + \frac{CF_3}{(1+IRR)^3}$$

$$= \frac{-100}{1} + \frac{-20}{(1+IRR)^1} + \frac{0}{(1+IRR)^2} + \frac{142.64}{(1+IRR)^3}$$

$$IRR = 6.28\%$$

Solution to 3:

In this example, the time-weighted return (21.03 percent) is greater than the money-weighted return (20 percent). The Walbright Fund's performance was relatively poorer during the eight-month period, when the fund owned more shares, than it was overall. This fact is reflected in a lower money-weighted rate of return compared with time-weighted rate of return, as the money-weighted return is sensitive to the timing and amount of withdrawals and additions to the portfolio.

The accurate measurement of portfolio returns is important to the process of evaluating portfolio managers. In addition to considering returns, however, analysts must also weigh risk. When we worked through Example 2, we stopped short of suggesting that in-house management was superior to Super Trust because it earned a higher time-weighted rate of return. A judgement as to whether performance was "better" or "worse" must include the risk dimension, which will be covered later in your study materials.

2.1.6 *Annualized Return*

The period during which a return is earned or computed can vary and often we have to annualize a return that was calculated for a period that is shorter (or longer) than one year. You might buy a short-term treasury bill with a maturity of 3 months, or you might take a position in a futures contract that expires at the end of the next quarter. How can we compare these returns? In, many cases, it is most convenient to annualize all available returns. Thus, daily weekly, monthly, and quarterly returns are converted to annualize all available returns. Many formulas used for calculating certain values or prices also require all returns and periods to be expressed as annualized rates of return. For example, the most common version of the Black–Scholes option-pricing model requires annualized returns and periods to be in years.

To annualize any return for a period shorter than one year, the return for the period must be compounded by the number of periods in a year. A monthly return is compounded 12 times, a weekly return is compounded 52 times, and a quarterly return is compounded 4 times. Daily returns are normally compounded 365 times. For an uncommon number of days, we compound by the ratio of 365 to the number of days.

If the weekly return is 0.2 percent, then the compound annual return is computed as shown because there are 52 weeks in a year:

$$r_{annual} = \left(1 + r_{weekly}\right)^{52} - 1 = \left(1 + 0.2\%\right)^{52} - 1$$
$$= \left(1.002\right)^{52} - 1 = 0.1095 = 10.95\%$$

---

3 By convention, we denote outflow with a negative sign, and we need 0 as a placeholder for the $t = 2$.

If the return for 15 days is 0.4 percent, the annualized return is computed assuming 365 days in a year. Thus,

$$r_{annual} = \left(1 + r_{15}\right)^{365/15} - 1 = \left(1 + 0.4\%\right)^{365/15} - 1$$
$$= \left(1.004\right)^{365/15} - 1 = 0.1020 = 10.20\%$$

A general equation to annualize returns is given, where c is the number of periods in a year. For a quarter, $c = 4$ and for a month, $c = 12$:

$$r_{annual} = \left(1 + r_{period}\right)^{c} - 1$$

How can we annualize a return when the holding period return is more than one year? For example, how do we annualize an 18-month holding period return? Because one year contains two-thirds of 18-month periods, $c = 2/3$ in the above equation. An 18-month return of 20 percent can be annualized, as shown:

$$r_{annual} = \left(1 + r_{18month}\right)^{2/3} - 1 = \left(1 + 0.20\right)^{2/3} - 1 = 0.1292 = 12.92\%$$

Similar expressions can be constructed when quarterly or weekly returns are needed for comparison instead of annual returns. In such cases, c is equal to the number of holding periods in a quarter or in a week. For example, assume that you want to convert daily returns to weekly returns or annual returns to weekly returns for comparison between weekly returns. For converting daily returns to weekly returns, $c = 5$, assuming that there are five trading days in a week. For converting annual returns to weekly returns, $c = 1/52$. The expressions for annual returns can then be rewritten as expressions for weekly returns, as shown:

$$r_{weekly} = \left(1 + r_{daily}\right)^{5} - 1;\ r_{weekly} = \left(1 + r_{annual}\right)^{1/52} - 1$$

One major limitation of annualizing returns is the implicit assumption that returns can be repeated precisely, that is, money can be reinvested repeatedly while earning a similar return. This type of return is not always possible. An investor may earn a return of 5 percent during a week because the market went up that week or he got lucky with his stock, but it is highly unlikely that he will earn a return of 5 percent every week for the next 51 weeks, resulting in an annualized return of 1,164.3 percent ($= 1.05^{52} - 1$). Therefore, it is important to annualize short-term returns with this limitation in mind.

EXAMPLE 4

Annualized Returns

An analyst is trying to evaluate three securities that have been in her portfolio for different periods of time.

- In the last 100 days, Security A has earned a return of 6.2 percent.
- Security B has earned 2 percent over the last 4 weeks.
- Security C has earned a return of 5 percent over the last 3 months

The analyst is trying to assess the relative performance of the 3 securities.

Solution:

Annualized return for Security A: $R_{SA} = (1 + 0.062)^{365/100} - 1 = 0.2455 =$ 24.55%

Annualized return for Security B: $R_{SB} = (1 + 0.02)^{52/4} - 1 = 0.2936 = 29.36\%$

Annualized return for Security C: $R_{SC} = (1 + 0.05)^{4} - 1 = 0.2155 = 21.55\%$

Security B has the highest annualized return.

2.2 Other Major Return Measures and their Applications

The statistical measures of return discussed in the previous section are generally applicable across a wide range of assets and time periods. Special assets, however, such as mutual funds, and other considerations, such as taxes or inflation, may require return measures that are specific to a particular application.

Although it is not possible to consider all types of special applications, we will discuss the effect of fees (gross versus net returns), taxes (pre-tax and after-tax returns), inflation (nominal and real returns), and **leverage**. Many investors use mutual funds or other external entities (i.e., investment vehicles) for investment. In those cases, funds charge management fees and expenses to the investors. Consequently, gross and net-of-fund-expense returns should also be considered. Of course, an investor may be interested in the net-of-expenses after-tax real return, which is in fact what an investor truly receives. We consider these additional return measures in the following sections.

2.2.1 *Gross and Net Return*

A gross return is the return earned by an asset manager prior to deductions for management expenses, custodial fees, taxes, or any other expenses that are not directly related to the generation of returns but rather related to the management and administration of an investment. These expenses are not deducted from the gross return because they may vary with the amount of assets under management or may vary because of the tax status of the investor. Trading expenses, however, such as commissions, *are* accounted for in (i.e., deducted from) the computation of gross return because trading expenses contribute directly to the return earned by the manager. Thus, gross return is an appropriate measure for evaluating and comparing the investment skill of asset managers because it does not include any fees related to the management and administration of an investment.

Net return is a measure of what the investment vehicle (mutual fund, etc.) has earned for the investor. Net return accounts for (i.e., deducts) all managerial and administrative expenses that reduce an investor's return. Because individual investors are most concerned about the net return (i.e., what they actually receive), small mutual funds with a limited amount of assets under management are at a disadvantage compared with the larger funds that can spread their largely fixed administrative expenses over a larger asset base. As a result, many small mutual funds waive part of the expenses to keep the funds competitive.

2.2.2 *Pre-tax and After-tax Nominal Return*

All return measures discussed previously are pre-tax nominal returns—that is, no adjustment has been made for taxes or inflation. In general, all returns are pre-tax nominal returns unless they are otherwise designated.

Many investors are concerned about the possible tax liability associated with their returns because taxes reduce the net return that they receive. Capital gains and income may be taxed differently, depending on the jurisdiction. Capital gains come in two forms: short-term capital gains and long-term capital gains. Long-term capital gains receive preferential tax treatment in a number of countries. Interest income is taxed as ordinary income in most countries. Dividend income may be taxed as ordinary income, may have a lower tax rate, or may be exempt from taxes depending on the country and the type of investor. The after-tax nominal return is computed as the total return minus any allowance for taxes on dividends, interest and realized gains.[4]

Because taxes are paid on realized capital gains and income, the investment manager can minimize the tax liability by selecting appropriate securities (e.g., those subject to more favorable taxation, all other investment considerations equal) and reducing trading turnover. Therefore, taxable investors evaluate investment managers based on the after-tax nominal return.

2.2.3 *Real Returns*

A nominal return (r) consists of three components: a real risk-free return as compensation for postponing consumption (r_{rF}), inflation as compensation for loss of purchasing power (π), and a **risk premium** for assuming risk (RP). Thus, nominal return and real return can be expressed as:

$$(1 + r) = (1 + r_{rF}) \times (1 + \pi) \times (1 + RP)$$

$$(1 + r_{real}) = (1 + r_{rF}) \times (1 + RP) \text{ or}$$

$$(1 + r_{real}) = (1 + r) \div (1 + \pi)$$

Often the real risk-free return and the risk premium are combined to arrive at the real "risky" rate as given in the second equation above, simply referred to as the real return. Real returns are particularly useful in comparing returns across time periods because inflation rates may vary over time. Real returns are also useful in comparing returns among countries when returns are expressed in local currencies instead of a constant investor currency and when inflation rates vary between countries (which are usually the case). Finally, the after-tax real return is what the investor receives as compensation for postponing consumption and assuming risk after paying taxes on investment returns. As a result, the after-tax real return becomes a reliable benchmark for making investment decisions. Although it is a measure of an investor's benchmark return, it is not commonly calculated by asset managers because it is difficult to estimate a general tax component applicable to all investors. For example, the tax component depends on an investor's specific taxation rate (marginal tax rate), how long the investor holds an investment (long-term versus short-term), and the type of account the asset is held in (tax-exempt, tax-deferred, or normal).

EXAMPLE 5

Computation of Special Returns

Let's return to Example 1. After reading this section, Mr. Lohrmann decided that he was not being fair to the fund manager by including the asset management fee and other expenses because the small size of the fund would put it at a competitive disadvantage. He learns that the fund spends a fixed amount of €500,000 every year on expenses that are unrelated to the manager's performance.

Mr. Lohrmann has become concerned that both taxes and inflation may reduce his return. Based on the current tax code, he expects to pay 20 percent tax on the return he earns from his investment. Historically, inflation has been around 2 percent and he expects the same rate of inflation to be maintained.

1 Estimate the annual gross return for the first year by adding back the fixed expenses.

4 Bonds issued at a discount to the par value may be taxed based on accrued gains instead of realized gains.

2 What is the net return that investors in the Rhein Valley Superior Fund earned during the five-year period?

3 What is the after-tax net return for the first year that investors earned from the Rhein Valley Superior Fund? Assume that all gains are realized at the end of the year and the taxes are paid immediately at that time.

4 What is the anticipated after-tax real return that investors would have earned in the fifth year?

Solution to 1:

The gross return for the first year is higher by 1.67 percent (= €500,000/€30,000,000) than the investor return reported by the fund. Thus, the gross return is 16.67 percent (= 15% + 1.67%).

Solution to 2:

The investor return reported by the mutual fund is the net return of the fund after accounting for all direct and indirect expenses. The net return is also the pre-tax nominal return because it has not been adjusted for taxes or inflation. The net return for the five-year holding period was 42.35 percent.

Solution to 3:

The net return earned by investors during the first year was 15 percent. Applying a 20 percent tax rate, the after-tax return that accrues to the investors is 12 percent [= 15% – (0.20 × 15%)].

Solution to 4:

As in Part 3, the after-tax return earned by investors in the fifth year is 2.4 percent [= 3% – (0.20 × 3%)]. Inflation reduces the return by 2 percent so the after-tax real return earned by investors in the fifth year is 0.39 percent, as shown:

$$\frac{(1+2.40\%)}{(1+2.00\%)}-1=\frac{(1+0.0240)}{(1+0.0200)}-1=1.0039-1=0.0039=0.39\%$$

Note that taxes are paid before adjusting for inflation.

2.2.4 *Leveraged Return*

In the previous calculations, we have assumed that the investor's position in an asset is equal to the total investment made by an investor using his or her own money. This section differs in that the investor creates a leveraged position. There are two ways of creating a claim on asset returns that are greater than the investment of one's own money. First, an investor may trade futures contracts in which the money required to take a position may be as little as 10 percent of the notional value of the asset. In this case, the leveraged return, the return on the investor's own money, is 10 times the actual return of the underlying security. Both the gains and losses are amplified by a factor of 10.

Investors can also invest more than their own money by borrowing money to purchase the asset. This approach is easily done in stocks and bonds, and very common when investing in real estate. If half (50 percent) of the money invested is borrowed, then the gross return to the investor is doubled but the interest to be paid on borrowed money must be deducted in order to calculate the net return.

2.3 Historical Return and Risk

At this time, it is helpful to look at historical risk and returns for the three main asset categories: stocks, bonds, and Treasury bills. Stocks refer to corporate ownership, bonds refer to long-term fixed-income securities, and Treasury bills refer to short-term government debt securities. Although there is generally no expectation of default on government securities, long-term government bond prices are volatile (risky) because of possible future changes in interest rates. In addition, bondholders also face the risk that inflation will reduce the purchasing power of their cash flows.

2.3.1 *Historical Mean Return and Expected Return*

Before examining historical data, it is useful to distinguish between the historical mean return and expected return, which are very different concepts but easy to confuse. Historical return is what was actually earned in the *past*, whereas expected return is what an investor anticipates to earn in the *future*.

Expected return is the nominal return that would cause the marginal investor to invest in an asset based on the real risk-free interest rate (r_{rF}), expected inflation [$E(\pi)$], and expected risk premium for the risk of the asset [$E(RP)$]. The real risk-free interest rate is expected to be positive as compensation for postponing consumption. Similarly, the risk premium is expected to be positive in most cases.[5] The expected inflation rate is generally positive, except when the economy is in a deflationary state and prices are falling. Thus, expected return is generally positive. The relationship between the expected return and the real risk-free interest rate, inflation rate, and risk premium can be expressed by the following equation:

$$1 + E(R) = (1 + r_{rF}) \times [1 + E(\pi)] \times [1 + E(RP)]$$

The historical mean return for investment in a particular asset, however, is obtained from the actual return that was earned by an investor. Because the investment is risky, there is no guarantee that the actual return will be equal to the expected return. In fact, it is very unlikely that the two returns are equal for a specific time period being considered. Given a long enough period of time, we can *expect* that the future (expected) return will equal the average historical return. Unfortunately, we do not know how long that period is—10 years, 50 years, or 100 years. As a practical matter, we often assume that the historical mean return is an adequate representation of the expected return, although this assumption may not be accurate. For example, Exhibit 7 shows that the historical equity returns in the last eight years (2010–2017) for large US company stocks were positive whereas the actual return was negative the prior decade, but nearly always positive historically. Nonetheless, longer-term returns (1926–2017) were positive and could be consistent with expected return. Though it is unknown if the historical mean returns accurately represent expected returns, it is an assumption that is commonly made.

Exhibit 7 Risk and Return for US Asset Classes by Decade (%)

		1930s	1940s	1950s	1960s	1970s	1980s	1990s	2000s	2010s*	1926–2017
Large company stocks	Return	−0.1	9.2	19.4	7.8	5.9	17.6	18.2	−1.0	13.9	10.2
	Risk	41.6	17.5	14.1	13.1	17.2	19.4	15.9	16.3	13.6	19.8

(continued)

5 There are exceptions when an asset reduces overall risk of a portfolio. We will consider those exceptions in section 4.3.

Exhibit 7 (Continued)

		1930s	1940s	1950s	1960s	1970s	1980s	1990s	2000s	2010s*	1926–2017
Small company stocks	Return	1.4	20.7	16.9	15.5	11.5	15.8	15.1	6.3	14.8	12.1
	Risk	78.6	34.5	14.4	21.5	30.8	22.5	20.2	26.1	19.4	31.7
Long-term corporate bonds	Return	6.9	2.7	1	1.7	6.2	13	8.4	7.7	8.3	6.1
	Risk	5.3	1.8	4.4	4.9	8.7	14.1	6.9	11.7	8.8	8.3
Long-term government bonds	Return	4.9	3.2	−0.1	1.4	5.5	12.6	8.8	7.7	6.8	5.5
	Risk	5.3	2.8	4.6	6	8.7	16	8.9	12.4	10.8	9.9
Treasury bills	Return	0.6	0.4	1.9	3.9	6.3	8.9	4.9	2.8	0.2	3.4
	Risk	0.2	0.1	0.2	0.4	0.6	0.9	0.4	0.6	0.1	3.1
Inflation	Return	−2.0	5.4	2.2	2.5	7.4	5.1	2.9	2.5	1.7	2.9
	Risk	2.5	3.1	1.2	0.7	1.2	1.3	0.7	1.6	1.1	4.0

* Through 31 December 2017
Note: Returns are measured as annualized geometric mean returns.
Risk is measured by annualizing monthly standard deviations.
Source: 2018 SBBI Yearbook (Exhibits 1.2,1.3, 2.3 and 6.2).

Going forward, be sure to distinguish between expected return and historical mean return. We will alert the reader whenever historical returns are used to estimate expected returns.

2.3.2 *Nominal Returns of Major US Asset Classes*

We focus on three major asset categories in Exhibit 7: stocks, bonds, and T-bills. The mean nominal returns for US asset classes are reported decade by decade since the 1930s. The total for the 1926–2017 period is in the last column. All returns are annual geometric mean returns. Large company stocks had an overall annual return of 10.2 percent during the 92-year period. The return was negative in the 1930s and 2000s, and positive in all remaining decades. The 1950s and 1990s were the best decades for large company stocks. Small company stocks fared even better. The nominal return was never negative for any decade, and had double-digit growth in all decades except two, leading to an overall 92-year annual return of 12.1 percent.

Long-term corporate bonds and long-term government bonds earned overall returns of 6.1 percent and 5.5 percent, respectively. The corporate bonds did not have a single negative decade, although government bonds recorded a negative return in the 1950s when stocks were doing extremely well. Bonds also had some excellent decades, earning double-digit returns in the 1980s and 2000s.

Treasury bills (short-term government securities) did not earn a negative return in any decade. In fact, Treasury bills earned a negative return only in 1938 (−0.02 percent) when the inflation rate was −2.78 percent. Consistently positive returns for Treasury bills are not surprising because nominal interest rates are almost never negative and the Treasury bills suffer from little interest rate or inflation risk. Since the Great Depression, there has been no deflation in any decade, although inflation rates were highly negative in 1930 (−6.03 percent), 1931 (−9.52 percent), and 1932 (−10.30 percent). Conversely, inflation rates were very high in the late 1970s and early 1980s, reaching 13.31 percent in 1979. Inflation rates have been largely range bound between 1 and 3 percent from 1991 to 2017. Overall, the inflation rate was 2.9 percent for the 92-year period.

2.3.3 *Real Returns of Major US Asset Classes*

Because annual inflation rates can vary greatly, from −10.30 percent to +13.31 percent in the last 92 years, comparisons across various time periods is difficult and misleading using nominal returns. Therefore, it is more effective to rely on real returns. Real returns on stocks, bonds, and T-bills are reported from 1900 in Exhibits 8 and 9.

Exhibit 8 Cumulative Returns on US Asset Classes in Real Terms, 1900–2017

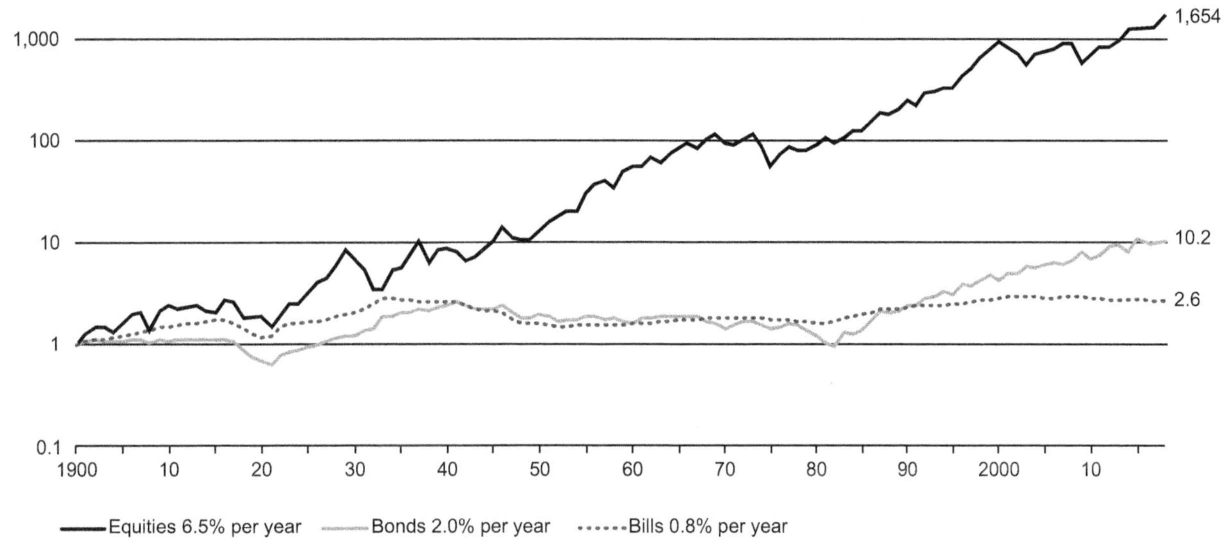

Source: E. Dimson, P. Marsh, and M. Staunton, *Credit Suisse Global Investment Returns Yearbook 2018*, Credit Suisse Research Institute (February 2018). This chart is updated annually and can be found at https://www.credit-suisse.com/media/assets/corporate/docs/about-us/media/media-release/2018/02/giry-summary-2018.pdf.

Exhibit 8 shows that $1 would have grown to $1,654 if invested in stocks, to only $10.20 if invested in bonds, and to $2.60 if invested in T-bills. The difference in growth among the three asset categories is huge, although the difference in real returns does not seem that large: 6.5 percent per year for equities compared with 2.0 percent per year for bonds. This difference represents the effect of compounding over a 118-year period.

Exhibit 9 reports real rates of return. As we discussed earlier and as shown in the table, geometric mean is never greater than the arithmetic mean. Our analysis of returns focuses on the geometric mean because it is a more accurate representation of returns for multiple holding periods than the arithmetic mean. We observe that the real returns for stocks are higher than the real returns for bonds.

Exhibit 9 Real Returns and Risk Premiums for Asset Classes (1900–2017)

		United States			World			World excluding United States		
	Asset	*GM* (%)	*AM* (%)	*SD* (%)	*GM* (%)	*AM* (%)	*SD* (%)	*GM* (%)	*AM* (%)	*SD* (%)
Real Returns	Equities	6.5	8.4	20.0	5.2	6.6	17.4	4.5	6.2	18.9
	Bonds	2.0	2.5	10.4	2.0	2.5	11.0	1.7	2.7	14.4
Premiums	Equities vs. bonds	4.4	6.5	20.7	3.2	4.4	15.3	2.8	3.8	14.4

Note: All returns are in percent per annum measured in US$. GM = geometric mean, AM = arithmetic mean, SD = standard deviation. "World" consists of 21 developed countries: Australia, Austria, Belgium, Canada, Denmark, Finland, France, Germany, Ireland, Italy, Japan, the Netherlands, New Zealand, Norway, Portugal, South Africa, Spain, Sweden, Switzerland, United Kingdom, and the United States. Weighting is by each country's relative market capitalization size.
Source: Credit Suisse Global Investment Returns Sourcebook, 2018.

2.3.4 *Nominal and Real Returns of Asset Classes in Major Countries*

Along with US returns, real returns of major asset classes for a 21-country world and the world excluding the United States are also presented in Exhibit 9. Equity returns are weighted by each country's GDP before 1968 because of a lack of reliable market capitalization data. Returns are weighted by a country's market capitalization beginning with 1968. Similarly, bond returns are defined by a 21-country bond index, except GDP is used to create the weights because equity market capitalization weighting is inappropriate for a bond index and bond market capitalizations were not readily available.

The real geometric mean return for the world stock index over the last 117 years was 5.2 percent, and bonds had a real geometric mean return of 2.0 percent. The real geometric mean return for the world excluding the United States were 4.5 percent for stocks and 1.7 percent for bonds. For both stocks and bonds, the United States earned higher returns than the world excluding the United States. Similarly, real returns for stocks and bonds in the United States were higher than the real returns for rest of the world.

2.3.5 *Risk of Major Asset Classes*

Risk for major asset classes in the United States is reported for 1926–2017 in Exhibit 7, and the risk for major asset classes for the United States, the world, and the world excluding the United States are reported for 1900–2017 in Exhibit 9. Exhibit 7 shows that US small company stocks had the highest risk, 31.7 percent, followed by US large company stocks, 19.8 percent. Long-term government bonds and long-term corporate bonds had lower risk at 9.9 percent and 8.3 percent, with Treasury bills having the lowest risk at about 3.1 percent.

Exhibit 9 shows that the risk for world stocks is 17.4 percent and for world bonds is 11.0 percent. The world excluding the United States has risks of 18.9 percent for stocks and 14.4 percent for bonds. The effect of diversification is apparent when world risk is compared with US risk and world excluding US risk. Although the risk of US stocks is 20.0 percent and the risk of world excluding US stocks is 18.9 percent, the combination gives a risk of only 17.4 percent for world stocks.

2.3.6 Risk–Return Trade-off

The expression "risk–return trade-off" refers to the positive relationship between expected risk and return. In other words, a higher return is not possible to attain in **efficient markets** and over long periods of time without accepting higher risk. Expected returns should be greater for assets with greater risk.

The historical data presented above show the risk–return trade-off. Exhibit 7 shows for the United States that small company stocks had higher risk and higher return than large company stocks. Large company stocks had higher returns and higher risk than both long-term corporate bonds and government bonds. Bonds had higher returns and higher risk than Treasury bills. Uncharacteristically, however, long-term government bonds had higher total risk than long-term corporate bonds, although the returns of corporate bonds were slightly higher. These factors do not mean that long-term government bonds had greater default risk, just that they were more variable than corporate bonds during this historic period.

Exhibit 9 reveals that the risk and return for stocks were the highest of the asset classes, and the risk and return for bonds were lower than stocks for the United States, the world, and the world excluding the United States.

Another way of looking at the risk–return trade-off is to focus on the **risk premium**, which is the extra return investors can expect for assuming additional risk, after accounting for the nominal risk-free interest rate (includes both compensation for expected inflation and the real risk-free interest rate). Worldwide equity risk premiums reported at the bottom of Exhibit 9 show that equities outperformed bonds. Investors in equities earned a higher return than investors in bonds because of the higher risk in equities.

A more dramatic representation of the risk–return trade-off is shown in Exhibit 8, which shows the cumulative returns of US asset classes in real terms. The line representing T-bills is much less volatile than the other lines. Adjusted for inflation, the average real return on T-bills was 0.8 percent per year. The line representing bonds is more volatile than the line for T-bills but less volatile than the line representing stocks. The total return for equities including dividends and capital gains shows how $1 invested at the beginning of 1900 grows to $1,654, generating an annualized return of 6.5 percent in real terms.

Over long periods of time, we observe that higher risk does result in higher mean returns. Thus, it is reasonable to claim that, over the long term, market prices reward higher risk with higher returns, which is a characteristic of a risk-averse investor, a topic that we discuss in Section 3.

2.4 Other Investment Characteristics

In evaluating investments using only the mean (expected return) and variance (risk), we are implicitly making two important assumptions: 1) that the returns are normally distributed and can be fully characterized by their means and variances and 2) that markets are not only informationally efficient but that they are also operationally efficient. To the extent that these assumptions are violated, we need to consider additional investment characteristics. These are discussed below.

2.4.1 *Distributional Characteristics*

As explained in an earlier reading, a **normal distribution** has three main characteristics: its mean and median are equal; it is completely defined by two parameters, mean and variance; and it is symmetric around its mean with:

- 68 percent of the observations within $\pm 1\sigma$ of the mean,
- 95 percent of the observations within $\pm 2\sigma$ of the mean, and
- 99 percent of the observations within $\pm 3\sigma$ of the mean.

Using only mean and variance would be appropriate to evaluate investments if returns were distributed normally. Returns, however, are not normally distributed; deviations from normality occur both because the returns are skewed, which means they are not symmetric around the mean, and because the probability of extreme events is significantly greater than what a normal distribution would suggest. The latter deviation is referred to as kurtosis or fat tails in a return distribution. The next sections discuss these deviations more in-depth.

Skewness **Skewness** refers to asymmetry of the return distribution, that is, returns are not symmetric around the mean. A distribution is said to be left skewed or negatively skewed if most of the distribution is concentrated to the right, and right skewed or positively skewed if most is concentrated to the left. Exhibit 10 shows a typical representation of negative and positive skewness, whereas Exhibit 11 demonstrates the negative skewness of stock returns by plotting a histogram of US large company stock returns for 1926–2017.

Exhibit 10 Skewness

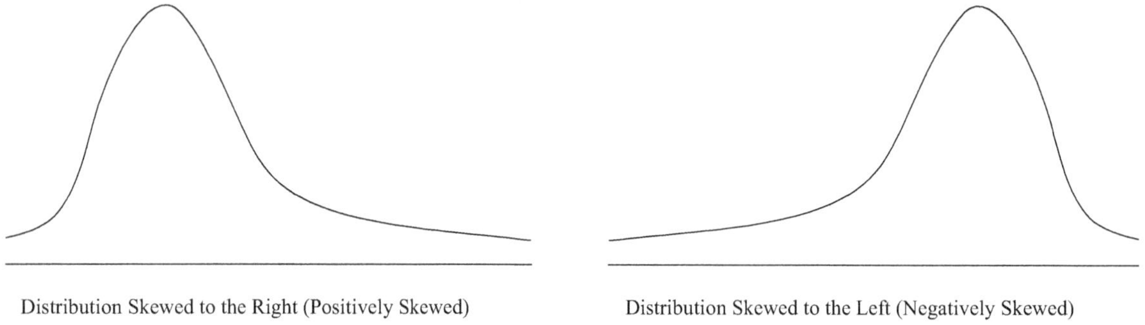

Source: Reprinted from *Fixed Income Readings for the Chartered Financial Analyst® Program.* Copyright CFA Institute.

Exhibit 11 Histogram of US Large Company Stock Returns, 1926–2017 (Percent)

						2016				
						2014				
						2012				
						2010				
					2015	2006	2017			
					2011	2004	2009	2013		
				2000	2007	1988	2003	1997		
				1990	2005	1986	1999	1995		
				1981	1994	1979	1998	1991		
				1977	1993	1972	1996	1989		
				1969	1992	1971	1983	1985		
				1962	1987	1968	1982	1980		
				1953	1984	1965	1976	1975		
				1946	1978	1964	1967	1955		
			2001	1940	1970	1959	1963	1950		
			1973	1939	1960	1952	1961	1945		
		2002	1966	1934	1956	1949	1951	1938	1958	
	2008	1974	1957	1932	1948	1944	1943	1936	1935	1954
1931	1937	1939	1941	1929	1947	1926	1942	1927	1928	1933

–60 –50 –40 –30 –20 –10 0 10 20 30 40 50 60 70

Source: 2018 SBBI Yearbook (Appendix A1)

Kurtosis **Kurtosis** refers to fat tails or higher than normal probabilities for extreme returns and has the effect of increasing an asset's risk that is not captured in a mean–variance framework, as illustrated in Exhibit 12. Investors try to evaluate the effect of kurtosis by using such statistical techniques as value at risk (VaR) and conditional tail expectations.[6] Several market participants note that the probability and the magnitude of extreme events is underappreciated and was a primary contributing factor to the financial crisis of 2008.[7] The higher probability of extreme negative outcomes among stock returns can also be observed in Exhibit 11.

Exhibit 12 Kurtosis

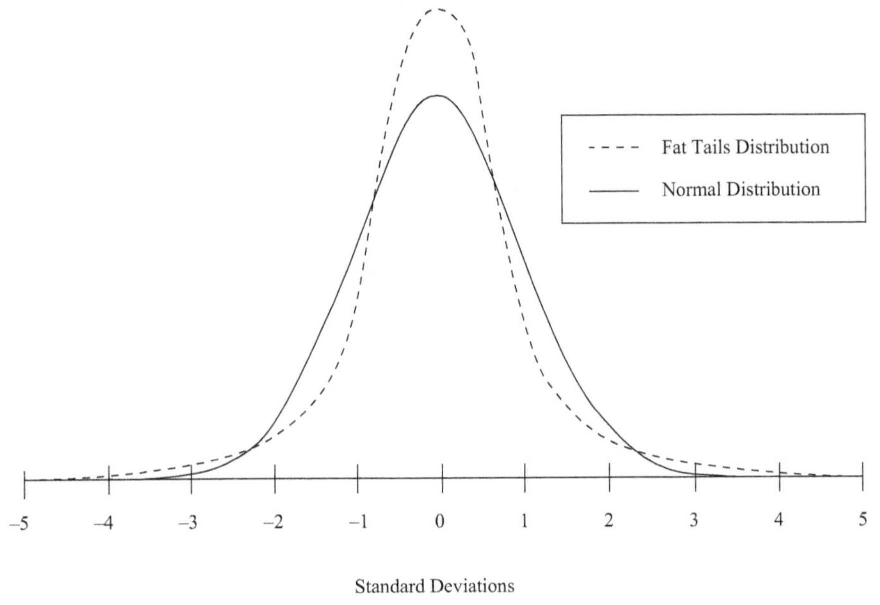

Source: Reprinted from *Fixed Income Readings for the Chartered Financial Analyst® Program.* Copyright CFA Institute.

2.4.2 *Market Characteristics*

In the previous analysis, we implicitly assumed that markets are both informationally and operationally efficient. Although informational efficiency of markets is a topic beyond the purview of this reading, we should highlight certain operational limitations of the market that affect the choice of investments. One such limitation is **liquidity**.

The cost of trading has three main components—brokerage commission, bid–ask spread, and price impact. Liquidity affects the latter two. Stocks with low liquidity can have wide bid–ask spreads. The bid–ask spread, which is the difference between the buying price and the selling price, is incurred as a cost of trading a security. The larger the bid–ask spread, the higher the cost of trading. If a $100 stock has a spread of 10 cents, the bid–ask spread is only 0.1 percent ($0.10/$100). On the other hand, if

6 Value at risk is a money measure of the minimum losses expected on a portfolio during a specified time period at a given level of probability. It is commonly used to measure the losses a portfolio can suffer under normal market conditions. For example, if a portfolio's one-day 10 percent VaR is £200,000, it implies that there is a 10 percent probability that the value of the portfolio will decrease by more than £200,000 over a single one-day period (under normal market conditions). This probability implies that the portfolio will experience a loss of at least £200,000 on one out of every ten days.

7 For example, see Bogle (2008) and Taleb (2007).

a $10 stock has a spread of 10 cents, the bid–ask spread is 1 percent. Clearly, the $10 stock is more expensive to trade and an investor will need to earn 0.9 percent extra to make up the higher cost of trading relative to the $100 stock.

Liquidity also has implications for the price impact of trade. Price impact refers to how the price moves in response to an order in the market. Small orders usually have little impact, especially for liquid stocks. For example, an order to buy 100 shares of a $100 stock with a spread of 1 cent may have no effect on the price. On the other hand, an order to buy 100,000 shares may have a significant impact on the price as the buyer has to induce more and more stockholders to tender their shares. The extent of the price impact depends on the liquidity of the stock. A stock that trades millions of shares a day may be less affected than a stock that trades only a few hundred thousand shares a day. Investors, especially institutional investors managing large sums of money, must keep the liquidity of a stock in mind when making investment decisions.

Liquidity is a bigger concern in emerging markets than in developed markets because of the smaller volume of trading in those markets. Similarly, liquidity is a more important concern in corporate bond markets and especially for bonds of lower credit quality than in equity markets because an individual corporate bond issue may not trade for several days or weeks. This certainly became apparent during the global financial crisis.

There are other market-related characteristics that affect investment decisions because they might instill greater confidence in the security or might affect the costs of doing business. These include analyst coverage, availability of information, firm size, etc. These characteristics about companies and financial markets are essential components of investment decision making.

3 RISK AVERSION AND PORTFOLIO SELECTION

As we have seen, stocks, bonds, and T-bills provide different levels of returns and have different levels of risk. Although investment in equities may be appropriate for one investor, another investor may not be inclined to accept the risk that accompanies a share of stock and may prefer to hold more cash. In the last section, we considered investment characteristics of assets in understanding their risk and return. In this section, we consider the characteristics of investors, both individual and institutional, in an attempt to pair the right kind of investors with the right kind of investments.

First, we discuss risk aversion and utility theory. Later we discuss their implications for portfolio selection.

3.1 The Concept of Risk Aversion

The concept of **risk aversion** is related to the behavior of individuals under uncertainty. Assume that an individual is offered two alternatives: one where he will get £50 for sure and the other is a gamble with a 50 percent chance that he gets £100 and 50 percent chance that he gets nothing. The expected value in both cases is £50, one with certainty and the other with uncertainty. What will an investor choose? There are three possibilities: an investor chooses the gamble, the investor chooses £50 with certainty, or the investor is indifferent. Let us consider each in turn. However, please understand that this is only a representative example, and a single choice does not determine the risk aversion of an investor.

Risk Seeking

If an investor chooses the gamble, then the investor is said to be risk loving or risk seeking. The gamble has an uncertain outcome, but with the same expected value as the guaranteed outcome. Thus, an investor choosing the gamble means that the investor gets extra "utility" from the uncertainty associated with the gamble. How much is that extra utility worth? Would the investor be willing to accept a smaller expected value because he gets extra utility from risk? Indeed, risk seekers will accept less return because of the risk that accompanies the gamble. For example, a risk seeker may choose a gamble with an expected value of £45 in preference to a guaranteed outcome of £50.

There is a little bit of gambling instinct in many of us. People buy lottery tickets although the expected value is less than the money they pay to buy it. Or people gamble at casinos with the full knowledge that the expected return is negative, a characteristic of risk seekers. These or any other isolated actions, however, cannot be taken at face value except for compulsive gamblers.

Risk Neutral

If an investor is indifferent about the gamble or the guaranteed outcome, then the investor may be risk neutral. Risk neutrality means that the investor cares only about return and not about risk, so higher return investments are more desirable even if they come with higher risk. Many investors may exhibit characteristics of risk neutrality when the investment at stake is an insignificant part of their wealth. For example, a billionaire may be indifferent about choosing the gamble or a £50 guaranteed outcome.

Risk Averse

If an investor chooses the guaranteed outcome, he/she is said to be **risk averse** because the investor does not want to take the chance of not getting anything at all. Depending on the level of aversion to risk, an investor may be willing to accept a guaranteed outcome of £45 instead of a gamble with an expected value of £50.

In general, investors are likely to shy away from risky investments for a lower, but guaranteed return. That is why they want to minimize their risk for the same amount of return, and maximize their return for the same amount of risk. The risk–return trade-off discussed earlier is an indicator of risk aversion. A risk-neutral investor would maximize return irrespective of risk and a risk-seeking investor would maximize both risk and return.

Data presented in the last section illustrate the historically positive relationship between risk and return, which demonstrates that market prices were based on transactions and investments by risk-averse investors and reflect risk aversion. Therefore, for all practical purposes and for our future discussion, we will assume that the representative investor is a risk-averse investor. This assumption is the standard approach taken in the investment industry globally.

Risk Tolerance

Risk tolerance refers to the amount of risk an investor can tolerate to achieve an investment goal. The higher the risk tolerance, the greater is the willingness to take risk. Thus, risk tolerance is negatively related to risk aversion.

3.2 Utility Theory and Indifference Curves

Continuing with our previous example, a risk-averse investor would rank the guaranteed outcome of £50 higher than the uncertain outcome with an expected value of £50. We can say that the utility that an investor or an individual derives from the guaranteed outcome of £50 is greater than the utility or satisfaction or happiness he/

she derives from the alternative. In general terms, utility is a measure of relative satisfaction from consumption of various goods and services or in the case of investments, the satisfaction that an investor derives from a portfolio.

Because individuals are different in their preferences, all risk-averse individuals may not rank investment alternatives in the same manner. Consider the £50 gamble again. All risk-averse individuals will rank the guaranteed outcome of £50 higher than the gamble. What if the guaranteed outcome is only £40? Some risk-averse investors might consider £40 inadequate, others might accept it, and still others may now be indifferent about the uncertain £50 and the certain £40.

A simple implementation of utility theory allows us to quantify the rankings of investment choices using risk and return. There are several assumptions about individual behavior that we make in the definition of utility given in the equation below. We assume that investors are risk averse. They always prefer more to less (greater return to lesser return). They are able to rank different portfolios in the order of their preference and that the rankings are internally consistent. If an individual prefers X to Y and Y to Z, then he/she must prefer X to Z. This property implies that the indifference curves (see Exhibit 13) for the same individual can never touch or intersect. An example of a utility function is given below

$$U = E(r) - \frac{1}{2}A\sigma^2$$

where, U is the utility of an investment, $E(r)$ is the expected return, and σ^2 is the variance of the investment.

In the above equation, A is a measure of risk aversion, which is measured as the marginal reward that an investor requires to accept additional risk. More risk-averse investors require greater compensation for accepting additional risk. Thus, A is higher for more risk-averse individuals. As was mentioned previously, a risk-neutral investor would maximize return irrespective of risk and a risk-seeking investor would maximize both risk and return.

We can draw several conclusions from the utility function. First, utility is unbounded on both sides. It can be highly positive or highly negative. Second, higher return contributes to higher utility. Third, higher variance reduces the utility but the reduction in utility gets amplified by the risk aversion coefficient, A. Utility can always be increased, albeit marginally, by getting higher return or lower risk. Fourth, utility does not indicate or measure satisfaction itself—it can be useful only in ranking various investments. For example, a portfolio with a utility of 4 is not necessarily two times better than a portfolio with a utility of 2. The portfolio with a utility of 4 could increase our happiness 10 times or just marginally. But we do prefer a portfolio with a utility of 4 to a portfolio with a utility of 2. Utility cannot be compared among individuals or investors because it is a very personal concept. From a societal point of view, by the same argument, utility cannot be summed among individuals.

Let us explore the utility function further. The risk aversion coefficient, A, is greater than zero for a risk-averse investor. So any increase in risk reduces his/her utility. The risk aversion coefficient for a risk-neutral investor is 0, and changes in risk do not affect his/her utility. For a risk lover, the risk aversion coefficient is negative, creating an inverse situation so that additional risk contributes to an increase in his/her utility. Note that a risk-free asset ($\sigma^2 = 0$) generates the same utility for all individuals.

3.2.1 *Indifference Curves*

An **indifference curve** plots the combinations of risk–return pairs that an investor would accept to maintain a given level of utility (i.e., the investor is indifferent about the combinations on any one curve because they would provide the same level of overall utility). Indifference curves are thus defined in terms of a trade-off between expected rate of return and variance of the rate of return. Because an infinite number of combinations of risk and return can generate the same utility for the same investor, indifference curves are continuous at all points.

Exhibit 13 Indifference Curves for Risk-Averse Investors

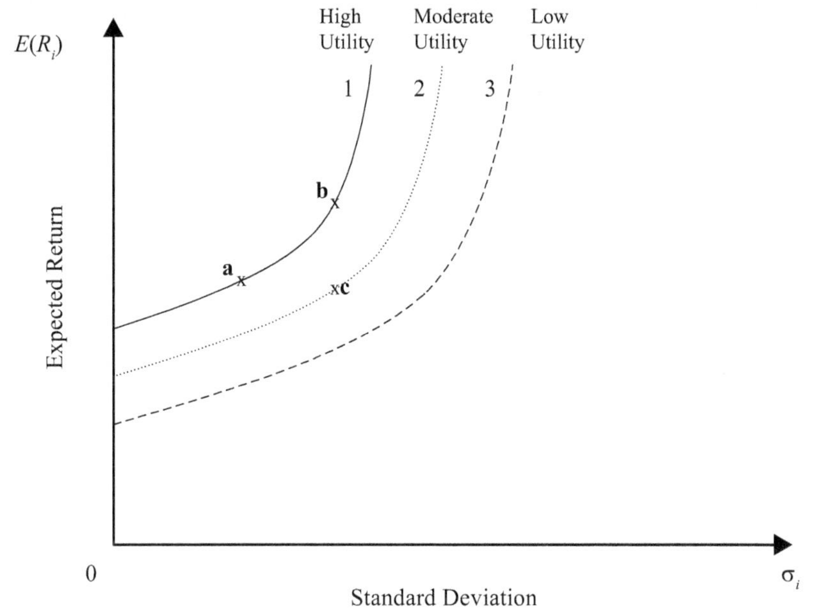

A set of indifference curves is plotted in Exhibit 13. By definition, all points on any one of the three curves have the same utility. An investor does not care whether he/she is at Point **a** or Point **b** on indifference Curve 1. Point **a** has lower risk and lower return than Point **b**, but the utility of both points is the same because the higher return at Point **b** is offset by the higher risk.

Like Curve 1, all points on Curve 2 have the same utility and an investor is indifferent about where he/she is on Curve 2. Now compare Point **c** with Point **b**. Point **c** has the same risk but significantly lower return than Point **b**, which means that the utility at Point **c** is less than the utility at Point **b**. Given that all points on Curve 1 have the same utility and all points on Curve 2 have the same utility and Point **b** has higher utility than Point **c**, Curve 1 has higher utility than Curve 2. Therefore, a risk-averse investor with indifference Curves 1 and 2 will prefer Curve 1 to Curve 2. The utility of a risk-averse investor always increases as you move northwest—higher return with lower risk. Because all investors prefer more utility to less, investors want to move northwest to the indifference curve with the highest utility.

The indifference curve for risk-averse investors runs from the southwest to the northeast because of the risk–return trade-off. If risk increases (going east) then it must be compensated by higher return (going north) to generate the same utility. The indifference curves are convex because of diminishing marginal utility of return (or wealth). As risk increases, an investor needs greater return to compensate for higher risk at an increasing rate (i.e., the curve gets steeper). The upward-sloping convex indifference curve has a slope coefficient closely related to the risk aversion coefficient. The greater the slope, the higher is the risk aversion of the investor as a greater increment in return is required to accept a given increase in risk.

Indifference curves for investors with different levels of risk aversion are plotted in Exhibit 14. The most risk-averse investor has an indifference curve with the greatest slope. As volatility increases, this investor demands increasingly higher returns to compensate for risk. The least risk-averse investor has an indifference curve with the least slope and so the demand for higher return as risk increases is not as acute as for the more risk-averse investor. The risk-loving investor's indifference curve, however, exhibits a negative slope, implying that the risk-lover is happy to substitute risk for return. For a risk lover, the utility increases both with higher risk and higher return. Finally, the indifference curves of risk-neutral investors are horizontal because the utility is invariant with risk.

Exhibit 14 Indifference Curves for Various Types of Investors

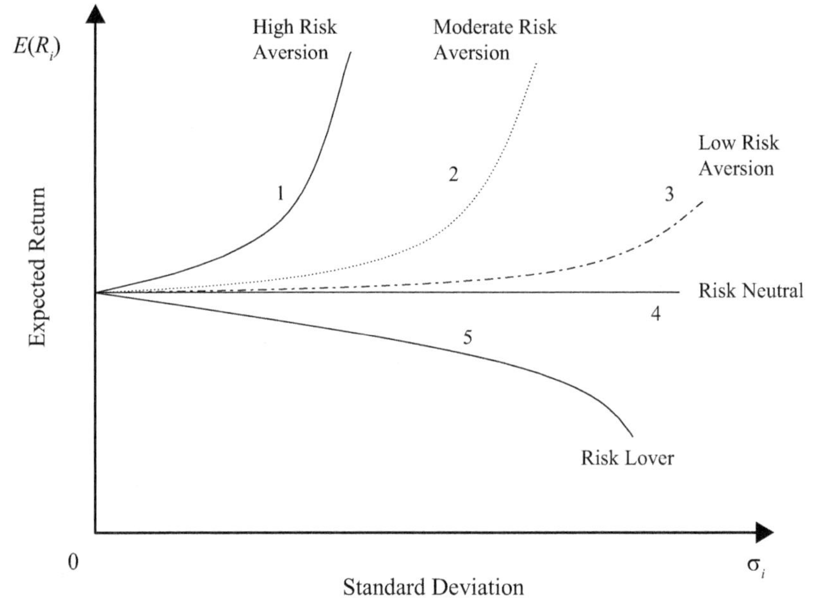

In the remaining parts of this reading, all investors are assumed to be risk averse unless stated otherwise.

EXAMPLE 6

Comparing a Gamble with a Guaranteed Outcome

Assume that you are given an investment with an expected return of 10 percent and a risk (standard deviation) of 20 percent, and your risk aversion coefficient is 3.

1 What is your utility of this investment?

2 What must be the minimum risk-free return you should earn to get the same utility?

Solution to 1:

$$U = 0.10 - 0.5 \times 3 \times 0.20^2 = 0.04.$$

Solution to 2:

A risk-free return's σ is zero, so the second term disappears. To get the same utility (0.04), the risk-free return must be at least 4 percent. Thus, in your mind, a risky return of 10 percent is equivalent to a risk-free return or a guaranteed outcome of 4 percent.

EXAMPLE 7

Computation of Utility

Based on investment information given below and the utility formula $U = E(r) - 0.5A\sigma^2$, answer the following questions. Returns and standard deviations are both expressed as percent per year. When using the utility formula, however, returns and standard deviations must be expressed in decimals.

Investment	Expected Return $E(r)$	Standard Deviation σ
1	12%	30%
2	15	35
3	21	40
4	24	45

1 Which investment will a risk-averse investor with a risk aversion coefficient of 4 choose?

2 Which investment will a risk-averse investor with a risk aversion coefficient of 2 choose?

3 Which investment will a risk-neutral investor choose?

4 Which investment will a risk-loving investor choose?

Solutions to 1 and 2:

The utility for risk-averse investors with $A = 4$ and $A = 2$ for each of the four investments are shown in the following table. Complete calculations for Investment 1 with $A = 4$ are as follows: $U = 0.12 - 0.5 \times 4 \times 0.30^2 = -0.06$.

Investment	Expected Return $E(r)$	Standard Deviation σ	Utility $A = 4$	Utility $A = 2$
1	12%	30%	−0.0600	0.0300
2	15	35	−0.0950	0.0275
3	21	40	−0.1100	0.0500
4	24	45	−0.1650	0.0375

The risk-averse investor with a risk aversion coefficient of 4 should choose Investment 1. The risk-averse investor with a risk aversion coefficient of 2 should choose Investment 3.

Solution to 3:

A risk-neutral investor cares only about return. In other words, his risk aversion coefficient is 0. Therefore, a risk-neutral investor will choose Investment 4 because it has the highest return.

Solution to 4:

A risk-loving investor likes both higher risk and higher return. In other words, his risk aversion coefficient is negative. Therefore, a risk-loving investor will choose Investment 4 because it has the highest return and highest risk among the four investments.

3.3 Application of Utility Theory to Portfolio Selection

The simplest application of utility theory and risk aversion is to a portfolio of two assets, a risk-free asset and a risky asset. The risk-free asset has zero risk and a return of R_f. The risky asset has a risk of σ_i (> 0) and an expected return of $E(R_i)$. Because the risky asset has risk that is greater than that of the risk-free asset, the expected return from the risky asset will be greater than the return from the risk-free asset, that is, $E(R_i) > R_f$.

We can construct a portfolio of these two assets with a portfolio expected return, $E(R_p)$, and portfolio risk, σ_p, based on the formulas provided below. In the equations given below, w_1 is the weight in the risk-free asset and $(1 - w_1)$ is the weight in the risky asset. Because $\sigma_f = 0$ for the risk-free asset, the first and third terms in the formula for variance are zero leaving only the second term. We arrive at the last equation by taking the square root of both sides, which shows the expression for standard deviation for a portfolio of two assets when one asset is the risk-free asset:

$$E(R_p) = w_1 R_f + (1 - w_1) E(R_i)$$

$$\sigma_p^2 = w_1^2 \sigma_f^2 + (1 - w_1)^2 \sigma_i^2 + 2 w_1 (1 - w_1) \rho_{12} \sigma_f \sigma_i = (1 - w_1)^2 \sigma_i^2$$

$$\sigma_p = (1 - w_1) \sigma_i$$

The two-asset portfolio is drawn in Exhibit 15 by varying w_1 from 0 percent to 100 percent. The portfolio standard deviation is on the horizontal axis and the portfolio return is on the vertical axis. If only these two assets are available in the economy and the risky asset represents the market, the line in Exhibit 15 is called the **capital allocation line**. The capital allocation line represents the portfolios available to an investor. The equation for this line can be derived from the above two equations by rewriting the second equation as $w_1 = 1 - \frac{\sigma_p}{\sigma_i}$. Substituting the value of w_1 in the equation for expected return, we get the following equation for the capital allocation line:

$$E(R_p) = \left(1 - \frac{\sigma_p}{\sigma_i}\right) R_f + \frac{\sigma_p}{\sigma_i} E(R_i)$$

This equation can be rewritten in a more usable form:

$$E(R_p) = R_f + \frac{\left(E(R_i) - R_f\right)}{\sigma_i} \sigma_p$$

The capital allocation line has an intercept of R_f, and a slope of $\frac{\left(E(R_i) - R_f\right)}{\sigma_i}$, which is the additional required return for every increment in risk, and is sometimes referred to as the market price of risk.

Exhibit 15 Capital Allocation Line with Two Assets

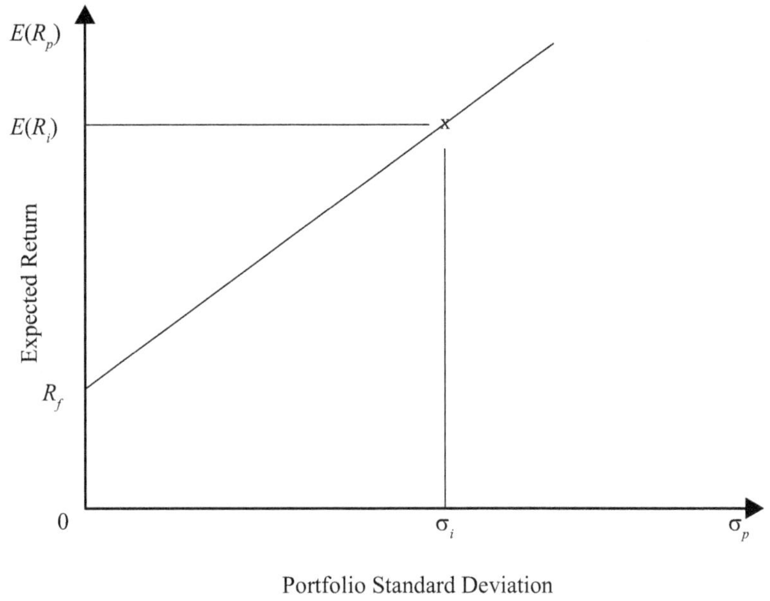

Because the equation is linear, the plot of the capital allocation line is a straight line. The line begins with the risk-free asset as the leftmost point with zero risk and a risk-free return, R_f. At that point, the portfolio consists of only the risk-free asset. If 100 percent is invested in the portfolio of all risky assets, however, we have a return of $E(R_i)$ with a risk of σ_i.

We can move further along the line in pursuit of higher returns by borrowing at the risk-free rate and investing the borrowed money in the portfolio of all risky assets. If 50 percent is borrowed at the risk-free rate, then $w_1 = -0.50$ and 150 percent is placed in the risky asset, giving a return $= 1.50E(R_i) - 0.50R_f$, which is $> E(R_i)$ because $E(R_i) > R_f$.

The line plotted in Exhibit 15 is comprised of an unlimited number of risk–return pairs or portfolios. Which *one* of these portfolios should be chosen by an investor? The answer lies in combining indifference curves from utility theory with the capital allocation line from portfolio theory. Utility theory gives us the utility function or the indifference curves for an individual, as in Exhibit 13, and the capital allocation line gives us the set of feasible investments. Overlaying each individual's indifference curves on the capital allocation line will provide us with the optimal portfolio for that investor. Exhibit 16 illustrates this process of portfolio selection.

Exhibit 16 Portfolio Selection

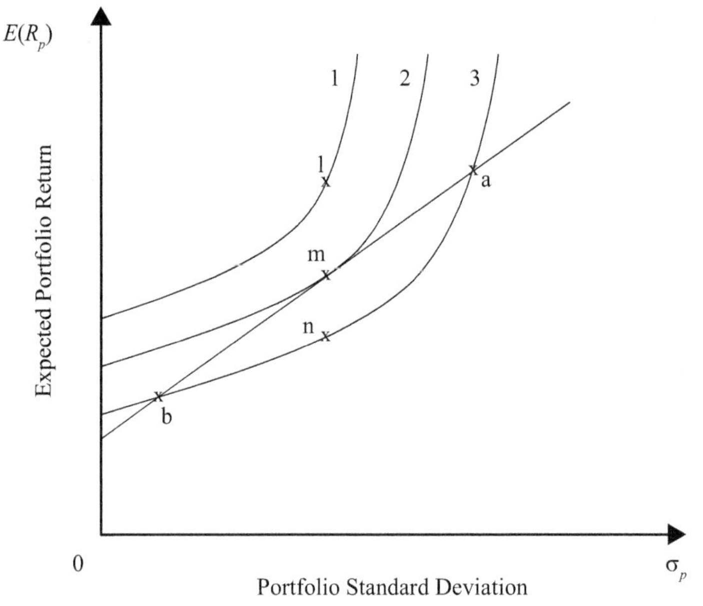

The capital allocation line consists of the set of feasible portfolios. Points under the capital allocation line may be attainable but are not preferred by any investor because the investor can get a higher return for the same risk by moving up to the capital allocation line. Points above the capital allocation line are desirable but not achievable with available assets.

Three indifference curves for the same individual are also shown in Exhibit 16. Curve 1 is above the capital allocation line, Curve 2 is tangential to the line, and Curve 3 intersects the line at two points. Curve 1 has the highest utility and Curve 3 has the lowest utility. Because Curve 1 lies completely above the capital allocation line, points on Curve 1 are not achievable with the available assets on the capital allocation line. Curve 3 intersects the capital allocation line at two Points, **a** and **b**. The investor is able to invest at either Point **a** or **b** to derive the risk–return trade-off and utility associated with Curve 3. Comparing points with the same risk, observe that Point **n** on Curve 3 has the same risk as Point **m** on Curve 2, yet Point **m** has the higher expected return. Therefore, all investors will choose Curve 2 instead of Curve 3. Curve 2 is tangential to the capital allocation line at Point **m**. Point **m** is on the capital allocation line and investable. Point **m** and the utility associated with Curve 2 is the best that the investor can do because he/she cannot move to a higher utility indifference curve. Thus, we have been able to select the optimal portfolio for the investor with indifference Curves 1, 2, and 3. Point **m**, the optimal portfolio for one investor, may not be optimal for another investor. We can follow the same process, however, for finding the optimal portfolio for other investors: the optimal portfolio is the point of tangency between the capital allocation line and the indifference curve for that investor. In other words, the optimal portfolio maximizes the return per unit of risk (as it is on the capital allocation line), and it simultaneously supplies the investor with the most satisfaction (utility).

As an illustration, Exhibit 17 shows two indifference curves for two different investors: Kelly with a risk aversion coefficient of 2 and Jane with a risk aversion coefficient of 4. The indifference curve for Kelly is to the right of the indifference curve for Jane because Kelly is less risk averse than Jane and can accept a higher amount of risk, i.e. has a higher tolerance for risk. Accordingly, their optimal portfolios are different: Point **k** is the optimal portfolio for Kelly and Point **j** is the optimal portfolio for Jane.

In addition, for the same return, the slope of Jane's curve is higher than Kelly's suggesting that Jane needs greater incremental return as compensation for accepting an additional amount of risk compared with Kelly.

Exhibit 17 Portfolio Selection for Two Investors with Various Levels of Risk Aversion

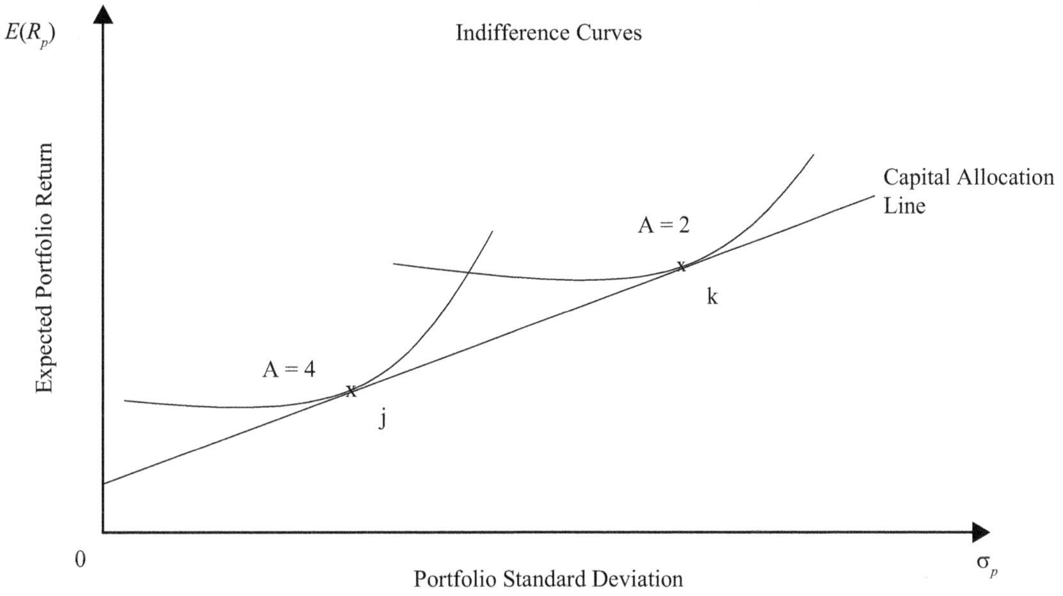

PORTFOLIO RISK

4

We have seen before that investors are risk averse and demand a higher return for a riskier investment. Therefore, ways of controlling portfolio risk without affecting return are valuable. As a precursor to managing risk, this section explains and analyzes the components of portfolio risk. In particular, it examines and describes how a portfolio consisting of assets with low correlations have the potential of reducing risk without necessarily reducing return.

4.1 Portfolio of Two Risky Assets

The return and risk of a portfolio of two assets was introduced in Section 2 of this reading. In this section, we briefly review the computation of return and extend the concept of portfolio risk and its components.

4.1.1 *Portfolio Return*

When several individual assets are combined into a portfolio, we can compute the portfolio return as a weighted average of the returns in the portfolio. The portfolio return is simply a weighted average of the returns of the individual investments, or assets. If Asset 1 has a return of 20 percent and constitutes 25 percent of the portfolio's investment, then the contribution to the portfolio return is 5 percent (= 25% of 20%). In general, if Asset i has a return of R_i and has a weight of w_i in the portfolio, then the portfolio return, R_P, is given as:

$$R_P = \sum_{i=1}^{N} w_i R_i, \quad \sum_{i=1}^{N} w_i = 1$$

Note that the weights must add up to 1 because the assets in a portfolio, including cash, must account for 100 percent of the investment. Also, note that these are single period returns, so there are no cash flows during the period and the weights remain constant.

When two individual assets are combined in a portfolio, we can compute the portfolio return as a weighted average of the returns of the two assets. Consider Assets 1 and 2 with weights of 25 percent and 75 percent in a portfolio. If their returns are 20 percent and 5 percent, the weighted average return = (0.25 × 20%) + (0.75 × 5%) = 8.75%. More generally, the portfolio return can be written as below, where R_p is return of the portfolio, w_1 and w_2 are the weights of the two assets, and R_1, R_2 are returns on the two assets:

$$R_p = w_1 R_1 + (1 - w_1) R_2$$

4.1.2 *Portfolio Risk*

Like a portfolio's return, we can calculate a portfolio's variance. Although the return of a portfolio is simply a weighted average of the returns of each security, this is not the case with the standard deviation of a portfolio (unless all securities are perfectly correlated—that is, correlation equals one). Variance can be expressed more generally for N securities in a portfolio using the notation from the portfolio return calculation above:

$$\sum_{i=1}^{N} w_i = 1$$

$$\sigma_P^2 = \text{Var}(R_P) = \text{Var}\left(\sum_{i=1}^{N} w_i R_i\right)$$

Note that the weights must add up to 1. The right side of the equation is the variance of the weighted average returns of individual securities. Weight is a constant, but the returns are variables whose variance is shown by Var(R_i). We can rewrite the equation as shown next. Because the covariance of an asset with itself is the variance of the asset, we can separate the variances from the covariances in the second equation:

$$\sigma_P^2 = \sum_{i,j=1}^{N} w_i w_j \text{Cov}(R_i, R_j)$$

$$\sigma_P^2 = \sum_{i=1}^{N} w_i^2 \text{Var}(R_i) + \sum_{i,j=1, i \neq j}^{N} w_i w_j \text{Cov}(R_i, R_j)$$

Cov(R_i,R_j) is the covariance of returns, R_i and R_j, and can be expressed as the product of the correlation between the two returns ($\rho_{1,2}$) and the standard deviations of the two assets. Thus, Cov(R_i,R_j) = $\rho_{ij}\sigma_i\sigma_j$.

For a two asset portfolio, the expression for portfolio variance simplifies to the following using covariance and then using correlation:

$$\sigma_P^2 = w_1^2\sigma_1^2 + w_2^2\sigma_2^2 + 2w_1w_2\text{Cov}(R_1, R_2)$$

$$\sigma_P^2 = w_1^2\sigma_1^2 + w_2^2\sigma_2^2 + 2w_1w_2\rho_{12}\sigma_1\sigma_2$$

The standard deviation of a two asset portfolio is given by the square root of the portfolio's variance:

$$\sigma_P = \sqrt{w_1^2\sigma_1^2 + w_2^2\sigma_2^2 + 2w_1w_2\text{Cov}(R_1,R_2)}$$

or,

$$\sigma_P = \sqrt{w_1^2\sigma_1^2 + w_2^2\sigma_2^2 + 2w_1w_2\rho_{12}\sigma_1\sigma_2}$$

EXAMPLE 8

Return and Risk of a Two-Asset Portfolio

Assume that as a US investor, you decide to hold a portfolio with 80 percent invested in the S&P 500 US stock index and the remaining 20 percent in the MSCI Emerging Markets index. The expected return is 9.93 percent for the S&P 500 and 18.20 percent for the Emerging Markets index. The risk (standard deviation) is 16.21 percent for the S&P 500 and 33.11 percent for the Emerging Markets index. What will be the portfolio's expected return and risk given that the covariance between the S&P 500 and the Emerging Markets index is 0.5 percent or 0.0050? Note that units for covariance and variance are written as $\%^2$ when not expressed as a fraction. These are units of measure like squared feet and the numbers themselves are not actually squared.

Solution:

Portfolio return, $R_P = w_1R_1 + (1 - w_1)$, $R_2 = (0.80 \times 0.0993) + (0.20 \times 0.1820) = 0.1158 = 11.58\%$.

$$\text{Portfolio risk} = \sigma_P = \sqrt{w_1^2\sigma_1^2 + w_2^2\sigma_2^2 + 2w_1w_2Cov(R_1,R_2)}$$

$$\sigma_p^2 = w_{US}^2\sigma_{US}^2 + w_{EM}^2\sigma_{EM}^2 + 2w_{US}w_{EM}Cov_{US,EM}$$

$$\sigma_p^2 = \left(0.80^2 \times 0.1621^2\right) + \left(0.20^2 \times 0.3311^2\right) + \left(2 \times 0.80 \times 0.20 \times 0.0050\right)$$

$$\sigma_p^2 = 0.01682 + 0.00439 + 0.00160 = 0.02281$$

$$\sigma_p = 0.15103 = 15.10\%$$

The portfolio's expected return is 11.58 percent and the portfolio's risk is 15.10 percent. Look at this example closely. It shows that we can take the portfolio of a US investor invested only in the S&P 500, combine it with a *riskier* portfolio consisting of emerging markets securities, and the return of the US investor increases from 9.93 percent to 11.58 percent while the risk of the portfolio actually falls from 16.21 percent to 15.10 percent. Exhibit 18 depicts how the combination of the two assets results in a superior risk–return trade-off. Not only does the investor get a higher return, but he also gets it at a lower risk. That is the power of diversification as you will see later in this reading.

Exhibit 18 Combination of Two Assets

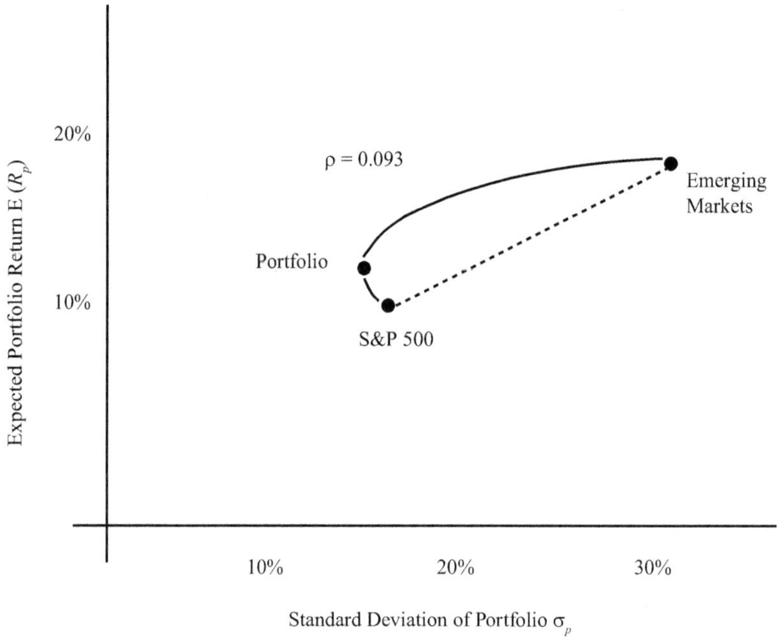

4.1.3 *Covariance and Correlation*

The **covariance** in the formula for portfolio standard deviation can be expanded as $\text{Cov}(R_1,R_2) = \rho_{12}\sigma_1\sigma_2$ where ρ_{12} is the correlation between returns, R_1, R_2. Although covariance is important, it is difficult to interpret because it is unbounded on both sides. It is easier to understand the **correlation coefficient** (ρ_{12}), which is bounded but provides similar information.

Correlation is a measure of the consistency or tendency for two investments to act in a similar way. The correlation coefficient, ρ_{12}, can be positive or negative and ranges from –1 to +1. Consider three different values of the correlation coefficient:

- $\rho_{12} = +1$: Returns of the two assets are perfectly *positively* correlated. Assets 1 and 2 move together 100 percent of the time.
- $\rho_{12} = -1$: Returns of the two assets are perfectly *negatively* correlated. Assets 1 and 2 move in opposite directions 100 percent of the time.
- $\rho_{12} = 0$: Returns of the two assets are *uncorrelated.* Movement of Asset 1 provides no prediction regarding the movement of Asset 2.

The correlation coefficient between two assets determines the effect on portfolio risk when the two assets are combined. To see how this works, consider two different values of ρ_{12}. You will find that portfolio risk is unaffected when the two assets are perfectly correlated ($\rho_{12} = +1$). In other words, the portfolio's standard deviation is simply a weighted average of the standard deviations of the two assets and as such a portfolio's risk is unchanged with the addition of assets with the same risk parameters. Portfolio risk falls, however, when the two assets are not perfectly correlated ($\rho_{12} <$ +1). Sufficiently low values of the correlation coefficient can make the portfolio riskless under certain conditions.

First, let $\rho_{12} = +1$

$$\sigma_p^2 = w_1^2\sigma_1^2 + w_2^2\sigma_2^2 + 2w_1w_2\rho_{12}\sigma_1\sigma_2 = w_1^2\sigma_1^2 + w_2^2\sigma_2^2 + 2w_1w_2\sigma_1\sigma_2$$
$$= \left(w_1\sigma_1 + w_2\sigma_2\right)^2$$
$$\sigma_p = w_1\sigma_1 + w_2\sigma_2$$

The first set of terms on the right side of the first equation contain the usual terms for portfolio variance. Because the correlation coefficient is equal to +1, the right side can be rewritten as a perfect square. The third row shows that portfolio risk is a weighted average of the risks of the individual assets' risks. We showed earlier that the portfolio return is a weighted average of the assets' returns. Because both risk and return are just weighted averages of the two assets in the portfolio there is no reduction in risk when $\rho_{12} = +1$.

Now let $\rho_{12} < +1$

The above analysis showed that portfolio risk is a weighted average of asset risks when $\rho_{12} = +1$. When $\rho_{12} < +1$, the portfolio risk is less than the weighted average of the individual assets' risks.

To show this, we begin by reproducing the general formula for portfolio risk, which is expressed by the terms to the left of the "<" sign below. The term to the right of "<" shows the portfolio risk when $\rho_{12} = +1$:

$$\sigma_p = \sqrt{w_1^2\sigma_1^2 + w_2^2\sigma_2^2 + 2w_1w_2\rho_{12}\sigma_1\sigma_2} < \sqrt{w_1^2\sigma_1^2 + w_2^2\sigma_2^2 + 2w_1w_2\sigma_1\sigma_2}$$
$$= \left(w_1\sigma_1 + w_2\sigma_2\right)$$
$$\sigma_p < \left(w_1\sigma_1 + w_2\sigma_2\right)$$

The left side is smaller than the right side because the correlation coefficient on the left side for the new portfolio is <1. Thus, the portfolio risk is less than the weighted average of risks while the portfolio return is still a weighted average of returns.

As you can see, we have achieved diversification by combining two assets that are not perfectly correlated. For an extreme case in which $\rho_{12} = -1$ (that is, the two asset returns move in opposite directions), the portfolio can be made risk free.

EXAMPLE 9

Effect of Correlation on Portfolio Risk

Two stocks have the same return and risk (standard deviation): 10 percent return with 20 percent risk. You form a portfolio with 50 percent each of Stock 1 and Stock 2 to examine the effect of correlation on risk.

1 Calculate the portfolio return and risk if the correlation is 1.0.
2 Calculate the portfolio return and risk if the correlation is 0.0.
3 Calculate the portfolio return and risk if the correlation is –1.0.
4 Compare the return and risk of portfolios with different correlations.

Solution to 1:

$R_1 = R_2 = 10\% = 0.10$; $\sigma_1 = \sigma_2 = 20\% = 0.20$; $w_1 = w_2 = 50\% = 0.50$. Case 1: $\rho_{12} = +1$

$$R_p = w_1 R_1 + w_2 R_2$$

$$R_p = (0.5 \times 0.1) + (0.5 \times 0.1) = 0.10 = 10\%$$

$$\sigma_p^2 = w_1^2 \sigma_1^2 + w_2^2 \sigma_2^2 + 2 w_1 w_2 \sigma_1 \sigma_2 \rho_{12}$$

$$\sigma_p^2 = \left(0.5^2 \times 0.2^2\right) + \left(0.5^2 \times 0.2^2\right) + \left(2 \times 0.5 \times 0.5 \times 0.2 \times 0.2 \times 1\right) = 0.04$$

$$\sigma_p = \sqrt{0.04} = 0.20 = 20\%$$

This equation demonstrates the earlier point that with a correlation of 1.0 the risk of the portfolio is the same as the risk of the individual assets.

Solution to 2:

$$\rho_{12} = 0$$

$$R_p = w_1 R_1 + w_2 R_2 = 0.10 = 10\%$$

$$\sigma_p^2 = w_1^2 \sigma_1^2 + w_2^2 \sigma_2^2 + 2 w_1 w_2 \sigma_1 \sigma_2 \rho_{12}$$

$$\sigma_p^2 = \left(0.5^2 \times 0.2^2\right) + \left(0.5^2 \times 0.2^2\right) + \left(2 \times 0.5 \times 0.5 \times 0.2 \times 0.2 \times 0\right) = 0.02$$

$$\sigma_p = \sqrt{0.02} = 0.14 = 14\%$$

This equation demonstrates the earlier point that, when assets have correlations of less than 1.0, they can be combined in a portfolio that has less risk than either of the assets individually.

Solution to 3:

$$\rho_{12} = -1$$

$$R_p = w_1 R_1 + w_2 R_2 = 0.10 = 10\%$$

$$\sigma_p^2 = w_1^2 \sigma_1^2 + w_2^2 \sigma_2^2 + 2 w_1 w_2 \sigma_1 \sigma_2 \rho_{12}$$

$$\sigma_p^2 = \left(0.5^2 \times 0.2^2\right) + \left(0.5^2 \times 0.2^2\right) + \left(2 \times 0.5 \times 0.5 \times 0.2 \times 0.2 \times -1\right) = 0$$

$$\sigma_p = 0\%$$

This equation demonstrates the earlier point that, if the correlation of assets is low enough, in this case 100 percent negative correlation or −1.00 (exactly inversely related), a portfolio can be designed that eliminates risk. The individual assets retain their risk characteristics, but the portfolio is risk free.

Solution to 4:

The expected return is 10 percent in all three cases; however, the returns will be more volatile in Case 1 and least volatile in Case 3. In the first case, there is no diversification of risk (same risk as before of 20 percent) and the return remains the same. In the second case, with a correlation coefficient of 0, we have achieved diversification of risk (risk is now 14 percent instead of 20 percent), again with the same return. In the third case with a correlation coefficient of

−1, the portfolio is risk free, although we continue to get the same return of 10 percent. This example shows the power of diversification that we expand on further in Section 4.3.

4.1.4 *Relationship between Portfolio Risk and Return*

The previous example illustrated the effect of correlation on portfolio risk while keeping the weights in the two assets equal and unchanged. In this section, we consider how portfolio risk and return vary with different portfolio weights and different correlations.

Asset 1 has an annual return of 7 percent and annualized risk of 12 percent, whereas Asset 2 has an annual return of 15 percent and annualized risk of 25 percent. The relationship is tabulated in Exhibit 19 for the two assets and graphically represented in Exhibit 20.

Exhibit 19 Relationship between Risk and Return

Weight in Asset 1 (%)	Portfolio Return	Portfolio Risk with Correlation of			
		1.0	0.5	0.2	−1.0
0	15.0	25.0	25.0	25.0	25.0
10	14.2	23.7	23.1	22.8	21.3
20	13.4	22.4	21.3	20.6	17.6
30	12.6	21.1	19.6	18.6	13.9
40	11.8	19.8	17.9	16.6	10.2
50	11.0	18.5	16.3	14.9	6.5
60	10.2	17.2	15.0	13.4	2.8
70	9.4	15.9	13.8	12.3	0.9
80	8.6	14.6	12.9	11.7	4.6
90	7.8	13.3	12.2	11.6	8.3
100	7.0	12.0	12.0	12.0	12.0

Exhibit 20 Relationship between Risk and Return

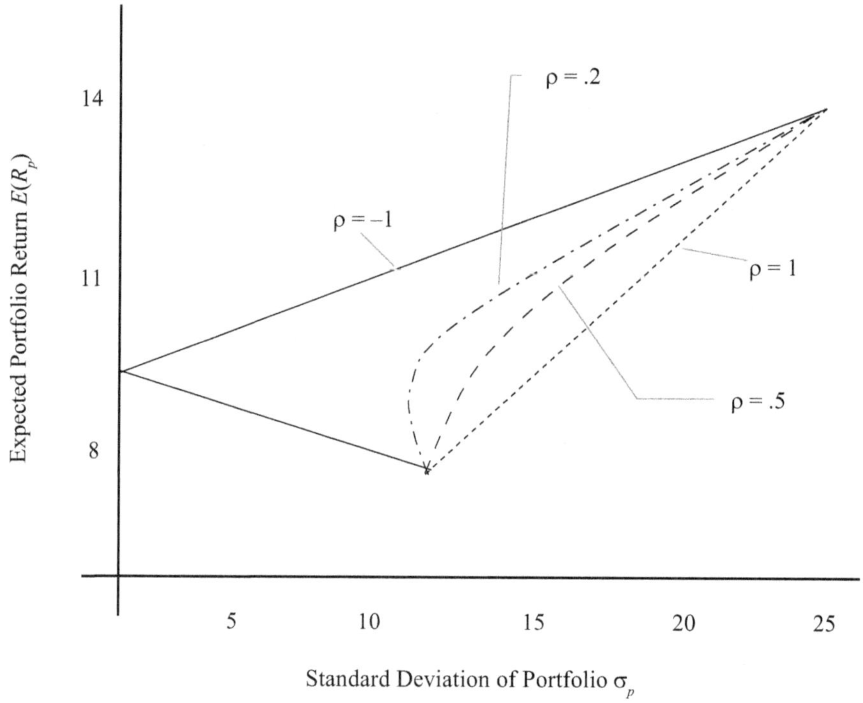

The table shows the portfolio return and risk for four correlation coefficients ranging from +1.0 to −1.0 and 11 weights ranging from 0 percent to 100 percent. The portfolio return and risk are 15 percent and 25 percent, respectively, when 0 percent is invested in Asset 1, versus 7 percent and 12 percent when 100 percent is invested in Asset 1. The portfolio return varies with weights but is unaffected by the correlation coefficient.

Portfolio risk becomes smaller with each successive decrease in the correlation coefficient, with the smallest risk when $\rho_{12} = -1$. The graph in Exhibit 20 shows that the risk–return relationship is a straight line when $\rho_{12} = +1$. As the correlation falls, the risk becomes smaller and smaller as in the table. The curvilinear nature of a portfolio of assets is recognizable in all investment opportunity sets (except at the extremes where $\rho_{12} = -1$ or $+1$).

EXAMPLE 10

Portfolio of Two Assets

An investor is considering investing in a small-cap stock fund and a general bond fund. Their returns and standard deviations are given below and the correlation between the two fund returns is 0.10.

	Expected Annual Return (%)	Standard Deviation of Returns (%)
Small-cap fund, S	19	33
Bond fund, B	8	13

1 If the investor requires a portfolio return of 12 percent, what should the proportions in each fund be?

2 What is the standard deviation of the portfolio constructed in Part 1?

Solution to 1:

We can calculate the weights by setting the portfolio return equal to 12 percent. $12\% = w_1 \times 19\% + (1 - w_1) \times 8\%$; $w_1 = 36.4\%$, $(1 - w_1) = 63.6\%$. Thus, 36.4 percent should be invested in the small-cap fund and 63.6 percent should be invested in the bond fund.

Solution to 2:

$$\sigma_p = \sqrt{w_1^2\sigma_1^2 + w_2^2\sigma_2^2 + 2w_1w_2\rho_{12}\sigma_1\sigma_2}$$

$$= \sqrt{\left(0.364^2 \times 0.33^2\right) + \left(0.636^2 \times 0.13^2\right) + (2 \times 0.364 \times 0.636 \times 0.10 \times 0.33 \times 0.13)}$$

$$= 15.23\%$$

The portfolio risk is 15.23 percent, which is much less than a weighted average of risks of 20.28% (63.6% × 13% + 36.4% × 33%).

4.2 Portfolio of Many Risky Assets

In the previous section, we discussed how the correlation between two assets can affect the risk of a portfolio and the smaller the correlation the lower is the risk. The above analysis can be extended to a portfolio with many risky assets (N). Recall the previous equations for portfolio return and variance:

$$E(R_p) = \sum_{i=1}^{N} w_i E(R_i),\ \sigma_P^2 = \left(\sum_{i=1}^{N} w_i^2\sigma_i^2 + \sum_{i,j=1,i\neq j}^{N} w_i w_j \mathrm{Cov}(i,j)\right),\ \sum_{i=1}^{N} w_i = 1$$

To examine how a portfolio with many risky assets works and the ways in which we can reduce the risk of a portfolio, assume that the portfolio has equal weights ($1/N$) for all N assets. In addition, assume that $\bar{\sigma}^2$ and $\overline{\mathrm{Cov}}$ are the average variance and average covariance. Given equal weights and average variance/covariance, we can rewrite the portfolio variance as below (intermediate steps are omitted to focus on the main result):

$$\sigma_P^2 = \left(\sum_{i=1}^{N} w_i^2\sigma_i^2 + \sum_{i,j=1,i\neq j}^{N} w_i w_j \mathrm{Cov}(i,j)\right)$$

$$\sigma_P^2 = \frac{\bar{\sigma}^2}{N} + \frac{(N-1)}{N}\overline{\mathrm{Cov}}$$

The equation in the second line shows that as N becomes large, the first term on the right side with the denominator of N becomes smaller and smaller, implying that the contribution of one asset's variance to portfolio variance gradually becomes negligible.

The second term, however, approaches the average covariance as N increases. It is reasonable to say that for portfolios with a large number of assets, covariance among the assets accounts for almost all of the portfolio's risk.

4.2.1 *Importance of Correlation in a Portfolio of Many Assets*

The analysis becomes more instructive and interesting if we assume that all assets in the portfolio have the same variance and the same correlation among assets. In that case, the portfolio risk can then be rewritten as:

$$\sigma_p = \sqrt{\frac{\sigma^2}{N} + \frac{(N-1)}{N}\rho\sigma^2}$$

The first term under the root sign becomes negligible as the number of assets in the portfolio increases leaving the second term (correlation) as the main determining factor for portfolio risk. If the assets are unrelated to one another, the portfolio can have close to zero risk. In the next section, we review these concepts to learn how portfolios can be diversified.

4.3 The Power of Diversification

Diversification is one of the most important and powerful concepts in investments. Because investors are risk averse, they are interested in reducing risk preferably without reducing return. In other cases, investors may accept a lower return if it will reduce the chance of catastrophic losses. In previous sections of this reading, you learned the importance of correlation and covariance in managing risk. This section applies those concepts to explore ways for risk diversification. We begin with a simple but intuitive example.

EXAMPLE 11

Diversification with Rain and Shine

Assume a company Beachwear rents beach equipment. The annual return from the company's operations is 20 percent in years with many sunny days but falls to 0 percent in rainy years with few sunny days. The probabilities of a sunny year and a rainy year are equal at 50 percent. Thus, the average return is 10 percent, with a 50 percent chance of 20 percent return and a 50 percent chance of 0 percent return. Because Beachwear can earn a return of 20 percent or 0 percent, its average return of 10 percent is risky.

You are excited about investing in Beachwear but do not like the risk. Having heard about diversification, you decide to add another business to the portfolio to reduce your investment risk.

- There is a snack shop on the beach that sells all the healthy food you like. You estimate that the annual return from the Snackshop is also 20 percent in years with many sunny days and 0 percent in other years. As with the Beachwear shop, the average return is 10 percent.

You decide to invest 50 percent each in Snackshop and Beachwear. The average return is still 10 percent, with 50 percent of 10 percent from Snackshop and 50 percent of 10 percent from Beachwear. In a sunny year, you would earn 20 percent (= 50% of 20% from Beachwear + 50% of 20% from Snackshop). In a rainy year, you would earn 0 percent (=50% of 0% from Beachwear + 50% of 0% from Snackshop). The results are tabulated in Exhibit 21.

Exhibit 21

Type	Company	Percent Invested	Return in Sunny Year (%)	Return in Rainy Year (%)	Average Return (%)
Single stock	Beachwear	100	20	0	10
Single stock	Snackshop	100	20	0	10
Portfolio of two stocks	Beachwear	50	20	0	10
	Snackshop	50	20	0	10
	Total	100	20	0	10

These results seem counterintuitive. You thought that by adding another business you would be able to diversify and reduce your risk, but the risk is exactly the same as before. What went wrong? Note that both businesses do well when it is sunny and both businesses do poorly when it rains. The correlation between the two businesses is +1.0. No reduction in risk occurs when the correlation is +1.0.

- To reduce risk, you must consider a business that does well in a rainy year. You find a company that rents DVDs. DVDrental company is similar to the Beachwear company, except that its annual return is 20 percent in a rainy year and 0 percent in a sunny year, with an average return of 10 percent. DVDrental's 10 percent return is also risky just like Beachwear's return.

If you invest 50 percent each in DVDrental and Beachwear, then the average return is still 10 percent, with 50 percent of 10 percent from DVDrental and 50 percent of 10 percent from Beachwear. In a sunny year, you would earn 10 percent (= 50% of 20% from Beachwear + 50% of 0% from DVDrental). In a rainy year also, you would earn 10 percent (=50% of 0% from Beachwear + 50% of 20% from DVDrental). You have no risk because you earn 10 percent in both sunny and rainy years. Thus, by adding DVDrental to Beachwear, you have reduced (eliminated) your risk without affecting your return. The results are tabulated in Exhibit 22.

Exhibit 22

Type	Company	Percent Invested	Return in Sunny Year (%)	Return in Rainy Year (%)	Average Return (%)
Single stock	Beachwear	100	20	0	10
Single stock	DVDrental	100	0	20	10
Portfolio of two stocks	Beachwear	50	20	0	10
	DVDrental	50	0	20	10
	Total	100	10	10	10

In this case, the two businesses have a correlation of −1.0. When two businesses with a correlation of −1.0 are combined, risk can always be reduced to zero.

4.3.1 *Correlation and Risk Diversification*

Correlation is the key in diversification of risk. Notice that the returns from Beachwear and DVDRental always go in the opposite direction. If one of them does well, the other does not. Therefore, adding assets that do not behave like other assets in your portfolio is good and can reduce risk. The two companies in the above example have a correlation of −1.0.

Even when we expand the portfolio to many assets, correlation among assets remains the primary determinant of portfolio risk. Lower correlations are associated with lower risk. Unfortunately, most assets have high positive correlations. The challenge in diversifying risk is to find assets that have a correlation that is much lower than +1.0.

4.3.2 *Historical Risk and Correlation*

When we previously discussed asset returns, we were careful to distinguish between historical or past returns and expected or future returns because historical returns may not be a good indicator of future returns. Returns may be highly positive in one period and highly negative in another period depending on the risk of that asset. Exhibit 7 showed that returns for large US company stocks were high in the 1990s but were very low in the 2000s.

Risk for an asset class, however, does not usually change dramatically from one period to the next. Stocks have been risky even in periods of low returns. T-bills are always less risky even when they earn high returns. From Exhibit 7, we can see that risk has typically not varied much from one decade to the next, except that risk for bonds has been much higher in recent decades when compared with earlier decades. Therefore, it is not unreasonable to assume that historical risk can work as a good proxy for future risk.

As with risk, correlations are quite stable among assets of the same country. Intercountry correlations, however, have been on the rise in the last few decades as a result of globalization and the liberalization of many economies. A correlation above 0.90 is considered high because the assets do not provide much opportunity for diversification of risk Low correlations—generally less than 0.50—are desirable for portfolio diversification.

4.3.3 *Historical Correlation among Asset Classes*

Correlations among major US asset classes and international stocks are reported in Exhibit 23 for 1970–2017. The highest correlation is between US large company stocks and US small company stocks at about 70 percent, whereas the correlation between US large company stocks and international stocks is approximately 66 percent. Although these are the highest correlations, they still provide diversification benefits because the correlations are less than 100 percent. The correlation between international stocks and US small company stocks is lower, at 50 percent. The lowest correlations are between stocks and bonds, with some correlations being negative, such as that between US small company stocks and US long-term government bonds. Similarly, the correlation between T-bills and stocks is close to zero and is negative for international stocks.[8]

Exhibit 23 Correlation Among US Assets and International Stocks (1970–2017)

Series	International Stocks	US Large Company Stocks	US Small Company Stocks	US Long-Term Corporate Bonds	US Long-Term Treasury Bonds	US T-Bills	US Inflation
International stocks	1.00						
US large company stocks	0.66	1.00					
US small company stocks	0.50	0.72	1.00				
US long-term corporate bonds	0.02	0.23	0.06	1.00			
US long-term Treasury bonds	–0.13	0.01	–0.15	0.89	1.00		
US T-bills	0.01	0.04	0.02	0.05	0.09	1.00	
US inflation	–0.06	–0.11	0.04	–0.32	–0.26	0.69	1.00

Source: 2018 SBBI Yearbook (Exhibit 12.13).

The low correlations between stocks and bonds are attractive for portfolio diversification. Similarly, including international securities in a portfolio can also control portfolio risk. It is not surprising that most diversified portfolios of investors contain domestic stocks, domestic bonds, foreign stocks, foreign bonds, real estate, cash, and other asset classes.

4.3.4 *Avenues for Diversification*

The reason for diversification is simple. By constructing a portfolio with assets that do not move together, you create a portfolio that reduces the ups and downs in the short term but continues to grow steadily in the long term. Diversification thus makes a portfolio more resilient to gyrations in financial markets.

We describe a number of approaches for diversification, some of which have been discussed previously and some of which might seem too obvious. Diversification, however, is such an important part of investing that it cannot be emphasized enough, especially when we continue to meet and see many investors who are not properly diversified.

- *Diversify with asset classes.* Correlations among major asset classes[9] are not usually high, as can be observed from the few US asset classes listed in Exhibit 23. Correlations for other asset classes and other countries are also typically low, which provides investors the opportunity to benefit from diversifying among many asset classes to achieve the biggest benefit from diversification. A partial list of asset classes includes domestic large caps, domestic small caps,

8 In any short period, T-bills are riskless and uncorrelated with other asset classes. For example, a 3-month US Treasury bill is redeemable at its face value upon maturity irrespective of what happens to other assets. When we consider multiple periods, however, returns on T-bills may be related to other asset classes because short-term interest rates vary depending on the strength of the economy and outlook for inflation.

9 Major asset classes are distinguished from sub-classes, such as US value stocks and US growth stocks.

growth stocks, value stocks, domestic corporate bonds, long-term domestic government bonds, domestic Treasury bills (cash), emerging market stocks, emerging market bonds, developed market stocks (i.e., developed markets excluding domestic market), developed market bonds, real estate, and gold and other commodities. In addition, industries and sectors are used to diversify portfolios. For example, energy stocks may not be well correlated with health care stocks. The exact proportions in which these assets should be included in a portfolio depend on the risk, return, and correlation characteristics of each and the home country of the investor.

- *Diversify with index funds.* Diversifying among asset classes can become costly for small portfolios because of the number of securities required. For example, creating diversified exposure to a single category, such as a domestic large company asset class, may require a group of at least 30 stocks. Exposure to 10 asset classes may require 300 securities, which can be expensive to trade and track. Instead, it may be effective to use exchange-traded funds or mutual funds that track the respective indexes, which could bring down the costs associated with building a well-diversified portfolio. Therefore, many investors should consider index mutual funds as an investment vehicle as opposed to individual securities.
- *Diversification among countries.* Countries are different because of industry focus, economic policy, and political climate. The US economy produces many financial and technical services and invests a significant amount in innovative research. The Chinese and Indian economies, however, are focused on manufacturing. Countries in the European Union are vibrant democracies whereas East Asian countries are experimenting with democracy. Thus, financial returns in one country over time are not likely to be highly correlated with returns in another country. Country returns may also be different because of different currencies. In other words, the return on a foreign investment may be different when translated to the home country's currency. Because currency returns are uncorrelated with stock returns, they may help reduce the risk of investing in a foreign country even when that country, in isolation, is a very risky emerging market from an equity investment point of view. Investment in foreign countries is an essential part of a well-diversified portfolio.
- *Diversify by* not *owning your employer's stock.* Companies encourage their employees to invest in company stock through employee stock plans and retirement plans. You should evaluate investing in your company, however, just as you would evaluate any other investment. In addition, you should consider the nonfinancial investments that you have made, especially the human capital you have invested in your company. Because you work for your employer, you are already heavily invested in it—your earnings depend on your employer. The level of your earnings, whether your compensation improves or whether you get a promotion, depends on how well your employer performs. If a competitor drives your employer out of the market, you will be out of a job. Additional investments in your employer will concentrate your wealth in one asset even more so and make you less diversified.
- *Evaluate each asset before adding to a portfolio.* Every time you add a security or an asset class to the portfolio, recognize that there is a cost associated with diversification. There is a cost of trading an asset as well as the cost of tracking a larger portfolio. In some cases, the securities or assets may have different names

but belong to an asset class in which you already have sufficient exposure. A general rule to evaluate whether a new asset should be included to an existing portfolio is based on the following risk–return trade-off relationship:

$$E(R_{new}) = R_f + \frac{\sigma_{new}\rho_{new,p}}{\sigma_p} \times \left[E(R_p) - R_f\right]$$

where $E(R)$ is the return from the asset, R_f is the return on the risk-free asset, σ is the standard deviation, ρ is the correlation coefficient, and the subscripts *new* and *p* refer to the new stock and existing portfolio. If the new asset's risk-adjusted return benefits the portfolio, then the asset should be included. The condition can be rewritten using the Sharpe ratio on both sides of the equation as:

$$\frac{E(R_{new}) - R_f}{\sigma_{new}} > \frac{E(R_p) - R_f}{\sigma_p} \times \rho_{new,p}$$

If the Sharpe ratio of the new asset is greater than the Sharpe ratio of the current portfolio times the correlation coefficient, it is beneficial to add the new asset.

- *Buy insurance for risky portfolios.* It may come as a surprise, but insurance is an investment asset—just a different kind of asset. Insurance has a negative correlation with your assets and is thus very valuable. Insurance gives you a positive return when your assets lose value, but pays nothing if your assets maintain their value. Over time, insurance generates a negative average return. Many individuals, however, are willing to accept a small negative return because insurance reduces their exposure to an extreme loss. In general, it is reasonable to add an investment with a negative return if that investment significantly reduces risk (an example of a classic case of the risk–return trade-off).

  Alternatively, investments with negative correlations also exist. Historically, gold has a negative correlation with stocks; however, the expected return is usually small and sometimes even negative. Investors often include gold and other commodities in their portfolios as a way of reducing their overall portfolio risk, including currency risk and inflation risk.

  Buying put options is another way of reducing risk. Because put options pay when the underlying asset falls in value (negative correlation), they can protect an investor's portfolio against catastrophic losses. Of course, put options cost money, and the expected return is zero or marginally negative.

5 EFFICIENT FRONTIER AND INVESTOR'S OPTIMAL PORTFOLIO

In this section, we formalize the effect of diversification and expand the set of investments to include all available risky assets in a mean–variance framework. The addition of a risk-free asset generates an optimal risky portfolio and the capital allocation line. We can then derive an investor's optimal portfolio by overlaying the capital allocation line with the indifference curves of investors.

5.1 Investment Opportunity Set

If two assets are perfectly correlated, the risk–return opportunity set is represented by a straight line connecting those two assets. The line contains portfolios formed by changing the weight of each asset invested in the portfolio. This correlation was depicted by the straight line (with $\rho = 1$) in Exhibit 20. If the two assets are not perfectly correlated, the portfolio's risk is less than the weighted average risk of the components, and the portfolio formed from the two assets bulges on the left as shown by curves with the correlation coefficient (ρ) less than 1.0 in Exhibit 20. All of the points connecting the two assets are achievable (or feasible). The addition of new assets to this portfolio creates more and more portfolios that are either a linear combination of the existing portfolio and the new asset or a curvilinear combination, depending on the correlation between the existing portfolio and the new asset.

As the number of available assets increases, the number of possible combinations increases rapidly. When all investable assets are considered, and there are hundreds and thousands of them, we can construct an opportunity set of investments. The opportunity set will ordinarily span all points within a frontier because it is also possible to reach every possible point within that curve by judiciously creating a portfolio from the investable assets.

We begin with individual investable assets and gradually form portfolios that can be plotted to form a curve as shown in Exhibit 24. All points on the curve and points to the right of the curve are attainable by a combination of one or more of the investable assets. This set of points is called the investment opportunity set. Initially, the opportunity set consists of domestic assets only and is labeled as such in Exhibit 24.

Exhibit 24 Investment Opportunity Set

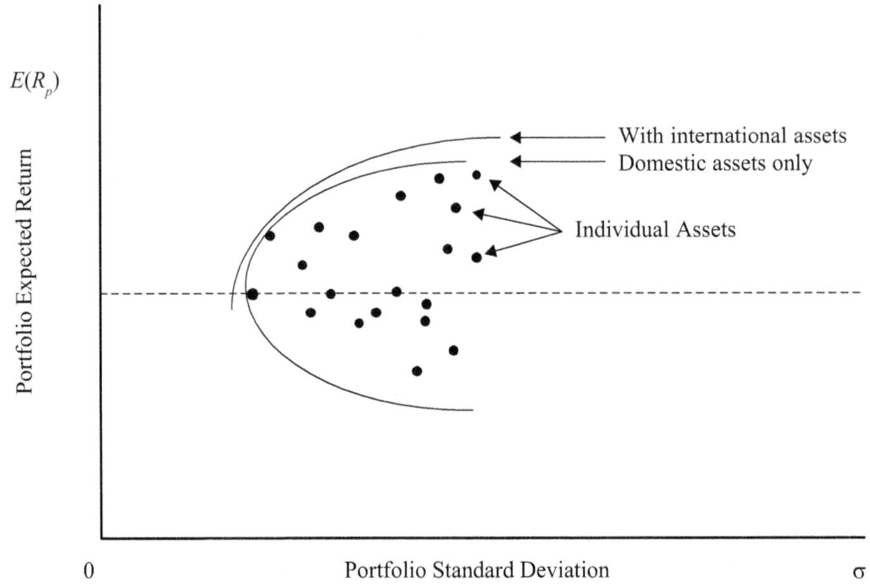

5.1.1 *Addition of Asset Classes*

Exhibit 24 shows the effect of adding a new asset class, such as international assets. As long as the new asset class is not perfectly correlated with the existing asset class, the investment opportunity set will expand out further to the northwest, providing a superior risk–return trade-off.

The investment opportunity set with international assets dominates the opportunity set that includes only domestic assets. Adding other asset classes will have the same impact on the opportunity set. Thus, we should continue to add asset classes until they do not further improve the risk–return trade-off. The benefits of diversification can be fully captured in this way in the construction of the investment opportunity set, and eventually in the selection of the optimal portfolio.

In the discussion that follows in this section, we will assume that *all* investable assets available to an investor are included in the investment opportunity set and no special attention needs to be paid to new asset classes or new investment opportunities.

5.2 Minimum-Variance Portfolios

The investment opportunity set consisting of all available investable sets is shown in Exhibit 25. There are a large number of portfolios available for investment, but we must choose a single optimal portfolio. In this subsection, we begin the selection process by narrowing the choice to fewer portfolios.

Exhibit 25 Minimum-Variance Frontier

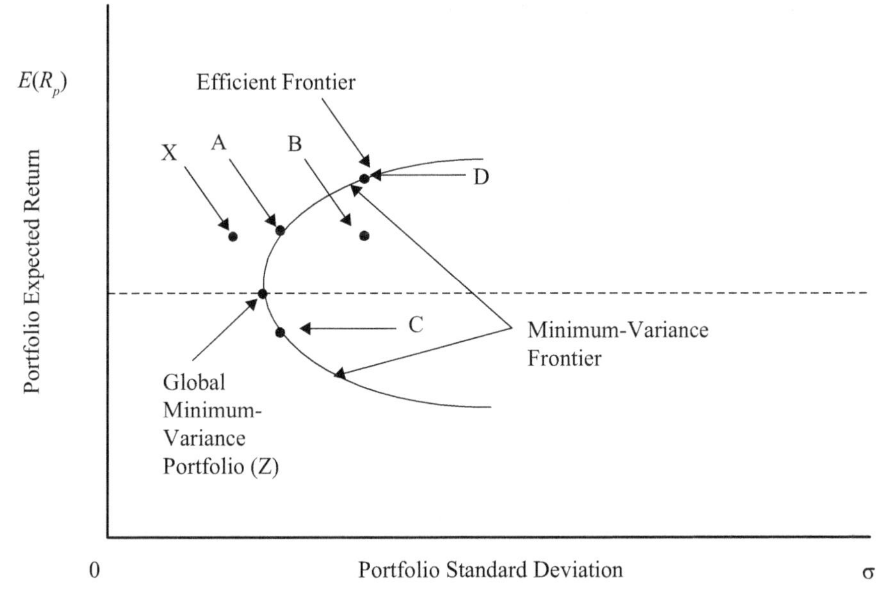

5.2.1 *Minimum-Variance Frontier*

Risk-averse investors seek to minimize risk for a given return. Consider Points A, B, and X in Exhibit 25 and assume that they are on the same horizontal line by construction. Thus, the three points have the same expected return, $E(R_1)$, as do all other points on the imaginary line connecting A, B, and X. Given a choice, an investor will choose the point with the minimum risk, which is Point X. Point X, however, is unattainable because it does not lie within the investment opportunity set. Thus, the minimum risk that we can attain for $E(R_1)$ is at Point A. Point B and all points to the right of Point A are feasible but they have higher risk. Therefore, a risk-averse investor will choose only Point A in preference to any other portfolio with the same return.

Similarly, Point C is the minimum variance point for the return earned at C. Points to the right of C have higher risk. We can extend the above analysis to all possible returns. In all cases, we find that the **minimum-variance portfolio** is the one that lies on the solid curve drawn in Exhibit 25. The entire collection of these minimum-variance portfolios is referred to as the minimum-variance frontier. The minimum-variance frontier defines the smaller set of portfolios in which investors would want to invest. Note that no risk-averse investor will choose to invest in a portfolio to the right of the minimum-variance frontier because a portfolio on the minimum-variance frontier can give the same return but at a lower risk.

5.2.2 *Global Minimum-Variance Portfolio*

The left-most point on the minimum-variance frontier is the portfolio with the minimum variance among all portfolios of risky assets, and is referred to as the **global minimum-variance portfolio**. An investor cannot hold a portfolio consisting of *risky* assets that has less risk than that of the global minimum-variance portfolio. Note the emphasis on "risky" assets. Later, the introduction of a risk-free asset will allow us to relax this constraint.

5.2.3 *Efficient Frontier of Risky Assets*

The minimum-variance frontier gives us portfolios with the minimum variance for a given return. However, investors also want to maximize return for a given risk. Observe Points A and C on the minimum-variance frontier shown in Exhibit 25. Both of them have the same risk. Given a choice, an investor will choose Portfolio A because it has a higher return. No one will choose Portfolio C. The same analysis applies to all points on the minimum-variance frontier that lie below the global minimum-variance portfolio. Thus, portfolios on the curve below the global minimum-variance portfolio and to the right of the global minimum-variance portfolio are not beneficial and are inefficient portfolios for an investor.

The curve that lies above and to the right of the global minimum-variance portfolio is referred to as the **Markowitz efficient frontier** because it contains all portfolios of risky assets that rational, risk-averse investors will choose.

An important observation that is often ignored is the slope at various points on the efficient frontier. As we move right from the global minimum-variance portfolio (Point Z) in Exhibit 25, there is an increase in risk with a concurrent increase in return. The increase in return with every unit increase in risk, however, keeps decreasing as we move from left to the right because the slope continues to decrease. The slope at Point D is less than the slope at Point A, which is less than the slope at Point Z. The increase in return by moving from Point Z to Point A is the same as the increase in return by moving from Point A to Point D. It can be seen that the additional risk in moving from Point A to Point D is 3 to 4 times more than the additional risk in moving from Point Z to Point A. Thus, investors obtain decreasing increases in returns as they assume more risk.

5.3 A Risk-Free Asset and Many Risky Assets

Until now, we have only considered risky assets in which the return is risky or uncertain. Most investors, however, have access to a risk-free asset, most notably from securities issued by the government. The addition of a risk-free asset makes the investment opportunity set much richer than the investment opportunity set consisting only of risky assets.

5.3.1 *Capital Allocation Line and Optimal Risky Portfolio*

By definition, a risk-free asset has zero risk so it must lie on the y-axis in a mean-variance graph. A risk-free asset with a return of R_f is plotted in Exhibit 26. This asset can now be combined with a portfolio of risky assets. The combination of a risk-free asset with a portfolio of risky assets is a straight line, such as in Section 3.3 (see Exhibit 15). Unlike in Section 3.3, however, we have many risky portfolios to choose from instead of a single risky portfolio.

Exhibit 26 Optimal Risky Portfolio

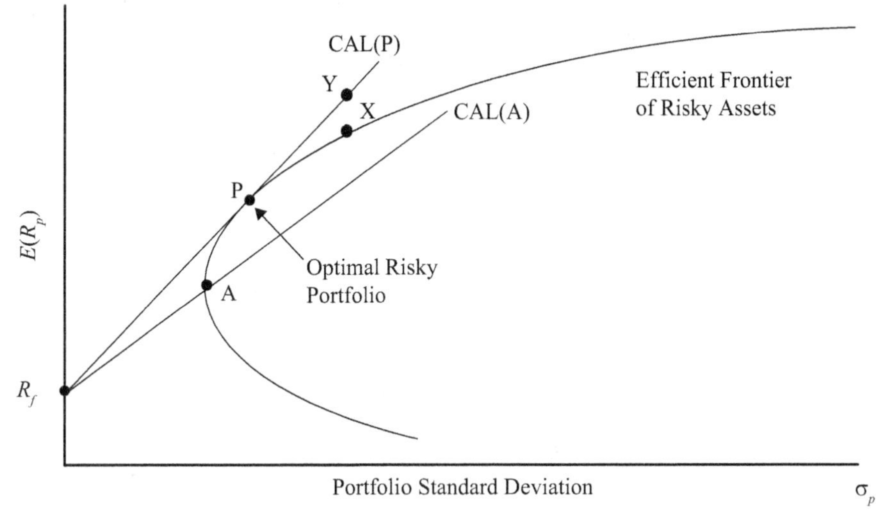

All portfolios on the efficient frontier are candidates for being combined with the risk-free asset. Two combinations are shown in Exhibit 26: one between the risk-free asset and efficient Portfolio A and the other between the risk-free asset and efficient Portfolio P. Comparing capital allocation line A and capital allocation line P reveals that there is a point on CAL(P) with a higher return and same risk for each point on CAL(A). In other words, the portfolios on CAL(P) dominate the portfolios on CAL(A). Therefore, an investor will choose CAL(P) over CAL(A). We would like to move further northwest to achieve even better portfolios. None of those portfolios, however, is attainable because they are above the efficient frontier.

What about other points on the efficient frontier? For example, Point X is on the efficient frontier and has the highest return of all risky portfolios for its risk. However, Point Y on CAL(P), achievable by leveraging Portfolio P as seen in Section 3.3, lies above Point X and has the same risk but higher return. In the same way, we can observe that not only does CAL(P) dominate CAL(A) but it also dominates the Markowitz efficient frontier of risky assets.

CAL(P) is the optimal capital allocation line and Portfolio P is the optimal risky portfolio. Thus, with the addition of the risk-free asset, we are able to narrow our selection of risky portfolios to a single optimal risky portfolio, P, which is at the tangent of CAL(P) and the efficient frontier of risky assets.

5.3.2 *The Two-Fund Separation Theorem*

The **two-fund separation theorem** states that all investors regardless of taste, risk preferences, and initial wealth will hold a combination of two portfolios or funds: a risk-free asset and an optimal portfolio of risky assets.[10]

The separation theorem allows us to divide an investor's investment problem into two distinct steps: the investment decision and the financing decision. In the first step, as in the previous analysis, the investor identifies the optimal risky portfolio. The

10 In the next reading, you will learn that the optimal portfolio of risky assets is the market portfolio.

optimal risky portfolio is selected from numerous risky portfolios without considering the investor's preferences. The investment decision at this step is based on the optimal risky portfolio's (a single portfolio) return, risk, and correlations.

The capital allocation line connects the optimal risky portfolio and the risk-free asset. All optimal investor portfolios must be on this line. Each investor's optimal portfolio on the CAL(P) is determined in the second step. Considering each individual investor's risk preference, using indifference curves, determines the investor's allocation to the risk-free asset (lending) and to the optimal risky portfolio. Portfolios beyond the optimal risky portfolio are obtained by borrowing at the risk-free rate (i.e., buying on margin). Therefore, the individual investor's risk preference determines the amount of financing (i.e., lending to the government instead of investing in the optimal risky portfolio or borrowing to purchase additional amounts of the optimal risky portfolio).

EXAMPLE 12

Choosing the Right Portfolio

In Exhibit 27, the risk and return of the points marked are as follows:

Point	Return (%)	Risk (%)	Point (%)	Return (%)	Risk (%)
A	15	10	B	11	10
C	15	30	D	25	30
F	4	0	G (gold)	10	30
P	16	17			

Exhibit 27

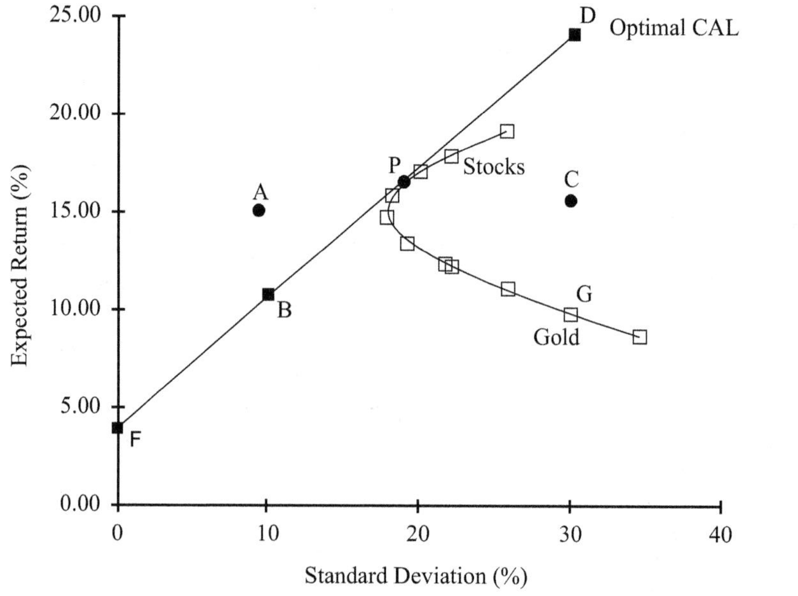

Answer the following questions with reference to the points plotted on Exhibit 27 and explain your answers. The investor is choosing one portfolio based on the graph.

1 Which of the above points is not achievable?

2 Which of these portfolios will not be chosen by a rational, risk-averse investor?

3 Which of these portfolios is most suitable for a risk-neutral investor?

4 Gold is on the inefficient part of the feasible set. Nonetheless, gold is owned by many rational investors as part of a larger portfolio. Why?

5 What is the utility of an investor at point P with a risk aversion coefficient of 3?

Solution to 1:

Portfolio A is not attainable because it lies outside the feasible set and not on the capital allocation line.

Solution to 2:

Portfolios G and C will not be chosen because D provides higher return for the same risk. G and C are the only investable points that do not lie on the capital allocation line.

Solution to 3:

Portfolio D is most suitable because a risk-neutral investor cares only about return and portfolio D provides the highest return. A = 0 in the utility formula.

Solution to 4:

Gold may be owned as part of a portfolio (not as *the* portfolio) because gold has low or negative correlation with many risky assets, such as stocks. Being part of a portfolio can thus reduce overall risk even though its standalone risk is high and return is low. Note that gold's price is not stable—its return is very risky (30 percent). Even risk seekers will choose D over G, which has the same risk but higher return.

Solution to 5:

$$U = E(r) - 0.5A\sigma^2 = 0.16 - 0.5 \times 3 \times 0.0289 = 0.1167 = 11.67\%.$$

5.4 Optimal Investor Portfolio

The CAL(P) in Exhibits 26 and 28 contains the best possible portfolios available to investors. Each of those portfolios is a linear combination of the risk-free asset and the optimal risky portfolio. Among the available portfolios, the selection of each investor's optimal portfolio depends on the risk preferences of an investor. In Section 3, we discussed that the individual investor's risk preferences are incorporated into their indifference curves. These can be used to select the optimal portfolio.

Exhibit 28 shows an indifference curve that is tangent to the capital allocation line, CAL(P). Indifference curves with higher utility than this one lie above the capital allocation line, so their portfolios are not achievable. Indifference curves that lie below this one are not preferred because they have lower utility. Thus, the optimal portfolio for the investor with this indifference curve is portfolio C on CAL(P), which is tangent to the indifference curve.

Exhibit 28 Optimal Investor Portfolio

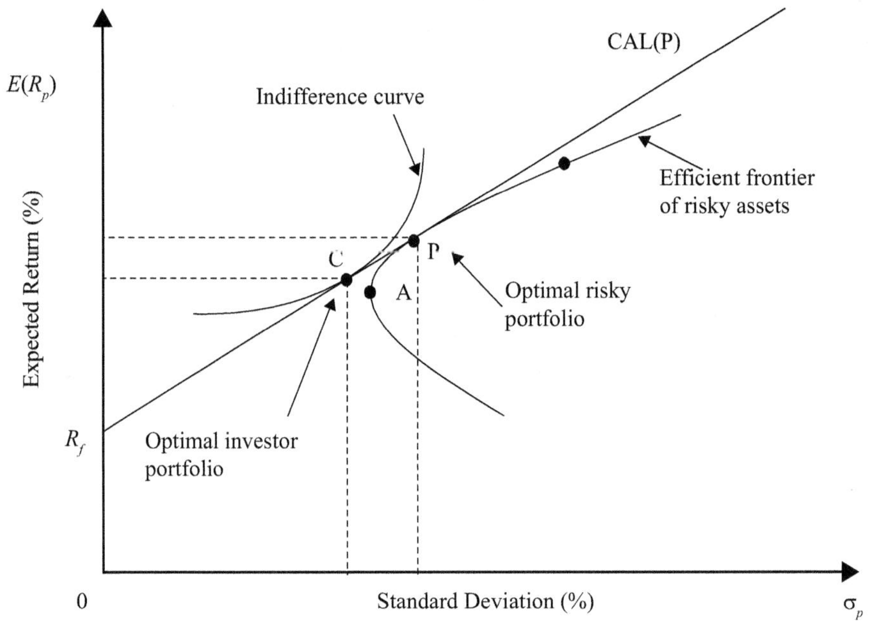

EXAMPLE 13

Comprehensive Example on Portfolio Selection

This comprehensive example reviews many concepts learned in this reading. The example begins with simple information about available assets and builds an optimal investor portfolio for the Lohrmanns.

Suppose the Lohrmanns can invest in only two risky assets, A and B. The expected return and standard deviation for asset A are 20 percent and 50 percent, and the expected return and standard deviation for asset B are 15 percent and 33 percent. The two assets have zero correlation with one another.

1 Calculate portfolio expected return and portfolio risk (standard deviation) if an investor invests 10 percent in A and the remaining 90 percent in B.

Solution to 1:

The subscript "*rp*" means risky portfolio.

$$R_{rp} = [0.10 \times 20\%] + [(1 - 0.10) \times 15\%] = 0.155 = 15.50\%$$

$$\sigma_{rp} = \sqrt{w_A^2\sigma_A^2 + w_B^2\sigma_B^2 + 2w_A w_B \rho_{AB}\sigma_A\sigma_B}$$

$$= \sqrt{(0.10^2 \times 0.50^2) + (0.90^2 \times 0.33^2) + (2 \times 0.10 \times 0.90 \times 0.0 \times 0.50 \times 0.33)}$$

$$= 0.3012 = 30.12\%$$

Note that the correlation coefficient is 0, so the last term for standard deviation is zero.

2 Generalize the above calculations for portfolio return and risk by assuming an investment of w_A in Asset A and an investment of $(1 - w_A)$ in Asset B.

Solution to 2:

$$R_{rp} = w_A \times 20\% + (1 - w_A) \times 15\% = 0.05w_A + 0.15$$

$$\sigma_{rp} = \sqrt{w_A^2 \times 0.5^2 + (1 - w_A)^2 \times 0.33^2} = \sqrt{0.25w_A^2 + 0.1089(1 - 2w_A + w_A^2)}$$

$$= \sqrt{0.3589w_A^2 - 0.2178w_A + 0.1089}$$

The investment opportunity set can be constructed by using different weights in the expressions for $E(R_{rp})$ and σ_{rp} in Part 1 of this example. Exhibit 29 shows the combination of Assets A and B.

Exhibit 29

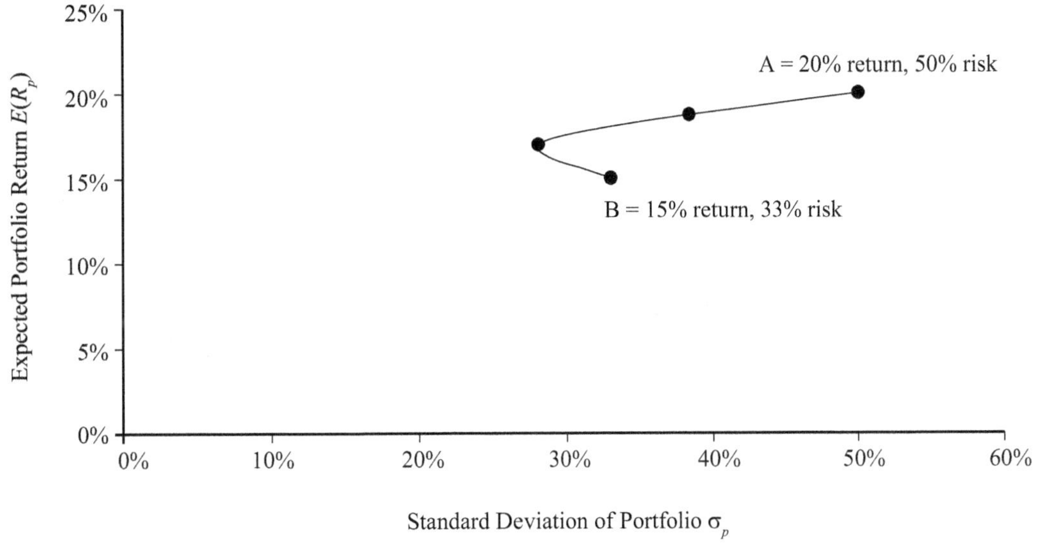

3 Now introduce a risk-free asset with a return of 3 percent. Write an equation for the capital allocation line in terms of w_A that will connect the risk-free asset to the portfolio of risky assets. (Hint: use the equation in Section 3.3 and substitute the expressions for a risky portfolio's risk and return from Part 2 above).

Solution to 3:

The equation of the line connecting the risk-free asset to the portfolio of risky assets is given below (see Section 3.3), where the subscript "rp" refers to the risky portfolio instead of "i," and the subscript "p" refers to the new portfolio of two risky assets and one risk-free asset.

$$E(R_p) = R_f + \frac{E(R_i) - R_f}{\sigma_i}\sigma_p,$$

Rewritten as

$$E(R_p) = R_f + \frac{E(R_{rp}) - R_f}{\sigma_{rp}}\sigma_p$$

$$= 0.03 + \frac{0.05w_A + 0.15 - 0.03}{\sqrt{0.3589w_A^2 - 0.2178w_A + 0.1089}}\sigma_p$$

$$= 0.03 + \frac{0.05w_A + 0.12}{\sqrt{0.3589w_A^2 - 0.2178w_A + 0.1089}}\sigma_p$$

The capital allocation line is the line that has the maximum slope because it is tangent to the curve formed by portfolios of the two risky assets. Exhibit 30 shows the capital allocation line based on a risk-free asset added to the group of assets.

Exhibit 30

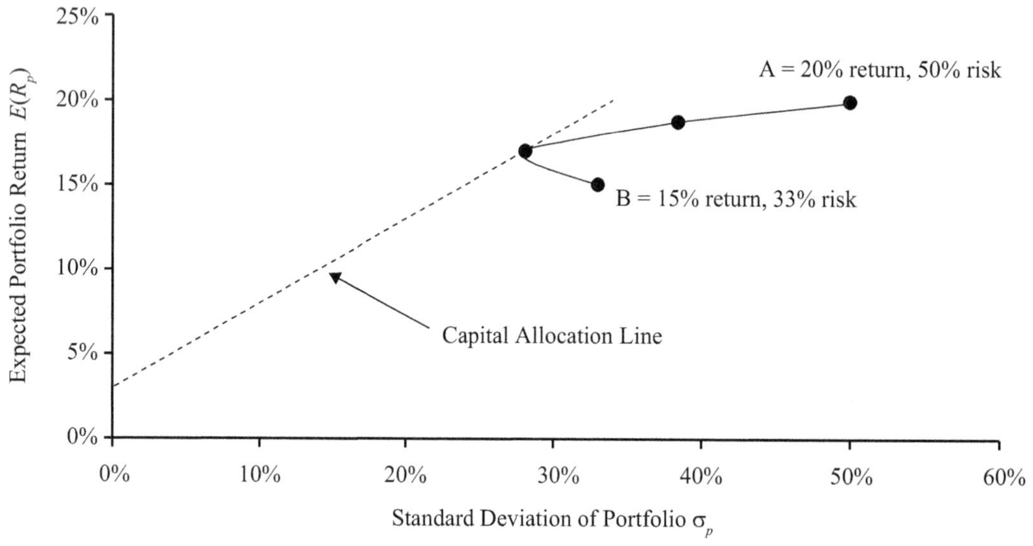

4 The slope of the capital allocation line is maximized when the weight in Asset A is 38.20 percent.[11] What is the equation for the capital allocation line using w_A of 38.20 percent?

---

11 You can maximize $\frac{0.05w_A + 0.12}{\sqrt{0.3589w_A^2 - 0.2178w_A + 0.1089}}$ by taking the first derivative of the slope with respect to w_A and setting it to 0.

Solution to 4:

By substituting 38.20 percent for w_A in the equation in Part 3, we get $E(R_p) = 0.03 + 0.4978\sigma_p$ as the capital allocation line.

5 Having created the capital allocation line, we turn to the Lohrmanns. What is the standard deviation of a portfolio that gives a 20 percent return and is on the capital allocation line? How does this portfolio compare with asset A?

Solution to 5:

Solve the equation for the capital allocation line to get the standard deviation: $0.20 = 0.03 + 0.4978\sigma_p$. $\sigma_p = 34.2\%$. The portfolio with a 20 percent return has the same return as Asset A but a lower standard deviation, 34.2 percent instead of 50.0 percent.

6 What is the risk of portfolios with returns of 3 percent, 9 percent, 15 percent, and 20 percent?

Solution to 6:

You can find the risk of the portfolio using the equation for the capital allocation line: $E(R_p) = 0.03 + 0.4978\sigma_p$.

For a portfolio with a return of 15 percent, write $0.15 = 0.03 + 0.4978\sigma_p$. Solving for σ_p gives 24.1 percent. You can similarly calculate risks of other portfolios with the given returns.

The risk of the portfolio for a return of 3 percent is 0.0 percent, for a return of 9 percent is 12.1 percent, for a return of 15 percent is 24.1 percent, and for a return of 20 percent is 34.2 percent. The points are plotted in Exhibit 31.

Exhibit 31

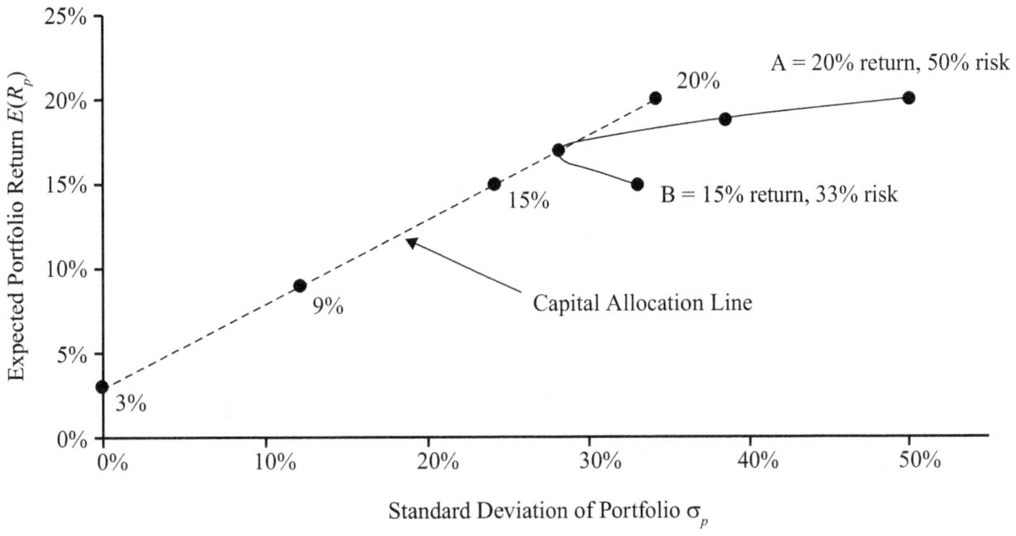

7 What is the utility that the Lohrmanns derive from a portfolio with a return of 3 percent, 9 percent, 15 percent, and 20 percent? The risk aversion coefficient for the Lohrmanns is 2.5.

Solution to 7:

To find the utility, use the utility formula with a risk aversion coefficient of 2.5:

$$\text{Utility} = E\left(R_p\right) - 0.5 \times 2.5\sigma_p^2$$

$$\text{Utility}\ (3\%) = 0.0300$$

$$\text{Utility}\ (9\%) = 0.09 - 0.5 \times 2.5 \times 0.121^2 = +0.0717$$

$$\text{Utility}\ (15\%) = 0.15 - 0.5 \times 2.5 \times 0.241^2 = +0.0774$$

$$\text{Utility}\ (20\%) = 0.20 - 0.5 \times 2.5 \times 0.341^2 = +0.0546$$

Based on the above information, the Lohrmanns choose a portfolio with a return of 15 percent and a standard deviation of 24.1 percent because it has the highest utility: 0.0774. Finally, Exhibit 32 shows the indifference curve that is tangent to the capital allocation line to generate Lohrmanns' optimal investor portfolio.

Exhibit 32

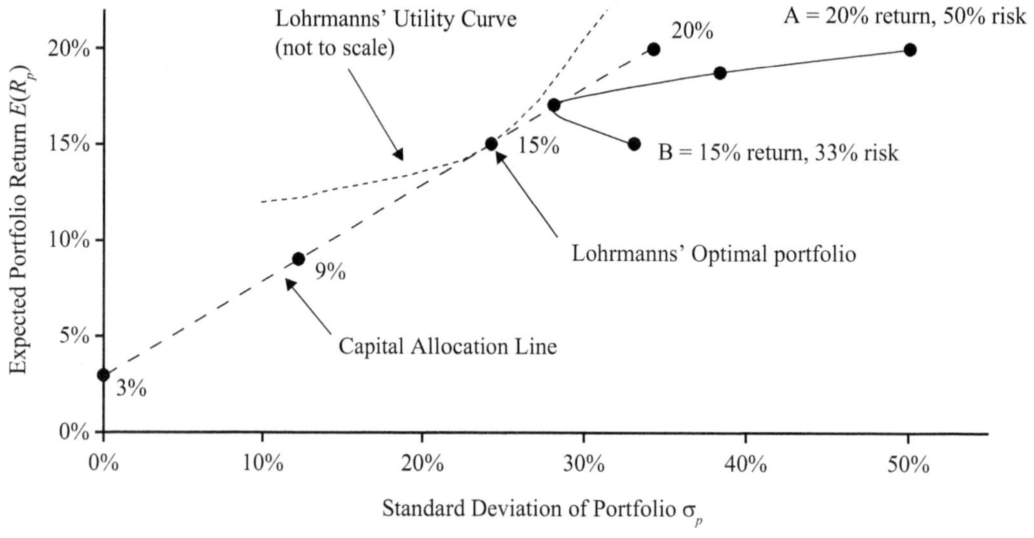

5.4.1 *Investor Preferences and Optimal Portfolios*

The location of an optimal investor portfolio depends on the investor's risk preferences. A highly risk-averse investor may invest a large proportion, even 100 percent, of his/her assets in the risk-free asset. The optimal portfolio in this investor's case will be located close to the *y*-axis. A less risk-averse investor, however, may invest a large portion of his/her wealth in the optimal risky asset. The optimal portfolio in this investor's case will lie closer to Point P in Exhibit 28.

Some less risk-averse investors (i.e., with a high risk tolerance) may wish to accept even more risk because of the chance of higher return. Such an investor may borrow money to invest more in the risky portfolio. If the investor borrows 25 percent of his wealth, he/she can invest 125 percent in the optimal risky portfolio. The optimal investor portfolio for such an investor will lie to the right of Point P on the capital allocation line.

Thus, moving from the risk-free asset along the capital allocation line, we encounter investors who are willing to accept more risk. At Point P, the investor is 100 percent invested in the optimal risky portfolio. Beyond Point P, the investor accepts even more risk by borrowing money and investing in the optimal risky portfolio.

Note that we are able to accommodate all types of investors with just two portfolios: the risk-free asset and the optimal risky portfolio. Exhibit 28 is also an illustration of the two-fund separation theorem. Portfolio P is the optimal risky portfolio that is selected without regard to investor preferences. The optimal investor portfolio is selected on the capital allocation line by overlaying the indifference curves that incorporate investor preferences.

SUMMARY

This reading provides a description and computation of investment characteristics, such as risk and return, that investors use in evaluating assets for investment. This was followed by sections about portfolio construction, selection of an optimal risky portfolio, and an understanding of risk aversion and indifference curves. Finally, the tangency point of the indifference curves with the capital allocation line allows identification of the optimal investor portfolio. Key concepts covered in the reading include the following:

- Holding period return is most appropriate for a single, predefined holding period.
- Multiperiod returns can be aggregated in many ways. Each return computation has special applications for evaluating investments.
- Risk-averse investors make investment decisions based on the risk–return trade-off, maximizing return for the same risk, and minimizing risk for the same return. They may be concerned, however, by deviations from a normal return distribution and from assumptions of financial markets' operational efficiency.
- Investors are risk averse, and historical data confirm that financial markets price assets for risk-averse investors.
- The risk of a two-asset portfolio is dependent on the proportions of each asset, their standard deviations and the correlation (or covariance) between the asset's returns. As the number of assets in a portfolio increases, the correlation among asset risks becomes a more important determinate of portfolio risk.
- Combining assets with low correlations reduces portfolio risk.
- The two-fund separation theorem allows us to separate decision making into two steps. In the first step, the optimal risky portfolio and the capital allocation line are identified, which are the same for all investors. In the second step, investor risk preferences enable us to find a unique optimal investor portfolio for each investor.
- The addition of a risk-free asset creates portfolios that are dominant to portfolios of risky assets in all cases except for the optimal risky portfolio.

By successfully understanding the content of this reading, you should be comfortable calculating an investor's optimal portfolio given the investor's risk preferences and universe of investable assets available.

REFERENCES

2009 Ibbotson Stocks, Bonds, Bills, and Inflation (SBBI) Classic Yearbook. 2009. Chicago, IL: Morningstar.

Bogle, John C. 2008. "Black Monday and Black Swans." *Financial Analysts Journal*, vol. 64, no. 2: 30–40.

Dimson, Elroy, Paul Marsh, and Mike Staunton. 2009. *Credit Suisse Global Investment Returns Sourcebook*. 2009. Zurich, Switzerland: Credit Suisse Research Institute.

Taleb, Nassim N. 2007. *The Black Swan: The Impact of the Highly Improbable*. New York: Random House Inc.

PRACTICE PROBLEMS

1 An investor purchased 100 shares of a stock for $34.50 per share at the beginning of the quarter. If the investor sold all of the shares for $30.50 per share after receiving a $51.55 dividend payment at the end of the quarter, the holding period return is *closest* to:

A −13.0%.

B −11.6%.

C −10.1%.

2 An analyst obtains the following annual rates of return for a mutual fund:

Year	Return (%)
2008	14
2009	−10
2010	−2

The fund's holding period return over the three-year period is *closest* to:

A 0.18%.

B 0.55%.

C 0.67%.

3 An analyst observes the following annual rates of return for a hedge fund:

Year	Return (%)
2008	22
2009	−25
2010	11

The hedge fund's annual geometric mean return is *closest* to:

A 0.52%.

B 1.02%.

C 2.67%.

4 Which of the following return calculating methods is *best* for evaluating the annualized returns of a buy-and-hold strategy of an investor who has made annual deposits to an account for each of the last five years?

A Geometric mean return.

B Arithmetic mean return.

C Money-weighted return.

5 An investor performs the following transactions on the shares of a firm.

- At $t = 0$, she purchases a share for $1,000.
- At $t = 1$, she receives a dividend of $25 and then purchases three additional shares for $1,055 each.
- At $t = 2$, she receives a total dividend of $100 and then sells the four shares for $1,100 each.

The money-weighted rate of return is *closest* to:

A 4.5%.

B 6.9%.

C 7.3%.

6 A fund receives investments at the beginning of each year and generates returns as shown in the table.

Year of Investment	Assets Under Management at the beginning of each year	Return during Year of Investment
1	$1,000	15%
2	$4,000	14%
3	$45,000	–4%

Which return measure over the three-year period is negative?

A Geometric mean return

B Time-weighted rate of return

C Money-weighted rate of return

7 At the beginning of Year 1, a fund has $10 million under management; it earns a return of 14% for the year. The fund attracts another $100 million at the start of Year 2 and earns a return of 8% for that year. The money-weighted rate of return is *most likely*:

A less than the time-weighted rate of return.

B the same as the time-weighted rate of return.

C greater than the time-weighted rate of return.

8 An investor evaluating the returns of three recently formed exchange-traded funds gathers the following information:

ETF	Time Since Inception	Return Since Inception (%)
1	146 days	4.61
2	5 weeks	1.10
3	15 months	14.35

The ETF with the highest annualized rate of return is:

A ETF 1.

B ETF 2.

C ETF 3.

9 With respect to capital market theory, which of the following asset characteristics is *least likely* to impact the variance of an investor's equally weighted portfolio?

A Return on the asset.

B Standard deviation of the asset.

C Covariances of the asset with the other assets in the portfolio.

10 A portfolio manager creates the following portfolio:

Security	Security Weight (%)	Expected Standard Deviation (%)
1	30	20
2	70	12

If the correlation of returns between the two securities is 0.40, the expected standard deviation of the portfolio is *closest* to:

A 10.7%.

B 11.3%.

C 12.1%.

11 A portfolio manager creates the following portfolio:

Security	Security Weight (%)	Expected Standard Deviation (%)
1	30	20
2	70	12

If the covariance of returns between the two securities is −0.0240, the expected standard deviation of the portfolio is *closest* to:

A 2.4%.

B 7.5%.

C 9.2%.

The following information relates to Questions 12–13

A portfolio manager creates the following portfolio:

Security	Security Weight (%)	Expected Standard Deviation (%)
1	30	20
2	70	12

12 If the standard deviation of the portfolio is 14.40%, the correlation between the two securities is equal to:

A −1.0.

B 0.0.

C 1.0.

13 If the standard deviation of the portfolio is 14.40%, the covariance between the two securities is equal to:

A 0.0006.

B 0.0240.

C 1.0000.

The following information relates to Questions 14–17

An analyst observes the following historic geometric returns:

Asset Class	Geometric Return (%)
Equities	8.0
Corporate Bonds	6.5
Treasury bills	2.5
Inflation	2.1

14 The real rate of return for equities is *closest* to:

A 5.4%.

B 5.8%.

C 5.9%.

15 The real rate of return for corporate bonds is *closest* to:

A 4.3%.

B 4.4%.

C 4.5%.

16 The risk premium for equities is *closest* to:

A 5.4%.

B 5.5%.

C 5.6%.

17 The risk premium for corporate bonds is *closest* to:

A 3.5%.

B 3.9%.

C 4.0%.

---

18 With respect to trading costs, liquidity is *least likely* to impact the:

A stock price.

B bid–ask spreads.

C brokerage commissions.

19 Evidence of risk aversion is *best* illustrated by a risk–return relationship that is:

A negative.

B neutral.

C positive.

20 With respect to risk-averse investors, a risk-free asset will generate a numerical utility that is:

A the same for all individuals.

B positive for risk-averse investors.

C equal to zero for risk seeking investors.

21 With respect to utility theory, the most risk-averse investor will have an indifference curve with the:

A most convexity.

B smallest intercept value.

C greatest slope coefficient.

22 With respect to an investor's utility function expressed as: $U = E(r) - \frac{1}{2}A\sigma^2$, which of the following values for the measure for risk aversion has the *least* amount of risk aversion?

A −4.

B 0.

C 4.

The following information relates to Questions 23–26

A financial planner has created the following data to illustrate the application of utility theory to portfolio selection:

Investment	Expected Return (%)	Expected Standard Deviation (%)
1	18	2
2	19	8
3	20	15
4	18	30

23 A risk-neutral investor is *most likely* to choose:

A Investment 1.

B Investment 2.

C Investment 3.

24 If an investor's utility function is expressed as $U = E(r) - \frac{1}{2}A\sigma^2$ and the measure for risk aversion has a value of −2, the risk-seeking investor is *most likely* to choose:

A Investment 2.

B Investment 3.

C Investment 4.

25 If an investor's utility function is expressed as $U = E(r) - \frac{1}{2}A\sigma^2$ and the measure for risk aversion has a value of 2, the risk-averse investor is *most likely* to choose:

A Investment 1.

B Investment 2.

C Investment 3.

26 If an investor's utility function is expressed as $U = E(r) - \frac{1}{2}A\sigma^2$ and the measure for risk aversion has a value of 4, the risk-averse investor is *most likely* to choose:

A Investment 1.

B Investment 2.

C Investment 3.

---

27 With respect to the mean–variance portfolio theory, the capital allocation line, CAL, is the combination of the risk-free asset and a portfolio of all:

A risky assets.

B equity securities.

C feasible investments.

28 Two individual investors with different levels of risk aversion will have optimal portfolios that are:

A below the capital allocation line.

B on the capital allocation line.

C above the capital allocation line.

The following information relates to Questions 29–31

A portfolio manager creates the following portfolio:

Security	Expected Annual Return (%)	Expected Standard Deviation (%)
1	16	20
2	12	20

29 If the portfolio of the two securities has an expected return of 15%, the proportion invested in Security 1 is:

A 25%.

B 50%.

C 75%.

30 If the correlation of returns between the two securities is −0.15, the expected standard deviation of an equal-weighted portfolio is *closest* to:

A 13.04%.

B 13.60%.

C 13.87%.

31 If the two securities are uncorrelated, the expected standard deviation of an equal-weighted portfolio is *closest* to:

A 14.00%.

B 14.14%.

C 20.00%.

---

32 As the number of assets in an equally-weighted portfolio increases, the contribution of each individual asset's variance to the volatility of the portfolio:

A increases.

B decreases.

C remains the same.

33 With respect to an equally-weighted portfolio made up of a large number of assets, which of the following contributes the *most* to the volatility of the portfolio?

A Average variance of the individual assets.

B Standard deviation of the individual assets.

C Average covariance between all pairs of assets.

34 The correlation between assets in a two-asset portfolio increases during a market decline. If there is no change in the proportion of each asset held in the portfolio or the expected standard deviation of the individual assets, the volatility of the portfolio is *most likely* to:

A increase.

B decrease.

C remain the same.

The following information relates to Questions 35–37

An analyst has made the following return projections for each of three possible outcomes with an equal likelihood of occurrence:

Asset	Outcome 1 (%)	Outcome 2 (%)	Outcome 3 (%)	Expected Return (%)
1	12	0	6	6
2	12	6	0	6
3	0	6	12	6

35 Which pair of assets is perfectly negatively correlated?

A Asset 1 and Asset 2.

B Asset 1 and Asset 3.

C Asset 2 and Asset 3.

36 If the analyst constructs two-asset portfolios that are equally-weighted, which pair of assets has the *lowest* expected standard deviation?

A Asset 1 and Asset 2.

B Asset 1 and Asset 3.

C Asset 2 and Asset 3.

37 If the analyst constructs two-asset portfolios that are equally weighted, which pair of assets provides the *least* amount of risk reduction?

A Asset 1 and Asset 2.

B Asset 1 and Asset 3.

C Asset 2 and Asset 3.

---

38 Which of the following statements is *least* accurate? The efficient frontier is the set of all attainable risky assets with the:

A highest expected return for a given level of risk.

B lowest amount of risk for a given level of return.

C highest expected return relative to the risk-free rate.

39 The portfolio on the minimum-variance frontier with the lowest standard deviation is:

A unattainable.

B the optimal risky portfolio.

C the global minimum-variance portfolio.

40 The set of portfolios on the minimum-variance frontier that dominates all sets of portfolios below the global minimum-variance portfolio is the:

A capital allocation line.

B Markowitz efficient frontier.

C set of optimal risky portfolios.

41 The dominant capital allocation line is the combination of the risk-free asset and the:

A optimal risky portfolio.

B levered portfolio of risky assets.

C global minimum-variance portfolio.

42 Compared to the efficient frontier of risky assets, the dominant capital allocation line has higher rates of return for levels of risk greater than the optimal risky portfolio because of the investor's ability to:

A lend at the risk-free rate.

B borrow at the risk-free rate.

C purchase the risk-free asset.

43 With respect to the mean–variance theory, the optimal portfolio is determined by each individual investor's:

A risk-free rate.

B borrowing rate.

C risk preference.

SOLUTIONS

1 C is correct. −10.1% is the holding period return, which is calculated as: (3,050 − 3,450 + 51.55)/3,450, which is comprised of a dividend yield of 1.49% = 51.55/(3,450) and a capital loss yield of −11.59% = −400/(3,450).

2 B is correct. [(1 + 0.14)(1 − 0.10)(1 − 0.02)] − 1 = 0.0055 = 0.55%.

3 A is correct. $[(1 + 0.22)(1 - 0.25)(1 + 0.11)]^{(1/3)} - 1 = 1.0157^{(1/3)} - 1 = 0.0052 =$ 0.52%

4 A is correct. The geometric mean return compounds the returns instead of the amount invested.

5 B is correct. Computation of the money-weighted return, *r*, requires finding the discount rate that sums the present value of cash flows to zero.

The first step is to group net cash flows by time. For this example, we have −\$1,000 for the $t = 0$ net cash flow, −\$3,140 = −\$3,165 + \$25 for the $t = 1$ net cash flow, and \$4,500 = \$4,400 + \$100 for the $t = 2$ net cash flow

Solving for *r*,

$$CF_0 = -1{,}000$$
$$CF_1 = -3{,}140$$
$$CF_2 = +4{,}500$$

$$\frac{CF_0}{(1+IRR)^0} + \frac{CF_1}{(1+IRR)^1} + \frac{CF_2}{(1+IRR)^2}$$
$$= \frac{-1{,}000}{1} + \frac{-3{,}140}{(1+IRR)^1} + \frac{4{,}500}{(1+IRR)^2} = 0$$

results in a value of $r = 6.91\%$

6 C is correct. The money-weighted rate of return considers both the timing and amounts of investments into the fund. To calculate the money-weighted rate of return, tabulate the annual returns and investment amounts to determine the cash flows

Year	1	2	3
Balance from previous year	0	\$1,150	\$4,560
New investment	\$1,000	\$2,850	\$40,440
Net balance at the beginning of year	\$1,000	\$4,000	\$45,000
Investment return for the year	15%	14%	−4%
Investment gain (loss)	\$150	\$560	−\$1,800
Balance at the end of year	\$1,150	\$4,560	\$43,200

$$CF_0 = -\$1{,}000,\ CF_1 = -\$2{,}850,\ CF_2 = -\$40{,}440,\ CF_3 = +\$43{,}200$$

Each cash inflow or outflow occurs at the end of each year. Thus, CF_0 refers to the cash flow at the end of Year 0 or beginning of Year 1, and CF_3 refers to the cash flow at end of Year 3 or beginning of Year 4. Because cash flows are being discounted to the present—that is, end of Year 0 or beginning of Year 1—the period of discounting CF_0 is zero whereas the period of discounting for CF_3 is 3 years.

Solving for r,

$CF_0 = -1{,}000$

$CF_1 = -2{,}850$

$CF_2 = -40{,}440$

$CF_3 = +43{,}200$

$$\frac{CF_0}{(1+IRR)^0} + \frac{CF_1}{(1+IRR)^1} + \frac{CF_2}{(1+IRR)^2} + \frac{CF_3}{(1+IRR)^3}$$

$$= \frac{-1{,}000}{1} + \frac{-2{,}850}{(1+IRR)^1} + \frac{-40{,}440}{(1+IRR)^2} + \frac{43{,}200}{(1+IRR)^3} = 0$$

results in a value of $r = -2.22\%$

Note that B is incorrect because the time-weighted rate of return (TWR) of the fund is the same as the geometric mean return of the fund and is thus positive:

$$TWR = \sqrt[3]{(1.15)(1.14)(0.96)} - 1 = 7.97\%$$

7 A is correct. Computation of the money-weighted return, r, requires finding the discount rate that sums the present value of cash flows to zero. Because most of the investment came during Year 2, the measure will be biased toward the performance of Year 2. The cash flows are as follows:

$CF_0 = -10$

$CF_1 = -100$

$CF_2 = +120.31$

The terminal value is determined by summing the investment returns for each period [(10 × 1.14 × 1.08) + (100 × 1.08)]

$$\frac{CF_0}{(1+IRR)^0} + \frac{CF_1}{(1+IRR)^1} + \frac{CF_2}{(1+IRR)^2}$$

$$= \frac{-10}{1} + \frac{-100}{(1+IRR)^1} + \frac{120.31}{(1+IRR)^2}$$

results in a value of $r = 8.53\%$

The time-weighted return of the fund is $= \sqrt[2]{(1.14)(1.08)} - 1 = 10.96\%$.

8 B is correct. The annualized rate of return for ETF 2 is 12.05% = $(1.0110^{52/5}) - 1$, which is greater than the annualized rate of ETF 1, 11.93% = $(1.0461^{365/146}) - 1$, and ETF 3, 11.32% = $(1.1435^{12/15}) - 1$. Despite having the lowest value for the periodic rate, ETF 2 has the highest annualized rate of return because of the reinvestment rate assumption and the compounding of the periodic rate.

9 A is correct. The asset's returns are not used to calculate the portfolio's variance [only the assets' weights, standard deviations (or variances), and covariances (or correlations) are used].

10 C is correct.

$$\sigma_{port} = \sqrt{w_1^2\sigma_1^2 + w_2^2\sigma_2^2 + 2w_1w_2\rho_{1,2}\sigma_1\sigma_2}$$

$$= \sqrt{(0.3)^2(20\%)^2 + (0.7)^2(12\%)^2 + 2(0.3)(0.7)(0.40)(20\%)(12\%)}$$

$$= (0.3600\% + 0.7056\% + 0.4032\%)^{0.5} = (1.4688\%)^{0.5} = 12.11\%$$

11 A is correct.

$$\sigma_{port} = \sqrt{w_1^2\sigma_1^2 + w_2^2\sigma_2^2 + 2w_1w_2Cov(R_1R_2)}$$
$$= \sqrt{(0.3)^2(20\%)^2 + (0.7)^2(12\%)^2 + 2(0.3)(0.7)(-0.0240)}$$
$$= (0.3600\% + 0.7056\% - 1.008\%)^{0.5} = (0.0576\%)^{0.5} = 2.40\%$$

12 C is correct. A portfolio standard deviation of 14.40% is the weighted average, which is possible only if the correlation between the securities is equal to 1.0.

13 B is correct. A portfolio standard deviation of 14.40% is the weighted average, which is possible only if the correlation between the securities is equal to 1.0. If the correlation coefficient is equal to 1.0, then the covariance must equal 0.0240, calculated as: $Cov(R_1,R_2) = \rho_{12}\sigma_1\sigma_2 = (1.0)(20\%)(12\%) = 2.40\% = 0.0240$.

14 B is correct. (1 + 0.080)/(1 + 0.0210) – 1 = 5.8%

15 A is correct. (1 + 0.065)/(1 + 0.0210) – 1 = 4.3%

16 A is correct. (1 + 0.080)/(1 + 0.0250) – 1 = 5.4%

17 B is correct. (1 + 0.0650)/(1 + 0.0250) – 1 = 3.9%

18 C is correct. Brokerage commissions are negotiated with the brokerage firm. A security's liquidity impacts the operational efficiency of trading costs. Specifically, liquidity impacts the bid–ask spread and can impact the stock price (if the ability to sell the stock is impaired by the uncertainty associated with being able to sell the stock).

19 C is correct. Historical data over long periods of time indicate that there exists a positive risk–return relationship, which is a reflection of an investor's risk aversion.

20 A is correct. A risk-free asset has a variance of zero and is not dependent on whether the investor is risk neutral, risk seeking or risk averse. That is, given that the utility function of an investment is expressed as $U = E(r) - \frac{1}{2}A\sigma^2$, where A is the measure of risk aversion, then the sign of A is irrelevant if the variance is zero (like that of a risk-free asset).

21 C is correct. The most risk-averse investor has the indifference curve with the greatest slope.

22 A is correct. A negative value in the given utility function indicates that the investor is a risk seeker.

23 C is correct. Investment 3 has the highest rate of return. Risk is irrelevant to a risk-neutral investor, who would have a measure of risk aversion equal to 0. Given the utility function, the risk-neutral investor would obtain the greatest amount of utility from Investment 3.

Investment	Expected Return (%)	Expected Standard Deviation (%)	Utility $A = 0$
1	18	2	0.1800
2	19	8	0.1900
3	20	15	0.2000
4	18	30	0.1800

24 C is correct. Investment 4 provides the highest utility value (0.2700) for a risk-seeking investor, who has a measure of risk aversion equal to –2.

Investment	Expected Return (%)	Expected Standard Deviation (%)	Utility $A = -2$
1	18	2	0.1804
2	19	8	0.1964
3	20	15	0.2225
4	18	30	0.2700

25 B is correct. Investment 2 provides the highest utility value (0.1836) for a risk-averse investor who has a measure of risk aversion equal to 2.

Investment	Expected Return (%)	Expected Standard Deviation (%)	Utility $A = 2$
1	18	2	0.1796
2	19	8	0.1836
3	20	15	0.1775
4	18	30	0.0900

26 A is correct. Investment 1 provides the highest utility value (0.1792) for a risk-averse investor who has a measure of risk aversion equal to 4.

Investment	Expected Return (%)	Expected Standard Deviation (%)	Utility $A = 4$
1	18	2	0.1792
2	19	8	0.1772
3	20	15	0.1550
4	18	30	0.0000

27 A is correct. The CAL is the combination of the risk-free asset with zero risk and the portfolio of all risky assets that provides for the set of feasible investments. Allowing for borrowing at the risk-free rate and investing in the portfolio of all risky assets provides for attainable portfolios that dominate risky assets below the CAL.

28 B is correct. The CAL represents the set of all feasible investments. Each investor's indifference curve determines the optimal combination of the risk-free asset and the portfolio of all risky assets, which must lie on the CAL.

29 C is correct.

$$R_p = w_1 \times R_1 + (1 - w_1) \times R_2$$

$$R_p = w_1 \times 16\% + (1 - w_1) \times 12\%$$

$$15\% = 0.75(16\%) + 0.25(12\%)$$

30 A is correct.

$$\sigma_{port} = \sqrt{w_1^2\sigma_1^2 + w_2^2\sigma_2^2 + 2w_1w_2\rho_{1,2}\sigma_1\sigma_2}$$

$$= \sqrt{(0.5)^2(20\%)^2 + (0.5)^2(20\%)^2 + 2(0.5)(0.5)(-0.15)(20\%)(20\%)}$$

$$= (1.0000\% + 1.0000\% - 0.3000\%)^{0.5} = (1.7000\%)^{0.5} = 13.04\%$$

31 B is correct.

$$\begin{aligned}\sigma_{port} &= \sqrt{w_1^2\sigma_1^2 + w_2^2\sigma_2^2 + 2w_1w_2\rho_{1,2}\sigma_1\sigma_2}\\ &= \sqrt{(0.5)^2(20\%)^2 + (0.5)^2\left(20\%^2\right) + 2(0.5)(0.5)(0.00)(20\%)(20\%)}\\ &= (1.0000\% + 1.0000\% + 0.0000\%)^{0.5} = (2.0000\%)^{0.5} = 14.14\%\end{aligned}$$

32 B is correct. The contribution of each individual asset's variance (or standard deviation) to the portfolio's volatility decreases as the number of assets in the equally weighted portfolio increases. The contribution of the co-movement measures between the assets increases (i.e., covariance and correlation) as the number of assets in the equally weighted portfolio increases. The following equation for the variance of an equally weighted portfolio illustrates these points: $\sigma_p^2 = \frac{\bar{\sigma}^2}{N} + \frac{N-1}{N}\overline{COV} = \frac{\bar{\sigma}^2}{N} + \frac{N-1}{N}\bar{\rho}\bar{\sigma}^2$.

33 C is correct. The co-movement measures between the assets increases (i.e., covariance and correlation) as the number of assets in the equally weighted portfolio increases. The contribution of each individual asset's variance (or standard deviation) to the portfolio's volatility decreases as the number of assets in the equally weighted portfolio increases. The following equation for the variance of an equally weighted portfolio illustrates these points:

$$\sigma_p^2 = \frac{\bar{\sigma}^2}{N} + \frac{N-1}{N}\overline{COV} = \frac{\bar{\sigma}^2}{N} + \frac{N-1}{N}\bar{\rho}\bar{\sigma}^2$$

34 A is correct. Higher correlations will produce less diversification benefits provided that the other components of the portfolio standard deviation do not change (i.e., the weights and standard deviations of the individual assets).

35 C is correct. Asset 2 and Asset 3 have returns that are the same for Outcome 2, but the exact opposite returns for Outcome 1 and Outcome 3; therefore, because they move in opposite directions at the same magnitude, they are perfectly negatively correlated.

36 C is correct. An equally weighted portfolio of Asset 2 and Asset 3 will have the lowest portfolio standard deviation, because for each outcome, the portfolio has the same expected return (they are perfectly negatively correlated).

37 A is correct. An equally weighted portfolio of Asset 1 and Asset 2 has the highest level of volatility of the three pairs. All three pairs have the same expected return; however, the portfolio of Asset 1 and Asset 2 provides the least amount of risk reduction.

38 C is correct. The efficient frontier does not account for the risk-free rate. The efficient frontier is the set of all attainable risky assets with the highest expected return for a given level of risk or the lowest amount of risk for a given level of return.

39 C is correct. The global minimum-variance portfolio is the portfolio on the minimum-variance frontier with the lowest standard deviation. Although the portfolio is attainable, when the risk-free asset is considered, the global minimum-variance portfolio is not the optimal risky portfolio.

40 B is correct. The Markowitz efficient frontier has higher rates of return for a given level of risk. With respect to the minimum-variance portfolio, the Markowitz efficient frontier is the set of portfolios above the global minimum-variance portfolio that dominates the portfolios below the global minimum-variance portfolio.

41 A is correct. The use of leverage and the combination of a risk-free asset and the optimal risky asset will dominate the efficient frontier of risky assets (the Markowitz efficient frontier).

42 B is correct. The CAL dominates the efficient frontier at all points except for the optimal risky portfolio. The ability of the investor to purchase additional amounts of the optimal risky portfolio by borrowing (i.e., buying on margin) at the risk-free rate makes higher rates of return for levels of risk greater than the optimal risky asset possible.

43 C is correct. Each individual investor's optimal mix of the risk-free asset and the optimal risky asset is determined by the investor's risk preference.

READING

53

Portfolio Risk and Return: Part II

by Vijay Singal, PhD, CFA

Vijay Singal, PhD, CFA, is at Virginia Tech (USA).

LEARNING OUTCOMES

Mastery	*The candidate should be able to:*
☐	**a.** describe the implications of combining a risk-free asset with a portfolio of risky assets;
☐	**b.** explain the capital allocation line (CAL) and the capital market line (CML);
☐	**c.** explain systematic and nonsystematic risk, including why an investor should not expect to receive additional return for bearing nonsystematic risk;
☐	**d.** explain return generating models (including the market model) and their uses;
☐	**e.** calculate and interpret beta;
☐	**f.** explain the capital asset pricing model (CAPM), including its assumptions, and the security market line (SML);
☐	**g.** calculate and interpret the expected return of an asset using the CAPM;
☐	**h.** describe and demonstrate applications of the CAPM and the SML;
☐	**i.** calculate and interpret the Sharpe ratio, Treynor ratio, M^2, and Jensen's alpha.

INTRODUCTION

1

Our objective in this reading is to identify the optimal risky portfolio for all investors by using the capital asset pricing model (CAPM). The foundation of this reading is the computation of risk and return of a portfolio and the role that correlation plays in diversifying portfolio risk and arriving at the efficient frontier. The efficient frontier and the capital allocation line consist of portfolios that are generally acceptable to all investors. By combining an investor's individual indifference curves with the market-determined capital allocation line, we are able to illustrate that the only optimal risky portfolio for an investor is the portfolio of all risky assets (i.e., the market).

Additionally, we discuss the capital market line, a special case of the capital allocation line that is used for passive investor portfolios. We also differentiate between systematic and nonsystematic risk, and explain why investors are compensated for bearing systematic risk but receive no compensation for bearing nonsystematic risk. We discuss in detail the CAPM, which is a simple model for estimating asset returns based only on the asset's systematic risk. Finally, we illustrate how the CAPM allows security selection to build an optimal portfolio for an investor by changing the asset mix beyond a passive market portfolio.

The reading is organized as follows. In Section 2, we discuss the consequences of combining a risk-free asset with the market portfolio and provide an interpretation of the capital market line. Section 3 decomposes total risk into systematic and nonsystematic risk and discusses the characteristics of and differences between the two kinds of risk. We also introduce return-generating models, including the single-index model, and illustrate the calculation of beta. In Section 4, we introduce the capital asset pricing model and the security market line. Our focus on the CAPM does not suggest that the CAPM is the only viable asset pricing model. Although the CAPM is an excellent starting point, more advanced readings expand on these discussions and extend the analysis to other models that account for multiple explanatory factors. Section 5 covers several post-CAPM developments in theory. Section 6 covers measures for evaluating the performance of a portfolio which take account of risk. Section 7 covers some applications of the CAPM in portfolio construction. A summary and practice problems conclude the reading.

2 CAPITAL MARKET THEORY

You have learned how to combine a risk-free asset with one risky asset and with many risky assets to create a capital allocation line. In this section, we will expand our discussion of multiple risky assets and consider a special case of the capital allocation line, called the capital market line. While discussing the capital market line, we will define the market and its role in passive portfolio management. Using these concepts, we will illustrate how leveraged portfolios can enhance both risk and return.

2.1 Portfolio of Risk-Free and Risky Assets

Although investors desire an asset that produces the highest return and carries the lowest risk, such an asset does not exist. As the risk–return capital market theory illustrates, one must assume higher risk in order to earn a higher return. We can improve an investor's portfolio, however, by expanding the opportunity set of risky assets because this allows the investor to choose a superior mix of assets.

Similarly, an investor's portfolio improves if a risk-free asset is added to the mix. In other words, a combination of the risk-free asset and a risky asset can result in a better risk–return trade-off than an investment in only one type of asset because the risk-free asset has zero correlation with the risky asset. The combination is called the **capital allocation line** (and is depicted in Exhibit 2). Superimposing an investor's indifference curves on the capital allocation line will lead to the optimal investor portfolio.

Investors with different levels of risk aversion will choose different portfolios. Highly risk-averse investors choose to invest most of their wealth in the risk-free asset and earn low returns because they are not willing to assume higher levels of risk. Less risk-averse investors, in contrast, invest more of their wealth in the risky asset, which is expected to yield a higher return. Obviously, the higher return cannot come without higher risk, but the less risk-averse investor is willing to accept the additional risk.

2.1.1 *Combining a Risk-Free Asset with a Portfolio of Risky Assets*

We can extend the analysis of one risky asset to a portfolio of risky assets. For convenience, assume that the portfolio contains all available risky assets (*N*), although an investor may not wish to include all of these assets in the portfolio because of the investor's specific preferences. If an asset is not included in the portfolio, its weight will be zero. The risk–return characteristics of a portfolio of *N* risky assets are given by the following equations:

$$E(R_p) = \sum_{i=1}^{N} w_i E(R_i)$$

$$\sigma_p^2 = \left(\sum_{i=1,j=1}^{N} w_i w_j \text{Cov}(i,j) \right), \text{ and } \sum_{i=1}^{N} w_i = 1$$

The expected return on the portfolio, $E(R_p)$, is the weighted average of the expected returns of individual assets, where w_i is the fractional weight in asset i and R_i is the expected return of asset i. The risk of the portfolio (σ_p), however, depends on the weights of the individual assets, the risk of the individual assets, and their interrelationships. The **covariance** between assets i and j, Cov(i,j), is a statistical measure of the interrelationship between each pair of assets in the portfolio and can be expressed as follows, where ρ_{ij} is the **correlation** between assets i and j and σ_i is the risk of asset i:

$$\text{Cov}(i,j) = \rho_{ij}\sigma_i\sigma_j$$

Note from the equation below that the correlation of an asset with itself is 1; therefore:

$$\text{Cov}(i,i) = \rho_{ii}\sigma_i\sigma_i = \sigma_i^2$$

By substituting the above expressions for covariance, we can rewrite the portfolio variance equation as

$$\sigma_p^2 = \left(\sum_{i=1}^{N} w_i^2\sigma_i^2 + \sum_{i,j=1, i\neq j}^{N} w_i w_j \rho_{ij}\sigma_i\sigma_j \right)$$

The suggestion that portfolios have lower risk than the assets they contain may seem counterintuitive. These portfolios can be constructed, however, as long as the assets in the portfolio are not perfectly correlated. As an illustration of the effect of asset weights on portfolio characteristics, consider a simple two-asset portfolio with zero weights in all other assets. Assume that Asset 1 has a return of 10 percent and a standard deviation (risk) of 20 percent. Asset 2 has a return of 5 percent and a standard deviation (risk) of 10 percent. Furthermore, the correlation between the two assets is zero. Exhibit 1 shows risks and returns for Portfolio X with a weight of 25 percent in Asset 1 and 75 percent in Asset 2, Portfolio Y with a weight of 50 percent in each of the two assets, and Portfolio Z with a weight of 75 percent in Asset 1 and 25 percent in Asset 2.

Exhibit 1 Portfolio Risk and Return

Portfolio	Weight in Asset 1 (%)	Weight in Asset 2 (%)	Portfolio Return (%)	Portfolio Standard Deviation (%)
X	25.0	75.0	6.25	9.01
Y	50.0	50.0	7.50	11.18
Z	75.0	25.0	8.75	15.21
Return	10.0	5.0		
Standard deviation	20.0	10.0		
Correlation between Assets 1 and 2		0.0		

From this example we observe that the three portfolios are quite different in terms of their risk and return. Portfolio X has a 6.25 percent return and only 9.01 percent standard deviation, whereas the standard deviation of Portfolio Z is more than two-thirds higher (15.21 percent), although the return is only slightly more than one-third higher (8.75 percent). These portfolios may become even more dissimilar as other assets are added to the mix.

Consider three portfolios of risky assets, A, B, and C, as in Exhibit 2, that may have been presented to a representative investor by three different investment advisers. Each portfolio is combined with the risk-free asset to create three capital allocation lines, CAL(A), CAL(B), and CAL(C). The exhibit shows that Portfolio C is superior to the other two portfolios because it has a greater expected return for any given level of risk. As a result, an investor will choose the portfolio that lies on the capital allocation line for Portfolio C. The combination of the risk-free asset and the risky Portfolio C that is selected for an investor depends on the investor's degree of risk aversion.

Exhibit 2 Risk-Free Asset and Portfolio of Risky Assets

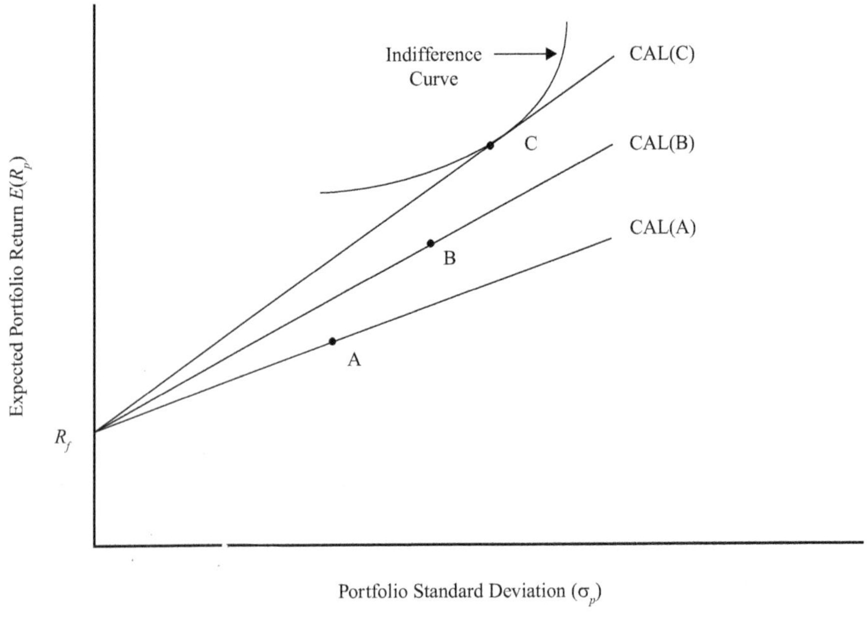

2.1.2 *Does a Unique Optimal Risky Portfolio Exist?*

We assume that all investors have the same economic expectation and thus have the same expectations of prices, cash flows, and other investment characteristics. This assumption is referred to as **homogeneity of expectations**. Given these investment characteristics, everyone goes through the same calculations and should arrive at the same optimal risky portfolio. Therefore, assuming homogeneous expectations, only one optimal portfolio exists. If investors have different expectations, however, they might arrive at different optimal risky portfolios. To illustrate, we begin with an expression for the price of an asset:

$$P = \sum_{t=0}^{T} \frac{\text{CF}_t}{\left(1 + r_t\right)^t}$$

where CF_t is the cash flow at the end of period t and r_t is the discount rate or the required rate of return for that asset for period t. Period t refers to all periods beginning from now until the asset ceases to exist at the end of time T. Because the current time is the end of period 0, which is the same as the beginning of period 1, there are $(T + 1)$ cash flows and $(T + 1)$ required rates of return. These conditions are based on the assumption that a cash flow, such as an initial investment, can occur now (t = 0). Ordinarily, however, CF_0 is zero.

We use the formula for the price of an asset to estimate the intrinsic value of an asset. Assume that the asset we are valuing is a share of Siemens AG which trades on Xetra. In the case of corporate stock, there is no expiration date, so T could be extremely large, meaning we will need to estimate a large number of cash flows and rates of return. Fortunately, the denominator reduces the importance of distant cash flows, so it may be sufficient to estimate, say, 20 annual cash flows and 20 rates of returns. How much will Siemens earn next year and the year after next? What will the product markets Siemens operates in look like in five years' time? Different analysts and investors will have their own estimates that may be quite different from one another. Also, as we delve further into the future, more serious issues in estimating future revenue, expenses, and growth rates arise. Therefore, to assume that cash flow estimates for Siemens will vary among these investors is reasonable. In addition to the numerator (cash flows), it is also necessary to estimate the denominator, the required rates of return. We know that riskier companies will require higher returns because risk and return are positively correlated. Siemens stock is riskier than a risk-free asset, but by how much? And what should the compensation for that additional risk be? Again, it is evident that different analysts will view the riskiness of Siemens differently and, therefore, arrive at different required rates of return.

Siemens closed at €111.84 on Xetra on 31 August 2018. The traded price represents the value that a marginal investor attaches to a share of Siemens, say, corresponding to Analyst A's expectation. Analyst B may think that the price should be €95, however, and Analyst C may think that the price should be €125. Given a price of €111.84, the expected returns of Siemens are quite different for the three analysts. Analyst B, who believes the price should be €95, concludes that Siemens is overvalued and may assign a weight of zero to Siemens in the recommended portfolio even though the market capitalization of Siemens was in excess of €100 billion as of the date of the quotation. In contrast, Analyst C, with a valuation of €125, thinks Siemens is undervalued and may significantly overweight Siemens in a portfolio.

Our discussion illustrates that analysts can arrive at different valuations that necessitate the assignment of different asset weights in a portfolio. Given the existence of many asset classes and numerous assets in each asset class, one can visualize that each investor will have his or her own optimal risky portfolio depending on his or her assumptions underlying the valuation computations. Therefore, market participants will have their own and possibly different optimal risky portfolios.

If investors have different valuations of assets, then the construction of a unique optimal risky portfolio is not possible. If we make a simplifying assumption of homogeneity in investor expectations, we will have a single optimal risky portfolio as previously mentioned. Even if investors have different expectations, market prices are a proxy of what the marginal, informed investor expects, and the market portfolio becomes the base case, the benchmark, or the reference portfolio that other portfolios can be judged against. For Siemens, the market price was €111.84 per share and the market capitalization was about €108 billion. In constructing the market portfolio, Siemens's weight in the market portfolio will be equal to its market value divided by the value of all other assets included in the market portfolio.

2.2 The Capital Market Line

In the previous section, we discussed how the risk-free asset could be combined with a risky portfolio to create a capital allocation line (CAL). In this section, we discuss a specific CAL that uses the market portfolio as the optimal risky portfolio and is known as the capital market line. We also discuss the significance of the market portfolio and applications of the capital market line (CML).

2.2.1 *Passive and Active Portfolios*

In the above subsection, we hypothesized three possible valuations for each share of Siemens: €95, €111.84, and €125. Which one is correct?

If the market is an **informationally efficient market**, the price in the market, €111.84, is an unbiased estimate of all future discounted cash flows (recall the formula for the price of an asset). In other words, the price aggregates and reflects all information that is publicly available, and investors cannot expect to earn a return that is greater than the required rate of return for that asset. If, however, the price reflects all publicly available information and there is no way to outperform the market, then there is little point in investing time and money in evaluating Siemens to arrive at your price using your own estimates of cash flows and rates of return.

In that case, a simple and convenient approach to investing is to rely on the prices set by the market. Portfolios that are based on the assumption of unbiased market prices are referred to as passive portfolios. Passive portfolios most commonly replicate and track market indexes, which are passively constructed on the basis of market prices and market capitalizations. Examples of market indexes are the S&P 500 Index, the Nikkei 300, and the CAC 40. Passive portfolios based on market indexes are called index funds and generally have low costs because no significant effort is expended in valuing securities that are included in an index.

In contrast to passive investors' reliance on market prices and index funds, active investors may not rely on market valuations. They have more confidence in their own ability to estimate cash flows, growth rates, and discount rates. Based on these estimates, they value assets and determine whether an asset is fairly valued. In an actively managed portfolio, assets that are undervalued, or have a chance of offering above-normal returns, will have a positive weight (i.e., overweight compared to the market weight in the benchmark index), whereas other assets will have a zero weight, or even a negative weight if short selling is permitted (i.e., some assets will be underweighted compared with the market weight in the benchmark index). (**Short selling** is a transaction in which borrowed securities are sold with the intention to repurchase them at a lower price at a later date and return them to the lender.) This style of investing is called active investment management, and the portfolios are referred to as active portfolios. Most open-end mutual funds and hedge funds practice active investment management, and most analysts believe that active investing adds value. Whether these analysts are right or wrong is the subject of continuing debate.

2.2.2 *What Is the "Market"?*

In the previous discussion, we referred to the "market" on numerous occasions without actually defining the market. The optimal risky portfolio and the capital market line depend on the definition of the market. So what is the market?

Theoretically, the market includes all risky assets or anything that has value, which includes stocks, bonds, real estate, and even human capital. Not all assets are tradable, however, and not all tradable assets are investable. For example, the Taj Mahal in India is an asset but is not a tradable asset. Similarly, human capital is an asset that is not tradable. Moreover, assets may be tradable but not investable because of restrictions placed on certain kinds of investors. For example, all stocks listed on the Shanghai Stock Exchange are tradable. However, whereas Class A shares are listed in RMB and open to domestic investors and qualified foreign investors, Class B shares are listed in USD and open to foreign investors and domestic investors holding foreign currency dealing accounts.

If we consider all stocks, bonds, real estate assets, commodities, etc., probably hundreds of thousands of assets are tradable and investable. The "market" should contain as many assets as possible; we emphasize the word "possible" because it is not practical to include all assets in a single risky portfolio. Even though advancements in technology and interconnected markets have made it much easier to span the major equity markets, we are still not able to easily invest in other kinds of assets like bonds and real estate except in the most developed countries.

For the rest of this reading, we will define the "market" quite narrowly because it is practical and convenient to do so. Typically, a local or regional stock market index is used as a proxy for the market because of active trading in stocks and because a local or regional market is most visible to the local investors. For our purposes, we will use the S&P 500 Index as the market's proxy. The S&P 500 is commonly used by analysts as a benchmark for market performance throughout the United States. It contains 500 of the largest stocks that are domiciled in the United States, and these stocks are weighted by their market capitalization (price times the number of outstanding shares).

As of mid-2018, the stocks in the S&P 500 account for approximately 80 percent of the total equity market capitalization in the United States, and because the US stock markets represent about 40 percent of the world markets, the S&P 500 represents roughly 32 percent of worldwide publicly traded equity. Our definition of the market does not include non-US stock markets, bond markets, real estate, and many other asset classes, and therefore, "market" return and the "market" risk premium refer to US equity return and the US equity risk premium, respectively. The use of this proxy, however, is sufficient for our discussion, and is relatively easy to expand to include other tradable assets.

2.2.3 *The Capital Market Line (CML)*

A capital allocation line includes all possible combinations of the risk-free asset and an investor's optimal risky portfolio. The **capital market line** is a special case of the capital allocation line, where the risky portfolio is the market portfolio. The risk-free asset is a debt security with no default risk, no inflation risk, no liquidity risk, no interest rate risk, and no risk of any other kind. US Treasury bills are usually used as a proxy of the risk-free return, R_f.

The S&P 500 is a proxy of the market portfolio, which is the optimal risky portfolio. Therefore, the expected return on the risky portfolio is the expected market return, expressed as $E(R_m)$. The capital market line is shown in Exhibit 3, where the standard deviation (σ_p), or total risk, is on the x-axis and expected portfolio return, $E(R_p)$, is on the y-axis. Graphically, the market portfolio is the point on the Markowitz efficient frontier where a line from the risk-free asset is tangent to the Markowitz efficient frontier. All points on the interior of the Markowitz efficient frontier are inefficient portfolios in that they provide the same level of return with a higher level of risk or a lower level of return with the same amount of risk. When plotted together, the point at which the CML is tangent to the Markowitz efficient frontier is the optimal combination of risky assets, on the basis of market prices and market capitalizations. The optimal risky portfolio is the market portfolio.

Exhibit 3 Capital Market Line

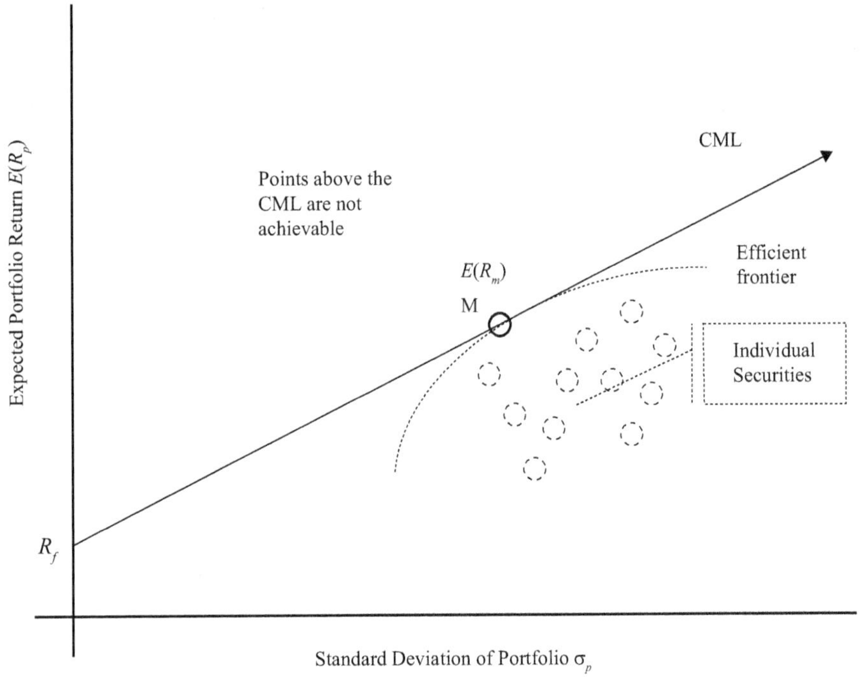

The CML's intercept on the y-axis is the risk-free return (R_f) because that is the return associated with zero risk. The CML passes through the point represented by the market return, $E(R_m)$. With respect to capital market theory, any point above the CML is not achievable and any point below the CML is dominated by and inferior to any point on the CML.

Note that we identify the CML and CAL as lines even though they are a combination of two assets. Unlike a combination of two risky assets, which is usually not a straight line, a combination of the risk-free asset and a risky portfolio is a straight line, as illustrated below by computing the combination's risk and return.

Risk and return characteristics of the portfolio represented by the CML can be computed by using the return and risk expressions for a two-asset portfolio:

$$E(R_p) = w_1 R_f + (1 - w_1)E(R_m),$$

and

$$\sigma_p = \sqrt{w_1^2\sigma_f^2 + (1 - w_1)^2\sigma_m^2 + 2w_1(1 - w_1)\text{Cov}(R_f, R_m)}$$

The proportion invested in the risk-free asset is given by w_1, and the balance is invested in the market portfolio, $(1 - w_1)$. The risk of the risk-free asset is given by σ_f, the risk of the market is given by σ_m, the risk of the portfolio is given by σ_p, and the covariance between the risk-free asset and the market portfolio is represented by $\text{Cov}(R_f, R_m)$.

By definition, the standard deviation of the risk-free asset is zero. Because its risk is zero, the risk-free asset does not co-vary or move with any other asset. Therefore, its covariance with all other assets, including the market portfolio, is zero, making the first and third terms under the square root sign zero. As a result, the portfolio return and portfolio standard deviation can be simplified and rewritten as:

$$E(R_p) = w_1 R_f + (1 - w_1)E(R_m),$$

and

$$\sigma_p = (1 - w_1)\sigma_m$$

By substitution, we can express $E(R_p)$ in terms of σ_p. Substituting for w_1, we get:

$$E(R_p) = R_f + \left(\frac{E(R_m) - R_f}{\sigma_m}\right) \times \sigma_p$$

Note that the expression is in the form of a line, $y = a + bx$. The y-intercept is the risk-free rate, and the slope of the line referred to as the market price of risk is $[E(R_m) - R_f]/\sigma_m$. The CML has a positive slope because the market's risky return is larger than the risk-free return. As the amount of the total investment devoted to the market increases—that is, as we move up the line—both standard deviation (risk) and expected return increase.

EXAMPLE 1

Risk and Return on the CML

Mr. Miles is a first time investor and wants to build a portfolio using only US T-bills and an index fund that closely tracks the S&P 500 Index. The T-bills have a return of 5 percent. The S&P 500 has a standard deviation of 20 percent and an expected return of 15 percent.

1 Draw the CML and mark the points where the investment in the market is 0 percent, 25 percent, 75 percent, and 100 percent.

2 Mr. Miles is also interested in determining the exact risk and return at each point.

Solution to 1:

We calculate the equation for the CML as $E(R_p) = 5\% + 0.50 \times \sigma_p$ by substituting the given information into the general CML equation. The intercept of the line is 5 percent, and its slope is 0.50. We can draw the CML by arbitrarily taking any two points on the line that satisfy the above equation.

Alternatively, the CML can be drawn by connecting the risk-free return of 5 percent on the y-axis with the market portfolio at (20 percent, 15 percent). The CML is shown in Exhibit 4.

Exhibit 4 Risk and Return on the CML

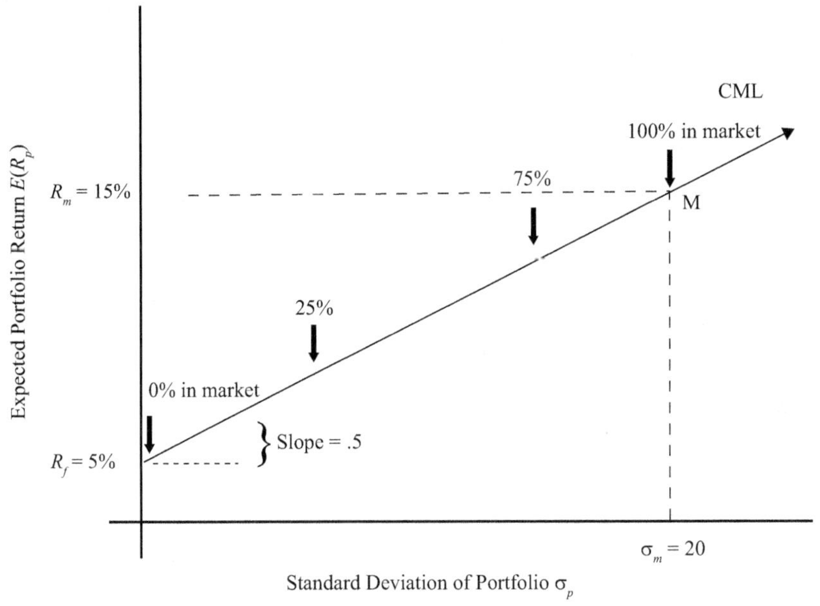

Solution to 2:

Return with 0 percent invested in the market = 5 percent, which is the risk-free return.

Standard deviation with 0 percent invested in the market = 0 percent because T-bills are not risky.

Return with 25 percent invested in the market = (0.75 × 5%) + (0.25 × 15%) = 7.5%.

Standard deviation with 25 percent invested in the market = 0.25 × 20% = 5%.

Return with 75 percent invested in the market = (0.25 × 5%) + (0.75 × 15%) = 12.50%.

Standard deviation with 75 percent invested in the market = 0.75 × 20% = 15%.

Return with 100 percent invested in the market = 15 percent, which is the return on the S&P 500.

Standard deviation with 100 percent invested in the market = 20 percent, which is the risk of the S&P 500.

2.2.4 *Leveraged Portfolios*

In the previous example, Mr. Miles evaluated an investment of between 0 percent and 100 percent in the market and the balance in T-bills. The line connecting R_f and M (market portfolio) in Exhibit 4 illustrates these portfolios with their respective levels of investment. At R_f, an investor is investing all of his or her wealth into risk-free securities, which is equivalent to lending 100 percent at the risk-free rate. At Point M he or she is holding the market portfolio and not lending any money at the risk-free rate. The combinations of the risk-free asset and the market portfolio, which may be achieved by the points between these two limits, are termed "lending" portfolios. In effect, the investor is lending part of his or her wealth at the risk-free rate.

If Mr. Miles is willing to take more risk, he may be able to move to the right of the market portfolio (Point M in Exhibit 4) by borrowing money and purchasing more of Portfolio M. Assume that he is able to borrow money at the same risk-free rate of interest, R_f, at which he can invest. He can then supplement his available wealth with borrowed money and construct a borrowing portfolio. If the straight line joining R_f and M is extended to the right of Point M, this extended section of the line represents borrowing portfolios. As one moves further to the right of Point M, an increasing amount of borrowed money is being invested in the market. This means that there is *negative* investment in the risk-free asset, which is referred to as a *leveraged position* in the risky portfolio. The particular point chosen on the CML will depend on the individual's utility function, which, in turn, will be determined by his risk and return preferences.

EXAMPLE 2

Risk and Return of a Leveraged Portfolio with Equal Lending and Borrowing Rates

Mr. Miles decides to set aside a small part of his wealth for investment in a portfolio that has greater risk than his previous investments because he anticipates that the overall market will generate attractive returns in the future. He assumes that he can borrow money at 5 percent and achieve the same return on the S&P 500 as before: an expected return of 15 percent with a standard deviation of 20 percent.

Calculate his expected risk and return if he borrows 25 percent, 50 percent, and 100 percent of his initial investment amount.

Solution:

The leveraged portfolio's standard deviation and return can be calculated in the same manner as before with the following equations:

$$E(R_p) = w_1 R_f + (1 - w_1)E(R_m)$$

and

$$\sigma_p = (1 - w_1)\sigma_m$$

The proportion invested in T-bills becomes negative instead of positive because Mr. Miles is borrowing money. If 25 percent of the initial investment is borrowed, $w_1 = -0.25$, and $(1 - w_1) = 1.25$, etc.

Return with $w_1 = -0.25 = (-0.25 \times 5\%) + (1.25 \times 15\%) = 17.5\%$.

Standard deviation with $w_1 = -0.25 = 1.25 \times 20\% = 25\%$.

Return with $w_1 = -0.50 = (-0.50 \times 5\%) + (1.50 \times 15\%) = 20.0\%$.

Standard deviation with $w_1 = -0.50 = 1.50 \times 20\% = 30\%$.

Return with $w_1 = -1.00 = (-1.00 \times 5\%) + (2.00 \times 15\%) = 25.0\%$.

Standard deviation with $w_1 = -1.00 = 2.00 \times 20\% = 40\%$.

Note that negative investment (borrowing) in the risk-free asset provides a higher expected return for the portfolio but that higher return is also associated with higher risk.

Leveraged Portfolios with Different Lending and Borrowing Rates Although we assumed that Mr. Miles can borrow at the same rate as the US government, it is more likely that he will have to pay a higher interest rate than the government because his ability to repay is not as certain as that of the government. Now consider that although Mr. Miles can invest (lend) at R_f, he can borrow at only R_b, a rate that is higher than the risk-free rate.

With different lending and borrowing rates, the CML will no longer be a single straight line. The line will have a slope of $[E(R_m) - R_f]/\sigma_m$ between Points R_f and M, where the lending rate is R_f, but will have a smaller slope of $[E(R_m) - R_b]/\sigma_m$ at points to the right of M, where the borrowing rate is R_b. Exhibit 5 illustrates the CML with different lending and borrowing rates.

Exhibit 5 CML with Different Lending and Borrowing Rates

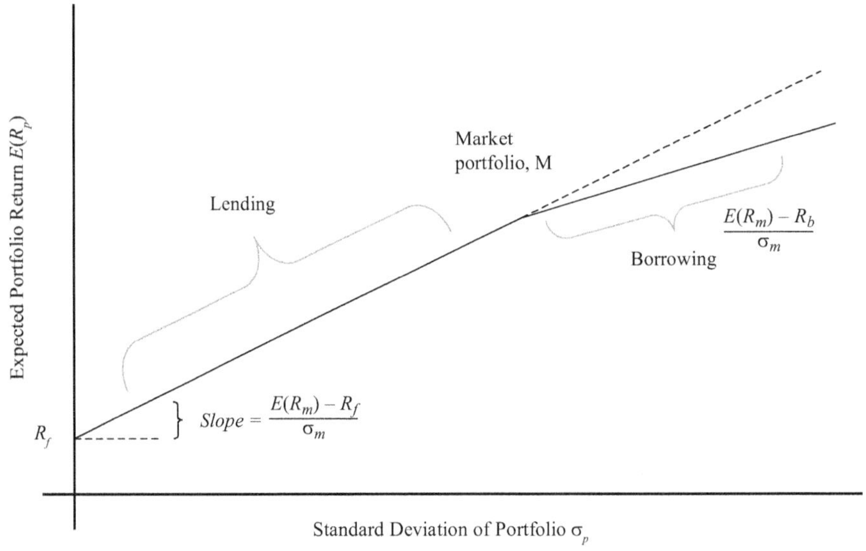

The equations for the two lines are given below.

$$w_1 \geq 0: E(R_p) = R_f + \left(\frac{E(R_m) - R_f}{\sigma_m}\right) \times \sigma_p$$

and

$$w_1 < 0: E(R_p) = R_b + \left(\frac{E(R_m) - R_b}{\sigma_m}\right) \times \sigma_p$$

The first equation is for the line where the investment in the risk-free asset is zero or positive—that is, at M or to the left of M in Exhibit 5. The second equation is for the line where borrowing, or negative investment in the risk-free asset, occurs. Note that the only difference between the two equations is in the interest rates used for borrowing and lending.

All passive portfolios will lie on the kinked CML, although the investment in the risk-free asset may be positive (lending), zero (no lending or borrowing), or negative (borrowing). Leverage allows less risk-averse investors to increase the amount of risk they take by borrowing money and investing more than 100 percent in the passive portfolio.

EXAMPLE 3

Leveraged Portfolio with Different Lending and Borrowing Rates

Mr. Miles approaches his broker to borrow money against securities held in his portfolio. Even though Mr. Miles' loan will be secured by the securities in his portfolio, the broker's rate for lending to customers is 7 percent. Assuming a risk-free rate of 5 percent and a market return of 15 percent with a standard deviation of 20 percent, estimate Mr. Miles' expected return and risk if he invests 25 percent and 75 percent in the market and if he decides to borrow 25 percent and 75 percent of his initial investment and invest the money in the market.

Solution:

The unleveraged portfolio's standard deviation and return are calculated using the same equations as before:

$$E(R_p) = w_1 R_f + (1 - w_1)E(R_m),$$

and

$$\sigma_p = (1 - w_1)\sigma_m$$

The results are unchanged. The slope of the line for the unleveraged portfolio is 0.50, just as before:

Return with 25 percent invested in the market = (0.75 × 5%) + (0.25 × 15%) = 7.5%.

Standard deviation with 25 percent invested in the market = 0.25 × 20% = 5%.

Return with 75 percent invested in the market = (0.25 × 5%) + (0.75 × 15%) = 12.5%.

Standard deviation with 75 percent invested in the market = 0.75 × 20% = 15%.

For the leveraged portfolio, everything remains the same except that R_f is replaced with R_b.

$$E(R_p) = w_1 R_b + (1 - w_1)E(R_m),$$

and

$$\sigma_p = (1 - w_1)\sigma_{m.}$$

Return with $w_1 = -0.25$ = (−0.25 × 7%) + (1.25 × 15%) = 17.0%.

Standard deviation with $w_1 = -0.25$ = 1.25 × 20% = 25%.

Return with $w_1 = -0.275$ = (−0.75 × 7%) + (1.75 × 15%) = 21.0%.

Standard deviation with $w_1 = -0.75$ = 1.75 × 20% = 35%.

The risk and return of the leveraged portfolio is higher than that of the unleveraged portfolio. As Mr. Miles borrows more money to invest in the market, the expected return increases but so does the standard deviation of the portfolio. The slope of the line for the leveraged portfolio is 0.40, compared with 0.50 for the unleveraged portfolio, which means that for every 1 percent increase in risk, the investor gets a 0.40 percent increase in expected return in the leveraged part of the portfolio, compared with a 0.50 percent increase in expected return in the unleveraged part of the portfolio. Only investors who are less risk averse will choose leveraged portfolios.

3 PRICING OF RISK AND COMPUTATION OF EXPECTED RETURN

In constructing a portfolio, it is important to understand the concept of correlation and how less than perfect correlation can diversify the risk of a portfolio. As a consequence, the risk of an asset held alone may be greater than the risk of that same asset when it is part of a portfolio. Because the risk of an asset varies from one environment to another, which kind of risk should an investor consider and how should that risk be priced? This section addresses the question of pricing of risk by decomposing the total risk of a security or a portfolio into systematic and nonsystematic risk. The meaning of these risks, how they are computed, and their relevance to the pricing of assets are also discussed.

3.1 Systematic Risk and Nonsystematic Risk

Systematic risk, also known as non-diversifiable or market risk, is the risk that affects the entire market or economy. In contrast, nonsystematic risk is the risk that pertains to a single company or industry and is also known as company-specific, industry-specific, diversifiable, or idiosyncratic risk.

Systematic risk is risk that cannot be avoided and is inherent in the overall market. It is non-diversifiable because it includes risk factors that are innate within the market and affect the market as a whole. Examples of factors that constitute systematic risk include interest rates, inflation, economic cycles, political uncertainty, and widespread natural disasters. These events affect the entire market, and there is no way to avoid their effect. Systematic risk can be magnified through selection or by using leverage, or diminished by including securities that have a low correlation with the portfolio, assuming they are not already part of the portfolio.

Nonsystematic risk is risk that is local or limited to a particular asset or industry that need not affect assets outside of that asset class. Examples of nonsystematic risk could include the failure of a drug trial or an airliner crash. All these events will directly affect their respective companies and possibly industries, but have no effect on assets that are far removed from these industries. Investors can avoid nonsystematic risk through diversification by forming a portfolio of assets that are not highly correlated with one another.

We will derive expressions for each kind of risk later in this reading. You will see that the sum of systematic variance and nonsystematic variance equals the total variance of the security or portfolio:

Total variance = Systematic variance + Nonsystematic variance

Although the equality relationship is between variances, you will find frequent references to total risk as the sum of systematic risk and nonsystematic risk. In those cases, the statements refer to variance, not standard deviation.

3.1.1 *Pricing of Risk*

Pricing or valuing an asset is equivalent to estimating its expected rate of return. If an asset has a known terminal value, such as the face value of a bond, then a lower current price implies a higher future return and a higher current price implies a lower future return. The relationship between price and return can also be observed in the valuation expression shown in Section 2.1.2. Therefore, we will occasionally use price and return interchangeably when discussing the price of risk.

Consider an asset with both systematic and nonsystematic risk. Assume that both kinds of risk are priced—that is, you receive a return for both systematic risk and nonsystematic risk. What will you do? Realizing that nonsystematic risk can be diversified away, you would buy assets that have a large amount of nonsystematic risk. Once you have bought those assets with nonsystematic risk, you would diversify, or reduce that risk, by including other assets that are not highly correlated. In the process, you will minimize nonsystematic risk and eventually eliminate it altogether from your portfolio. You would now have a diversified portfolio with only systematic risk, yet you would be compensated for nonsystematic risk that you no longer have. Just like everyone else, you would have an incentive to take on more and more diversifiable risk because you are compensated for it even though you can get rid of it. The demand for diversifiable risk would keep increasing until its price becomes infinite and its expected return falls to zero. This means that our initial assumption of a non-zero return for diversifiable risk was incorrect and that the correct assumption is zero return for diversifiable risk. Therefore, according to theory, in an efficient market no incremental reward is earned for taking on diversifiable risk.

We have argued that investors should not be compensated for taking on nonsystematic risk. Therefore, investors who have nonsystematic risk must diversify it away by investing in many industries, many countries, and many asset classes. Because future returns are unknown and it is not possible to pick only winners, diversification helps in offsetting poor returns in one asset class by garnering good returns in another asset class, thereby reducing the overall risk of the portfolio. In contrast, investors must be compensated for accepting systematic risk because that risk cannot be diversified away. If investors do not receive a return commensurate with the amount of systematic risk they are taking, they will refuse to accept systematic risk.

In summary, according to theory, systematic or non-diversifiable risk is priced and investors are compensated for holding assets or portfolios based only on that investment's systematic risk. Investors do not receive any return for accepting non-systematic or diversifiable risk. Therefore, it is in the interest of risk-averse investors to hold only well-diversified portfolios.

EXAMPLE 4

Systematic and Nonsystematic Risk

1 Describe the systematic and nonsystematic risk components of the following assets:
   - **A** A risk-free asset, such as a three-month Treasury bill
   - **B** The market portfolio, such as the S&P 500.

2 Consider two assets, A and B. Asset A has twice the amount of total risk as Asset B. For Asset A, systematic risk comprises two-thirds of total risk. For Asset B, all of total risk is systematic risk. Which asset should have a higher expected rate of return?

Solution to 1A:

By definition, a risk-free asset has no risk. Therefore, a risk-free asset has zero systematic risk and zero nonsystematic risk.

Solution to 1B:

As we mentioned earlier, a market portfolio is a diversified portfolio, one in which no more risk can be diversified away. We have also described it as an efficient portfolio. Therefore, a market portfolio does not contain any nonsystematic risk.

Solution to 2:

Based on the facts given, Asset A's systematic risk is one-third greater than Asset B's systematic risk. Because only systematic risk is priced or receives a return, the expected rate of return must be higher for Asset B.

3.2 Calculation and Interpretation of Beta

As previously mentioned, in order to form the market portfolio, you should combine all available risky assets. Knowledge of the correlations among those assets allows us to estimate portfolio risk. You also learned that a fully diversified portfolio will include all asset classes and essentially all assets in those asset classes. The work required for construction of the market portfolio is formidable. For example, for a portfolio of 1,000 assets, we will need 1,000 return estimates, 1,000 standard deviation estimates, and 499,500 (1,000 × 999 ÷ 2) correlations. Other related questions that arise with this analysis are whether we really need all 1,000 assets and what happens if there are errors in these estimates.

An alternate method of constructing an optimal portfolio is simpler and easier to implement. An investor begins with a known portfolio, such as the S&P 500, and then adds other assets one at a time on the basis of the asset's standard deviation, expected return, and impact on the portfolio's risk and return. This process continues until the addition of another asset does not have a significant impact on the performance of the portfolio. The process requires only estimates of systematic risk for each asset because investors will not be compensated for nonsystematic risk. Expected returns can be calculated by using return-generating models, as we will discuss in this section. In addition to using return-generating models, we will also decompose total variance into systematic variance and nonsystematic variance and establish a formal relationship between systematic risk and return. In the next section, we will expand on this discussion and introduce the CAPM as the preferred return-generating model.

3.2.1 *Return-Generating Models*

A **return-generating model** is a model that can provide an estimate of the expected return of a security given certain parameters. If systematic risk is the only relevant parameter for return, then the return-generating model will estimate the expected return for any asset given the level of systematic risk.

As with any model, the quality of estimates of expected return will depend on the quality of input estimates and the accuracy of the model. Because it is difficult to decide which factors are appropriate for generating returns, the most general form of a return-generating model is a multi-factor model. A **multi-factor model** allows more than one variable to be considered in estimating returns and can be built using different kinds of factors, such as macroeconomic, fundamental, and statistical factors.

Macroeconomic factor models use economic factors that are correlated with security returns. These factors may include economic growth, the interest rate, the inflation rate, productivity, employment, and consumer confidence. Past relationships with returns are estimated to obtain parameter estimates, which are, in turn, used for computing expected returns. Fundamental factor models analyze and use relationships between security returns and the company's underlying fundamentals, such as, for example, earnings, earnings growth, cash flow generation, investment in research, advertising, and number of patents. Finally, in a statistical factor model, historical and cross-sectional return data are analyzed to identify factors that explain variance or covariance in observed returns. These statistical factors, however, may or may not have an economic or fundamental connection to returns. For example, the conference to which the American football Super Bowl winner belongs, whether the American Football Conference or the National Football Conference, may be a factor in US stock returns, but no obvious economic connection seems to exist between the winner's conference and US stock returns. Moreover, data mining may generate many spurious factors that are devoid of any economic meaning. Because of this limitation, analysts prefer the macroeconomic and fundamental factor models for specifying and estimating return-generating models.

A general return-generating model is expressed in the following manner:

$$E(R_i) - R_f = \sum_{j=1}^{k} \beta_{ij} E(F_j) = \beta_{i1}\left[E(R_m) - R_f\right] + \sum_{j=2}^{k} \beta_{ij} E(F_j)$$

The model has k factors, $E(F_1)$, $E(F_2)$, ... $E(F_k)$. The coefficients, β_{ij}, are the factor weights (sometimes called factor loadings) associated with each factor. The left-hand side of the model has the expected excess return (i.e., the expected return over the risk-free rate). The right-hand side provides the risk factors that would generate the return or premium required to assume that risk. We have separated out one factor, $E(R_m)$, which represents the market return. All models contain return on the market portfolio as a key factor.

Three-Factor and Four-Factor Models Eugene Fama and Kenneth French[1] suggested that a return-generating model for stock returns should include relative size of the company and relative book-to-market value of the company in addition to beta. Fama and French found that past returns could be explained better with their model than with other models available at that time, most notably, the capital asset pricing model. Mark Carhart (1997) extended the Fama and French model by adding another factor: momentum, defined as relative past stock returns.

The Single-Index Model The simplest form of a return-generating model is a single-factor linear model, in which only one factor is considered. The most common implementation is a single-index model, which uses the market factor in the following form: $E(R_i) - R_f = \beta_i[E(R_m) - R_f]$.

Although the single-index model is simple, it fits nicely with the capital market line. Recall that the CML is linear, with an intercept of R_f and a slope of $[E(R_m) - R_f]/\sigma_m$. We can rewrite the CML by moving the intercept to the left-hand side of the equation, rearranging the terms, and generalizing the subscript from p to i, for any security:

$$E(R_i) - R_f = \left(\frac{\sigma_i}{\sigma_m}\right)\left[E(R_m) - R_f\right]$$

The factor loading or factor weight, σ_i/σ_m, refers to the ratio of total security risk to total market risk. To obtain a better understanding of factor loading and to illustrate that the CML reduces to a single-index model, we decompose total risk into its components.

3.2.2 *Decomposition of Total Risk for a Single-Index Model*

With the introduction of return-generating models, particularly the single-index model, we are able to decompose total variance into systematic and nonsystematic variances. Instead of using expected returns in the single index, let us use realized returns. The difference between expected returns and realized returns is attributable to non-market changes, as an error term, e_i, in the second equation below:

$$E(R_i) - R_f = \beta_i[E(R_m) - R_f]$$

and

$$R_i - R_f = \beta_i(R_m - R_f) + e_i$$

1 Fama and French (1992).

The variance of realized returns can be expressed in the equation below (note that R_f is a constant). We can further drop the covariance term in this equation because, by definition, any non-market return is uncorrelated with the market. Thus, we are able to decompose total variance into systematic and nonsystematic variances in the second equation below:

$$\sigma_i^2 = \beta_i^2\sigma_m^2 + \sigma_e^2 + 2\text{Cov}(R_m, e_i)$$

Total variance = Systematic variance + Nonsystematic variance, which can be written as

$$\sigma_i^2 = \beta_i^2\sigma_m^2 + \sigma_e^2$$

Total risk can be expressed as

$$\sigma_i = \sqrt{\beta_i^2\sigma_m^2 + \sigma_e^2}$$

Because nonsystematic risk is zero for well-diversified portfolios, such as the market portfolio, the total risk of a market portfolio and other similar portfolios is only systematic risk, which is $\beta_i\sigma_m$. We can now return to the CML discussed in the previous subsection and replace σ_i with $\beta_i\sigma_m$ because the CML assumes that the market is a diversified portfolio. By making this substitution for the above equation, we get the following single-index model:

$$E(R_i) - R_f = \left(\frac{\sigma_i}{\sigma_m}\right) \times \left[E(R_m) - R_f\right] = \left(\frac{\beta_i\sigma_m}{\sigma_m}\right) \times \left[E(R_m) - R_f\right],$$

$$E(R_i) - R_f = \beta_i[E(R_m) - R_f]$$

Thus, the CML, which holds only for well-diversified portfolios, is fully consistent with a single-index model.

In summary, total variance may be decomposed into systematic and nonsystematic variances and the CML is the same as a single-index model for diversified portfolios.

3.2.3 *Return-Generating Models: The Market Model*

The most common implementation of a single-index model is the **market model**, in which the market return is the single factor or single index. In principle, the market model and the single-index model are similar. The difference is that the market model is easier to work with and is normally used for estimating beta risk and computing abnormal returns. The market model is

$$R_i = \alpha_i + \beta_i R_m + e_i$$

To be consistent with the previous section, $\alpha_i = R_f(1 - \beta)$. The intercept, α_i, and slope coefficient, β_i, can be estimated by using historical security and market returns. These parameter estimates are then used to predict company-specific returns that a security may earn in a future period. Assume that a regression of Wal-Mart's historical daily returns on S&P 500 daily returns gives an α_i of 0.0001 and a β_i of 0.9. Thus, Wal-Mart's expected daily return = 0.0001 + 0.90 × R_m. If, on a given day the market rises by 1 percent and Wal-Mart's stock rises by 2 percent, then Wal-Mart's company-specific return (e_i) for that day = $R_i - E(R_i) = R_i - (\alpha_i + \beta_i R_m)$ = 0.02 – (0.0001 + 0.90 × 0.01) = 0.0109, or 1.09%. In other words, Wal-Mart earned an abnormal return of 1.09 percent on that day.

3.2.4 *Calculation and Interpretation of Beta*

We begin with the single-index model introduced earlier using realized returns and rewrite it as

$$R_i = (1 - \beta_i)R_f + \beta_i \times R_m + e_i$$

Because systematic risk depends on the correlation between the asset and the market, we can arrive at a measure of systematic risk from the covariance between R_i and R_m, where R_i is defined using the above equation. Note that the risk-free rate is a constant, so the first term in R_i drops out.

$$\begin{aligned}\text{Cov}(R_i,R_m) &= \text{Cov}(\beta_i \times R_m + e_i,R_m)\\ &= \beta_i\text{Cov}(R_m,R_m) + \text{Cov}(e_i,R_m)\\ &= \beta_i\sigma_m^2 + 0\end{aligned}$$

The first term is beta multiplied by the variance of R_m. Because the error term is uncorrelated with the market, the second term drops out. Then, we can rewrite the equation in terms of beta as follows:

$$\beta_i = \frac{\text{Cov}(R_i,R_m)}{\sigma_m^2} = \frac{\rho_{i,m}\sigma_i\sigma_m}{\sigma_m^2} = \frac{\rho_{i,m}\sigma_i}{\sigma_m}$$

The above formula shows the expression for beta, β_i, which is similar to the factor loading in the single-index model presented earlier. For example, if the correlation between an asset and the market is 0.70 and the asset and market have standard deviations of return of 0.25 and 0.15, respectively, the asset's beta would be (0.70)(0.25)/0.15 = 1.17. If the asset's covariance with the market and market variance were given as 0.026250 and 0.02250, respectively, the calculation would be 0.026250/0.02250 = 1.17. The beta in the market model includes an adjustment for the correlation between asset *i* and the market because the market model covers all assets whereas the CML works only for fully diversified portfolios.

As shown in the above equation, **beta** is a measure of how sensitive an asset's return is to the market as a whole and is calculated as the covariance of the return on *i* and the return on the market divided by the variance of the market return; that expression is equivalent to the product of the asset's correlation with the market with a ratio of standard deviations of return (i.e., the ratio of the asset's standard deviation to the market's). As we have shown, beta captures an asset's systematic risk, or the portion of an asset's risk that cannot be eliminated by diversification. The variances and correlations required for the calculation of beta are usually based on historical returns.

A positive beta indicates that the return of an asset follows the general market trend, whereas a negative beta shows that the return of an asset generally follows a trend that is opposite to that of the market. In other words, a positive beta indicates that the return of an asset moves in the same direction of the market, whereas a negative beta indicates that the return of an asset moves in the opposite direction of the market. A risk-free asset's beta is zero because its covariance with other assets is zero. In other words, a beta of zero indicates that the asset's return has no correlation with movements in the market. The market's beta can be calculated by substituting σ_m for σ_i in the numerator. Also, any asset's correlation with itself is 1, so the beta of the market is 1:

$$\beta_i = \frac{\rho_{i,m}\sigma_i}{\sigma_m} = \frac{\rho_{m,m}\sigma_m}{\sigma_m} = 1$$

Because the market's beta is 1, the average beta of stocks in the market, by definition, is 1. In terms of correlation, most stocks, especially in developed markets, tend to be highly correlated with the market, with correlations in excess of 0.70. Some US broad market indexes, such as the S&P 500, the Dow Jones 30, and the NASDAQ 100, have even higher correlations that are in excess of 0.90. The correlations among different sectors are also high, which shows that companies have similar reactions to the same economic and market changes. As a consequence and as a practical matter, finding assets that have a consistently negative beta is unusual because of the market's broad effects on all assets.

EXAMPLE 5

Calculation of Beta

Assuming that the risk (standard deviation) of the market is 25 percent, calculate the beta for the following assets:

1 A short-term US Treasury bill.

2 Gold, which has a standard deviation equal to the standard deviation of the market but a zero correlation with the market.

3 A new emerging market that is not currently included in the definition of "market"—the emerging market's standard deviation is 60 percent, and the correlation with the market is –0.1.

4 An initial public offering or new issue of stock with a standard deviation of 40 percent and a correlation with the market of 0.7 (IPOs are usually very risky but have a relatively low correlation with the market).

We use the formula for beta in answering the above questions: $\beta_i = \dfrac{\rho_{i,m}\sigma_i}{\sigma_m}$

Solution to 1:

By definition, a short-term US Treasury bill has zero risk. Therefore, its beta is zero.

Solution to 2:

Because the correlation of gold with the market is zero, its beta is zero.

Solution to 3:

Beta of the emerging market is $-0.1 \times 0.60 \div 0.25 = -0.24$.

Solution to 4:

Beta of the initial public offering is $0.7 \times 0.40 \div 0.25 = 1.12$.

3.2.5 *Estimation of Beta*

An alternative and more practical approach is to estimate beta directly by using the market model described above. The market model, $R_i = \alpha_i + \beta_i R_m + e_i$, is estimated by using regression analysis, which is a statistical process that evaluates the relationship between a given variable (the dependent variable) and one or more other (independent) variables. Historical security returns (R_i) and historical market returns (R_m) are inputs used for estimating the two parameters α_i and β_i.

Regression analysis is similar to plotting all combinations of the asset's return and the market return (R_i, R_m) and then drawing a line through all points such that it minimizes the sum of squared linear deviations from the line. Exhibit 6 illustrates the market model and the estimated parameters. The intercept, α_i (sometimes referred to as the constant), and the slope term, β_i, are all that is needed to define the security characteristic line and obtain beta estimates.

Exhibit 6 Beta Estimation Using a Plot of Security and Market Returns

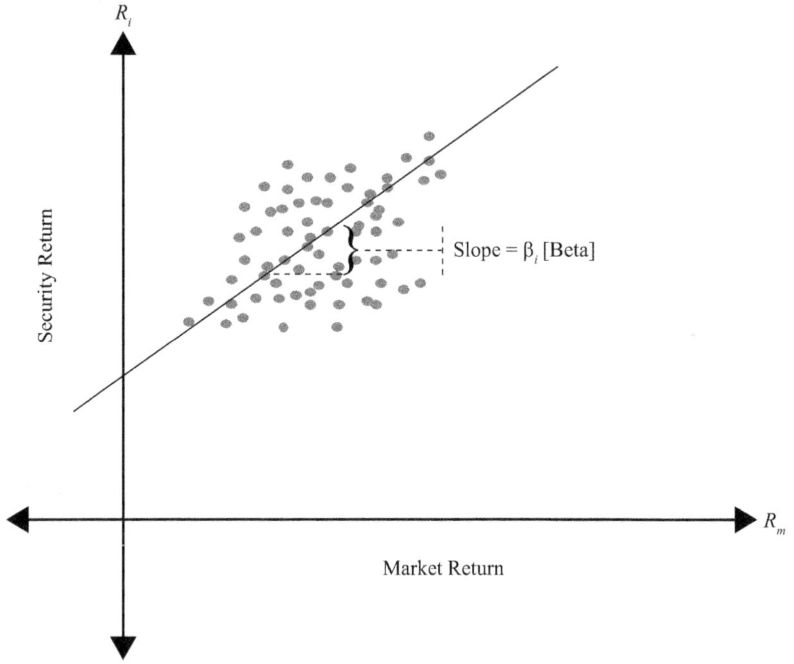

Although beta estimates are important for forecasting future levels of risk, there is much concern about their accuracy. In general, shorter periods of estimation (e.g., 12 months) represent betas that are closer to the asset's current level of systematic risk. Shorter period beta estimates, however, are also less accurate than beta estimates measured over three to five years because they may be affected by special events in that short period. Although longer period beta estimates are more accurate, they may be a poor representation of future expectations, especially if major changes in the asset have occurred. Therefore, it is necessary to recognize that estimates of beta, whether obtained through calculation or regression analysis, may or may not represent current or future levels of an asset's systematic risk.

3.2.6 *Beta and Expected Return*

Although the single-index model, also called the **capital asset pricing model** (CAPM), will be discussed in greater detail in the next section, we will use the CAPM in this section to estimate returns, given asset betas. The CAPM is usually written with the risk-free rate on the right-hand side:

$$E(R_i) = R_f + \beta_i[E(R_m) - R_f]$$

The model shows that the primary determinant of expected return for a security is its beta, or how well the security correlates with the market. The higher the beta of an asset, the higher its expected return will be. Assets with a beta greater than 1 have an expected return that is higher than the market return, whereas assets with a beta of less than 1 have an expected return that is less than the market return.

In certain cases, assets may require a return less than the risk-free return. For example, if an asset's beta is negative, the required return will be less than the risk-free rate. When combined with the market, the asset reduces the risk of the overall portfolio, which makes the asset very valuable. Insurance is one such asset. Insurance gives a positive return when the insured's wealth is reduced because of a catastrophic loss. In the absence of such a loss or when the insured's wealth is growing, the insured is required to pay an insurance premium. Thus, insurance has a negative beta and a negative expected return, but helps in reducing overall risk.

EXAMPLE 6

Calculation of Expected Return

1 Alpha Natural Resources (ANR), a coal producer, buys a large but privately held coal producer in China. As a result of the cross-border acquisition of a private company, ANR's standard deviation of returns is reduced from 50 percent to 30 percent and its correlation with the market falls from 0.95 to 0.75. Assume that the standard deviation and return of the market remain unchanged at 25 percent and 10 percent, respectively, and that the risk-free rate is 3 percent.

A Calculate the beta of ANR stock and its expected return before the acquisition.

B Calculate the expected return after the acquisition.

Solution to 1A:

Using the formula for β_i, we can calculate β_i and then the return.

$$\beta_i = \frac{\rho_{i,m}\sigma_i}{\sigma_m} = \frac{0.95 \times 0.50}{0.25} = 1.90$$

$$E(R_i) = R_f + \beta_i[E(R_m) - R_f] = 0.03 + 1.90 \times (0.10 - 0.03) = 0.163 = 16.3\%$$

Solution to 1B:

We follow the same procedure but with the after-acquisition correlation and risk.

$$\beta_i = \frac{\rho_{i,m}\sigma_i}{\sigma_m} = \frac{0.75 \times 0.30}{0.25} = 0.90$$

$$E(R_i) = R_f + \beta_i[E(R_m) - R_f] = 0.03 + 0.90 \times (0.10 - 0.03) = 0.093 = 9.3\%$$

The market risk premium is 7 percent (10% – 3%). As the beta changes, the change in the security's expected return is the market risk premium multiplied by the change in beta. In this scenario, ANR's beta decreased by 1.0, so the new expected return for ANR is 7 percentage points lower.

2 Mr. Miles observes the strong demand for iPods and iPhones and wants to invest in Apple stock. Unfortunately, Mr. Miles doesn't know the return he should expect from his investment. He has been given a risk-free rate of 3 percent, a market return of 10 percent, and Apple's beta of 1.5.

A Calculate Apple's expected return.

B An analyst looking at the same information decides that the past performance of Apple is not representative of its future performance. He decides that, given the increase in Apple's market capitalization, Apple acts much more like the market than before and thinks Apple's beta should be closer to 1.1. What is the analyst's expected return for Apple stock?

Solution to 2A:

$$E(R_i) = R_f + \beta_i[E(R_m) - R_f] = 0.03 + 1.5 \times (0.10 - 0.03) = 0.135 = 13.5\%$$

Solution to 2B:

$$E(R_i) = R_f + \beta_i[E(R_m) - R_f] = 0.03 + 1.1 \times (0.10 - 0.03) = 0.107 = 10.7\%$$

This example illustrates the lack of connection between estimation of past returns and projection into the future. Investors should be aware of the limitations of using past returns for estimating future returns.

THE CAPITAL ASSET PRICING MODEL

4

The capital asset pricing model is one of the most significant innovations in portfolio theory. The model is simple, yet powerful; is intuitive, yet profound. The CAPM was introduced independently by William Sharpe, John Lintner, Jack Treynor, and Jan Mossin and builds on Harry Markowitz's earlier work on diversification and modern portfolio theory.[2] The model provides a linear expected return–beta relationship that precisely determines the expected return given the beta of an asset. In doing so, it makes the transition from total risk to systematic risk, the primary determinant of expected return. Recall the following equation:

$$E(R_i) = R_f + \beta_i[E(R_m) - R_f]$$

The CAPM asserts that the expected returns of assets vary only by their systematic risk as measured by beta. Two assets with the same beta will have the same expected return irrespective of the nature of those assets. Given the relationship between risk and return, all assets are defined only by their beta risk, which we will explain as the assumptions are described.

In the remainder of this section, we will examine the assumptions made in arriving at the CAPM and the limitations those assumptions entail. Second, we will implement the CAPM through the security market line to price any portfolio or asset, both efficient and inefficient. Finally, we will discuss ways in which the CAPM can be applied to investments, valuation, and capital budgeting.

4.1 Assumptions of the CAPM

Similar to all other models, the CAPM ignores many of the complexities of financial markets by making simplifying assumptions. These assumptions allow us to gain important insights into how assets are priced without complicating the analysis. Once the basic relationships are established, we can relax the assumptions and examine how our insights need to be altered. Some of these assumptions are constraining, whereas others are benign. And other assumptions affect only a particular set of assets or only marginally affect the hypothesized relationships.

1 ***Investors are risk-averse, utility-maximizing, rational individuals.***

Risk aversion means that investors expect to be compensated for accepting risk. Note that the assumption does not require investors to have the same degree of risk aversion; it only requires that they are averse to risk. Utility maximization implies that investors want higher returns, not lower returns, and that investors always want more wealth (i.e., investors are never satisfied). Investors are understood to be rational in that they correctly evaluate and analyze available information to arrive at rational decisions. Although rational investors may

2 See, for example, Markowitz (1952), Sharpe (1964), Lintner (1965a, 1965b), Treynor (1961, 1962), and Mossin (1966).

use the same information to arrive at different estimates of expected risk and expected returns, homogeneity among investors (see Assumption 4) requires that investors be rational individuals.

Risk aversion and utility maximization are generally accepted as reflecting a realistic view of the world. Yet, rationality among investors has been questioned because investors may allow their personal biases and experiences to disrupt their decision making, resulting in suboptimal investments. Nonetheless, the model's results are unaffected by such irrational behavior as long as it does not affect prices in a significant manner (i.e., the trades of irrational investors cancel each other or are dominated by the trades of rational investors).

2 ***Markets are frictionless, including no transaction costs and no taxes.***

Frictionless markets allow us to abstract the analysis from the operational characteristics of markets. In doing so, we do not allow the risk–return relationship to be affected by, for example, the trading volume on the New York Stock Exchange or the difference between buying and selling prices. Specifically, frictionless markets do not have transaction costs, taxes, or any costs or restrictions on short selling. We also assume that borrowing and lending at the risk-free rate is possible.

The transaction costs of many large institutions are negligible, and many institutions do not pay taxes. Even the presence of non-zero transaction costs, taxes, or the inability to borrow at the risk-free rate does not materially affect the general conclusions of the CAPM. Costs of short selling or restrictions on short selling, however, can introduce an upward bias in asset prices, potentially jeopardizing important conclusions of the CAPM.

3 ***Investors plan for the same single holding period.***

The CAPM is a single-period model, and all investor decisions are made on the basis of that one period. The assumption of a single period is applied for convenience because working with multi-period models is more difficult. A single-period model, however, does not allow learning to occur, and bad decisions can persist. In addition, maximizing utility at the end of a multi-period horizon may require decisions in certain periods that may seem suboptimal when examined from a single-period perspective. Nonetheless, the single holding period does not severely limit the applicability of the CAPM to multi-period settings.

4 ***Investors have homogeneous expectations or beliefs.***

This assumption means that all investors analyze securities in the same way using the same probability distributions and the same inputs for future cash flows. In addition, given that they are rational individuals, the investors will arrive at the same valuations. Because their valuations of all assets are identical, they will generate the same optimal risky portfolio, which we call the market portfolio.

The assumption of homogeneous beliefs can be relaxed as long as the differences in expectations do not generate significantly different optimal risky portfolios.

5 ***All investments are infinitely divisible.***

This assumption implies that an individual can invest as little or as much as he or she wishes in an asset. This supposition allows the model to rely on continuous functions rather than on discrete jump functions. The assumption is made for convenience only and has an inconsequential impact on the conclusions of the model.

6 ***Investors are price takers.***

The CAPM assumes that there are many investors and that no investor is large enough to influence prices. Thus, investors are price takers, and we assume that security prices are unaffected by investor trades. This assumption is generally true because even though investors may be able to affect prices of small stocks, those stocks are not large enough to affect the primary results of the CAPM.

The main objective of these assumptions is to create a marginal investor who rationally chooses a mean–variance-efficient portfolio in a predictable fashion. We assume away any inefficiency in the market from both operational and informational perspectives. Although some of these assumptions may seem unrealistic, relaxing most of them will have only a minor influence on the model and its results. Moreover, the CAPM, with all its limitations and weaknesses, provides a benchmark for comparison and for generating initial return estimates.

4.2 The Security Market Line

In this subsection, we apply the CAPM to the pricing of securities. The **security market line** (SML) is a graphical representation of the capital asset pricing model with beta, reflecting systematic risk, on the *x*-axis and expected return on the *y*-axis. Using the same concept as the capital market line, the SML intersects the *y*-axis at the risk-free rate of return, and the slope of this line is the market risk premium, $R_m - R_f$. Recall that the capital market line (CML) does not apply to all securities or assets but only to portfolios on the efficient frontier. The efficient frontier gives optimal combinations of expected return and total risk. In contrast, the security market line applies to any security, efficient or not. Total risk and systematic risk are equal only for efficient portfolios because those portfolios have no diversifiable risk remaining.

Exhibit 7 is a graphical representation of the CAPM, the security market line. As shown earlier in this reading, the beta of the market is 1 (*x*-axis) and the market earns an expected return of R_m (*y*-axis). Using this line, it is possible to calculate the expected return of an asset. The next example illustrates the beta and return calculations.

Exhibit 7 The Security Market Line

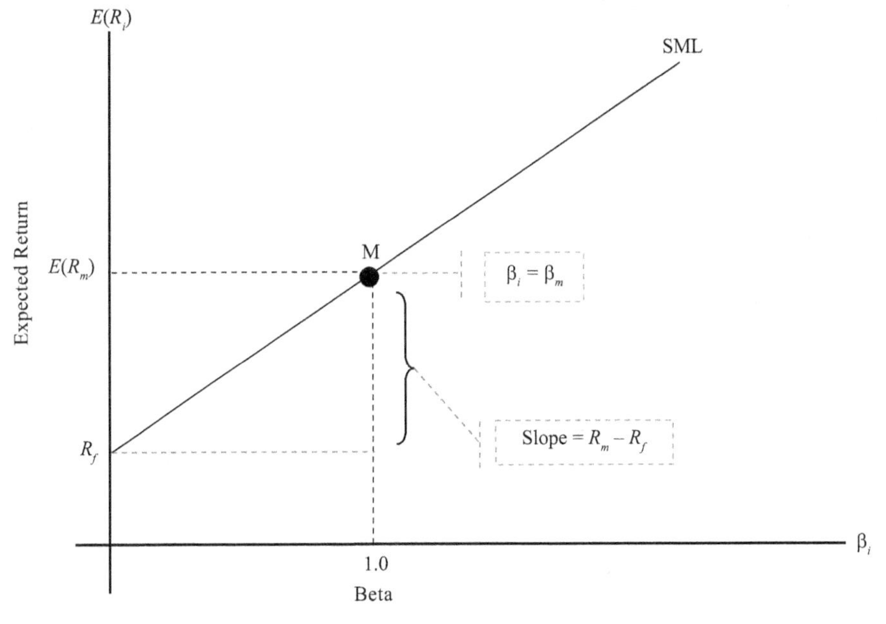

EXAMPLE 7

Security Market Line and Expected Return

1 Suppose the risk-free rate is 3 percent, the expected return on the market portfolio is 13 percent, and its standard deviation is 23 percent. An Indian company, Bajaj Auto, has a standard deviation of 50 percent but is uncorrelated with the market. Calculate Bajaj Auto's beta and expected return.

2 Suppose the risk-free rate is 3 percent, the expected return on the market portfolio is 13 percent, and its standard deviation is 23 percent. A German company, Mueller Metals, has a standard deviation of 50 percent and a correlation of 0.65 with the market. Calculate Mueller Metal's beta and expected return.

Solution to 1:

Using the formula for β_i, we can calculate β_i and then the return.

$$\beta_i = \frac{\rho_{i,m}\sigma_i}{\sigma_m} = \frac{0.0 \times 0.50}{0.23} = 0$$

$$E(R_i) = R_f + \beta_i[E(R_m) - R_f] = 0.03 + 0 \times (0.13 - 0.03) = 0.03 = 3.0\%$$

Because of its zero correlation with the market portfolio, Bajaj Auto's beta is zero. Because the beta is zero, the expected return for Bajaj Auto is the risk-free rate, which is 3 percent.

Solution to 2:

Using the formula for β_i, we can calculate β_i and then the return.

$$\beta_i = \frac{\rho_{i,m}\sigma_i}{\sigma_m} = \frac{0.65 \times 0.50}{0.23} = 1.41$$

$$E(R_i) = R_f + \beta_i[E(R_m) - R_f] = 0.03 + 1.41 \times (0.13 - 0.03) = 0.171 = 17.1\%$$

Because of the high degree of correlation with the market, the beta for Mueller Metals is 1.41 and the expected return is 17.1 percent. Because Mueller Metals has systematic risk that is greater than that of the market, it has an expected return that exceeds the expected return of the market.

4.2.1 *Portfolio Beta*

As we stated above, the security market line applies to all securities. But what about a combination of securities, such as a portfolio? Consider two securities, 1 and 2, with a weight of w_i in Security 1 and the balance in Security 2. The return for the two securities and return of the portfolio can be written as:

$$E(R_1) = R_f + \beta_1\left[E(R_m) - R_f\right]$$

$$E(R_2) = R_f + \beta_2\left[E(R_m) - R_f\right]$$

$$\begin{aligned} E(R_p) &= w_1 E(R_1) + w_2 E(R_2) \\ &= w_1 R_f + w_1\beta_1\left[E(R_m) - R_f\right] + w_2 R_f + w_2\beta_2\left[E(R_m) - R_f\right] \\ &= R_f + (w_1\beta_1 + w_2\beta_2)\left[E(R_m) - R_f\right] \end{aligned}$$

The last equation gives the expression for the portfolio's expected return. From this equation, we can conclude that the portfolio's beta = $w_1\beta_1 + w_2\beta_2$. In general, the portfolio beta is a weighted sum of the betas of the component securities and is given by:

$$\beta_p = \sum_{i=1}^{n} w_i\beta_i;\ \sum_{i=1}^{n} w_i = 1$$

The portfolio's return given by the CAPM is

$$E(R_p) = R_f + \beta_p[E(R_m) - R_f]$$

This equation shows that a linear relationship exists between the expected return of a portfolio and the systematic risk of the portfolio as measured by β_p.

EXAMPLE 8

Portfolio Beta and Return

You invest 20 percent of your money in the risk-free asset, 30 percent in the market portfolio, and 50 percent in RedHat, a US stock that has a beta of 2.0. Given that the risk-free rate is 4 percent and the market return is 16 percent, what are the portfolio's beta and expected return?

Solution:

The beta of the risk-free asset = 0, the beta of the market = 1, and the beta of RedHat is 2.0. The portfolio beta is

$$\beta_p = w_1\beta_1 + w_2\beta_2 + w_3\beta_3 = (0.20 \times 0.0) + (0.30 \times 1.0) + (0.50 \times 2.0) = 1.30$$

$$E(R_i) = R_f + \beta_i[E(R_m) - R_f] = 0.04 + 1.30 \times (0.16 - 0.04) = 0.196 = 19.6\%$$

The portfolio beta is 1.30, and its expected return is 19.6 percent.

Alternate Method:

Another method for calculating the portfolio's return is to calculate individual security returns and then use the portfolio return formula (i.e., weighted average of security returns) to calculate the overall portfolio return.

Return of the risk-free asset = 4 percent; return of the market = 16 percent

RedHat's return based on its beta = 0.04 + 2.0 × (0.16 – 0.04) = 0.28

Portfolio return = (0.20 × 0.04) + (0.30 × 0.16) + (0.50 × 0.28) = 0.196 = 19.6%

Not surprisingly, the portfolio return is 19.6 percent, as calculated in the first method.

4.3 Applications of the CAPM

The CAPM offers powerful and intuitively appealing predictions about risk and the relationship between risk and return. The CAPM is not only important from a theoretical perspective but is also used extensively in practice. In this section, we will discuss some common applications of the model. When applying these tools to different scenarios, it is important to understand that the CAPM and the SML are functions that give an indication of what the return in the market *should* be, given a certain level of risk. The actual return may be quite different from the expected return.

Applications of the CAPM include estimates of the expected return for capital budgeting, comparison of the actual return of a portfolio or portfolio manager with the CAPM return for performance appraisal, and the analysis of alternate return estimates and the CAPM returns as the basis for security selection. The applications are discussed in more detail in this section.

4.3.1 *Estimate of Expected Return*

Given an asset's systematic risk, the expected return can be calculated using the CAPM. Recall that the price of an asset is the sum of all future cash flows discounted at the required rate of return, where the discount rate or the required rate of return is commensurate with the asset's risk. The expected rate of return obtained from the CAPM is normally the first estimate that investors use for valuing assets, such as stocks, bonds, real estate, and other similar assets. The required rate of return from the CAPM is also used for capital budgeting and determining the economic feasibility of projects. Again, recall that when computing the net present value of a project, investments and net revenues are considered cash flows and are discounted at the required rate of return. The required rate of return, based on the project's risk, is calculated using the CAPM.

Because risk and return underlie almost all aspects of investment decision making, it is not surprising that the CAPM is used for estimating expected return in many scenarios. Other examples include calculating the cost of capital for regulated companies by regulatory commissions and setting fair insurance premiums. The next example shows an application of the CAPM to capital budgeting.

EXAMPLE 9

Application of the CAPM to Capital Budgeting

GlaxoSmithKline Plc is examining the economic feasibility of developing a new medicine. The initial investment in Year 1 is \$500 million. The investment in Year 2 is \$200 million. There is a 50 percent chance that the medicine will be developed and will be successful. If that happens, GlaxoSmithKline must spend another \$100 million in Year 3, but its income from the project in Year 3 will be \$500 million, not including the third-year investment. In Years 4, 5, and 6, it will earn \$400 million a year if the medicine is successful. At the end of Year 6, it intends to sell all rights to the medicine for \$600 million. If the medicine is unsuccessful, none of GlaxoSmithKline's investments can be salvaged. Assume that the market return is 12 percent, the risk-free rate is 2 percent, and the beta risk of the project is 2.3. All cash flows occur at the end of each year.

1 Calculate the expected annual cash flows using the probability of success.

2 Calculate the expected return.

3 Calculate the net present value.

Solution to 1:

There is a 50 percent chance that the cash flows in Years 3–6 will occur. Taking that into account, the expected annual cash flows are:

Year 1: –\$500 million (outflow)

Year 2: –\$200 million (outflow)

Year 3: 50% of –\$100 million (outflow) + 50% of \$500 million = \$200 million

Year 4: 50% of \$400 million = \$200 million

Year 5: 50% of \$400 million = \$200 million

Year 6: 50% of $400 million + 50% of $600 million = $500 million

Solution to 2:

The expected or required return for the project can be calculated using the CAPM, which is = 0.02 + 2.3 × (0.12 – 0.02) = 0.25.

Solution to 3:

The net present value is the discounted value of all cash flows:

$$NPV = \sum_{t=0}^{T} \frac{CF_t}{(1 + r_t)^t}$$

$$= \frac{-500}{(1+0.25)} + \frac{-200}{(1+0.25)^2} + \frac{200}{(1+0.25)^3} + \frac{200}{(1+0.25)^4}$$

$$+ \frac{200}{(1+0.25)^5} + \frac{500}{(1+0.25)^6}$$

$$= -400 - 128 + 102.40 + 81.92 + 65.54 + 131.07 = -147.07.$$

Because the net present value is negative (–$147.07 million), the project should not be accepted by GlaxoSmithKline.

5 BEYOND THE CAPITAL ASSET PRICING MODEL

In general, return-generating models allow us to estimate an asset's return given its characteristics, where the asset characteristics required for estimating the return are specified in the model. Estimating an asset's return is important for investment decision making. These models are also important as a benchmark for evaluating portfolio, security, or manager performance. The return-generating models were briefly introduced in Section 3.2.1, and one of those models, the capital asset pricing model, was discussed in detail in Section 4.

The purpose of this section is to make readers aware that, although the CAPM is an important concept and model, the CAPM is not the only return-generating model. In this section, we revisit and highlight the limitations of the CAPM and preview return-generating models that address some of those limitations.

5.1 Limitations of the CAPM

The CAPM is subject to theoretical and practical limitations. Theoretical limitations are inherent in the structure of the model, whereas practical limitations are those that arise in implementing the model.

5.1.1 *Theoretical Limitations of the CAPM*

- Single-factor model: Only systematic risk or beta risk is priced in the CAPM. Thus, the CAPM states that no other investment characteristics should be considered in estimating returns. As a consequence, it is prescriptive and easy to understand and apply, although it is very restrictive and inflexible.
- Single-period model: The CAPM is a single-period model that does not consider multi-period implications or investment objectives of future periods, which can lead to myopic and suboptimal investment decisions. For example, it may be optimal to default on interest payments in the current period to

maximize current returns, but the consequences may be negative in the next period. A single-period model like the CAPM is unable to capture factors that vary over time and span several periods.

5.1.2 *Practical Limitations of the CAPM*

In addition to the theoretical limitations, implementation of the CAPM raises several practical concerns, some of which are listed below.

- Market portfolio: The true market portfolio according to the CAPM includes all assets, financial and nonfinancial, which means that it also includes many assets that are not investable, such as human capital and assets in closed economies. Richard Roll[3] noted that one reason the CAPM is not testable is that the true market portfolio is unobservable.
- Proxy for a market portfolio: In the absence of a true market portfolio, market participants generally use proxies. These proxies, however, vary among analysts, the country of the investor, etc. and generate different return estimates for the same asset, which is impermissible in the CAPM.
- Estimation of beta risk: A long history of returns (three to five years) is required to estimate beta risk. The historical state of the company, however, may not be an accurate representation of the current or future state of the company. More generally, the CAPM is an *ex ante* model, yet it is usually applied using *ex post* data. In addition, using different periods for estimation results in different estimates of beta. For example, a three-year beta is unlikely to be the same as a five-year beta, and a beta estimated with daily returns is unlikely to be the same as the beta estimated with monthly returns. Thus, we are likely to estimate different returns for the same asset depending on the estimate of beta risk used in the model.
- The CAPM is a poor predictor of returns: If the CAPM is a good model, its estimate of asset returns should be closely associated with realized returns. However, empirical support for the CAPM is weak.[4] In other words, tests of the CAPM show that asset returns are not determined only by systematic risk. Poor predictability of returns when using the CAPM is a serious limitation because return-generating models are used to estimate future returns.
- Homogeneity in investor expectations: The CAPM assumes that homogeneity exists in investor expectations for the model to generate a single optimal risky portfolio (the market) and a single security market line. Without this assumption, there will be numerous optimal risky portfolios and numerous security market lines. Clearly, investors can process the same information in a rational manner and arrive at different optimal risky portfolios.

5.2 Extensions to the CAPM

Given the limitations of the CAPM, it is not surprising that other models have been proposed to address some of these limitations. These new models are not without limitations of their own, which we will mention while discussing the models. We divide the models into two categories—theoretical models and practical models—and provide one example of each type.

3 Roll (1977).
4 See, for example, Fama and French (1992).

5.2.1 *Theoretical Models*

Theoretical models are based on the same principle as the CAPM but expand the number of risk factors. The best example of a theoretical model is the arbitrage pricing theory (APT), which was developed by Stephen Ross.[5] Like the CAPM, APT proposes a linear relationship between expected return and risk:

$$E(R_p) = R_F + \lambda_1\beta_{p,1} + \ldots + \lambda_K\beta_{p,K}$$

where

$E(R_p)$ = the expected return of portfolio p
R_F = the risk-free rate
λ_j = the risk premium (expected return in excess of the risk-free rate) for factor j
$\beta_{p,j}$ = the sensitivity of the portfolio to factor j
K = the number of risk factors

Unlike the CAPM, however, APT allows numerous risk factors—as many as are relevant to a particular asset. Moreover, other than the risk-free rate, the risk factors need not be common and may vary from one asset to another. A no-arbitrage condition in asset markets is used to determine the risk factors and estimate betas for the risk factors.

Although it is theoretically elegant, flexible, and superior to the CAPM, APT is not commonly used in practice because it does not specify any of the risk factors and it becomes difficult to identify risk factors and estimate betas for each asset in a portfolio. So from a practical standpoint, the CAPM is preferred to APT.

5.2.2 *Practical Models*

If beta risk in the CAPM does not explain returns, which factors do? Practical models seek to answer this question through extensive research. As mentioned in Section 3.2.1, the best example of such a model is the four-factor model proposed by Fama and French (1992) and Carhart (1997).

Based on an analysis of the relationship between past returns and a variety of different factors, Fama and French (1992) proposed that three factors seem to explain asset returns better than just systematic risk. Those three factors are relative size, relative book-to-market value, and beta of the asset. With Carhart's (1997) addition of relative past stock returns, the model can be written as follows:

$$E(R_{it}) = \alpha_i + \beta_{i,MKT}MKT_t + \beta_{i,SMB}SMB_t + \beta_{i,HML}HML_t + \beta_{i,UMD}UMD_t$$

where

$E(R_i)$ = the return on an asset in excess of the one-month T-bill return
MKT = the excess return on the market portfolio
SMB = the difference in returns between small-capitalization stocks and large-capitalization stocks (size)
HML = the difference in returns between high-book-to-market stocks and low-book-to-market stocks (value versus growth)
UMD = the difference in returns of the prior year's winners and losers (momentum)

5 Ross (1976).

Historical analysis shows that the coefficient on *MKT* is not significantly different from zero, which implies that stock return is unrelated to the market. The factors that explain stock returns are size (smaller companies outperform larger companies), book-to-market ratio (value companies outperform glamour companies), and momentum (past winners outperform past losers).

The four-factor model has been found to predict asset returns much better than the CAPM and is extensively used in estimating returns for US stocks.

Two observations are in order. First, the model is not underpinned by a theory of market equilibrium, as is the case for the CAPM. Second, there is no assurance that the model will continue to work well in the future.

6 PORTFOLIO PERFORMANCE APPRAISAL MEASURES

In the investment industry, **performance evaluation** refers to the measurement, attribution, and appraisal of investment results. In particular, performance evaluation provides information about the return and risk of investment portfolios over specified investment period(s). By providing accurate data and analysis on investment decisions and their consequences, performance evaluation allows portfolio managers to take corrective measures to improve investment decision-making and management processes. Performance evaluation information helps in understanding and controlling investment risk and should, therefore, lead to improved risk management. Performance evaluation seeks to answer the following questions:

- What was the investment portfolio's past performance, and what may be expected in the future?

Answering this question is the subject of performance measurement. *Performance measurement is concerned with the measurement of return and risk.*

- How did the investment portfolio produce its observed performance, and what are the expected sources of expected future performance?

Answering this question is the subject of performance attribution. *Performance attribution is concerned with identifying and quantifying the sources of performance of a portfolio.*

- Was the observed investment portfolio's performance the result of investment skill or luck?

Answering this question is the subject of performance appraisal. *Performance appraisal is concerned with identifying and measuring investment skill.*

The information provided by performance evaluation is of great interest to all stakeholders in the investment management process because of its value in evaluating the overall quality of the investment management process as well as individual investment decisions.

In this reading, performance appraisal is based only on the CAPM. However, it is easy to extend this analysis to multi-factor models that may include industry or other special factors. Four ratios are commonly used in performance appraisal.

6.1 The Sharpe Ratio

Performance has two components, risk and return. Although return maximization is a laudable objective, comparing just the return of a portfolio with that of the market is not sufficient. Because investors are risk averse, they will require compensation for higher risk in the form of higher returns. A commonly used measure of performance is the **Sharpe ratio**, which is defined as the portfolio's risk premium divided by its risk. An appealing feature of the Sharpe ratio is that its use can be justified on a theoretical *ex ante* (before the fact) basis and *ex post* (after the fact) values can easily be determined by using readily available market data. The Sharpe ratio is also easy to interpret, essentially being an efficiency ratio relating reward to risks taken. It is the most widely recognized and used appraisal measure.

The equation below defines the *ex ante* Sharpe ratio in terms of three inputs: (1) the portfolio's expected return, $E(R_p)$; (2) the risk-free rate of interest, R_f; and (3) the portfolio's *ex ante* standard deviation of returns (return volatility), σ_p, a quantitative measure of total risk.

$$\text{SR} = \frac{E(R_p) - R_F}{\sigma_p}$$

The Sharpe ratio can also be used on an *ex post* basis to evaluate historical risk-adjusted returns. Assume we have a sample of historical data that can be used to determine the sample mean portfolio return, $\overline{R}_p$; the standard deviation of the sample returns, here denoted by $\hat{\sigma}_p$ (s_p is a familiar notation in other contexts); and the sample mean risk-free rate, $\overline{R}_f$. The *ex post* (or realized or historical) Sharpe ratio can then be determined by using the following:

$$\widehat{\text{SR}} = \frac{\overline{R}_p - \overline{R}_F}{\hat{\sigma}_p}$$

Recalling the CAL from earlier in the reading, one can see that the Sharpe ratio, also called the reward-to-variability ratio, is simply the slope of the capital allocation line. Note, however, that the ratio uses the *total risk* of the portfolio, not its systematic risk. The use of total risk is appropriate if the portfolio is an investor's total portfolio—that is, the investor does not own any other assets. Sharpe ratios of the market and other portfolios can also be calculated in a similar manner. The portfolio with the highest Sharpe ratio has the best risk-adjusted performance, and the one with the lowest Sharpe ratio has the worst risk-adjusted performance, provided that the numerator is positive for all comparison portfolios. If the numerator is negative, the ratio will be less negative for riskier portfolios, resulting in incorrect rankings.

The Sharpe ratio, however, suffers from two limitations. First, it uses total risk as a measure of risk when only systematic risk is priced. Second, the ratio itself (e.g., 0.2 or 0.3) is not informative. To rank portfolios, the Sharpe ratio of one portfolio must be compared with the Sharpe ratio of another portfolio. Nonetheless, the ease of computation makes the Sharpe ratio a popular tool.

6.2 The Treynor Ratio

The **Treynor ratio** is a simple extension of the Sharpe ratio and resolves the Sharpe ratio's first limitation by substituting beta (systematic risk) for total risk. The *ex ante* and *ex post* Treynor ratios are provided below.

$$\text{TR} = \frac{E(R_p) - R_f}{\beta_p}$$

$$\widehat{\text{TR}} = \frac{\overline{R}_p - \overline{R}_f}{\hat{\beta}_p}$$

Just like the Sharpe ratio, the numerators must be positive for the Treynor ratio to give meaningful results. In addition, the Treynor ratio does not work for negative-beta assets—that is, the denominator must also be positive for obtaining correct estimates and rankings. Although both the Sharpe and Treynor ratios allow for ranking of portfolios, neither ratio gives any information about the economic significance of differences in performance. For example, assume the Sharpe ratio of one portfolio is 0.75 and the Sharpe ratio for another portfolio is 0.80. The second portfolio is superior, but is that difference meaningful? In addition, we do not know whether either of the portfolios is better than the passive market portfolio. The remaining two measures, M^2 and Jensen's alpha, attempt to address that problem by comparing portfolios while also providing information about the extent of the overperformance or underperformance.

6.3 M^2: Risk-Adjusted Performance (RAP)

M^2 provides a measure of portfolio return that is adjusted for the total risk of the portfolio relative to that of some benchmark. In 1997, Nobel Prize winner Franco Modigliani and his granddaughter, Leah Modigliani, developed what they called a risk-adjusted performance measure, or RAP. The RAP measure has since become more commonly known as M^2 reflecting the Modigliani names. It is related to the Sharpe ratio and ranks portfolios identically, but it has the useful advantage of being denominated in familiar terms of percentage return advantage assuming the same level of total risk as the market

M^2 borrows from capital market theory by assuming a portfolio is leveraged or de-leveraged until its volatility (as measured by standard deviation) matches that of the market. This adjustment produces a portfolio-specific leverage ratio that equates the portfolio's risk to that of the market. The portfolio's excess return times the leverage ratio plus the risk-free rate is then compared with the markets actual return to determine whether the portfolio has outperformed or underperformed the market on a risk-adjusted basis.

The equations below provide the *ex ante* and *ex post* formulas for M^2, where σ_m is the standard deviation of the market portfolio and σ_m/σ_p is the portfolio-specific leverage ratio. Because the Sharpe ratio is defined as $\frac{E(R_p) - R_f}{\sigma_p}$, the equation shows that M^2 can be thought of as a rescaling of the Sharpe ratio that allows for easier comparisons among different portfolios. The reason that M^2 and Sharpe ratios rank portfolios identically is because, in a given time period—and for any given comparison of the market portfolio—both the risk-free rate and the market volatility are constant across all comparisons. Only the Sharpe ratio differs, so it determines all rankings.

$$\text{M}^2 = \left[E(R_p) - R_f\right]\frac{\sigma_m}{\sigma_p} + R_f = \text{SR} \times \sigma_m + R_f \text{ (ex ante)}$$

$$\widehat{\text{M}^2} = \left(\bar{R}_p - \bar{R}_f\right)\frac{\hat{\sigma}_m}{\hat{\sigma}_p} + R_f = \widehat{\text{SR}} \times \hat{\sigma}_m + R_f \text{ (ex post)}$$

For example, assume that $\bar{R}_f = 4.0\%$, $\bar{R}_p = 14.0\%$, $\hat{\sigma}_p = 25.0\%$ and $\hat{\sigma}_m = 20.0\%$. The Sharpe ratio is 0.4, $\widehat{\text{SR}} = \frac{0.14 - 0.04}{0.25} = 0.4$, and $\widehat{M^2}$ is 12.0%, $\widehat{M^2} = 0.4(0.2) + 0.04 = 0.12 = 12.0\%$. If the market return was 10%, then the portfolio outperformed the market on a risk-adjusted basis by 12.0% – 10.0% = 2.0%. This difference between the risk-adjusted performance of the portfolio and the performance of the market is frequently referred to as **M^2 alpha**.

The Sharpe ratio of the market portfolio is $\widehat{SR} = \frac{0.10 - 0.04}{0.20} = 0.3$. Comparing the Sharpe ratio of the portfolio with the Sharpe ratio of the market portfolio shows that the fund outperformed the market. But the 2.0% difference between M^2 and the market's return tells us the risk-adjusted outperformance as a percentage return.

6.4 Jensen's Alpha

Like the Treynor ratio, Jensen's alpha is based on systematic risk. We can measure a portfolio's systematic risk by estimating the market model, which is done by regressing the portfolio's daily return on the market's daily return. The coefficient on the market return is an estimate of the beta risk of the portfolio. We can calculate the risk-adjusted return of the portfolio using the beta of the portfolio and the CAPM. The difference between the actual portfolio return and the calculated risk-adjusted return is a measure of the portfolio's performance relative to the market portfolio and is called Jensen's alpha. By definition, α_m of the market is zero. Jensen's alpha is also the vertical distance from the SML measuring the excess return for the same risk as that of the market and is given by

$$\alpha_p = R_p - \{R_f + \beta_p[E(R_m) - R_f]\}$$

If the period is long, it may contain different risk-free rates, in which case R_f represents the average risk-free rate. Furthermore, the returns in the equation are all realized, actual returns. The sign of α_p indicates whether the portfolio has outperformed the market. If α_p is positive, then the portfolio has outperformed the market; if α_p is negative, the portfolio has underperformed the market. Jensen's alpha is commonly used for evaluating most institutional managers, pension funds, and mutual funds. Values of alpha can be used to rank different managers and the performance of their portfolios, as well as the magnitude of underperformance or overperformance. For example, if a portfolio's alpha is 2 percent and another portfolio's alpha is 5 percent, the second portfolio has outperformed the first portfolio by 3 percentage points and the market by 5 percentage points. Jensen's alpha is the maximum amount that you should be willing to pay the manager to manage your money. As with other performance appraisal measures, Jensen's alpha has *ex ante* and *ex post* forms. The use context usually clarifies which one is being referred to. Where we want to underscore a reference to *ex post* Jensen's alpha based on an estimated beta, $\hat{\beta}_p$, and an average market return, the notation $\hat{\alpha}_p$ is used.

EXAMPLE 10

Portfolio Performance Evaluation

A British pension fund has employed three investment managers, each of whom is responsible for investing in one-third of all asset classes so that the pension fund has a well-diversified portfolio. Information about the managers is given below.

Manager	Average Return	$\hat{\sigma}$	$\hat{\beta}$
X	10%	20%	1.1
Y	11	10	0.7
Z	12	25	0.6
Market (M)	9	19	
Risk-free rate (R_f)	3		

Calculate the expected return for each manager, based on using the average market return and the CAPM. Then also calculate for the managers (ex post) Sharpe ratio, Treynor ratio, M^2 alpha, and Jensen's alpha. Analyze your results and plot the returns and betas of these portfolios.

Solution:

In each case, the calculations are shown only for Manager X. All answers are tabulated below. Note that the β of the market is 1 and the σ and β of the risk-free rate are both zero.

$$\text{Expected return: } E(R_X) = R_f + \beta_X\left[E(R_m) - R_f\right] = 0.03 + 1.10 \times (0.09 - 0.03) = 0.096 = 9.6\%$$

$$\widehat{\text{SR}} = \frac{\bar{R}_x - \bar{R}_f}{\hat{\sigma}_x} = \frac{0.10 - 0.03}{0.20} = 0.35$$

$$\widehat{\text{TR}} = \frac{\bar{R}_x - \bar{R}_f}{\hat{\beta}_x} = \frac{0.10 - 0.03}{1.1} = 0.064$$

$$\widehat{M^2} = \left(\bar{R}_x - \bar{R}_f\right)\frac{\hat{\sigma}_m}{\hat{\sigma}_x} + \bar{R}_f = \widehat{SR} \times \hat{\sigma}_m + \bar{R}_f$$

$$= 0.35 \times 0.19 + 0.03 = 0.0965 = 9.65\%$$

Since the market return is 9%, M^2 alpha is 0.65% (9.65% – 9%).

$$\hat{\alpha}_X = R_X - \left[\bar{R}_f + \hat{\beta}_X\left(\bar{R}_m - \bar{R}_f\right)\right] = 0.10 - (0.03 + 1.1 \times 0.06)$$

$$= 0.004 = 0.40\%$$

Exhibit 8 Measures of Portfolio Performance Evaluation

Manager	$\bar{R}_i$	$\hat{\sigma}_i$	$\hat{\beta}_i$	$E(R_i)$	Sharpe Ratio	Treynor Ratio	M^2 alpha	$\hat{\alpha}_i$
X	10.0%	20.0%	1.10	9.6%	0.35	0.064	0.65%	0.40%
Y	11.0	10.0	0.70	7.2	0.80	0.114	9.20	3.80
Z	12.0	25.0	0.60	6.6	0.36	0.150	0.84	5.40
M	9.0	19.0	1.00	9.0	0.32	0.060	0.00	0.00
R_f	3.0	0.0	0.00	3.0	–	–	–	0.00

Let us begin with an analysis of the risk-free asset. Because the risk-free asset has zero risk and a beta of zero, calculating the Sharpe ratio, Treynor ratio, or M^2 is not possible because they all require the portfolio risk in the denominator. The risk-free asset's alpha, however, is zero. Turning to the market portfolio, we see that the absolute measures of performance, the Sharpe ratio and the Treynor ratio, are positive for the market portfolio. These ratios are positive as long as the portfolio earns a return that is in excess of that of the risk-free asset. $\widehat{M}^2$ and $\hat{\alpha}_i$ are performance measures relative to the market, so they are both equal to zero for the market portfolio.

All three managers have Sharpe and Treynor ratios greater than those of the market, and all three managers' M^2 alpha and α_i are positive; therefore, the pension fund should be satisfied with their performance. Among the three managers, Manager X has the worst performance, irrespective of whether total risk or systematic risk is considered for measuring performance. The relative rankings are depicted in Exhibit 9.

Exhibit 9 Ranking of Portfolios by Performance Measure

Rank	Sharpe Ratio	Treynor Ratio	M^2 alpha	α_i
1	Y	Z	Y	Z
2	Z	Y	Z	Y
3	X	X	X	X
4	M	M	M	M
5	–	–	–	R_f

Comparing Y and Z, we can observe that Y performs much better than Z when total risk is considered. Y has a Sharpe ratio of 0.80, compared with a Sharpe ratio of 0.36 for Z. Similarly, M^2 alpha is higher for Y (9.20 percent) than for Z (0.84 percent). In contrast, when systematic risk is used, Z outperforms Y. The Treynor ratio is higher for Z (0.150) than for Y (0.114), and Jensen's alpha is also higher for Z (5.40 percent) than for Y (3.80 percent), which indicates that Z has done a better job of generating excess return relative to systematic risk than Y.

Exhibit 10 confirms these observations in that all three managers outperform the benchmark because all three points lie above the SML. Among the three portfolios, Z performs the best when we consider risk-adjusted returns because it is the point in Exhibit 10 that is located northwest relative to the portfolios X and Y.

Exhibit 10 Portfolios Along the SML

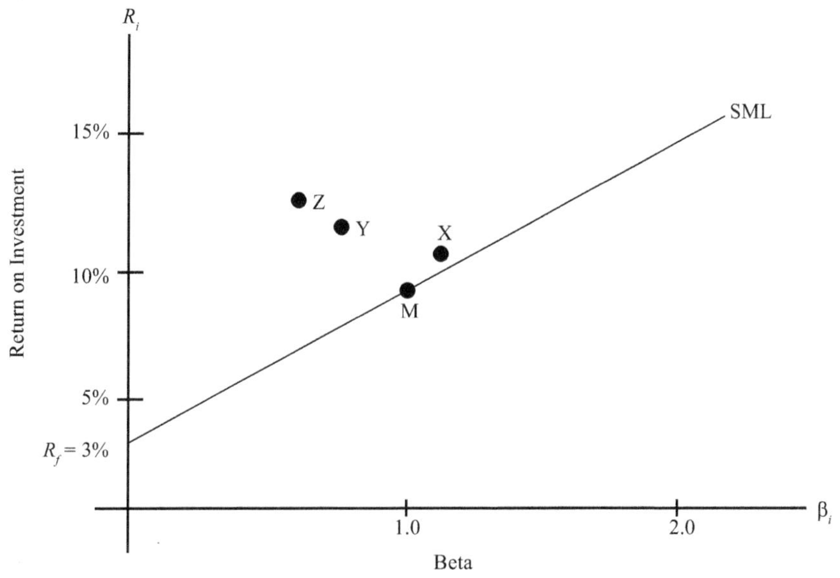

When do we use total risk performance measures like the Sharpe ratio and M^2, and when do we use beta risk performance measures like the Treynor ratio and Jensen's alpha? Total risk is relevant for an investor when he or she holds a portfolio that is not fully diversified, which is not a desirable portfolio. In such cases, the Sharpe ratio and M^2 are appropriate performance measures. Thus, if the pension fund were to choose only one fund manager to manage all its assets, it should choose Manager Y. Performance measures relative to beta risk—Treynor ratio and Jensen's alpha—are relevant when the investor holds a well-diversified portfolio with negligible diversifiable risk. In other words, if the pension fund is well diversified and only the systematic risk of the portfolio matters, the fund should choose Manager Z.

The measures of performance evaluation assume that the market portfolio is the correct benchmark. As a result, an error in the benchmark may cause the results to be misleading. For example, evaluating a real estate fund against the S&P 500 is incorrect because real estate has different characteristics than equity. In addition to errors in benchmarking, errors could occur in the measurement of risk and return of the market portfolio and the portfolios being evaluated. Finally, many estimates are based on historical data. Any projections based on such estimates assume that this level of performance will continue in the future.

7 APPLICATIONS OF THE CAPM IN PORTFOLIO CONSTRUCTION

This section introduces applications of the CAPM in portfolio construction. First, the security characteristic line, which graphically indicates *ex post* Jensen's alpha, is described. If we relax the assumption that investors have the same expectations about risk and return, a positive Jensen's alpha can be interpreted as an indication of superior information or investment ability. The section on security selection covers that possibility. The last section summarizes how the CAPM and related concepts can be applied to portfolio construction.

7.1 Security Characteristic Line

Similar to the SML, we can draw a **security characteristic line** (SCL) for a security. The SCL is a plot of the excess return of the security on the excess return of the market. In Exhibit 8, Jensen's alpha is the intercept and the beta is the slope. The equation of the line can be obtained by rearranging the terms in the expression for Jensen's alpha and replacing the subscript p with i:

$$R_i - R_f = \alpha_i + \beta_i(R_m - R_f)$$

As an example, the SCL is drawn in Exhibit 11 using Manager X's portfolio from Exhibit 8. The security characteristic line can also be estimated by regressing the excess security return, $R_i - R_f$, on the excess market return, $R_m - R_f$.

Exhibit 11 The Security Characteristic Line

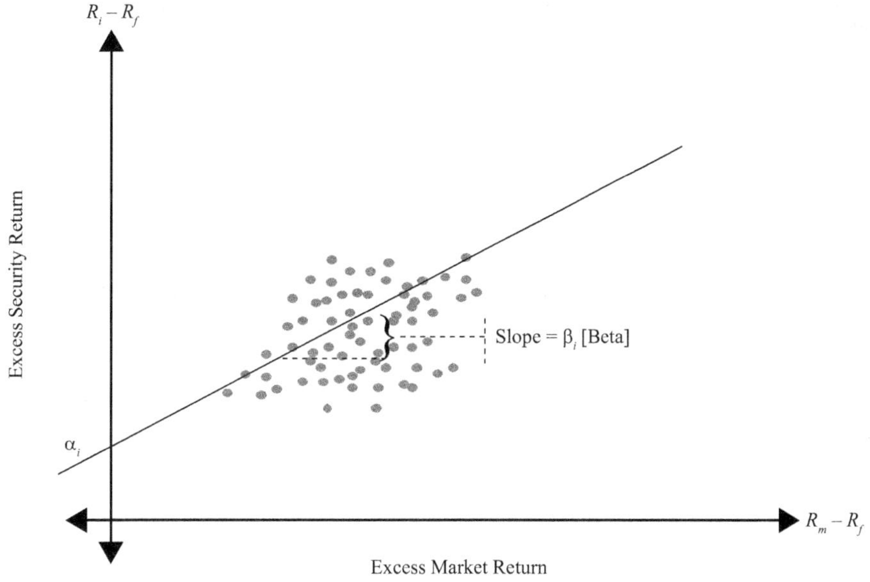

7.2 Security Selection

When discussing the CAPM, we assumed that investors have homogeneous expectations and are rational, risk-averse, utility-maximizing investors. With these assumptions, we were able to state that all investors assign the same value to all assets and, therefore, have the same optimal risky portfolio, which is the market portfolio. In other words, we assumed that there is commonality among beliefs about an asset's future cash flows and the required rate of return. Given the required rate of return, we can discount the future cash flows of the asset to arrive at its current value, or price, which is agreed upon by all or most investors.

In this section, we introduce heterogeneity in beliefs of investors. Because investors are price takers, it is assumed that such heterogeneity does not significantly affect the market price of an asset. The difference in beliefs can relate to future cash flows, the systematic risk of the asset, or both. Because the current price of an asset is the discounted value of the future cash flows, the difference in beliefs could result in an investor-estimated price that is different from the CAPM-calculated price. The CAPM-calculated price is the current market price because it reflects the beliefs of all other investors in the market. If the investor-estimated current price is higher (lower) than the market price, the asset is considered undervalued (overvalued). Therefore, the CAPM is an effective tool for determining whether an asset is undervalued or overvalued and whether an investor should buy or sell the asset.

Although portfolio performance evaluation is backward looking and security selection is forward looking, we can apply the concepts of portfolio evaluation to security selection. The best measure to apply is Jensen's alpha because it uses systematic risk and is meaningful even on an absolute basis. A positive Jensen's alpha indicates a superior security, whereas a negative Jensen's alpha indicates a security that is likely to underperform the market when adjusted for risk.

Another way of presenting the same information is with the security market line. Potential investors can plot a security's expected return and beta against the SML and use this relationship to decide whether the security is overvalued or undervalued in the market.[6] Exhibit 12 shows a number of securities along with the SML. All securities that reflect the consensus market view are points directly on the SML (i.e., properly valued). If a point representing the estimated return of an asset is above the SML (Points A and C), the asset has a low level of risk relative to the amount of expected return and would be a good choice for investment. In contrast, if the point representing a particular asset is below the SML (Point B), the stock is considered overvalued. Its return does not compensate for the level of risk and should not be considered for investment. Of course, a short position in Asset B can be taken if short selling is permitted.

Exhibit 12 Security Selection Using SML

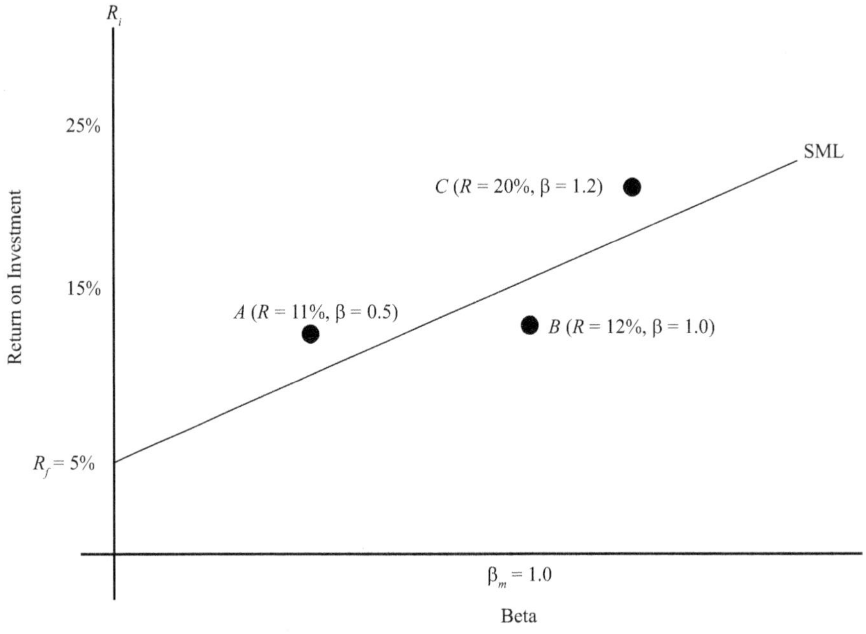

7.3 Implications of the CAPM for Portfolio Construction

Based on the CAPM, investors should hold a combination of the risk-free asset and the market portfolio. The true market portfolio consists of a large number of securities, and an investor would have to own all of them in order to be completely diversified. Because owning all existing securities is not practical, in this section, we will consider an alternate method of constructing a portfolio that may not require a large number of securities and will still be sufficiently diversified. Exhibit 13 shows the reduction in risk as we add more and more securities to a portfolio. As can be seen from the exhibit, much of the nonsystematic risk can be diversified away in as few as 30 securities. These securities, however, should be randomly selected and represent different asset classes for the portfolio to effectively diversify risk. Otherwise, one may be better off using an index (e.g., the S&P 500 for a diversified large-cap equity portfolio and other indexes for other asset classes).

6 In this reading, we do not consider transaction costs, which are important whenever deviations from a passive portfolio are considered. Thus, the magnitude of undervaluation or overvaluation should be considered in relation to transaction costs prior to making an investment decision.

Exhibit 13 Diversification with Number of Stocks

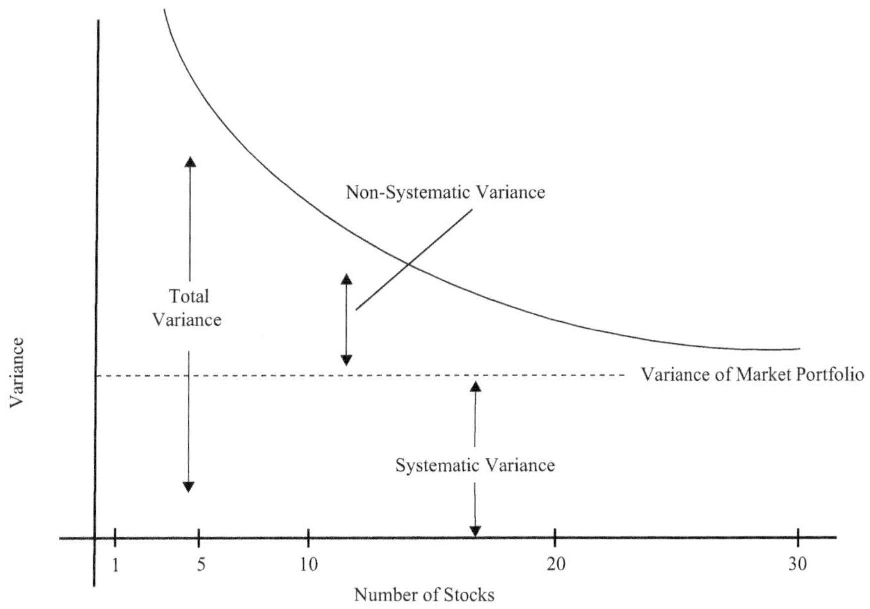

Let's begin constructing the optimal portfolio with a portfolio of securities like the S&P 500. Although the S&P 500 is a portfolio of 500 securities, it is a good starting point because it is readily available as a single security for trading. In contrast, it represents only the large corporations that are traded on the US stock markets and, therefore, does not encompass the global market entirely. Because the S&P 500 is the base portfolio, however, we treat it is as the market for the CAPM.

Any security not included in the S&P 500 can be evaluated to determine whether it should be integrated into the portfolio. That decision is based on the α_i of the security, which is calculated using the CAPM with the S&P 500 as the market portfolio. Note that security i may not necessarily be priced incorrectly for it to have a non-zero α_i; α_i can be positive merely because it is not well correlated with the S&P 500 and its return is sufficient for the amount of systematic risk it contains. For example, assume a new stock market, ABC, opens to foreign investors only and is being considered for inclusion in the portfolio. We estimate ABC's model parameters relative to the S&P 500 and find an α_i of approximately 3 percent, with a β_i of 0.60. Because α_i is positive, ABC should be added to the portfolio. Securities with a significantly negative α_i may be short sold to maximize risk-adjusted return. For convenience, however, we will assume that negative positions are not permitted in the portfolio.

In addition to the securities that are correctly priced but enter the portfolio because of their risk–return superiority, securities already in the portfolio (S&P 500) may be undervalued or overvalued based on investor expectations that are incongruent with the market. Securities in the S&P 500 that are overvalued (negative α_i) should be dropped from the S&P 500 portfolio, if it is possible to exclude individual securities, and positions in securities in the S&P 500 that are undervalued (positive α_i) should be increased.

This brings us to the next question: What should the relative weight of securities in the portfolio be? Because we are concerned with maximizing risk-adjusted return, securities with a higher α_i should have a higher weight, and securities with greater nonsystematic risk should be given less weight in the portfolio. A complete analysis of portfolio optimization is beyond the scope of this reading, but the following principles are helpful. The weight in each nonmarket security should be proportional to $\frac{\alpha_i}{\sigma_{ei}^2}$, where the denominator is the nonsystematic variance of security i. The total weight of nonmarket securities in the portfolio is proportional to $\frac{\sum_{i=1}^{N} w_i\alpha_i}{\sum_{i=1}^{N} w_i^2\sigma_{ei}^2}$. The weight in the market portfolio is a function of $\frac{E(R_m)}{\sigma_m^2}$. The information ratio, $\frac{\alpha_i}{\sigma_{ei}}$ (i.e., alpha divided by nonsystematic risk), measures the abnormal return per unit of risk added by the security to a well-diversified portfolio. The larger the information ratio is, the more valuable the security.

EXAMPLE 11

Optimal Investor Portfolio with Heterogeneous Beliefs

A Japanese investor is holding the Nikkei 225 index, which is her version of the market. She thinks that three stocks, P, Q, and R, which are not in the Nikkei 225, are undervalued and should form a part of her portfolio. She has the following information about the stocks, the Nikkei 225, and the risk-free rate (the information is given as expected return, standard deviation, and beta):

P: 15%, 30%, 1.5

Q: 18%, 25%, 1.2

R: 16%, 23%, 1.1

Nikkei 225: 12%, 18%, 1.0

Risk-free rate: 2%, 0%, 0.0

1 Calculate Jensen's alpha for P, Q, and R.
2 Calculate nonsystematic variance for P, Q, and R.
3 Should any of the three stocks be included in the portfolio? If so, which stock should have the highest weight in the portfolio?

Solution to 1:

Stock P's α: $R_i - [R_f + \beta_i(R_m - R_f)] = 0.15 - (0.02 + 1.5 \times 0.10) = -0.02$

Stock Q's α: $R_i - [R_f + \beta_i(R_m - R_f)] = 0.18 - (0.02 + 1.2 \times 0.10) = 0.04$

Stock R's α: $R_i - [R_f + \beta_i(R_m - R_f)] = 0.16 - (0.02 + 1.1 \times 0.10) = 0.03$

Solution to 2:

Total variance = Systematic variance + Nonsystematic variance. From Section 3.2.2, we write the equation as $\sigma_{ei}^2 = \sigma_i^2 - \beta_i^2\sigma_m^2$.

Stock P's nonsystematic variance = $(0.30 \times 0.30) - (1.5 \times 1.5 \times 0.18 \times 0.18) = 0.09 - 0.0729 = 0.0171$

Stock Q's nonsystematic variance = $(0.25 \times 0.25) - (1.2 \times 1.2 \times 0.18 \times 0.18) = 0.0625 - 0.0467 = 0.0158$

Stock R's nonsystematic variance = $(0.23 \times 0.23) - (1.1 \times 1.1 \times 0.18 \times 0.18) = 0.0529 - 0.0392 = 0.0137$

Solution to 3:

Stock P has a negative α and should not be included in the portfolio, unless a negative position can be assumed through short selling. Stocks Q and R have a positive α; therefore, they should be included in the portfolio with positive weights.

The relative weight of Q is 0.04/0.0158 = 2.53.

The relative weight of R is 0.03/0.0137 = 2.19.

Stock Q will have the largest weight among the nonmarket securities to be added to the portfolio. In relative terms, the weight of Q will be 15.5 percent greater than the weight of R (2.53/2.19 = 1.155). As the number of securities increases, the analysis becomes more complex. However, the contribution of each additional security toward improvement in the risk–return trade-off will decrease and eventually disappear, resulting in a well-diversified portfolio.

SUMMARY

In this reading, we discussed the capital asset pricing model in detail and covered related topics such as the capital market line. The reading began with an interpretation of the CML, uses of the market portfolio as a passive management strategy, and leveraging of the market portfolio to obtain a higher expected return. Next, we discussed systematic and nonsystematic risk and why one should not expect to be compensated for taking on nonsystematic risk. The discussion of systematic and nonsystematic risk was followed by an introduction to beta and return-generating models. This broad topic was then broken down into a discussion of the CAPM and, more specifically, the relationship between beta and expected return. The final section included applications of the CAPM to capital budgeting, portfolio performance evaluation, and security selection. The highlights of the reading are as follows.

- The capital market line is a special case of the capital allocation line, where the efficient portfolio is the market portfolio.
- Obtaining a unique optimal risky portfolio is not possible if investors are permitted to have heterogeneous beliefs because such beliefs will result in heterogeneous asset prices.
- Investors can leverage their portfolios by borrowing money and investing in the market.
- Systematic risk is the risk that affects the entire market or economy and is not diversifiable.
- Nonsystematic risk is local and can be diversified away by combining assets with low correlations.
- Beta risk, or systematic risk, is priced and earns a return, whereas nonsystematic risk is not priced.
- The expected return of an asset depends on its beta risk and can be computed using the CAPM, which is given by $E(R_i) = R_f + \beta_i[E(R_m) - R_f]$.
- The security market line is an implementation of the CAPM and applies to all securities, whether they are efficient or not.
- Expected return from the CAPM can be used for making capital budgeting decisions.

- Portfolios can be evaluated by several CAPM-based measures, such as the Sharpe ratio, the Treynor ratio, M^2, and Jensen's alpha.
- The SML can assist in security selection and optimal portfolio construction.

By successfully understanding the content of this reading, you should feel comfortable decomposing total variance into systematic and nonsystematic variance, analyzing beta risk, using the CAPM, and evaluating portfolios and individual securities.

REFERENCES

Carhart, Mark. 1997. "On Persistence in Mutual Fund Performance." *Journal of Finance*, vol. 52, no. 1:57–82.

Fama, Eugene, and Kenneth French. 1992. "The Cross-Section of Expected Stock Returns." *Journal of Finance*, vol. 47, no. 2:427–466.

Lintner, John. 1965a. "Security Prices, Risk, and Maximal Gains from Diversification." *Journal of Finance*, vol. 20, no. 4:587–615.

Lintner, John. 1965b. "The Valuation of Risk Assets and the Selection of Risky Investments in Stock Portfolios and Capital Budgets." *Review of Economics and Statistics*, vol. 47, no. 1:13–37.

Markowitz, Harry. 1952. "Portfolio Selection." *Journal of Finance*, vol. 7, no. 1:77–91.

Mossin, Jan. 1966. "Equilibrium in a Capital Asset Market." *Econometrica*, vol. 34, no. 4:768–783.

Roll, Richard. 1977. "A Critique of the Asset Pricing Theory's Tests Part I: On Past and Potential Testability of the Theory." *Journal of Financial Economics*, vol. 4, no. 2:129–176.

Ross, Stephen A. 1976. "The Arbitrage Theory of Capital Asset Pricing." *Journal of Economic Theory*, vol. 13, no. 3:341–360.

Sharpe, William F. 1964. "Capital Asset Prices: A Theory Of Market Equilibrium under Conditions of Risk." *Journal of Finance*, vol. 19, no. 3:425–442.

Treynor, Jack L. 1961. *Market Value, Time, and Risk*. Unpublished manuscript.

Treynor, Jack L. 1962. *Toward a Theory of Market Value of Risky Assets*. Unpublished manuscript.

PRACTICE PROBLEMS

1 The line depicting the total risk and expected return of portfolio combinations of a risk-free asset and any risky asset is the:

A security market line.

B capital allocation line.

C security characteristic line.

2 The portfolio of a risk-free asset and a risky asset has a better risk-return tradeoff than investing in only one asset type because the correlation between the risk-free asset and the risky asset is equal to:

A −1.0.

B 0.0.

C 1.0.

3 With respect to capital market theory, an investor's optimal portfolio is the combination of a risk-free asset and a risky asset with the highest:

A expected return.

B indifference curve.

C capital allocation line slope.

4 Highly risk-averse investors will *most likely* invest the majority of their wealth in:

A risky assets.

B risk-free assets.

C the optimal risky portfolio.

5 The capital market line (CML) is the graph of the risk and return of portfolio combinations consisting of the risk-free asset and:

A any risky portfolio.

B the market portfolio.

C the leveraged portfolio.

6 Which of the following statements *most accurately* defines the market portfolio in capital market theory? The market portfolio consists of all:

A risky assets.

B tradable assets.

C investable assets.

7 With respect to capital market theory, the optimal risky portfolio:

A is the market portfolio.

B has the highest expected return.

C has the lowest expected variance.

8 Relative to portfolios on the CML, any portfolio that plots above the CML is considered:

A inferior.

B inefficient.

C unachievable.

9 A portfolio on the capital market line with returns greater than the returns on the market portfolio represents a(n):

A lending portfolio.

B borrowing portfolio.

C unachievable portfolio.

10 With respect to the capital market line, a portfolio on the CML with returns less than the returns on the market portfolio represents a(n):

A lending portfolio.

B borrowing portfolio.

C unachievable portfolio.

11 Which of the following types of risk is *most likely* avoided by forming a diversified portfolio?

A Total risk.

B Systematic risk.

C Nonsystematic risk.

12 Which of the following events is *most likely* an example of nonsystematic risk?

A A decline in interest rates.

B The resignation of chief executive officer.

C An increase in the value of the US dollar.

13 With respect to the pricing of risk in capital market theory, which of the following statements is *most accurate*?

A All risk is priced.

B Systematic risk is priced.

C Nonsystematic risk is priced.

14 The sum of an asset's systematic variance and its nonsystematic variance of returns is equal to the asset's:

A beta.

B total risk.

C total variance.

15 With respect to return-generating models, the intercept term of the market model is the asset's estimated:

A beta.

B alpha.

C variance.

16 With respect to return-generating models, the slope term of the market model is an estimate of the asset's:

A total risk.

B systematic risk.

C nonsystematic risk.

17 With respect to return-generating models, which of the following statements is *most accurate*? Return-generating models are used to directly estimate the:

A expected return of a security.

B weights of securities in a portfolio.

C parameters of the capital market line.

The following information relates to Questions 18–20

An analyst gathers the following information:

Security	Expected Annual Return (%)	Expected Standard Deviation (%)	Correlation between Security and the Market
Security 1	11	25	0.6
Security 2	11	20	0.7
Security 3	14	20	0.8
Market	10	15	1.0

18 Which security has the *highest* total risk?

A Security 1.

B Security 2.

C Security 3.

19 Which security has the *highest* beta measure?

A Security 1.

B Security 2.

C Security 3.

20 Which security has the *least* amount of market risk?

A Security 1.

B Security 2.

C Security 3.

---

21 With respect to capital market theory, the average beta of all assets in the market is:

A less than 1.0.

B equal to 1.0.

C greater than 1.0.

22 The slope of the security characteristic line is an asset's:

A beta.

B excess return.

C risk premium.

23 The graph of the capital asset pricing model is the:

A capital market line.

B security market line.

C security characteristic line.

24 With respect to capital market theory, correctly priced individual assets can be plotted on the:

A capital market line.

B security market line.

C capital allocation line.

25 With respect to the capital asset pricing model, the primary determinant of expected return of an individual asset is the:

A asset's beta.

B market risk premium.

C asset's standard deviation.

26 With respect to the capital asset pricing model, which of the following values of beta for an asset is *most likely* to have an expected return for the asset that is less than the risk-free rate?

A –0.5

B 0.0

C 0.5

27 With respect to the capital asset pricing model, the market risk premium is:

A less than the excess market return.

B equal to the excess market return.

C greater than the excess market return.

The following information relates to Questions 28–31

An analyst gathers the following information:

Security	Expected Standard Deviation (%)	Beta
Security 1	25	1.50
Security 2	15	1.40
Security 3	20	1.60

28 With respect to the capital asset pricing model, if the expected market risk premium is 6% and the risk-free rate is 3%, the expected return for Security 1 is *closest* to:

A 9.0%.

B 12.0%.

C 13.5%.

29 With respect to the capital asset pricing model, if expected return for Security 2 is equal to 11.4% and the risk-free rate is 3%, the expected return for the market is *closest* to:

A 8.4%.

B 9.0%.

C 10.3%.

30 With respect to the capital asset pricing model, if the expected market risk premium is 6% the security with the *highest* expected return is:

A Security 1.

B Security 2.

C Security 3.

31 With respect to the capital asset pricing model, a decline in the expected market return will have the *greatest* impact on the expected return of:

A Security 1.

B Security 2.

C Security 3.

---

32 Three equity fund managers have performance records summarized in the following table:

	Mean Annual Return (%)	Standard Deviation of Return (%)
Manager 1	14.38	10.53
Manager 2	9.25	6.35
Manager 3	13.10	8.23

Given a risk-free rate of return of 2.60%, which manager performed best based on the Sharpe ratio?

A Manager 1

B Manager 2

C Manager 3

33 Which of the following performance measures is consistent with the CAPM?

A *M*-squared.

B Sharpe ratio.

C Jensen's alpha.

34 Which of the following performance measures does *not* require the measure to be compared to another value?

A Sharpe ratio.

B Treynor ratio.

C Jensen's alpha.

35 Which of the following performance measures is *most* appropriate for an investor who is *not* fully diversified?

A *M*-squared.

B Treynor ratio.

C Jensen's alpha.

36 Analysts who have estimated returns of an asset to be greater than the expected returns generated by the capital asset pricing model should consider the asset to be:

A overvalued.

B undervalued.

C properly valued.

37 With respect to capital market theory, which of the following statements *best* describes the effect of the homogeneity assumption? Because all investors have the same economic expectations of future cash flows for all assets, investors will invest in:

A the same optimal risky portfolio.

B the Standard and Poor's 500 Index.

C assets with the same amount of risk.

38 With respect to capital market theory, which of the following assumptions allows for the existence of the market portfolio? All investors:

A are price takers.

B have homogeneous expectations.

C plan for the same, single holding period.

39 The intercept of the best fit line formed by plotting the excess returns of a manager's portfolio on the excess returns of the market is *best* described as Jensen's:

A beta.

B ratio.

C alpha.

40 Portfolio managers who are maximizing risk-adjusted returns will seek to invest *more* in securities with:

A lower values of Jensen's alpha.

B values of Jensen's alpha equal to 0.

C higher values of Jensen's alpha.

41 Portfolio managers, who are maximizing risk-adjusted returns, will seek to invest *less* in securities with:

A lower values for nonsystematic variance.

B values of nonsystematic variance equal to 0.

C higher values for nonsystematic variance.

SOLUTIONS

1 B is correct. A capital allocation line (CAL) plots the expected return and total risk of combinations of the risk-free asset and a risky asset (or a portfolio of risky assets).

2 B is correct. A portfolio of the risk-free asset and a risky asset or a portfolio of risky assets can result in a better risk-return tradeoff than an investment in only one type of an asset, because the risk-free asset has zero correlation with the risky asset.

3 B is correct. Investors will have different optimal portfolios depending on their indifference curves. The optimal portfolio for each investor is the one with highest utility; that is, where the CAL is tangent to the individual investor's highest possible indifference curve.

4 B is correct. Although the optimal risky portfolio is the market portfolio, highly risk-averse investors choose to invest most of their wealth in the risk-free asset.

5 B is correct. Although the capital allocation line includes all possible combinations of the risk-free asset and any risky portfolio, the capital market line is a special case of the capital allocation line, which uses the market portfolio as the optimal risky portfolio.

6 A is correct. The market includes all risky assets, or anything that has value; however, not all assets are tradable, and not all tradable assets are investable.

7 A is correct. The optimal risky portfolio is the market portfolio. Capital market theory assumes that investors have homogeneous expectations, which means that all investors analyze securities in the same way and are rational. That is, investors use the same probability distributions, use the same inputs for future cash flows, and arrive at the same valuations. Because their valuations of all assets are identical, all investors will invest in the same optimal risky portfolio (i.e., the market portfolio).

8 C is correct. Theoretically, any point above the CML is not achievable and any point below the CML is dominated by and inferior to any point on the CML.

9 B is correct. As one moves further to the right of point M on the capital market line, an increasing amount of borrowed money is being invested in the market portfolio. This means that there is negative investment in the risk-free asset, which is referred to as a leveraged position in the risky portfolio.

10 A is correct. The combinations of the risk-free asset and the market portfolio on the CML where returns are less than the returns on the market portfolio are termed 'lending' portfolios.

11 C is correct. Investors are capable of avoiding nonsystematic risk by forming a portfolio of assets that are not highly correlated with one another, thereby reducing total risk and being exposed only to systematic risk.

12 B is correct. Nonsystematic risk is specific to a firm, whereas systematic risk affects the entire economy.

13 B is correct. Only systematic risk is priced. Investors do not receive any return for accepting nonsystematic or diversifiable risk.

14 C is correct. The sum of systematic variance and nonsystematic variance equals the total variance of the asset. References to total risk as the sum of systematic risk and nonsystematic risk refer to variance, not to risk.

15 B is correct. In the market model, $R_i = \alpha_i + \beta_i R_m + e_i$, the intercept, α_i, and slope coefficient, β_i, are estimated using historical security and market returns.

16 B is correct. In the market model, $R_i = \alpha_i + \beta_i R_m + e_i$, the slope coefficient, β_i, is an estimate of the asset's systematic or market risk.

17 A is correct. In the market model, $R_i = \alpha_i + \beta_i R_m + e_i$, the intercept, α_i, and slope coefficient, β_i, are estimated using historical security and market returns. These parameter estimates then are used to predict firm-specific returns that a security may earn in a future period.

18 A is correct. Security 1 has the highest total risk = 0.25 compared to Security 2 and Security 3 with a total risk of 0.20.

19 C is correct. Security 3 has the highest beta value; $1.07 = \dfrac{\rho_{3,m}\sigma_3}{\sigma_m} = \dfrac{(0.80)(20\%)}{15\%}$ compared to Security 1 and Security 2 with beta values of 1.00 and 0.93, respectively.

20 B is correct. Security 2 has the lowest beta value; $0.93 = \dfrac{\rho_{2,m}\sigma_2}{\sigma_m} = \dfrac{(0.70)(20\%)}{15\%}$ compared to Security 1 and 3 with beta values of 1.00 and 1.07, respectively.

21 B is correct. The average beta of all assets in the market, by definition, is equal to 1.0.

22 A is correct. The security characteristic line is a plot of the excess return of the security on the excess return of the market. In such a graph, Jensen's alpha is the intercept and the beta is the slope.

23 B is correct. The security market line (SML) is a graphical representation of the capital asset pricing model, with beta risk on the x-axis and expected return on the y-axis.

24 B is correct. The security market line applies to any security, efficient or not. The CAL and the CML use the total risk of the asset (or portfolio of assets) rather than its systematic risk, which is the only risk that is priced.

25 A is correct. The CAPM shows that the primary determinant of expected return for an individual asset is its beta, or how well the asset correlates with the market.

26 A is correct. If an asset's beta is negative, the required return will be less than the risk-free rate in the CAPM. When combined with a positive market return, the asset reduces the risk of the overall portfolio, which makes the asset very valuable. Insurance is an example of a negative beta asset.

27 B is correct. In the CAPM, the market risk premium is the difference between the return on the market and the risk-free rate, which is the same as the return in excess of the market return.

28 B is correct. The expected return of Security 1, using the CAPM, is 12.0% = 3% + 1.5(6%); $E(R_i) = R_f + \beta_i[E(R_m) - R_f]$.

29 B is correct. The expected risk premium for Security 2 is 8.4%, (11.4% − 3%), indicates that the expected market risk premium is 6%; therefore, since the risk-free rate is 3% the expected rate of return for the market is 9%. That is, using the CAPM, $E(R_i) = R_f + \beta_i[E(R_m) - R_f]$, 11.4% = 3% + 1.4(X%), where X% = (11.4% − 3%)/1.4 = 6.0% = market risk premium.

30 C is correct. Security 3 has the highest beta; thus, regardless of the value for the risk-free rate, Security 3 will have the highest expected return:

$$E(R_i) = R_f + \beta_i[E(R_m) - R_f]$$

31 C is correct. Security 3 has the highest beta; thus, regardless of the risk-free rate the expected return of Security 3 will be most sensitive to a change in the expected market return.

32 C is correct. The Sharpe ratio $\left(\widehat{SR}\right)$ is the mean excess portfolio return per unit of risk, where a higher Sharpe ratio indicates better performance:

$$\widehat{SR_1} = \frac{\overline{R}_p - \overline{R}_f}{\hat{\sigma}_p} = \frac{14.38 - 2.60}{10.53} = 1.12$$

$$\widehat{SR_2} = \frac{\overline{R}_p - \overline{R}_f}{\hat{\sigma}_p} = \frac{9.25 - 2.60}{6.35} = 1.05$$

$$\widehat{SR_3} = \frac{\overline{R}_p - \overline{R}_f}{\hat{\sigma}_p} = \frac{13.10 - 2.60}{8.23} = 1.28$$

33 C is correct. Jensen's alpha adjusts for systematic risk, and M-squared and the Sharpe Ratio adjust for total risk.

34 C is correct. The sign of Jensen's alpha indicates whether or not the portfolio has outperformed the market. If alpha is positive, the portfolio has outperformed the market; if alpha is negative, the portfolio has underperformed the market.

35 A is the correct. M-squared adjusts for risk using standard deviation (i.e., total risk).

36 B is correct. If the estimated return of an asset is above the SML (the expected return), the asset has a lower level of risk relative to the amount of expected return and would be a good choice for investment (i.e., undervalued).

37 A is correct. The homogeneity assumption refers to all investors having the same economic expectation of future cash flows. If all investors have the same expectations, then all investors should invest in the same optimal risky portfolio, therefore implying the existence of only one optimal portfolio (i.e., the market portfolio).

38 B is correct. The homogeneous expectations assumption means that all investors analyze securities in the same way and are rational. That is, they use the same probability distributions, use the same inputs for future cash flows, and arrive at the same valuations. Because their valuation of all assets is identical, they will generate the same optimal risky portfolio, which is the market portfolio.

39 C is correct. This is because of the plot of the excess return of the security on the excess return of the market. In such a graph, Jensen's alpha is the intercept and the beta is the slope.

40 C is correct. Since managers are concerned with maximizing risk-adjusted returns, securities with a higher value of Jensen's alpha, α_i, should have a higher weight.

41 C is correct. Since managers are concerned with maximizing risk-adjusted returns, securities with greater nonsystematic risk should be given less weight in the portfolio.

PORTFOLIO MANAGEMENT

STUDY SESSION

19

Portfolio Management (2)

This study session introduces the portfolio planning and construction process, including the development of an investment policy statement (IPS). A discussion of risk management, including the various types and measures of risk, follows, and a risk management framework is provided. Technical analysis, a set of tools that uses asset price, trading volume, and other similar data for making investment decisions, is then examined. The session concludes with coverage on how financial technology (fintech) is impacting areas within the investment industry, such as investment analysis, automated advice, and risk management.

READING ASSIGNMENTS

Reading 54	Basics of Portfolio Planning and Construction by Alistair Byrne, PhD, CFA, and Frank E. Smudde, MSc, CFA
Reading 55	Introduction to Risk Management by Don M. Chance, PhD, CFA, and Michael E. Edleson, PhD, CFA
Reading 56	Technical Analysis by Barry M. Sine and Robert A. Strong, PhD, CFA
Reading 57	Fintech in Investment Management by Robert Kissell, PhD, and Barbara J. Mack

READING

54

Basics of Portfolio Planning and Construction

by Alistair Byrne, PhD, CFA, and Frank E. Smudde, MSc, CFA

Alistair Byrne, PhD, CFA, is at State Street Global Advisors (United Kingdom). Frank E. Smudde, MSc, CFA, is at APG Asset Management (Netherlands).

LEARNING OUTCOMES

Mastery	*The candidate should be able to:*
☐	a. describe the reasons for a written investment policy statement (IPS);
☐	b. describe the major components of an IPS;
☐	c. describe risk and return objectives and how they may be developed for a client;
☐	d. distinguish between the willingness and the ability (capacity) to take risk in analyzing an investor's financial risk tolerance;
☐	e. describe the investment constraints of liquidity, time horizon, tax concerns, legal and regulatory factors, and unique circumstances and their implications for the choice of portfolio assets;
☐	f. explain the specification of asset classes in relation to asset allocation;
☐	g. describe the principles of portfolio construction and the role of asset allocation in relation to the IPS;
☐	h. describe how environmental, social, and governance (ESG) considerations may be integrated into portfolio planning and construction.

INTRODUCTION

1

To build a suitable portfolio for a client, investment advisers should first seek to understand the client's investment goals, resources, circumstances, and constraints. Investors can be categorized into broad groups based on shared characteristics with respect to these factors (e.g., various types of individual investors and institutional investors). Even investors within a given type, however, will invariably have a number of distinctive requirements. In this reading, we consider in detail the planning for investment success based on an individualized understanding of the client.

This reading is organized as follows: Section 2 discusses the investment policy statement, a written document that captures the client's investment objectives and the constraints. Section 3 discusses the portfolio construction process, including the first step of specifying a strategic asset allocation for the client. Section 4 concludes and summarizes the reading.

2 PORTFOLIO PLANNING

Portfolio planning can be defined as a program developed in advance of constructing a portfolio that is expected to define the client's investment objectives. The written document governing this process is the investment policy statement (IPS). The IPS is sometimes complemented by a document outlining policy on **sustainable investing**—distinguishing between companies (or sectors) that either can or cannot efficiently manage their financial, environmental, and human capital resources to generate attractive long-term profitability.[1] Policies on sustainable investing may also be integrated within the IPS itself. In the remainder of this reading, the integration of sustainable investing within the IPS will be our working assumption.

2.1 The Investment Policy Statement

The IPS is the starting point of the portfolio management process. Without a full understanding of the client's situation and requirements, it is unlikely that successful results will be achieved. "Success" can be defined as a client achieving his or her important investment goals using means that he or she is comfortable with (in terms of risks taken and other concerns). The IPS essentially communicates a plan for achieving investment success.

The IPS is typically developed following a fact-finding discussion with the client. This fact-finding discussion can include the use of a questionnaire designed to articulate the client's risk tolerance as well as specific circumstances. In the case of institutional clients, the fact finding may involve asset–liability management studies, identification of liquidity needs, and a wide range of tax and legal considerations.

The IPS can take a variety of forms.[2] A typical format will include the client's investment objectives and the constraints that apply to the client's portfolio.

The client's objectives are specified in terms of risk tolerance and return requirements. These must be consistent with each other: a client is unlikely to be able to find a portfolio that offers a relatively high expected return without taking on a relatively high level of expected risk. As part of their financial planning, clients may specify specific spending goals, each of which could have different risk tolerance and return objectives.

1 In practice, the term "sustainable investing" is sometimes synonymous with "responsible investing" or 'socially responsible investing."

2 In this Reading, an IPS is assumed to be a document governing investment management activities covering all or most of the financial wealth of a client. In many practical contexts, investment professionals work with investment mandates that only cover parts of a client's wealth or financial risk. Governance documents such as "Limited Partnership Agreements" and "Investment Management Agreements" will govern such mandates. Their contents are to a large degree comparable to the contents of the IPS as described in this Reading.

The constraints section covers factors that need to be taken into account when constructing a portfolio for the client that meets the objectives. The typical categories are liquidity requirements, time horizon, regulatory requirements, tax status, and unique needs. The constraints may be internal (i.e., set by the client), or external (i.e., set by law or regulation). These are discussed in detail below.

Having a well constructed IPS for all clients should be standard procedure for an investment manager. The investment manager should build the portfolio with reference to the IPS and be able to refer to it to assess the suitability of a particular investment for the client. In some cases, the need for the IPS goes beyond simply being a matter of standard procedure. In some countries, the IPS (or an equivalent document) is a legal or regulatory requirement. For example, UK pension schemes must have a statement of investment principles under the Pensions Act 1995 (Section 35), and this statement is in essence an IPS. The UK Financial Services Authority also has requirements for investment firms to "know their customers." The European Union's Markets in Financial Instruments Directive ("MiFID") requires firms to assign clients to categories, such as eligible counterparties, institutional clients and retail clients.

In the case of an institution, such as a pension plan or university endowment, the IPS may set out the governance arrangements that apply to the investment funds. For example, this information could cover the investment committee's approach to appointing and reviewing investment managers for the portfolio, and the discretion that those managers have.

The IPS should be reviewed on a regular basis to ensure that it remains consistent with the client's circumstances and requirements. For example, the UK Pensions Regulator suggests that a pension scheme's statements of investment principles—a form of IPS—should be reviewed at least every three years. The IPS should also be reviewed if the manager becomes aware of a material change in the client's circumstances, or on the initiative of the client when his or her objectives, time horizon, or liquidity needs change.

2.2 Major Components of an IPS

There is no single standard format for an IPS. Many IPS and investment governance documents with a similar purpose (as noted previously), however, include the following sections:

- *Introduction.* This section describes the client.
- *Statement of Purpose.* This section states the purpose of the IPS.
- *Statement of Duties and Responsibilities.* This section details the duties and responsibilities of the client, the custodian of the client's assets, and the investment managers.
- *Procedures.* This section explains the steps to take to keep the IPS current and the procedures to follow to respond to various contingencies.
- *Investment Objectives.* This section explains the client's objectives in investing.
- *Investment Constraints.* This section presents the factors that constrain the client in seeking to achieve the investment objectives.
- *Investment Guidelines.* This section provides information about how policy should be executed (e.g., on the permissible use of leverage and derivatives) and on specific types of assets excluded from investment, if any.

- *Evaluation and Review.* This section provides guidance on obtaining feedback on investment results.
- *Appendices*: (A) Strategic Asset Allocation (B) Rebalancing Policy. Many investors specify a strategic asset allocation (SAA), also known as the policy portfolio, which is the baseline allocation of portfolio assets to asset classes in view of the investor's investment objectives and the investor's policy with respect to rebalancing asset class weights. This SAA may include a statement of policy concerning hedging risks such as currency risk and interest rate risk.

The sections that are most closely linked to the client's distinctive needs, and probably the most important from a planning perspective, are those dealing with investment objectives and constraints. An IPS focusing on these two elements has been called an IPS in an "objectives and constraints" format.

In the following sections, we discuss the investment objectives and constraints format of an IPS beginning with risk and return objectives. The process of developing the IPS is the basic mechanism for evaluating and trying to improve an investor's overall expected return–risk stance. In a portfolio context, return objectives and expectations must be tailored to be consistent with risk objectives. The risk and return objectives must also be consistent with the constraints that apply to the portfolio. In recent years, a large proportion of investors explicitly included non-financial considerations when formulating their investment policies. This is often referred to as sustainable investing (which we discussed earlier, as well as related terms) whereby environmental, social, and governance (ESG) considerations are reflected. Sustainable investing both recognizes that ESG considerations may eventually affect the financial risk-return profile of the portfolio and expresses societal convictions of the investor. In a survey by CFA Institute,[3] 73% of respondents indicated they take ESG factors in consideration in their investment decisions on behalf of their clients. In this reading, we discuss sustainable investing aspects of investment policy, where relevant.

2.2.1 *Risk Objectives*

When constructing a portfolio for a client, it is important to ensure that the risk of the portfolio is suitable for the client. The IPS should state clearly the risk tolerance of the client. Risk objectives are specifications for portfolio risk that reflect the risk tolerance of the client. Quantitative risk objectives can be absolute or relative or a combination of the two.

Examples of an absolute risk objective would be a desire not to suffer any loss of capital or not to lose more than a given percent of capital in any 12-month period. Note that these objectives are not related to investment market performance, good or bad, and are absolute in the sense of being self-standing. The fulfillment of such objectives could be achieved by not taking any risk; for example, by investing in an insured bank certificate of deposit at a creditworthy bank. If investments in risky assets are undertaken, however, such statements would need to be restated as a probability statement to be operational (i.e., practically useful). For example, the desire not to lose more than 4 percent of capital in any 12-month period might be restated as an objective that with 95 percent probability the portfolio not lose more than 4 percent in any 12-month period. Measures of absolute risk include the variance or standard deviation of returns and value at risk.[4]

---

3 Environmental, Societal, and Governance Issues in Investing: A Guide for Investment Professionals, CFA Institute, 2015

4 **Value at risk** is a money measure of the minimum value of losses expected during a specified time period at a given level of probability.

Some clients may choose to express relative risk objectives, which relate risk relative to one or more benchmarks perceived to represent appropriate risk standards. For example, investments in large-cap UK equities could be benchmarked to an equity market index, such as the FTSE 100 Index. The S&P 500 Index could be used as a benchmark for large-cap US equities, or for investments with cash-like characteristics, the benchmark could be an interest rate such as Libor or a Treasury bill rate. For risk relative to a benchmark, the measure could be tracking risk, or tracking error.[5] In practice, such risk objectives are used in situations where the total wealth management activities on behalf of a client are divided into partial mandates.

For institutional clients, the benchmark may be linked to some form of liability the institution has. For example, a pension plan must meet the pension payments as they come due and the risk objective will be to minimize the probability that it will fail to do so. A related return objective might be to outperform the discount rate used in finding the present value of liabilities over a multi-year time horizon.

When a policy portfolio (that is, a specified set of long-term asset class weightings and hedge ratios) is used, the risk objective may be expressed as a desire for the portfolio return to be within a band of plus or minus X percent of the benchmark return calculated by assigning an index or benchmark to represent each asset class present in the policy portfolio. Again, this objective has to be interpreted as a statement of probability; for example, a 95 percent probability that the portfolio return will be within X percent of the benchmark return over a stated time period. Example 1 reviews this material.

EXAMPLE 1

Types of Risk Objectives

A Japanese institutional investor has a portfolio valued at ¥10 billion. The investor expresses his first risk objective as a desire not to lose more than ¥1 billion in the coming 12-month period. The investor specifies a second risk objective of achieving returns within 4 percent of the return to the TOPIX stock market index, which is the investor's benchmark. Based on this information, address the following:

1 **A** Characterize the first risk objective as absolute or relative.

B Give an example of how the risk objective could be restated in a practical manner.

2 **A** Characterize the second risk objective as absolute or relative.

B Identify a measure for quantifying the risk objective.

Solutions:

1 **A** This is an absolute risk objective.

B This risk objective could be restated in a practical manner by specifying that the 12-month 95 percent value at risk of the portfolio must not be more than ¥1 billion.

2 **A** This is a relative risk objective.

B This risk objective could be quantified using the tracking risk as a measure. For example, assuming returns follow a normal distribution, an expected tracking risk of 2 percent would imply a return within

5 **Tracking risk** (sometimes called **tracking error**) is the standard deviation of the differences between a portfolio's returns and its benchmark's returns.

4 percent of the index return approximately 95 percent of the time. Remember that tracking risk is stated as a one standard deviation measure.

A client's overall risk tolerance is a function of the client's ability to bear (accept) risk and his or her "risk attitude," which might be considered as the client's willingness to take risk. For ease of expression, from this point on we will refer to ability to bear risk and willingness to take risk as the two components of risk tolerance. Above average ability to bear risk and above average willingness to take risk imply above average risk tolerance. Below average ability to bear risk and below average willingness to take risk imply below average risk tolerance. These interactions are shown in Exhibit 1.

Exhibit 1 Risk Tolerance

	Ability to Bear Risk	
Willingness to Take Risk	**Below Average**	**Above Average**
Below Average	Below-average risk tolerance	Resolution needed
Above Average	Resolution needed	Above-average risk tolerance

The *ability* to bear risk is measured mainly in terms of objective factors, such as time horizon, expected income, and the level of wealth relative to liabilities. For example, an investor with a 20-year time horizon can be considered to have a greater ability to bear risk, other things being equal, than an investor with a 2-year horizon. This difference is because over 20 years there is more scope for losses to be recovered or other adjustments to circumstances to be made than there is over two years.

Similarly, an investor whose assets are comfortably in excess of their liabilities has more ability to bear risk than an investor whose wealth and expected future expenditure are more closely balanced. For example, a wealthy individual who can sustain a comfortable lifestyle after a very substantial investment loss has a relatively high ability to bear risk. A pension plan that has a large surplus of assets over liabilities has a relatively high ability to bear risk.

The *willingness* to take risk, or risk attitude, is a more subjective factor based on the client's psychology and perhaps also his or her current circumstances. Although the list of factors that are related to an individual's risk attitude remains open to debate, it is believed that some psychological factors, such as personality type, self esteem, and inclination to independent thinking, are correlated with risk attitude. Some individuals are comfortable taking financial and investment risk, whereas others find it distressing. Although there is no single agreed-upon method for measuring risk tolerance, a willingness to take risk may be gauged by discussing risk with the client or by asking the client to complete a psychometric questionnaire. For example, financial planning academic John Grable and collaborators have developed 13-item and 5-item risk attitude questionnaires that have undergone some level of technical validation. The five-item questionnaire is shown in Exhibit 2.

Exhibit 2 A Five-Item Risk Assessment Instrument

1 Investing is too difficult to understand.

Exhibit 2 (Continued)

- **a** Strongly agree
- **b** Tend to agree
- **c** Tend to disagree
- **d** Strongly disagree

2 I am more comfortable putting my money in a bank account than in the stock market.

- **a** Strongly agree
- **b** Tend to agree
- **c** Tend to disagree
- **d** Strongly disagree

3 When I think of the word "risk" the term "loss" comes to mind immediately.

- **a** Strongly agree
- **b** Tend to agree
- **c** Tend to disagree
- **d** Strongly disagree

4 Making money in stocks and bonds is based on luck.

- **a** Strongly agree
- **b** Tend to agree
- **c** Tend to disagree
- **d** Strongly disagree

5 In terms of investing, safety is more important than returns.

- **a** Strongly agree
- **b** Tend to agree
- **c** Tend to disagree
- **d** Strongly disagree

Source: Grable and Joo (2004).

The responses, a), b), c), and d), are coded 1, 2, 3, and 4, respectively, and summed. The lowest score is 5 and the highest score is 20, with higher scores indicating greater risk tolerance. For two random samples drawn from the faculty and staff of large US universities (n = 406), the mean score was 12.86 with a standard deviation of 3.01 and a median (i.e., most frequently observed) score of 13.

Note that a question, such as the first one in Exhibit 2, indicates that risk attitude may be associated with non-psychological factors (such as level of financial knowledge and understanding and decision making style) as well as psychological factors.

The adviser needs to examine whether a client's ability to accept risk is consistent with the client's willingness to take risk. For example, a wealthy investor with a 20-year time horizon, who is thus able to take risk, may also be comfortable taking risk; in this case the factors are consistent. If the wealthy investor has a low willingness to take risk, there would be a conflict.

In the institutional context, there could also be conflict between ability and willingness to take risk. In addition, different stakeholders within the institution may take different views. For example, the trustees of a well-funded pension plan may desire a low-risk approach to safeguard the funding of the scheme and beneficiaries of the scheme may take a similar view. The sponsor, however, may wish a higher-risk/higher-return approach in an attempt to reduce future funding costs. When a trustee bears a fiduciary responsibility to pension beneficiaries and the interests of the pension sponsor and the pension beneficiaries conflict, the trustee should act in the best interests of the beneficiaries.

When ability to take risk and willingness to take risk are consistent, the investment adviser's task is the simplest. When ability to take risk is below average and willingness to take risk is above average, the investor's risk tolerance should be assessed as below average overall. When ability to take risk is above average but willingness is below average, the portfolio manager or adviser may seek to counsel the client and explain the conflict and its implications. For example, the adviser could outline the reasons why the client is considered to have a high ability to take risk and explain the likely consequences, in terms of reduced expected return, of not taking risk. The investment adviser, however, should not aim to change a client's willingness to take risk that is not a result of a miscalculation or misperception. Modification of elements of personality is not within the purview of the investment adviser's role. The prudent approach is to reach a conclusion about risk tolerance consistent with the lower of the two factors (ability and willingness) and to document the decisions made.

Example 2 is the first of a set that follows the analysis of an investment client through the preparation of the major elements of an IPS.

EXAMPLE 2

The Case of Henri Gascon: Risk Tolerance

Henri Gascon is an energy trader who works for a major French oil company based in Paris. He is 30-years old and married with one son, aged 5. Gascon has decided that it is time to review his financial situation and consults a financial adviser. The financial adviser notes the following aspects of Gascon's situation:

- Gascon's annual salary of €250,000 is more than sufficient to cover the family's outgoings.
- Gascon owns his apartment outright and has €1,000,000 of savings.
- Gascon perceives that his job is reasonably secure.
- Gascon has a good knowledge of financial matters and is confident that equity markets will deliver positive returns over the longer term.
- In the risk tolerance questionnaire, Gascon strongly disagrees with the statements that "making money in stocks and bonds is based on luck" and that "in terms of investing, safety is more important than returns."
- Gascon expects that most of his savings will be used to fund his retirement, which he hopes to start at age 50.

Based only on the information given, which of the following statements is *most* accurate?

A Gascon has a low ability to take risk, but a high willingness to take risk.

B Gascon has a high ability to take risk, but a low willingness to take risk.

C Gascon has a high ability to take risk, and a high willingness to take risk.

Solution:

C is correct. Gascon has a high income relative to outgoings, a high level of assets, a secure job, and a time horizon of 20 years. This information suggests a high *ability* to take risk. At the same time, Gascon is knowledgeable and confident about financial markets and responds to the questionnaire with answers that suggest risk tolerance. This result suggests he also has a high *willingness* to take risk.

EXAMPLE 3

The Case of Jacques Gascon: Risk Tolerance

Henri Gascon is so pleased with the services provided by the financial adviser, that he suggests to his brother Jacques that he should also consult the adviser. Jacques thinks it is a good idea. Jacques is a self-employed computer consultant also based in Paris. He is 40-years old and divorced with four children, aged between 12 and 16. The financial adviser notes the following aspects of Jacques' situation:

- Jacques' consultancy earnings average €40,000 per annum, but are quite volatile.
- Jacques is required to pay €10,000 per year to his ex-wife and children.
- Jacques has a mortgage on his apartment of €100,000 and €10,000 of savings.
- Jacques has a good knowledge of financial matters and expects that equity markets will deliver very high returns over the longer term.
- In the risk tolerance questionnaire, Jacques strongly disagrees with the statements "I am more comfortable putting my money in a bank account than in the stock market" and "When I think of the word "risk" the term "loss" comes to mind immediately."
- Jacques expects that most of his savings will be required to support his children at university.

Based on the above information, which statement is correct?

A Jacques has a low ability to take risk, but a high willingness to take risk.

B Jacques has a high ability to take risk, but a low willingness to take risk.

C Jacques has a high ability to take risk, and a high willingness to take risk.

Solution:

A is correct. Jacques does not have a particularly high income, his income is unstable, and he has reasonably high outgoings for his mortgage and maintenance payments. His investment time horizon is approximately two to six years given the ages of his children and his desire to support them at university. This finely balanced financial situation and short time horizon suggests a low ability to take risk. In contrast, his expectations for financial market returns and risk tolerance questionnaire answers suggest a high willingness to take risk. The financial adviser may wish to explain to Jacques how finely balanced his financial situation is and suggest that, despite his desire to take more risk, a relatively cautious portfolio might be the most appropriate approach to take.

2.2.2 *Return Objectives*

A client's return objectives can be stated in a number of ways. Similar to risk objectives, return objectives may be stated on an absolute or a relative basis.

As an example of an absolute objective, the client may want to achieve a particular percentage rate of return, for example, X percent. This could be a nominal rate of return or be expressed in real (inflation-adjusted) terms.

Alternatively, the return objective can be stated on a relative basis, for example, relative to a benchmark return. The benchmark could be an equity market index, such as the S&P 500 or the FTSE 100, or a cash rate of interest such as Libor. A relative return objective might be stated as, for example, a desire to outperform the benchmark index by one percentage point per year.

Some institutions also set their return objective relative to a peer group or universe of managers; for example, an endowment aiming for a return that is in the top 50 percent of returns of similar institutions, or a private equity mandate aiming for returns in the top quartile among the private equity universe. This objective can be problematic when limited information is known about the investment strategies or the returns calculation methodology being used by peers, and we must bear in mind the impossibility of *all* institutions being "above average." Furthermore, a good benchmark should be investable—that is, able to be replicated by the investor—and a peer benchmark typically does not meet that criterion.

In each case, the return requirement can be stated before or after fees. Care should be taken that the fee basis used is clear and understood by both the manager and client. The return can also be stated on either a pre- or post-tax basis when the investor is required to pay tax. For a taxable investor, the baseline is to state and analyze returns on an after-tax basis.

The return objective could be a required return—that is, the amount the investor needs to earn to meet a particular future goal—such as a certain level of retirement income.

The manager or adviser must ensure that the return objective is realistic. Care should be taken that client and manager are in agreement on whether the return objective is nominal (which is more convenient for measurement purposes) or real (i.e., inflation-adjusted, which usually relates better to the objective). It must be consistent with the client's risk objective (high expected returns are unlikely to be possible without high levels of risk) and also with the current economic and market environment. For example, 15 percent nominal returns might be possible when inflation is 10 percent, but will be unlikely when inflation is 3 percent.

When a client has unrealistic return expectations, the manager or adviser will need to counsel them about what is achievable in the current market environment and within the client's tolerance for risk.

EXAMPLE 4

The Case of Henri Gascon: Return Objectives

Having assessed his risk tolerance, Henri Gascon now begins to discuss his retirement income needs with the financial adviser. He wishes to retire at age 50, which is 20 years from now. His salary meets current and expected future expenditure requirements, but he does not expect to be able to make any additional pension contributions to his fund. Gascon sets aside €100,000 of his savings as an emergency fund to be held in cash. The remaining €900,000 is invested for his retirement.

Gascon estimates that a before-tax amount of €2,000,000 in today's money will be sufficient to fund his retirement income needs. The financial adviser expects inflation to average 2 percent per year over the next 20 years. Pension fund contributions and pension fund returns in France are exempt from tax, but pension fund distributions are taxable upon retirement.

1 Which of the following is closest to the amount of money Gascon will have to accumulate in nominal terms by his retirement date to meet his retirement income objective (i.e., expressed in money of the day in 20 years)?

 A €900,000

 B €2,000,000

 C €3,000,000

2 Which of the following is closest to the annual rate of return that Gascon must earn on his pension portfolio to meet his retirement income objective?

 A 2.0%

 B 6.2%

 C 8.1%

Solution to 1.

C is correct. At 2 percent annual inflation, €2,000,000 in today's money equates to €2,971,895 in 20 years measured in money of the day [$2\text{m} \times (1 + 2\%)^{20}$].

Solution to 2.

B is correct. €900,000 growing at 6.2 percent per year for 20 years will accumulate to €2,997,318, which is just above the required amount. (The solution of 6.2 percent comes from $€2{,}997{,}318/€900{,}000 = (1 + X)^{20}$, where X is the required rate of return.)

In the following sections, we analyze five major types of constraints on portfolio selection: liquidity, time horizon, tax concerns, legal and regulatory factors, and unique circumstances.

2.2.3 *Liquidity Requirements*

The IPS should state what the likely requirements are to withdraw funds from the portfolio. Examples for an individual investor would be outlays for covering healthcare payments or tuition fees. For institutions, it could be spending rules and requirements for endowment funds, the existence of claims coming due in the case of property and casualty insurance, or benefit payments for pension funds and life insurance companies.

When the client does have such a requirement, the manager should allocate part of the portfolio to cover the liability. This part of the portfolio will be invested in assets that are liquid—that is, easily converted to cash—and have low risk when the liquidity need is actually present (e.g., a bond maturing at the time when private education expenses will be incurred), so that their value is known with reasonable certainty. For example, the asset allocation in the insurance portfolios of US insurer Progressive Corporation (see Exhibit 3) shows a large allocation to fixed-income investments (called "Fixed maturities" by the company), some of which are either highly liquid or have a short maturity. These investments enable the company, in the case of automobile insurance, to pay claims for which the timing is unpredictable.

Exhibit 3 Asset Allocation of Progressive Corporation

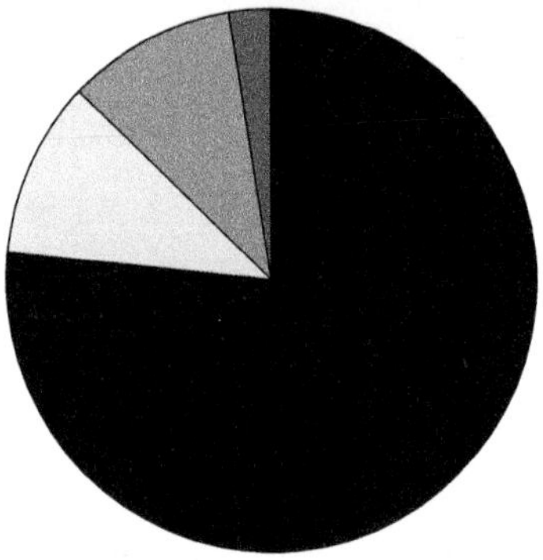

Source: Progressive Corporation, 2018 Second Quarter Report.

2.2.4 *Time Horizon*

The IPS should state the time horizon over which the investor is investing. It may be the period over which the portfolio is accumulating before any assets need to be withdrawn; it could also be the period until the client's circumstances are likely to change. For example, a 55-year-old pension plan investor hoping to retire at age 65 has a ten-year horizon. The portfolio may not be liquidated at age 65, but its structure may need to change, for example, as the investor begins to draw an income from the fund.

The time horizon of the investor will affect the nature of investments used in the portfolio. Illiquid or risky investments may be unsuitable for an investor with a short time horizon because the investor may not have enough time to recover from investment losses, for example. Such investments, however, may be suitable for an investor with a longer horizon, especially if the risky investments are expected to have higher returns.

EXAMPLE 5

Investment Time Horizon

1 Frank Johnson is investing for retirement and has a 20-year horizon. He has an average risk tolerance. Which investment is likely to be the *least* suitable for a major allocation in Johnson's portfolio?

   A Listed equities

   B Private equity

   C US Treasury bills

2 Al Smith has to pay a large tax bill in six months and wants to invest the money in the meantime. Which investment is likely to be the *least* suitable for a major allocation in Smith's portfolio?

   A Listed equities

   B Private equity

   C US Treasury bills

Solution to 1:

C is correct. With a 20-year horizon and average risk tolerance, Johnson can accept the additional risk of listed equities and private equity compared with US Treasury bills.

Solution to 2:

B is correct. Private equity is risky, has no public market, and is the least liquid among the assets mentioned.

2.2.5 *Tax Concerns*

Tax status varies among investors. Some investors will be subject to taxation on investment returns and some will not. For example, in many countries returns to pension funds are exempt from tax. Some investors will face a different tax rate on income (dividends and interest payments) than they do on capital gains (associated with increases in asset prices). Typically, when there is a differential, income is taxed more highly than gains. Gains may be subject to a lower rate of tax or part or all of the gain may be exempt from taxation. Furthermore, income may be taxed as it is earned, whereas gains may be taxed when they are realized. Hence, in such cases there is a time value of money benefit in the deferment of taxation of gains relative to income.

In many cases, the portfolio should reflect the tax status of the client. For example, a taxable investor may wish to hold a portfolio that emphasizes capital gains and receives little income. A taxable investor based in the United States is also likely to consider including U.S. municipal bonds ("munis") in his or her portfolio because interest income from munis, unlike from treasuries and corporate bonds, is exempt from taxes. A tax-exempt investor, such as a pension fund, will be relatively indifferent to the form of returns.

2.2.6 *Legal and Regulatory Factors*

The IPS should state any legal and regulatory restrictions that constrain how the portfolio is invested.

In some countries, such institutional investors as pension funds are subject to restrictions on the composition of the portfolio. For example, there may be a limit on the proportion of equities or other risky assets in the portfolio, or on the proportion of the portfolio that may be invested overseas. The United States has no limits on pension fund asset allocation but some countries do, examples of which are shown in Exhibit 4. Pension funds also often face restrictions on the percentage of assets that can be invested in securities issued by the plan sponsor, so called **self-investment limits**.

Exhibit 4 Examples of Pension Fund Investment Restrictions

Country	Listed Equity	Real Estate	Government Bonds	Corporate Bonds	Foreign Currency Exposure
Switzerland	50%	30%	100%	100%	Unhedged 30%
Japan	100%	Not permitted	100%	100%	No limits
South Africa	75%	25%	100%	75%	25%

Source: OECD 'Survey of Investment Regulations of Pension Funds', July 2018.

When an individual has access to material nonpublic information about a particular security, this situation may also form a constraint. For example, the directors of a public company may need to refrain from trading the company's stock at certain points of the year before financial results are published. The IPS should note this constraint so that the portfolio manager does not inadvertently trade the stock on the client's behalf.

2.2.7 *Unique Circumstances*

This section of the IPS should cover any other aspect of the client's circumstances, including beliefs and values, that is likely to have a material impact on the composition of the portfolio. A client may have considerations derived from his or her religion or ethical values that could constrain investment choices. For instance, an investor seeking compliance with Shari'a (the Islamic law) will avoid investing in businesses and financial instruments inconsistent with Shari'a, such as casinos and bonds, because Shari'a prohibits gambling and lending money on interest. Similarly, an investor may wish to avoid investments that he or she believes are inconsistent with their faith. Charitable and pension fund investors may have constituencies that want to express their values in an investment portfolio.

Whether rooted in religious beliefs or not, a client may have personal objections to certain products (e.g., weapons, tobacco, gambling) or practices (e.g., environmental impact of business activities, human impact of government policies, labor standards), which could lead to the exclusion of certain companies, countries, or types of securities (e.g., interest-bearing debt) from the investable universe as well as the client's benchmark. Such considerations are often referred to as ESG (environmental, social, governance), and investing in accordance with such considerations is referred to as SRI (socially responsible investing).

There are several implementation approaches in which ESG considerations can be expressed in an investment portfolio. The oldest form is **negative screening** (or **exclusionary screening**), which refers to the practice of excluding certain sectors or excluding companies that deviate from accepted standards or norms. Exclusion based on *values*, such as exclusion of gambling, alcohol and tobacco-related companies, relate to an investor's moral or ethical beliefs in a company's or sector's business. Exclusion based on standards and norms refers to business practices that an investor does not want to be associated with from either a reputational or financial risk point of view. These practices may include harmful production processes, corruption and land ownership issues.

Another common approach is **best-in-class**, whereby investors seek to identify companies within an industry that rank (or score) most favorably based on ESG considerations. Under this approach, investor portfolios would include only securities of those companies that exceed a certain threshold when evaluating ESG considerations. **Shareholder engagement** (sometimes call *active ownership*) is the practice of entering into a dialogue with companies (including with respect to ESG issues). Note that this is a different approach than best-in-class selection, where securities companies that do not meet investor standards are excluded. Generally speaking, the IPS should contain guidelines on shareholder voting behavior.

While exclusionary screening and best-in-class eliminate investment options, **thematic investing** and **impact investing** focus on investment in objectives, themes, and trends that relate positively to ESG issues. An example of a thematic investment (i.e., related to a business theme or societal trend) that considers ESG would be investments in alternative energy providers. In impact investing, an investment is selected primarily on its expected social or environmental benefits with measurable investment returns.

The final ESG implementation approach, **ESG integration**, refers to the integration of qualitative and quantitative ESG factors into traditional security and industry analysis. The focus of ESG integration is to identify risks and opportunities arising from ESG factors and to determine whether a company is properly managing its ESG resources in accordance with a sustainable business model. Examples of ESG integration may include potential earnings per share dilution due to a company's overly generous options program for key executives; a company's poor environmental safety or labor standards potentially resulting in a large future liability that affects the company's profitability and financial condition; or a company's technology leadership position in a certain production process technology may give a company a competitive advantage once new regulations come into place.

These ESG implementation approaches may impact a portfolio manager's investment universe and, in some cases, the manner in which investment management firms operate. The growth of ESG investing has resulted in the development of new investment management services, such as data providers specializing in quantitative and qualitative data on sustainability and governance aspects of businesses. Data quality, however, needs to be judged carefully in each case: disclosure standards differ across jurisdictions; data services companies may have limited coverage of a relevant investment universe; and data item definitions may differ. Nevertheless, the availability of such data makes it possible to estimate certain ESG considerations (e.g., the CO_2 footprint of an investment portfolio) and implement these considerations as a constraint in the portfolio construction process.

EXAMPLE 6

Ethical Preferences

The F&C Responsible UK Equity Growth Fund is designed for investors who wish to have ethical and environmental principles applied to the selection of their investments. The fund's managers apply both positive (characteristics to be emphasized in the portfolio) and negative (characteristics to be avoided in the portfolio) screening criteria:

Positive criteria

- Supplies the basic necessities of life (e.g., healthy food, housing, clothing, water, energy, communication, healthcare, public transport, safety, personal finance, education)
- Offers product choices for ethical and sustainable lifestyles (e.g. fair trade, organic)
- Improves quality of life through the responsible use of new technologies
- Shows good environmental management
- Actively addresses climate change (e.g., renewable energy, energy efficiency)
- Promotes and protects human rights
- Supports good employment practices
- Provides a positive impact on local communities
- Maintains good relations with customers and suppliers
- Applies effective anti-corruption controls
- Uses transparent communication

Negative criteria

- Tobacco production
- Alcohol production

- Gambling
- Violent material
- Manufacture and sale of weapons
- Unnecessary exploitation of animals
- Nuclear power generation
- Poor environmental practices
- Human rights abuses
- Poor relations with employees, customers or suppliers

[Excerpted from F&C documents; www.fandc.com/new/Advisor/Default.aspx?ID=79620.]

When the portfolio represents only part of the client's total wealth, there may be aspects or portions of wealth not under the control of the manager that have implications for the portfolio. For example, an employee of a public company whose labor income and retirement income provision are reliant on that company and who may have substantial investment exposure to the company through employee share options and stock holdings, may decide that their portfolio should not invest additional amounts in that stock. An entrepreneur may be reluctant to see his or her portfolio invested in the shares of competing businesses or in any business that has risk exposures aligned with his or her entrepreneurial venture.

A client's income may rely on a particular industry or asset class. Appropriate diversification requires that industry or asset class to be de-emphasized in the client's investments. For example, a stockbroker should consider having a relatively low weighting in equities, as his skills and thus income-generating ability are worth less when equities do not perform well. Employees should similarly be wary of having concentrated share positions in the equity of the company they work for. If the employer encounters difficulties, not only may the employee lose his or her job, but their investment portfolio could also suffer a significant loss of value.

2.3 Gathering Client Information

As noted above, it is important for portfolio managers and investment advisers to know their clients. For example, in the EU, MiFID II requires financial intermediaries to undertake substantial fact finding. This is required not only in the case of full service wealth management or in the context of an IPS, but also in "lighter" forms of financial intermediation, such as advisory relationships (in which clients make investment decisions after consultation with their investment adviser or broker) or execution-only relationships (in which the client makes his investment decisions independently).

An exercise in fact finding about the customer should take place at the beginning of the client relationship. This will involve gathering information about the client's circumstances as well as discussing the client's objectives and requirements.

Important data to gather from a client should cover family and employment situation as well as financial information. If the client is an individual, it may also be necessary to know about the situation and requirements of the client's spouse or other family members. The health of the client and his or her dependents is also relevant information. In an institutional relationship, it will be important to know about key stakeholders in the organization and what their perspective and requirements are. Information gathering may be done in an informal way or may involve structured interviews or questionnaires or analysis of data. Many advisers will capture data electronically and use special systems that record data and produce customized reports.

Good record keeping is very important, and may be crucial in a case in which any aspect of the client relationship comes into dispute at a later stage.

EXAMPLE 7

Henri Gascon: Description of Constraints

Henri Gascon continues to discuss his investment requirements with the financial adviser. The financial adviser begins to draft the constraints section of the IPS.

Gascon expects that he will continue to work for the oil company and that his relatively high income will continue for the foreseeable future. Gascon and his wife do not plan to have any additional children, but expect that their son will go to a university at age 18. They expect that their son's education costs can be met out of their salary income.

Gascon's emergency reserve of €100,000 is considered to be sufficient as a reserve for unforeseen expenditures and emergencies. His retirement savings of €900,000 has been contributed to his defined-contribution pension plan account to fund his retirement. Under French regulation, pension fund contributions are paid from gross income (i.e., income prior to deduction of tax) and pension fund returns are exempt from tax, but pension payments from a fund to retirees are taxed as income to the retiree.

With respect to Gascon's retirement savings portfolio, refer back to Example 2 as needed and address the following:

1 As concerns liquidity,
   - **A** a maximum of 50 percent of the portfolio should be invested in liquid assets.
   - **B** the portfolio should be invested entirely in liquid assets because of high spending needs.
   - **C** the portfolio has no need for liquidity because there are no short-term spending requirements.

2 The investment time horizon is closest to
   - **A** 5 years.
   - **B** 20 years.
   - **C** 40 years.

3 As concerns taxation, the portfolio
   - **A** should emphasize capital gains because income is taxable.
   - **B** should emphasize income because capital gains are taxable.
   - **C** is tax exempt and thus indifferent between income and capital gains.

4 The principle legal and regulatory factors applying to the portfolio are
   - **A** US Securities laws.
   - **B** European banking laws.
   - **C** French pension fund regulations.

5 As concerns unique needs, the portfolio should
   - **A** have a high weighting in oil and other commodity stocks.
   - **B** be invested only in responsible and sustainable investments.
   - **C** not have significant exposure to oil and other commodity stocks.

Solution to 1.

C is correct. The assets are for retirement use, which is 20 years away. Any short-term spending needs will be met from other assets or income.

Solution to 2.

B is correct. The relevant time horizon is to the retirement date, which is 20 years away. The assets may not be liquidated at that point, but a restructuring of the portfolio is to be expected as Gascon starts to draw an income from it.

Solution to 3.

C is correct. Because no tax is paid in the pension fund, it does not matter whether returns come in the form of income or capital gains.

Solution to 4.

C is correct. The management of the portfolio will have to comply with any rules relating the French pension funds.

Solution to 5.

C is correct. Gascon's human capital (i.e., future labor income) is affected by the prospects of the oil industry. If his portfolio has significant exposure to oil stocks, he would be increasing a risk exposure he already has.

Example 8, the final one based on Henri Gascon, shows how the information obtained from the fact-finding exercises might be incorporated into the objectives and constraints section of an IPS.

EXAMPLE 8

Henri Gascon: Outline of an IPS

Following is a simplified excerpt from the IPS the adviser prepares for Henri Gascon, covering objectives and constraints.

Risk Objectives:

- The portfolio may take on relatively high amounts of risk in seeking to meet the return requirements. With a 20-year time horizon and significant assets and income, the client has an above average ability to take risk. The client is a knowledgeable investor, with an above average willingness to take risk. Hence, the client's risk tolerance is above average, explaining the above portfolio risk objective.
- The portfolio should be well diversified with respect to asset classes and concentration of positions within an asset class. Although the client has above average risk tolerance, his investment assets should be diversified to control the risk of catastrophic loss.

Return Objectives:

- The portfolio's long-term return requirement is 6.2 percent per year, in nominal terms and net of fees, to meet the client's retirement income goal.

Constraints:

- *Liquidity*: The portfolio consists of pension fund assets and there is no need for liquidity in the short to medium term.
- *Time Horizon*: The portfolio will be invested with a 20-year time horizon. The client intends to retire in 20 years, at which time an income will be drawn from the portfolio.
- *Tax Status*: Under French law, contributions to the fund are made gross of tax and returns in the fund are tax-free. Hence, the client is indifferent between income and capital gains in the fund.
- *Legal and Regulatory Factors*: The management of the portfolio must comply with French pension fund regulations.
- *Unique Needs*: The client is executive in the oil industry. The portfolio should strive to minimize additional exposures to oil and related stocks.

PORTFOLIO CONSTRUCTION

3

Once the IPS has been compiled, the investment manager can construct a suitable portfolio. Strategic asset allocation is a traditional focus of the first steps in portfolio construction. The strategic asset allocation is stated in terms of percent allocations to asset classes. An **asset class** is a category of assets that have similar characteristics, attributes, and risk/return relationships. The **strategic asset allocation** (SAA) is the set of exposures to IPS-permissible asset classes that is expected to achieve the client's long-term objectives given the client's risk profile and investment constraints. An SAA could include a policy of hedging portfolio risks not explicitly covered by asset class weights. The obvious examples are hedge ratios for foreign currency exposure, or the management of interest rate risk resulting from asset-liability mismatch, and the hedging of inflation risk. So-called "overlay" portfolios of derivatives are often used for this purpose.

The focus on the SAA is the result of a number of important investment principles. One principle is that a portfolio's systematic risk accounts for most of its change in value over the long term. **Systematic risk** is risk related to the economic system (e.g., risk related to business cycle) that cannot be eliminated by holding a diversified portfolio. This risk is different from **nonsystematic risk**, which is the unique risks of particular assets, which may be avoided by holding other assets with offsetting risks. A second principle is that the returns to groups of similar assets (e.g., long-term debt claims) predictably reflect exposures to certain sets of systematic factors (e.g., for the debt claims, unexpected changes in the interest rate). Thus, the SAA is a means of providing the investor with exposure to the systematic risks of asset classes in proportions that meet the risk and return objectives.

The process of formulating a strategic asset allocation is based on the IPS, already discussed, and capital market expectations, introduced in Section 3.1. How to make the strategic asset allocation operational with a rebalancing policy and a translation into actual investment portfolios will be described in Section 3.3. Section 3.4 lists some alternatives to the approach chosen and describes some portfolio construction techniques.

3.1 Capital Market Expectations

Capital market expectations are the investor's expectations concerning the risk and return prospects of asset classes, however broadly or narrowly the investor defines those asset classes. When associated with the client's investment objectives, the result is the strategic asset allocation that is expected to allow the client to achieve his or her investment objectives (at least under normal capital market conditions).

Traditionally, capital market expectations are quantified in terms of asset class expected returns, standard deviation of returns, and correlations among pairs of asset classes. Formally, the expected return of an asset class consists of the risk-free rate and one or more risk premium(s) associated with the asset class. Expected returns are in practice developed in a variety of ways, including the use of historical estimates, economic analysis, and various kinds of valuation models. Standard deviations and correlation estimates are frequently based on historical data and risk models.

3.2 The Strategic Asset Allocation

Traditionally, investors have distinguished cash, equities, bonds (government and corporate), and real estate as the major asset classes. In recent years, this list has been expanded with private equity, hedge funds, high yield and emerging market bonds and commodities. In addition, such assets as art and intellectual property rights may be considered asset classes for those investors prepared to take a more innovative approach and to accept some illiquidity. Combining such new asset classes as well as hedge funds and private equity under the header "alternative investments" has become accepted practice.

As the strategic asset allocation is built up by asset classes, the decision about how to define those asset classes is an important one. Defining the asset classes also determines the extent to which the investor controls the risk and return characteristics of the eventual investment portfolio. For example, separating bonds into government bonds and corporate bonds, and then further separating corporate bonds into investment grade and non-investment grade (high yield) and government bonds into domestic and foreign government bonds, creates four bond categories for which risk–return expectations can be expressed and correlations with other asset classes (and, in an asset–liability management context, with the liabilities) can be estimated. An investment manager who wants to explicitly consider the risk–return characteristics of those bond categories in the strategic asset allocation may choose to treat them as distinct asset classes. Similarly, in equities some investors distinguish between emerging market and developed market equities, between domestic and international equities, or between large-cap and small-cap equities. In some regulatory environments for institutional investors, asset class definitions are mandatory, thereby forcing investment managers to articulate risk–return expectations (and apply risk management) on the asset classes specified. Conversely, a broader categorization of asset classes leaves the allocation between different categories of bonds and equities, for example, to managers responsible for these asset classes.

When defining asset classes, a number of criteria apply. Intuitively, an asset class should contain relatively homogeneous assets while providing diversification relative to other asset classes. In statistical terms, risk and return expectations should be similar and paired correlations of assets should be relatively high within an asset class but should be lower versus assets in other asset classes. Also, the asset classes, while being mutually exclusive, should add up to a sufficient approximation of the relevant investable universe. Applying these criteria ensures that the strategic asset allocation process has considered all available investment alternatives.

EXAMPLE 9

Specifying Asset Classes

The strategic asset allocations of many institutional investors make a distinction between domestic equities and international equities, or between developed market equities and emerging market equities. Often, equities are separated into different market capitalization brackets, resulting, for example, in an asset class such as domestic small-cap equity.

The correlation matrix in Exhibit 5 shows the paired correlations of monthly returns between different equity asset classes and other asset classes. Specifically, these correlations are measured over the period from December 2000 through August 2018. In addition, the exhibit shows the annualized volatility of monthly returns.

Exhibit 5 Asset Class Correlation Matrix

Correlations	US Equities	Emerging Markets	European Equities	Japanese Equities	US Small-Cap Equities	Commodities	European Gov't. Bonds	US Treasuries	US Credits	US High-Yield Credit
US Equities	1.00	0.78	0.88	0.59	0.89	0.32	0.08	−0.37	0.19	0.66
Emerging Markets Equities	0.78	1.00	0.84	0.64	0.75	0.46	0.21	−0.24	0.34	0.70
European Equities	0.88	0.84	1.00	0.64	0.79	0.43	0.16	−0.28	0.29	0.68
Japanese Equities	0.59	0.64	0.64	1.00	0.57	0.32	0.24	−0.18	0.29	0.52
US Small-Cap Equities	0.89	0.75	0.79	0.57	1.00	0.32	0.09	−0.36	0.19	0.69
Commodities	0.32	0.46	0.43	0.32	0.32	1.00	0.13	−0.18	0.12	0.36
European Gov't. Bonds	0.08	0.21	0.16	0.24	0.09	0.13	1.00	0.45	0.60	0.30
US Treasuries	−0.37	−0.24	−0.28	−0.18	−0.36	−0.18	0.45	1.00	0.58	−0.19
US Credits	0.19	0.34	0.29	0.29	0.19	0.12	0.60	0.58	1.00	0.54
US High-Yield Credit	0.66	0.70	0.68	0.52	0.69	0.36	0.30	−0.19	0.54	1.00
Volatility	14.3%	21.6%	18.4%	15.6%	18.4%	22.3%	4.9%	4.4%	5.5%	9.3%

Correlations and volatilities have been calculated using monthly returns from December 2000 through August 2018, unhedged, in USD.
Source: MSCI Bloomberg, S&P

Based only on the information given, address the following:

1 Contrast the correlations between equity asset classes with the correlations between equity asset classes and US Treasuries.

2 The monthly returns of which equity asset class differ the most from US equities?

Solution to 1:

The matrix reveals very strong correlation between the equity asset classes. For example, the correlation between European equities and US equities is 0.88. The correlation of equities with bonds, however, is much lower. For example, US equities, emerging markets equities, European equities, and Japanese equities all have negative correlation with US government bonds (–0.37, –0.24 and –0.28, and –0.18, respectively). It is worth noting, however, that correlations can vary through time and the values shown may be specific to the sample period used.

Solution to 2:

Among equity asset classes as listed in the table, the correlation between US and Japanese equities is the lowest, at 0.59. By contrast, correlations between US equities and emerging markets, European and US small cap equities are 0.78 or higher.

Using correlation as a metric, Example 9 tends to indicate that only emerging markets were well differentiated from European equities. So, why do investors still often subdivide equities? Apart from any regulatory reasons, one explanation might be that this decomposition into smaller asset classes corresponds to the way the asset allocation is structured in portfolios. Many investment managers have expertise exclusively in specific areas of the market, such as emerging market equities, US small-cap equity, or international investment-grade credit. Bringing the asset class definitions of the asset allocation in line with investment products actually available in the market may simplify matters from an organizational perspective.

The risk–return profile of the strategic asset allocation depends on the expected returns and risks of the individual asset classes, as well as the correlation between those asset classes. In general, adding assets classes with low correlation improves the risk–return trade-off (more return for similar risk). Typically, the strategic asset allocation for risk-averse investors will have a large weight in government bonds and cash, whereas those with more willingness and ability to take risk will have more of their assets in risky asset classes, such as equities and many types of alternative investments.

It is customary to represent asset classes using benchmarks and universes calculated by providers such as FTSE, MSCI or Bloomberg. An exclusionary screening or a best-in-class policy (discussed previously) limits the number of securities to choose from, potentially impacting the risk and expected return estimates for these asset classes. Some examples of exclusions may be controversial weaponry or tobacco companies, or investments in certain countries. When such exclusions apply, risk and return estimates based on non-traditional ("off-the-shelf") asset class benchmarks may not be applicable. Separate benchmark indices reflecting the exclusions may available from the providers to mitigate this issue.

ABP is the pension fund for the Dutch government sector employees. The fund offers teachers, police officers, the military and other civil servants a defined benefit pension plan, aiming for a pension of 70% of the average career real income for employees. As of the first quarter of 2018, ABP had €405 billion under management. The strategic asset allocation[6] as of this period is shown in Exhibit 6.

6 ABP defines an asset class category called "real assets," which contains asset classes (not fixed-income securities) that are expected to perform well in times of inflation, but considered a major risk. The use of the term "real assets" differs from the use elsewhere in the CFA curriculum.

Exhibit 6 Strategic Asset Allocation for ABP

Real assets	
Equities, developed countries	27%
Equities, emerging markets	9%
Real estate	10%
Private Equity	5%
Hedge Funds	4%
Commodities	5%
Infrastructure	3%
Total real assets	***63%***

Fixed income securities	
Government bonds	13%
Corporate bonds	13%
Inflation-linked bonds	8%
Emerging market bonds	3%
Total fixed income securities	***37%***
Total	100%

Source: ABP Quarterly Report Q1 2018

A strategic asset allocation results from combining the constraints and objectives articulated in the IPS and long-term capital market expectations regarding the asset classes. The strategic asset allocation or policy portfolio will subsequently be implemented into real portfolios. Exhibit 7 illustrates conceptually how investment objectives and constraints and long-term capital market expectations combine into a policy portfolio.

Exhibit 7 Strategic Asset Allocation Process

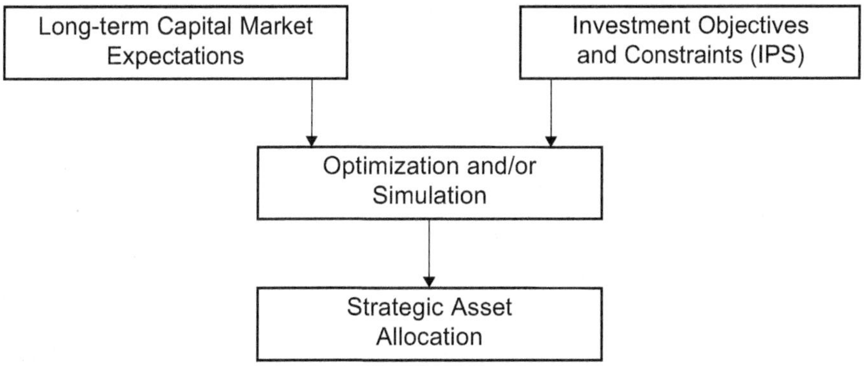

In some frameworks used in practice, the asset allocation is an integral part of the investment policy statement. This presentation, however, keeps the asset allocation separate from the investment policy statement because clients' investment objectives and constraints qualitatively differ in nature from capital market expectations, thus requiring different types of analysis, different sources of information, and different review cycles.

The combination of investment objectives/constraints and capital market expectations theoretically occurs using optimization techniques. In this section we apply mean–variance optimization to an sample set of investment objectives and constraints, using an investment universe with associated market expectations. We assume that investors choosing from a range of asset allocations with similar returns would prefer those with lower risk. Choosing from allocations with similar levels of risk, investors would prefer those with the highest return. Formally, investors' risk and return objectives can be described as a utility function, in which utility increases with higher expected returns and lower risk. This assumption could yield an expected utility equation such as that shown in Equation 1.[7]

$$U_p = E(R_p) - \lambda\sigma_p^2 \tag{1}$$

where

U_p = the investor's expected utility from the portfolio

$E(R_p)$ = the expected return of the portfolio

σ_p = the standard deviation of returns of the portfolio

λ = a measure of the investor's risk aversion

This utility function expresses a positive relationship between utility and expected portfolio return (i.e., higher expected return increases utility, all else equal) and a negative relationship between utility and volatility of portfolio return as measured by the variance of portfolio returns. The stronger the negative relationship, the greater the investor's risk aversion. The portfolio is understood to represent a particular asset allocation. The asset allocation providing the highest expected utility is the one that is optimal for the investor given his or her risk aversion.

For different values of U_p, a line can be plotted that links those combinations of risk and expected return that produces that level of utility: an indifference curve. An investor would attain equal utility from all risk/return combinations on that curve.

Capital market expectations, specified in asset classes' expected returns, standard deviations of return, and correlations, translate into an efficient frontier of portfolios. A multi-asset class portfolio's expected return is given by

$$E(R_p) = \sum_{i=1}^{n} w_i E(R_i) \tag{2}$$

where w_i equals the weight of asset class i in the portfolio, and its risk is given by

$$\sigma_p = \sqrt{\sum_{i=1}^{n}\sum_{j=1}^{n} w_{p,i} w_{p,j} \text{Cov}(R_i, R_j)} \tag{3}$$

The covariance between the returns on asset classes i and j is given by the product of the correlation between the two asset classes and their standard deviations of return:

$$\text{Cov}(R_i, R_j) = \rho_{i,j}\sigma_i\sigma_j \tag{4}$$

where

$\text{Cov}(R_i, R_j)$ = the covariance between the return of asset classes i and j

$\rho_{i,j}$ = the correlation between the returns of asset classes i and j

7 Sharpe, Chen, Pinto, and McLeavey (2007).

The resulting portfolios can be represented as a scatter of dots in a chart depicting their risk and expected return. As a portfolio's risk is a positive function of the risk of its assets and the correlations among them, a portfolio consisting of lowly correlated risky assets has lower risk than one with similarly risky assets with high correlation. It is therefore possible to construct different portfolios with equal expected returns but with different levels of risk. The line that connects those portfolios with the minimal risk for each level of expected return (above that of the **minimum-variance portfolio**—the portfolio with the minimum variance for each given level of expected return) is the efficient frontier. Clearly, the efficient frontier will move "upward" as more lowly correlated assets with sufficient expected return are added to the mix because it lowers the risk in the portfolios for equal expected returns. Similarly, when return expectations increase for asset classes while volatility and correlation assumptions remain unchanged, the efficient frontier will move upward because each portfolio is able to generate higher returns for the same level of risk.

Both the efficient frontier and a range of indifference curves can be plotted in the risk–return space. In Exhibit 8, the dark curves that are concave from below represent efficient frontiers associated with different assumed expected returns. The lighter colored curves are indifference curves. The point where the efficient frontier intersects with the indifference curve with the highest utility attainable (i.e., the point of tangency) represents the optimal asset allocation for the client/investor. In Exhibit 8, efficient frontier 1 has a point of tangency with indifference curve 1. Higher levels of utility, such as those associated with indifference curve 0, can apparently not be reached with the assets underlying the efficient frontier. It is clear that when capital market expectations change, this change moves the efficient frontier away from its original location. In the chart, this movement is illustrated by efficient frontier 2, which incorporates different capital market expectations. This new efficient frontier has a point of tangency with indifference curve 2, which is associated with a lower level of expected utility. Because the point of tangency represents the strategic asset allocation, it implies the asset allocation should be adjusted. Similarly, should investment objectives or constraints change, the indifference curves will change their shape and location. This change will again move the point of tangency, and hence change the asset allocation.

Exhibit 8 Strategic Asset Allocation Efficient Frontier

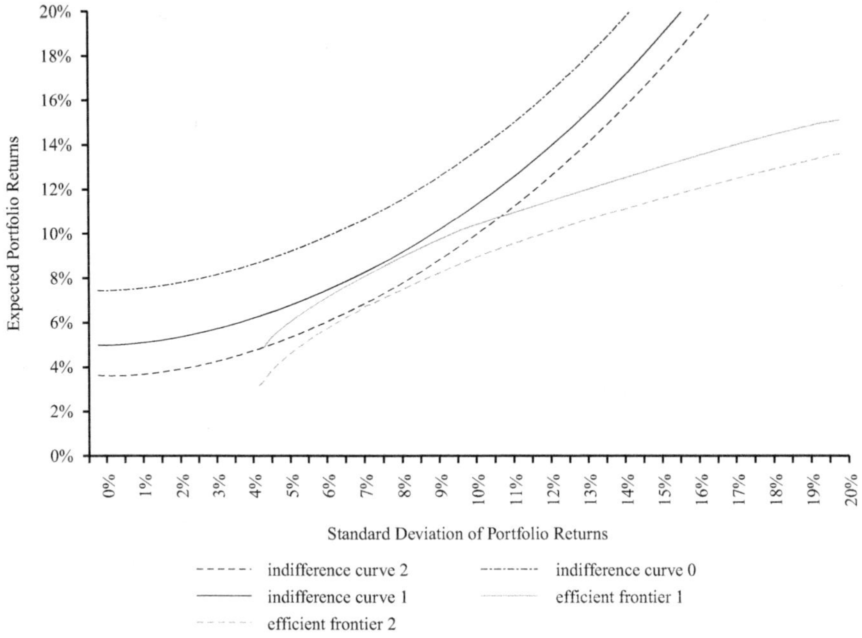

This framework describes how investor objectives and capital market expectations should theoretically be reconciled. It will, however, not be the exact procedure that in practice will be followed. First, an IPS does not necessarily translate the client's investment objectives and constraint into a utility function. Rather, an IPS gives threshold levels for risk and expected return, combined with a number of additional constraints that cannot be captured in this model. Second, the model illustrated is a single-period model, whereas in practice, the constraints from the IPS will make it more appropriate to use multi-period models. Multi-period problems can be more effectively addressed using simulation.

EXAMPLE 10

Approaching a SAA for a Private Investor

Rainer Gottschalk recently sold his local home construction company in the south of Germany to a large homebuilder with a nationwide reach. Upon selling his company, he accepted a job as regional manager for that nationwide homebuilder. He is now considering his and his family's financial future. He looks forward to his new job, where he likes his new role, and which provides him with income to fulfill his family's short-term and medium-term liquidity needs. He feels strongly that he should not invest the proceeds of the sale of his company in real estate because his income already depends on the state of the real estate market. Also, reflecting family values, he feels strongly his savings should not support the tobacco industry. He therefore wants his equity allocation to exclude any stocks of tobacco product manufacturers or retailers. He consults a financial adviser from his bank about how to invest his money to retire in good wealth in 20 years.

The IPS they develop suggests a return objective of 5 percent, with a standard deviation of 10 percent. The bank's asset management division provides Gottschalk and his adviser with the following data (Exhibit 9, Panel 1) on market expectations. The advisor estimates that excluding the tobacco industry from the investment universe affects expected equity returns of European equities by −0.2% and annual standard deviation by +0.1%. The impact on emerging market equities, and on the correlation structure, was considered negligible. Gottschalk accepts the results of these calculations as shown in Exhibit 9, Panel 2.

Exhibit 9 Risk, Return, and Correlation Estimates

			Correlation Matrix		
	Expected Return	Standard Deviation	European Equities	Emerging Mkt Equities	European Govt Bonds
Panel 1					
European equities	6.0%	15.0%	1.00	0.78	−0.08
Emerging market equities	8.0%	20.1%	0.78	1.00	−0.07
European government bonds	2.0%	7.8%	−0.08	−0.07	1.00
Panel 2					
European equities	5.8%	15.1%	1.00	0.78	−0.08
Emerging market equities	8.0%	20.1%	0.78	1.00	−0.07
European government bonds	2.00%	7.8%	−0.08	−0.07	1.00

Standard deviation and correlation calculated over the period March 1999–August 2018. All data in unhedged euros.
Sources: MSCI, Bloomberg

To illustrate the possibilities, the adviser presents Gottschalk with the following plot (Exhibit 10), in which the points forming the shaded curve outline the risk–return characteristics of the portfolios that can be constructed out of the three asset classes. An imaginary line linking the points with the lowest standard deviation for each attainable level of return would be the efficient frontier. The two straight lines show the risk and return objectives. Gottschalk should aim for portfolios that offer an expected return of at least 6 percent (the straight horizontal line or above) and a standard deviation of return of 12 percent or lower (the straight vertical line to the left).

Exhibit 10 Efficient Frontier

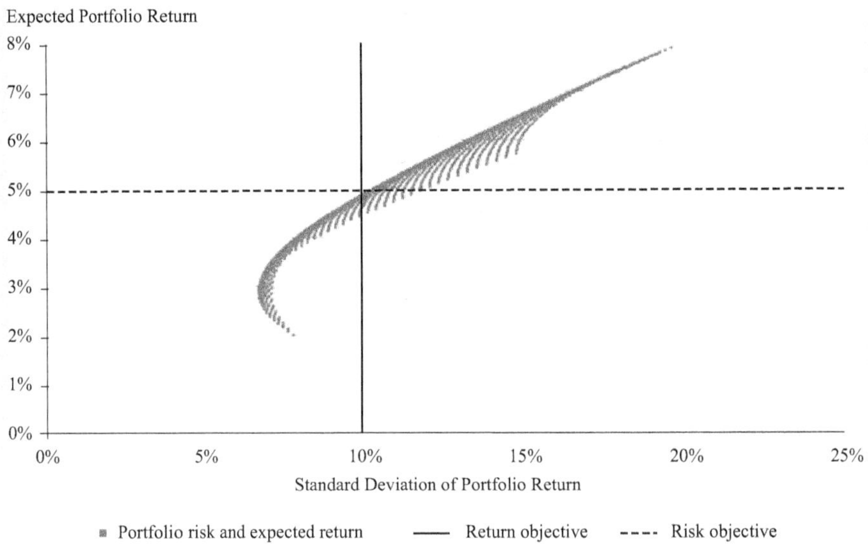

Exhibit 10 shows that no portfolio satisfies the two objectives (return of 5% and standard deviation of 10%) exactly, as the highest expected return that can be attained at a maximum volatility of 10% is 4.9%. This difference, Gottschalk and the advisor agree, is acceptable. The portfolio that would correspond with this expected return consists of 16 percent European stocks, 38 percent emerging market equities, and 46 percent government bonds.

3.3 Steps Toward an Actual Portfolio

The strategic asset allocation in itself does not yet represent an actual investment portfolio. It is the first step in implementing an investment strategy. For quantitatively oriented portfolio managers, the next step is often risk budgeting.

As used in this reading, **risk budgeting** is the process of deciding on the amount of risk to assume in a portfolio (the overall risk budget), and subdividing that risk over the sources of investment return (e.g., strategic asset allocation, tactical asset allocation, and security selection). Because the decision about the total amount of risk to be taken is made in constructing the IPS, at this stage we are concerned about the subdivision of that risk.

Apart from the exposures to systematic risk factors specified in the strategic asset allocation, the returns of an investment strategy depend on two other sources: tactical asset allocation and security selection. **Tactical asset allocation** is the decision to deliberately deviate from the policy exposures to systematic risk factors (i.e., the policy weights of asset classes) with the intent to add value based on forecasts of the near-term returns of those asset classes. For instance, an investor may decide to temporarily invest more of the portfolio in equities than the SAA prescribes if the investor anticipates that equities will deliver a higher return over the short term than other asset classes. **Security selection** is an attempt to generate higher returns than the asset class benchmark by selecting securities with a higher expected return. For example, an investment manager may decide to add more IBM stock in his portfolio than the weight in his equity benchmark if he expects this stock to do better than the benchmark. To fund this purchase, he may sell another stock expected to do worse than either the benchmark or IBM. Obviously, deciding to deviate from policy weights or to select securities aiming to beat the benchmark creates additional uncertainty about returns. This risk is over and above the risk inherent in the policy portfolio. Hence, an investment policy should set risk limits and desired payoffs for each of these three activities.

Risk budgeting implies that the portfolio manager has to choose, for every asset class, whether to deploy security selection as a return generator. This choice is generally referred to as the choice between active or passive management. Contrary to strategic asset allocation, where exposures to sources of systematic risk are selected and sized, security selection is not rewarded with a long-run payoff to risk. Security selection is a zero-sum game: All investors in an asset class are competing with each to identify a typically limited number of assets that are misvalued. In total, the gross returns of all market participants average out to the market return (the reward for taking systematic risk). This implies that the average active investor will match the market return, and that one investor's gain versus the market return is the other investor's loss versus the market return. However, because active managers tend to trade more and have to pay people (including themselves) to generate investment ideas or information leading to such ideas, the average active manager will underperform the market, net of costs. This does not imply, however, that there are no skillful investment managers who, with some consistency, beat their benchmarks. Neither does it imply that all passive managers will be able to match the benchmark. The higher the turnover of an index, the more trading costs a passive manager will incur, making the task of matching the return of an index more difficult.

The likelihood of adding a significant amount of value from security selection depends on the skills of the manager and the informational efficiency of the market for the asset class his skill relates to. The more efficient an asset class or a subset of that asset class (such as a regional stock, bond, or real estate market or a size category within the stock market), the more skillful an asset manager has to be to add value. Broadly speaking, an efficient market is a market in which prices, on average, very quickly reflect newly available information. That requires a sizeable participation of investors trading risk against expected return, acting on rational expectations, using the same or similar pricing models, and having equal opportunities to access relevant information. Clearly, the market for US large-capitalization equities would be quite efficient. By contrast, some regional bond and equity markets do not have the technical and regulatory systems for information dissemination that are sufficient to serve all investors on a timely basis. Skilled managers should be able to exploit the resulting inefficiencies.

Sometimes the choice between active and passive management is actually made implicitly when the asset class is included in the asset allocation. The markets for some assets—such as those for non-listed real estate and infrastructure assets—are so illiquid that it is very difficult to buy a diversified exposure. As a result, participating in that market is not possible without engaging in security selection.

As the portfolio is constructed and its value changes with the returns of the asset classes and securities in which it is invested, the weights of the asset classes will gradually deviate from the policy weights in the strategic asset allocation. This process is referred to as drift. Periodically, or when a certain threshold deviation from the policy weight (the bandwidth) has been breached, the portfolio should be rebalanced back to the policy weights. The set of rules that guide the process of restoring the portfolio's original exposures to systematic risk factors is known as the **rebalancing policy**. Even absent a formal risk budget, formulating a rebalancing policy is an important element of risk management, as the following example illustrates.

EXAMPLE 11

Strategic and Tactical Asset Allocation for a European Charity

A European charity has an asset allocation at the beginning of the year consisting of the asset classes and weights shown in Exhibit 11.

Exhibit 11 Asset Allocation of a European Charity (beginning of year)

Asset Class	Policy Weight	Corridor (+/–)	Upper Limit	Lower Limit
European equities	30.0%	2.0%	32.0%	28.0%
International equities	15.0%	2.0%	17.0%	13.0%
European government bonds	20.0%	2.0%	22.0%	18.0%
Corporate bonds	20.0%	2.0%	22.0%	18.0%
Cash and money market instruments	15.0%	2.0%	17.0%	13.0%
Total	100.0%			

As Exhibit 11 reveals, the charity has a policy that the asset class weights cannot deviate from the policy weights by more than 2 percent (the corridor). The resulting upper and lower limits for the asset class weights are shown in the rightmost columns of the table. There are two reasons for asset class actual weights to deviate from policy weights: by deliberate choice (tactical asset allocation or market timing) and as a result of divergence of the returns of the different asset classes (drift). In this example, the asset class weights start the year exactly in line with policy weights.

After half a year, the investment portfolio is as shown in Exhibit 12.

Exhibit 12 Asset Allocation for a European Charity (6 months later)

Asset Class	Policy Weight	Corridor (+/–)	Upper Limit	Lower Limit	Period Return	Ending Weight
European equities	30.0%	2.0%	32.0%	28.0%	15.0%	32.4%
International equities	15.0%	2.0%	17.0%	13.0%	10.0%	15.5%
European government bonds	20.0%	2.0%	22.0%	18.0%	0.5%	18.9%
Corporate bonds	20.0%	2.0%	22.0%	18.0%	1.5%	19.1%
Cash and money market instruments	15.0%	2.0%	17.0%	13.0%	1.0%	14.2%
Total	100.0%				6.6%	100.0%

1 Discuss the returns of the portfolio and comment on the main asset weight changes.

Solution to 1:

The investment portfolio generated a return calculated on beginning (policy) weights of 6.55 percent or 6.6 percent (= 0.30 × 15% + 0.15 × 10% + 0.20 × 0.5% + 0.20 × 1.5% + 0.15 × 1.0%), mainly driven by a strong equity market. Bond returns were more subdued, leading to considerable drift in asset class weights. In particular, the European equity weight breached the upper limit of its allowed actual weight.

The investment committee decides against reducing European equities back to policy weight and adding to the fixed income and cash investments toward policy weights. Although this rebalancing would be prudent, the committee decides to engage in tactical asset allocation based on the view that this market will continue to be strong over the course of the year. It decides to just bring European equities back to within its bandwidth (a 32 percent portfolio weight) and add the proceeds to cash. Exhibit 13 shows the outcome after another half year.

Exhibit 13 Asset Allocation for a European Charity (an additional 6 months later)

Asset Class	Policy Weight	Starting Weight	Corridor (+/–)	Upper Limit	Lower Limit	Period Return	Ending Weight
European equities	30.0%	32.0%	2.0%	32.0%	28.0%	–9.0%	29.7%
International equities	15.0%	15.5%	2.0%	17.0%	13.0%	–6.0%	14.9%
European government bonds	20.0%	18.9%	2.0%	22.0%	18.0%	4.0%	20.0%
Corporate bonds	20.0%	19.1%	2.0%	22.0%	18.0%	4.0%	20.2%
Cash and money market instruments	15.0%	14.6%	2.0%	17.0%	13.0%	2.0%	15.2%
Total	100.0%					–2.0%	100.0%

The prior decision not to rebalance to policy weights did not have a positive result. Contrary to the expectations of the investment committee, both European and international equities performed poorly while bonds recovered. The return of the portfolio was –2.0 percent.

2 How much of this return can be attributed to tactical asset allocation?

Solution to 2:

Because tactical asset allocation is the deliberate decision to deviate from policy weights, the return contribution from tactical asset allocation is equal to the difference between the actual return, and the return that would have been made if the asset class weights were equal to the policy weights. Exhibit 14 shows the difference to be –0.30 percent.

Exhibit 14 Returns to Tactical Asset Allocation

Asset Class	Policy Weight I	Starting Weight II	Weights Difference III (= II – I)	Period Return IV	TAA Contribution V(= III × IV)
European equities	30.0%	32.0%	2.0%	–9.0%	–0.18%
International equities	15.0%	15.5%	0.5%	–6.0%	–0.03%
European government bonds	20.0%	18.9%	–1.1%	4.0%	–0.05%
Corporate bonds	20.0%	19.1%	–0.9%	4.0%	–0.04%
Cash and money market instruments	15.0%	14.6%	–0.4%	2.0%	–0.01%
Total	100.0%			–2.0%	–0.30%

The process of executing an investment strategy continues with selecting the appropriate manager(s) for each asset class and allocating funds to them. The investment portfolio management process is then well into the execution stage.

The investment managers' performance will be monitored, as well as the results of the tactical and strategic asset allocation. When asset class weights move outside their corridors, money is transferred from the asset classes that have become too large compared with the SAA to those that fall short. Managers as well as the strategic asset allocation will be reviewed on the basis of the outcome of the monitoring process. In addition, capital market expectations may change, as may the circumstances and objectives of the client. These changes could result in an adjustment of the strategic asset allocation.

3.4 ESG Considerations in Portfolio Planning and Construction

The implementation of a policy on sustainable investing affects both strategic asset allocation and implementation of the portfolio construction process. The ESG implementation approaches described previously require a set of instructions for investment managers with regards to the selection of securities, the exercise of shareholder rights and the selection of investment strategies. Typical examples of ESG issues that help formulate a sustainable investing policy are shown in Exhibit 15.

Exhibit 15 Examples of ESG Issues

Environmental Issues	Social Issues	Governance Issues
■ Climate change and carbon emissions	■ Customer satisfaction	■ Board composition
■ Air and water pollution	■ Data protection and privacy	■ Audit committee structure
■ Biodiversity	■ Gender and diversity	■ Bribery and corruption
■ Deforestation	■ Employee engagement	■ Executive compensation
■ Energy efficiency	■ Community relations	■ Lobbying
■ Waste management	■ Human rights	■ Political contributions
■ Water scarcity	■ Labor standards	■ Whistleblower schemes

The list of ESG issues in Exhibit 15 is not exhaustive. Structured, numeric data can be processed for most of these issues (e.g., executive salaries and bonuses, carbon footprint, employee turnover, and employee absenteeism). However, such data is often not required to be disclosed by companies. Many organizations and regulatory bodies have derived frameworks setting out standards on a number of these issues—examples include the Principles of Responsible Investment, the UN Global Compact, and the OECD Guidelines for Multinational Enterprises. Such standards help form the basis of SRI policies for asset owners. In turn, asset owners may exclude or engage with companies in accordance with these issues, or demand from their selected investment managers consider these issues in their investment process.

We previously discussed that the limitation in the investment universe using either exclusionary screening or best-in-class policies affects the expected returns and risk. When selecting or instructing active or passive managers, these managers will clearly want to see their performance measured against a benchmark that reflects the limited universe. There are benchmarks and investment vehicles (both active and passive) available, particularly in equities, that reflect many commonly excluded companies or sectors. For best-in-class inclusion policy, there is no established set of broadly agreed rules; thus asset management products associated with such a policy are customized.

Shareholder engagement requires good cooperation between investor (client) and investment manager. Engagement efforts are time-consuming and the interest in such efforts is often that of clients, rather than that of the investment managers. Clients and investment managers have to be clear with each other about the exercise of voting rights, filing shareholder proposals or entering into conversations with company management. It may be that the engagement and voting is delegated by the client to the investment manager and implemented according to the manager's stewardship policy. Alternatively, the client may instruct some proxy agent to vote on its behalf and according to its own stewardship policies.

Selecting thematic investments, particularly in liquid asset classes, requires finding specialist managers who can identify the right opportunities and manage thematic investment portfolios. In particular, an allocation to thematic investments will bias the total asset class portfolio towards a particular theme, so it is important for the investment manager to demonstrate the impact of the thematic investment on the total risk-return profile of the portfolio. Impact investing specifically selects investment opportunities based on their potential to positively affect ESG issues.

The effort and costs associated with limiting the investment universe as part of sustainable investing suggests a negative impact on investment returns. Sustainable investing proponents argue, however, that potential improvements in governance and the avoidance of risks by companies that screen favorably improve returns. Significant empirical research has been conducted on the performance of ESG factors in equities, including the return differences of ESG equity portfolios relative to mainstream equity portfolios. Academic research remains mixed on the impact of ESG factors on portfolio returns.

3.5 Alternative Portfolio Organizing Principles

The portfolio planning and construction framework presented so far relies on a somewhat rigid process. Nonetheless, there are two newer, less structured developments that deserve specific mention.

The first development is the growth in the offering of exchange traded funds, or ETFs, in combination with algorithm-based financial advice (or robo-advice). ETFs are funds that track the performance of an asset class index or sub-index, are easily tradeable and relatively cheap compared to actively managed funds or managed accounts. The broad array of ETF offerings, covering the main equity and fixed income indices as well as commodities, enable retail investors to obtain fast, inexpensive, and liquid exposure to asset classes. Robo-advice has further reduced the costs for retail investors to create a well-diversified portfolio.

The second development relates to criticism of asset class return forecasts over relevant time horizons, and the perceived instability of asset class correlations and volatilities. Some market participants argue that poor investment portfolio results reflect the sensitivity of modern portfolio theory-based portfolio construction methodologies to small errors in return forecasts or estimated correlations. In response, practitioners developed an investment approach where asset classes were weighted according to risk contribution. This approach is known as *risk parity investing.* Proponents of risk parity investing argue that traditionally constructed portfolios have considerable risk from equities. That is, the typically high (60% or more) weight of equities in institutional portfolios understates the risk impact: equities tend to be much more volatile than fixed income. Opponents of risk parity argue that following the global financial crisis of 2007–2009, favorable results of risk parity portfolios were caused by the long period of decline in interest rates that benefited bond market performance.

4 CONCLUSION AND SUMMARY

In this reading, we have discussed construction of a client's investment policy statement, including discussion of risk and return objectives and the various constraints that will apply to the portfolio. We have also discussed the portfolio construction process, with emphasis on the strategic asset allocation decisions that must be made.

- The IPS is the starting point of the portfolio management process. Without a full understanding of the client's situation and requirements, it is unlikely that successful results will be achieved.
- The IPS can take a variety of forms. A typical format will include the client's investment objectives and also list the constraints that apply to the client's portfolio.
- The client's objectives are specified in terms of risk tolerance and return requirements.
- The constraints section covers factors that need to be considered when constructing a portfolio for the client that meets the objectives. The typical constraint categories are liquidity requirements, time horizon, regulatory requirements, tax status, and unique needs.
- Clients may have personal objections to certain products or practices, which could lead to the exclusion of certain companies, countries, or types of securities from the investable universe as well as the client's benchmark. Such considerations are often referred to as ESG (environmental, social, governance).
- ESG considerations can be integrated into an investment policy by exclusionary screening, best-in-class selection, active ownership, thematic and impact investing and ESG integration in security analysis.
- Risk objectives are specifications for portfolio risk that reflect the risk tolerance of the client. Quantitative risk objectives can be absolute or relative or a combination of the two.
- The client's overall risk tolerance is a function of the client's ability to accept risk and their "risk attitude," which can be considered the client's willingness to take risk.

- The client's return objectives can be stated on an absolute or a relative basis. As an example of an absolute objective, the client may want to achieve a particular percentage rate of return. Alternatively, the return objective can be stated on a relative basis, for example, relative to a benchmark return.
- The liquidity section of the IPS should state what the client's requirements are to draw cash from the portfolio.
- The time horizon section of the IPS should state the time horizon over which the investor is investing. This horizon may be the period during which the portfolio is accumulating before any assets need to be withdrawn.
- Tax status varies among investors and a client's tax status should be stated in the IPS.
- The IPS should state any legal or regulatory restrictions that constrain the investment of the portfolio.
- The unique circumstances section of the IPS should cover any other aspect of a client's circumstances that is likely to have a material impact on the composition of the portfolio. Certain ESG implementation approaches, such as negative (exclusionary) screening, best-in-class, thematic investing, impact investing, and ESG integration may be discussed in this section.
- Asset classes are the building blocks of an asset allocation. An asset class is a category of assets that have similar characteristics, attributes, and risk/return relationships. Traditionally, investors have distinguished cash, equities, bonds, and real estate as the major asset classes.
- A strategic asset allocation results from combining the constraints and objectives articulated in the IPS and capital market expectations regarding the asset classes.
- As time goes on, a client's asset allocation will drift from the target allocation, and the amount of allowable drift as well as a rebalancing policy should be formalized.
- In addition to taking systematic risk, an investment committee may choose to take tactical asset allocation risk or security selection risk. The amount of return attributable to these decisions can be measured.
- ESG considerations may be integrated into the portfolio planning and construction process. Such considerations can be difficult given that ESG data is often not required to be disclosed by companies. ESG implementation approaches require a set of instructions for investment managers with regards to the selection of securities, the exercise of shareholder rights and the selection of investment strategies.

REFERENCES

Grable, John E., and Soo-Hyun Joo. 2004. "Environmental and Biopsychosocial Factors Associated with Financial Risk Tolerance." *Financial Counseling and Planning* 15 (1): 73–82.

Sharpe, William F., Peng Chen, Jerald E. Pinto, and Dennis W. McLeavey. 2007. "Asset Allocation." In *Managing Investment Portfolios: A Dynamic Process*. 3rd ed. New York: Wiley.

Waring, M. Barton, and Laurence B. Siegel. 2003. "The Dimensions of Active Management." *Journal of Portfolio Management* 29 (3): 35–51.

Waring, M. Barton, Duane Whitney, John Pirone, and Charles Castille. 2000. "Optimizing Manager Structure and Budgeting Manager Risk." *Journal of Portfolio Management* 26 (3): 90–104.

PRACTICE PROBLEMS

1 Which of the following is *least* important as a reason for a written investment policy statement (IPS)?

A The IPS may be required by regulation.

B Having a written IPS is part of best practice for a portfolio manager.

C Having a written IPS ensures the client's risk and return objectives can be achieved.

2 Which of the following *best* describes the underlying rationale for a written investment policy statement (IPS)?

A A written IPS communicates a plan for trying to achieve investment success.

B A written IPS provides investment managers with a ready defense against client lawsuits.

C A written IPS allows investment managers to instruct clients about the proper use and purpose of investments.

3 A written investment policy statement (IPS) is *most* likely to succeed if:

A it is created by a software program to assure consistent quality.

B it is a collaborative effort of the client and the portfolio manager.

C it reflects the investment philosophy of the portfolio manager.

4 The section of the investment policy statement (IPS) that provides information about how policy may be executed, including investment constraints, is *best* described as the:

A *Investment Objectives.*

B *Investment Guidelines.*

C *Statement of Duties and Responsibilities.*

5 Which of the following is *least* likely to be placed in the appendices to an investment policy statement (IPS)?

A *Rebalancing Policy.*

B *Strategic Asset Allocation.*

C *Statement of Duties and Responsibilities.*

6 Which of the following typical topics in an investment policy statement (IPS) is *most* closely linked to the client's "distinctive needs"?

A *Procedures.*

B *Investment Guidelines.*

C *Statement of Duties and Responsibilities.*

7 An investment policy statement that includes a return objective of outperforming the FTSE 100 by 120 basis points is *best* characterized as having a(n):

A relative return objective.

B absolute return objective.

C arbitrage-based return objective.

8 Risk assessment questionnaires for investment management clients are *most* useful in measuring:

A value at risk.

B ability to take risk.

C willingness to take risk.

9 Which of the following is *best* characterized as a relative risk objective?

A Value at risk for the fund will not exceed US$3 million.

B The fund will not underperform the DAX by more than 250 basis points.

C The fund will not lose more than €2.5 million in the coming 12-month period.

10 In preparing an investment policy statement, which of the following is *most* difficult to quantify?

A Time horizon.

B Ability to accept risk.

C Willingness to accept risk.

11 After interviewing a client in order to prepare a written investment policy statement (IPS), you have established the following:

- The client has earnings that vary dramatically between £30,000 and £70,000 (pre-tax) depending on weather patterns in Britain.
- In three of the previous five years, the after-tax income of the client has been less than £20,000.
- The client's mother is dependent on her son (the client) for approximately £9,000 per year support.
- The client's own subsistence needs are approximately £12,000 per year.
- The client has more than 10 years' experience trading investments including commodity futures, stock options, and selling stock short.
- The client's responses to a standard risk assessment questionnaire suggest he has above average risk tolerance.

The client is *best* described as having a:

A low ability to take risk, but a high willingness to take risk.

B high ability to take risk, but a low willingness to take risk.

C high ability to take risk and a high willingness to take risk.

12 After interviewing a client in order to prepare a written investment policy statement (IPS), you have established the following:

- The client has earnings that have exceeded €120,000 (pre-tax) each year for the past five years.
- She has no dependents.
- The client's subsistence needs are approximately €45,000 per year.
- The client states that she feels uncomfortable with her lack of understanding of securities markets.
- All of the client's current savings are invested in short-term securities guaranteed by an agency of her national government.
- The client's responses to a standard risk assessment questionnaire suggest she has low risk tolerance.

The client is *best* described as having a:

A low ability to take risk, but a high willingness to take risk.

B high ability to take risk, but a low willingness to take risk.

C high ability to take risk and a high willingness to take risk.

13 A client who is a 34-year old widow with two healthy young children (aged 5 and 7) has asked you to help her form an investment policy statement. She has been employed as an administrative assistant in a bureau of her national government for the previous 12 years. She has two primary financial goals—her retirement and providing for the college education of her children. This client's time horizon is *best* described as being:

A long term.

B short term.

C medium term.

14 The timing of payouts for property and casualty insurers is unpredictable ("lumpy") in comparison with the timing of payouts for life insurance companies. Therefore, in general, property and casualty insurers have:

A lower liquidity needs than life insurance companies.

B greater liquidity needs than life insurance companies.

C a higher return objective than life insurance companies.

15 A client who is a director of a publicly listed corporation is required by law to refrain from trading that company's stock at certain points of the year when disclosure of financial results are pending. In preparing a written investment policy statement (IPS) for this client, this restriction on trading:

A is irrelevant to the IPS.

B should be included in the IPS.

C makes it illegal for the portfolio manager to work with this client.

16 Consider the pairwise correlations of monthly returns of the following asset classes:

	Brazilian Equities	East Asian Equities	European Equities	US Equities
Brazilian equities	1.00	0.70	0.85	0.76
East Asian equities	0.70	1.00	0.91	0.88
European equities	0.85	0.91	1.00	0.90
US equities	0.76	0.88	0.90	1.00

Based solely on the information in the above table, which equity asset class is *most* sharply distinguished from US equities?

A Brazilian equities.

B European equities.

C East Asian equities.

17 Returns on asset classes are *best* described as being a function of:

A the failure of arbitrage.

B exposure to the idiosyncratic risks of those asset classes.

C exposure to sets of systematic factors relevant to those asset classes.

18 In defining asset classes as part of the strategic asset allocation decision, pairwise correlations within asset classes should generally be:

A equal to correlations among asset classes.

B lower than correlations among asset classes.

C higher than correlations among asset classes.

19 Tactical asset allocation is *best* described as:

A attempts to exploit arbitrage possibilities among asset classes.

B the decision to deliberately deviate from the policy portfolio.

C selecting asset classes with the desired exposures to sources of systematic risk in an investment portfolio.

SOLUTIONS

1 C is correct. Depending on circumstances, a written IPS or its equivalent may be required by law or regulation and a written IPS is certainly consistent with best practices. The mere fact that a written IPS is prepared for a client, however, does not *ensure* that risk and return objectives will in fact be achieved.

2 A is correct. A written IPS is best seen as a communication instrument allowing clients and portfolio managers to mutually establish investment objectives and constraints.

3 B is correct. A written IPS, to be successful, must incorporate a full understanding of the client's situation and requirements. As stated in the reading, "The IPS will be developed following a fact finding discussion with the client."

4 B is correct. The major components of an IPS are listed in Section 2.2 of the reading. *Investment Guidelines* are described as the section that provides information about how policy may be executed, including investment constraints. *Statement of Duties and Responsibilities* "detail[s] the duties and responsibilities of the client, the custodian of the client's assets, the investment managers, and so forth." *Investment Objectives* is "a section explaining the client's objectives in investing."

5 C is correct. The major components of an IPS are listed in Section 2.2 of the reading. Strategic Asset Allocation (also known as the policy portfolio) and Rebalancing Policy are often included as appendices to the IPS. The *Statement of Duties and Responsibilities*, however, is an integral part of the IPS and is unlikely to be placed in an appendix.

6 B is correct. According to the reading, "The sections of an IPS that are most closely linked to the client's distinctive needs are those dealing with investment objectives and constraints." *Investment Guidelines* "[provide] information about how policy may be executed, including investment constraints." *Procedures* "[detail] the steps to be taken to keep the IPS current and the procedures to follow to respond to various contingencies." *Statement of Duties and Responsibilities* "detail[s] the duties and responsibilities of the client, the custodian of the client's assets, the investment managers, and so forth."

7 A is correct. Because the return objective specifies a target return *relative to* the FTSE 100 Index, the objective is best described as a relative return objective.

8 C is correct. Risk attitude is a subjective factor and measuring risk attitude is difficult. Oftentimes, investment managers use psychometric questionnaires, such as those developed by Grable and Joo (2004), to assess a client's willingness to take risk.

9 B is correct. The reference to the DAX marks this response as a relative risk objective. Value at risk establishes a minimum value of loss expected during a specified time period at a given level of probability. A statement of maximum allowed absolute loss (€2.5 million) is an absolute risk objective.

10 C is correct. Measuring willingness to take risk (risk tolerance, risk aversion) is an exercise in applied psychology. Instruments attempting to measure risk attitudes exist, but they are clearly less objective than measurements of ability to take risk. Ability to take risk is based on relatively objective traits such as expected income, time horizon, and existing wealth relative to liabilities.

11 A is correct. The volatility of the client's income and the significant support needs for his mother and himself suggest that the client has a low ability to take risk. The client's trading experience and his responses to the risk assessment questionnaire indicate that the client has an above average willingness to take risk.

12 B is correct. On the one hand, the client has a stable, high income and no dependents. On the other hand, she exhibits above average risk aversion. Her ability to take risk is high, but her willingness to take risk is low.

13 A is correct. The client's financial objectives are long term. Her stable employment indicates that her immediate liquidity needs are modest. The children will not go to college until 10 or more years later. Her time horizon is best described as being long term.

14 B is correct. The unpredictable nature of property and casualty (P&C) claims forces P&C insurers to allocate a substantial proportion of their investments into liquid, short maturity assets. This need for liquidity also forces P&C companies to accept investments with relatively low expected returns. Liquidity is of less concern to life insurance companies given the greater predictability of life insurance payouts.

15 B is correct. When a client has a restriction in trading, such as this obligation to refrain from trading, the IPS "should note this constraint so that the portfolio manager does not inadvertently trade the stock on the client's behalf."

16 A is correct. The correlation between US equities and Brazilian equities is 0.76. The correlations between US equities and East Asian equities and the correlation between US equities and European equities both exceed 0.76. Lower correlations indicate a greater degree of separation between asset classes. Therefore, using solely the data given in the table, returns on Brazilian equities are most sharply distinguished from returns on US equities.

17 C is correct. Strategic asset allocation depends on several principles. As stated in the reading, "One principle is that a portfolio's systematic risk accounts for most of its change in value over the long run." A second principle is that, "the returns to groups of like assets… predictably reflect exposures to certain sets of systematic factors." This latter principle establishes that returns on asset classes primarily reflect the systematic risks of the classes.

18 C is correct. As the reading states, "an asset class should contain homogeneous assets… paired correlations of securities would be high within an asset class, but should be lower versus securities in other asset classes."

19 B is correct. Tactical asset allocation allows actual asset allocation to deviate from that of the strategic asset allocation (policy portfolio) of the IPS. Tactical asset allocation attempts to take advantage of temporary dislocations from the market conditions and assumptions that drove the policy portfolio decision.

READING

55

Introduction to Risk Management

by Don M. Chance, PhD, CFA, and Michael E. Edleson, PhD, CFA

Don M. Chance, PhD, CFA, is at Louisiana State University (USA). Michael E. Edleson, PhD, CFA, is at the University of Chicago (USA).

LEARNING OUTCOMES

Mastery	The candidate should be able to:
☐	a. define risk management;
☐	b. describe features of a risk management framework;
☐	c. define risk governance and describe elements of effective risk governance;
☐	d. explain how risk tolerance affects risk management;
☐	e. describe risk budgeting and its role in risk governance;
☐	f. identify financial and non-financial sources of risk and describe how they may interact;
☐	g. describe methods for measuring and modifying risk exposures and factors to consider in choosing among the methods.

INTRODUCTION

1

Risk—and risk management—is an inescapable part of economic activity. People generally manage their affairs to be as happy and secure as their environment and resources will allow. But regardless of how carefully these affairs are managed, there is risk because the outcome, whether good or bad, is seldom predictable with complete certainty. There is risk inherent in nearly everything we do, but this reading will focus on economic and financial risk, particularly as it relates to investment management.

All businesses and investors manage risk, whether consciously or not, in the choices they make. At its core, business and investing are about allocating resources and capital to chosen risks. In their decision process, within an environment of uncertainty, these organizations may take steps to avoid some risks, pursue the risks that provide the highest rewards, and measure and mitigate their exposure to these risks as necessary. Risk management processes and tools make difficult business and financial problems easier to address in an uncertain world. Risk is not just a matter of fate; it is something that organizations can actively manage with their decisions, within a risk management framework. Risk is an integral part of the business or investment process. Even in the earliest models of modern portfolio theory, such as mean–variance portfolio optimization and the capital asset pricing model, investment return is linked directly to risk but requires that risk be managed optimally. Proper identification and measurement of risk, and keeping risks aligned with the goals of the enterprise, are key factors in managing businesses and investments. Good risk management results in a higher chance of a preferred outcome—more value for the company or portfolio or more utility for the individual.

Portfolio managers need to be familiar with risk management not only to improve the portfolio's risk–return outcome, but also because of two other ways in which they use risk management at an enterprise level. First, they help to manage their own companies that have their own enterprise risk issues. Second, many portfolio assets are claims on companies that have risks. Portfolio managers need to evaluate the companies' risks and how those companies are addressing them.

This reading takes a broad approach that addresses both the risk management of enterprises in general and portfolio risk management. The principles underlying portfolio risk management are generally applicable to the risk management of financial and non-financial institutions as well.

The concept of risk management is also relevant to individuals. Although many large organizations formally practice risk management, most individuals practice it more informally and some practice it haphazardly, oftentimes responding to risk events after they occur. Although many individuals do take reasonable precautions against unwanted risks, these precautions are often against obvious risks. The more subtle risks are often ignored. Unfortunately, many individuals do not view risk management as a formal, systematic process that would help them achieve not only their financial goals but also the ultimate goal, or maximum utility as economists like to call it, but they should.

Although the primary focus of this reading is on institutions, we will also cover risk management as it applies to individuals. We will show that many common themes underlie risk management—themes that are applicable to both organizations and individuals.

Although often viewed as defensive, risk management is a valuable offensive weapon in the manager's arsenal. In the quest for preferred outcomes, such as higher profit, returns, or share price, management does not usually get to choose the outcomes but does choose the risks it takes in pursuit of those outcomes. The choice of which risks to undertake through the allocation of its scarce resources is the key tool available to management. An organization with a comprehensive risk management culture in place, in which risk is integral to every key strategy and decision, should perform better in the long-term, in good times and bad, as a result of better decision making.

The fact that all businesses and investors engage in risky activities (i.e., activities with uncertain outcomes) raises a number of important questions. The questions that this reading will address include the following:

- What is risk management, and why is it important?
- What risks does an organization (or individual) face in pursuing its objectives?
- How are an organization's goals affected by risk, and how does it make risk management decisions to produce better results?
- How does risk governance guide the risk management process and risk budgeting to integrate an organization's goals with its activities?
- How does an organization measure and evaluate the risks it faces, and what tools does it have to address these risks?

The answers to these questions collectively help to define the process of risk management. This reading is organized along the lines of these questions. Section 2 describes the risk management process, and Section 3 discusses risk governance and risk tolerance. Section 4 covers the identification of various risks, and Section 5 addresses the measurement and management of risks. Section 6 provides a summary.

THE RISK MANAGEMENT PROCESS

2

Risk, broadly speaking, is exposure to uncertainty. Risk is also the concept used to describe all of the uncertain environmental variables that lead to variation in and unpredictability of outcomes. More colloquially, risk is about the chance of a loss or adverse outcome as a result of an action, inaction, or external event.

This last view may make it sound as if risk is something to be avoided. But that is not at all the case. Risk is a key ingredient in the recipe for business or investment success; return without risk is generally a false hope and usually a prescription for falling short of one's goals. Risks taken must be carefully chosen, understood, and well-managed to have a chance at adding value through decisions. Risk and return are the interconnected forces of the financial universe. Many decision makers focus on return, which is not something that is easily controlled, as opposed to risk, or exposure to risk, which may actually be managed or controlled.

Risk exposure is the extent to which the underlying environmental or market risks result in actual risk borne by a business or investor who has assets or liabilities that are sensitive to those risks. It is the state of being exposed or vulnerable to a risk. Risk exposure results from the decisions of an organization or investor to take on risk-sensitive assets and liabilities.

Suppose there is an important announcement in Japan that will result in the yen either appreciating or depreciating by 1%. The range of possible outcomes in real situations is clearly not as simple as the up-or-down 1% case used here, but we will use a simplified example to make an important point. The risk is the uncertain outcome of this event, and the currency risk to a non-Japanese business is the uncertain return or variation in return in domestic currency terms that results from the event. The risk can be described as the range of resulting outcomes and is often thought of in terms of a probability distribution of future returns. Suppose that the underlying amount is ¥1,000,000. The risk exposure of a business may be zero or it could be sizable, depending on whether the business has assets or liabilities tied to this risk—in this case, exposure to that currency. One million yen would, in this example, result in ¥10,000 of risk exposure (1% of ¥1,000,000). Risk management would include, among other things, quantifying and understanding this risk exposure, deciding how and why to have the exposure and how much risk the participant can bear, and possibly mitigating this risk by tailoring the exposure in several ways. The risk management process would inform the decision of whether to operate or invest in this risky currency.

The word "risk" can be is confusing because it is used by different people at different times to mean so many different things. Even when used properly, the term has three related but different meanings, which this example illustrates well. Risk can mean, in turn, the underlying uncertainty, the extent of the risky action taken, or the resulting range of risky outcomes to the organization. In this example, the first meaning is the uncertain +1% or −1% movement of the currency. The second meaning is the ¥1,000,000 worth of risky currency, the position taken by the business. The third meaning is the +¥10,000 or −¥10,000 risky outcome that might accrue to the business for having engaged in this risky activity. A common way of more precisely distinguishing among these three "risks" in usage is: *risk driver* for the underlying risk, *risk position* to describe or quantify the risky action taken, and *risk exposure* for the potential valuation change that may result. In the oversimplified example above, the risk exposure is simply the risk position multiplied by the risk driver. In practice the term "risk" is used interchangeably for all three meanings.

> ***Risk management*** *is the process by which an organization or individual defines the level of risk to be taken, measures the level of risk being taken, and adjusts the latter toward the former, with the goal of maximizing the company's or portfolio's value or the individual's overall satisfaction, or utility.*

Said differently, risk management comprises all the decisions and actions needed to *best* achieve organizational or personal objectives while bearing a tolerable level of risk. Risk management is *not* about minimizing risk; it is about actively understanding and embracing those risks that best balance the achievement of goals with an acceptable chance of failure, quantifying the exposure, and continually monitoring and modifying it. A company that shied away from all risk would find that it could not operate. In trying to create wealth, all organizations will find themselves "in the risk business." Risk management is not about avoiding risks any more than a practical diet is about avoiding calories. Risk management is not even about predicting risks. "The Doctrine of No Surprises" is a key mantra among many risk managers, but it does not mean they are expected to predict what will happen. Instead, it means that if an unpredictable event, either positive or negative, happens in an uncertain world, the *impact* of that event on the organization or portfolio would not be a surprise and would have been quantified and considered in advance.

For example, a risk manager of a bank would not have been expected to know that a real estate crisis was going to occur and cause significant defaults on the bank's real estate securities. But a good risk manager would help the bank's management decide how much exposure it should have in these securities by quantifying the potential financial impact of such a crisis destroying, say, 60% of the bank's capital. A good risk management process would include a deep discussion at the governance level about the balance between the likely returns and the unlikely—but sizable—losses and whether such losses are tolerable. Management would ensure that the risk analysis and discussion actively affects their investment decisions, that the potential loss is continuously quantified and communicated, and that it will take actions to mitigate or transfer any portion of the risk exposure that cannot be tolerated.[1] The only surprise here should be the market shock itself; the risk manager should have prepared the organization through stress-testing and scenario analysis, continuously reporting in advance on the potential impact of this sizable risk exposure.

A poor risk management process would have ignored the possibility, though small, of such a significant market event and not quantified the potential loss from exposure to a real estate crisis. As such, the bank's management would have had no idea that more than half of the bank's capital could be at risk, not addressed this risk in any governance/risk appetite discussion, ignored these risks in its investment decisions, and not taken any action to mitigate this risk. In a good risk management process, most of the work is done before an adverse event happens; in a poor risk management process, perhaps just as much work gets done, but it all comes after the event, which is after the damage has been done.

Good risk management does not prevent losses, but provides a full top-to-bottom framework that rigorously informs the decision-making process—before, during, and after a risk event. Because risks and exposures are dynamic, risk management

1 For example, hedges may be used to limit loss of capital to 20%.

is a continuous process that is always being reevaluated and revised. If this process is done well, it provides management and staff with the knowledge to navigate as efficiently as possible toward the goals set by the governing body. In turn, this effort increases *ex ante* the value of the business or investment decisions undertaken. Good risk management may allow managers to more quickly or effectively act in the face of a crisis. But *ex post*, even the best risk management may not stop a portfolio from losing money in a market crash nor prevent a business from reduced profits in an economic downturn.

A **risk management framework** flows logically from the definition of risk management that was previously given: It is the infrastructure, process, and analytics needed to support effective risk management in an organization. This process should fully integrate the "risk" and "return" aspects of the enterprise into decisions in support of best achieving its goals within its tolerance for risk. Risk management is not a "one size fits all" solution; it is integral to the enterprise's goals and needs. Thus, it is best achieved through a custom solution. Despite customization, every risk management system or framework should address the following key factors:

- Risk governance
- Risk identification and measurement
- Risk infrastructure
- Defined policies and processes
- Risk monitoring, mitigation, and management
- Communications
- Strategic analysis or integration

Not surprisingly, these factors often overlap in practice. They are defined and discussed here.

Governance is the top-level system of structures, rights, and obligations by which organizations are directed and controlled. Normally performed at the board level, governance is how goals are defined, authority is granted, and top-level decisions are made. The foundation for risk management in the organization is set at the board level as well. **Risk governance** is the top-down process and guidance that directs risk management activities to align with and support the overall enterprise and is addressed in more detail in Section 3. Good governance should include defining an organization's risk tolerance and providing risk oversight. Governance is often driven by regulatory concerns, as well as by the fiduciary role of the governing body. A risk management committee is another facet of governance; it provides top decision makers with a forum for regularly considering risk management issues. To achieve the best results for an organization, risk governance should take an enterprise-wide view. **Enterprise risk management** is an overarching governance approach applied throughout the organization and consistent with its strategy, guiding the risk management framework to focus risk activities on the objectives, health, and value of the *entire* organization.

Risk identification and measurement is the main quantitative core of risk management; but more than that, it must include the qualitative assessment and evaluation of all potential sources of risk and the organization's risk exposures. This ongoing work involves analyzing the environment for relevant risk drivers, which is the common term used for any fundamental underlying factor that results in a risk that is relevant or important to an organization, analyzing the business or portfolio to ascertain risk exposures, tracking changes in those risk exposures, and calculating risk metrics to size these risks under various scenarios and stresses.

Risks are not limited to what is going on in the financial markets. There are many types of risk that can potentially impact a business, portfolio, or individual.

The power of technology has allowed for risk management to be more quantitative and timely. Management can measure and monitor risk, run scenarios, conduct statistical analysis, work with more complex models, and examine more dimensions and risk drivers as well as do it faster. This use of technology needs to be balanced with and supplement—not supplant—experienced business judgment. Technology has made risk infrastructure even more important and beneficial in managing risks.

Risk infrastructure refers to the people and systems required to track risk exposures and perform most of the quantitative risk analysis to allow an assessment of the organization's risk profile. Infrastructure would include risk capture (the important operational process by which a risk exposure gets populated into a risk system), a database and data model, analytic models and systems, a stress or scenario engine, and an ability to generate reports, as well as some amount of skilled and empowered personnel resources dedicated to building and executing the risk framework. With increased reliance on technology, more time and effort must be allotted to test data, models, and results in order to avoid the ironic outcome of the risk of errors coming from within risk systems.

Obviously, the scope of risk infrastructure will be related to the resources, or potential losses, of the organization. Individuals and smaller businesses may rely heavily on an external partner or provider for much of their risk infrastructure and analysis.

Policies and processes are the extension of risk governance into both the day-to-day operation and decision-making processes of the organization. There may be limits, requirements, constraints, and guidelines—some quantitative, some procedural—to ensure risky activities are in line with the organization's predetermined risk tolerance and regulatory requirements. Much of this is just common-sense business practice: updating and protecting data, controlling cash flows, conducting due diligence on investments, handling exceptions and escalations, and making checklists to support important decisions. In a good risk framework, processes would naturally evolve to consider risk at all key decision points, such as investment decisions and asset allocation. Risk management should become an integrated part of the business and not just a policing or regulatory function.

The process of *risk monitoring, mitigation, and management* is the most obvious facet of a risk framework, but also one of the most difficult. Actively monitoring and managing risk requires pulling together risk governance, identification and measurement, infrastructure, and policies and processes and continually reviewing and reevaluating in the face of changing risk exposures and risk drivers. It requires recognizing when risk exposure is not aligned with risk tolerance and then taking action to bring them back into alignment.[2]

Communication of critical risk issues must happen continually and across all levels of the organization. Governance parameters, such as risk tolerances and associated constraints, must be clearly communicated to, and understood by, managers. Risk metrics must be reported in a clear and timely manner. Risk issues must be reviewed and discussed as a standard part of decision making. Changes in exposure must be discussed so that action can be taken as appropriate. There should also be a feedback loop with the governance body so that top-level risk guidance can be validated or updated and communicated back to the rest of the organization.

Strategic analysis and integration help turn risk management into an offensive weapon to improve performance. Good risk management is a key to increasing the value of the overall business or portfolio. A risk management framework should provide the tools to better understand the how and why of performance and help sort out which activities are adding value, and which are not. In investing, rigorous analysis can support better investment decisions and improve strategy and risk-adjusted returns.

---

2 Risk mitigation and management is discussed in more detail in Section 5.

Exhibit 1 The Risk Management Framework in an Enterprise Context

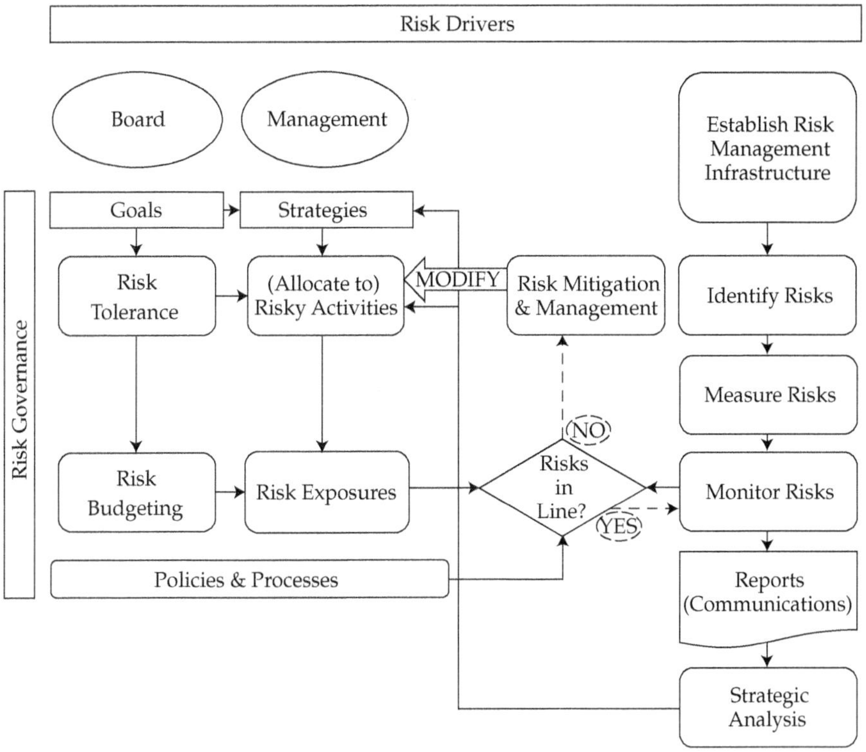

Exhibit 1 illustrates the process of risk management for an enterprise, pulling all the described elements of the risk framework together. Although there are a very high number of risks faced by every organization, most organizations are primarily affected by a small number of key risk drivers, or primary underlying factors that create risk. Along the left side is risk governance, which represents board-level decisions and encompasses and affects the boxes immediately to its right. The governance body, often called a board, defines the goals of the organization and, in turn, decides on its risk tolerance. It may additionally provide guidance on how or where that risk is taken (risk budgeting). The board is also involved in setting high-level policies that will affect most risk management processes. These risk governance activities are a crucial keystone of the risk framework and will be discussed in detail in the next section. When the rest of the risk framework hinges off of these top-down governance elements and is focused on the goals of the entire enterprise (as shown here), the end result is effective enterprise risk management.

The role of management, shown in the middle column, is to plan and execute value-maximizing strategies consistent with their governance guidance. Each management activity in the framework flows not only from management (shown with the arrows) but also from the governance activities on the left. Thus, not only are management's strategies designed to achieve the board's goals, but management also allocates capital to risky activities (its business or investing choices) to execute its strategies consistent with the defined risk tolerance. The risk exposures that result from management's choice of activities should also be aligned with the governing body's risk budget. In addition, management participates actively in setting or implementing policies and establishing procedures that relate to when, how, how much, and by whom each of the other elements of the risk framework are performed.[3]

The rest of the risk management framework comprises a number of important risk activities to help the business achieve all of its strategic and governance goals and mandates. These other elements to implement risk management are shown in the far right column of the illustration. Driven by its need to establish a risk management program to support the enterprise's goals, management would provide the requisite resources for risk management activities by establishing a risk management infrastructure. With risk processes defined and risk infrastructure in place, risks are then identified and measured, which is a regular and continual process of translating risk exposures (produced by the risky activities) into meaningful and generally quantitative risk metrics.

The next major steps—risk monitoring, mitigation, and management—are where much of a firm's day-to-day risk management activity is focused. These activities are split across three boxes in the illustration. Risk levels are continuously monitored, having just been measured.[4] There is a major decision at the monitoring stage: Management must check that all the risks are in line and not outside the limits of the defined risk tolerance or budget.[5] This process involves evaluating the actual risk exposures compared with the organization's risk policies and procedures to ensure that everything is in compliance. If the answer is "no," then risk mitigation and management actions need to be taken to modify risk levels and to bring them back into compliance. There are a variety of methods to accomplish this task, which are addressed in Section 5. Whatever the method, management's allocation of the risk budget to risky activities will be altered by this modification, which includes changing the organization's risk exposures, starting the circle again through the steps on the right, and re-checking to see if risk levels are now consistent with risk policies.

When risks *are* in line with limits, policies, tolerances, mandates, and so on, then the process moves back to continuous monitoring followed by communicating risk levels.[6] This communication, at a minimum, includes reporting key risk metrics on a regular and timely basis across the organization to assist management in its decision-making process and the board in fulfilling its governance duties. Finally, strategic analysis is supported by the risk measurement, reporting, and other steps of the enterprise risk management process. By analyzing all of the enterprise's strategies and risky activities via the risk measurement lens, management can improve its decision-making process and ascertain where to invest its limited capital and risk budget most fruitfully. This step is generally underappreciated and is an inexpensive and beneficial by-product of having built a risk framework. The last two boxes or steps (reports and strategic analysis) represent important feedback loops to inform and improve both governance and the portfolio of risky activities that make up the business.

---

3 In essence, there could be an arrow from policies and processes to every other box to the right, but these rather obvious relationships are intentionally omitted in the diagram to avoid clutter. Likewise, risk exposures inform nearly all the boxes to the right. Risk management is innately quite interrelated.

4 Continuous usually does not mean real-time; the frequency of monitoring is based on the resources available, the level of systems support, and the need for risk information in the decision process. At large financial firms, this monitoring will generally be daily; for small businesses and individuals it might be quarterly.

5 This task is generally delegated to a risk manager; but whatever the title, someone must be accountable for this important check.

6 While not obvious in the illustration, communication and reporting should happen whether or not risk levels are in compliance; such communications are even more important when risk levels are out of alignment with tolerances.

There are many feedback loops in properly executed risk management. In practice, most of these steps overlap most of the time and are being performed simultaneously. Good risk management ties together all these steps from the highest governance decisions to lower-level specifics, such as models, reports, and operational checklists.

The risk environment is dynamic, and many of our notions of probabilities and likely risk outcomes change in ways we probably could not predict. The risk management framework should be robust enough to anticipate this dynamism—to expect the unexpected. It should be evolutionary—flexible enough to grow with a company or individual and its new challenges.

The complexity of the risk management framework depends on the complexity of an organization's risk exposures and their resources. But that does not mean that smaller organizations or individuals should skip the risk management process; they may simply be able to do less, or have to work with external partners to assist with large portions of the framework, or be less formal about the process. Ultimately, the key principles just covered are still important even to the smallest organization, even if the specific components do not get assembled as described.

THE RISK MANAGEMENT PROCESS FOR AN INDIVIDUAL

Although an individual has neither the resources nor the organizational overhead of a large business, the importance of risk management is not diminished and the risk management framework still applies, albeit most likely in a scaled-down form. Though nearly all of the essential elements of the process illustrated in Exhibit 1 are still useful, the individual can reduce the recipe to six essential ingredients, consistent with the reduced scope of the individual's risk exposures.

The first step for an individual is much like that shown in Exhibit 1 for the most complex organization: the determination of goals or objectives. This step would include most of the elements associated with risk governance, just without all the organizational complexity.

The next functional step involves choosing investments (or other assets) and identifying their risks. Lacking any risk infrastructure, the individual may at this stage already require the services of an investment professional or financial adviser. This step and subsequent steps will probably be executed by the adviser, although the individual principal still needs to stay knowledgeable and involved. In the context of the illustration in Exhibit 1, the individual is effectively their own governance body and the adviser serves the role of management.

The next steps for the individual are equivalent to the heart of the risk management process: risk monitoring and risk mitigation and management. The individual would first evaluate their risk exposure (like the diamond or decision step in the illustration), then consider various alternative approaches to modify the risk if necessary, followed by implementing the risk management solution (insuring, hedging, trading, etc.).

The final functional step for an individual's risk management process would be evaluation and review. This step is parallel to the back-end of the risk management illustration, the boxes at the bottom right. This process may occur with much less frequency for an individual—but it is no less important.

Each individual should simplify the risk management process as required so that they do not end up considering it "too esoteric and complicated to worry about" and thus ignoring risk management altogether. The potential costs of avoiding risk management are essentially the same for an individual as for a large corporation or a hedge fund, although perhaps with less money involved.

At its core, business and investing are about allocating resources and capital to chosen risks. Understanding which risks drive better outcomes should be one of the goals of risk management, and it makes good *risk* management inextricably linked with good management generally. When effective risk management is truly integrated at all levels of the decision-making process and the overall management process, the organization has developed an effective *risk culture.* This culture generally produces better results than just considering risk issues as a separate afterthought, and, in turn, it produces *much* better results than ignoring risk issues altogether in the decision-making process. For individuals, the adoption of a risk culture should result in a personal awareness of the many types of risks, their rewards, the costs, the relationships between them, and the methods of aligning the risks borne with the risks and outcomes desired. This awareness should lead to better investment return and/or smaller losses for the risk taken, resulting in higher satisfaction.

There are a number of other benefits from establishing good risk management: (1) Most obvious is less frequent surprises and a better notion of what the damage would be in the event of a surprise; (2) more decision discipline leading to better consideration of trade-offs and better risk–return relationships; (3) better response and risk mitigation stemming from more awareness and active monitoring, which should trim some of the worst losses; (4) better efficiency and fewer operational errors from policies and procedures, transparency, and risk awareness; (5) better relations, with more trust, between the governing body and management, which generally results in more effective delegation; (6) a better image or reputation because analysts and investors perceive a company as prudent and value-focused. Together, all these benefits should lead to higher value for the enterprise.

EXAMPLE 1

Risk Management and Risk Management Framework

1. Which of the following is *not* a goal of risk management?
   - **A** Measuring risk exposures
   - **B** Minimizing exposure to risk
   - **C** Defining the level of risk appetite
2. Which element of a risk management framework sets the overall context for risk management in an organization?
   - **A** Governance
   - **B** Risk infrastructure
   - **C** Policies and processes
3. Which element of risk management makes up the analytical component of the process?
   - **A** Communication
   - **B** Risk governance
   - **C** Risk identification and measurement
4. Which element of risk management involves action when risk exposures are found to be out of line with risk tolerance?
   - **A** Risk governance
   - **B** Risk identification and measurement
   - **C** Risk monitoring, mitigation, and management

Solution to 1:

B is correct. The definition of risk management includes both defining the level of risk desired and measuring the level of risk taken. Risk management means taking risks actively and in the best, most value-added way possible and is not about minimizing risks.

Solution to 2:

A is correct. Governance is the element of the risk management framework that is the top-level foundation for risk management. Although policies, procedures, and infrastructure are necessary to implement a risk management framework, it is governance that provides the overall context for an organization's risk management.

Solution to 3:

C is correct. Risk identification and measurement is the quantitative part of the process. It involves identifying the risks and summarizing their potential quantitative impact. Communication and risk governance are largely qualitative.

Solution to 4:

C is correct. Risk monitoring, mitigation, and management require recognizing and taking action when these (risk exposure and risk tolerance) are not in line, as shown in the middle of Exhibit 1. Risk governance involves setting the risk tolerance. Risk identification and measurement involves identifying and measuring the risk exposures.

RISK GOVERNANCE

3

Risk governance is the foundation for risk management. As defined earlier, it is the top-down process and guidance that directs risk management activities to align with and support the goals of the overall enterprise. It typically emanates from a board of directors with fiduciary obligations and risk oversight and who prescribe goals and authorities. Referring back to the definition of risk management, note that risk management is keenly focused on the risk and value of the overall enterprise.

3.1 An Enterprise View of Risk Governance

In addition to the responsibility for risk oversight, there are two other important areas in which the governing body drives the risk framework. First, it determines the organization's goals, direction, and priorities, which combined serve as a key foundation for enterprise risk management. Recall that enterprise risk management is an overarching governance approach applied across the organization that focuses risk activities on the objectives, health, and value of the whole organization. Second, it spells out the risk appetite or tolerance, meaning which risks are acceptable, which risks are to be mitigated and to what extent, and which risks are unacceptable. Risk governance should also provide a sense of the worst losses that could be tolerated in various scenarios, and management should manage risk accordingly. These considerations should flow naturally into decisions about risk budgeting to guide implementation of an optimal program that is consistent with that risk tolerance.

Risk governance is the impact of the governing body of an organization on the risk management framework. It provides context for and clarity on an organization's value drivers and risk appetite, specifies clear authority to management to execute risk management, and ensures risk oversight to continually determine whether risk management is functioning well and consistent with the organization's value maximization. It is the governing body's job to tie the organizational goals and risk framework together; thus, risk governance happens within an enterprise context. Risk governance and risk oversight also entail compliance with regulatory requirements. Risk governance is a difficult and demanding discipline, and if it is going to flourish in an organization, it needs visible commitment from the top.

Providing clear guidance with sufficient leeway to execute strategy is often a difficult balance. Even more challenging is providing for advance discussion and a clear decision and statement of organizational risk appetite. There is usually substantial discussion about this risk appetite *after* a crisis, but too often there is very little discussion during periods of normalcy, when it would be much more beneficial. Because risk is one of the main strategic tools that management can regulate, it is especially important for governing bodies to openly discuss risk, consider scenarios, understand the impact of negative outcomes on the organization, and make it clear where they are not willing to venture. Much like an automobile that comes with a red zone on some dials to establish boundaries for safe operation, risk governance bodies should likewise establish hypothetical red zones to ensure the safe operation of their enterprise.

Enterprise risk management (focusing risk activities on the objectives, health, and value of the *whole* organization) requires that the entire economic balance sheet of the business be considered, not just the assets or one part of the business in isolation. A narrower view of risk management is unlikely to meet the goal of maximizing the value of the entire enterprise.

Pension fund management provides a classic example of the importance of considering enterprise risk management: "Funds" are the assets and "pension" is the liability. But a true enterprise view requires an even broader outlook. A corporate pension fund's manager might try to maximize only the fund's assets, but this would generally do a disservice to the corporation. The assets and liabilities of a pension fund are both sensitive to market variables, so ignoring the liabilities would be ignoring half the risk. With liabilities that are quite bond-like, a pension fund manager using all equities for maximum growth would potentially make the overall fund insolvent in a market collapse with declining interest rates because, in such a situation, the liabilities would increase substantially in value while the assets fell. Risk tolerance for the assets in isolation would be far different from the risk tolerance of the entire enterprise. One should look beyond just the pension liabilities, which are likely to be a small part of the overall enterprise. Broader still, a true enterprise risk view in this case would *also* consider the parent corporation's business risk profile and not just the pension assets and liabilities. In a market collapse, the overall business might be in a recessionary phase, rendering increasing contributions from the corporation to its pension fund quite painful. Factoring the corporate risk profile into the pension fund investment strategy may cause the risk tolerance to be lower in this case.

Risk governance that focuses on the entire enterprise will result in risk management that is much less likely to be at odds with the goals of the organization and more likely to enhance long-run value. Likewise, consideration of a full spectrum of risks, and not just the most obvious quantitative risks, will result in better risk governance.

The enterprise view of risk management is equally applicable and important to an individual, even if the term "enterprise" is not often used in an individual context.[7] The appropriate set of risks for an individual must be viewed not in isolation, but in consideration of the goals and characteristics of the individual in a holistic view. For example, an adviser may be designing an investment portfolio to maximize a client's wealth and optimize the risk–return trade-off at some perceived comfortable level of risk.[8] But the client, whose wealth consists not only of financial assets but also of

7 Enterprise risk management is an easier concept for an individual; compared with an organization in which deciding, coordinating, and communicating goals can be a big challenge, the scope of risk management efforts for an individual is smaller and more manageable.

8 Here, the individual is the governing body, setting individual goals and risk appetite; the financial professional or wealth manager is the "management team" executing much of the rest of the risk framework.

valuable **human capital**, might prefer that risk allocation decisions be made in view of both forms of capital, optimizing her total wealth. For example, a client with a career in real estate would most likely benefit if her financial portfolio is invested in a way that considers her earnings exposure to real estate related risks. Holdings of real estate securities above a certain level, even if optimal from an isolated portfolio perspective, might make this individual less than optimally diversified from a total wealth perspective. In another example, Investor X, who has substantial inflation-adjusted pension benefits, is different from Investor Y, who has a fixed pension benefit, and different still from Investor Z, who has no pension benefit and retires with solely his own investment portfolio. These three investors will require remarkably different investment solutions, not only to deal with inflation but also to deal with the uncertainty surrounding lifespans. Individuals with different goals and characteristics will need differing investment and risk solutions that are best suited to their individual situations. In fact, because of the extremely variable life cycle of an individual and the discrete nature of many individuals' goals, the enterprise view is even more important to risk management for individuals than it is for institutions.

Risk governance extends into management to include ways to ensure that the risk framework of an organization stays consistent with top-level guidance. One useful approach is to provide a regular forum to discuss the risk framework and key risk issues at the management level. In other words, a risk management committee would be a key element of good risk governance. Its activities could parallel the governance body's risk deliberations, but at an operational level as opposed to high-level oversight. In this forum, governance overlaps with many of the other aspects of the organization's risk framework as discussed in Section 2. In fact, if done well, it integrates all of them.

In the same vein, another element of good risk governance is the formal appointment of a responsible executive as chief risk officer (CRO). This officer should be responsible for building and implementing the risk framework for the enterprise and managing the many activities therein. In the same manner that risks are inextricably linked with the core business activities, the CRO is likewise a key participant in the strategic decisions of the enterprise—this position is not solely a policing role. Although the chief executive is responsible for risk as well as all other aspects of an enterprise, it makes no more sense for the CEO to perform the role of the CRO than it would be for the CEO to perform the role of the CFO. Many financial firms now have a CRO in executive management,[9] which had become best practice even in the years prior to the 2008 crisis.

3.2 Risk Tolerance

Perhaps the most important element of good risk governance is the **risk tolerance** discussion and decision within the governing body. Business and investment strategy centers on selecting a portfolio of acceptable risk activities that will maximize value and produce the highest returns possible for the given risk level. At the governance level, the duty is generally not to select these activities—a job that usually falls to management—but to establish the organization's risk appetite. Certain risks or levels of risks may be deemed acceptable, other risks deemed unacceptable, and in the middle are risks that may be pursued in a risk-limited fashion. Said differently, risk tolerance identifies the extent to which the organization is willing to experience losses or opportunity costs and to fail in meeting its objectives.

9 Although this is common for financial firms or other large organizations, many less-complex companies will forgo a formal risk structure. The board still maintains its risk governance responsibilities; and it is up to them to work out with management as to how, and to what extent, to meet these responsibilities.

The risk tolerance decision *for an individual* is similar, but not identical, to that of a business enterprise. In traditional finance theory, the individual focuses on maximizing unobservable utility, whereas the business maximizes a generally observable value—the market value or equity price of the company. Although individuals are facing life and certain death on an uncertain timetable, most businesses tend to be relatively short-lived organizations, but with an expectation of immortality. The decisions about risk tolerance from those two very different viewpoints can be expected to differ—for example, risk tolerance in organizations often treats its continued existence as a major consideration. In many ways, the individual's risk tolerance decision is the harder one.

The enterprise risk management perspective is the right lens through which to view the risk appetite question. The risk tolerance decision begins with two different analyses that must be integrated—an "inside" view and an "outside" view. First, what shortfalls within an organization would cause it to fail, or at least fail to achieve some critical goals? Second, what uncertain forces is the organization exposed to? That is, what are its risk drivers? With the answers to these two difficult questions in hand, a board could begin defining dimensions and levels of risk that it finds too uncomfortable to take on. This risk tolerance should be formally chosen and communicated *before* a crisis, and will serve as the high-level guidance for management in its strategic selection of risks. Many organizations will do this *after* a crisis, which is better than not doing it at all but is much like buying insurance after the loss occurs. It is best to take care of it when there seems to be no particularly pressing reason to do so. Similarly, some individuals may not give much thought to their own risk tolerance until after a crisis occurs, when they belatedly decide that the risk was not worth taking.

For example, suppose a Spanish construction equipment manufacturing company's board is determining its risk tolerance. From the inside perspective, it has two main concerns: revenue and liquidity. It determines that it can tolerate a 5%–10% drop in revenue, but that a 20% drop would trigger its debt covenants and put the launch of its new flagship product at risk. Related to this strategy, it needs €40 million of cash flow annually for the next three years for critical capital expenditures and can leave almost none of this cash flow at risk. From the outside perspective, it realizes that there are three main uncertainties or risk drivers over which it has no control: changes in the value of the US dollar, interest rate changes, and market returns on industrial sector equities. Both its business results and its own stock price are strongly correlated with these three risks and could be adversely affected by any of them.

Rather than taking a passive approach as a risk observer, the board in this example uses a top-level analysis to formulate its risk tolerance. In this case, it may decide to limit maximum cash flow variation to €10 million annually and revenue exposure to −10% in a global recession. In addition, it may specify other stated limits, such as the maximum exposure to currency or other risks. This guidance may affect the riskiness of other product strategies that management may pursue. The company may require more expensive financing options to reduce cash flow uncertainty. The governance restrictions may drive risk mitigation programs, such as a hedging strategy, especially for the primary risk drivers that are stated areas of concern.

Governance guidance is important in helping an enterprise target where it should actively pursue risk and where it should mitigate or modify risk. Strategic goals centered on core competencies should be pursued, which leads the company into taking risks that best position the enterprise for success and value creation. Companies sometimes take risks in areas where they have no expertise, which puts their core value creation and their entire organization at peril. A well-functioning risk program would limit or hedge those non-core risks in areas where they have no comparative advantage. Modifying risk is covered in detail in Section 5.

How does a company determine its risk tolerance? There is certainly no formula. Most importantly, a company's goals, its expertise in certain areas, and its strategies will help a board determine which risks the company may pursue and with how much intensity. The ability of a company to respond dynamically to adverse events may allow for a higher risk tolerance. The amount of loss a company can sustain without impairing its status as a going concern should factor into its risk tolerance; some companies are more fragile than others. The competitive landscape matters because both the board's and investors' expectations are usually developed in the context of how a company is positioned in its industry. The government and regulatory landscape is important too, both in their *ex ante* demands on how companies approach risk and in the likely *ex post* reaction in the event of disasters. Quantitative analyses such as scenario analysis, economic models, and sensitivities to macro risk drivers might be used to assess where a board's zone of comfort is bounded. There are other factors that should *not* determine risk tolerance, but in many cases they do. Personal motivations, beliefs, and agendas of board members (the agency problem); company size; whether the market environment seems stable; short-term pressures; and management compensation often affect risk tolerance in ways that might not be in line with the owners' best interests.

Once risk tolerance is determined, the overall risk framework should be geared toward measuring, managing, and communicating compliance with this risk tolerance—getting the risk exposure in line with the enterprise's risk appetite.

This sort of governance exercise not only helps ensure that the organization survives through the worst of times, but also helps ensure a strategic trade-off between risk and return in the decision process, which, in turn, improves potential returns for the given level of risk and value. It is quite easy to find business strategies and investment approaches that produce apparently outsized returns, but they might be at the cost of putting the organization at extreme risk. A somewhat extreme example would be a company selling put options on its own equity, which could produce higher short-term profits but would dramatically increase the chance of the company failing in a steep market decline. Excessive leverage is another risky strategy for boosting short-term profits that may decrease value or lead to failure in the long run. A formal risk governance process with a stated risk tolerance would naturally result in avoidance of many easier, less well-reasoned strategies that entail excessive risk compared with the firm's risk tolerance. Instead, it would lead the strategic discussion into alternative strategies that are more likely to add value while taking reasonable risk within the enterprise's risk tolerance and not simply trade ruin for return. Sincere, good risk governance and risk culture can avoid excessively risky strategies that might put the long-term enterprise value at risk. This approach should produce enhanced value for the enterprise.

3.3 Risk Budgeting

Risk budgeting picks up where risk tolerance leaves off. Whereas risk tolerance focuses on the appetite for risk and what is and is not acceptable, risk budgeting has a more specific focus on how that risk is taken. Risk budgeting quantifies and allocates the tolerable risk by specific metrics; it extends and guides implementation of the risk tolerance decision.

Risk budgeting applies to both business management and portfolio management. Its foundation is the perspective that business or portfolio management involves assembling a number of risk activities or securities, which can be collated into an assemblage of various risk characteristics. For example, a traditional view of a portfolio might be that it is allocated 20% to hedge funds, 30% to private equity, and the remaining 50% is split between stocks and bonds. An alternative risk view of the same portfolio might be 70% driven by global equity returns, 20% by domestic equity returns, with the remaining 10% driven by interest rates. The equity component might be allocated 65% to value and 35% to growth. The portfolio might also have 45% illiquid securities and the remainder liquid. Other allocations can be stated in terms of exposures to inflation, long-term interest rates, currencies, and so on. These multiple dimensions for viewing the allocation of a portfolio are not mutually exclusive: they co-exist. If one is evaluating the risk exposure of a portfolio and trying to keep it in line with a stated risk tolerance, one would be far more concerned with the risk characteristics of the investment assets and portfolio rather than their common classifications of stocks, hedge funds, real estate, private equity, and so on. These terms tell us a little about risk but not enough. Equity is traditionally riskier than hedge funds, but some equities are of quite low risk and some hedge funds are of quite high risk. The risk view may be more meaningful and useful in understanding the portfolio risk than the traditional asset allocation view.

Risk budgeting is any means of allocating a portfolio based on some risk characteristics of the investments. In the purest sense, the term "budget" implies that there is a total risk limit for the organization. Although this approach is not formally required,[10] it would certainly be good practice to have a risk budget that is consistent with the organization's risk tolerance. A risk budget provides a means of implementing the risk tolerance at a strategic level, or in other words, a means of bridging from the high-level governance risk decision to the many management decisions, large and small, that result in the actual risk exposures.

A risk budget can be complex and multi-dimensional, or it can be a simple, one-dimensional risk measure. Even the simplest measure can provide significant benefits in developing an effective risk culture. Four well-known single-dimension measures that are often used are standard deviation, beta, value at risk (VaR), and scenario loss, but there are many others. It is common for some hedge funds to budget risk using standard deviation, managing to a fixed-risk fund target, and evaluating individual investments based on their returns and risks as they affect the *ex ante* standard deviation.

More complex forms of risk budgeting use multiple dimensions of risk. One popular approach evaluates risks by their underlying risk classes, such as equity, fixed income, commodity risk, and so on, and then allocates investments by their risk class. Also common are risk factor approaches to risk budgeting, in which exposure to various factors is used to attempt to capture associated risk premiums. An example would be to budget an allocation to give greater emphasis to value stocks based on the belief that they may provide a higher risk-adjusted return than growth stocks. This tactic might be layered over a strategic budget with a certain "beta" as the overall equity risk, supplemented with value and additional factor tilts specified up to some level.

Risk budgeting, although a desirable element of risk governance, cuts across the entire risk management framework, providing a focal point for each of the facets of risk management described in Section 2. And although it is true that in practice many organizations operate without a risk budget, it is generally because there has been no specific declaration of their risk tolerance. If a board has a clear understanding of its risk appetite, both the board and management will want some means of implementing a strategic allocation that is consistent with it. Thus, the risk budget becomes a critical overarching construct for the organization's risk framework.

Some individuals may, often through the assistance of a financial planner, engage in some form of risk budgeting, but many do not execute it well or carry it far enough. A classic example of this failure is the tendency of many individuals to invest their financial portfolios in their employers. The risk budget for their total wealth—financial

---

10 One could do risk budgeting even if there were no other risk governance guidance.

and human capital—is extremely concentrated in one firm and/or one industry. Not surprisingly, such risk budgets typically occur not through formal planning because most formal plans would recognize the problem, but through inaction or inattention.

One major benefit of even the most basic risk budgeting is that it forces risk trade-offs and supports a culture in which risk is considered as a part of all key decisions. Suppose that all the activities a business wants to pursue are in excess of the risk budget. The budgeting of risk should result in an approach, whether explicit or not, of choosing to invest where the return per unit of risk is the highest. Better still, it should also result in a market-benchmarked choice of risk intensity, between possibly doing less of each risky investment or doing more, but with a risk-mitigating hedge. This benefit is extremely important. By choosing between a market hedge or less of a risky investment, one ends up evaluating the investment directly against the market risk–return benchmark. Thus, one is not only comparing risk–return relationships among one's investment choices, but also comparing active versus passive strategies; that is, evaluating investment choices as a whole against the "market return" on a risk-equivalent basis. In other words, one ends up attempting to add active value in each of one's decisions while still staying within the confines of the organization's risk tolerance. The result is even more powerful than merely ensuring that the business is compensated well for the risks they decide to accept. Just having a risk budget in place, forces decision makers to try to add value to the enterprise in every risky decision they make. The risk-budgeting framework makes this consideration innate to the decision process.

EXAMPLE 2

Risk Governance

1 Which of the following approaches is *most* consistent with an enterprise view of risk governance?

   A Separate strategic planning processes for each part of the enterprise

   B Considering an organization's risk tolerance when developing its asset allocation

   C Trying to achieve the highest possible risk-adjusted return on a company's pension fund's assets

2 Which of the following statements about risk tolerance is *most* accurate?

   A Risk tolerance is best discussed after a crisis, when awareness of risk is heightened.

   B The risk tolerance discussion is about the actions management will take to minimize losses.

   C The organization's risk tolerance describes the extent to which the organization is willing to experience losses.

3 Which of the following is *not* consistent with a risk-budgeting approach to portfolio management?

   A Limiting the beta of the portfolio to 0.75

   B Allocating investments by their amount of underlying risk sources or factors

   C Limiting the amount of money available to be spent on hedging strategies by each portfolio manager

4 Who would be the *least* appropriate for controlling the risk management function in a large organization?

A Chief risk officer
B Chief financial officer
C Risk management committee

Solution to 1:

B is correct. The enterprise view is characterized by a focus on the organization as a whole—its goals, value, and risk tolerance. It is not about strategies or risks at the individual business line level.

Solution to 2:

C is correct. Risk tolerance identifies the extent to which the organization is willing to experience losses or opportunity costs and fail in meeting its objectives. It is best discussed before a crisis and is primarily a risk governance or oversight issue at the board level, not a management or tactical one.

Solution to 3:

C is correct. Risk budgeting is any means of allocating a portfolio by some risk characteristics of the investments. This approach could be a strict limit on beta or some other risk measure or an approach that uses risk classes or factors to allocate investments. Risk budgeting does not require nor prohibit hedging, although hedging is available as an implementation tool to support risk budgeting and overall risk governance.

Solution to 4:

B is correct. A chief risk officer or a risk management committee is an individual or group that specializes in risk management. A chief financial officer may have considerable knowledge of risk management, may supervise a CRO, and would likely have some involvement in a risk management committee, but a CFO has broader responsibilities and cannot provide the specialization and attention to risk management that is necessary in a large organization.

4 IDENTIFICATION OF RISKS

Having laid the framework for understanding the concept of risk management and risk governance, we now move into the implementation of the process. One of the first important parts of the process is the identification of risks. In this reading, we identify two general categorizations of risks. The first is the set of risks that originate from the financial markets. Accordingly, we refer to this type of risk as **financial risks**. The second group of risks includes those that emanate from outside the financial markets. As such, we refer to these as **non-financial risks**. Although most risks ultimately have monetary consequences, we reserve the term "financial risks" to refer to the risks that arise from events occurring in the financial markets, such as changes in prices or interest rates.[11] In this reading, we will consider the types of financial and non-financial risks faced by organizations and individuals.

11 We use the term "financial markets" in a very broad sense. A company may also be exposed to commodity price risk, which we would include as a financial risk.

4.1 Financial Risks

The risk management industry has come to classify three types of risks as primarily financial in nature. The three primary types of financial risks are market risk, credit risk, and liquidity risk. **Market risk** is the risk that arises from movements in interest rates, stock prices, exchange rates, and commodity prices. This categorization is not to say that these four main factors are the underlying drivers of market risks. Market risks typically arise from certain fundamental economic conditions or events in the economy or industry or developments in specific companies. These are the underlying risk drivers, which we will cover later.

Market risks are among the most obvious and visible risks faced by most organizations and many individuals. The financial markets receive considerable attention in the media, and information on financial market activity is abundant. Institutional investors and many corporations devote considerable resources to processing this information with the objective of optimizing performance. Many individuals also devote considerable attention to market risk, and financial publications and television and radio shows are widely followed in the general population. The state of knowledge in risk management is probably greatest in the area of market risk.

The second primary financial risk is credit risk. **Credit risk** is the risk of loss if one party fails to pay an amount owed on an obligation, such as a bond, loan, or derivative, to another party. In a loan, only one party owes money to the other. In some types of derivatives, only one party owes money to the other, and in other types of derivatives, either party can owe the other. This type of risk is also sometimes called default risk and sometimes counterparty risk. As with market risk, the root source of the risk can arise from fundamental conditions in the economy, industry, or weakness in the market for a company's products. Ultimately, default is an asset-specific risk. Bond and derivatives investors must consider credit risk as one of their primary decision tools.[12] Similar to market risk, credit risk is also a highly visible risk with considerable attention paid to defaults, bankruptcies, and the stresses arising from inadequate cash flow in relation to leverage. Credit risk is a particularly significant risk in that although market prices can go down and bounce back up, defaults and bankruptcies have extremely long-term implications for borrowers.

Although market and credit risk are extremely common risks to institutions, they are also assumed by individuals in their personal investments. One other financial risk, however, is much more common to institutions, although it can be faced by individuals, often unknowingly. This third risk is **liquidity risk**, which is the risk of a significant downward valuation adjustment when selling a financial asset. In order to sell an asset, a party may need to reduce the price to a level that is less than the marked value or the seller's assessment of the asset's true value based on the fundamentals of the asset. In certain market conditions, the seller must make a significant price concession. Having to make price concessions is not necessarily unusual and does not imply a poorly functioning market. Indeed, given no shift in demand, a rightward shift of a supply curve in order to sell a larger quantity is entirely consistent with the notion that a seller must lower the price to sell a greater quantity.

All assets have transaction costs in the market, such as the bid–ask spread. The existence of a sell price that is less than a buy price, however, is not a risk but simply a cost. It is the *uncertainty* of that valuation spread that creates this type of risk. Thus, liquidity risk could also be called "transaction cost risk." The liquidity risk of a \$10 stock purchased for \$10 is not the risk that one would receive the "bid" price of only \$9.99 right after one bought it. That \$0.01 spread is a known cost when the stock is

12 With certain derivatives (swaps and forwards), either party could be forced to pay off to the other, so each party is concerned about whether its counterparty will pay off, meaning that for some products, credit risk is bilateral.

purchased, so it is not a risk. The risk is that this spread cost might increase dramatically as a result of either changing market conditions or attempting to maintain a position significantly larger than the normal trading volume for the stock. This problem becomes a serious issue for risk management when the liquidation price falls to less than the seller's estimate of the fundamental value of the asset. Although this risk is often associated with illiquid assets,[13] it really stems from a couple of sources. First, market liquidity varies over time and the market for specific assets may become less liquid; second, as the size of a position increases, the cost and uncertainty associated with liquidating it will increase. In some extreme cases, there may be no price above zero at which the seller can sell the asset.

Of course, one might argue that the cost of illiquidity, and liquidity risk, should thus be part of the investor's assessment of fundamental value, and indeed it is for many analysts. If not, liquidity risk can sometimes be confused with a form of valuation denial in which investors believe that they paid an appropriate price and that the market has not converged to its true value. But less liquidity means a thin market and a lack of investor interest, which may be fertile ground for investment opportunities. Although lack of liquidity can offer benefits, such as the opportunity to buy an asset well before everyone else sees that it is an attractive investment, liquidity risk is generally considered to be a negative factor with which risk managers and indeed all investors must contend.

4.2 Non-Financial Risks

Recall that we refer to financial risks as those arising primarily from events occurring in the financial markets. Although most risks have monetary consequences, there are a number of risks that are typically classified as non-financial in nature. These risks arise from a variety of sources, such as from actions within the organization or from external origins, such as the environment as well as from the relationship between the organization and counterparties, regulators, governments, suppliers, and customers.

One important risk of this type is closely related to default risk but deals more with the settling of payments that occur just before a default. This risk is called settlement risk. As an example, suppose Party A enters into a forward contract to purchase ¥200 million of Japanese government bonds from Party B. At expiration if all goes well, Party A would wire the money and Party B would transfer the bonds. Each party fulfills its obligation expecting that the other will do so as well. However, suppose Party A wires the money but Party B does not send the bonds because it has declared bankruptcy. At this point, Party A cannot get the money back, except possibly much later through the potentially slow and cumbersome bankruptcy process.[14] Although the financial consequences are very high, the root source of this risk is the timing of the payment process itself.

Organizations face two types of risks related to the law, and as such, this risk is referred to as legal risk. One risk is simply the risk of being sued over a transaction or for that matter, anything an organization does or fails to do. In financial risk management, however, the major legal concern is that the terms of a contract will not be upheld by the legal system. For example, suppose Bank E enters into a derivatives contract with Party F. Assume that as the underlying changes in price, Party F incurs

13 The illiquid nature of an asset is not itself the risk because that is a direct cost borne immediately upon purchase. Still, uncertainty around the valuation of illiquid assets is a pervasive issue, so it is natural to associate liquidity risk with liquidity characteristics. More importantly, though, the term *liquidity risk* also commonly refers to a much broader set of risks for the organization, which are addressed in the next section.

14 This type of risk often arises because of significant time zone differences. Settlement risk is also called Herstatt risk; Herstatt was the name of a German bank that failed in 1974 after receiving "overnight" payments and then defaulting.

a loss, whereas there is a corresponding gain to Bank E. But suppose that Party F then identifies a legal issue that it interprets as giving it the right to refuse to pay. If the court upholds Party F's position, Bank E could incur a loss. Litigation always involves uncertainty because even a seemingly weak case can prevail in court.

The following three non-financial risks are related: regulatory risk, accounting risk, and tax risk. They could even be collectively referred to as compliance risk because they all deal with the matter of conforming to policies, laws, rules, and regulations as set forth by governments and authoritative bodies, such as accounting governing boards. Obviously the regulatory, accounting, and tax environment is always subject to change, but the rapid expansion of financial products and strategies in relation to the relatively slow manner in which government and private regulators are able to respond means that laws and regulations are nearly always catching up with the financial world. When these laws and regulations are updated, it can result in significant unexpected costs, back taxes, financial restatements, and penalties.

Another type of non-financial risk is model risk, which is the risk of a valuation error from improperly using a model. This risk arises when an organization uses the wrong model or uses the right model incorrectly. A simple example applicable to both a portfolio manager and a corporate analyst is the assumption of constant dividend growth in the dividend discount model when, in fact, growth is not constant.

Closely related to model risk is tail risk—more events in the tail of the distribution than would be expected by probability models. This risk is a facet of market risk, but it also infects valuations and models when it is ignored or mishandled. Tail risk is known to be especially severe for the normal distribution, which tends to be overused in modeling. As an example, consider the monthly returns on the S&P 500 Index from January 1950 to October 2018. The monthly average return was 0.70%, and the monthly standard deviation was 4.10%. If we rank the monthly returns, we would find that the largest negative return was −21.76%, which occurred in the well-known market crash of October 1987. With a normal distribution, we would find that a return that low would occur only once every 2,199,935 years.[15] The second and third worst monthly returns of −16.94% (October 2008) and −14.58% (August 1998) would occur only once every 6,916 and 654 years respectively. If the normal distribution is a realistic descriptor of returns, results of these magnitudes should *never* have occurred in recorded market history, and yet we have seen three such instances. Interestingly, according to the normal distribution, the largest positive return of 16.30% in October 1974 would occur only once every 888 years. Technically, one could argue that if we go another 2,199,935 years and do not observe a monthly return as low as −21.76%, then the assumption of a normal distribution might seem reasonable, but it seems safe to reject the normal distribution for at least another two million years. Similar comments can apply to the second and third worst returns albeit over shorter periods.

Many quantitative models (e.g., option models) and decision models (e.g., portfolio construction and asset allocation, relying on variances and covariances in analysis and decisions) ignore the existence of fat tails in returns; as a result, market risk is often considered and dealt with in an oversimplified fashion. Tail risk, as the term is used in practice, is important and is discussed separately because financial professionals realize the implicit failure of modeling market risk. More plainly, ignoring tail risk is a form of model risk. And although tail risk might seem more of a financial risk than a non-financial risk, the mistake occurs internally, arising from poor choices made in modeling.

Most of the internal risks faced by an organization are often grouped together and referred to as operational risk. **Operational risk** is the risk that arises inadequate or failed people, systems, and internal policies, procedures, and processes, as well as

15 This calculation and those that follow are based on determining the probability of the given return or less.

from external events that are beyond the control of the organization but that affect its operations. Although the factors that give rise to such risks can arise externally, the risks themselves are largely internal to an organization because it would be expected to have its people, systems and internal policies, procedures, and processes functioning effectively regardless of pressures placed on it by external forces.

Employees themselves are major sources of potential internal risks. Banks are keenly aware of the vulnerability to employee theft, given the ease with which so many employees have access to accounts and systems for making entries. But even perfectly honest employees make mistakes, and some can be quite costly. The employee who credits someone's account $100,000 for a $100 deposit may have made an honest mistake, but it is a mistake that could quickly lead to the rapid disappearance of money. In the past, employees up to senior management have been guilty of perpetrating accounting fraud, not necessarily for their own direct benefit but to make the company look better.

In banks and other companies that trade in the financial markets, there is the risk that a trader or portfolio manager will fail to follow laws, rules, or guidelines and put the company at great financial risk. This individual is commonly described as a "rogue trader." Personified by Nick Leeson of Barings Bank, who in 1995 destroyed the 200-year old company by engaging in a series of highly speculative trades to cover up losses, the rogue trader has become a standard concern of risk managers. Although it was never clear if Leeson's trades were truly unauthorized, his legacy left the fear that institutions bear the risk that one trader can imperil the entire organization by making large and highly speculative trades that put the bank's entire capital base at risk. In essence, a rogue trader is a trader who engages in risky transactions without regard for the organization's limits or conforming to its controls.

Organizations are also threatened by business interruptions, such as those caused by extreme weather and natural disasters. Events such as floods, earthquakes, or hurricanes can cause significant damage and temporarily shut down an organization. Although extreme weather and natural disasters are external forces that are completely out of the control of an organization, it does not excuse the organization from having the appropriate internal procedures for managing problems caused by their external environment. Simple and fairly low-cost actions, such as having generators, backup facilities, or providing employees the option to work remotely, can go a long way toward keeping employees working during extreme weather events and when natural disasters strike. Yet, some organization have not heeded inclement weather forecasts. Failing to react to warnings can result in considerable loss.

In a world that is increasingly digital, cyber risk is a major operational risk that spares no organization and that can have significant consequences. Organizations are expected to understand and manage the risk associated with the disruption of or failure related to their information technology (IT) systems. For example, a hacker breaking into a company's IT system and stealing customer or client data is an external threat. Hacking, however, is not simply a random act of mischief. Companies are aware of the threat of hackers, and hackers can break in to a system only if that system is vulnerable. An organization is responsible for ensuring cyber security and establishing sufficiently robust IT safeguards, such as data encryption, to deter hackers from breaking in and either stealing or causing disruption. Cyber-attacks and data breaches can have serious reputational and compliance consequences. For example, all organizations targeting European citizens must comply with the General Data Protection Regulation (GDPR) and notify regulators and data subjects of any data breaches regarding sensitive personal information within 72 hours. Failure to do so can lead to fines of several million euros, including for organizations based outside the European Union. In addition to the threats posed by hackers and viruses, even secure IT systems themselves are a particular source of risk. Programming errors and bugs can create the possibility of costly mistakes.

Terrorism is another form of operational risks that poses a threat to organizations and individuals. The 1993 attacks on the World Trade Center led many companies to recognize that the New York City financial district was a major terrorist target and that, as such, their operations could be shut down by these acts of violence. When the more destructive attacks of 11 September 2001 occurred, many organizations had already established backup facilities sufficiently far away from that area. Of course, such risk is not confined to major financial centers, and indeed, organizations worldwide have begun to take security measures that address this operational risk.

Some of these operational risks are insurable, at least to a modest extent. We will briefly discuss insurance later, but most companies would much prefer to take proactive steps toward prevention than to incur the inconvenience of losses and then have an outside organization compensate them for their losses.

Solvency risk is the risk that the organization does not survive or succeed because it runs out of cash, even though it might otherwise be solvent.[16] This was probably the most underappreciated component of risk prior to the financial crisis of 2008.[17] The collapse of Lehman Brothers was often associated with an excess of leverage, which was certainly a key factor in its failure. But it was solvency risk that forced the company into bankruptcy. Almost overnight, Lehman's liquidity disappeared because most funding sources would no longer willingly bear Lehman's counterparty risk. Even if it had experienced large market gains on the day it went under, it had already been destroyed by solvency risk. Across the entire financial industry, from hedge funds to pension funds, painful but valuable lessons were learned about the critical importance of funds availability and solvency risk, even if all other risks were well-aligned. Solvency risk is now viewed as one of the key factors in running a successful hedge fund because investors are extremely sensitive to not recovering their investment in the event of a "run on the fund."

Solvency, in the personal or institutional sense, is the availability of funding to continue to operate without liquidating—or at a less extreme level, to be able to make good on liabilities and meet one's cash flow requirements. Solvency risk is the ultimate example of the importance of taking an enterprise view of risk management. For example, a university's investment officer might have a perfectly well-balanced set of risks in the endowment portfolio when viewed in isolation. But as a part of a university, the portfolio may be affected by a deep recession because the university's professional degree revenue, grant money, and donations will fall at the same time as the portfolio's investment value and cash distributions are in decline. Although the endowment and university may survive, it might be necessary for the endowment to take many emergency actions that impair its value, simply attributable to the overall solvency risk and the ultimate need of the enterprise to not run out of cash.

Solvency risk is easily mitigated, though never eliminated, by a large number of possible safeguards, none of which is free. Many businesses produce short-term higher returns by essentially ignoring solvency risk, but in doing so, they are not managing risk very well. Since the 2008 crisis, most businesses are keenly aware of the consequences of bad solvency management, and have taken such steps as using less leverage, securing more stable sources of financing, investing in models to provide more transparency on solvency risk, incorporating solvency risk at an enterprise level in risk governance, and holding more cash equivalents and assets with less liquidity risk.

---

16 Solvency risk is often referred to as liquidity risk by industry professionals, even though the expression *liquidity risk* was used earlier to refer to the risk of valuation shock when selling a security. Although the term "liquidity risk" is used in practice in both contexts, in this reading we will refer to the risk relating to the cash position of an organization as "solvency risk."

17 Bank runs are perhaps the simplest example of solvency risk. An otherwise solvent bank can easily be ruined by a bank run that wipes out its ability to make good on short-term liabilities.

Individuals can also face a number of risks of an operational nature. These include hackers breaking into one's computer and the threat of burglary and robbery. One of the most commonly cited risks for individuals is identity theft. For individuals, however, we consider their primary non-financial risks to be related to their life and health as well as other life-changing events.

Obviously, the health of an individual is an extremely important risk. Poor health can result from poor choices in life, but it can also arise from factors that are outside the control of the individual. These risks can result in direct health care expenses, reduced income because of disability, and reduced lifespan or quality of life. People vary widely in the risk management strategies they undertake to control their health, such as in their choices in diet, exercise, preventive health care, and avoidance of undue health risks. Some individuals address only their financial exposure to health risks, and still others do not take proactive steps to address this risk at all.

Closely related to health risk is mortality risk—the risk of dying relatively young—and longevity risk—the risk of outliving one's financial resources. Not only are these risks a primary determinant of the quality of life, they are also critical factors in investment planning. Although it is probably desirable not to know when one will die, financial planning for one's years in retirement is heavily dependent on one's mortality assumption. Insurance companies, defined benefit pension plans, and vendors of retirement annuities need only know the group average mortality. Mortality tables are reasonably accurate, so these institutions have relatively precise estimates of death rates for groups as a whole. Individuals themselves, however, clearly do not know how long they will live. People who use defined contribution plans must therefore build portfolios and control retirement distributions so that their assets outlive them, which is difficult to do when they do not know when they will die. No one wants to outlive their money, but with an increasingly aging population and good health care, this problem is becoming a greater concern.

There are a number of other major non-financial risks that individuals face, which are generally involved with some sort of life-changing disaster. The largest ones—fire, natural disaster, or massive liability stemming from harming others, such as in a car accident—are generally considered "property and casualty" risks and are insured as such.

4.3 Interactions between Risks

In some cases, a risk classified into one category could easily have been classified into another. Indeed, the interactions between risks are numerous. It has been said that market risk begets credit risk, which begets operational risk. That is, given unexpected market moves, one party then owes the other party money. Given the debtor–creditor nature of the relationship, the two parties must have internal operations that process the transactions and pay or collect the money. Thus, whenever there is credit risk, there is settlement risk. If there were no market risk, the other risks in the chain would likely be relatively minor. Legal risk often arises from market or credit risk. Large market moves create losses for one party. There is a long history of parties searching for loopholes in contracts and suing to avoid incurring the loss.

One simple example of an adverse risk interaction is counterparty risk. When trading a derivative contract, it is important to consider the cost of counterparty risk. Suppose Party A buys an out-of-the-money put option with a strike price of ¥1000—a contract theoretically worth ¥100 entitling him to as much as ¥1000 from Counterparty C if an underlying equity index is down. But there is a 2% chance that C could default; and assume that the possibility of default is considered independent of the performance of the equity market. This transaction, with payoffs adjusted for the possibility of default, might price at, say, ¥98 to A. But in reality, the credit risk of C's default is likely dependent on the equity market return. If the probability distribution of default risk overlaps substantially with that of the market being down, which is a likely scenario, then the risks interact, and the cost of risk is higher. In this example, perhaps the probability of C defaulting is 10% or more when the put option is in the money. So, A's expected payoff is lower as a result of facing a credit risk that is compounded by market risk. In fact, it is quite likely that in the extreme event—a deep decline in the equity market when A would presumably receive ¥1000—Party A will in all likelihood get nothing. Thus, the investor bears much more risk than initially thought as a result of the failure to consider the interaction of the two risks. And in doing so, Party A overpaid for the contract. This sort of risk interaction is so common in markets that practitioners have given it a very fitting term—"wrong-way risk." In fact, it was extremely common in the financial crisis of 2008, when holders of many securities based on mortgage credit believed that the risks were well-diversified when in truth, the risks were quite systematic.

Another example of interacting risks was experienced by many banks, funds, and private investment partnerships in 2008, as well as the hedge fund Long-Term Capital Management in 1998. Leverage, which manifested itself in higher market risk, interacted in an extremely toxic manner with liquidity risk and solvency risk and impaired or shuttered many investment firms.[18]

In most adverse financial risk interactions, the whole is much worse than the sum of its parts; the combined risk compounds the individual risks in a non-linear manner. For this example, a 2× levered organization might produce a 2% loss when its unlevered twin or baseline risk bears a 1% loss. If liquidity is a serious issue for the organization, then at a 10% baseline loss, the organization might face some moderate distress from liquidity or funding problems that it ends up losing 25% instead of 20%. It would not be surprising if this organization failed at a 30% baseline loss because of the toxic interplay between levered risk and liquidity problems. This resulting non-linear reaction to risk drivers exists across many risk interactions in many markets, making up-front scenario planning even more valuable to the risk process, a point we will return to later.

Earlier, we briefly described a common example of interacting risks for individuals. Suppose an individual works for a publicly traded company and, through an incentive program, receives shares of the company in her company retirement portfolio or for her personal holdings. Company policies may require that employees hold on to these shares for a number of years. When that time has elapsed, however, many individuals fail to recognize the incredibly concentrated risk they are assuming, so they hold on to their shares. An employee's reasoning for not selling the shares is often that the company she works for has been a solid performing company for many years, so she feels no reason to worry. Moreover, the team spirit often imbued in employees generates pride that can make employees believe that there is no better place in which to work and to invest their money. But if something goes wrong in the company or the industry, the employee may lose her job *and* her savings—an incredibly adverse interaction between market risk and human capital risk. The 2003 collapse of Enron remains a powerful historical example, with many loyal and honest employees losing virtually all of their retirement savings by failing to recognize this risk.

In sum, it is important to recognize that risks do not usually arise independently, but generally interact with one another, a problem that is even more critical in stressed market conditions. The resulting combined risk is practically always non-linear in that the total risk faced is worse than the sum of the risks of the separate components. Most risk models and systems do not directly account for risk interactions, which makes the consequences of the risk interaction even worse. Governance bodies,

18 This example illustrates yet another risk, systemic risk, that is a significant concern to regulators and governments. Stresses and failures in one sector transmit to stresses and failures in other sectors, which can ultimately impact an entire economy. Systemic risk is the ultimate example of interactions among risks.

company management, and financial analysts should be keenly aware of the potential risk and damage of risks in combination, and be aware of the dangers of treating risks as separate and unrelated.

EXAMPLE 3

Financial and Non-Financial Sources of Risk

1 Which of the following is *not* a financial risk?

  A Credit risk

  B Market risk

  C Operational risk

2 Which of the following *best* describes an example of interactions among risks?

  A A stock in Russia declines at the same time as a stock in Japan declines.

  B Political events cause a decline in economic conditions and an increase in credit spreads.

  C A market decline makes a derivative counterparty less creditworthy while causing it to owe more money on that derivative contract.

3 Which of the following *best* describes a financial risk?

  A The risk of an increase in interest rates.

  B The risk that regulations will make a transaction illegal.

  C The risk of an individual trading without limits or controls.

4 Which of the following is *not* an example of model risk?

  A Assuming the tails of a returns distribution are thin when they are, in fact, fat.

  B Using standard deviation to measure risk when the returns distribution is asymmetric.

  C Using the one-year risk-free rate to discount the face value of a one-year government bond.

5 Which of the following is the risk that arises when it becomes difficult to sell a security in a highly stressed market?

  A Liquidity risk

  B Systemic risk

  C Wrong-way risk

6 The risks that individuals face based on mortality create which of the following problems?

  A The risk of loss of income to their families.

  B Covariance risk associated with their human capital and their investment portfolios.

  C The interacting effects of solvency risk and the risk of being taken advantage of by an unscrupulous financial adviser.

Solution to 1:

C is correct. Operational risk is the only risk listed that is considered non-financial, even though it may have financial consequences. Credit and market risks derive from the possibility of default and market movements, respectively, and along with liquidity risk, are considered financial risks.

Solution to 2:

C is correct. Although most risks are likely to be interconnected in some way, in some cases the risks an organization is exposed to will *interact* in such a way that a loss (or gain) in one exposure will lead directly to a loss in a different exposure as well, such as with many counterparty contracts. Conditions in A and B are much more directly linked in that market participants fully expect what follows—for example, in B, an outbreak of war in one region of the world could well cause widespread uncertainty; a flight to quality, such as to government-backed securities; and a widening in spreads for credit-risky securities. In C, in contrast, the reduction in creditworthiness following the market decline may be expected, but owing more money on an already existing contract as a result comes from the interaction of risks.

Solution to 3:

A is correct because this risk arises from the financial markets.

Solution to 4:

C is correct. The risk-free rate is generally the appropriate rate to use in discounting government bonds. Although government bonds are generally default free, their returns are certainly risky. Assuming a returns distribution has thin tails when it does not and assuming symmetry in an asymmetric distribution are both forms of model risk.

Solution to 5:

A is correct. Securities vary highly in how liquid they are. Those with low liquidity are those for which either the number of agents willing to invest or the amount of capital these agents are willing to invest is limited. When markets are stressed, these limited number of investors or small amount of capital dry up, leading to the inability to sell the security at any price the seller feels is reasonable. Systemic risk is the risk of failure of the entire financial system and a much broader risk than liquidity risk. Wrong-way risk is the extent to which one's exposure to a counterparty is positively related to the counterparty's credit risk.

Solution to 6:

A is correct. The uncertainty about death creates two risks: mortality risk and longevity risk. The mortality risk (risk of dying relatively young) is manifested by a termination of the income stream generated by the person. In contrast, longevity risk is the risk of outliving one's financial resources.

MEASURING AND MODIFYING RISKS 5

The core element of risk management is the measurement and modification of risk. One cannot modify risk without measuring it. The primary purpose of measuring risk is to determine whether the risk being taken, or being considered, is consistent with the pre-defined risk tolerance. To understand how risk is measured, it is important to understand the basic elements that drive risk.

5.1 Drivers

This section illustrates the origins of risk. Risk is a part of life itself. None of us knows from one day to the next everything that will happen to us in the next 24 hours, let alone over a longer period. We may get a phone call that a relative is extremely sick, or we may be contacted by a head-hunter about an attractive job possibility. We may learn that we are going to be given an award from a prestigious organization, or we may find that our identity has been stolen. All of us can almost surely name something that happened the previous day that was not anticipated. Most of these happenings are minor and often quickly forgotten. Others are serious. Some are good. Some are bad. Some are unpredictable outcomes of known events, such as whether we get an offer following a job interview or whether a medical test reveals that we are healthy or ill. Some events are completely unanticipated, such as getting a phone call from an old friend we have not talked to in many years or having a flat tire on the drive home. Fortunately, the vast majority of risks in life are minor. The ones that are not minor, however, have the potential to be highly unpredictable and financially, and sometimes physically and emotionally, quite costly.

In a conceptual sense, financial risks are no different from the other risks we face in life. All risks arise from the fact that the future is unknown. Financial risks largely emanate from economic risks, and economic risks emanate from the uncertainties of life.

Financial markets generate prices that fluctuate as investors absorb information about the global and domestic state of the economy, the company's industry, and the idiosyncratic characteristics of the company itself. Global and domestic macroeconomies are driven by the companies that operate within them, but much of the tone as well as the ground rules are set by governments and quasi-governmental agencies, such as central banks. Taxes, regulations, laws, and monetary and fiscal policy establish a legal and economic environment and a set of ground rules that greatly affect the degree and quality of economic activity that takes place. Attempts by governments and central banks of different countries to coordinate economic policies can lead to some degrees of success if harmonized, but if not, they can create an environment in which companies engage in practices designed to seek favorable treatment in some countries and avoid unfavorable treatment in others.[19]

All economies, in turn, are composed of industries. Government policies also affect industries, in some cases encouraging economic activity in some industries while discouraging it in others. Some industries are stable, weathering macroeconomic storms quite well, whereas others are highly cyclical.

The uncertainties of global and domestic macroeconomic and central bank policies create risks for economies and industries that we often treat as systematic. Seemingly minor events, such as filling the position of central bank chairperson, are often viewed by investors as major events, signaling possibly a change in policy that can greatly affect the macroeconomy and possibly certain industries.

Moving down to a more fundamental level, investors face the unsystematic or idiosyncratic risks of individual companies. Modern investment analysis prescribes that diversified portfolios bear no unsystematic risk. We are then led to believe that unsystematic risk does not matter in a well-diversified portfolio. But unsystematic risk does matter to the management of a company. It also matters to poorly diversified investors. And it certainly matters to the financial analysts who cover specific

19 This practice is sometimes called regulatory arbitrage. The policies of certain countries can be more conducive to establishing operations. Examples are the flow of money into countries whose banking laws are less restrictive and more conducive to secrecy and incorporation in or moving a company to a country with lighter regulations or more favorable tax treatment.

companies. And what would appear to be unsystematic risk can oftentimes actually be systematic. For example, poor credit risk management by a major bank can turn into a global financial crisis if that bank is "too big to fail."

In sum, the basic drivers of risk arise from global and domestic macroeconomies, industries, and individual companies. Risk management can control some of this risk, but it cannot control all of it. For example, the risk manager of a company may be able to reduce the likelihood that his company will default, but he cannot control movements in interest rates. For the latter risk, he must accept that interest rate volatility is a given and that he can only position the company to be able to ensure that its risk exposure is aligned with its objective and risk tolerance. In order to do so, he must first be able to measure the risk.

5.2 Metrics

The notion of metrics in the context of risk refers to the quantitative measures of risk exposure. The most basic metric associated with risk is probability. Probability is a measure of the relative frequency with which one would expect an outcome, series of outcomes, or range of outcomes to occur. One can speak about the probability of rolling a six in one roll of a die as 1/6, the chance of rain in the next 24 hours as 20%, or the odds of a central bank taking actions to increase interest rates of 50%. These are all probabilities, differing in concept by the fact that the die roll is associated with an objective probability measure, whereas the other two examples are subjective probabilities. It is important to note that probability, in and of itself, is not a sufficient metric of risk. A chance of financial loss of 25% does not tell us everything we need to know. There are other measures of risk that incorporate probability but give us more information.

The standard deviation is a measure of the dispersion in a probability distribution. Although there is a formal mathematical definition of standard deviation, at this point we need only understand the conceptual definition. Standard deviation measures a range over which a certain percentage of the outcomes would be expected to occur. For example, in a normal distribution, about 68% of the time the outcomes will lie within plus or minus one standard deviation of the expected value. Two standard deviations in both directions would cover about 95% of the outcomes, whereas three would encompass 99% of the outcomes. Although standard deviation, or volatility, is widely used in the financial world, it does have significant limitations. In particular, standard deviation may not be an appropriate measure of risk for non-normal distributions. Standard deviation may not exist for return distributions with fat tails.

Moreover, according to modern portfolio theory, the risk captured by an asset's standard deviation overstates the risk of that asset's returns in the context of a diversified portfolio. Investors can easily diversify their holdings, thereby eliminating a portion of the risk in their portfolios by diversifying away the security-specific risk. As a result, most financial valuation theories assert that the ability of investors to eliminate security-specific risk, or non-systematic risk, means that investors should not expect to earn a premium to compensate them for the assumption of this risk. As a consequence, the risk of a security may be better measured by its **beta**, a measure of the sensitivity of a security's returns to the returns on the market portfolio. Beta measures relative risk, meaning how much market risk an asset contributes to a well-diversified portfolio.[20]

Beta describes risk well for a portfolio of equities, but other sources of risk may require other descriptive risk metrics. The risk associated with derivatives is one example of this. Although derivatives are widely used to manage risk, they do so by assuming other risks. Even if the derivative is being used to establish a hedge of an existing exposure to risk, it would still result in the assumption of additional risk because the assumed risk is being used to offset an existing risk. For example, if one purchases a call option denominated in euros to buy Russian rubles, one would be assuming the risk of the ruble/euro exchange rate. Because most derivatives exposures are highly leveraged, it is critical that the risk of derivatives be properly measured. There are several specialized measures of derivatives risk.

The sensitivity of the derivative price to a small change in the value of the underlying asset is called the **delta**. It is perhaps the most important measure of derivatives risk. Yet delta is limited to capturing only small changes in the value of the underlying. Large changes are captured by the concept of **gamma**. Whereas delta is a first-order risk, gamma is considered a second-order risk because it reflects the risk of changes in delta.[21] Some derivatives, such as options, are also sensitive to changes in the volatility of the underlying. This risk is captured by a concept called **vega**, which is a first-order measure of the change in the derivative price for a change in the volatility of the underlying. Derivatives are also sensitive to changes in interest rates, which are reflected in a measure called **rho**. Most options have relatively low sensitivity to interest rates.[22] These, and other mathematically derived derivatives metrics, are collectively referred to as "the Greeks."

Other asset classes may have their own special metrics to describe risk. One well-known example, **duration**, is a measure of the interest rate sensitivity of a fixed-income instrument. Analogous to delta, it is a first-order risk. The wide variety of financial instrument types and asset classes leads to a proliferation of terminology and risk measures, with most of them having no meaning outside their asset class. As financial organizations and asset risk modeling became more sophisticated and computer power increased, an approach was needed to measure and describe financial risk across the broad spectrum of asset classes. Spurred by the onset of global bank capital regulation, this led to the development of value at risk.

Value at risk or **VaR** is a measure of the size of the tail of the distribution of profits on a portfolio or for an organization. A VaR measure contains three elements: an amount stated in units of currency, a time period, and a probability. For example, assume a London bank determines that its VaR is £3 million at 5% for one day. This statement means that the bank expects to lose a minimum of £3 million in one day 5% of the time. A critical, and often overlooked word, is *minimum*. In this example, the bank expects that its losses will be at least £3 million in one day with 5% probability. In a VaR measure, there is no ultimate maximum that one can state. VaR is thus a minimum extreme loss metric. With a probability of 5% and a measurement period of

20 Earlier, we discussed the fact that unsystematic risk matters to some parties. Here we seem to be saying that it should not matter to anyone. Capital market models almost always assume that investors can diversify quite easily and, as a result, they should not expect to earn a premium for bearing diversifiable risk. This assumption does not mean that everyone's wealth is well-diversified. Investors who do not diversify probably cannot expect to earn a return for bearing diversifiable risk, but it does not mean that these investors should not care about measuring the risk they choose to assume by not diversifying.

21 The notion of a first-order risk versus a second-order risk can be seen by considering the following. Suppose A affects B and B, in turn, affects C. A does not affect C directly but does so only indirectly. A is a first-order risk for B and a second-order risk for C.

22 Options on interest rates, however, have a high sensitivity to interest rates, but only because interest rates are the underlying, and thus, the source of market risk.

one day, we can interpret the bank's VaR as expecting a minimum loss of £3 million once every 20 business days. VaR can also be used to measure credit losses, although the construction of the measure is considerably more difficult given the extreme asymmetry of the risk.

VaR is a simple but controversial measure. There are several ways to estimate VaR, each of which has its own advantages and disadvantages. The different measures can lead to highly diverse estimates. Moreover, VaR is subject to the same model risk as derivative pricing models. VaR is based on a particular assumption about the probability distribution of returns or profits. If that assumption is incorrect, the VaR estimate will be incorrect. VaR also requires certain inputs. If those inputs are incorrect, the VaR estimate will be incorrect. Many critics of VaR have argued that naive users of VaR can be lulled into a false sense of security. A presumably tolerable VaR can give the illusion that the risk is under control, when in fact, it is not. Yet, VaR is accepted as a risk measure by most banking regulators and is approved for disclosure purposes in typical accounting standards. As with any risk measure, one should supplement it with other measures.

As emphasized earlier, VaR does not tell the maximum loss. The maximum loss is the entire equity of an organization or the entire value of a portfolio, but the statistics used to estimate VaR can be used to gauge average extreme losses. Conditional VaR or **CVaR** is a common tail loss measure, defined as the weighted average of all loss outcomes in the statistical distribution that exceed the VaR loss. Another tail risk metric in the credit risk space that is analogous to CVaR is expected loss given default, which answers the question for a debt security, "If the underlying company or asset defaults, how much do we lose on average?"

VaR focuses on the left tail of the distribution and purports to tell us the expected frequency of extreme negative returns, but it can understate the actual risk. For example, the normal distribution gives us a well-defined measure of extreme negative returns, which are balanced by extreme positive returns. Yet, actual historical return distributions have shown that there are more extreme negative returns than would be expected under the normal distribution. We previously described this concern in the form of tail risk. In response to this concern, statisticians have developed a branch of study that focuses primarily on extreme outcomes, which is called **extreme value theory**, and leads to measures of the statistical characteristics of outcomes that occur in the tails of the distribution. There are mathematical rules that define the statistical properties of such large outcomes, and these rules have been widely used for years in the insurance business. In the past 20 years or so, risk managers have taken to using them to help gauge the likelihood of outcomes that exceed those that would normally be expected.

Two measures in particular that are often used to complement VaR are **scenario analysis** and **stress testing**. These are common sense approaches that ask "If this happens, then how are we affected?" Scenario analysis can be thought of as a package of stress tests, usually with some common underlying theme. A scenario defines a set of conditions or market movements that could occur and would put some pressure on a portfolio. An example might be a sharp increase in interest rates coupled with a significant decline in the value of a currency. The portfolio is then evaluated to determine its expected loss under these scenarios. A different means of posing a scenario analysis is stress testing, which is done by proposing specific asset price moves generally involving extremely large and high pressure scenarios that would occur only rarely but would have the potential for destabilizing the entire organization. The US Federal Reserve and other central banks have begun requiring major banks to stress test their portfolios. Although scenario analysis and stress testing can provide some information, they are, as noted previously for other measures, subject to model risk.

Of course, the measures just mentioned focus primarily on market risk. Credit risk, which is covered in more detail in readings on fixed-income analysis, has long relied heavily on the credit ratings provided by private companies, such as Moody's Analytics, Standard & Poor's, and Fitch Ratings. In effect, a large part of credit analysis for many lenders has been outsourced since the early part of the 20th century. Most lenders, however, do not rely exclusively on these rating companies. They do their own analysis, which focuses on the creditor's liquidity, profitability, and leverage. Liquidity measures, such as the current ratio, may indicate how well a borrower can cover short-term obligations. Solvency ratios, such as cash flow coverage or interest coverage, may reveal whether a borrower generates enough cash or earnings to make its promised interest payments. Profitability measures, such as return on assets, estimate whether a company is sufficiently profitable so that it can easily accommodate debt. Leverage measures, such as the ratio of debt to total assets, reflect whether a company has sufficient equity capital in relation to its debt to absorb losses and negative cash flows without defaulting. Credit analysis also examines the strength and cyclicality of the macroeconomy and the company's industry. Other widely used measures of credit risk include credit VaR, probability of default, expected loss given default, and the probability of a credit rating change.

One of the problems of credit risk measurement is that credit events, such as a ratings downgrade or a default, are relatively rare for a particular organization. Certainly, in the aggregate there are many credit losses, but very few companies that default have a history of defaulting. Without a history to go by, estimating the likelihood of an event that has never actually occurred is extremely difficult. Imagine the challenge of assigning a default probability to Lehman Brothers in 2007. It had been in operation since 1850 and had never defaulted. Yet in 2008, Lehman Brothers, one of the most successful financial companies of all time, filed for bankruptcy. Because of the infrequency of default, risk managers normally attempt to assess default probability by aggregating companies with similar characteristics.[23]

Another useful source of information for risk managers about these rare events is the *ex ante* risk cost that is implied by the market pricing of derivatives. A **credit default swap (CDS)** on an issuing company has an observable price that acts as a signal to a bondholder of the risk cost of a default. Put options, exotic options, insurance contracts, and other financial instruments may contain valuable signals of the cost of rare adverse events, or at least the price of hedging them.

Operational risk is one of the most difficult risks to measure. Consider the operational risk event reported in 2014 in which hackers broke into Home Depot's credit card data base. Assessing the likelihood of such an event and estimating the potential losses would be almost impossible. The threat of litigation alone for years afterward is difficult to quantify. As with credit risk, significant operational risk events are rare but usually quite costly if they do occur. Hence, attempts to quantify the risk usually involve a third party aggregating operational risk events across numerous companies and publishing the statistics.

As mentioned, there are numerous other risks that would likewise be difficult to measure. For example, there is always the possibility of changes in accounting rules, laws, tax rates, and regulatory requirements that can result in significant costs as companies adapt their policies and actions from one regulatory environment to a new one. How would one measure such risks? Moreover, the time period spanned by these risks is extremely long, and in fact, theoretically infinite. Changes in these rules and

23 In some sense, aggregating companies with similar characteristics is what credit ratings do. Companies rated BAA/Baa+ can be quite diverse but all are considered similar with respect to their ability to pay their debts.

laws are often motivated by politics. How does one quantify such risks when there are no real numeric measures? Analysis invariably reverts to subjective evaluation of the likelihood of such threats and their potential losses.

As we have described, many risks are measurable, at least on an *ex post* basis. Market-related risks are blessed with large quantities of data, so they are relatively measurable. Credit, operational, and other risks are somewhat rare events. Although it is probably a good thing that such events are indeed rare, their infrequency makes measurement more difficult. Nonetheless, virtually any risk manager will attempt to obtain at least a subjective sense of the expected frequency, likelihood, and cost of these events. With either objective or subjective measurements in mind, risk managers can then proceed to modify these risks accordingly.

5.3 Methods of Risk Modification

The notion of risk modification presumes that an analysis has been conducted in the risk governance stage that defines how much risk is acceptable. Coupled with measurements of the actual risk, as discussed in the previous section, the risk manager then proceeds to align the actual risk with the acceptable risk.

It is important to understand, however, that risk modification is not strictly risk reduction. For example, a portfolio with the strategic objective of maintaining a 50/50 split between equity and cash will naturally find that in a market in which cash outperforms equity, the split between equity and cash will tilt toward cash. Thus, the portfolio becomes less risky. Beyond a certain point, the risk of the portfolio is unacceptably low given the return target. Thus, risk modification would take the form of rebalancing by increasing the risk. For the most part, however, risk management focuses more on reducing the risk. Risk reduction is commonly referred to as hedging. A hedge is a transaction put in place to reduce risk. Some hedges are designed to lead to the ultimate in risk reduction—the complete elimination of risk. Others are simply designed to lower the risk to an acceptable level.[24] For some companies, risk management is primarily concerned with keeping the organization solvent. Regardless of the focus, much of what is done to manage risk is the same. In this section, we will examine four broad categories of risk modification: risk prevention and avoidance, risk acceptance, risk transfer, and risk shifting.

5.3.1 *Risk Prevention and Avoidance*

One method of managing risk is taking steps to avoid it altogether; however, avoiding risk may not be as simple as it appears. It is difficult to completely avoid risk, but more importantly, it is unclear that every risk should be completely avoided particularly if there are high costs associated with eliminating the risk. Instead we choose a trade-off between cost and benefits. The actual trade-off may be subject to debate because risk assessment and risk management are subject to variation from one person to another.

We could nearly eliminate the risk of being injured or killed in an automobile accident if we choose to never drive or ride in a car. Like any risk-avoidance strategy, however, there would more than likely be a trade-off in terms of the loss of the benefits provided by the activity. We could try to protect our children from all harm, but that may come at the expense of preparing them poorly for adult life. We could invest our entire retirement savings in cash, but would most likely give up protection against inflation and lose out on the opportunity to benefit from long-term economic growth and the performance of investable assets that benefit from that growth.

---

24 For example, in the case of the portfolio with a strategic target of 50/50 equity and cash, if equity outperforms cash, the portfolio will tilt toward equity. At some point, a risk-reducing strategy would then be in order. This type of hedge would reduce the risk but not eliminate it.

Insurance companies rely heavily on the techniques of risk prevention and avoidance. An automobile insurance company would prefer that their policyholders never drive their cars. Although it cannot prohibit them from doing so, it can reward them with lower premiums if they drive less and have safe driving records. A life insurance company would prefer that their policyholders do not smoke, and it can reward non-smokers with lower rates.

Nearly every risk we take has an upside, at least as perceived by the person taking the risk. Some counterexamples might seem to belie this point, but not if viewed from the point of view of the risk taker. One could argue that there are no benefits from smoking, but people who smoke may have the opinion that the pleasure they receive exceeds the costs. Casino gambling incurs the risk of significant financial loss and addiction, but it is risk that is acceptable to the consumers who incur it relative to the perceived benefits they receive. The risks of extreme sports, such as skydiving, would seem to be exceeded by the benefits obtained by participants, and yet participants engage in them with apparently much enjoyment. People undertake all types of risky behaviors because they obtain commensurate benefits. These examples are simply cases in which the decision maker chooses to bear a certain degree of risk. They are conceptually the same as an investor who chooses to accept a relatively high degree of risk. Likewise, those who live their lives engaging in very few risky activities are conceptually the same as the investor who keeps only a modest exposure to risky assets.

In organizations, the decision to avoid risk is generally made at the governance level as a part of setting the risk tolerance. Boards will often decide that there are some business or investment activities simply not worth pursuing based on either the goals of the organization or the perceived risk–return trade-off. These are strategic decisions. Boards may exclude some areas or activities to allow management to focus on choosing risks in other areas where they presumably have a better chance of adding value.

We recap this section by noting that risk prevention and avoidance is simply an element of the decision of how much risk to accept, given the trade-off between the risk of loss and the benefit of gain. This could be a direct benefit or an indirect benefit of avoiding or eliminating a risk. Most decisions in life involve a trade-off between benefits and costs, neither of which is necessarily easy to measure. Thus, risk management is an ongoing process of fine-tuning exposure to achieve the level of risk that is desired in relation to the benefits.

If the risk measurement process shows that the risk exceeds the acceptable level, there are three approaches to managing the risk: self-insuring, risk transfer, and risk shifting.

5.3.2 *Risk Acceptance: Self-Insurance and Diversification*

In many cases, from both a risk tolerance and a strategic standpoint, it makes sense to keep a risk exposure—but to do so in the most efficient manner possible. Self-insurance is the notion of bearing a risk that is considered undesirable but too costly to eliminate by external means. In some cases, self-insuring means simply to bear the risk. In other cases, it may involve the establishment of a reserve to cover losses. Choosing to not have health insurance can be an optimal choice for some young, healthy adults without responsibility for children. Setting aside some money to cover potential health costs completes the picture of an individual who completely self-insures. Similarly, a young healthy individual who does not buy life insurance but engages in a systematic, well-conceived savings and investment plan is engaging in self-insurance.

One must be careful with this approach, however, because there is a fine line between self-insurance and denial. To the extent that self-insurance results in risks that are completely in line with the enterprise's risk tolerance, it would be an example of good governance. But if there is a risk that is outside the enterprise's risk tolerance, and management decides to bear that risk anyway, saying it is self-insuring, management is basically ignoring that risk, disregarding and violating its risk tolerance, and practicing bad risk governance. For example, an investment management firm, via its risk tolerance decision, may decide that it cannot bear any investment loss exceeding €1 billion and may apply a variety of risk management tools to limit its market and credit risk accordingly. But suppose that the firm makes no move to limit or insure its risks from fraud or a rogue trader on the grounds that it is "self-insuring" this risk, which could result in a loss as high as €3 billion. By leaving itself open to a loss that far exceeds its stated risk tolerance, management is violating the firm's risk governance.

From the perspective of a business organization, self-insurance is obtained by setting aside sufficient capital to cover losses. The banking industry is a classic example of self-insurance. Although in many countries government insurance may protect depositors, banks self-insure to some extent by maintaining capital and loan loss reserves.

Another form of accepting risk, but doing so in the most efficient manner possible, is diversification. Technically, it is a risk-mitigation technique. But diversification and "the efficient frontier" are so central to modern portfolio analysis that capturing the full benefits of diversification seems the obvious thing for all organizations to pursue—a starting point at which other risk modification could be appended. Although diversification is one form of risk management, it is usually not effective if used in isolation.

In the next two subsections, we discuss how undesired risk can be modified or eliminated by selling the risk to another party. We make two subtle classifications of these methods: risk transfer and risk shifting.

5.3.3 *Risk Transfer*

Risk transfer is the process of passing on a risk to another party, often, but not always, in the form of an insurance policy. Insurance is a legal contract in which one party, the insurer, agrees to cover some percentage of a loss incurred by another party, the insured, from a specific event in return for the payment of a premium by the insured. Insurance as a method of risk modification has been in existence for very long time, and in fact, is even mentioned in the Code of Hammurabi almost 4,000 years ago. Insurance has been widely used in the commercial shipping and farming industries going back hundreds of years. Insurance is almost as old as commerce itself.[25]

From the point of view of the insurer, insurance almost always works on the basis of diversification or pooling of risks. An insurer attempts to sell many policies with risks that have low correlations. The insurer assesses the pooled risks and charges a premium that covers the expected aggregate losses and the insurer's operating costs as well as leaves a profit. Insurers need accurate statistics on aggregate risks, but these are often not difficult to obtain. These actuarial data are widely available on accidents, illnesses, property and casualty damage, and death. In principle, a well-diversified insurer does not care if a single insured party has significantly larger-than-average claims as long as there is no reason to believe that the claims are correlated. There will be other parties that have smaller-than-average claims.

Insurers do have to manage their risks carefully. Some risks can be correlated. In the US Gulf Coast region, property insurance, which includes coverage for loss by hurricanes, is typically more expensive than property insurance in other regions. Even with a higher premium, an insurer has to avoid providing too much property coverage in an area where a systemic event, such as a hurricane, can occur in order to diversify its risk exposure.

Although insurers carefully assess their risk and charge premiums that they believe accurately reflect expected losses, they nonetheless remain responsible for potentially large claims. Insurers also manage their risk by avoiding writing too many policies

25 It is worth noting that the insurance industry has for a long time referred to itself using the term "risk management." A department of risk management in a large organization is often the group that manages the organization's insurance policies. But since around 1990 or so, the term "risk management" has increasingly come to refer to far more than insurance.

with similar and potentially correlated risks and by selling some of the risk to another insurer, a practice known as reinsurance. A company that primarily insures property in the US Midwest, which is highly subject to tornado risk, might be willing to accept some Gulf Coast hurricane risk for a reasonable premium. Insurers often write provisions into contracts to exclude coverage of special cases. For example, a war might nullify insurance coverage in an area. Most insurance policies also contain provisions to guard against moral hazards, such as suicide or destroying one's own property. In the last 20 years or so, some insurance companies have issued bonds that permit them to legally avoid paying principal and/or interest if insurance claims exceed a certain amount. These instruments, known as catastrophe bonds, essentially pass some of the insurance risk on to the investors who buy the bonds.

Most insurance policies do not cover *all* of the risk that is insured. It is common for policies to contain a provision known as a deductible. A deductible is a monetary amount of the loss that will be covered by the insured before any claims are paid. Thus, both the insured and the insurer bear some of the risk, although the insurer usually bears the greater amount. Deductibles serve several purposes. Because insurers incur fixed costs for each claim, deductibles reduce the number of small claims. Deductibles also encourage good risk management by the insured parties. Finally, deductibles offer the insured the opportunity to combine risk transfer with self-insurance and thereby achieve a potentially better trade-off of risk and reward.

As noted, the concept of insurance relies on the diversification or pooling of risks. In a few cases, however, the risks are not easy to pool. For example, suppose a volatile but extremely successful actor is signed to star in a movie. The production company knows that it runs the risk that the actor will engage in behavior that damages the ability of the company to finish the movie. The number of volatile and extremely successful actors for whom policies could be written at the same time is somewhat limited. Thus, an insurer would have to bear that risk without the benefit of diversification.

For example, suppose a television network plans to cover the Olympics but is concerned about a possible cancellation or boycott. It might want an insurance policy to cover it against loss. Specialized coverage is possible through such companies as Lloyd's of London. The approximately 350-year old Lloyd's is famous for covering unusual risks. It does so by organizing groups of investors who are willing to bear a risk for a premium. These groups, called syndicates, are subject to the full extent of losses. In many cases, investors in these syndicates have been required to pay substantial amounts of money to cover losses.[26] These examples illustrate how syndicates work. Although there is only one Olympics to insure, there may also be only one actor to insure. Because the two risks are uncorrelated, a company could write policies on both risks and would achieve some diversification. Moreover, there are other unusual risks that can be covered such that the aggregate pool would represent a highly diverse set of risks that have low correlations.

A very slight variation of insurance is a surety bond. With a surety bond, an insurer promises to pay an insured a certain amount of money if a third party fails to fulfill its obligation. For example, if a party engages the services of another party, the first party is covered if the party obligated to provide the service fails to perform to a satisfactory degree. Surety bonds are widely used in commercial activity when one party bears the risk of the potentially high cost of non-performance by another party. A slight variation of a surety bond is a fidelity bond, which is often used to cover against losses that result from employee dishonesty. Bonds of this type work very similarly to

---

26 NBC insured the 1980 Summer Olympics in Moscow through Lloyd's of London to the extent that if a US boycott occurred, Lloyd's would pay NBC for losses that it incurred by prepaying the Soviet Union for broadcasting rights. The United States did boycott the Olympics and NBC collected on its policy.

insurance and rely on the pooling of uncorrelated risks.[27] Other similar arrangements include indemnity clauses and hold harmless arrangements, such as when two parties sign a contract and one party agrees to hold the other harmless and/or indemnify the other in the event of loss.

The use of insurance by so many as a risk management tool suggests that the cost of risk exceeds the actuarial cost to many individuals and enterprises. *Ex ante* consideration of the cost of a risk in terms of the organization's value or utility ties risk mitigation back to the risk tolerance decision and the most fundamental governance decisions on which value-added strategies to pursue. As an alternative to *ignoring* the cost of risk, the impact on enterprise value should be quite positive.

5.3.4 *Risk Shifting*

Whereas risk transfer refers to actions taken that pass the risk on to other parties, **risk shifting** refers to actions that change the distribution of risk outcomes. Risk transfer is often associated with insurance, whereas risk shifting generally involves derivatives as the risk modification vehicle. Although insurance is a form of risk management based on the pooling or diversification of risks, risk shifting diverts some portion of the risk distribution to another market participant who either bears the risk or intermediates that risk by moving it to yet another party. The organization may want to adjust its probability distribution of returns, essentially adjusting the payoff diagram of its risk exposures. An example is a company that is willing to make slightly less profit than it otherwise would if the stock market is up to prevent it from losing too much money if the stock market is down, for example, more than 20% next year. It is adjusting its potential economic outcomes by shifting the probability distribution of its profits conditional on market performance. Risk shifting represents the bulk of hedging and is the most common form of risk modification for financial organizations.

The principal device through which risk shifting is performed is a derivative. We briefly mentioned derivatives earlier in this reading. By definition, a derivative is a financial instrument that derives its price from the price of an underlying asset or rate. Because the price of the underlying and the price of the derivative are so closely related, derivatives can provide essentially the same exposure as the underlying but can do so at lower cost and capital requirements. As such, derivatives permit the efficient shifting of risk across the probability distribution and from one party to another. One can hold the underlying and take an offsetting position in the derivative or vice versa. Whereas insurance can be designed to perform similarly, insurance functions primarily through the pooling of diverse risks. With derivatives, risks are shifted across probability distributions or payoffs and across parties, to leave specific outcomes of the conditional probability distribution with the parties most willing to bear the risk.

There are several types of derivatives, and the manner in which they provide risk shifting varies by type. Derivatives are classified into two categories: forward commitments or contingent claims. Forward commitments are agreements that obligate two parties to undertake a transaction at a future date at a price or rate agreed on when the commitment is made. Forward commitments include such instruments as forward contracts, futures contracts, and swaps. Forward commitments can be used to lock in a future interest rate for a borrower or lender, the purchase or sale price of an asset, or an exchange rate for a currency. Parties who engage in forward commitments do not pay any money at the initiation of the contract. In lieu of any up-front payment from one party to the other, the two parties agree on the terms of the transaction that will be consummated at the end of the contract. Depending on

---

27 In the context of surety and fidelity bonds, the word "bond" does not mean a debt obligation issued by one party, the borrower, and bought by another, the lender. In this context, the word refers to assuring one party that it bears no risk for the actions of a specific other party.

movements in the price or rate of the underlying, one party will ultimately gain from the transaction while the other will lose or, in the less likely case, both parties could breakeven. For example, a corporate treasurer can use a forward contract to lock in the rate at which a foreign cash flow will be converted into the company's domestic currency. Regardless of movements in the exchange rate during the life of the contract, the foreign cash flow will convert to the domestic currency at a rate that is locked in when the contract is initiated. On the opposite side of the transaction, the party can be a speculator who simply bears the risk, or it can be a dealer who intermediates the risk between the hedger and the speculator. We will discuss dealers in more detail in a few paragraphs.

The other type of derivative is a contingent claim, which is commonly known as an option. An option is a contract between two parties that gives one party the right to buy or sell an underlying asset or to pay or receive a known underlying rate. An option takes the form of either a call option, which provides the right to buy the underlying or to pay a known rate, or a put option, which provides the right to sell the underlying or to receive a known rate.

With a forward commitment, both parties are mutually obligated to each other. Because an option grants the right, but not the obligation, to one party, that party has an advantage over the other. Consequently, that party, the buyer of the option, must pay cash, called the premium, to the seller of the option at the start of the contract. Once the premium is paid, the option buyer has no further obligation. He can either exercise the option or he can let the option expire unexercised. In the latter case, the option buyer incurs a loss equal to the premium. If the option is a call and it is exercised, the buyer pays the fixed price or rate and receives the underlying. If the option is a put and it is exercised, the buyer receives the fixed price or rate and delivers the underlying.[28] If the buyer of the option does exercise it, he may achieve a gain that exceeds the premium paid but the gain could also be less than the premium paid, thereby resulting in a net overall loss. An option buyer could be using the option to speculate on an upward move in the underlying if a call or downward move if a put. Alternatively, the option buyer could be hedging. In the example used earlier for forward commitments, the corporate treasurer anticipating an inflow of cash in a foreign currency could buy a put option to sell that currency, thereby converting it into his domestic cash flow at a known fixed rate. The option gives the treasurer the flexibility to not exercise it if the underlying currency rises in value. This flexibility comes at the cost of having to pay a premium at the start of the transaction, thus shifting the financial outcome across the entire probability distribution of that uncertain currency rate. In contrast, with the forward contract, the treasurer does not have to pay cash at the start but is obligated to convert at the agreed-upon rate.

Derivatives can be created in public forums, such as on derivatives exchanges, or privately between two parties. On derivatives exchanges, there are a large number of individual and institutional traders that make markets in derivatives. For private derivatives transactions, there is an extensive market of large bank and non-bank dealers willing to buy and sell derivatives. In both types of markets, these dealers assume the risk being transferred from parties who originate the transactions. These dealers almost always restructure and transfer some portion, if not all, of the risk by finding other parties that are willing to take on that risk. Ultimately, the risk is assumed by some party willing to accept the risk, producing an economically efficient outcome for all parties.

28 Instead of one party delivering the underlying, some options call for settlement in cash of an equivalent amount. Some forward commitments also settle in cash.

5.3.5 *How to Choose Which Method for Modifying Risk*

Choosing which risk mitigation method to use—risk prevention and avoidance, self-insuring, risk transfer, or risk shifting—is a critical part of the risk management process. Fortunately, the methods are not mutually exclusive, and many organizations use all methods to some extent. No single method provides a clear-cut advantage over the others. As with all decisions, the trade-off is one of costs versus benefits that are weighed in light of the risk tolerance of the organization or individual.

For example, many companies that have extensive foreign operations and are, therefore, highly exposed to exchange rate risk, hedge that risk using derivatives. Some companies prefer forwards, some prefer swaps, some prefer options, and some use multiple instruments. Some companies attempt to hedge currency risk by setting up operations in foreign countries rather than manufacturing domestically and shipping the goods to foreign countries.[29] Some companies manage their currency risk by attempting to balance currency assets and liabilities. Some airlines hedge the risk of oil price changes and others do not. Some airlines that do hedge this risk do so to a far greater degree than others. Additionally, some prefer the certainty of forwards and swaps, whereas others prefer the flexibility of options, even with the up-front cost that options require. Most insurance companies rely on their actuarial knowledge but supplement it with proactive measures, such as selling risk to other parties.

To the extent possible, most organizations should avoid risks that provide few benefits and potentially extreme costs. Reasonable, low-cost precautions against risks with few benefits should always be taken. Thus, risk prevention and risk avoidance are probably the first choice of measures, especially for risks that lie outside the core competencies of the organization and have little reasonable expectation of adding value. Nonetheless, avoidance may not be the best value for its cost. Moreover, avoiding risk may mean avoiding opportunity. Thus, an organization often cannot simply decide not to take a risk, at least not for all undesirable risks.

Organizations that have large amounts of free cash flow may choose to self-insure some risks, but few organizations have so much cash that they can afford to self-insure all risks. Some risks can potentially imperil the entire capital base. Most companies would, however, prefer to self-insure to the extent possible because self-insurance reduces the costs associated with external monitoring and gives the organization the greatest flexibility. Self-insurance and avoidance should generally be clearly addressed at the governance level and be consistent with stated risk tolerance.

Risk transfer, or the use of insurance, is a widely used risk management tactic, but it may not be suitable for many types of risks. Some risks simply are not insurable, at least not in a cost-effective way. Insurance works best when risks can be pooled, and that is not the case for many types of risks, particularly those that can affect a large number of parties at the same time. The use of risk shifting tools, such as derivatives, may not be available for all types of risks, thus limiting their use in risk mitigation. For financial risks that exceed risk appetite, risk shifting is a very common choice.

The various risk management methods are not equal in terms of the risk reduction and the risk profile that remains. For example, contingent claims, such as insurance, provide the flexibility in the form of offering opportunity to profit in one direction and have a loss reduced in the other, but they require payment of cash up front. In contrast, forward commitments lock in an outcome. In other words, they provide little flexibility, but they require no cash payment up front. The risk profile that exists when

29 Here is another example of the interactions of risks. A decision to manufacture products in a foreign country involves trade-offs between exchange rate risk, political risk, and a variety of other risks germane to that country's economy, not to mention a potentially different degree of operational risk, in the pursuit of higher profits.

a contingent claim hedge is put in place differs significantly from the risk profile that exists when a forward commitment hedge is placed. This process requires significant understanding and discussion at all levels of the organization.

To recap, risk takers should identify risks that offer few rewards in light of potential costs and avoid those risks when possible. They should self-insure where it makes sense and diversify to the extent possible. They should consider insurance when risks can be pooled effectively if the cost of the insurance is less than the expected benefit. If derivatives are used, they must consider the trade-off of locking in outcomes with forward commitments versus the flexibility relative to cash cost of contingent claims, which can tailor the desired outcomes or payoffs by shifting the risk. Ultimately, the decision is always one of balancing costs against benefits while producing a risk profile that is consistent with the risk management objectives of the organization.

EXAMPLE 4

Measuring and Modifying Risk

1 From the perspective of an organization, which of the following *best* describes risk drivers?

   A The probabilities of adverse events

   B The statistical methods that measure risk

   C Factors that influence macroeconomies and industries

2 Which of the following concepts directly measures the risk of derivatives?

   A Probability

   B Delta and gamma

   C Beta and standard deviation

3 The *best* definition of value at risk is:

   A the expected loss if a counterparty defaults.

   B the maximum loss an organization would expect to incur over a holding period.

   C the minimum loss expected over a holding period a certain percentage of the time.

4 Which of the following are methods commonly used to supplement VaR to measure the risk of extreme events?

   A Standard deviation

   B Loss given default

   C Scenario analysis and stress testing

5 Which of the following is a true statement about insurable risks?

   A Insurable risks are less costly.

   B Insurable risks have smaller loss limits.

   C Insurable risks are typically diversifiable by the insurer.

Solution to 1:

C is correct. Risks (and risk drivers) arise from fundamental factors in macroeconomies and industries.

Solution to 2:

B is correct. Delta and gamma are measures of the movement in an option price, given a movement in the underlying. The other answers can reflect some elements of derivatives risk, but they are not direct measures of the risk.

Solution to 3:

C is correct. VaR measures a minimum loss expected over a holding period a certain percentage of the time. It is not an expected loss nor does it reflect the maximum possible loss, which is the entire equity of the organization.

Solution to 4:

C is correct. Scenario analysis and stress testing both examine the performance of a portfolio subject to extreme events. The other two answers are metrics used in portfolio analysis but are not typically associated with extreme events.

Solution to 5:

C is correct. Insurance works by pooling risks. It is not necessarily less costly than derivatives nor does it have lower loss limits.

SUMMARY

Success in business and investing requires the skillful selection and management of risks. A well-developed risk management process ties together an organization's goals, strategic competencies, and tools to create value to help it both thrive and survive. Good risk management results in better decision making and a keener assessment of the many important trade-offs in business and investing, helping managers maximize value.

- Risk and risk management are critical to good business and investing. Risk management is *not* only about avoiding risk.
- Taking risk is an active choice by boards and management, investment managers, and individuals. Risks must be understood and carefully chosen and managed.
- Risk exposure is the extent to which an organization's value may be affected through sensitivity to underlying risks.
- Risk management is a process that defines risk tolerance and measures, monitors, and modifies risks to be in line with that tolerance.
- A risk management framework is the infrastructure, processes, and analytics needed to support effective risk management; it includes risk governance, risk identification and measurement, risk infrastructure, risk policies and processes, risk mitigation and management, communication, and strategic risk analysis and integration.
- Risk governance is the top-level foundation for risk management, including risk oversight and setting risk tolerance for the organization.
- Risk identification and measurement is the quantitative and qualitative assessment of all potential sources of risk and the organization's risk exposures.
- Risk infrastructure comprises the resources and systems required to track and assess the organization's risk profile.

- Risk policies and processes are management's complement to risk governance at the operating level.
- Risk mitigation and management is the active monitoring and adjusting of risk exposures, integrating all the other factors of the risk management framework.
- Communication includes risk reporting and active feedback loops so that the risk process improves decision making.
- Strategic risk analysis and integration involves using these risk tools to rigorously sort out the factors that are and are not adding value as well as incorporating this analysis into the management decision process, with the intent of improving outcomes.
- Employing a risk management committee, along with a chief risk officer (CRO), are hallmarks of a strong risk governance framework.
- Governance and the entire risk process should take an enterprise risk management perspective to ensure that the value of the entire enterprise is maximized.
- Risk tolerance, a key element of good risk governance, delineates which risks are acceptable, which are unacceptable, and how much risk the overall organization can be exposed to.
- Risk budgeting is any means of allocating investments or assets by their risk characteristics.
- Financial risks are those that arise from activity in the financial markets.
- Non-financial risks arise from actions within an organization or from external origins, such as the environment, the community, regulators, politicians, suppliers, and customers.
- Financial risks consist of market risk, credit risk, and liquidity risk.
- Market risk arises from movements in stock prices, interest rates, exchange rates, and commodity prices.
- Credit risk is the risk that a counterparty will not pay an amount owed.
- Liquidity risk is the risk that, as a result of degradation in market conditions or the lack of market participants, one will be unable to sell an asset without lowering the price to less than the fundamental value.
- Non-financial risks consist of a variety of risks, including settlement risk, legal risk, regulatory risk, accounting risk, tax risk, model risk, tail risk, and operational risk.
- Operational risk is the risk that arises either from within the operations of an organization or from external events that are beyond the control of the organization but affect its operations. Operational risk can be caused by employees, the weather and natural disasters, vulnerabilities of IT systems, or terrorism.
- Solvency risk is the risk that the organization does not survive or succeed because it runs out of cash to meet its financial obligations.
- Individuals face many of the same organizational risks outlined here but also face health risk, mortality or longevity risk, and property and casualty risk.
- Risks are not necessarily independent because many risks arise as a result of other risks; risk interactions can be extremely non-linear and harmful.
- Risk drivers are the fundamental global and domestic macroeconomic and industry factors that create risk.
- Common measures of risk include standard deviation or volatility; asset-specific measures, such as beta or duration; derivative measures, such as delta, gamma, vega, and rho; and tail measures such as value at risk, CVaR and expected loss given default.

- Risk can be modified by prevention and avoidance, risk transfer (insurance), or risk shifting (derivatives).
- Risk can be mitigated internally through self-insurance or diversification.
- The primary determinants of which method is best for modifying risk are the benefits weighed against the costs, with consideration for the overall final risk profile and adherence to risk governance objectives.

PRACTICE PROBLEMS

1 Risk management in the case of individuals is *best* described as concerned with:

A hedging risk exposures.

B maximizing utility while bearing a tolerable level of risk.

C maximizing utility while avoiding exposure to undesirable risks.

2 Which of the following may be controlled by an investor?

A Risk

B Raw returns

C Risk-adjusted returns

3 The process of risk management includes:

A minimizing risk.

B maximizing returns.

C defining and measuring risks being taken.

4 Risk governance:

A aligns risk management activities with the goals of the overall enterprise.

B defines the qualitative assessment and evaluation of potential sources of risk in an organization.

C delegates responsibility for risk management to all levels of the organization's hierarchy.

5 The factors a risk management framework should address include all of the following *except*:

A communications.

B policies and processes.

C names of responsible individuals.

6 Which of the following is the correct sequence of events for risk governance and management that focuses on the entire enterprise? Establishing:

A risk tolerance, then risk budgeting, and then risk exposures.

B risk exposures, then risk tolerance, and then risk budgeting.

C risk budgeting, then risk exposures, and then risk tolerance.

7 Which of the following *best* describes activities that are supported by a risk management infrastructure?

A Risk tolerance, budgeting, and reporting

B Risk tolerance, measurement, and monitoring

C Risk identification, measurement, and monitoring

8 Effective risk governance in an enterprise provides guidance on all of the following *except*:

A unacceptable risks.

B worst losses that may be tolerated.

C specific methods to mitigate risk for each subsidiary in the enterprise.

9 A firm's risk management committee would be expected to do all of the following *except*:

A approving the governing body's proposed risk policies.

B deliberating the governing body's risk policies at the operational level.
C providing top decision-makers with a forum for considering risk management issues.

10 Once an enterprise's risk tolerance is determined, the role of risk management is to:
A analyze risk drivers.
B align risk exposures with risk appetite.
C identify the extent to which the enterprise is willing to fail in meeting its objectives.

11 Which factor should *most* affect a company's ability to tolerate risk?
A A stable market environment
B The beliefs of the individual board members
C The ability to dynamically respond to adverse events

12 Risk budgeting includes all of the following *except*:
A determining the target return.
B quantifying tolerable risk by specific metrics.
C allocating a portfolio by some risk characteristics of the investments.

13 A benefit of risk budgeting is that it:
A considers risk tradeoffs.
B establishes a firm's risk tolerance.
C reduces uncertainty facing the firm.

14 Which of the following risks is *best* described as a financial risk?
A Credit
B Solvency
C Operational

15 Liquidity risk is *most* associated with:
A the probability of default.
B a widening bid–ask spread.
C a poorly functioning market.

16 An example of a non-financial risk is:
A market risk.
B liquidity risk.
C settlement risk.

17 If a company has a one-day 5% Value at Risk of $1 million, this means:
A 5% of the time the firm is expected to lose at least $1 million in one day.
B 95% of the time the firm is expected to lose at least $1 million in one day.
C 5% of the time the firm is expected to lose no more than $1 million in one day.

18 An organization choosing to accept a risk exposure may:
A buy insurance.
B enter into a derivative contract.
C establish a reserve fund to cover losses.

19 The choice of risk-modification method is based on:
A minimizing risk at the lowest cost.

B maximizing returns at the lowest cost.

C weighing costs versus benefits in light of the organization's risk tolerance.

SOLUTIONS

1 B is correct. For individuals, risk management concerns maximizing utility while taking risk consistent with individual's level of risk tolerance.

2 A is correct. Many decision makers focus on return, which is not something that is easily controlled, as opposed to risk, or exposure to risk, which may actually be managed or controlled

3 C is correct. Risks need to be defined and measured so as to be consistent with the organization's chosen level of risk tolerance and target for returns or other outcomes.

4 A is correct. Risk governance is the top-down process that defines risk tolerance, provides risk oversight and guidance to align risk with enterprise goals.

5 C is correct. While risk infrastructure, which a risk management framework must address, refers to the people and systems required to track risk exposures, there is no requirement to actually name the responsible individuals.

6 A is correct. In establishing a risk management system, determining risk tolerance must happen before specific risks can be accepted or reduced. Risk tolerance defines the appetite for risk. Risk budgeting determine how or where the risk is taken and quantifies the tolerable risk by specific metrics. Risk exposures can then be measured and compared against the acceptable risk.

7 C is correct. *Risk infrastructure* refers to the people and systems required to track risk exposures and perform most of the quantitative risk analysis to allow an assessment of the organization's risk profile. The risk management infrastructure identifies, measures, and monitors risks (among other things).

8 C is correct. Risk governance is not about specifying methods to mitigate risk at the business line level. Rather, it is about establishing an appropriate level of risk for the entire enterprise. Specifics of dealing with risk fall under risk management and the risk infrastructure framework.

9 A is correct. The risk management committee is a part of the risk governance structure at the operational level—as such, it does not approve the governing body's policies.

10 B is correct. When risk tolerance has been determined, the risk framework should be geared toward measuring, managing, and complying with the risk tolerance, or aligning risk exposure with risk tolerance. The risk tolerance decision begins by looking at what shortfalls within an organization would cause it to fail to achieve some critical goals and what are the organization's risk drivers.

11 C is correct. If a company has the ability to adapt quickly to adverse events may allow for a higher risk tolerance. There are other factors, such as beliefs of board members and a stable market environment, which may but should not affect risk tolerance.

12 A is correct. Risk budgeting does not include determining the target return. Risk budgeting quantifies and allocates the tolerable risk by specific metrics.

13 A is correct. The process of risk budgeting forces the firm to consider risk tradeoffs. As a result, the firm should choose to invest where the return per unit of risk is the highest.

14 A is correct. A financial risk originates from the financial markets. Credit risk is one of three financial risks identified in the reading: Credit risk is the chance of loss due to an outside party defaulting on an obligation. Solvency risk depends at least in part on factors internal to the organization and operational risk is an *internal* risk arising from the people and processes within the organization.

15 B is correct. Liquidity risk is also called transaction cost risk. When the bid–ask spread widens, purchase and sale transactions become increasingly costly. The risk arises from the uncertainty of the spread.

16 C is correct. Settlement risk is related to default risk, but deals with the timing of payments rather than the risk of default.

17 A is correct. The VaR measure indicates the probability of a loss of at least a certain level in a time period.

18 C is correct. Risk acceptance is similar to self-insurance. An organization choosing to self-insure may set up a reserve fund to cover losses. Buying insurance is a form of risk transfer and using derivatives is a form of risk-shifting, not risk acceptance.

19 C is correct. Among the risk-modification methods of risk avoidance, risk acceptance, risk transfer, and risk shifting none has a clear advantage. One must weigh benefits and costs in light of the firm's risk tolerance when choosing the method to use.

READING

56

Technical Analysis

by Barry M. Sine and Robert A. Strong, PhD, CFA

Barry M. Sine is at Drexel Hamilton, LLC (USA). Robert A. Strong, PhD, CFA, is at the University of Maine (USA).

LEARNING OUTCOMES

Mastery	*The candidate should be able to:*
☐	a. explain principles of technical analysis, its applications, and its underlying assumptions;
☐	b. describe the construction of different types of technical analysis charts and interpret them;
☐	c. explain uses of trend, support, resistance lines, and change in polarity;
☐	d. describe common chart patterns;
☐	e. describe common technical analysis indicators (price-based, momentum oscillators, sentiment, and flow of funds);
☐	f. explain how technical analysts use cycles;
☐	g. describe the key tenets of Elliott Wave Theory and the importance of Fibonacci numbers;
☐	h. describe intermarket analysis as it relates to technical analysis and asset allocation.

INTRODUCTION

1

Technical analysis has been used by traders and analysts for centuries, but it has only recently achieved broad acceptance among regulators and the academic community. This reading gives a brief overview of the field, compares technical analysis with other schools of analysis, and describes some of the main tools in technical analysis. Some applications of technical analysis are subjective. That is, although certain aspects, such as the calculation of indicators, have specific rules, the interpretation of findings is often subjective and based on the long-term context of the security being analyzed. This aspect is similar to fundamental analysis, which has specific rules for calculating ratios, for example, but introduces subjectivity in the evaluation phase.

The reading is organized as follows. Section 2 addresses the definition and scope of technical analysis. Section 3 explains the technical analysis toolkit in sections on trend, technical indicators, and cycles. Illustrations are drawn from specific examples of historical market action within the timeframe from 2005 to mid-2018. Section 4 addresses a theory of longer term price movements known as Elliot Wave Theory. Section 5 covers intermarket analysis related to interactions between multiple markets. Section 6 concludes.

2 TECHNICAL ANALYSIS: DEFINITION AND SCOPE

Technical analysis is a form of security analysis that uses price and volume data, which is often graphically displayed, in decision making. Technical analysis can be used for securities in any freely traded market around the globe. A freely traded market is one in which willing buyers trade with willing sellers without external intervention or impediment. Prices are the result of the interaction of supply and demand in real time. Technical analysis is used on a wide range of financial instruments, including equities, bonds, commodity futures, and currency futures.

The underlying logic of technical analysis is simple:

- Supply and demand determine prices.
- Changes in supply and demand cause changes in prices.
- Prices can be projected with charts and other technical tools.

Technical analysis of any financial instrument does not require detailed knowledge of that instrument. As long as the chart represents the action in a freely traded market, a technician does not even need to know the name or type of the security to conduct the analysis. Technical analysis can also be applied over any time frame—from short-term price movements to long-term movements of annual closing prices. Trends that are apparent in short-term charts may also appear over longer time frames. Because fundamental analysis is more time consuming than technical analysis, investors with short-term time horizons, such as traders, tend to prefer technical analysis—but not always. For example, fundamental analysts with long time frames often perform technical analysis to time the purchase and sale of the securities they have analyzed.

2.1 Principles and Assumptions

Technical analysis can be thought of as the study of collective investor psychology, or sentiment. Prices in any freely traded market are set by human beings or their automated proxies (such as computerized trading programs), and price is set at the equilibrium between supply and demand at any instant in time. Various fundamental theorists have proposed that markets are efficient and rational, but technicians believe that humans are often irrational and emotional and that they tend to behave similarly in similar circumstances.

Although fundamental data are key inputs into the determination of value, these data are analyzed by humans, who may be driven, at least partially, by factors other than rational factors.[1] Human behavior is often erratic and driven by emotion in many aspects of one's life, so technicians conclude that it is unreasonable to believe that investing is the one exception where humans always behave rationally. Technicians

1 Fundamental analysts use a wide variety of inputs, including financial statements, legal documents, economic data, first-hand observations from visiting the facilities of subject companies, and interviews with corporate managers, customers, suppliers, and competitors.

believe that market trends and patterns reflect this irrational human behavior. Thus, technical analysis is the study of market trends or patterns. And technicians believe the trends and patterns tend to repeat themselves and are, therefore, somewhat predictable. So, technicians rely on recognition of patterns that have occurred in the past in an attempt to project future patterns of security prices.

Another tenet of technical analysis is that the market reflects the collective knowledge and sentiment of many varied participants and the amount of buying and selling activity in a particular security. In a freely traded market, only those market participants who actually buy or sell a security have an impact on price. And the greater the volume of a participant's trades, the more impact that market participant will have on price. Those with the best information and most conviction have more say in setting prices than others because the informed traders trade higher volumes. To make use of their information, however, they must trade. Technical analysis relies on knowledgeable market participants putting this knowledge to work by trading in the market, thereby influencing prices and volume. Without trading, the information is not captured in the charts. Arguably, although insider trading is illegal for a variety of reasons, it improves the efficiency of technical analysis.

Trades determine volume and price. The impact occurs instantaneously and frequently anticipates fundamental developments correctly. So, by studying market technical data—price and volume trends—the technician is seeking to understand investor sentiment. The technician is benefiting from the wide range of knowledge of market participants and the collective conclusion of market participants about a security. In contrast, the fundamental analyst must wait for the release of financial statements to conduct financial statement analysis, so a time lag occurs between the market's activities and the analyst's conclusions.

Charles Dow, creator in 1896 of what is now known as the Dow Jones Industrial Average, described the collective action of participants in the markets as follows:

> The market reflects all the jobber knows about the condition of the textile trade; all the banker knows about the money market; all that the best-informed president knows of his own business, together with his knowledge of all other businesses; it sees the general condition of transportation in a way that the president of no single railroad can ever see; it is better informed on crops than the farmer or even the Department of Agriculture. In fact, the market reduces to a bloodless verdict all knowledge bearing on finance, both domestic and foreign.

A similar notion was expressed by George A. Akerlof and Robert J. Shiller:

> To understand how economies work and how we can manage them and prosper, we must pay attention to the thought patterns that animate people's ideas and feelings, their animal spirits. We will never really understand important economic events unless we confront the fact that their causes are largely mental in nature.[2]

Market participants use many inputs and analytical tools before trading. Fundamental analysis is a key input in determining security prices, but it is not the only one. Technical analysts believe that emotions play a role. Investors with a favorable fundamental view may nonetheless sell a financial instrument for other reasons, including pessimistic investor sentiment, margin calls, and requirements for their capital—for example, to pay for a child's college tuition. Technicians do not care why market participants are buying or selling, just that they are doing so.

---

2 See Akerlof and Shiller (2009).

Some financial instruments have an associated income stream that contributes to the security's intrinsic value. Bonds have regular coupon payments, and equity shares may have underlying cash flows or dividend streams. A fundamental analyst can adjust these cash flows for risk and use standard time value of money techniques to determine a present value. Other assets, such as a bushel of wheat, gallon of crude oil, or ounce of silver, do not have underlying financial statements or an income stream, so valuation models cannot be used to derive their fundamental intrinsic values. For these assets, technical analysis is the only form of analysis possible. So, whereas fundamental analysis is widely used in the analysis of fixed-income and equity securities, technical analysis is widely used in the analysis of commodities, currencies, and futures.

Market participants attempt to anticipate economic developments and enter into trades to profit from them. Technicians believe that security price movements occur before fundamental developments unfold—certainly before they are reported. This belief is reflected in the fact that stock prices are one of the 12 components of the National Bureau of Economic Research's Index of Leading Economic Indicators. A key tenet of technical analysis is that the equity market moves roughly six months ahead of inflection points in the broad economy.

2.2 Technical and Fundamental Analysis

Technical analysis and fundamental analysis are both useful and valid, but they approach the market in different ways. Technicians focus solely on analyzing markets and the trading of financial instruments. Fundamental analysis is a much wider field, encompassing financial and economic analysis as well as analysis of societal and political trends. Technicians analyze the result of this extensive fundamental analysis in terms of how it affects market prices. A technician's analysis is derived solely from price and volume data, whereas a fundamental equity analyst analyzes a company and incorporates data that are external to the market and then uses this analysis to predict security price movements. As the quotation from Dow in Section 2.1 illustrates, technical analysis assumes that all of the factors considered by a fundamental analyst are reflected in the price of a financial instrument through buying and selling activity.

A key distinction between technical analysis and fundamental analysis is that the technician has more concrete data, primarily price and volume data, to work with. The financial statements analyzed by fundamental analysts are not objective data but are the result of numerous estimates and assumptions that have been added together to arrive at the line items in the financial statements. Even the cash line on a balance sheet is subject to corporate management's opinion about which securities are liquid enough to be considered "cash." This opinion must be agreed to by auditors and, in many countries, regulators (who sometimes differ with the auditors). Financial statements are subject to restatements because of such issues as changes in accounting assumptions and even fraud. But the price and volume data used in technical analysis are objective. When the data become subject to analysis, however, both types of analysis become subjective because judgment is exercised when a technician analyzes a price chart and when a fundamental analyst analyzes an income statement.

Fundamental analysis can be considered to be the more theoretical approach because it seeks to determine the underlying long-term (or intrinsic) value of a security. Technical analysis can be considered to be the more practical because a technician studies the markets and financial instruments as they exist, even if trading activity appears, at times, to be irrational. Technicians seek to project the level at which a financial instrument *will* trade, whereas fundamental analysts seek to predict where it *should* trade.

Being a fundamental analyst can be lonely if the analyst is the first to arrive at a fundamental conclusion, even though it is correct, because deviations from intrinsic value can persist for long periods. The reason these deviations may persist is that it takes buying activity to raise (or lower) the price of a security in a freely traded market.

A drawback of technical analysis is that technicians are limited to studying market movements and do not use other predictive analytical methods, such as interviewing the customers of a subject company, to determine future demand for a company's products. Technicians study market trends and are mainly concerned with a security's price trend: Is the security trading up, down, or sideways? Trends are driven by collective investor psychology, however, and can change without warning. Additionally, it can take some time for a trend to become evident. Thus, technicians may make wrong calls and have to change their opinions. Technicians are better at identifying market moves after the moves are already under way.

Moreover, trends and patterns must be in place for some time before they are recognizable, so a key shortcoming of technical analysis is that it can be late in identifying changes in trends or patterns. This shortcoming mirrors a key shortcoming of fundamental analysis in that securities often overshoot fundamental fair values in an uptrend and undershoot fundamental fair values in a downtrend. Strictly relying on price targets obtained by fundamental analysis can lead to closing profitable investment positions too early because investors may irrationally bid securities prices well above or well below intrinsic value.

Fundamental analysis is a younger field than technical analysis because reliable fundamental data are a relatively new phenomenon. In contrast, the first recorded use of technical analysis was in Japan in the 1700s, where it was used to analyze trading in the rice market. The Japanese developed a detailed field of technical analysis with their own chart design and patterns. These tools were translated and widely understood outside Japan only in the 1980s.

Western use of technical analysis was pioneered by Dow, who was also the first editor of the *Wall Street Journal*, in the 1890s. At the time, publicly traded companies were under no requirement to release their financial information even to shareholders, and insider trading was common and legal. Dow created the Dow Jones Industrial Average and the Dow Jones Railroad Average (now the Transportation Average) as a proxy to gauge the health of the economy, because fundamental data were not available. By his logic, if industrial stocks were doing well, industrial companies themselves must be doing well and if railroad stocks were doing well, railroad companies must be doing well. And if both manufacturers and the companies that transported goods to market were prospering, the economy as a whole must be prospering.

Not until the Securities Exchange Act of 1934 were public companies in the United States required to regularly file financial statements that were available to the public. In that year, Benjamin Graham published his seminal work, *Security Analysis*, and three years later, he and several others founded one of the first societies devoted to fundamental analysis, the New York Society of Security Analysts.[3] Fundamental analysis quickly overtook technical analysis in terms of acceptance by practitioners, regulators, and academics.

Acceptance of technical analysis by practitioners was revived in the 1970s with the creation of the Market Technicians Association in New York and the International Federation of Technical Analysts a few years later. Only in the last decade, however, has the field started to achieve widespread acceptance by regulators and academics. An important impediment to acceptance by academics is the difficulty of capturing the

3 The New York Society of Security Analysts was a successor to the New York Society of Financial Statisticians, which was founded in 1916.

subjectivity involved in technical analysis. The human brain can recognize, analyze, and interpret technical information that is difficult for statistical computer models to recognize and test.

Although technical analysis can be applied to any freely traded security, it does have its limits. In markets that are subject to large outside manipulation, the application of technical analysis is limited. For example, the central banks of many countries intervene in their currency markets from time to time to maintain exchange rate stability. Interestingly, traders claim to have been able to successfully predict interventions in some countries, especially those where the central bank is itself using technical analysis. Technical analysis is also limited in illiquid markets, where even modestly sized trades can have an inordinate impact on prices. For example, in considering a thinly traded American Depositary Receipt (ADR), analyzing the more heavily traded local security frequently yields a better analysis.[4] Another example of when technical analysis may give an incorrect reading is in the case of a company that has declared bankruptcy and announced that its shares will have zero value in a restructuring. A positive technical trend may appear in such cases as investors who hold short positions buy shares to close out their positions.

A good example of when technical analysis is a superior tool to fundamental analysis is in the case of securities fraud, such as occurred at Enron Corporation and WorldCom. These companies were issuing fraudulent financial statements, but many fundamental analysts continued to hold favorable views of the companies' equity securities even as the share prices declined. Simultaneously, a small group of investors came to the opposite view and expressed this view through high-volume sales of the securities. The result was clearly negative chart patterns that could then be discerned by technical analysis.

3 TECHNICAL ANALYSIS TOOLS

The primary tools used in technical analysis are charts and indicators. Charts are the graphical display of price and volume data, and the display may be done in a number of ways. Charts are then subjected to various analyses, including the identification of trends, patterns, and cycles. Technical indicators include a variety of measures of relative price level—for example, price momentum, market sentiment, and funds flow. We will discuss charts first.

3.1 Charts

Charts are an essential component of the technical analyst's toolkit. Charts provide information about past price behavior and provide a basis for inferring likely future price behavior. A variety of charts can be useful in studying the markets. The selection of the chart to use in technical analysis is determined by the intended purpose of the analysis.

3.1.1 *Line Chart*

Line charts are familiar to all types of analysts and are a simple graphic display of price trends over time. Usually, the chart is a plot of data points, such as share price, with a line connecting these points. Line charts are typically drawn with closing prices

4 An American Depositary Receipt is a negotiable certificate issued by a depositary bank that represents ownership in a non-US company's deposited equity (i.e., equity held in custody by the depositary bank in the company's home market).

as the data points. The vertical axis (y-axis) reflects price level, and the horizontal axis (x-axis) is time. Even though the line chart is the simplest chart, an analyst can quickly glean information from this chart.

The chart in Exhibit 1 is a quarterly chart of the FTSE 100 Index from 1984 through mid-2018. Up years and down years are clearly evident. The strong rally from 1984 through 1999 and the market decline from late 1999 to late 2002 are also clearly visible. The 2003–2007 rally did not exceed the high reached in 1999, which suggests that investors were not willing to pay as high a price for stocks on the London Stock Exchange during that rally as they were in the prior rally. The 2007–2009 decline didn't reach the lows of 2002, suggesting that investors viewed the prior recessionary period as a support level. From 2009 through mid-2018, the market has been in a general uptrend with some pull-back in 2015. This visual information from the price chart, provides a broad overview of investor sentiment and can lead to further analysis. Importantly, the analyst can access and analyze this information quickly. Collecting and analyzing the full array of data normally incorporated in fundamental analysis would take much longer.

Exhibit 1 Line Chart: FTSE 100 Quarterly Price Data, 1984–mid-2018 (Price in British Pounds Sterling)

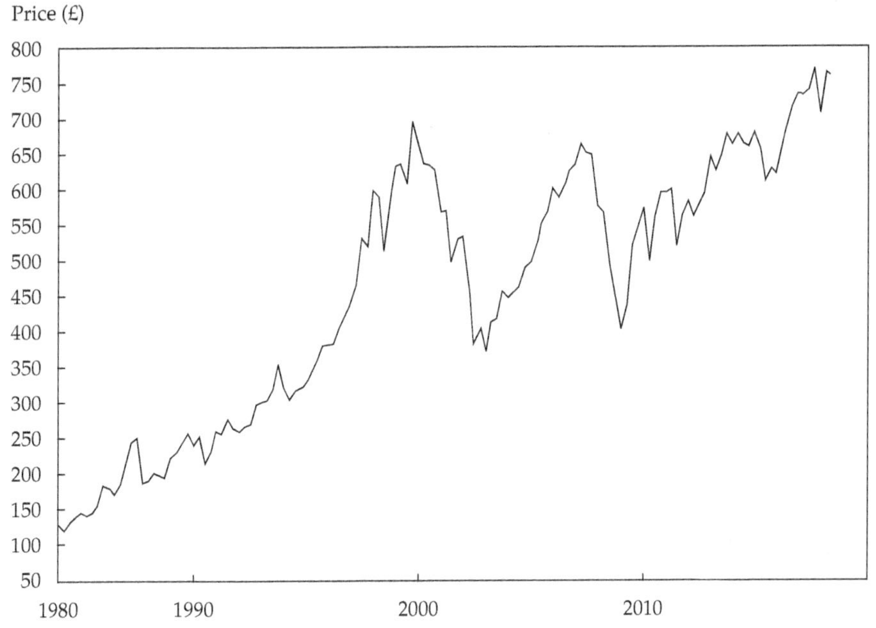

3.1.2 *Bar Chart*

A line chart has one data point per time interval. A **bar chart**, in contrast, has four bits of data in each entry—the high and low price encountered during the time interval plus the opening and closing prices. Such charts can be constructed for any time period, but they are customarily constructed from daily data.

As Exhibit 2 shows, a vertical line connects the high and low price of the day; a cross-hatch to the right indicates the closing price, and a cross-hatch to the left indicates the opening price. The appeal of this chart is that the analyst immediately gets a sense of the nature of that day's trading. A short bar indicates little price movement during the day; that is, the high, low, and close were near the opening price. A long bar indicates a wide divergence between the high and the low for the day.

Exhibit 2 Bar Chart Notation

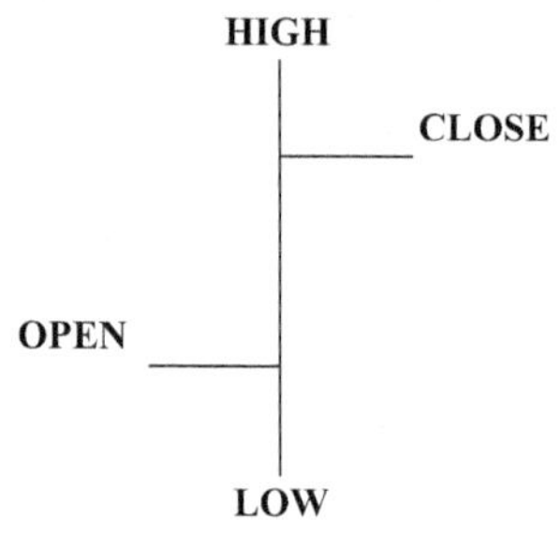

Exhibit 3 shows daily performance of the Brazilian Bovespa Index (BVSP) from late 2007 through late 2009. The top part provides the price open, close, high, and low; the bottom part shows volume, which will be discussed in section 3.1.6. The downturn in the second half of 2008 is obvious, but also notable are the extreme price movements in the fourth quarter of 2008. There were 40 trading days from 29 September to 24 November. On 20 of those days, the closing value of the index changed from the previous close by at least 4 percent, a huge move by historical standards. During the same period, the average daily price range (high to low) was 7 percent, compared with 3.7 percent in the previous two months. This potentially important information would not be captured in a line chart.

Exhibit 3 Bar Chart: Bovespa Index, November 2007–November 2009 (Price in Brazilian Reais)

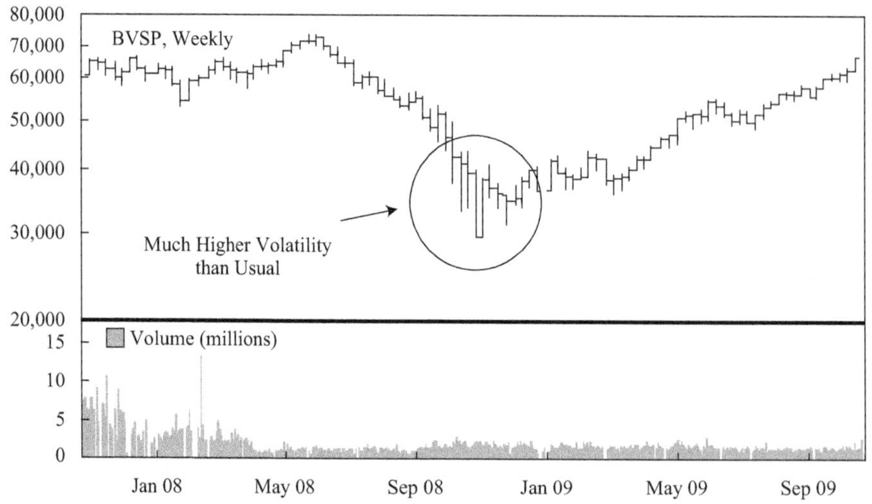

3.1.3 *Candlestick Chart*

Candlestick charts trace their roots to Japan, where technical analysis has been in use for centuries. Like a bar chart, a **candlestick chart** also provides four prices per data point entry: the opening and closing prices and the high and low prices during the period. As shown in Exhibit 4, a vertical line represents the range through which the security price traveled during the time period. The line is known as the wick or shadow. The body of the candle is shaded if the opening price was higher than the closing price, and the body is clear if the opening price was lower than the closing price.

Exhibit 4 Construction of a Candlestick Chart

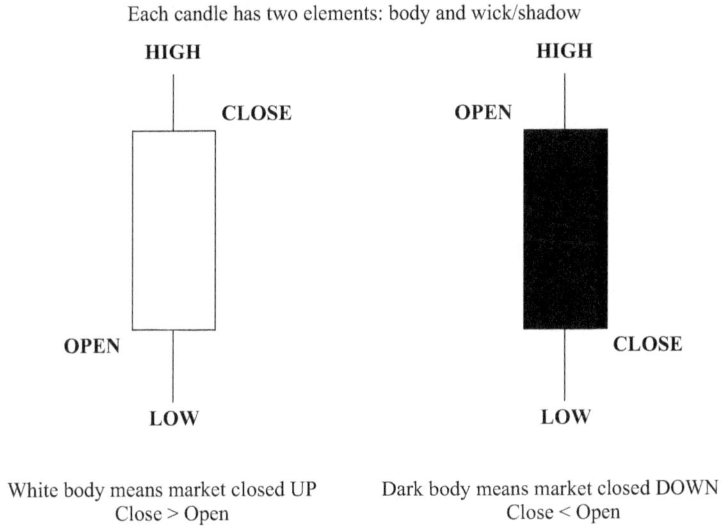

Exhibit 5 shows a weekly candlestick chart for Companhia Vale do Rio Doce for the period 1 January through 15 June 2009.

Exhibit 5 Candlestick Chart: Companhia Vale do Rio Doce, 1 January–15 June 2009 (Price in US Dollars)

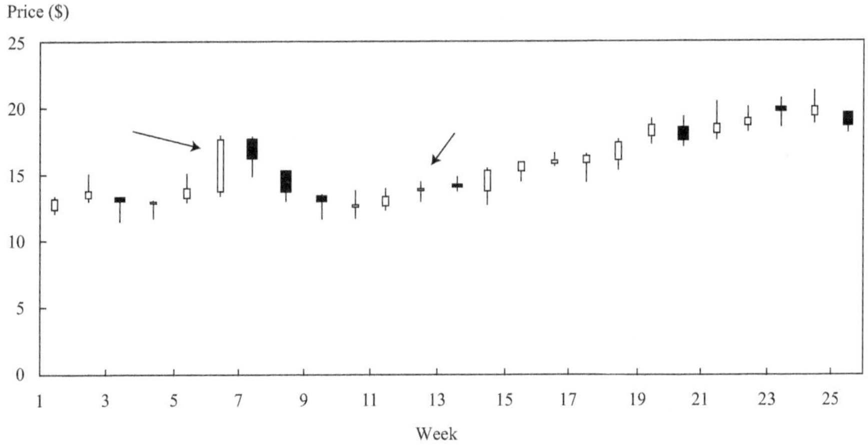

The advantage of the candlestick chart over the bar chart is that price moves are much more visible in the candlestick chart, which allows faster analysis. The bar chart indicates market volatility only by the height of each bar, but in candlestick charts, the difference between opening and closing prices and their relationship to the highs and lows of the day are clearly apparent. Compare the sixth candle with the twelfth in Exhibit 5. In the sixth candle, the analyst can see significant volatility because the high of the day and low of the day are so far apart. The stock opened near the low of the day and closed near the high, suggesting a steady rally during the day. In contrast, the twelfth candle shows that the shares opened and closed at the same price, creating a cross-pattern. In Japanese terminology used in candlestick charting, this pattern is called a "doji." The doji signifies that after a full day of trading, the positive price influence of buyers and the negative price influence of sellers exactly counteracted each other, which tells the analyst that this market is in balance. If a doji occurs at the end of a long uptrend or downtrend, it signals that the trend will probably reverse.

3.1.4 *Point and Figure Chart*

Point and figure charts were widely used in the United States in the early 1900s and were favored because they were easy to create and update manually in the era before computers. As with any technical analysis tool, these charts can be used with equities, fixed-income securities, commodities, or foreign exchange.

Who originated the **point and figure chart** is unclear; they are referred to in a number of books in the United States dating back to 1898. The methodology evolved until 1934 when the first book was published on the topic: *The Point and Figure Method of Anticipating Stock Price Movements* by Victor de Villiers and Owen Taylor. With the advent of powerful charting software and internet websites, complex chart types, such as the candlestick chart, have become more popular. But point and figure charts still offer tremendous value if one knows their limitations and their advantages. The key reason this knowledge is necessary, as explained below, is that point and figure charts are constructed differently from other charts; they have a clear focus on entry and exit levels but no focus on holding periods.

As illustrated in Exhibit 6, a point and figure chart is drawn on a grid and consists of columns of X's alternating with columns of O's. Neither time nor volume are represented on this type of chart, and *the horizontal axis represents the number of changes in price, not time.* Movement along the horizontal axis does reflect the passage of time, but not in any uniform fashion. The analyst makes entries on a point and figure chart only when the price changes by the "box size," which is explained below. This lack of a normal time dimension is perhaps the most unusual characteristic of a point and figure chart.

Exhibit 6 Point and Figure Chart: Wharf Holdings Daily Price Chart, 2007–2009 (in Hong Kong Dollars)

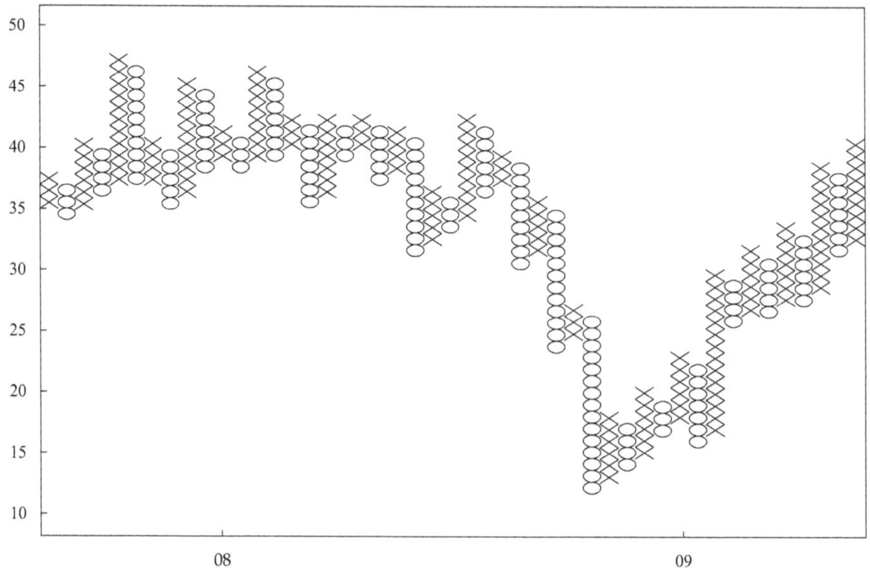

Note: The box size is HK$1, and the reversal size is three.

To construct a point and figure chart, the analyst must determine both the box size and the reversal size. Box size refers to the change in price represented by the height of each box (boxes are generally square, but the width has no meaning). In Exhibit 6, the box size is HK$1. The reversal size is used to determine when to create a new column. In Exhibit 6, the reversal size is three, meaning a reversal in price of three or more boxes.

Although a point and figure chart can be constructed in several ways, these charts are always drawn on graph paper to facilitate seeing the "columns and rows" nature of the data. The vertical axis measures *discrete increments of price*. For example, an analyst in Europe might draw a €1 chart, a €2 chart, or any other increment. In a €1 chart, boxes would be €1 apart (e.g. €40, €41, €42), whereas in a €2 chart they would be €2 apart (€40, €42, €44). The most commonly used box size is 1 unit of currency, which is used when prices range from 20 to 100 per share of the currency.

The next decision the technician needs to make is the reversal size. The most common size is three, meaning a reversal in price of three or more boxes (€3 in the case of a box size of €1). This use of a multibox reversal helps eliminate "noise" in the price data. (*Noise* refers to short-term trading volatility that does not alter the long-term trend of the security.)

In a point and figure chart, X represents an increase in price and O represents a decline in price. In constructing a chart, the technician draws an X in a column of boxes every time the security price closes up by the amount of the box size. (Ideally, all security prices are considered on an intraday basis, but this practice has given way to using closing prices only.) If the price increases by twice the box size, the technician draws two X's to fill in two boxes, one on top of the other. The technician fills in more boxes for larger price moves. The resulting column starts at the opening price level and extends to the closing price level. As long as the security keeps closing at higher prices, the technician keeps filling in boxes with X's, which makes the column higher and higher. If the price does not increase by at least the box size, no indication is made on the chart. Thus, in some cases, the chart is not updated for long periods, but no indication of this passage of time is made on the chart.

The reversal size determines when to create a new column. In the case of a €1 box size, and three-box reversal size, a decline of €3 or more would result in the technician shifting to the next column over and beginning a column of O's. The first box to be filled in is to the right and below the highest X in the prior column. The technician then fills in an O to bring the column down to the price level at the close. Again, each filled-in box (if the box size is €1) represents a €1 decline in the security price. As long as the downtrend continues, without a €3 increase in price, the technician continues adding O's to the column below the prior O's. A reversal in the downtrend by at least the amount of the reversal size prompts the technician to move to the next column and begin drawing a series of X's again. Computer technology makes the process easy, but many technicians prefer to keep point and figure charts on their wall and update them manually because doing so provides a vivid reminder of the market trend.

Point and figure charts are particularly useful for making trading decisions because they clearly illustrate price levels that may signal the end of a decline or advance. They also clearly show price levels at which a security may frequently trade. In using the point size and reversal size to make trading decisions, for uptrends, or columns of X's, the practitioner would maintain long positions. The reversal size could be considered the amount of loss that would prompt the closing of a long position and the establishment of a new short position. The larger the reversal size, the fewer columns in the chart and the longer uptrends and downtrends will run.

The box size can be varied in relation to the security price. For a security with a very low price—say, below €5—a €1 box size might mean few or no updates on the chart because the price would only rarely change by this amount. Thus, the technician could reduce the box size to cents. For highly priced securities, much larger box sizes could be used. The reversal size is a multiple of the box size, so if the box size is changed, the reversal size changes. Practitioners who want fewer columns or trade signals can use a large reversal size.

Analysis of a point and figure chart is relatively straightforward as long as the technician understands its construction and limitations. The chart is relatively simple, and repeated high and low prices are evident. Congestion areas, where a security trades up and down in a narrow range, are evidenced by a series of short columns of X's and O's spanning roughly the same price range. Major, sustained price moves are represented by long columns of X's (when prices are moving up) or O's (when prices are moving down).

3.1.5 *Scale*

For any chart—line, bar, or candlestick—the vertical axis can be constructed with either a **linear scale** (also known as an arithmetic scale) or a **logarithmic scale**, depending on how you want to view the data. With a logarithmic scale, equal vertical distances on the chart correspond to an equal percentage change. A logarithmic scale is appropriate when the data move through a range of values representing several orders of magnitude (e.g., from 10 to 10,000); a linear scale is better suited for narrower ranges (e.g., prices from \$35 to \$50). The share price history of a particular company, for instance, is usually best suited to a linear scale because the data range is usually narrow.

The horizontal axis shows the passage of time. The appropriate time interval depends on the nature of the underlying data and the specific use of the chart. An active trader, for instance, may find 10-minute, 5-minute, or even tick-by-tick data useful, but other technical analysts may prefer daily or weekly data. In general, the greater the volatility of the data, the greater the likelihood that an analyst can find useful information in more-frequent data sampling.

Consider Exhibits 7 and 8, which both show the yearly history of the Dow Jones Industrial Average (DJIA) from 1928 to 2018. Plotting the index on a linear scale, as in Exhibit 7, makes it difficult to gather much information from the first 60 years of the data series. Analysts can see a slight uptrend but not much else. The eye is drawn to the bull market of the 1980s, the subsequent dot-com bubble, the subprime crisis, and a sustained recovery. When plotted on a logarithmic scale, as in Exhibit 8, however, many people would find that the data tell a more comprehensive story. The Great Depression of the 1930s stands out, but over the following 80 years, the data follow a relatively stable upward trend.

Exhibit 7 Dow Jones Industrial Average on Linear Scale, 1920–2018 (in US Dollars)

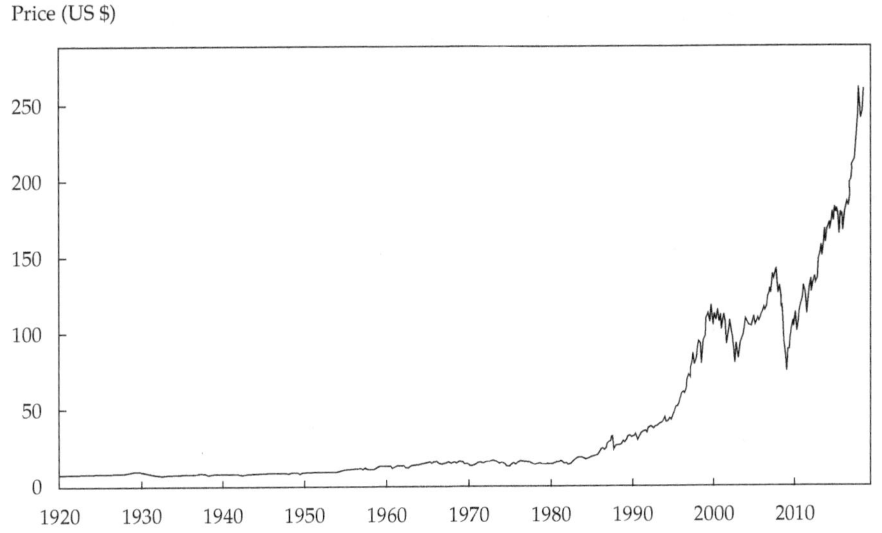

Exhibit 8 Dow Jones Industrial Average on Logarithmic Scale, 1920–2018 (in US Dollars)

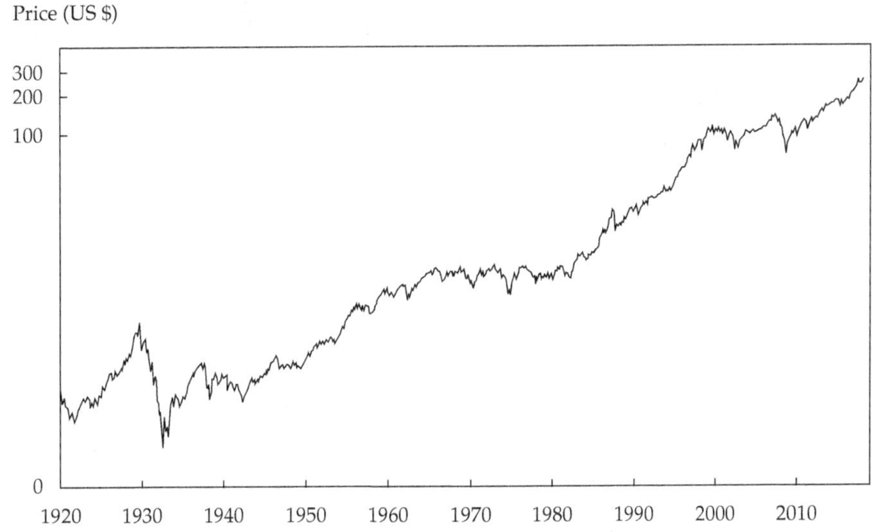

3.1.6 *Volume*

Volume is an important characteristic that is included at the bottom of many charts; see, for example Exhibit 3. Volume is used to assess the strength or conviction of buyers and sellers in determining a security's price. For example, on a daily price chart, below the price section would be a column chart showing the volume traded for that day.

Some technicians consider volume information to be crucial. If volume increases during a time frame in which price is also increasing, that combination is considered positive and the two indicators are said to "confirm" each other. The signal would be interpreted to mean that over time, more and more investors are buying the financial instrument and they are doing so at higher and higher prices. This pattern is considered a positive technical development.

Conversely, if volume and price diverge—for example, if a stock's price rises while its volume declines—the implication is that fewer and fewer market participants are willing to buy that stock at the new price. If this trend in volume continues, the price rally will soon end because demand for the security at higher prices will cease. Exhibit 9 shows a chart for Toronto-Dominion Bank (TD Bank) with volume displayed separately.

Exhibit 9 Daily Candlestick Price Chart and Volume Bar Chart: TD Bank, March 2015–June 2016 (Price in Canadian Dollars)

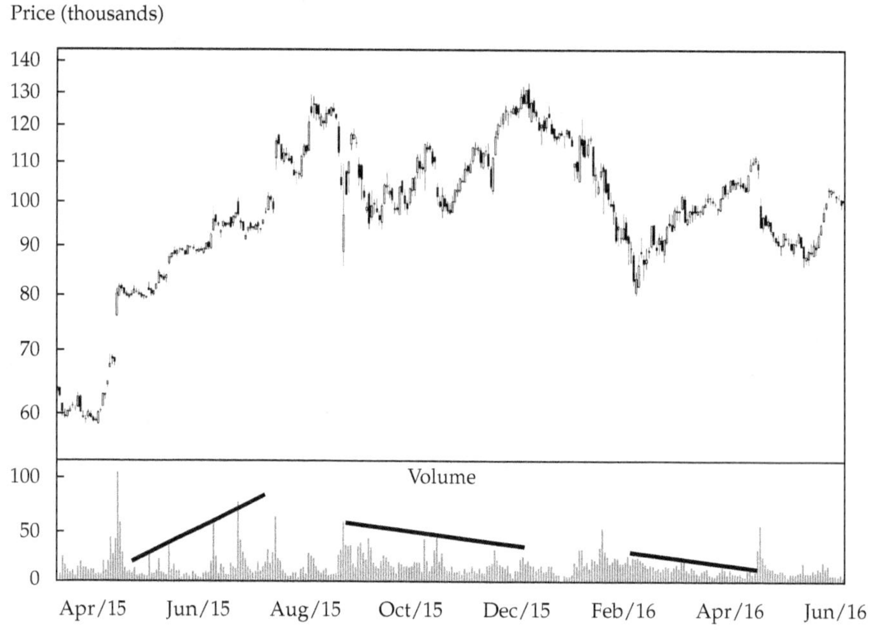

3.1.7 *Time Intervals*

Most of the chart examples in this reading are daily price charts in that they show the price and volume on a daily basis. Daily frequency is not required, however, because charts can be constructed by using any time interval. For short-term trading, the analyst can create charts with one-minute or shorter intervals. For long-term investing, the analyst can use weekly, monthly, or even annual intervals. The same analytical approach applies irrespective of the time interval. Using long intervals allows the analyst to chart longer time periods than does using short time intervals for the simple reason that long intervals contain fewer data points, so a longer time frame can be presented on the chart. Using short intervals allows the analyst to see more detail. A useful step for many analysts is to begin the analysis of a security with the chart for a long time frame, such as a weekly or monthly chart, and then construct charts with shorter and shorter time intervals, such as daily or hourly charts.

3.1.8 *Relative Strength Analysis*

Relative strength analysis is widely used to compare the performance of a particular asset, such as a common stock, with that of some benchmark—such as, in the case of common stocks, the FTSE 100, the Nikkei 225, or the S&P 500 Index—or the performance of another security. The intent is to show out- or underperformance of the individual issue relative to some other index or asset. Typically, the analyst prepares a line chart of the ratio of two prices, with the asset under analysis as the numerator and with the benchmark or other security as the denominator. A rising line shows the asset is performing better than the index or other stock; a declining line shows the opposite. A flat line shows neutral performance.

Suppose a private investor wants to understand changing market trends between two investment ideas she read about. Amazon Inc. (AMZN) is a well-known technology enabled retail company; and Walmart Inc. (WMT) a US multinational retail company. The investor wants to determine which of the stocks of these two companies has been the stronger performer (relative to the S&P 500) over the roughly seven-year period ending August 2018. Exhibit 10 shows relative strength lines for the two stocks between 2011 and 2018. For ease of comparison, the ratio of Amazon Inc. price data versus the S&P 500 Index is indexed to 1.00 in the beginning of 2011. A move from 1.00 to 1.50 would indicate a 50% outperformance for Amazon Inc. versus the S&P 500 Index. Likewise, a drop from 1.00 to 0.80 on the Walmart vs. S&P 500 Index charts would indicate a 20% underperformance for Walmart vs. the S&P 500 Index.

Exhibit 10 Relative Strength Analysis of Two Retail Giants: AMZN vs. the S&P 500 and WMT vs. the S&P 500, January 2011–August 2018

A. Amazon.com Inc. vs. S&P 500

B. Walmart vs. S&P 500

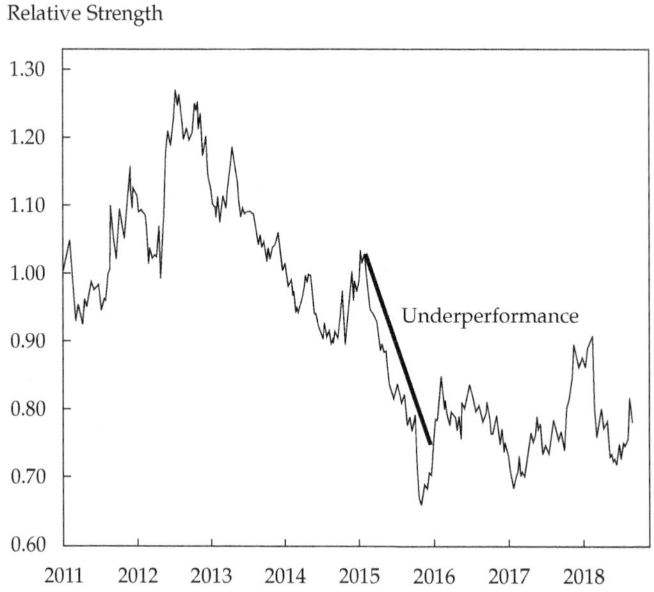

The units on the vertical axis are not significant; the ratio is a function of the relative prices of the assets under consideration. The important information is how the ratio has changed. This type of chart allows an analyst to make a visual determination of that change. As Exhibit 10 illustrates, Amazon Inc. was a strong performer starting in 2015 but its relative performance wasn't as strong prior to that. In contrast, the stock of Walmart Inc. lost its leadership in the beginning of 2013 and from that point up to mid-2018 its stock has clearly lagged the performance of the S&P 500 Index.

3.2 Trend

The concept of a **trend** is perhaps the most important aspect of technical analysis. Trend analysis is based on the observation that market participants tend to act in herds and that trends tend to stay in place for some time. A security can be considered to be in an upward trend, a downward trend, a sideways trend, or no apparent trend. Not all securities are in a trend, and little useful forecasting information can be gleaned from technical analysis when a security is not in a trend. Not every chart will have obvious or clear implications, so the analyst must avoid the temptation to force a conclusion from every chart and thus reach a wrong interpretation.

An uptrend for a security is when the price goes to higher highs and higher lows. As the security moves up in price, each subsequent new high is higher than the prior high and each time there is a **retracement**, which is a reversal in the movement of the security's price, it must stop at a higher low than the prior lows in the trend period. To draw an uptrend line, a technician draws a line connecting the lows of the price chart. Major breakdowns in price, however, when the price drops through and below the trendline by a significant amount (many technicians use 5–10 percent below the trendline) indicate that the uptrend is over and may signal a further decline in the price. Minor breakthroughs below previous lows simply call for the line to be moderately adjusted over time. Time is also a consideration in trends: The longer the security price stays below the trendline, the more meaningful the breakdown is considered to be.

In an uptrend, the forces of demand are greater than the forces of supply. So, traders are willing to pay higher and higher prices for the same asset over time. Presumably, the strong demand indicates that investors believe the intrinsic value of the security is increasing.

A downtrend is when a security makes lower lows and lower highs. As the security moves down in price, each subsequent new high must be lower than the prior high and each time there is a retracement, it must stop at a lower low than the prior lows in the trend period. To draw a downtrend line, a technician draws a line connecting the highs of the price chart. Major breakouts above the downtrend line (e.g., 5–10 percent) indicate that the downtrend is over and a rise in the security's price may occur. And as with an uptrend, the longer the security price stays above the trendline, the more meaningful the breakout is considered to be.

In a downtrend, supply overwhelms demand. Over time, sellers are willing to accept lower and lower prices to exit long positions or enter new short positions. Both motives of the sellers generally indicate deteriorating investor sentiment about the asset. However, selling may be prompted by factors not related to the fundamental or intrinsic value of the stock. For example, investors may be forced to sell to meet margin calls in their portfolios. From a purely technical standpoint, the reason is irrelevant. The downtrend is assumed to continue until contrary technical evidence appears. Combining fundamental analysis with technical analysis in such a case, however, might reveal a security that has attractive fundamentals but a currently negative technical position. In uptrends, however, a security with an attractive technical position but unattractive fundamentals is rare because most buying activity is driven by traders who expect the security price to increase in the future. The rare exception is covering short positions after a sizable decline in the share price.

A security may trade in a fairly narrow range, moving sideways on the price chart without much upward or downward movement. This pattern indicates a relative balance between supply and demand. A technical analyst may not expect to profit from long or short trades in such securities but might devise profitable option strategies for short-term investors with the ability to accept the risks.

Exhibit 11 shows the application of trend analysis. Depicted is an uptrend line for the shares of British American Tobacco PLC. Note that from late 2008 to early 2018 there was generally an upward trend. The first sign of trouble came in the first quarter of 2018 when the rally terminated at a lower price point than the prior rally, of 2017. This movement was followed by the shares breaking through the trendline.

Exhibit 11 Trend Analysis: British American Tobacco PLC Price Chart, 2008–2018 (Prices in British Pound)

The chart in Exhibit 11 covers roughly eleven years and would most likely be used by investors with a long time horizon. Investors with a shorter horizon might use a chart with a shorter time frame and would thus obtain a different trendline as well as a different trendline breakdown.

Two concepts related to trend are support and resistance. **Support** is defined as a low price range in which buying activity is sufficient to stop the decline in price. It is the opposite of **resistance**, which is a price range in which selling is sufficient to stop the rise in price. The psychology behind the concepts of support and resistance is that investors have come to a collective consensus about the price of a security. Support and resistance levels can be sloped lines, as in trendlines, or horizontal lines.

A key tenet of support and resistance as a part of technical analysis is the **change in polarity principle**, which states that once a support level is breached, it becomes a resistance level. The same holds true for resistance levels; once breached, they become support levels. For example, if the price of a security never rises above SFr10 over a long period of time and begins to decline each time it reaches this level but then finally breaks through this level by a significant amount, the point to which the price rises becomes a support level.

Support and resistance levels are commonly round numbers. Support indicates that at some price level, investors consider a security to be an attractive investment and are willing to buy, even in the wake of a sharp decline (and for resistance, at some level, investors are not willing to buy, even in an uptrend). The fact that these price points tend to be round numbers strongly suggests that human sentiment is at work.

One of the best-known historical examples of support and resistance is when the DJIA broke through the 1,000 mark in 1982, as shown in Exhibit 12. Previously, 1,000 had been viewed as a resistance line, but following the breakout in 1982, in 1984 it acted as a support level.

Exhibit 12 Support Level: DJIA Weekly Price Chart, 1955–1995 (Price in US Dollars)

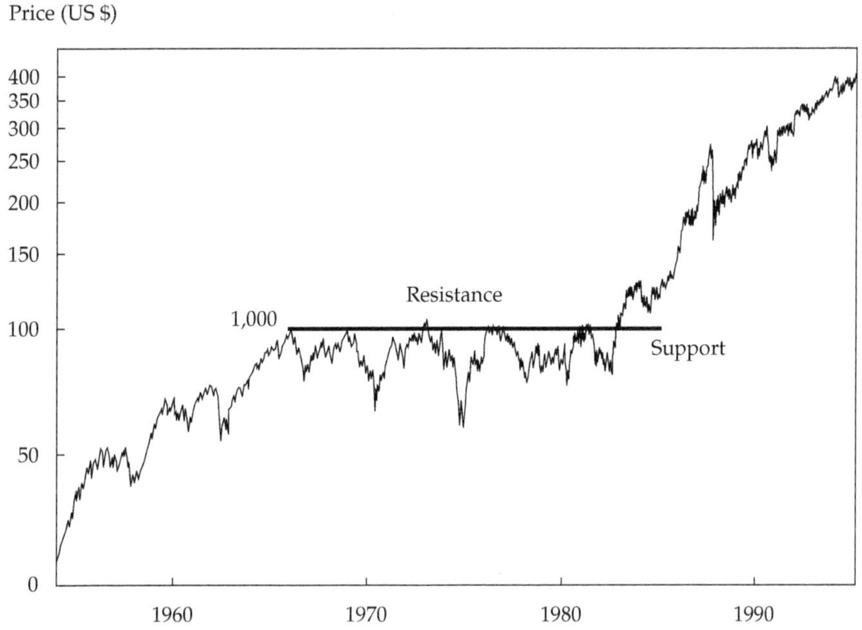

3.3 Chart Patterns

Chart patterns are formations that appear in price charts that create some type of recognizable shape. Common patterns appear repeatedly and often lead to similar subsequent price movements. Thus, the identification and analysis of chart patterns is a common aspect of technical analysis used to predict security prices. An important connection to understand is that patterns form as a result of the behavior of market participants and that these patterns represent graphical depictions of the collective psychology of the market at a given time.

The recurring patterns that appear in charts can be used as a basis for market forecasting. The reason chart patterns have predictive value is that they are graphic representations of human trading activity and human behavior is frequently repeated, especially trading activity that is driven by fear (in market sell-offs) or hope and greed (as evidenced in bubbles—that is, rallies that extend well beyond valuation levels that would be derived by fundamental values). An example of a rally driven by greed is the recent real estate bubble, which took home prices to unsustainably high levels. This bubble started a few years after the internet stock bubble of the 1990s, which also took prices to unsustainably high levels. In bubbles, investors, driven by hope and greed, drive the price of an asset to irrationally high levels, in the expectation that another buyer will be willing to pay an even higher price for the asset. The housing bubble was notable because it so closely followed the internet stock bubble, despite all that had been written about the "irrational exuberance" of the internet bubble of the 1990s.

Chart patterns can be divided into two categories: **reversal patterns** and **continuation patterns**. These terms refer to the trend for the security in question prior to the formation of the pattern. The most important concept to understand in using chart patterns is that without a clear trend in place prior to the pattern, the pattern has no predictive value. This aspect is frequently forgotten by investors who are so eager to identify and use patterns that they forget the proper application of charts.

3.3.1 *Reversal Patterns*

As the name implies, a reversal pattern signals the end of a trend, a change in direction of the financial instrument's price. Evidence that the trend is about to change direction is obviously important, so reversal patterns are noteworthy.

3.3.1.1 Head and Shoulders Perhaps the most widely recognized reversal pattern is the **head and shoulders pattern**. The pattern consists of three segments. Volume is an important characteristic in interpreting this pattern. Because head and shoulders indicates a trend reversal, a clear trend must exist prior to the formation of the pattern in order for the pattern to have predictive validity. For a head and shoulders pattern, the prior trend must be an uptrend. Later, we will discuss the *inverse* head and shoulders pattern (preceded by a downtrend).

Exhibit 13 depicts a head and shoulders pattern for Marvell Technology Group. The three parts of the pattern are as follows:

- Left shoulder: This part appears to show a strong rally, with the slope of the rally being greater than the prior uptrend, on strong volume. The rally then reverses back to the price level where it started, forming an inverted V pattern, but on lower volume.
- Head: The head is a more pronounced version of the left shoulder. A rally following the first shoulder takes the security to a higher high than the left shoulder by a significant enough margin to be clearly evident on the price chart. Volume is typically lower in this rally, however, than in the one that formed the first, upward side of the left shoulder. This second rally also fails, with price falling back to the same level at which the left shoulder began and ended. This price level is called the neckline. This price level also will be below the uptrend line formed by connecting the low prices in the uptrend preceding the beginning of the head and shoulders pattern. This head pattern is the first signal that the rally may be coming to an end and that a reversal may be starting.
- Right shoulder: The right shoulder is a mirror image (or close to a mirror image) of the left shoulder but on lower volume, signifying less buying enthusiasm. The price rallies up to roughly the same level as the first shoulder, but the rally reverses at a lower high price than the rally that formed the head.

Exhibit 13 Head and Shoulders Pattern: Marvell Technology Daily Price Chart, August 2005–August 2006 (Price in US Dollars)

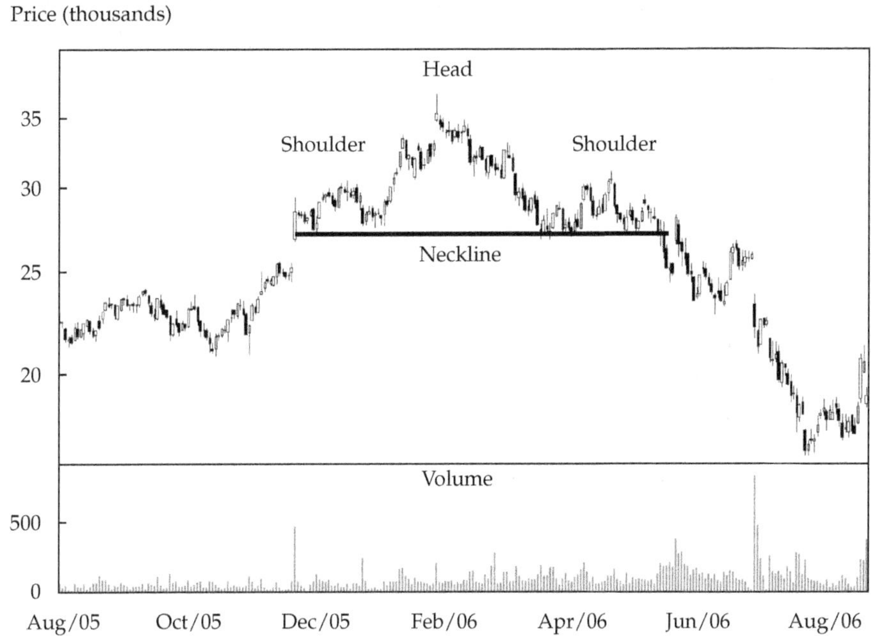

Rarely will an analyst see a perfectly formed head and shoulders pattern; variations include two tops on the shoulders or on the head. The head, however, should rise to a higher price level than either shoulder, whereas the shoulders should be roughly symmetrical. In terms of the neckline price level, the first rally should begin at this level and the left shoulder and head should also decline to roughly this level. But necklines may not always form exactly horizontal lines. These imperfect variations make this (and other) technical patterns difficult for quantitative analysts or academicians to model, but the human brain can detect the pattern even if it is imperfectly formed.

Volume is important in analyzing head and shoulders patterns. A new high in price at the top of the head without a new high in volume signals fewer bullish market participants. When one indicator is making a new high (or low) but another is not, this situation is called **divergence**. In divergence, the right shoulder will have even lower volume, signaling that buying interest or demand is tapering off and will soon be overwhelmed by supply. The result will be a price decline.

Once the head and shoulders pattern has formed, the expectation is that the share price will decline down through the neckline price. Technicians tend to use filtering rules to make sure that a clear breakdown of the neckline has occurred. These rules may take the form of waiting to trade until the price falls to a meaningful level below the neckline (3 percent or 5 percent are commonly used) and/or a time limit for the price to remain below the neckline before trading; when a daily price chart is used, the rule may be several days to a week. Prices commonly rebound to the neckline levels, even after a decline has exceeded the filter levels. Prices generally stop, however, at or around the neckline. The neckline was a support level, and under the change in polarity principle, once a support level is breached, it becomes a resistance level.

3.3.1.2 Inverse Head and Shoulders The head and shoulders pattern can also form upside down and act as a reversal pattern for a preceding downtrend. The three parts of the inverse head and shoulders are as follows:

- Left shoulder: This shoulder appears to show a strong decline, with the slope of the decline greater than the prior downtrend, on strong volume. The rally then reverses back to the price level where it started, forming a V pattern, but on lower volume.
- Head: The head is a more pronounced version of the left shoulder. Another decline follows but on diminishing volume, which takes the price to a lower low than the prior shoulder by a significant enough margin that it is clearly evident on the price chart. This second decline also reverses, with price rising to the same level at which the left shoulder began and ended. This price level, the neckline, will also be above the downtrend line formed by connecting the high prices in the downtrend preceding the beginning of the inverse head and shoulders pattern. This pattern is the first signal that the decline may be coming to an end and that a reversal may be near.
- Right shoulder: The right shoulder is roughly a mirror image of the left shoulder but on lower volume, signifying less selling enthusiasm. The price declines down to roughly the same level as the first shoulder, but the rally reverses at a higher low price than the rally that formed the head.

3.3.1.3 Setting Price Targets with Head and Shoulders Pattern As with all technical patterns, the head and shoulders pattern must be analyzed from the perspective of the security's long-term price trend. The rally that happened before the formation of the pattern must be large enough for there to be something to reverse. The stronger and more pronounced the rally was, the stronger and more pronounced the reversal is likely to be. Similarly, once the neckline is breached, the security is expected to decline by the same amount as the change in price from the neckline to the top of the head. If the preceding rally started at a price higher than the neckline, however, the correction is unlikely to bring the price lower than the price level at the start of the rally. Because a head and shoulders formation is a bearish indicator (i.e., a technician would expect the previously established uptrend to end and a downtrend to commence), a technician would seek to profit by shorting the security under analysis. When attempting to profit from the head and shoulders pattern, a technician will often use the price differences between the head and the neckline to set a price target, which is the price at which the technician anticipates closing the investment position. The price target for the head and shoulders pattern is calculated as follows:

$$\text{Price target} = \text{Neckline} - (\text{Head} - \text{Neckline})$$

For example, in Exhibit 14, the high price reached at the top of the head is roughly \$37 and the neckline formed at roughly \$27 for a difference of \$10. So a technician would expect the price to decline to a level \$10 below the neckline, or to \$17; that is,

$$\text{Price target} = \$27 - (\$37 - \$27) = \$17$$

Exhibit 14 Calculating a Price Target: Marvell Technology Daily Price Chart, August 2005–August 2006 (Price in US Dollars)

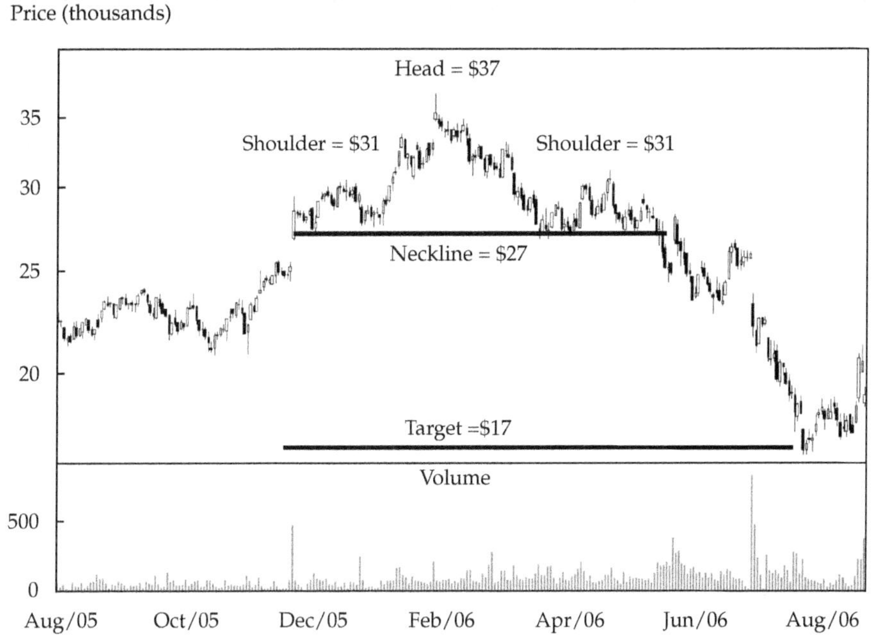

EXAMPLE 1

Determining a Price Target from a Head and Shoulders Pattern

Danielle Waterhouse is the technical analyst at Kanektok Securities. One of the companies her firm follows is LPA Petroleum. Waterhouse believes that a graph of LPA's share prices over the past six months reveals a classic head and shoulders pattern. The share price peaked at US$108, and she estimates the neckline at US$79. At today's close, the shares traded at US$78. Based on the head and shoulders pattern, what price target should Waterhouse estimate?

Solution:

Waterhouse estimates the neckline at US$79, which is US$108 minus US$79, or US$29 lower than the head. Her price target is thus US$79 minus US$29, which is US$50. Waterhouse would attempt to sell LPA short at today's price of US$78 and anticipate closing the position at US$50 for a profit of US$28 per share (not accounting for transaction costs).

3.3.1.4 Setting Price Targets with Inverse Head and Shoulders Pattern Calculating price targets for inverse head and shoulders patterns is similar to the process for head and shoulders patterns, but in this case, because the pattern predicts the end of a downtrend, the technician calculates how high the price is expected to rise once it breaches the neckline. Exhibit 15 illustrates an inverse head and shoulders pattern.

Exhibit 15 Calculating a Price Target for Inverse Head and Shoulders Pattern: DJIA Daily Price Chart, January 2002–January 2004 (Price in US Dollars)

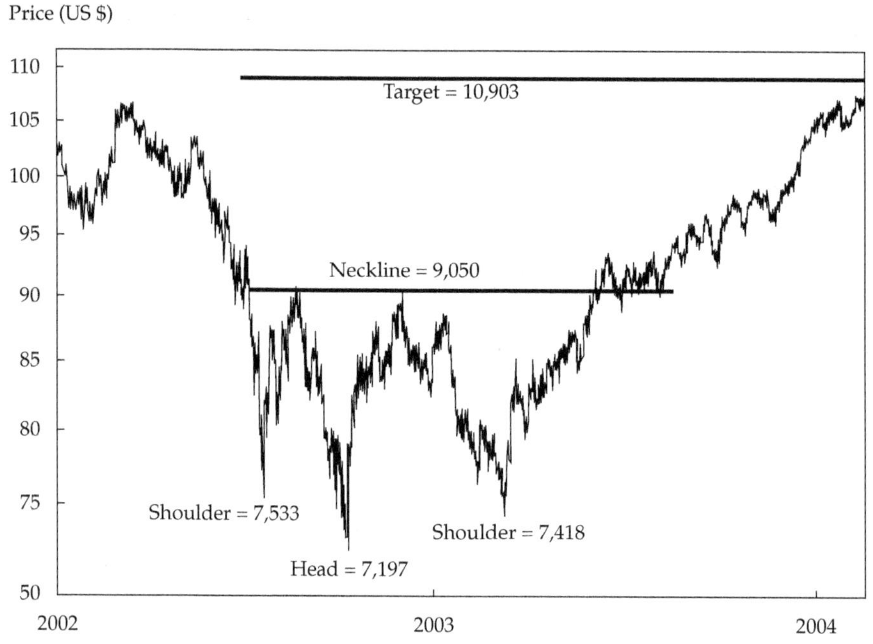

For an inverse head and shoulders pattern, the formula is similar to a head and shoulders pattern:

Price target = Neckline + (Neckline – Head)

For example, in the price chart in Exhibit 15, the low price reached at the bottom of the head is roughly US$7,197 and the neckline formed at roughly US$9,050. The target can thus be found as $9,050 + (9,050 – $7,197) = $10,903. In this case, a technician might have taken a long position in the summer of 2003 with the hope of eventually exiting the position at about US$10,903 for a profit.

3.3.1.5 Double Tops and Bottoms A **double top** is when an uptrend reverses twice at roughly the same high price level. Typically, volume is lower on the second high than on the first high, signaling a diminishing of demand. The longer the time is between the two tops and the deeper the sell-off is after the first top, the more significant the pattern is considered to be. Price targets can be calculated from this pattern in a manner similar to the calculation for the head and shoulders pattern. For a double top, price is expected to decline below the low of the valley between the two tops by at least the distance from the valley low to the high of the double tops.

EXAMPLE 2

Determining a Price Target from a Double-Top Pattern

Richard Dupuis is a technician who trades Eurodollar futures for his own account. He analyzes charts based on one-minute time intervals looking for short-term trading opportunities. Eurodollar futures contracts have been trending upward most of the morning, but Dupuis now observes what he believes is a double-top pattern: After peaking at US$97.00, the futures contract price fell to US$96.42, climbed again to US$97.02, and then started a decline. Because of the double top, Dupuis anticipates a reversal from the uptrend to a downtrend. Dupuis decides to open a short position to capitalize on the anticipated trend reversal. What price target should Dupuis estimate for closing the position?

Solution:

Dupuis estimates the price target as \$96.42 – (\$97.02 – \$96.42) = \$95.82.

Double bottoms are formed when the price reaches a low, rebounds, and then sells off back to the first low level. Exhibit 16 depicts a double-bottom pattern for Citigroup Inc. Technicians use the double bottom to predict a change from a downtrend to an uptrend in security prices. For double bottoms, the price is expected to appreciate above the peak between the two bottoms by at least the distance from the valley lows to the peak.

Exhibit 16 Double-Bottom Pattern: Citigroup Inc. Daily Price Chart, February 2012–February 2013 (Price in US Dollars)

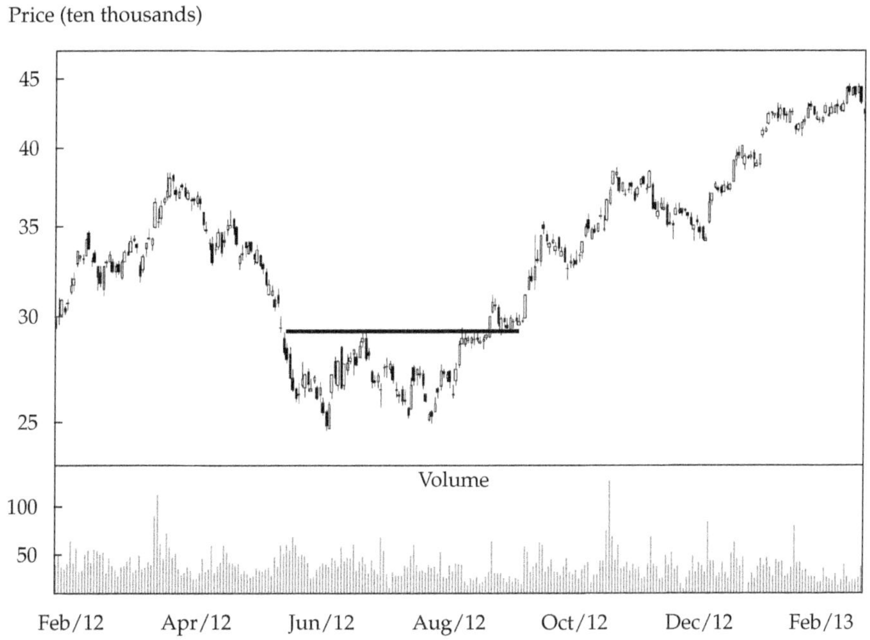

The reason these patterns are significant is that they show that at some price point, investors step in to reverse trends that are under way. For an uptrend, a double top implies that at some price point, enough traders are willing to either sell positions (or enter new short positions) that their activities overwhelm and reverse the uptrend created by demand for the shares. A reasonable conclusion is that this price level has been fundamentally derived and that it represents the intrinsic value of the security that is the consensus of investors. With double bottoms, if a security ceases to decline at the same price point on two separate occasions, the analyst can conclude that the market consensus is that at that price point, the security is now cheap enough that it is an attractive investment.

3.3.1.6 Triple Tops and Bottoms **Triple tops** consist of three peaks at roughly the same price level, and **triple bottoms** consist of three troughs at roughly the same price level. A triple top for Rockwell Automation during 1999 is shown in Exhibit 17.

Exhibit 17 Triple-Top Pattern: Rockwell Automation Daily Price Chart, 1999 (Price in US Dollars)

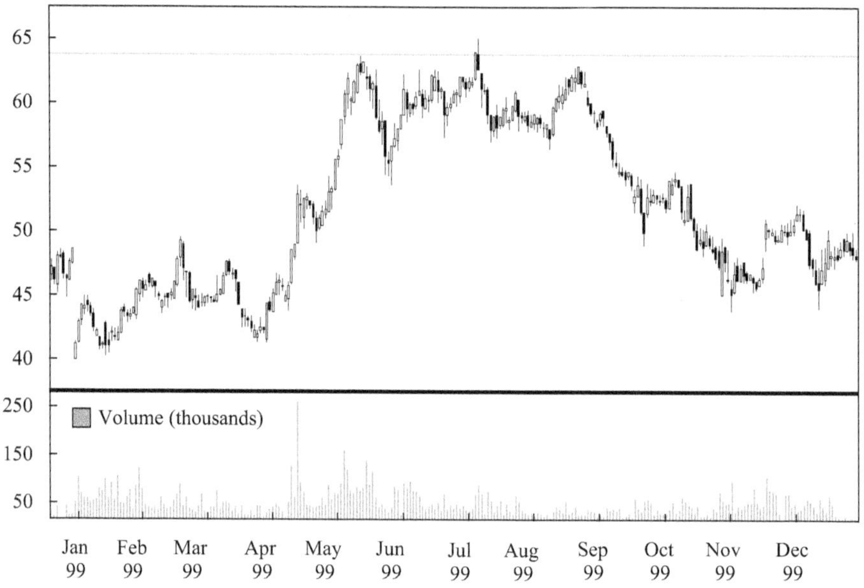

One of the challenges in double-top and triple-top patterns, and one of the valid criticisms of technical analysis in general, is that an analyst cannot know which pattern will result until after the fact. For example, after the broad equity market sell-off in the first quarter of 2009, a number of investment professionals were quoted as calling for a "retest of the lows"—in technical terms, a double bottom.

There is no evidence that market corrections (or rallies) must end with a double bottom (or double top in the case of an uptrend), and there is no generally accepted technical theory that predicts whether a low will be repeated once or even twice before a reversal occurs. A double bottom is considered to be a more significant pattern than a single bottom because traders have stepped in on two occasions to halt declines. However, traders have no way to determine whether a double top or bottom will be followed by a third top or bottom. Triple tops and triple bottoms are rare, but when they occur, they are more significant reversal patterns than double tops or double bottoms. On three separate occasions, traders stepped in to sell or buy shares with enough volume to end a rally or decline under way at the time. Nevertheless, the greater the number of times the price reverses at the same level, and the greater the time interval over which this pattern occurs, the greater the significance of the pattern.

3.3.2 *Continuation Patterns*

A **continuation pattern** is used to predict the resumption of a market trend that was in place prior to the formation of a pattern. From a supply-and-demand standpoint, a continuation pattern indicates a change in ownership from one group of investors to another. For example, if a positive trend was in place prior to a pattern and then one group of investors begins selling, the negative impact on price is quickly offset by other investors buying, so the forces of supply and demand go back and forth in terms of their impact on price. But neither has an overwhelming advantage. This type of pattern is often called "a healthy correction" because the long-term market trend does not change and because while one set of investors is seeking to exit, they are replaced by another set of investors willing to take their positions at roughly the same share price.

3.3.2.1 Triangles **Triangle patterns** are a type of continuation pattern. They come in three forms, symmetrical triangles, ascending triangles, and descending triangles. A triangle pattern forms as the range between high and low prices narrows, visually forming a triangle. In old terminology, triangles were referred to as "coils" (which was also synonymous with "springs") because a triangle was considered analogous to a spring being wound up tighter and tighter and storing energy that would at some point be released. In a triangle, a trendline connects the highs and a trendline connects the lows. As the distance between the highs and lows narrows, the trendlines meet, forming a triangle. In a daily price chart, a triangle pattern usually forms over a period of several weeks.

In an ascending triangle, as shown in Exhibit 18, the trendline connecting the high prices is horizontal and the trendline connecting the low prices forms an uptrend. What this pattern means is that market participants are selling the stock at the same price level over a period of time, putting a halt to rallies at the same price point, but that buyers are getting more and more bullish and stepping in at increasingly higher prices to halt sell-offs instead of waiting for further price declines. An ascending triangle typically forms in an uptrend. The horizontal line represents sellers taking profits at around the same price point, presumably because they believe that this price represents the fundamental, intrinsic value of the security. The fact that the rally continues beyond the triangle may be a bullish signal; it means that another set of investors is presumably willing to buy at an even higher price because their analysis suggests the intrinsic value of the security is higher. Alternatively, the fundamental facts themselves may have changed; that is, the security's fundamental value may be increasing over time. The technician does not care which explanation is true; the technician is relying solely on the information conveyed by the security price itself, not the underlying reason.

Exhibit 18 Ascending Triangle Pattern

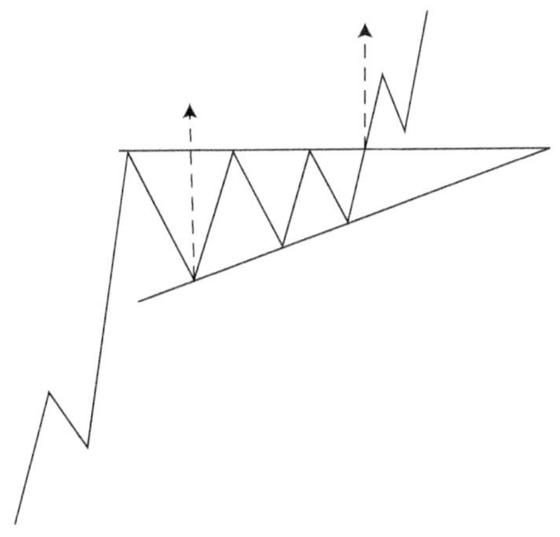

In the descending triangle, shown in Exhibit 19, the low prices form a horizontal trendline and the high prices form a series of lower and lower highs. Typically, a descending triangle will form in a downtrend. At some point in the sell-offs, buyers appear with enough demand to halt sell-offs each time they occur, at around the same price. Again, this phenomenon may be the result of fundamental analysts believing that the security has reached a price where it represents a significant discount to its intrinsic value and these analysts step in and buy. As the triangle forms, each rally ceases at a lower and lower high price point, suggesting the selling demand is exerting greater price influence than buying demand.

Exhibit 19 Descending Triangle

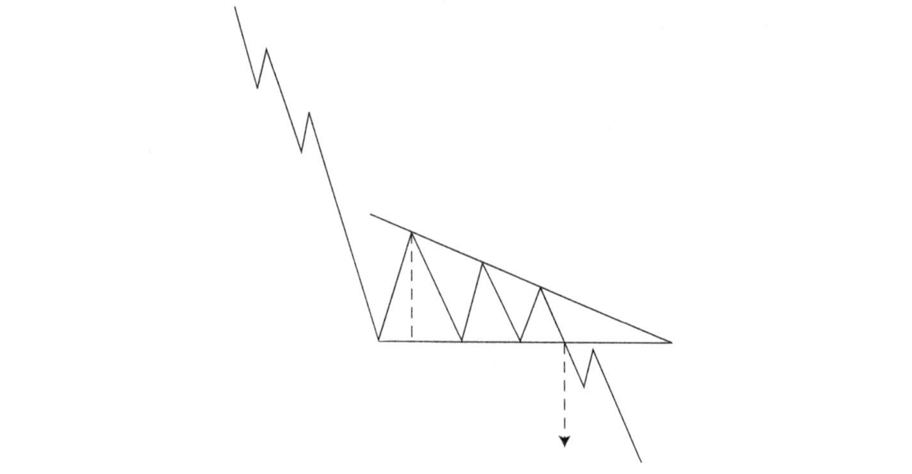

In a symmetrical triangle, the trendline formed by the highs angles down and the trendline formed by the lows angles up, both at roughly the same angle, forming a symmetrical pattern. Exhibit 20 contains a symmetrical triangle formed by the price for Bank of New York Mellon Corp. in early 2017. What this triangle indicates is that buyers are becoming more bullish while, simultaneously, sellers are becoming more bearish, so they are moving toward a point of consensus. Because the sellers are often dominated by long investors exiting positions (as opposed to short sellers creating new short positions), the pressure to sell diminishes once the sellers have sold the security. Thus, the pattern ends in the same direction as the trend that preceded it, either uptrend or downtrend.

Exhibit 20 Symmetrical Triangle Pattern: Bank of New York Mellon Corp. Daily Price Chart, August 2016–September 2017 (Price in US Dollars)

The term "measuring implication" refers to the height of a triangle, as illustrated with a dark vertical bar in Exhibit 20. The measuring implication is derived by calculating the difference in price from the two trendlines at the start of the triangle. Once the pattern is broken and the price breaks through one of the trendlines that form the triangle, the analyst expects the price to move by at least the amount of the breakthrough above or below the trendline. Typically, price breaks out of a triangle pattern between halfway and three-quarters of the way through the pattern. The longer the triangle pattern persists, the more volatile and sustained the subsequent price movement is likely to be.

3.3.2.2 Rectangle Pattern A rectangle pattern is a continuation pattern formed by two parallel trendlines, one formed by connecting the high prices during the pattern, and the other formed by the lows. Exhibit 21 shows two rectangle patterns. As is the case with other patterns, the rectangle pattern is a graphical representation of what has been occurring in terms of collective market sentiment. The horizontal resistance line that forms the top of the rectangle shows that investors are repeatedly selling shares at a specific price level, bringing rallies to an end. The horizontal support line forming the bottom of the rectangle indicates that traders are repeatedly making large enough purchases at the same price level to reverse declines. The support level in a bullish rectangle is natural because the long-term trend in the market is bullish. The resistance line may simply represent investors taking profits. Conversely, in a bearish rectangle, the support level may represent investors buying the security. Again, the technician is not concerned with why a pattern has formed, only with the likely next price movement once the price breaks out of the pattern.

Exhibit 21 Rectangle Patterns

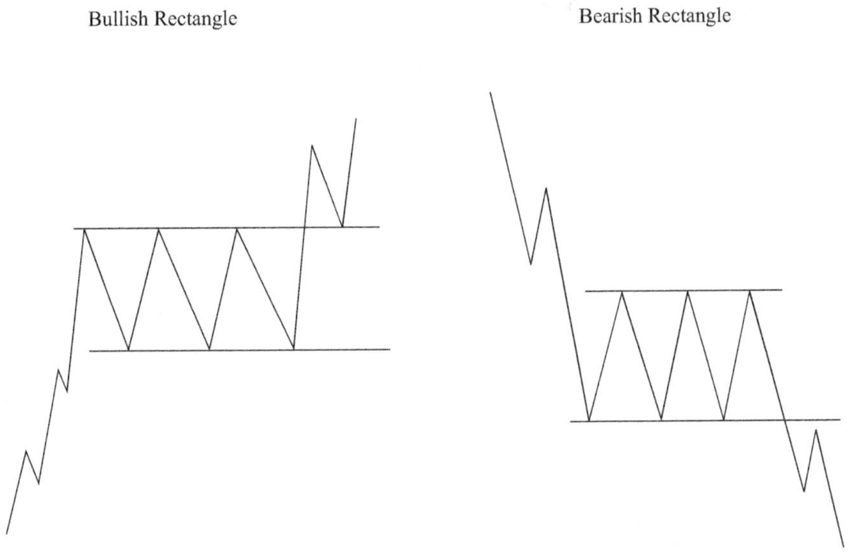

3.3.2.3 Flags and Pennants **Flags** and **pennants** are considered minor continuation patterns because they form over short periods of time—on a daily price chart, typically over a week. They are similar to each other and have the same uses. A flag is formed by parallel trendlines, in the same way that most countries' flags are rectangular and create a parallelogram. Typically, the trendlines slope in a direction opposite to the trend up to that time; for example, in an uptrend, they slope down. A pennant formation is similar except that the trendlines converge to form a triangle, similar to the pennants of many sports teams or pennants flown on ships. The key difference between a triangle and pennant is that a pennant is a short-term formation whereas a triangle is a long-term formation.

The expectation for both flags and pennants is that the trend will continue after the pattern in the same direction it was going prior to the pattern. The price is expected to change by at least the same amount as the price change from the start of the trend to the formation of the flag or pennant. In Exhibit 22, an uptrend begins at point A, which is $65.1. At point B, which is $71.9, a pennant begins to form. The distance from point A to point B is $6.8. The pennant ends at point C, which is $69.75. The price target is $69.75 plus $6.8, which is $76.55, the line labeled D.

Exhibit 22 Pennant Formation: Exxon Mobil Corp., September 2010–March 2011 (Price in US Dollars)

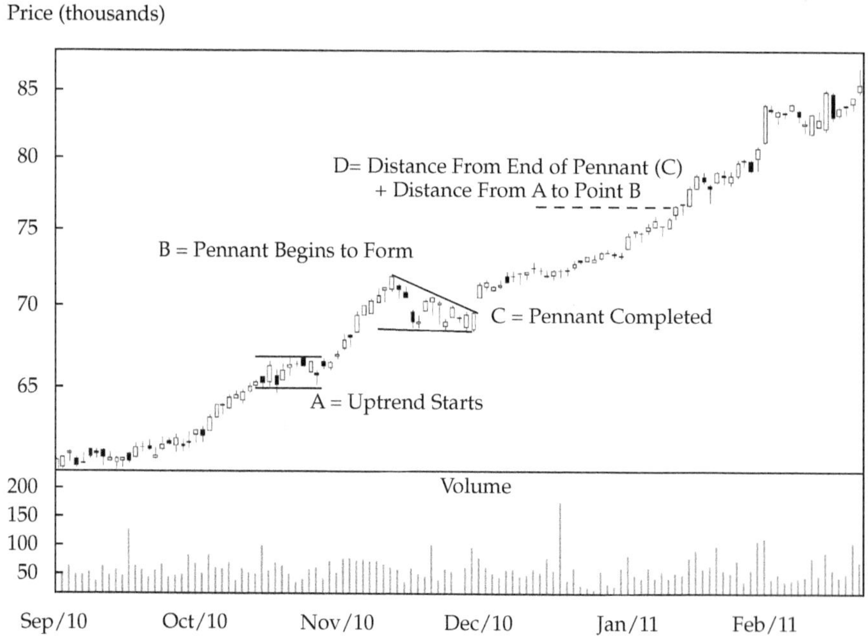

3.4 Technical Indicators

The technical analyst uses a variety of technical indicators to supplement the information gleaned from charts. A technical indicator is any measure based on price, market sentiment, or funds flow that can be used to predict changes in price. These indicators often have a supply-and-demand underpinning; that is, they measure how potential changes in supply and demand might affect a security's price.

3.4.1 *Price-Based Indicators*

Price-based indicators somehow incorporate information contained in the current and past history of market prices. Indicators of this type range from simple (e.g., a moving average) to complex (e.g., a stochastic oscillator).

3.4.1.1 Moving Average A **moving average** is the average of the closing price of a security over a specified number of periods. Moving averages smooth out short-term price fluctuations, giving the technician a clearer image of market trend. Technicians commonly use a simple moving average, which weights each price equally in the calculation of the average price. Some technicians prefer to use an exponential moving average (also called an exponentially smoothed moving average), which gives the greatest weight to recent prices while giving exponentially less weight to older prices.

The number of data points included in the moving average depends on the intended use of the moving average. A 20-day moving average is commonly used because a month contains roughly 20 trading days. Also, 60 days is commonly used because it represents a quarter year (three months) of trading activity.

Moving averages can be used in conjunction with a price trend or in conjunction with one another. Moving averages are also used to determine support and resistance.

Because a moving average is less volatile than price, this tool can be used in several ways. First, whether price is above or below its moving average is important. A security that has been trending down in price will trade below its moving average, and a security that has been trending up will trade above its moving average. Second, the distance between the moving-average line and price is also significant. Once price begins to move back up toward its moving-average line, this line can serve as a resistance level. The 65-day moving-average line is commonly cited in the press, and when the price approaches the moving-average line, many investors become concerned that a rally will stall, so they sell the security.

Two or more moving averages can be used in conjunction. Exhibit 23 shows the price chart of Gazprom SP European Depositary Receipts (EDRs) on the Frankfurt Stock Exchange overlaid with 20-day and 60-day EDR moving averages for late 2007 to mid-2009.[5] Note that the longer the time frame used in the creation of a moving average, the smoother and less volatile the line. Investors often use moving-average crossovers as a buy or sell signal. When a short-term moving average (ie 1 month) crosses from underneath a longer-term average (ie 3 months), this movement is considered bullish and is termed a **golden cross**. Conversely, when a short-term moving average crosses from above a longer-term moving average, this movement is considered bearish and is called a **death cross**. In the case shown in Exhibit 23, a trading strategy of buying on golden crosses and selling on dead crosses would have been profitable.

5 A European Depositary Receipt is a negotiable certificate issued by a depositary bank in one country against equity that is traded on the stock exchange of another country.

Exhibit 23 Daily Price Chart with 20-Day and 60-Day Moving Averages: Gazprom EDR, November 2007–August 2009 (Price in Euros)

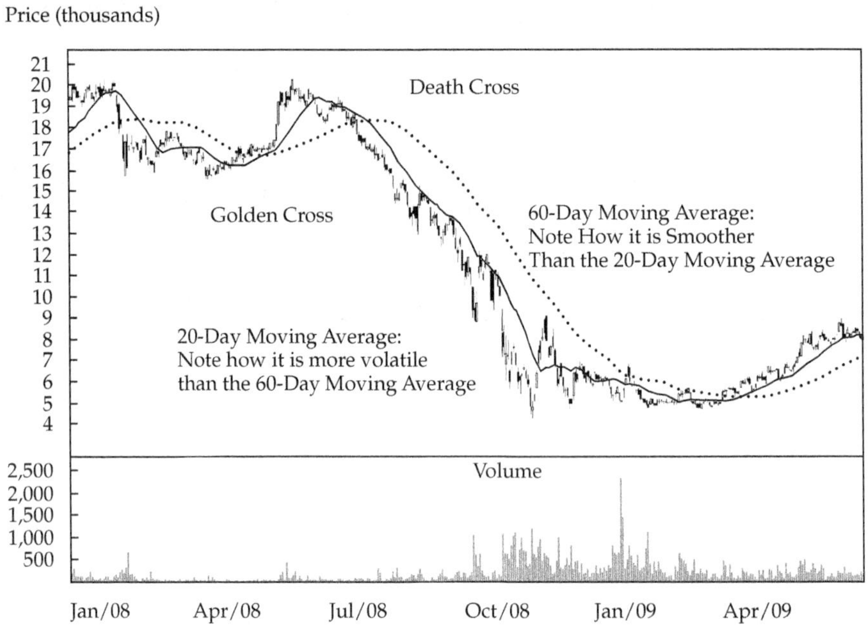

Moving averages are easy to construct, and simple trading rules can be derived for using them. Computers can optimize what time lengths to set when using two moving averages. This optimization may take the form of changing the number of days included in each moving average or adding filter rules, such as waiting several days after a trade signal is given to make a trade. Reasons for optimization include the desire to manage capital drawdowns, to maximize gains, or to minimize losses. Once the moving average is optimized, even if a profitable trading system is devised for that security, the strategy is unlikely to work for other securities, especially if they are dissimilar. Also, as market conditions change, a previously optimized trading system may no longer work.

3.4.1.2 Bollinger Bands Market veteran John Bollinger combined his knowledge of technical analysis with his knowledge of statistics to create an indicator called **Bollinger Bands**. Bollinger Bands consist of a moving average plus a higher line representing the moving average plus a set number of standard deviations from average price (for the same number of periods as used to calculate the moving average) and a lower line that is a moving average minus the same number of standard deviations. Exhibit 24 depicts Bollinger Bands for the Gazprom EDR.

Exhibit 24 Bollinger Band Using 60-Day Moving Average and Two Standard Deviations: Gazprom EDR Daily Price Chart, December 2007–July 2009 (Price in Euros)

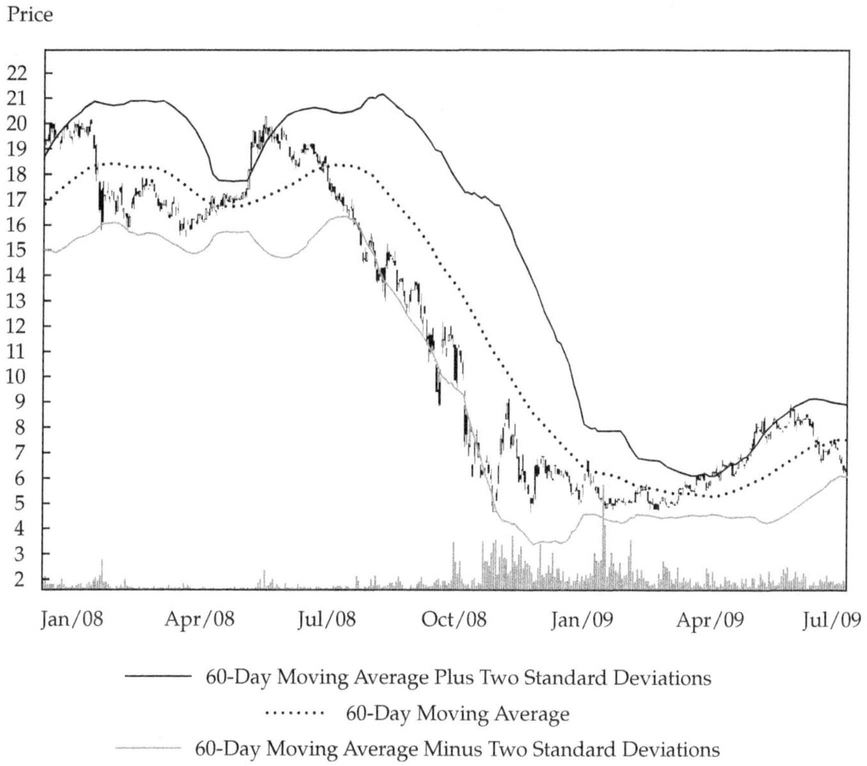

The more volatile the security being analyzed becomes, the wider the range becomes between the two outer lines or bands. Similar to moving averages, Bollinger Bands can be used to create trading strategies that can be easily computerized and tested. A common use is as a contrarian strategy, in which the investor sells when a security price reaches the upper band and buys when it reaches the lower band. This strategy assumes that the security price will stay within the bands.

This type of strategy is likely to lead to a large number of trades, but it also limits risk because the trader can quickly exit unprofitable trades. In the event of a sharp price move and a change in trend, however, a contrarian strategy based on Bollinger Bands would be unprofitable. So, long-term investors might actually buy on a significant breakout above the upper boundary band because a major breakout would imply a change in trend likely to persist for some time. The long-term investor would sell on a significant breakout below the lower band. In this strategy, significance would be defined as breaking above or below the band by a certain percentage (say, 5 percent or 10 percent) and/or for a certain period of time (say, a week for a daily price chart). Again, such rules can easily be computerized and tested.

3.4.2 *Momentum Oscillators*

One of the key challenges in using indicators overlaid on a price chart is the difficulty of discerning changes in market sentiment that are out of the ordinary. **Momentum oscillators** are intended to alleviate this problem. They are constructed from price data, but they are calculated so that they either oscillate between a high and low (typically 0 and 100) or oscillate around a number (such as 0 or 100). Because of this construction, extreme highs or lows are easily discernible. These extremes can be viewed as graphic representations of market sentiment when selling or buying activity is more aggressive than historically typical. Because they are price based, momentum oscillators also can be analyzed by using the same tools technicians use to analyze price, such as the concepts of trend, support, and resistance.

Technicians also look for **convergence** or **divergence** between oscillators and price. Convergence is when the oscillator moves in the same manner as the security being analyzed, and divergence is when the oscillator moves differently from the security. For example, when price reaches a new high, this sign is considered bullish, but if the momentum oscillator being used does not also reach a new high at the same time, this pattern is divergence. It is considered to be an early warning of weakness, an indication that the uptrend may soon end.

Momentum oscillators should be used in conjunction with an understanding of the existing market (price) trend. Oscillators alert a trader to **overbought** or **oversold** conditions. In an overbought condition, market sentiment is unsustainably bullish. In an oversold condition, market sentiment is unsustainably bearish. In other words, the oscillator *range* must be considered separately for every security. Some securities may experience wide variations, and others may experience only minor variations.

Oscillators have three main uses. First, oscillators can be used to determine the strength of a trend. Extreme overbought levels are warning signals for uptrends, and extreme oversold levels are warning signals for downtrends. Second, when oscillators reach historically high or low levels, they may be signaling a pending trend reversal. For oscillators that move above and below 0, crossing the 0 level signals a change in the direction of the trend. For oscillators that move above and below 100, crossing the 100 level signals a change in the direction of the trend. Third, in a non-trending market, oscillators can be used for short-term trading decisions—that is, to sell at overbought levels and to buy at oversold levels.

3.4.2.1 Momentum or Rate of Change Oscillator The terms *momentum oscillator* and *rate of change oscillator* are synonymous. "Rate of change" is often abbreviated ROC. The ROC oscillator is calculated by taking the most recent closing price, subtracting the closing price from a prior date that is a set number of days in the past, and multiplying the result by 100:

$$M = (V - Vx) \times 100$$

where

M = momentum oscillator value

V = last closing price

Vx = closing price x days ago, typically 10 days

When the ROC oscillator crosses zero in the same direction as the direction of the trend, this movement is considered a buy or sell signal. For example, if the ROC oscillator crosses into positive territory during an uptrend, it is a buy signal. If it enters into negative territory during a downtrend, it is considered a sell signal. The technician will ignore crossovers in opposition to the trend because the technician must *always* first take into account the general trend when using oscillators.

An alternative method of constructing this oscillator is to set it so that it oscillates above and below 100, instead of 0, as follows:

$$M = \frac{V}{Vx} \times 100$$

This approach is shown in Exhibit 25 for Toyota Motor Corporation.

Exhibit 25 Momentum Oscillator with 100 as Midpoint: Toyota Motor, May 2008–October 2009 (Price in Japanese Yen)

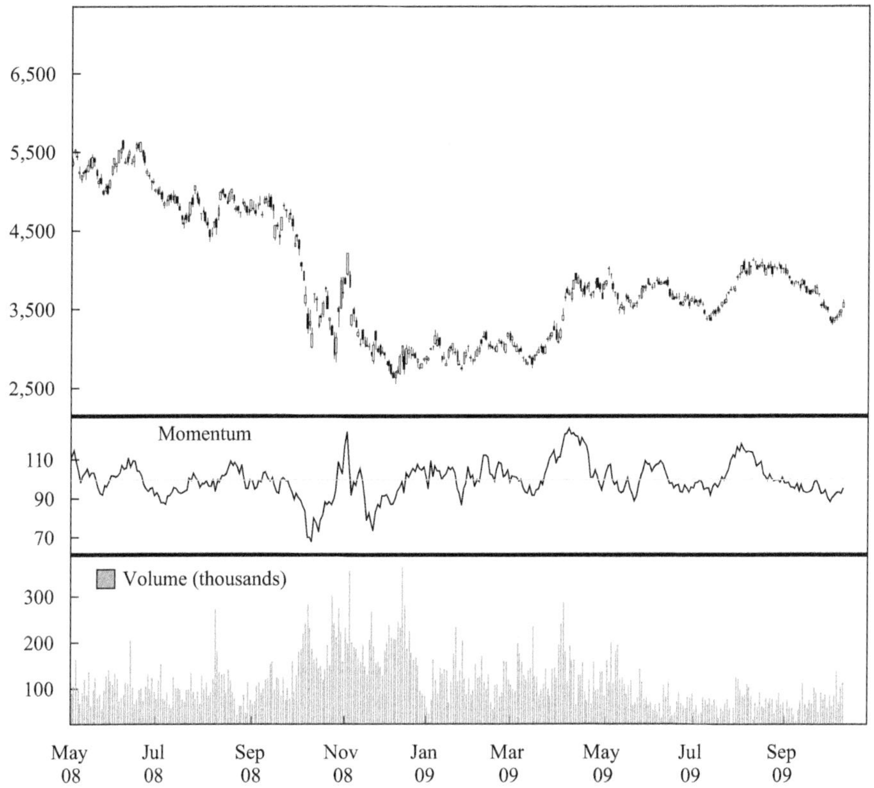

In Exhibit 25, the calculation method for the ROC oscillator for Toyota stock, traded on the Tokyo Stock Exchange, is for the oscillator to move around 100 and *x* is 12 days. Note that for this stock, the ROC oscillator tends to maintain a range between ¥85 and ¥115. So episodes when the oscillator moves outside this range are of particular interest to the technician. An extreme high means that the stock has posted its highest gain in any 12-day period at this point, and an extreme low reading means it has posted its greatest loss over any 12-day period. When investors bid up the price of a security too rapidly, the indication is that sentiment may be unduly bullish and the market may be overbought. Exhibit 25 shows that overbought levels of the ROC oscillator coincide with temporary highs in the stock price. So, those levels would have been signals to sell the stock. The other notable aspect of Exhibit 25 is the divergence when the share price hit a new low in December 2008 but the ROC oscillator did not. This divergence would have been a bullish signal and would have been interpreted to mean that, although the share price hit a new low, investor sentiment was actually higher than it had been previously. In itself, this information would not have been enough to warrant buying the shares because a downtrend in price was still in place, but it alerted the technician to the fact that the trend might end soon. The technician could then look for further indication of the trend's end and, with confirmation, might buy the stock.

3.4.2.2 Relative Strength Index A **relative strength index** (RSI) is computed over a rolling time period.[6] It graphically compares a security's gains with its losses over the set period. The creator of the RSI, Welles Wilder, suggested a 14-day time period, and

6 This indicator is sometimes called the Wilder RSI.

this period is generally the period used in most technical analysis software. The technician should understand that this variable can be changed and that the optimal time range should be determined by how the technician intends to use the RSI information. Factors that influence selection of the time period are similar to those that influence the selection of a time period for moving averages. Short time periods (such as 14 days) provide information about short-term price behavior. If 200 days is used, this short-term information will be smoothed out and, perhaps, will not be apparent at all.

RSI is a momentum oscillator and is not to be confused with the charting method called "relative strength analysis," in which the ratio of two security prices is plotted over time. The RSI provides information on whether or not an asset is overbought. The formula for the RSI is not intuitive and is best understood with an example. The formula is:

$$RSI = 100 - \frac{100}{1 + RS}$$

$$\text{where } RS = \frac{\sum(\text{Up changes for the period under consideration})}{\sum(|\text{Down changes for the period under consideration}|)}$$

Exhibit 26 shows closing prices for Ford Motor Company during the month of June 2009 for use in Exhibit 27.

Exhibit 26 Calculation of RSI: Ford, June 2009

Date	Close	Up Changes	Down Changes
6/1/2009	6.13		
6/2/2009	6.41	0.28	
6/3/2009	6.18		−0.23
6/4/2009	6.36	0.18	
6/5/2009	6.36		
6/8/2009	6.38	0.02	
6/9/2009	6.26		−0.12
6/10/2009	6.19		−0.07
6/11/2009	5.98		−0.21
6/12/2009	6.11	0.13	
6/15/2009	5.93		−0.18
6/16/2009	5.67		−0.26
6/17/2009	5.71	0.04	
6/18/2009	5.68		−0.03
6/19/2009	5.72	0.04	
6/22/2009	5.38		−0.34
6/23/2009	5.53	0.15	
6/24/2009	5.63	0.10	
6/25/2009	5.68	0.05	
6/26/2009	5.61		−0.07
6/29/2009	5.78	0.17	
6/30/2009	6.07	0.29	
		1.45	−1.51

During this time, markets were still rebounding from the subprime crisis; automobile company stocks were unusually volatile and, to some speculators, presented interesting short-term trading opportunities. Suppose a trader decided to compute an RSI for the month of June. It would be a 22-day RSI with 21 price changes—11 up, 9 down, and 1 unchanged. To calculate the RSI, the trader would sum the 11 up changes, which sum to US$1.45. The down changes total – US$1.51; the absolute value drops the minus sign. The ratio of these two numbers is 0.96, so the RSI is

$$\text{RSI} = 100 - \frac{100}{1 + 0.96} = 100 - 51.02 = 48.98$$

The index construction forces the RSI to lie within 0 and 100. A value above 70 represents an overbought situation. Values below 30 suggest the asset is oversold. Again, as is the case with most technical tools, an analyst cannot simply learn the default settings and use them in every case. The 30–70 range is a good rule of thumb, but because the oscillator is a measure of volatility, less volatile stocks (such as utilities) may normally trade in a much narrower range. More volatile stocks (such as small-capitalization technology stocks) may trade in a wider range. The range also does not have to be symmetrical around 50. For example, in an uptrend, one might see a range of 40–80 but in downtrends, a range of 20–60.

The RSI measure often appears at the bottom or top of a price chart. Exhibit 27 shows a candlestick chart of Ford stock in 2009 with the corresponding RSI.

Exhibit 27 Candlestick Chart with RSI: Ford, January–August 2009 (Price in US Dollars)

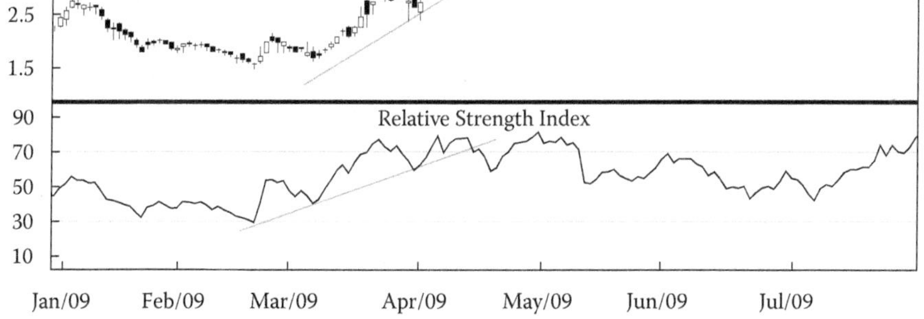

The candlestick chart of Ford stock prices in Exhibit 27 illustrates several aspects of the use of an RSI. For example, because the RSI oscillator was higher than 70 on 23 March so the stock was overbought at that time, a simple reading of the chart might have led to the conclusion that the trader should sell the stock. Doing so, however, would have caused the trader to miss a significant advance in the shares. A more careful technical analysis that took into account the trend would have indicated that the stock was in an uptrend, so RSI readings above 70 could be expected.

Because RSI is a price-based oscillator, the trader can also apply trend lines to analyze it. Note in Exhibit 27 that both the share price and the RSI oscillator were in uptrends from February until April but that the RSI uptrend was broken on 15 April, a potential warning that the uptrend in price might also break downward. In June, the share price broke its uptrend support line.

3.4.2.3 Stochastic Oscillator The stochastic oscillator is based on the observation that in uptrends, prices tend to close at or near the high end of their recent range and in downtrends, they tend to close near the low end. The logic behind these patterns is that if the shares of a stock are constantly being bid up during the day but then lose value by the close, continuation of the rally is doubtful. If sellers have enough supply to overwhelm buyers, the rally is suspect. If a stock rallies during the day and is able to hold on to some or most of those gains by the close, that sign is bullish.

The stochastic oscillator oscillates between 0 and 100 and has a default setting of a 14-day period, which, again, might be adjusted for the situation as we discussed for the RSI. The oscillator is composed of two lines, called %K and %D, that are calculated as follows:

$$\%\text{K} = 100\left(\frac{C - L14}{H14 - L14}\right)$$

where

C = latest closing price
$L14$ = lowest price in past 14 days
$H14$ = highest price in past 14 days
%D = average of the last three %K values calculated daily

Analysts should think about the %D in the same way they would a long-term moving-average line in conjunction with a short-term line. That is, %D, because it is the average of three %K values, is the slower moving, smoother line and is called the signal line. And %K is the faster moving line. The %K value means that the latest closing price (C) was in the %K percentile of the high–low range ($L14$ to $H14$).

The default oversold–overbought range for the stochastic oscillator is based on reading the signal line relative to readings of 20 and 80, but warnings about always using the default range for the RSI oscillator also apply in the case of the stochastic oscillator. In fact, noted technician Constance Brown has coined a term called the "stochastics default club" to refer to neophyte technicians who trade based solely on these defaults.[7] She has reported being able to develop successful trading strategies by using a time frame shorter than the 14-day default to calculate the stochastic oscillator. Apparently, enough traders are basing trades on the defaults to move the market for certain stocks. So, using shorter time frames than the default, she could trade ahead of the traders in the default stochastic club and generate a profit. Of course, other traders might be tempted to use an even shorter time frame, but there is a drawback to using a short time frame; namely, the shorter the time frame is, the more volatile the oscillator becomes and the more false signals it generates.

The stochastic oscillator should be used with other technical tools, such as trend analysis or pattern analysis. If both methods suggest the same conclusion, the trader has convergence (or confirmation), but if they give conflicting signals, the trader has divergence, which is a warning signal suggesting that further analysis is necessary.

The absolute level of the two lines should be considered in light of their normal range. Movements above this range indicate to a technician an overbought security and are considered bearish; movements below this range indicate an oversold security

7 See Brown (2012).

and are considered bullish. Crossovers of the two lines can also give trading signals the same way crossovers of two moving averages give signals. When the %K moves from below the %D line to above it, this move is considered a bullish short-term trading signal; conversely, when %K moves from above the %D line to below it, this pattern is considered bearish. In practice, a trader can use technical analysis software to adjust trading rules and optimize the calculation of the stochastic oscillator for a particular security and investment purpose (e.g., short-term trading or long-term investing).

The reason technicians use historical data to test their trading rules and find the optimal parameters for each security is that each security is different. The group of market participants actively trading differs from security to security. Just as each person has a different personality, so do groups of people. In effect, the groups of active market participants trading each security are imparting their personality on the trading activity for that security. As this group changes over time, the ideal parameters for a particular security may change.

Exhibit 28 provides a good example of how the stochastic oscillator can be used together with trend analysis. The exhibit provides the weekly price chart and stochastic oscillator for Petroleo Brasileiro ADRs, which are traded on the New York Stock Exchange, for June 2008 through June 2009. Note that during the downtrend on the left side of the chart the stochastic oscillator often moved below 20. Each time it reached 80, however, it provided a valid sell signal. When the downtrend ended in November 2008 and an uptrend began, the stochastic oscillator was regularly moving above 80, but each time the %K line moved above %D, a valid buy signal was given.

Exhibit 28 Daily Price Chart and Stochastic Oscillator: Petroleo Brasileiro ADR, June 2008–July 2009 (Price in US Dollars)

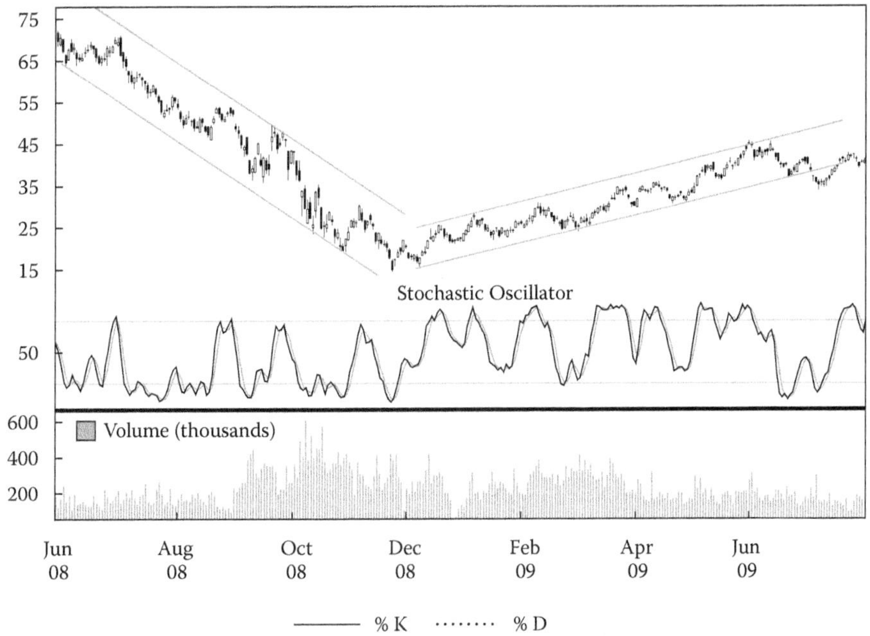

3.4.2.4 Moving-Average Convergence/Divergence Oscillator The **moving-average convergence/divergence oscillator** is commonly referred to as MACD, which is pronounced Mack Dee. The MACD is the difference between a short-term and a long-term moving average of the security's price. The MACD is constructed by calculating two lines, the MACD line and the signal line:

- MACD line: difference between two exponentially smoothed moving averages, generally 12 and 26 days.
- Signal line: exponentially smoothed average of MACD line, generally 9 days.

The indicator oscillates around zero and has no upper or lower limit. Rather than using a set overbought–oversold range for MACD, the analyst compares the current level with the historical performance of the oscillator for a particular security to determine when a security is out of its normal sentiment range.

MACD is used in technical analysis in three ways. The first is to note crossovers of the MACD line and the signal line, as discussed for moving averages and the stochastic oscillator. Crossovers of the two lines may indicate a change in trend. The second is to look for times when the MACD is outside its normal range for a given security. The third is to use trend lines on the MACD itself. When the MACD is trending in the same direction as price, this pattern is convergence, and when the two are trending in opposite directions, the pattern is divergence.

Exhibit 29 shows a daily price chart of Exxon Mobil (at the top) with the MACD oscillator for March through October of 2005. Note the convergence in the bottoming of both the oscillator and price in May, which provided confirmation of a change in trend. This change was further confirmed by the MACD line crossing above the signal line. A bearish signal was given in late-September with the change in trend of both price and the oscillator and the crossover of the signal line by the MACD line. The fact that the MACD oscillator was moving up to a level that was unusually high for this stock would have been an early warning signal in September.

Exhibit 29 MACD and Daily Price Chart: Exxon Mobil, March–November 2005 (Price in US Dollars)

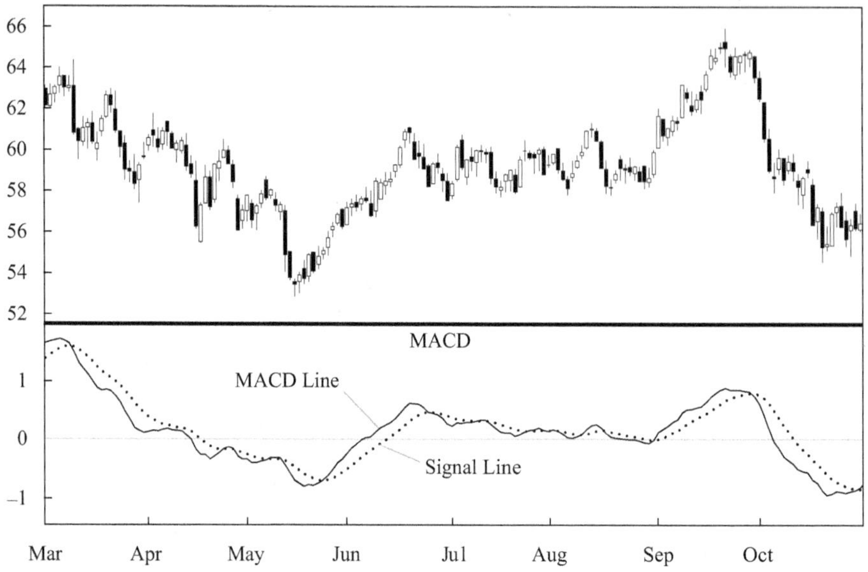

3.4.3 *Sentiment Indicators*

Sentiment indicators attempt to gauge investor activity for signs of increasing bullishness or bearishness. Sentiment indicators come in two forms—investor polls and calculated statistical indexes.

3.4.3.1 Opinion Polls A wide range of services conduct periodic polls of either individual investors or investment professionals to gauge their sentiment about the equity market. The most common of the polls are the Investors Intelligence Advisors Sentiment reports, Market Vane Bullish Consensus, Consensus Bullish Sentiment Index, and Daily Sentiment Index, all of which poll investment professionals, and reports of the American Association of Individual Investors (AAII), which polls individual investors. All but the AAII survey are subscription-based services. *Barron's* magazine publishes data from four of these surveys on a weekly basis.

By regularly polling, compiling these data over time, and presenting it graphically, these services provide technicians with an analyzable snapshot of investor sentiment over time. Technicians look at prior market activity and compare it with highs or lows in sentiment, as well as inflection points in sentiment, as a gauge when they are forecasting the future direction of the market.

The most widely used investor polls are all US-based. One reason is that interpretation of the surveys is determined by comparing the survey results with market performance over time. To gauge a survey's usefulness in predicting major market turns, the survey must have been published over several cycles, and each of the surveys mentioned here, based on US data, has been available for several decades.

3.4.3.2 Calculated Statistical Indexes The other category of sentiment indicators are indicators that are calculated from market data, such as security prices. The two most commonly used are derived from the options market; they are the put/call ratio and the volatility index. Additionally, many analysts look at margin debt and short interest.

The **put/call ratio** is the volume of put options traded divided by the volume of call options traded for a particular financial instrument. Investors who buy put options on a security are presumably bearish, and investors who buy call options are presumably bullish. The volume in call options is greater than the volume traded in put options over time, so the put/call ratio is normally below 1.0. The ratio is considered to be a contrarian indicator, meaning that higher values are considered bearish and lower values are considered bullish. But, its usefulness as a contrarian indicator is limited except at extreme low or high levels in relation to the historical trading level of the put/call ratio for a particular financial instrument. The actual value of the put/call ratio, and its normal range, differs for each security or market, so no standard definitions of overbought or oversold levels exist. At extreme lows where call option volume is significantly greater than put option volume, market sentiment is said to be so overly positive that a correction is likely. At extreme highs in the put/call ratio, market sentiment is said to be so extremely negative that an increase in price is likely.

The **CBOE Volatility Index** (VIX) is a measure of near-term market volatility calculated by the Chicago Board Options Exchange. Since 2003, it has been calculated from option prices on the stocks in the S&P 500. The VIX rises when market participants become fearful of an impending market decline. These participants then bid up the price of puts, and the result is an increase in the VIX level. Technicians use the VIX in conjunction with trend, pattern, or oscillator tools, and it is interpreted from a contrarian perspective. When other indicators suggest that the market is oversold and the VIX is at an extreme high, this combination is considered bullish. Exhibit 30 shows the VIX from March 2005 to August 2018.

Exhibit 30 VIX, March 2005–August 2018

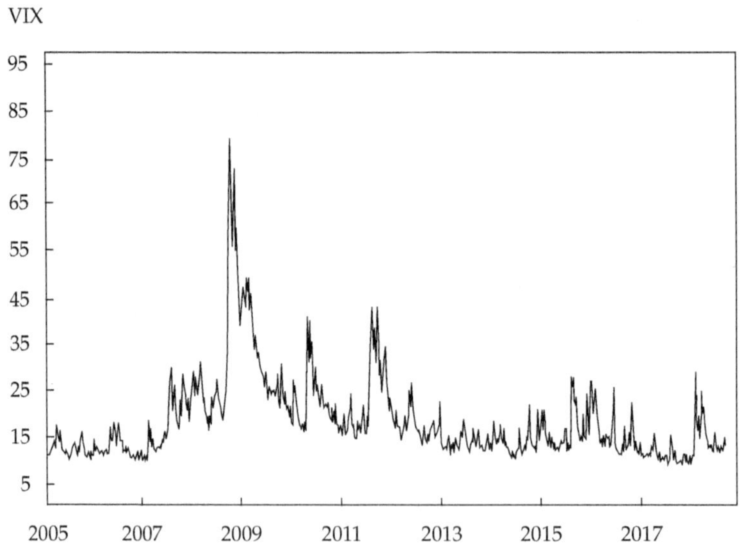

Margin debt is also often used as an indication of sentiment. As a group, investors have a history of buying near market tops and selling at the bottom. When the market is rising and indexes reach new highs, investors are motivated to buy more equities in the hope of participating in the market rally. A margin account permits an investor to borrow part of the investment cost from the brokerage firm. This debt magnifies the gains or losses resulting from the investment.

Investor psychology plays an important role in the intuition behind margin debt as an indicator. When stock margin debt is increasing, investors are aggressively buying and stock prices will move higher because of increased demand. Eventually, the margin traders use all of their available credit, so their buying power (and, therefore, demand) decreases, which fuels a price decline. Falling prices may trigger margin calls and forced selling, thereby driving prices even lower.

Brokerage firms must report activity in their customers' margin accounts, so keeping track of borrowing behavior is relatively easy. Exhibit 31 provides a 10-year comparison of margin debt with the S&P 500. The correlation is striking: Rising margin debt is generally associated with a rising index level, and falling margin debt is associated with a falling index level. In fact, for the 113 months shown in Exhibit 31, the correlation coefficient between the levels of margin debt and the S&P 500 is 80.2 percent. When margin debt peaked in the summer of 2007, the market also topped out. Margin debt dropped sharply during the latter part of 2008 as the subprime crisis took the market down. Investors began to use borrowed funds again in the first half of 2009 when heavily discounted shares became increasingly attractive. Margin debt was still well below the average of the last decade, but the upturn would be viewed as a bullish sign by advocates of this indicator.

Exhibit 31 Margin Debt in US Markets vs. S&P 500, 1997–2018

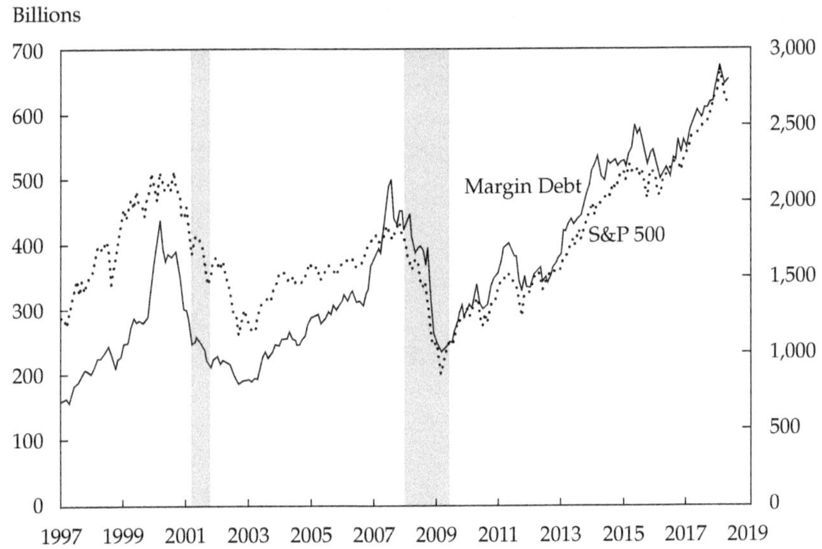

Source: FINRA.

Short interest is another commonly used sentiment indicator. Investors sell shares short when they believe the share prices will decline. Brokerage firms must report short-sale activity, and these statistics are aggregated and reported by the exchanges and the financial press on a monthly basis. The number of shares of a particular security that are currently sold short is called "short interest." The short interest ratio represents the number of days of trading activity represented by short interest. To facilitate comparisons of large and small companies, common practice is to "normalize" this value by dividing short interest by average daily trading volume to get the short interest ratio:

Short interest ratio = Short interest/Average daily trading volume

EXAMPLE 3

Short Interest Ratio

At the end of September 2009, *Barron's* reported short interest of 10,936,467 shares in Goldman Sachs, with average daily trading volume of 9,086,174. At the same time, the short interest in TD Bank was 20,420,166 on average trading volume of 1,183,558 shares. Calculate the short interest ratio for both firms.

Solution:

The short interest ratio for Goldman Sachs was 10,936,467 divided by 9,086,174, or 1.2 days. For TD Bank, the short interest ratio was 20,420,166 divided by 1,183,558, or 17.25 days.

There are differences of opinion about how to interpret short interest as an indicator. It is considered to show market sentiment and to be a contrarian indicator. Some people believe that if a large number of shares are sold short and the short interest ratio is high, the market should expect a falling price for the shares because of so much negative sentiment about them. A counter-argument is that, although the short sellers are bearish on the security, the effect of their short sales has already been felt in the security price. The short sellers' next action will be to buy shares back to cover their short positions. When the short sellers cover their positions, those actions will provide a boost to the share price. Therefore, the short interest ratio constitutes future (and known) demand for the shares.

Regardless of the analyst's perspective, in Example 3, the TD Bank short interest ratio of approximately 17 is more noteworthy than the much lower figure for Goldman Sachs.

3.4.4 *Flow-of-Funds Indicators*

Technicians look at fund flows as a way to gauge the potential supply and demand for equities. Demand can come in the form of margin borrowing against current holdings or cash holdings by mutual funds and other groups that are normally large holders of equities, such as insurance companies and pension funds. The more cash these groups hold, the more bullish is the indication for equities. One caveat in looking at potential sources of demand is that, although these data indicate the potential buying power of various large investor groups, the data say nothing about the likelihood that the groups will buy.

On the supply side, technicians look at new or secondary issuance of stock because these activities put more securities into the market and increase supply.

3.4.4.1 Arms Index A common flow of funds indicator is the **Arms Index**, also called the **TRIN** (for "short-term trading index").[8] This indicator is applied to a broad market (such as the S&P 500) to measure the relative extent to which money is moving into or out of rising and declining stocks. The index is a ratio of two ratios:

$$\text{Arms Index} = \frac{\text{Number of advancing issues} \div \text{Number of declining issues}}{\text{Volume of advancing issues} \div \text{Volume of declining issues}}$$

When this index is near 1.0, the market is in balance; that is, as much money is moving into rising stocks as into declining stocks. A value above 1.0 means that there is more volume in declining stocks; a value below 1.0 means that most trading activity is in rising stocks. Exhibit 32 shows the Arms Index for the NYSE Composite Index on a daily basis for the first six months of 2018. Most observations are evenly distributed around the 1.0 level, suggesting that the market continued to be in a choppy trading range with several sharp down and up spikes. Note that the up spikes are associated with large price decreases in the index level and the down spikes reflect the opposite.

8 This tool was first proposed by Richard W. Arms, Jr., a well-known technical analyst.

Exhibit 32 Arms Index for the NYSE Index, January–June 2018

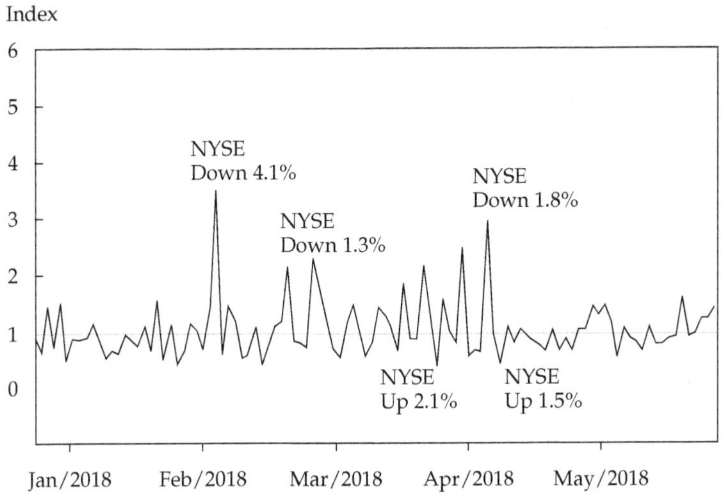

EXAMPLE 4

TRIN Indicator

Sarah Johannson, CFA, recently installed some investment software and is verifying the calculation of some of the statistics it produces. Her screen indicates a TRIN value of 1.02 for the NYSE and 1.80 for the NASDAQ market. These values seem to be unusually far apart to her, and she wonders whether they are both real-time statistics like the other market price data. To check whether they are real-time statistics, a few minutes later, she simultaneously captures the TRIN from her software display (slightly changed to 1.01 for the NYSE and 1.81 for NASDAQ) and on a separate monitor, she does a screen capture of NYSE and NASDAQ data, as follows:

		NYSE	NASDAQ
Number of issues	Advancing	850	937
	Declining	1,982	1,472
Volume	Advancing	76,921,200	156,178,475
	Declining	185,461,042	441,970,884

How does Johannson recalculate and interpret the TRIN value for the NYSE and NASDAQ?

Solution:

Johannson calculates the TRIN values for the NYSE and NASDAQ as follows:

$$\text{TRIN (NYSE)} = \frac{(850 \div 1{,}982)}{(76{,}921{,}200 \div 185{,}461{,}042)} = 1.03$$

$$\text{TRIN (NASDAQ)} = \frac{(937 \div 1{,}472)}{(156{,}178{,}475 \div 441{,}970{,}884)} = 1.80$$

Johannson concludes that her software is giving her current values and that the NASDAQ is having a much worse day than the NYSE.

3.4.4.2 Margin Debt The previous section discussed the use of margin debt as an indicator of market sentiment. Margin debt is also widely used as a flow-of-funds indicator because margin loans may increase the purchases of stocks and declining margin balances may force the selling of stocks.

3.4.4.3 Mutual Fund Cash Position Mutual funds hold a substantial proportion of all investable assets. Some analysts use the *percentage of mutual fund assets held in liquid assets (cash and cash equivalents)* as a predictor of market direction. It is called the "mutual fund cash position indicator." Mutual funds must hold some of their assets in cash in order to pay bills and send redemption checks to account holders. Cash arrives on a daily basis from customer deposits, interest earned, and dividends received. Cash also increases after a fund manager sells a position and holds the funds before reinvesting them. During a bull market, the manager wants to buy shares as quickly as possible to avoid having a cash "drag" hurt the fund's performance. If prices are trending lower, however, the manager may hold funds in cash to improve the fund's performance.

Exhibit 33 shows year-end mutual fund cash in the United States as a percentage of assets from 1984 through 2017. Over this period, the average cash percentage was 5.9 percent. An analyst's initial intuition might be that when cash is relatively low, fund managers are bullish and anticipate rising prices, but when fund managers are bearish, they conserve cash to wait for lower prices. Advocates of this technical indicator argue exactly the opposite: When the mutual fund cash position is low, fund managers have already bought, and the effects of their purchases are already reflected in security prices. When the cash position is high, however, that money represents buying power that will move prices higher when the money is used to add positions to the portfolio. The mutual fund cash position is another example of a contrarian indicator.

Exhibit 33 Mutual Fund Cash Position, 1984–2017

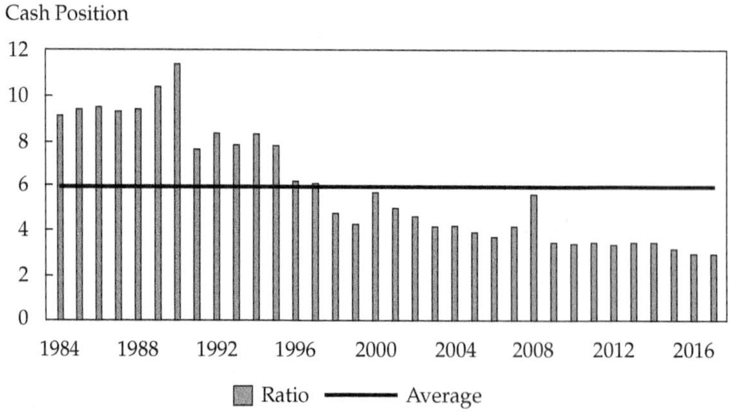

Source: http://www.icifactbook.org/data/18_fb_data (accessed 23 Nov 2018). Note: Data is the percentage of cash and cash equivalents held by equity mutual funds.

Some analysts modify the value of the cash percentage to account for differences in the level of interest rates. Cash is not sitting in a desk drawer; it is on deposit somewhere earning interest. When interest rates are low, holding cash can be a substantial drag on the fund's performance if the broad market advances. When interest rates are high, holding cash is less costly.

EXAMPLE 5

Market Indicators

At the request of a wealthy client, Erik Nielson is preparing a proprietary research report on the shares of a US company. He has completed the part of the report dealing with fundamental analysis and wants to include a section on technical analysis. Nielson has gathered the following information:

Company Information:

- The 20-day moving average of the share price just rose through the 200-day moving average.
- RSI = 40.6.

Market Information:

- TRIN = 1.9.
- Mutual fund cash position = 7.0%

Nielson has the data in Exhibit 33 available as a reference.

1 How should Nielson interpret each item of information?

2 Do these indicators, in the aggregate, lead Nielson to a buy, hold, or sell recommendation for the company's shares?

Solution to 1:

- Moving average: When a short-term moving average moves above a longer-term moving average, the movement is a golden cross and is a bullish signal.
- RSI: An RSI of 40.6 would be considered neutral. The RSI ranges between 0 and 100. Values greater than 70 are bearish; values below 30 are bullish.
- TRIN: A TRIN value above 1.0 means that there is more volume in declining stocks than in advancing stocks; therefore, a value of 1.9 is bearish.
- Mutual fund cash position: The 6.0 % figure is near the long-term average of 5.9% (based on exhibit 33), so it is a neutral signal.

Solution to 2:

Of the four indicators, one is bullish, one is bearish, and two are neutral. Most analysts would view this result as "net neutral" and would recommend continuing to hold the stock. An alternative point of view might be that seeing a bullish indicator for the stock while the indicator for the overall market is bearish could be an argument for overweighting the stock.

3.4.4.4 New Equity Issuance When a company's owners decide to take a company public and offer shares for sale, the owners want to put those shares on the market at a time when investors are eager to buy. That is, the owners want to offer the shares when they can sell them at a premium price. Premium prices occur near market tops. The new equity issuance indicator suggests that as the number of initial public offerings (IPOs) increases, the upward price trend may be about to turn down.

A supply-and-demand effect is also at work. Putting more shares on the market increases the aggregate supply of shares available for investors to purchase. The investment community has a finite quantity of cash to spend, so an increase in IPOs may be viewed as a bearish factor.

3.4.4.5 Secondary Offerings Technicians also monitor secondary offerings to gauge potential changes in the supply of equities. Although secondary offerings do not increase the supply of shares, because existing shares are sold by insiders to the general public, they do increase the supply available for trading or the float. So, from a market perspective, secondary offerings of shares have the potential to change the supply-and-demand equation as much as IPOs do.

3.5 Cycles

Over the centuries, technicians have noted recurring cycles of various frequencies in the capital markets. The study of cycles in the markets is part of broader cycle studies that exist in numerous fields of study. Many observed cycles, such as one in US equities tied to the cycle of US presidential elections, have an obvious and rational justification. Other cycles do not. However, why cycles in fields seemingly unrelated to finance, such as astronomy or weather patterns, may influence the economy (and thus the capital markets) may have a logical explanation. For example, sun spots affect weather patterns on earth, which in turn affect agriculture and, therefore, capital markets because they are related to agriculture.

3.5.1 *Kondratieff Wave*

The longest of the widely recognized cycles was identified by Nikolai Kondratieff in the 1920s. Kondratieff was an economist in the Soviet Union who suggested that Western economies had a 54-year cycle. He traced cycles from the 1780s to the time he published this theory in the 1920s, and the economic depression of the 1930s was consistent with the cycle he identified. His theory was mainly tied to economic cycles and commodity prices, but cycles can also be seen in the prices of equities during the time of his work.

Kondratieff's ideas have come into widespread acceptance, particularly since his works were translated into English in the 1980s. Two economists at the London School of Economics, E. H. Phelps Brown and Sheila Hopkins, identified a 50–52 year economic cycle in the United Kingdom. Together with Kondratieff, credit should be given to two Dutch economists, Jacob van Gelderen and Samuel de Wolff, who wrote about a 50–60 year economic cycle but published their work earlier, in 1913. Their work came to light only recently, however, so the long 54-year economic cycle is known as the **Kondratieff Wave** or K Wave.

3.5.2 *18-Year Cycle*

The 18-year cycle is interesting because three 18-year cycles make up the longer 54-year Kondratieff Wave. The 18-year cycle is most often mentioned in connection with real estate prices, but it can also be found in equities and other markets.

3.5.3 *Decennial Pattern*

The decennial pattern is the pattern of average stock market returns (based on the DJIA) broken down on the basis of the last digit in the year. Years ending with a 0 have had the worst performance, and years ending with a 5 have been by far the best. The DJIA was up every year ending in a 5 from 1885 until 1995. However, the DJIA declined by 0.6 percent in 2005 and by 2.2 percent in 2015.

3.5.4 *Presidential Cycle*

This cycle in the United States connects the performance of the DJIA with presidential elections. In this theory, years are grouped into categories on the basis of whether they were election years or the first, second, or third year following an election. The third year is the year prior to the next election. The third year shows the best performance; in fact, the DJIA experienced a positive return in every pre-election year from 1943 through 2011.[9] One explanation for this outcome is that with so many politicians up for re-election, they inject stimulus into the economy in an attempt to improve their chances to be re-elected.[10] Election years are also usually positive years for the stock market, but with less consistency. Post-election years and the so-called midterm year have the worst performance.

These long cycles are important to keep in mind when using other technical analysis tools. However, the long cycles described here and other theories about long cycles present a number of problems. The primary problem is the small sample size. Only 58 presidential elections have been held in the United States, and only 4 completed Kondratieff cycles have occurred in US history. Another problem is that even with the small number of cycles, the data do not always fit the cycle theory, and when they do, that fit may not be obvious.

ELLIOTT WAVE THEORY 4

In a theory proposed by R. N. Elliott in 1938, the market moves in regular, repeated waves or cycles. He identified and categorized these waves and wrote in detail about aspects of market cycles. Elliott was an accountant by training, but in 1929, after he contracted a progressive intestinal illness at age 58 while working in Latin America, he was forced to retire. Then, he turned his attention to a detailed study of equity prices in the United States.

A decade later, in 1938, he published his findings in a book titled *The Wave Principle.* In developing the concept that the market moves in waves, Elliott relied heavily on Charles Dow's early work. Elliott described how the market moved in a pattern of five waves moving up in a bull market in the following pattern: 1 = up, 2 = down, 3 = up, 4 = down and 5 = up. He called this wave the "impulse wave." The impulse wave was followed by a corrective wave with three components: a = down, b = up and c = down.

When the market is a bear market, as defined in Dow Theory—that is, with both of Dow's major indices in bear markets—the downward movements are impulse waves and are broken into five waves with upward corrections broken into three subwaves.

Elliott also noted that each wave could be broken down into smaller and smaller subwaves.

The longest of the waves is called the "grand supercycle" and takes place over centuries. Elliott traced grand supercycles back to the founding of the United States, and his successors have continued his work. Each grand supercycle can be broken down into subcycles until ending with the "subminuette," which unfolds over several minutes. The major cycles are:

- Grand supercycle
- Supercycle
- Cycle

9 In the 2015 pre-election year, the DJIA had its first loss in a pre-election year, with a decline of 2.2%.

10 In US presidential election years, all 435 House of Representatives seats, and 33 of the 100 Senate seats are also up for election.

- Primary
- Intermediate
- Minor
- Minute
- Minuette
- Subminuette

An important aspect of Elliott's work is that he discovered that market waves follow patterns that are ratios of the numbers in the **Fibonacci sequence**. Leonardo Fibonacci was an 11th century Italian mathematician who explained this sequence in his book *Liber Abaci,* but the sequence was known to mathematicians as far back as 200 BCE in India. The Fibonacci sequence starts with the numbers 0, 1, 1, and then each subsequent number in the sequence is the sum of the two preceding numbers:

0, 1, 1, 2, 3, 5, 8, 13, 21, 34 ...

Elliott was more interested in the ratios of the numbers in the sequence because he found that the ratio of the size of subsequent waves was generally a Fibonacci ratio. The ratios of one Fibonacci number to the next that Elliott considered most important are the following:

1/2 = 0.50, 2/3 = 0.6667, 3/5 = 0.6, 5/8 = 0.625, 8/13 = 0.6154

He also noticed that the ratio of a Fibonacci sequence number to its preceding number is important:

2/1 = 2, 3/2 = 1.5, 5/3 = 1.6667, 8/5 = 1.600, 13/8 = 1.6250

These ratios converge around 1.618. In mathematics, 1.618 is called the "golden ratio," and it can be found throughout nature—in astronomy, biology, botany, and many other fields. It is also widely used in art and architecture. The ancient Egyptians built the pyramids on the basis of this ratio, and the ancient Greeks used it widely.

As noted, Elliott numbered the impulse waves 1–5 and the corrective waves, a, b and c. Exhibit 34 depicts the impulse and corrective waves in a bull market.

Exhibit 34 Impulse Waves and Corrective Waves

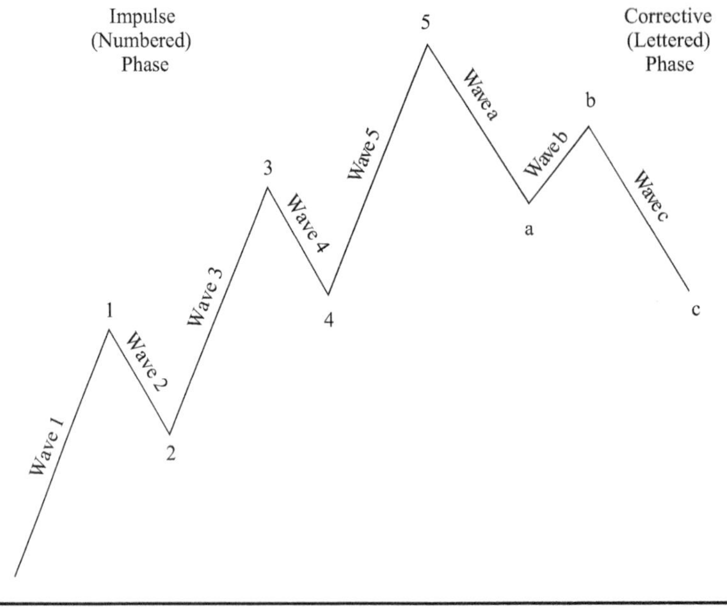

Elliott described the characteristics of each wave. Note the following, as shown in Exhibit 34:

- Wave 1 starts as a basing pattern and displays an increase in price, volume, and breadth.[11] Wave 1 consists of five smaller waves.
- Wave 2 moves down, retracing much of the gain in Wave 1 but not all of it. Common percentage retracements are Fibonacci ratios, such as 50 percent or 62 percent. Wave 2 never erases all of the gains from Wave 1. Wave 2 consists of three smaller waves.
- Wave 3 moves above the high of the first wave and has strong breadth, volume, and price movement. Most of the price movement in an uptrend typically occurs in Wave 3. Wave 3 consists of five smaller waves. Wave 3 often moves prices 1.618 times higher than the length of Wave 1, which is a Fibonacci ratio.
- Wave 4 is, again, a correction, and the ratio of the change in price during this wave to the price change during the third wave is also generally a Fibonacci ratio. Wave 4 commonly reverses 38 percent of the gain in Wave 3. Wave 5 is also an up wave. Generally, the price movement in Wave 5 is not as great as that in Wave 3. The exception to the rule is that Wave 5 may become extended, as when euphoria overtakes the market. Wave 5 consists of five smaller waves.

After Wave 5 is completed, the market traces out a series of three corrective waves, labeled a, b and c in Exhibit 34.

- Wave a is a down wave in a bull market; Wave a itself breaks down into three waves.
- Wave b is an upward movement and breaks down into five waves. Wave b is a false rally and is often called a "bull trap."
- Wave c is the final corrective wave. In a bull market, it does not move below the start of the prior Wave 1 pattern. Wave c breaks down into three subwaves.

This description of the waves applies to bull markets; in bear markets, the impulse waves are labeled A through E and the corrective waves are labeled 1, 2, and 3. Waves in the direction of the trend consist of five subwaves, and counter-waves consist of three subwaves.

In practice, a good deal of time is required to become proficient with **Elliott Wave Theory**. Wave counts may not become evident at first, and Elliotticians often have to renumber their wave counts on the basis of changes in market trends. This theory is widely used, however, and the patterns Elliott described can still be observed today.

As a technician begins to make initial judgments on wave counts, the next step is to draw lines representing Fibonacci ratios on the charts. These lines alert the technician to the levels at which trends may change in the future and can be used in conjunction with other technical tools for forecasting. Positive price movements generally take prices up by some Fibonacci ratio of prior highs (e.g., 1.5 or 1.62), and price declines generally reverse prices by a Fibonacci ratio (e.g., 0.50 or 0.667). Elliott Wave Theory is used in practice with Dow Theory, trend analysis, pattern analysis, and oscillator analysis to provide a sense of the general trend in the market. As Elliott's nine cycles imply, Elliott Wave Theory can be applied in both very short-term trading as well as in very long-term economic analysis, as is the case with most tools used in technical analysis.

11 Breadth is defined as the ratio of the number of advancing securities in an index or traded on a given stock market to the number of declining issues.

5 INTERMARKET ANALYSIS

Intermarket analysis is a field within technical analysis that combines analysis of major categories of securities—namely, equities, bonds, currencies, and commodities—to identify market trends and possible inflections in a trend. Intermarket analysis also looks at industry subsectors, such as the nine sectors the S&P 500 is divided into, and the relationships among the major stock markets of countries with the largest economies, such as the New York, London, and Tokyo stock exchanges.

Intermarket analysis relies heavily on the field of economic analysis for its theoretical underpinning. The field was pioneered by John Murphy with his 1991 book *Intermarket Technical Analysis*. Murphy noted that all markets are inter-related and that these relationships are strengthening with the globalization of the world economy.[12]

> Stock prices are affected by bond prices. High bond prices are a positive for stock prices since this means low interest rates. Lower interest rates benefit companies with lower borrowing costs and lead to higher equity valuations in the calculation of intrinsic value using discounted cash flow analysis in fundamental analysis. Thus rising bond prices are a positive for stock prices, and declining bond prices are a bearish indicator.
>
> Bond prices impact commodity prices. Bond prices move inversely to interest rates. Interest rates move in proportion to expectations to future prices of commodities or inflation. So declining bond prices are a signal of possible rising commodity prices.
>
> Currencies impact commodity prices. Most commodity trading is denominated in US dollars and so prices are commonly quoted in US dollars. As a result, a strong dollar results in lower commodity prices and vice versa.

In intermarket analysis, technicians often look for inflection points in one market as a warning sign to start looking for a change in trend in a related market. To identify these intermarket relationships, a commonly used tool is relative strength analysis, which charts the price of one security divided by the price of another.

Exhibit 35 shows the relative price of 10-year US Treasury bonds compared with the S&P 500. Major trends in periods of both outperformance and underperformance of the T-bond price relative to the S&P 500 can be clearly seen. The inflection points in this chart occur in 2000, 2003, 2007, and 2009. At each point, the relative performance ratio would signal that the time had come to move investments between asset classes.

12 See Murphy (1991).

Exhibit 35 Relative Strength of 10-Year T-Bonds vs. S&P 500, 1999–2018

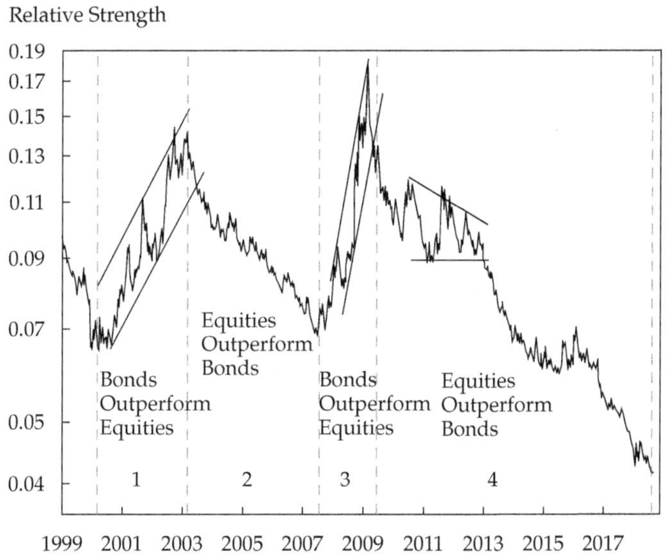

Exhibit 36 is a relative strength chart depicting the ratio between the S&P 500 and commodity prices. It shows a clear reversal of trend in mid-2008 from Commodities to Equities. This inflection point shows US stocks strengthening relative to commodities and would indicate that allocating funds away from commodities and into US equities might be appropriate.

Exhibit 36 Historical Example: S&P 500 Index vs. Commodity Prices, 2007–2010

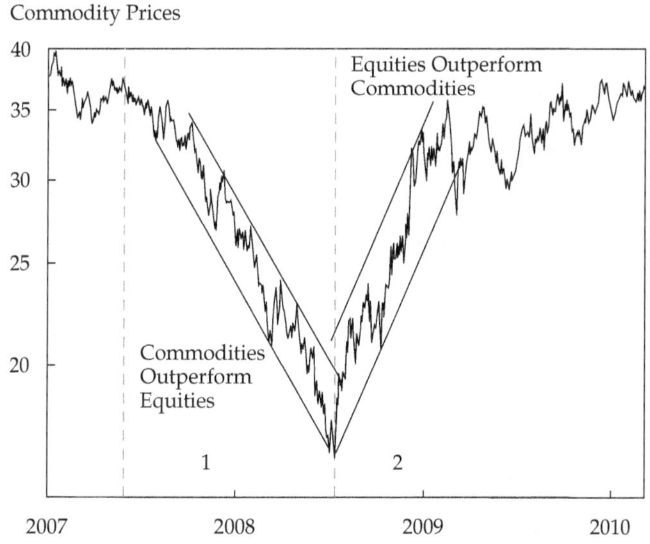

In addition to the preceding comparisons, once an asset category has been identified, relative strength analysis can be used to identify the strongest performing securities in a sector. For example, if commodities look promising, an investor can analyze each of the major commodities relative to a broad commodity index in order to find the strongest commodity.

Intermarket analysis can also be used to identify sectors of the equity market to invest in—often in connection with technical observations of the business cycle at any time. The equities of certain industry sectors tend to perform best at the beginning of an economic cycle. These sectors include utilities, financials, consumer nondurables, and transportation stocks. As an economic recovery gets under way, retailers, manufacturers, health care, and consumer durables tend to outperform. Lagging sectors include those tied to commodity prices, such as energy and basic industrial commodities, and also technology stocks.

Observations based on intermarket analysis can also help in allocating funds across national markets. Certain countries' economies are closely tied to commodities—for example, Australia, Canada, and South Africa. As economies evolve, these relationships change. So, the relationships must be monitored closely.

SUMMARY

This reading has introduced the investment tools known as technical analysis. Among the points made are the following:

- Technical analysis is a form of security analysis that uses price and volume market data, often graphically displayed.
- Technical analysis can be used for any freely traded security in the global market and is used on a wide range of financial instruments, such as equities, bonds, commodity futures, and currency futures.
- Technical analysis is the study of market trends or patterns and relies on recognition of patterns that have worked in the past in an attempt to predict future security prices. Technicians believe that market trends and patterns repeat themselves and are somewhat predictable because human behavior tends to repeat itself and is somewhat predictable.
- Another tenet of technical analysis is that the market brings together the collective wisdom of multiple participants, weights it according to the size of the trades they make, and allows analysts to understand this collective sentiment. Technical analysis relies on knowledgeable market participants putting this knowledge to work in the market and thereby influencing prices and volume.
- Technical analysis and fundamental analysis are equally useful and valid, but they approach the market in different ways. Technical analysis focuses solely on analyzing markets and the trading of financial instruments, whereas fundamental analysis is a much wider ranging field encompassing financial and economic analysis as well as analysis of societal and political trends.
- Technical analysis relies primarily on information gathered from market participants that is expressed through the interaction of price and volume. Fundamental analysis relies on information that is external to the market (e.g., economic data, company financial information) in an attempt to evaluate a security's value relative to its current price.
- The usefulness of technical analysis is diminished by any constraints on the security being freely traded, by large outside manipulation of the market, and in illiquid markets.
- Charts provide information about past price behavior and provide a basis for inferences about likely future price behavior. Various types of charts can be useful in studying the markets: line charts, bar charts, candlestick charts, and point and figure charts.

- Relative strength analysis is based on the ratio of the prices of a security to a benchmark and is used to compare the performance of one asset with the performance of another asset.
- Many technicians consider volume information to be very important and watch for the confirmation in volume of a price trend or the divergence of volume from a price trend.
- The concept of trend is perhaps the most important aspect of technical analysis. An uptrend is defined as a security making higher highs and higher lows. To draw an uptrend line, a technician draws a line connecting the lows of the price chart. A downtrend is defined as a security making lower highs and lower lows. To draw a downtrend line, a technician draws a line connecting the highs of the price chart.
- Support is defined as a low price range in which the price stops declining because of buying activity. It is the opposite of resistance, which is a price range in which price stops rising because of selling activity.
- Chart patterns are formations appearing in price charts that create some type of recognizable shape.
- Reversal patterns signal the end of a trend. Common reversal patterns are the head and shoulders, the inverse head and shoulders, double tops and bottoms, and triple tops and bottoms.
- Continuation patterns indicate that a market trend in place prior to the pattern formation will continue once the pattern is completed. Common continuation patterns are triangles, rectangles, flags, and pennants.
- Price-based indicators incorporate information contained in market prices. Common price-based indicators are the moving average and Bollinger Bands.
- Momentum oscillator indicators are constructed from price data, but they are calculated so that they fluctuate either between a high and low, typically 0 and 100, or around 0 or 100. Some examples are momentum (or rate of change) oscillators, the RSI, stochastic measures, and MACD.
- Sentiment indicators attempt to gauge investor activity for signs of increasing bullishness or bearishness. Sentiment indicators come in two forms—investor polls and calculated statistical indexes. Opinion polls to gauge investors' sentiment toward the equity market are conducted by a variety of services. Commonly used calculated statistical indexes are the put/call ratio, the VIX, margin debt, and the short interest ratio.
- Flow-of-funds indicators help technicians gauge potential changes in supply and demand for securities. Some commonly used indicators are the ARMS Index (also called the TRIN), margin debt (also a sentiment indicator), mutual fund liquidity positions, new equity issuance, and secondary equity offerings.
- Many technicians use various observed cycles to predict future movements in security prices; these cycles include Kondratieff waves, decennial patterns, and the US presidential cycle.
- Elliott Wave Theory is an approach to market forecasting that assumes that markets form repetitive wave patterns, which are themselves composed of smaller and smaller subwaves. The relationships among wave heights are frequently Fibonacci ratios.
- Intermarket analysis is based on the principle that all markets are interrelated and influence each other. This approach involves the use of relative strength analysis for different groups of securities (e.g., stocks versus bonds, sectors in an economy, and securities from different countries) to make allocation decisions.

REFERENCES

Akerlof, George A., and Robert J. Shiller. 2009. *Animal Spirits: How Human Psychology Drives the Economy, and Why It Matters for Global Capitalism*. Princeton, NJ: Princeton University Press.

Brown, Constance M. 2012. *Technical Analysis for the Trading Professional*, 2nd edition. McGraw-Hill.

Murphy, John J. 1991. I*ntermarket Technical Analysis: Trading Strategies for the Global Stock, Bond, Commodity, and Currency Markets*. John Wiley & Sons, Inc.

PRACTICE PROBLEMS

1 Technical analysis relies most importantly on:

A price and volume data.

B accurate financial statements.

C fundamental analysis to confirm conclusions.

2 Which of the following is *not* an assumption of technical analysis?

A Security markets are efficient.

B The security under analysis is freely traded.

C Market trends and patterns tend to repeat themselves.

3 Drawbacks of technical analysis include which of the following?

A It identifies changes in trends only after the fact.

B Deviations from intrinsic value can persist for long periods.

C It usually requires detailed knowledge of the financial instrument under analysis.

4 Why is technical analysis especially useful in the analysis of commodities and currencies?

A Valuation models cannot be used to determine fundamental intrinsic value for these securities.

B Government regulators are more likely to intervene in these markets.

C These types of securities display clearer trends than equities and bonds do.

5 A daily bar chart provides:

A a logarithmically scaled horizontal axis.

B a horizontal axis that represents changes in price.

C high and low prices during the day and the day's opening and closing prices.

6 A candlestick chart is similar to a bar chart *except* that the candlestick chart:

A represents upward movements in price with X's.

B also graphically shows the range of the period's highs and lows.

C has a body that is light or dark depending on whether the security closed higher or lower than its open.

7 In analyzing a price chart, high or increasing volume *most likely* indicates which of the following?

A Predicts a reversal in the price trend.

B Predicts that a trendless period will follow.

C Confirms a rising or declining trend in prices.

8 In constructing a chart, using a logarithmic scale on the vertical axis is likely to be *most useful* for which of the following applications?

A The price of gold for the past 100 years.

B The share price of a company over the past month.

C Yields on 10-year US Treasuries for the past 5 years.

9 A downtrend line is constructed by drawing a line connecting:

A the lows of the price chart.

B the highs of the price chart.

C the highest high to the lowest low of the price chart.

10 Exhibit 1 depicts GreatWall Information Industry Co., Ltd., ordinary shares, traded on the Shenzhen Stock Exchange, for late 2008 through late 2009 in renminbi (RMB).

Exhibit 1 Candlestick Chart: GreatWall Information Industry Co., Ltd. Price Data, November 2008–September 2009 (Price Measured in RMB × 10)

Based on Exhibit 1, the uptrend was *most likely* broken at a price level nearest to:

A 7 RMB.

B 8.5 RMB.

C 10 RMB.

11 The "change in polarity" principle states which of the following?

A Once an uptrend is broken, it becomes a downtrend.

B Once a resistance level is breached, it becomes a support level.

C The short-term moving average has crossed over the longer-term moving average.

12 Exhibit 2 depicts Barclays ordinary shares, traded on the London Stock Exchange, for 2009 in British pence.

Exhibit 2 Candlestick Chart: Barclays plc Price Data, January 2009–January 2010 (Price Measured in British Pence)

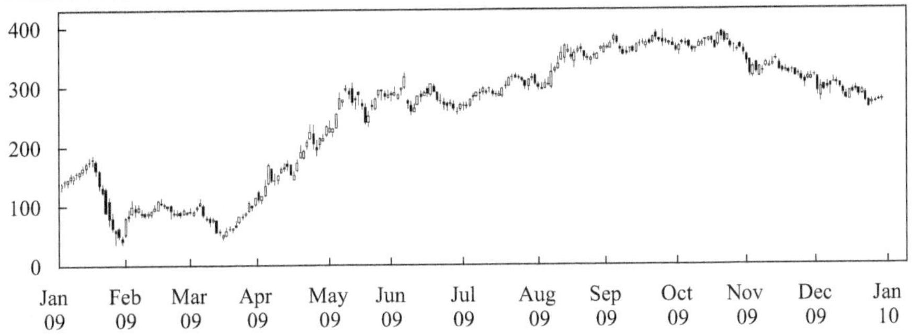

Based on Exhibit 2, Barclays appears to show resistance at a level nearest to:

A 50p.

B 275p.

C 390p.

13 Exhibit 3 depicts Archer Daniels Midland Company common shares, traded on the New York Stock Exchange, for 1996 to 2001 in US dollars.

Exhibit 3 Candlestick Chart: Archer Daniels Midland Company, February 1996–February 2001

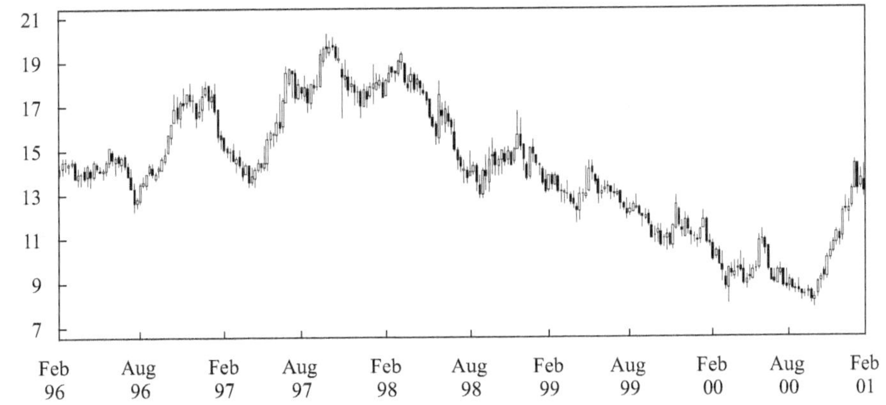

Exhibit 3 illustrates *most* clearly which type of pattern?

A Triangle.

B Triple top.

C Head and shoulders.

14 In an inverted head and shoulders pattern, if the neckline is at €100, the shoulders at €90, and the head at €75, the price target is *closest* to which of the following?

A €50.

B €110.

C €125.

15 Which flow-of-funds indicator is considered bearish for equities?

A A large increase in the number of IPOs.

B Higher-than-average cash balances in mutual funds.

C An upturn in margin debt but one that is still below the long-term average.

16 A TRIN with a value of less than 1.0 indicates:

A the market is in balance.

B there is more volume in rising shares.

C there is more volume in declining shares.

17 Bollinger Bands are constructed by plotting:

A a MACD line and a signal line.

B a moving-average line with an uptrend line above and downtrend line below.

C a moving-average line with upper and lower lines that are at a set number of standard deviations apart.

18 Which of the following is *not* a momentum oscillator?

A MACD.

B Stochastic oscillator.

C Bollinger Bands.

19 Which of the following is a continuation pattern?

A Triangle.

B Triple top.

C Head and shoulders.

20 Which of the following is a reversal pattern?

A Pennant.

B Rectangle.

C Double bottom.

21 Which of the following is generally true of the head and shoulders pattern?

A Volume is important in interpreting the data.

B The neckline, once breached, becomes a support level.

C Head and shoulders patterns are generally followed by an uptrend in the security's price.

22 Nikolai Kondratieff concluded in the 1920s that since the 1780s, Western economies have generally followed a cycle of how many years?

A 18.

B 54.

C 76.

23 Based on the decennial pattern of cycles, how would the return of the Dow Jones Industrial Average (DJIA) in the year 2015 compare with the return in 2020?

A The return would be better.

B The return would be worse.

C The answer cannot be determined because the theory does not apply to both of those years.

24 According to the US presidential cycle theory, the DJIA has the best performance during which year?

A The presidential election year itself.

B The first year following a presidential election.

C The third year following a presidential election.

25 What is a major problem with long-term cycle theories?

A The sample size is small.

B The data are usually hard to observe.

C They occur over such a long period that they are difficult to discern.

26 In 1938, R. N. Elliott proposed a theory that equity markets move:

A in stochastic waves.

B in cycles following Fibonacci ratios.

C in waves dependent on other securities.

27 All of the following are names of Elliott cycles *except*:

A presidential.

B supercycle.

C grand supercycle.

28 To identify intermarket relationships, technicians commonly use:

A stochastic oscillators.

B Fibonacci ratios.

C relative strength analysis.

SOLUTIONS

1 A is correct. Almost all technical analysis relies on these data inputs.

2 A is correct. Technical analysis works because markets are *not* efficient and rational and because human beings tend to behave similarly in similar circumstances. The result is market trends and patterns that repeat themselves and are somewhat predictable.

3 A is correct. Trends generally must be in place for some time before they are recognizable. Thus, some time may be needed for a change in trend to be identified.

4 A is correct. Commodities and currencies do not have underlying financial statements or an income stream; thus, fundamental analysis is useless in determining theoretical values for them or whether they are over- or undervalued.

5 C is correct. The top and bottom of the bars indicate the highs and lows for the day; the line on the left indicates the opening price and the line on the right indicates the closing price.

6 C is correct. Dark and light shading is a unique feature of candlestick charts.

7 C is correct. Rising volume shows conviction by many market participants, which is likely to lead to a continuation of the trend.

8 A is correct. The price of gold in nominal dollars was several orders of magnitude cheaper 100 years ago than it is today (roughly US$20 then versus US$1,100 today). Such a wide range of prices lends itself well to being graphically displayed on a logarithmic scale.

9 B is correct. A downtrend line is constructed by drawing a line connecting the highs of the price chart.

10 B is correct. It is demonstrated in the following chart:

Exhibit 1 Candlestick Chart: GreatWall Information Industry Co., Ltd. Price Data, November 2008–September 2009 (Price Measured in RMB × 10)

11 B is correct.

12 C is correct. As shown in the following chart, Barclays shares traded up to 390p on three occasions, each several weeks apart, and declined thereafter each time.

Exhibit 2 Candlestick Chart: Barclays plc Price Data, January 2009–January 2010 (Price Measured in British Pence)

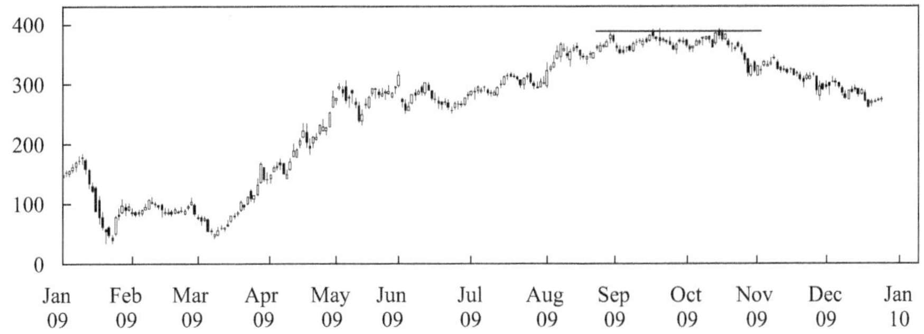

13 C is correct. The left shoulder formed at around US\$18.50, the head formed at around US\$20.50, and the second shoulder formed at around US\$19.

Exhibit 3 Candlestick Chart: Archer Daniels Midland Company, February 1996–February 2001

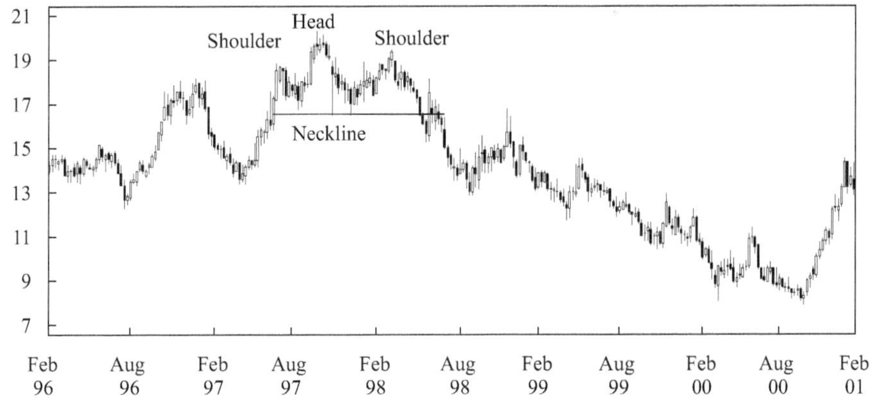

14 C is correct. Target = Neckline + (Neckline − Head): €100 + (€100 − €75) = €125

15 A is correct. A large increase in the number of IPOs increases the supply of equity and if overall demand remains the same, puts downward pressure on equities. Also, companies tend to issue shares of equity when the managers believe they will receive a premium price, which is also an indicator of a market top.

16 B is correct. A value below 1.0 is a bullish sign; it means more volume is in rising shares than in declining ones. The TRIN is calculated as: (Advancing issues/Declining issues)/(Volume of advancing issues/Volume of declining issues).

17 C is correct. Bollinger Bands consist of a moving average and a higher line representing the moving average plus a set number of standard deviations from average price (for the same number of periods as used to calculate the moving average) and a lower line that is a moving average minus the same number of standard deviations.

18 C is correct. Bollinger Bands are price-based indicators, *not* momentum oscillators, which are constructed so that they oscillate between a high and a low or around 0 or 100.

19 A is correct. Triangles are one of several continuation patterns.

20 C is correct. It is one of several reversal patterns.

21 A is correct. Volume is necessary to confirm the various market rallies and reversals during the formation of the head and shoulders pattern.

22 B is correct.

23 A is correct. The decennial pattern theory states that years ending with a 5 will have the best performance of any of the 10 years in a decade and that those ending with a zero will have the worst.

24 C is correct. A possible reason for the superior performance in the third year is that the US presidential election occurs, together with a number of other elections, in a four-year cycle, so the politicians desiring to be reelected inject money into the economy in the third year to improve their chances of winning the following year.

25 A is correct. Long-term cycles require many years to complete; thus, not many cycles are available to observe.

26 B is correct.

27 A is correct. This is the term for a separate cycle theory.

28 C is correct. Relative strength analysis is often used to compare two asset classes or two securities.

READING

57

Fintech in Investment Management

by Robert Kissell, PhD, and Barbara J. Mack

Robert Kissell, PhD, is at Molloy College and Kissell Research Group (USA). Barbara J. Mack is at Pingry Hill Enterprises, Inc. (USA).

LEARNING OUTCOMES

Mastery	*The candidate should be able to:*
☐	**a.** describe "fintech;"
☐	**b.** describe Big Data, artificial intelligence, and machine learning;
☐	**c.** describe fintech applications to investment management;
☐	**d.** describe financial applications of distributed ledger technology.

INTRODUCTION

1

The meeting of finance and technology, commonly known as *fintech*, is changing the landscape of investment management. Advancements include the use of Big Data, artificial intelligence, and machine learning to evaluate investment opportunities, optimize portfolios, and mitigate risks. These developments are affecting not only quantitative asset managers but also fundamental asset managers who make use of these tools and technologies to engage in hybrid forms of investment decision making.

Investment advisory services are undergoing changes with the growth of automated wealth advisers or "robo-advisers." Robo-advisers may assist investors without the intervention of a human adviser, or they may be used in combination with a human adviser. The desired outcome is the ability to provide tailored, actionable advice to investors with greater ease of access and at lower cost.

In the area of financial record keeping, blockchain and distributed ledger technology (DLT) are creating new ways to record, track, and store transactions for financial assets. An early example of this trend is the cryptocurrency bitcoin, but the technology is being considered in a broader set of applications.

This reading is divided into seven main sections, which together define fintech and outline some of its key areas of impact in the field of investment management. Section 2 explains the concept of and areas of fintech. Sections 3 and 4 discuss Big

Data, artificial intelligence, and machine learning. Section 5 discusses data science, and Section 6 provides applications of fintech to investment management. Section 7 examines DLT. A summary of key points completes the reading.

2 WHAT IS FINTECH?

In its broadest sense, the term "fintech" generally refers to technology-driven innovation occurring in the financial services industry. For the purposes of this reading, **fintech** refers to technological innovation in the design and delivery of financial services and products. Note, however, that in common usage, fintech can also refer to companies (often new, startup companies) involved in developing the new technologies and their applications, as well as the business sector that comprises such companies. Many of these innovations are challenging the traditional business models of incumbent financial services providers.

Early forms of fintech included data processing and the automation of routine tasks. Then followed systems that provided execution of decisions according to specified rules and instructions. Fintech has since advanced into decision-making applications based on complex machine-learning logic, where computer programs are able to "learn" how to complete tasks over time. In some applications, advanced computer systems are performing tasks at levels far surpassing human capabilities. Fintech has changed the financial services industry in many ways, giving rise to new systems for investment advice, financial planning, business lending, and payments.

Whereas fintech covers a broad range of services and applications, areas of fintech development that are more directly relevant to the investment industry include the following:

- **Analysis of large datasets.** In addition to growing amounts of traditional data, such as security prices, corporate financial statements, and economic indicators, massive amounts of alternative data generated from non-traditional data sources, such as social media and sensor networks, can now be integrated into a portfolio manager's investment decision-making process and used to help generate alpha and reduce losses.
- **Analytical tools.** For extremely large datasets, techniques involving **artificial intelligence** (AI)—computer systems capable of performing tasks that previously required human intelligence—may be better suited to identify complex, non-linear relationships than traditional quantitative methods and statistical analysis. Advances in AI-based techniques are enabling different data analysis approaches. For example, analysts are turning to artificial intelligence to sort through the enormous amounts of data from company filings, annual reports, and earnings calls to determine which data are most important and to help uncover trends and generate insights relating to human sentiment and behavior.
- **Automated trading.** Executing investment decisions through computer algorithms or automated trading applications may provide a number of benefits to investors, including more efficient trading, lower transaction costs, anonymity, and greater access to market liquidity.

- **Automated advice. Robo-advisers** or automated personal wealth management services provide investment services to a larger number of retail investors at lower cost than traditional adviser models can provide.
- **Financial record keeping.** New technology, such as DLT, may provide secure ways to track ownership of financial assets on a peer-to-peer (P2P) basis. By allowing P2P interactions—in which individuals or firms transact directly with each other without mediation by a third party—DLT reduces the need for financial intermediaries.

Drivers underlying fintech development in these areas include extremely rapid growth in data—including their quantity, types, sources, and quality—and technological advances that enable the capture and extraction of information from them. The data explosion is addressed in Section 3, and selected technological advances and data science are addressed in Sections 4 and 5, respectively.

BIG DATA

3

As noted, datasets are growing rapidly in terms of the size and diversity of data types that are available for analysis. The term **Big Data** has been in use since the late 1990s and refers to the vast amount of data being generated by industry, governments, individuals, and electronic devices. Big Data includes data generated from traditional sources—such as stock exchanges, companies, and governments—as well as non-traditional data types, also known as **alternative data**, arising from the use of electronic devices, social media, sensor networks, and company exhaust (data generated in the normal course of doing business).

Traditional data sources include corporate data in the form of annual reports, regulatory filings, sales and earnings figures, and conference calls with analysts. Traditional data also include data that are generated in the financial markets, including trade prices and volumes. Because the world has become increasingly connected, we can now obtain data from a wide range of devices, including smart phones, cameras, microphones, radio-frequency identification (RFID) readers, wireless sensors, and satellites that are now in use all over the world. As the internet and the presence of such networked devices have grown, the use of non-traditional data sources, or alternative data sources—including social media (posts, tweets, and blogs), email and text communications, web traffic, online news sites, and other electronic information sources—has risen.

The term *Big Data* typically refers to datasets having the following characteristics:

- **Volume**: The amount of data collected in files, records, and tables is very large, representing many millions, or even billions, of data points.
- **Velocity**: The speed with which the data are communicated is extremely great. Real-time or near-real-time data have become the norm in many areas.
- **Variety**: The data are collected from many different sources and in a variety of formats, including structured data (e.g., SQL tables or CSV files), semi-structured data (e.g., HTML code), and unstructured data (e.g., video messages).

Features relating to Big Data's volume, velocity, and variety are shown in Exhibit 1.

Exhibit 1 Big Data Characteristics: Volume, Velocity, and Variety

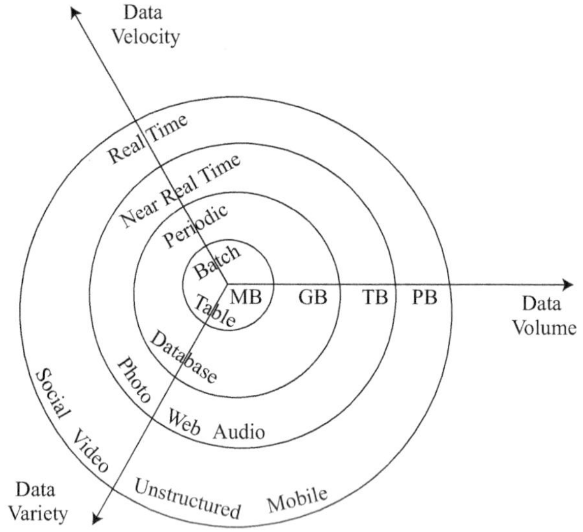

Data	Volume Key	Bytes of Information
MB	Megabyte	One Million
GB	Gigabyte	One Billion
TB	Terabyte	One Trillion
PB	Petabyte	One Quadrillion

Source: http://whatis.techtarget.com/definition/3Vs.

Exhibit 1 shows that data volumes are growing from megabytes (MB) and gigabytes (GB) to far larger sizes, such as terabytes (TB) and petabytes (PB), as more data are being generated, captured, and stored. At the same time, more data, traditional and non-traditional, are available on a real-time or near-real-time basis with far greater variety in data types than ever before.

Big Data may be structured, semi-structured, or unstructured data. Structured data items can be organized in tables and are commonly stored in a database where each field represents the same type of information. Unstructured data may be disparate, unorganized data that cannot be represented in tabular form. Unstructured data, such as those generated by social media, email, text messages, voice recordings, pictures, blogs, scanners, and sensors, often require different, specialized applications or custom programs before they can be useful to investment professionals. For example, in order to analyze data contained in emails or texts, specially developed or customized computer code may be required to first process these files. Semi-structured data may have attributes of both structured and unstructured data.

3.1 Sources of Big Data

Big Data, therefore, encompasses data generated by

- financial markets (e.g., equity, fixed income, futures, options, and other derivatives),
- businesses (e.g., corporate financials, commercial transactions, and credit card purchases),
- governments (e.g., trade, economic, employment, and payroll data),

- individuals (e.g., credit card purchases, product reviews, internet search logs, and social media posts),
- sensors (e.g., satellite imagery, shipping cargo information, and traffic patterns), and, in particular,
- the Internet of Things, or IoT (e.g., data generated by "smart" buildings, where the building is providing a steady stream of information about climate control, energy consumption, security, and other operational details).

In gathering business intelligence, historically, analysts have tended to draw on traditional data sources, employing statistical methods to measure performance, predict future growth, and analyze sector and market trends. In contrast, the analysis of Big Data incorporates the use of alternative data sources.

From retail sales data to social media sentiment to satellite imagery that may reveal information about agriculture, shipping, and oil rigs, alternative datasets may provide additional insights about consumer behavior, firm performance, trends, and other factors important for investment-related activities. Such information is having a significant effect on the way that professional investors, particularly quantitative investors, approach financial analysis and decision-making processes.

There are three main sources of alternative data:

- data generated by individuals,
- data generated by business processes, and
- data generated by sensors.

Data generated by individuals are often produced in text, video, photo, and audio formats and may also be generated through such means as website clicks or time spent on a webpage. This type of data tends to be unstructured. The volume of this type of data is growing dramatically as people participate in greater numbers and more frequently in online activities, such as social media and e-commerce, including online reviews of products, services, and entire companies, and as they make personal data available through web searches, email, and other electronic trails.

Business process data include information flows from corporations and other public entities. These data tend to be structured data and include direct sales information, such as credit card data, as well as corporate exhaust. Corporate exhaust includes corporate supply chain information, banking records, and retail point-of-sale scanner data. Business process data can be leading or real-time indicators of business performance, whereas traditional corporate metrics may be reported only on a quarterly or even yearly basis and are typically lagging indicators of performance.

Sensor data are collected from such devices as smart phones, cameras, RFID chips, and satellites that are usually connected to computers via wireless networks. Sensor data can be unstructured, and the volume of data is many orders of magnitude greater than that of individual or business process datastreams. This form of data is growing exponentially because microprocessors and networking technology are increasingly present in a wide array of personal and commercial electronic devices. Extended to office buildings, homes, vehicles, and many other physical forms, this culminates in a network arrangement, known as the **Internet of Things**, that is formed by the vast array of physical devices, home appliances, smart buildings, vehicles, and other items that are embedded with electronics, sensors, software, and network connections that enable the objects in the system to interact and share information.

Exhibit 2 shows a classification of alternative data sources and includes examples for each.

Exhibit 2 Classification of Alternative Data Sources

Individuals	Business Processes	Sensors
Social media	Transaction data	Satellites
News, reviews	Corporate data	Geolocation
Web searches, personal data		Internet of Things
		Other sensors

In the search to identify new factors that may affect security prices, enhance asset selection, improve trade execution, and uncover trends, alternative data are being used to support data-driven investment models and decisions. As interest in alternative data has risen, there has been a growth in the number of specialized firms that collect, aggregate, and sell alternative datasets.

While the marketplace for alternative data is expanding, investment professionals should understand potential legal and ethical issues related to information that is not in the public domain. For example, the scraping of web data could potentially capture personal information that is protected by regulations or that may have been published or provided without the explicit knowledge and consent of the individuals involved. Best practices are still in development in many jurisdictions, and because of varying approaches taken by national regulators, there may be conflicting forms of guidance.

3.2 Big Data Challenges

Big Data poses several challenges when it is used in investment analysis, including the quality, volume, and appropriateness of the data. Key issues revolve around the following questions, among others: Does the dataset have selection bias, missing data, or data outliers? Is the volume of collected data sufficient? Is the dataset well suited for the type of analysis? In most instances, the data must be sourced, cleansed, and organized before analysis can occur. This process can be extremely difficult with alternative data owing to the unstructured characteristics of the data involved, which are more often qualitative (e.g., texts, photos, and videos) than quantitative in nature.

Given the size and complexity of alternative datasets, traditional analytical methods cannot always be used to interpret and evaluate these datasets. To address this challenge, artificial intelligence and machine learning techniques have emerged that support work on such large and complex sources of information.

4 ADVANCED ANALYTICAL TOOLS: ARTIFICIAL INTELLIGENCE AND MACHINE LEARNING

Artificial intelligence computer systems are capable of performing tasks that have traditionally required human intelligence. AI technology has enabled the development of computer systems that exhibit cognitive and decision-making ability comparable or superior to that of human beings.

An early example of AI was the "expert system," a type of computer programming that attempted to simulate the knowledge base and analytical abilities of human experts in specific problem-solving contexts. This was often accomplished through the use of "if-then" rules. By the late 1990s, faster networks and more powerful processors enabled AI to be deployed in logistics, data mining, financial analysis, medical diagnosis, and other areas. Since the 1980s, financial institutions have made use of AI—particularly, **neural networks**, programming based on how our brain learns and processes information—to detect abnormal charges or claims in credit card fraud detection systems.

Machine learning (ML) involves computer-based techniques that seek to extract knowledge from large amounts of data without making any assumptions on the data's underlying probability distribution. The goal of ML algorithms is to automate decision-making processes by generalizing, or "learning," from known examples to determine an underlying structure in the data. The emphasis is on the ability of the algorithm to generate structure or predictions without any help from a human. Simply put, ML algorithms aim to "find the pattern, apply the pattern."

As it is currently used in the investing context, ML requires massive amounts of data for "training," so although some ML techniques have existed for years, insufficient data have historically limited broader application. Previously, these algorithms lacked access to the large amounts of data needed to model relationships successfully. The growth in Big Data has provided ML algorithms, such as neural networks, with sufficient data to improve modeling and predictive accuracy, and greater use of ML techniques is now possible.

In ML, the computer algorithm is given "inputs" (a set of variables or datasets) and may be given "outputs" (the target data). The algorithm "learns" from the data provided how best to model inputs to outputs (if provided) or how to identify or describe underlying data structure if no outputs are given. Training occurs as the algorithm identifies relationships in the data and uses that information to refine its learning process.

ML involves splitting the dataset into three distinct subsets: a training dataset, a validation dataset, and a test dataset. The training dataset allows the algorithm to identify relationships between inputs and outputs based on historical patterns in the data. These relationships are then validated, and the model tuned, using the validation dataset. The test dataset is used to test the model's ability to predict well on new data. Once an algorithm has been trained, validated, and tested, the ML model can be used to predict outcomes based on other datasets.

ML still requires human judgement in understanding the underlying data and selecting the appropriate techniques for data analysis. Before they can be used, the data must be clean and free of biases and spurious data. As noted, ML models also require sufficiently large amounts of data and may not perform well where there may not be enough available data to train and validate the model.

Analysts must also be cognizant of errors that may arise from **overfitting** the data, because models that overfit the data may discover "false" relationships or "unsubstantiated" patterns that will lead to prediction errors and incorrect output forecasts. Overfitting occurs when the ML model learns the input and target dataset too precisely. In such cases, the model has been "over-trained" on the data and treats noise in the data as true parameters. An ML model that has been overfitted is not able to accurately predict outcomes using a different dataset and may be too complex. When a model has been underfitted, the ML model treats true parameters as if they are noise and is not able to recognize relationships within the training data. In such cases, the model may be too simplistic. Underfitted models will typically fail to fully discover patterns that underlie the data.

In addition, since they are not explicitly programmed, ML techniques can appear to be opaque or "black box" approaches, which arrive at outcomes that may not be entirely understood or explainable.

4.1 Types of Machine Learning

ML approaches can help identify relationships between variables, detect patterns or trends, and create structure from data, including data classification. Machine learning can be broadly divided into three distinct classes of techniques: supervised learning, unsupervised learning, and deep learning.

In **supervised learning**, computers learn to model relationships based on labeled training data. In supervised learning, inputs and outputs are labeled, or identified, for the algorithm. After learning how best to model relationships for the labeled data, the trained algorithms are used to model or predict outcomes for new datasets. Trying to identify the best signal, or variable, to forecast future returns on a stock or trying to predict whether local stock market performance will be up, down, or flat during the next business day are problems that may be approached using supervised learning techniques.

In **unsupervised learning**, computers are not given labeled data but instead are given only data from which the algorithm seeks to describe the data and their structure. Trying to group companies into peer groups based on their characteristics rather than using standard sector or country groupings is a problem that may be approached using unsupervised learning techniques.

Underlying AI advances have been key developments relating to neural networks. In **deep learning**, (or **deep learning nets**), computers use neural networks, often with many hidden layers, to perform multistage, non-linear data processing to identify patterns. Deep learning may use supervised or unsupervised machine learning approaches. By taking a layered or multistage approach to data analysis, deep learning develops an understanding of simple concepts that informs analysis of more complex concepts. Neural networks have existed since 1958 and have been used for many applications, such as forecasting and pattern recognition, since the early 1990s. Improvements in the algorithms underlying neural networks are providing more accurate models that better incorporate and learn from data. As a result, these algorithms are now far better at such activities as image, pattern, and speech recognition. In many cases, the advanced algorithms require less computing power than the earlier neural networks, and their improved solution enables analysts to discover insights and identify relationships that were previously too difficult or too time consuming to uncover.

Advances in Artificial Intelligence outside Finance

Non-finance-related AI breakthroughs include victories in the general knowledge game-show Jeopardy (by IBM's Watson in 2011) and in the ancient Chinese board game Go (by Google's DeepMind in 2016). Not only is AI providing solutions where there is perfect information (all players have equal access to the same information), such as checkers, chess, and Go, but AI is also providing insight in cases where information may be imperfect and players have hidden information; AI successes at the game of poker (by DeepStack) are an example. AI has also been behind the rise of virtual assistants, such as Siri (from Apple), Google's Translate app, and Amazon's product recommendation engine.

The ability to analyze Big Data using ML techniques, alongside more traditional statistical methods, represents a significant development in investment research, supported by the presence of greater data availability and advances in the algorithms themselves. Improvements in computing power and software processing speeds and falling storage costs have further supported this evolution.

ML techniques are being used for Big Data analysis to help predict trends or market events, such as the likelihood of a successful merger or an outcome to a political election. Image recognition algorithms can now analyze data from satellite-imaging systems to provide intelligence on the number of consumers in retail store parking lots, shipping activity and manufacturing facilities, and yields on agricultural crops, to name just a few examples.

Such information may provide insights into individual firms or at national or global levels and may be used as inputs into valuation or economic models.

DATA SCIENCE: EXTRACTING INFORMATION FROM BIG DATA 5

Data science can be defined as an interdisciplinary field that harnesses advances in computer science (including machine learning), statistics, and other disciplines for the purpose of extracting information from Big Data (or data in general). Companies rely on the expertise of data scientists/analysts to extract information and insights from Big Data for a wide variety of business and investment purposes.

An important consideration for the data scientist is the structure of the data. As noted in the discussion on Big Data, because of their unstructured nature, alternative data often require specialized treatment before they can be used for analysis.

5.1 Data Processing Methods

To help determine the best data management technique needed for Big Data analysis, data scientists use various data processing methods, including capture, curation, storage, search, and transfer.

- Capture—Data capture refers to how the data are collected and transformed into a format that can be used by the analytical process. Low-latency systems—systems that operate on networks that communicate high volumes of data with minimal delay (latency)—are essential for automated trading applications that make decisions based on real-time prices and market events. In contrast, high-latency systems do not require access to real-time data and calculations.
- Curation—Data curation refers to the process of ensuring data quality and accuracy through a data cleaning exercise. This process consists of reviewing all data to detect and uncover data errors—bad or inaccurate data—and making adjustments for missing data when appropriate.
- Storage—Data storage refers to how the data will be recorded, archived, and accessed and the underlying database design. An important consideration for data storage is whether the data are structured or unstructured and whether analytical needs require low-latency solutions.
- Search—Search refers to how to query data. Big Data has created the need for advanced applications capable of examining and reviewing large quantities of data to locate requested data content.
- Transfer—Transfer refers to how the data will move from the underlying data source or storage location to the underlying analytical tool. This could be through a direct data feed, such as a stock exchange's price feed.

5.2 Data Visualization

Data visualization is an important tool for understanding Big Data. Visualization refers to how the data will be formatted, displayed, and summarized in graphical form. Traditional structured data can be visualized using tables, charts, and trends, whereas non-traditional unstructured data require new techniques of data visualization. These visualization tools include, for example, interactive three-dimensional (3D) graphics, where users can focus in on specified data ranges and rotate the data across 3D axes to help identify trends and uncover relationships. Multidimensional data analysis consisting of more than three variables requires additional data visualization techniques—for example, adding color, shapes, and sizes to the 3D charts. Further, a wide variety of solutions exists to reflect the structure of the data through the geometry of the visualization, with interactive graphics allowing for especially rich possibilities. Examples include heat maps, tree diagrams, and network graphs.

Another valuable Big Data visualization technique that is applicable to textual data is a "tag cloud," where words are sized and displayed on the basis of the frequency of the word in the data file. For example, words that appear more often are shown with a larger font, and words that appear less often are shown with a smaller font. A "mind map" is another data visualization technique; it is a variation of the tag cloud, but rather than displaying the frequency of words, a mind map shows how different concepts are related to each other.

Exhibit 3 shows an example of a "tag cloud" based on a section of this reading. The more frequently a word is found within the text, the larger it becomes in the tag cloud. As shown in the tag cloud, the words appearing most frequently in the section include "data," "ML," "learning," "AI," "techniques," "model," and "relationships."

Exhibit 3 Data Visualization Tag Cloud: Section 4, Advanced Analytical Tools

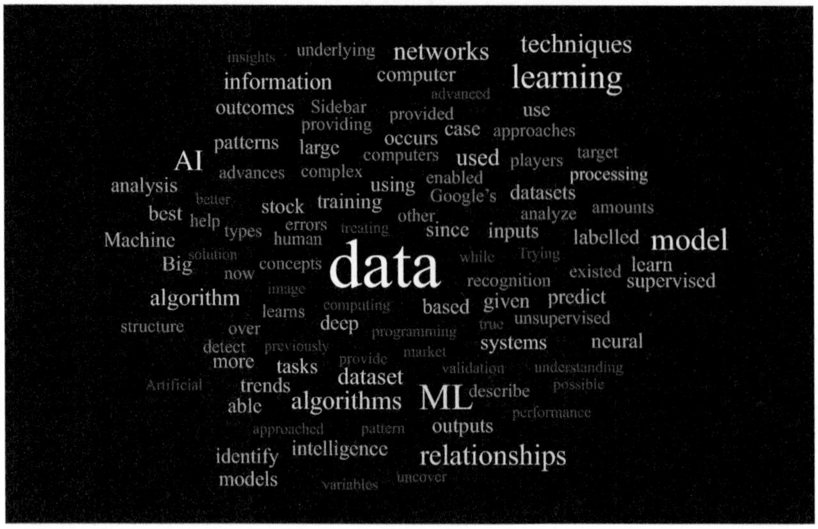

Source: https://worditout.com/word-cloud/create.

Programming Languages and Databases

Some of the more common programming languages used in data science include the following:

- **Python:** Python is an open source, free programming language that does not require an in-depth understanding of computer programming. Python allows individuals with little or no programming experience to develop computer applications for advanced analytical use and is the basis for many fintech applications.
- **R:** R is an open source, free programming language traditionally used for statistical analysis. R has mathematical packages for statistical analysis, machine learning, optimization, econometrics, and financial analysis.
- **Java:** Java is a programming language that can run on different computers, servers, and operating systems. Java is the underlying program language used in many internet applications.
- **C/C++:** C/C++ is a specialized programming language that provides the ability to optimize source code to achieve superior calculation speed and processing performance. C/C++ is used in applications for algorithmic and high-frequency trading.
- **Excel VBA:** Excel VBA helps bridge the gap between programming and manual data processing by allowing users to run macros to automate tasks, such as updating data tables and formulas, running data queries and collecting data from different web locations, and performing calculations. Excel VBA allows users to develop customized reports and analyses that rely on data that are updated from different applications and databases.

Some of the more common databases in use include the following:

- **SQL:** SQL is a database for structured data where the data can be stored in tables with rows and columns. SQL databases need to be run on a server that is accessed by users.
- **SQLite:** SQLite is a database for structured data. SQLite databases are embedded into the program and do not need to be run on a server. It is the most common database for mobile apps that require access to data.
- **NoSQL:** NoSQL is a database used for unstructured data where the data cannot be summarized in traditional tables with rows and columns.

SELECTED APPLICATIONS OF FINTECH TO INVESTMENT MANAGEMENT 6

Fintech is being used in numerous areas of investment management. Applications for investment management include text analytics and natural language processing, robo-advisory services, risk analysis, and algorithmic trading.

6.1 Text Analytics and Natural Language Processing

Text analytics involves the use of computer programs to analyze and derive meaning typically from large, unstructured text- or voice-based datasets, such as company filings, written reports, quarterly earnings calls, social media, email, internet postings, and surveys. Text analytics includes using computer programs to perform automated information retrieval from different, unrelated sources in order to aid the decision-making process. More analytical usage includes lexical analysis, or the analysis of word frequency in a document and pattern recognition based on key words and phrases. Text analytics may be used in predictive analysis to help identify indicators of future performance, such as consumer sentiment.

Natural language processing (NLP) is a field of research at the intersection of computer science, artificial intelligence, and linguistics that focuses on developing computer programs to analyze and interpret human language. Within the larger field of text analytics, NLP is an important application. Automated tasks using NLP include translation, speech recognition, text mining, sentiment analysis, and topic analysis. NLP may also be employed in compliance functions to review employee voice and electronic communications for adherence to company or regulatory policy, inappropriate conduct, or fraud or for ensuring private or customer information is kept confidential.

Consider that all the public corporations worldwide generate millions of pages of annual reports and tens of thousands of hours of earnings calls each year. This is more information than any individual analyst or team of researchers can assess. NLP, especially when aided by ML algorithms, can analyze annual reports, call transcripts, news articles, social media posts, and other text- and audio-based data to identify trends in shorter timespans and with greater scale and accuracy than is humanly possible.

For example, NLP may be used to monitor analyst commentary to aid investment decision making. Financial analysts may generate earnings-per-share (EPS) forecasts reflecting their views on a company's near-term prospects. Focusing on forecasted EPS numbers could mean investors miss subtleties contained in an analyst's written research report. Since analysts tend not to change their buy, hold, and sell recommendations for a company frequently, they may instead offer nuanced commentary without making a change in their investment recommendation. After analyzing analyst commentary, NLP can assign sentiment ratings ranging from very negative to very positive for each. NLP can, therefore, be used to detect, monitor, and tag shifts in sentiment, potentially ahead of an analyst's recommendation change. Machine capabilities enable this analysis to scale across thousands of companies worldwide, performing work previously done by humans.

Similarly, communications and transcripts from policymakers, such as the European Central Bank or the US Federal Reserve, offer an opportunity for NLP-based analysis, because officials at these institutions may send subtle messages through their choice of topics, words, and inferred tone. NLP can help analyze nuances within text to provide insights around trending or waning topics of interest, such as interest rate policy, aggregate output, or inflation expectations.

Models using NLP analysis may incorporate non-traditional information to evaluate what people are saying—via their preferences, opinions, likes, or dislikes—in an attempt to identify trends and short-term indicators about a company, a stock, or an economic event that might have a bearing on future performance. Past research has evaluated the predictive power of Twitter sentiment regarding IPO performance, for example.[1] The effect of positive and negative news sentiment on stock returns has also been researched.[2]

---

1 Jim Kyung-Soo Liew and Garrett Zhengyuan Wang, "Twitter Sentiment and IPO Performance: A Cross-Sectional Examination," *Journal of Portfolio Management*, vol. 42, no. 4 (Summer 2016): 129–135.

2 Steven L. Heston and Nitish Ranjan Sinha, "News vs. Sentiment: Predicting Stock Returns from News Stories," *Financial Analysts Journal*, vol. 73, no. 3 (Third Quarter 2017): 67–83. (https://www.cfapubs.org/doi/abs/10.2469/faj.v73.n3.3).

6.2 Robo-Advisory Services

Since their emergence in 2008, a number of startup firms, as well as large asset managers, have introduced robo-advisory services, which provide investment solutions through online platforms, reducing the need for direct interaction with financial advisers.

As robo-advisers have been incorporated into the investment landscape, they have drawn the attention of regulatory authorities. In the United States, robo-advisers must be established as registered investment advisers, and they are regulated by the Securities and Exchange Commission. In the United Kingdom, they are regulated by the Financial Conduct Authority. In Australia, all financial advisers must obtain an Australian Financial Services license, with guidance on digital advisers coming from the Australian Securities and Investments Commission. Robo-advisers are also on the rise in parts of Asia and the rest of the world. Although regulatory conditions vary, robo-advisers are likely to be held to a similar level of scrutiny and code of conduct as other investment professionals in the given region.

Robo-advice tends to start with an investor questionnaire, which may include many of the categories and subcategories shown in Exhibit 4. Exhibit 4 is a synthesis of questionnaires created by the researchers attributed in the source below. Once assets, liabilities, risk preferences, and target investment returns have been digitally entered by a client, the robo-adviser software produces recommendations, based on algorithmic rules and historical market data, that incorporate the client's stated investment parameters. According to research by Michael Tertilt and Peter Scholz, robo-advisers do not seem to incorporate the full range of available information into their recommendations;[3] further research will be necessary over time to see how this may affect performance and the evolution of digital advisory services. Nevertheless, current robo-advisory services include automated asset allocation, trade execution, portfolio optimization, tax-loss harvesting, and rebalancing for investor portfolios.

Exhibit 4 Categories and Subcategories for Investor Questionnaires

General Information	Risk Tolerance
Income	Age
Investment Amount	Association with Investing
Job Description	Association with Risk
Other	Choose Portfolio Risk Level
Source of Income	Comfort Investing in Stock
Spendings	Credit Based Investments
Time to Retirement	Dealing with Financial Decisions
Type of Account	Degree of Financial Risk Taken
Working Status	Education
Risk Capacity	Ever Interested in Risky Asset for Thrill
Dependence on Withdrawal of Investment Amount	Experience of Drop/Reaction on Drop/Max Drop before Selling
Income Prediction	Family and Household Status
Investment Amount/Savings Rate Ratio	Financial Knowledge
Investment Amount/Total Capital Ratio	Gender

(continued)

3 Michael Tertilt and Peter Scholz, To Advise, or Not to Advise — How Robo-Advisors Evaluate the Risk Preferences of Private Investors (June 12, 2017). Available at SSRN: https://ssrn.com/abstract=2913178 or http://dx.doi.org/10.2139/ssrn.2913178

Exhibit 4 (Continued)

Investment Horizon	Investment Experience
Liabilities	Investment Goal
Savings Rate	Investor Type/Self-Assessment Risk Tolerance
Total Capital	Preference Return vs. Risk

Source: Michael Tertilt and Peter Scholz, 2017 "To Advise, or Not to Advise—How Robo-Advisors Evaluate the Risk Preferences of Private Investors," working paper (13 June): Table 1: Categories and Subcategories for Questionnaires.

Although their analyses and recommendations can cover both active and passive management styles, most robo-advisers follow a passive investment approach. These robo-advisers typically have low fees and low account minimums, implementing their recommendations with low-cost, diversified index mutual funds or exchange-traded funds (ETFs). A diverse range of asset classes can be managed in this manner, including stocks, bonds, commodities, futures, and real estate. Because of their low-cost structure, robo-advisers can reach underserved populations, such as the mass affluent or mass market segments, which are less able to afford a traditional financial adviser.

Two types of wealth management services dominate the robo-advice sector: fully automated digital wealth managers and adviser-assisted digital wealth managers.

- **Fully Automated Digital Wealth Managers**

  The fully automated model does not rely on assistance from a human financial adviser. These services seek to offer a low-cost solution to investing and recommend an investment portfolio, which is often composed of ETFs. The service package may include direct deposits, periodic rebalancing, and dividend reinvestment options.

- **Adviser-Assisted Digital Wealth Managers**

  Adviser-assisted digital wealth managers provide automated investment services along with a virtual financial adviser, who is available to offer basic financial planning advice and periodic reviews by phone. Adviser-assisted digital wealth managers are capable of providing additional services that may involve a more holistic analysis of a client's assets and liabilities.

Wealthy and ultra-wealthy individuals typically have had access to human advisory teams, but there has been a gap in the availability and quality of advisers to serve investors with less wealth. The advent of robo-advisers offers a cost-effective and easily accessible form of financial guidance. In following a typically passive investment approach, research suggests that robo-advisers tend to offer fairly conservative advice.

However, critics of robo-advisers have wondered what would happen in a time of crisis, when people most often look to human expertise for guidance. It may not always be completely transparent why a robo-adviser chooses to make a recommendation or take a trading action that it did, unlike a human adviser who can provide his or her rationale. And finally, there may be trust issues in allowing computers to make these decisions, including worries of instances where robo-advisers might recommend inappropriate investments.

As the complexity and size of an investor's portfolio grows, robo-advisers may not be able to sufficiently address the particular preferences and needs of the investor. In the case of extremely affluent investors who may own a greater number of asset types—including alternative investments (e.g., venture capital, private equity, hedge funds, and real estate)—in addition to global stocks and bonds and have greater demands for customization, the need for a team of human advisers, each with particular areas of investment or wealth-management expertise, is likely to endure.

6.3 Risk Analysis

As mandated by regulators worldwide, the global investment industry has undertaken major steps in stress testing and risk assessment that involve the analysis of vast amounts of quantitative and qualitative risk data. Required data include information on the liquidity of the firm and its trading partners, balance sheet positions, credit exposures, risk-weighted assets, and risk parameters. Stress tests may also take qualitative information into consideration, such as capital planning procedures, expected business plan changes, business model sustainability, and operational risk.

There is increasing interest in monitoring risk in real time. To do so, relevant data must be taken by a firm, mapped to known risks, and identified as it moves within the firm. Data may be aggregated for reporting purposes or used as inputs to risk models. Big Data may provide insights into real-time and changing market circumstances to help identify weakening market conditions and adverse trends in advance, allowing managers to employ risk management techniques and hedging practices sooner to help preserve asset value. For example, evaluation of alternative data using ML techniques may help foreshadow declining company earnings and future stock performance. Furthermore, analysis of real-time market data and trading patterns may help analysts detect buying or selling pressure in the stock.

ML techniques may be used to help assess data quality. To help ensure accurate and reliable data that may originate from numerous alternative data sources, ML techniques can help validate data quality by identifying questionable data, potential errors, and data outliers before integration with traditional data for use in risk models and in risk management applications.

Portfolio risk management often makes use of scenario analysis—analyzing the likely performance of the portfolio and liquidation costs under a hypothetical stress scenario or the repeat of a historical stress event. For example, to understand the implications of holding or liquidating positions during adverse or extreme market periods, such as the financial crisis, fund managers may perform "what-if" scenario analysis and portfolio backtesting using point-in-time data to understand liquidation costs and portfolio consequences under differing market conditions. These backtesting simulations are often computationally intense and may be facilitated through the use of advanced AI-based techniques.

6.4 Algorithmic Trading

Algorithmic trading is the computerized buying and selling of financial instruments, in accordance with pre-specified rules and guidelines. Algorithmic trading is often used to execute large institutional orders, slicing orders into smaller pieces and executing across different exchanges and trading venues. Algorithmic trading provides investors with many benefits, including speed of execution, anonymity, and lower transaction costs. Over the course of a day, algorithms may continuously update and revise their execution strategy on the basis of changing prices, volumes, and market volatility. Algorithms may also determine the best way to price the order (e.g., limit or market order) and the most appropriate trading venue (e.g., exchange or dark pool) to route for execution.

High-frequency trading (HFT) is a form of algorithmic trading that makes use of vast quantities of granular financial data (tick data, for example) to automatically place trades when certain conditions are met. Trades are executed on ultra-high-speed, low-latency networks in fractions of a second. HFT algorithms decide what to buy or sell and where to execute on the basis of real-time prices and market conditions, seeking to earn a profit from intraday market mispricings.

Global financial markets have undergone substantial change as markets have fragmented into multiple trading destinations consisting of electronic exchanges, alternative trading systems, and so-called dark pools, and average trade sizes have fallen. In this environment, and with markets continuously reflecting real-time information, algorithmic trading has been viewed as an important tool.

7 DISTRIBUTED LEDGER TECHNOLOGY

Distributed ledger technology—technology based on a distributed ledger (defined below)—represents a fintech development that offers potential improvements in the area of financial record keeping. DLT networks are being considered as an efficient means to create, exchange, and track ownership of financial assets on a peer-to-peer basis. Potential benefits include greater accuracy, transparency, and security in record keeping; faster transfer of ownership; and peer-to-peer interactions. However, the technology is not fully secure, and breaches in privacy and data protection are possible. In addition, the processes underlying DLT generally require massive amounts of energy to verify transaction activity.

A **distributed ledger** is a type of database that may be shared among entities in a network. In a distributed ledger, entries are recorded, stored, and distributed across a network of participants so that each participant has a matching copy of the digital database. Basic elements of a DLT network include a digital ledger, a consensus mechanism used to confirm new entries, and a participant network.

The consensus mechanism is the process by which the computer entities (or nodes) in a network agree on a common state of the ledger. Consensus generally involves two steps: transaction validation and agreement on ledger update by network parties. These features enable the creation of records that are, for the most part, considered immutable, or unchangeable, yet they are transparent and accessible to network participants on a near-real-time basis.

Features of DLT include the use of **cryptography**—an algorithmic process to encrypt data, making the data unusable if received by unauthorized parties—which enables a high level of network security and database integrity. For example, DLT uses cryptographic methods of proof to verify network participant identity and for data encryption.

DLT has the potential to accommodate "**smart contracts**," which are computer programs that self-execute on the basis of pre-specified terms and conditions agreed to by the parties to a contract. Examples of smart contract use are the automatic execution of contingent claims for derivatives and the instantaneous transfer of collateral in the event of default.

Exhibit 5 illustrates a distributed ledger network in which all nodes are connected to one another, each having a copy of the distributed ledger. The term "Consensus" is shown in the center of the network and represents the consensus mechanism in which the nodes agree on new transactions and ledger updates.

Exhibit 5 Distributed Ledger Network Setup

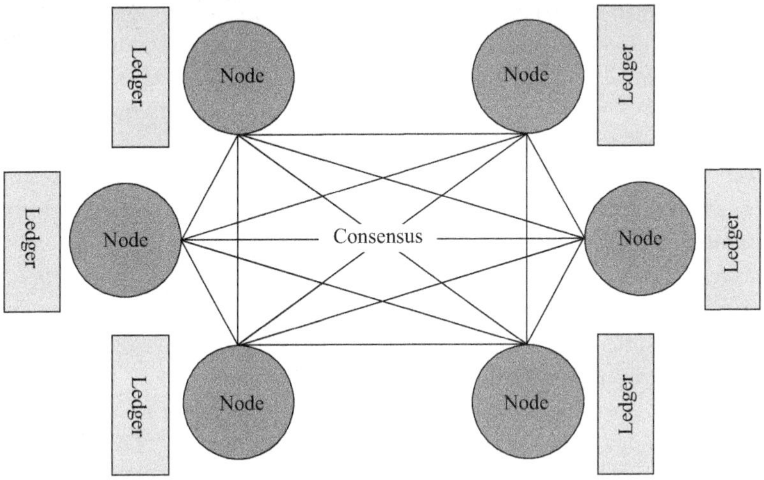

Source: https://blockgeeks.com/guides/what-is-hyperledger/.

Blockchain is a type of digital ledger in which information, such as changes in ownership, is recorded sequentially within blocks that are then linked or "chained" together and secured using cryptographic methods. Each block contains a grouping of transactions (or entries) and a secure link (known as a hash) to the previous block. New transactions are inserted into the chain only after validation via a consensus mechanism in which authorized members agree on the transaction and the preceding order, or history, in which previous transactions have occurred.

The consensus mechanism used to verify a transaction includes a cryptographic problem that must be solved by some computers on the network (known as miners) each time a transaction takes place. The process to update the blockchain can require substantial amounts of computing power, making it very difficult and extremely expensive for an individual third party to manipulate historical data. To manipulate historical data, an individual or entity would have to control the majority of nodes in the network. The success of the network, therefore, relies on broad network participation.

Blockchain (Distributed Ledger) Network—How Do Transactions Get Added?

Outlined below are the steps involved in adding a transaction to a blockchain distributed ledger.

1. Transaction takes place between buyer and seller
2. Transaction is broadcast to the network of computers (nodes)
3. Nodes validate the transaction details and parties to the transaction
4. Once verified, the transaction is combined with other transactions to form a new block (of predetermined size) of data for the ledger
5. This block of data is then added or linked (using a cryptographic process) to the previous block(s) containing data
6. Transaction is considered complete and ledger has been updated

7.1 Permissioned and Permissionless Networks

DLT can take the form of permissionless or permissioned networks. **Permissionless networks** are open to any user who wishes to make a transaction, and all users within the network can see all transactions that exist on the blockchain. In a permissionless, or open, DLT system, network participants can perform all network functions.

The main benefit of a permissionless network is that it does not depend on a centralized authority to confirm or deny the validity of transactions, because this takes place through the consensus mechanism. This means no single point of failure exists, since all transactions are recorded on a single distributed database and every node stores a copy of the database. Once a transaction has been added to the blockchain, it cannot be changed, barring manipulation; the distributed ledger becomes a permanent and immutable record of all previous transactions. In a permissionless network, trust is not a requirement between transacting parties.

A well-known example of an open, permissionless network is **bitcoin**. Using blockchain technology, Bitcoin was created in 2009 to serve as the public ledger for all transactions occurring on its virtual currency. Since the introduction of bitcoin, many more cryptocurrencies, or digital currencies, which use permissionless DLT networks, have been created.

In **permissioned networks**, network members may be restricted from participating in certain network activities. Controls, or permissions, may be used to allow varying levels of access to the ledger, from adding transactions (e.g., a participant) to viewing transactions only (e.g., a regulator) to viewing selective details of the transactions but not the full record.

7.2 Applications of Distributed Ledger Technology to Investment Management

Potential applications of DLT to investment management include cryptocurrencies, tokenization, post-trade clearing and settlement, and compliance.

7.2.1 *Cryptocurrencies*

A **cryptocurrency**, also known as a digital currency, operates as electronic currency and allows near-real-time transactions between parties without the need for an intermediary, such as a bank. As electronic mediums of exchange, cryptocurrencies lack physical form and are issued privately by individuals, companies, and other organizations. Most issued cryptocurrencies utilize open DLT systems in which a decentralized distributed ledger is used to record and verify all digital currency transactions. Cryptocurrencies have not traditionally been government backed or regulated. Central banks around the world, however, are recognizing potential benefits and examining use cases for their own cryptocurrency versions.

Many cryptocurrencies have a self-imposed limit on the total amount of currency they may issue. Although such limits could help maintain their store of value, it is important to note that many cryptocurrencies have experienced high levels of price volatility. A lack of clear fundamentals underlying these currencies has contributed to their volatility.

Cryptocurrencies have proven to be an attractive means for companies looking to raise capital. An **initial coin offering** (ICO) is an unregulated process whereby companies sell their crypto tokens to investors in exchange for fiat money or for another agreed upon cryptocurrency. An ICO is typically structured to issue digital tokens to investors that can be used to purchase future products or services being developed by the issuer. ICOs provide an alternative to traditional, regulated capital-raising processes, such as initial public offerings (IPOs). Compared to the regulated IPO market, ICOs may have lower associated issuance costs and shorter capital raising time frames.

However, most ICOs do not typically have attached voting rights. Regulation for ICOs is under consideration in a number of jurisdictions, and there have been numerous instances of investor loss resulting from fraudulent schemes.

7.2.2 *Tokenization*

Transactions involving physical assets, such as real estate, luxury goods, and commodities, often require substantial efforts in ownership verification and examination each time a transfer in ownership takes place. Through **tokenization**, the process of representing ownership rights to physical assets on a blockchain or distributed ledger, DLT has the potential to streamline this process by creating a single, digital record of ownership with which to verify ownership title and authenticity, including all historical activity. Real estate transactions that require ownership and identify verification may be one area to benefit from tokenization, because these transactions are typically labor intensive and costly, involving decentralized, paper-based records and multiple parties.

7.2.3 *Post-Trade Clearing and Settlement*

In the financial securities markets, post-trade processes to confirm, clear, and settle transactions are often complex and labor intensive, requiring multiple interactions between counterparties and financial intermediaries. DLT has the ability to streamline existing post-trade processes by providing near-real-time trade verification, reconciliation, and settlement, thereby reducing the complexity, time, and costs associated with processing transactions. A single distributed record of ownership between network peers would eliminate the need for independent and duplicative reconciliation efforts between parties and reduce the need for third-party facilitation. A shortened settlement time frame could lessen the time exposed to counterparty risk and associated collateral requirements while increasing the potential liquidity of assets and funds. Additionally, the use of automated contracts may also help to reduce post-trade time frames, lowering exposure to counterparty credit risk and trade fails.

7.2.4 *Compliance*

Regulators worldwide have imposed more stringent reporting requirements and demand greater transparency and access to data. To meet these requirements, many firms have added staff to their post-trade and compliance groups. But these functions remain predominantly manual. To comply with regulations, firms need to maintain and process large amounts of risk-related data. DLT may allow regulators and firms to maintain near-real-time review over transactions and other compliance-related processes. Improved post-trade reconciliation and automation through DLT could lead to more accurate record keeping and create operational efficiencies for a firm's compliance and regulatory reporting processes, while providing greater transparency and auditability for external authorities and regulators.

DLT-based compliance may better support shared information, communications, and transparency within and between firms, exchanges, custodians, and regulators. Closed or permissioned networks could offer advantages in security and privacy. These platforms could store highly sensitive information in a way that is secure but easily accessible to internal and external authorities. DLT could help uncover fraudulent activity and reduce compliance costs associated with know-your-customer and anti-money-laundering regulations, which entail verifying the identity of clients and business partners.

DLT Challenges

A number of challenges exist before DLT may be successfully adopted by the investment industry. These include the following:

- There is a lack of DLT network standardization, as well as difficulty integrating with legacy systems.
- DLT processing capabilities may not be financially competitive with existing solutions.
- Increasing the scale of DLT systems requires substantial (storage) resources.
- Immutability of transactions means accidental or "canceled" trades can be undone only by submitting an equal and offsetting trade.
- DLT requires huge amounts of computer power normally associated with high electricity usage.
- Regulatory approaches may differ by jurisdiction.

SUMMARY

- The term "fintech" refers to technological innovation in the design and delivery of financial services and products.
- Areas of fintech development include the analysis of large datasets, analytical techniques, automated trading, automated advice, and financial record keeping.
- Big Data is characterized by the three Vs—volume, velocity, and variety—and includes both traditional and non-traditional (or alternative) datasets.
- Among the main sources of alternative data are data generated by individuals, business processes, and sensors.
- Artificial intelligence computer systems are capable of performing tasks that traditionally required human intelligence at levels comparable (or superior) to those of human beings.
- Machine learning seeks to extract knowledge from large amounts of data by "learning" from known examples and then generating structure or predictions. Simply put, ML algorithms aim to "find the pattern, apply the pattern." Main types of ML include supervised learning, unsupervised learning, and deep learning.
- Natural language processing is an application of text analytics that uses insight into the structure of human language to analyze and interpret text- and voice-based data.
- Robo-advisory services are providing automated advisory services to increasing numbers of retail investors. Services include asset allocation, portfolio optimization, trade execution, rebalancing, and tax strategies.
- Big Data and ML techniques may provide insights into real-time and changing market circumstances to help identify weakening or adverse trends in advance, allowing for improved risk management and investment decision making.

- Algorithmic traders use automated trading programs to determine when, where, and how to trade an order on the basis of pre-specified rules and market conditions. Benefits include speed of executions, lower trading costs, and anonymity.
- Blockchain and distributed ledger technology (DLT) may offer a new way to store, record, and track financial assets on a secure, distributed basis. Applications include cryptocurrencies and tokenization. Additionally, DLT may bring efficiencies to post-trade and compliance processes through automation, smart contracts, and identity verification.

PRACTICE PROBLEMS

1 A correct description of fintech is that it:

A is driven by rapid growth in data and related technological advances.

B increases the need for intermediaries.

C is at its most advanced state using systems that follow specified rules and instructions.

2 A characteristic of Big Data is that:

A one of its traditional sources is business processes.

B it involves formats with diverse types of structures.

C real-time communication of it is uncommon due to vast content.

3 In the use of machine learning (ML):

A some techniques are termed "black box" due to data biases.

B human judgment is not needed because algorithms continuously learn from data.

C training data can be learned too precisely, resulting in inaccurate predictions when used with different datasets.

4 Text Analytics is appropriate for application to:

A economic trend analysis.

B large, structured datasets.

C public but not private information.

5 In providing investment services, robo-advisers are *most likely* to:

A rely on their cost effectiveness to pursue active strategies.

B offer fairly conservative advice as easily accessible guidance.

C be free from regulation when acting as fully-automated wealth managers.

6 Which of the following statements on fintech's use of data as part of risk analysis is correct?

A Stress testing requires precise inputs and excludes qualitative data.

B Machine learning ensures that traditional and alternative data are fully segregated.

C For real-time risk monitoring, data may be aggregated for reporting and used as model inputs.

7 A factor associated with the widespread adoption of algorithmic trading is increased:

A market efficiency.

B average trade sizes.

C trading destinations.

8 A benefit of distributed ledger technology (DLT) favoring its use by the investment industry is its:

A scalability of underlying systems.

B ease of integration with existing systems.

C streamlining of current post-trade processes.

9 What is a distributed ledger technology (DLT) application suited for physical assets?

A Tokenization

B Cryptocurrencies

C Permissioned networks

SOLUTIONS

1 A is correct. Drivers of fintech include extremely rapid growth in data (including their quantity, types, sources, and quality) and technological advances enabling the capture and extraction of information from it.

2 B is correct. Big Data is collected from many different sources and is in a variety of formats, including structured data (e.g., SQL tables or CSV files), semi-structured data (e.g., HTML code), and unstructured data (e.g., video messages).

3 C is correct. Overfitting occurs when the ML model learns the input and target dataset too precisely. In this case, the model has been "over trained" on the data and is treating noise in the data as true parameters. An ML model that has been overfitted is not able to accurately predict outcomes using a different dataset and may be too complex.

4 A is correct. Through the Text Analytics application of natural language processing (NLP), models using NLP analysis may incorporate non-traditional information to evaluate what people are saying—via their preferences, opinions, likes, or dislikes—in the attempt to identify trends and short-term indicators about a company, a stock, or an economic event that might have a bearing on future performance.

5 B is correct. Research suggests that robo-advisers tend to offer fairly conservative advice, providing a cost-effective and easily accessible form of financial guidance to underserved populations, such as the mass affluent and mass market segments.

6 C is correct. There is increasing interest in monitoring risk in real-time. To do so, relevant data must be taken by a firm, mapped to known risks, and identified while moving within the firm. Data may be aggregated for reporting purposes or used as inputs to risk models.

7 C is correct. Global financial markets have undergone substantial change as markets have fragmented into multiple trading destinations consisting of electronic exchanges, alternative trading systems, and so-called dark pools. In such an environment, when markets are continuously reflecting real-time information and continuously changing conditions, algorithmic trading has been viewed as an important tool.

8 C is correct. DLT has the potential to streamline the existing, often complex and labor intensive post-trade processes in securities markets by providing close to real-time trade verification, reconciliation, and settlement, thereby reducing related complexity, time, and costs.

9 A is correct. Through tokenization—the process of representing ownership rights to physical assets on a blockchain or distributed ledger—DLT has the potential to streamline this rights process by creating a single, digital record of ownership with which to verify ownership title and authenticity, including all historical activity.

Glossary

A priori probability A probability based on logical analysis rather than on observation or personal judgment.

Abnormal return The amount by which a security's actual return differs from its expected return, given the security's risk and the market's return.

Absolute advantage A country's ability to produce a good or service at a lower absolute cost than its trading partner.

Absolute dispersion The amount of variability present without comparison to any reference point or benchmark.

Absolute frequency The number of observations in a given interval (for grouped data).

Accelerated book build An offering of securities by an investment bank acting as principal that is accomplished in only one or two days.

Accelerated methods Depreciation methods that allocate a relatively large proportion of the cost of an asset to the early years of the asset's useful life.

Accounting costs Monetary value of economic resources used in performing an activity. These can be explicit, out-of-pocket, current payments, or an allocation of historical payments (depreciation) for resources. They do not include implicit opportunity costs.

Accounting profit Income as reported on the income statement, in accordance with prevailing accounting standards, before the provisions for income tax expense. Also called *income before taxes* or *pretax income.*

Accounts payable Amounts that a business owes to its vendors for goods and services that were purchased from them but which have not yet been paid.

Accounts receivable turnover Ratio of sales on credit to the average balance in accounts receivable.

Accrued expenses Liabilities related to expenses that have been incurred but not yet paid as of the end of an accounting period—an example of an accrued expense is rent that has been incurred but not yet paid, resulting in a liability "rent payable." Also called *accrued liabilities.*

Accrued interest Interest earned but not yet paid.

Acid-test ratio A stringent measure of liquidity that indicates a company's ability to satisfy current liabilities with its most liquid assets, calculated as (cash + short-term marketable investments + receivables) divided by current liabilities.

Acquisition method A method of accounting for a business combination where the acquirer is required to measure each identifiable asset and liability at fair value. This method was the result of a joint project of the IASB and FASB aiming at convergence in standards for the accounting of business combinations.

Action lag Delay from policy decisions to implementation.

Active investment An approach to investing in which the investor seeks to outperform a given benchmark.

Active return The return on a portfolio minus the return on the portfolio's benchmark.

Active strategy In reference to short-term cash management, an investment strategy characterized by monitoring and attempting to capitalize on market conditions to optimize the risk and return relationship of short-term investments.

Activity ratios Ratios that measure how efficiently a company performs day-to-day tasks, such as the collection of receivables and management of inventory. Also called *asset utilization ratios* or *operating efficiency ratios.*

Add-on rates Bank certificates of deposit, repos, and indexes such as Libor and Euribor are quoted on an add-on rate basis (bond equivalent yield basis).

Addition rule for probabilities A principle stating that the probability that *A* or *B* occurs (both occur) equals the probability that *A* occurs, plus the probability that *B* occurs, minus the probability that both *A* and *B* occur.

Agency bonds See *quasi-government bond.*

Agency RMBS In the United States, securities backed by residential mortgage loans and guaranteed by a federal agency or guaranteed by either of the two GSEs (Fannie Mae and Freddie Mac).

Aggregate demand The quantity of goods and services that households, businesses, government, and foreign customers want to buy at any given level of prices.

Aggregate demand curve Inverse relationship between the price level and real output.

Aggregate income The value of all the payments earned by the suppliers of factors used in the production of goods and services.

Aggregate output The value of all the goods and services produced in a specified period of time.

Aggregate supply The quantity of goods and services producers are willing to supply at any given level of price.

Aggregate supply curve The level of domestic output that companies will produce at each price level.

Aging schedule A breakdown of accounts into categories of days outstanding.

All-or-nothing (AON) orders An order that includes the instruction to trade only if the trade fills the entire quantity (size) specified.

Allocationally efficient A characteristic of a market, a financial system, or an economy that promotes the allocation of resources to their highest value uses.

Alternative data Non-traditional data types generated by the use of electronic devices, social media, satellite and sensor networks, and company exhaust.

Alternative investment markets Market for investments other than traditional securities investments (i.e., traditional common and preferred shares and traditional fixed income instruments). The term usually encompasses direct and indirect investment in real estate (including timberland and farmland) and commodities (including precious metals); hedge funds, private equity, and other investments requiring specialized due diligence.

Alternative trading systems Trading venues that function like exchanges but that do not exercise regulatory authority over their subscribers except with respect to the conduct of the subscribers' trading in their trading systems. Also called *electronic communications networks* or *multilateral trading facilities.*

American depository receipt A US dollar-denominated security that trades like a common share on US exchanges.

American depository share The underlying shares on which American depository receipts are based. They trade in the issuing company's domestic market.

American-style Type of option contract that can be exercised at any time up to the option's expiration date.

Amortisation The process of allocating the cost of intangible long-term assets having a finite useful life to accounting periods; the allocation of the amount of a bond premium or discount to the periods remaining until bond maturity.

Amortised cost The historical cost (initially recognised cost) of an asset, adjusted for amortisation and impairment.

Amortizing bond Bond with a payment schedule that calls for periodic payments of interest and repayments of principal.

Amortizing loan Loan with a payment schedule that calls for periodic payments of interest and repayments of principal.

Annual percentage rate The cost of borrowing expressed as a yearly rate.

Annuity A finite set of level sequential cash flows.

Annuity due An annuity having a first cash flow that is paid immediately.

Anticipation stock Excess inventory that is held in anticipation of increased demand, often because of seasonal patterns of demand.

Antidilutive With reference to a transaction or a security, one that would increase earnings per share (EPS) or result in EPS higher than the company's basic EPS—antidilutive securities are not included in the calculation of diluted EPS.

Arbitrage 1) The simultaneous purchase of an undervalued asset or portfolio and sale of an overvalued but equivalent asset or portfolio, in order to obtain a riskless profit on the price differential. Taking advantage of a market inefficiency in a risk-free manner. 2) The condition in a financial market in which equivalent assets or combinations of assets sell for two different prices, creating an opportunity to profit at no risk with no commitment of money. In a well-functioning financial market, few arbitrage opportunities are possible. 3) A risk-free operation that earns an expected positive net profit but requires no net investment of money.

Arbitrage-free pricing The overall process of pricing derivatives by arbitrage and risk neutrality. Also called the *principle of no arbitrage.*

Arbitrageurs Traders who engage in arbitrage. See *arbitrage.*

Arithmetic mean The sum of the observations divided by the number of observations.

Arms index A flow of funds indicator applied to a broad stock market index to measure the relative extent to which money is moving into or out of rising and declining stocks.

Artificial intelligence Computer systems that exhibit cognitive and decision-making ability comparable (or superior) to that of humans.

Asian call option A European-style option with a value at maturity equal to the difference between the stock price at maturity and the average stock price during the life of the option, or $0, whichever is greater.

Ask The price at which a dealer or trader is willing to sell an asset, typically qualified by a maximum quantity (ask size). See *offer.*

Ask size The maximum quantity of an asset that pertains to a specific ask price from a trader. For example, if the ask for a share issue is $30 for a size of 1,000 shares, the trader is offering to sell at $30 up to 1,000 shares.

Asset allocation The process of determining how investment funds should be distributed among asset classes.

Asset-backed securities A type of bond issued by a legal entity called a *special purpose entity* (SPE) on a collection of assets that the SPE owns. Also, securities backed by receivables and loans other than mortgages.

Asset-based loan A loan that is secured with company assets.

Asset-based valuation models Valuation based on estimates of the market value of a company's assets.

Asset beta The unlevered beta; reflects the business risk of the assets; the asset's systematic risk.

Asset class A group of assets that have similar characteristics, attributes, and risk/return relationships.

Asset swap Converts the periodic fixed coupon of a specific bond to a Libor plus or minus a spread.

Asset utilization ratios Ratios that measure how efficiently a company performs day-to-day tasks, such as the collection of receivables and management of inventory.

Assets Resources controlled by an enterprise as a result of past events and from which future economic benefits to the enterprise are expected to flow.

Assignment of accounts receivable The use of accounts receivable as collateral for a loan.

At the money An option in which the underlying's price equals the exercise price.

Auction A type of bond issuing mechanism often used for sovereign bonds that involves bidding.

Autarkic price The price of a good or service in an autarkic economy.

Autarky A state in which a country does not trade with other countries.

Automated Clearing House (ACH) An electronic payment network available to businesses, individuals, and financial institutions in the United States, US Territories, and Canada.

Automatic stabilizer A countercyclical factor that automatically comes into play as an economy slows and unemployment rises.

Available-for-sale Under US GAAP, debt securities not classified as either held-to-maturity or held-for-trading securities. The investor is willing to sell but not actively planning to sell. In general, available-for-sale debt securities are reported at fair value on the balance sheet, with unrealized gains included as a component of other comprehensive income.

Average accounting rate of return (ARR) Over the life of a project, the AAR can be defined as the average net income divided by the average book value.

Average fixed cost Total fixed cost divided by quantity produced.

Average life See *weighted average life.*

Average product Measures the productivity of inputs on average and is calculated by dividing total product by the total number of units for a given input that is used to generate that output.

Average revenue Total revenue divided by quantity sold.

Average total cost Total cost divided by quantity produced.

Average variable cost Total variable cost divided by quantity produced.

Back simulation Another term for the historical method of estimating VaR. This term is somewhat misleading in that the method involves not a *simulation* of the past but rather what *actually happened* in the past, sometimes adjusted to reflect the fact that a different portfolio may have existed in the past than is planned for the future.

Back-testing With reference to portfolio strategies, the application of a strategy's portfolio selection rules to historical data to assess what would have been the strategy's historical performance.

Backup lines of credit A type of credit enhancement provided by a bank to an issuer of commercial paper to ensure that the issuer will have access to sufficient liquidity to repay maturing commercial paper if issuing new paper is not a viable option.

Balance of payments A double-entry bookkeeping system that summarizes a country's economic transactions with the rest of the world for a particular period of time, typically a calendar quarter or year.

Balance of trade deficit When the domestic economy is spending more on foreign goods and services than foreign economies are spending on domestic goods and services.

Balance sheet The financial statement that presents an entity's current financial position by disclosing resources the entity controls (its assets) and the claims on those resources (its liabilities and equity claims), as of a particular point in time (the date of the balance sheet). Also called *statement of financial position* or *statement of financial condition.*

Balance sheet ratios Financial ratios involving balance sheet items only.

Balanced With respect to a government budget, one in which spending and revenues (taxes) are equal.

Balloon payment Large payment required at maturity to retire a bond's outstanding principal amount.

Bar chart A price chart with four bits of data for each time interval—the high, low, opening, and closing prices. A vertical line connects the high and low. A cross-hatch left indicates the opening price and a cross-hatch right indicates the close.

Barter economy An economy where economic agents as house-holds, corporations, and governments "pay" for goods and services with another good or service.

Base rates The reference rate on which a bank bases lending rates to all other customers.

Basic EPS Net earnings available to common shareholders (i.e., net income minus preferred dividends) divided by the weighted average number of common shares outstanding.

Basis point Used in stating yield spreads, one basis point equals one-hundredth of a percentage point, or 0.01%.

Basket of listed depository receipts An exchange-traded fund (ETF) that represents a portfolio of depository receipts.

Bearer bonds Bonds for which ownership is not recorded; only the clearing system knows who the bond owner is.

Behavioral finance A field of finance that examines the psychological variables that affect and often distort the investment decision making of investors, analysts, and portfolio managers.

Behind the market Said of prices specified in orders that are worse than the best current price; e.g., for a limit buy order, a limit price below the best bid.

Benchmark A comparison portfolio; a point of reference or comparison.

Benchmark issue The latest sovereign bond issue for a given maturity. It serves as a benchmark against which to compare bonds that have the same features but that are issued by another type of issuer.

Benchmark rate Typically the yield-to-maturity on a government bond having the same, or close to the same, time-to-maturity.

Benchmark spread The yield spread over a specific benchmark, usually measured in basis points.

Bernoulli random variable A random variable having the outcomes 0 and 1.

Bernoulli trial An experiment that can produce one of two outcomes.

Best bid The highest bid in the market.

Best effort offering An offering of a security using an investment bank in which the investment bank, as agent for the issuer, promises to use its best efforts to sell the offering but does not guarantee that a specific amount will be sold.

Best-in-class An ESG implementation approach that seeks to identify the most favorable companies in an industry based on ESG considerations.

Best offer The lowest offer (ask price) in the market.

Beta A measure of the sensitivity of a given investment or portfolio to movements in the overall market.

Bid The price at which a dealer or trader is willing to buy an asset, typically qualified by a maximum quantity.

Bid–ask spread The difference between the prices at which dealers will buy from a customer (bid) and sell to a customer (offer or ask). It is often used as an indicator of liquidity.

Bid–offer spread The difference between the prices at which dealers will buy from a customer (bid) and sell to a customer (offer or ask). It is often used as an indicator of liquidity.

Bid size The maximum quantity of an asset that pertains to a specific bid price from a trader.

Big Data The vast amount of data being generated by industry, governments, individuals, and electronic devices that arises from both traditional and non-traditional data sources.

Bilateral loan A loan from a single lender to a single borrower.

Binomial model A model for pricing options in which the underlying price can move to only one of two possible new prices.

Binomial random variable The number of successes in n Bernoulli trials for which the probability of success is constant for all trials and the trials are independent.

Binomial tree The graphical representation of a model of asset price dynamics in which, at each period, the asset moves up with probability p or down with probability $(1 - p)$.

Bitcoin A cryptocurrency using blockchain technology that was created in 2009.

Block brokers A broker (agent) that provides brokerage services for large-size trades.

Blockchain A type of digital ledger in which information is recorded sequentially and then linked together and secured using cryptographic methods.

Blue chip Widely held large market capitalization companies that are considered financially sound and are leaders in their respective industry or local stock market.

Bollinger Bands A price-based technical analysis indicator consisting of a moving average plus a higher line representing the moving average plus a set number of standard deviations from average price (for the same number of periods as used to calculate the moving average) and a lower line that is a moving average minus the same number of standard deviations.

Bond Contractual agreement between the issuer and the bondholders.

Bond equivalent yield A calculation of yield that is annualized using the ratio of 365 to the number of days to maturity. Bond equivalent yield allows for the restatement and comparison of securities with different compounding periods.

Bond indenture The governing legal credit agreement, typically incorporated by reference in the prospectus. Also called *trust deed.*

Bond market vigilantes Bond market participants who might reduce their demand for long-term bonds, thus pushing up their yields.

Bond yield plus risk premium approach An estimate of the cost of common equity that is produced by summing the before-tax cost of debt and a risk premium that captures the additional yield on a company's stock relative to its bonds. The additional yield is often estimated using historical spreads between bond yields and stock yields.

Bonus issue of shares A type of dividend in which a company distributes additional shares of its common stock to shareholders instead of cash.

Book building Investment bankers' process of compiling a "book" or list of indications of interest to buy part of an offering.

Book value The net amount shown for an asset or liability on the balance sheet; book value may also refer to the company's excess of total assets over total liabilities. Also called *carrying value.*

Boom An expansionary phase characterized by economic growth "testing the limits" of the economy.

Bottom-up analysis An investment selection approach that focuses on company-specific circumstances rather than emphasizing economic cycles or industry analysis.

Break point In the context of the weighted average cost of capital (WACC), a break point is the amount of capital at which the cost of one or more of the sources of capital changes, leading to a change in the WACC.

Breakeven point The number of units produced and sold at which the company's net income is zero (Revenues = Total cost); in the case of perfect competition, the quantity at which price, average revenue, and marginal revenue equal average total cost.

Bridge financing Interim financing that provides funds until permanent financing can be arranged.

Broad money Encompasses narrow money plus the entire range of liquid assets that can be used to make purchases.

Broker 1) An agent who executes orders to buy or sell securities on behalf of a client in exchange for a commission. 2) See *futures commission merchants.*

Broker–dealer A financial intermediary (often a company) that may function as a principal (dealer) or as an agent (broker) depending on the type of trade.

Brokered market A market in which brokers arrange trades among their clients.

Budget surplus/deficit The difference between government revenue and expenditure for a stated fixed period of time.

Bullet bond Bond in which the principal repayment is made entirely at maturity.

Business risk The risk associated with operating earnings. Operating earnings are uncertain because total revenues and many of the expenditures contributed to produce those revenues are uncertain.

Buy-side firm An investment management company or other investor that uses the services of brokers or dealers (i.e., the client of the sell side firms).

Buyback A transaction in which a company buys back its own shares. Unlike stock dividends and stock splits, share repurchases use corporate cash.

Call An option that gives the holder the right to buy an underlying asset from another party at a fixed price over a specific period of time.

Call market A market in which trades occur only at a particular time and place (i.e., when the market is called).

Call money rate The interest rate that buyers pay for their margin loan.

Call option An option that gives the holder the right to buy an underlying asset from another party at a fixed price over a specific period of time.

Call protection The time during which the issuer of the bond is not allowed to exercise the call option.

Callable bond A bond containing an embedded call option that gives the issuer the right to buy the bond back from the investor at specified prices on pre-determined dates.

Candlestick chart A price chart with four bits of data for each time interval. A candle indicates the opening and closing price for the interval. The body of the candle is shaded if the opening price was higher than the closing price, and the body is clear if the opening price was lower than the closing price. Vertical lines known as wicks or shadows extend from the top and bottom of the candle to indicate the high and the low prices for the interval.

Cannibalization Cannibalization occurs when an investment takes customers and sales away from another part of the company.

Capacity The ability of the borrower to make its debt payments on time.

Capital account A component of the balance of payments account that measures transfers of capital.

Capital allocation line (CAL) A graph line that describes the combinations of expected return and standard deviation of return available to an investor from combining the optimal portfolio of risky assets with the risk-free asset.

Capital asset pricing model (CAPM) An equation describing the expected return on any asset (or portfolio) as a linear function of its beta relative to the market portfolio.

Capital budgeting The process that companies use for decision making on capital projects—those projects with a life of one year or more.

Capital consumption allowance A measure of the wear and tear (depreciation) of the capital stock that occurs in the production of goods and services.

Capital deepening investment Increases the stock of capital relative to labor.

Capital expenditure Expenditure on physical capital (fixed assets).

Capital lease See *finance lease.*

Capital market expectations An investor's expectations concerning the risk and return prospects of asset classes.

Capital market line (CML) The line with an intercept point equal to the risk-free rate that is tangent to the efficient frontier of risky assets; represents the efficient frontier when a risk-free asset is available for investment.

Capital market securities Securities with maturities at issuance longer than one year.

Capital markets Financial markets that trade securities of longer duration, such as bonds and equities.

Capital rationing A capital rationing environment assumes that the company has a fixed amount of funds to invest.

Capital restrictions Controls placed on foreigners' ability to own domestic assets and/or domestic residents' ability to own foreign assets.

Capital stock The accumulated amount of buildings, machinery, and equipment used to produce goods and services.

Capital structure The mix of debt and equity that a company uses to finance its business; a company's specific mixture of long-term financing.

Captive finance subsidiary A wholly-owned subsidiary of a company that is established to provide financing of the sales of the parent company.

Carry The net of the costs and benefits of holding, storing, or "carrying" an asset.

Carrying amount The amount at which an asset or liability is valued according to accounting principles.

Carrying value The net amount shown for an asset or liability on the balance sheet; book value may also refer to the company's excess of total assets over total liabilities. For a bond, the purchase price plus (or minus) the amortized amount of the discount (or premium).

Cartel Participants in collusive agreements that are made openly and formally.

Cash collateral account Form of external credit enhancement whereby the issuer immediately borrows the credit-enhancement amount and then invests that amount, usually in highly rated short-term commercial paper.

Cash conversion cycle A financial metric that measures the length of time required for a company to convert cash invested in its operations to cash received as a result of its operations; equal to days of inventory on hand + days of sales outstanding − number of days of payables. Also called *net operating cycle.*

Cash flow additivity principle The principle that dollar amounts indexed at the same point in time are additive.

Cash flow from operating activities The net amount of cash provided from operating activities.

Cash flow from operations The net amount of cash provided from operating activities.

Cash flow yield The internal rate of return on a series of cash flows.

Cash market securities Money market securities settled on a "same day" or "cash settlement" basis.

Cash markets See *spot markets.*

Cash prices See *spot prices.*

Cash-settled forwards See *non-deliverable forwards.*

CBOE Volatility Index A measure of near-term market volatility as conveyed by S&P 500 stock index option prices.

Central bank funds market The market in which deposit-taking banks that have an excess reserve with their national central bank can loan money to banks that need funds for maturities ranging from overnight to one year. Called the Federal or Fed funds market in the United States.

Central bank funds rates Interest rates at which central bank funds are bought (borrowed) and sold (lent) for maturities ranging from overnight to one year. Called Federal or Fed funds rates in the United States.

Central banks The dominant bank in a country, usually with official or semi-official governmental status.

Certificate of deposit An instrument that represents a specified amount of funds on deposit with a bank for a specified maturity and interest rate. CDs are issued in various denominations and can be negotiable or non-negotiable.

Change in polarity principle A tenet of technical analysis that once a support level is breached, it becomes a resistance level. The same holds true for resistance levels; once breached, they become support levels.

Change of control put A covenant giving bondholders the right to require the issuer to buy back their debt, often at par or at some small premium to par value, in the event that the borrower is acquired.

Character The quality of a debt issuer's management.

Classified balance sheet A balance sheet organized so as to group together the various assets and liabilities into subcategories (e.g., current and noncurrent).

Clawback A requirement that the general partner return any funds distributed as incentive fees until the limited partners have received back their initial investment and a percentage of the total profit.

Clearing The process by which the exchange verifies the execution of a transaction and records the participants' identities.

Clearing instructions Instructions that indicate how to arrange the final settlement ("clearing") of a trade.

Clearinghouse An entity associated with a futures market that acts as middleman between the contracting parties and guarantees to each party the performance of the other.

Closed economy An economy that does not trade with other countries; an *autarkic economy.*

Closed-end fund A mutual fund in which no new investment money is accepted. New investors invest by buying existing shares, and investors in the fund liquidate by selling their shares to other investors.

Code of ethics An established guide that communicates an organization's values and overall expectations regarding member behavior. A code of ethics serves as a general guide for how community members should act.

Coefficient of variation (CV) The ratio of a set of observations' standard deviation to the observations' mean value.

Coincident economic indicators Turning points that are usually close to those of the overall economy; they are believed to have value for identifying the economy's present state.

Collateral manager Buys and sells debt obligations for and from the CDO's portfolio of assets (i.e., the collateral) to generate sufficient cash flows to meet the obligations to the CDO bondholders.

Collateral trust bonds Bonds secured by securities such as common shares, other bonds, or other financial assets.

Collateralized bond obligations A structured asset-backed security that is collateralized by a pool of bonds.

Collateralized debt obligation Generic term used to describe a security backed by a diversified pool of one or more debt obligations.

Collateralized loan obligations A structured asset-backed security that is collateralized by a pool of loans.

Collateralized mortgage obligation A security created through the securitization of a pool of mortgage-related products (mortgage pass-through securities or pools of loans).

Collaterals Assets or financial guarantees underlying a debt obligation that are above and beyond the issuer's promise to pay.

Combination A listing in which the order of the listed items does not matter.

Commercial paper A short-term, negotiable, unsecured promissory note that represents a debt obligation of the issuer.

Committed capital The amount that the limited partners have agreed to provide to the private equity fund.

Committed lines of credit A bank commitment to extend credit up to a pre-specified amount; the commitment is considered a short-term liability and is usually in effect for 364 days (one day short of a full year).

Commodity swap A swap in which the underlying is a commodity such as oil, gold, or an agricultural product.

Common market Level of economic integration that incorporates all aspects of the customs union and extends it by allowing free movement of factors of production among members.

Common shares A type of security that represent an ownership interest in a company.

Common-size analysis The restatement of financial statement items using a common denominator or reference item that allows one to identify trends and major differences; an example is an income statement in which all items are expressed as a percent of revenue.

Common stock See *common shares*.

Company analysis Analysis of an individual company.

Comparable company A company that has similar business risk; usually in the same industry and preferably with a single line of business.

Comparative advantage A country's ability to produce a good or service at a lower relative cost, or opportunity cost, than its trading partner.

Competitive strategy A company's plans for responding to the threats and opportunities presented by the external environment.

Complements Goods that tend to be used together; technically, two goods whose cross-price elasticity of demand is negative.

Complete markets Informally, markets in which the variety of distinct securities traded is so broad that any desired payoff in a future state-of-the-world is achievable.

Component cost of capital The rate of return required by suppliers of capital for an individual source of a company's funding, such as debt or equity.

Compounding The process of accumulating interest on interest.

Comprehensive income The change in equity of a business enterprise during a period from nonowner sources; includes all changes in equity during a period except those resulting from investments by owners and distributions to owners; comprehensive income equals net income plus other comprehensive income.

Conditional expected value The expected value of a stated event given that another event has occurred.

Conditional probability The probability of an event given (conditioned on) another event.

Conditional variances The variance of one variable, given the outcome of another.

Consistent With reference to estimators, describes an estimator for which the probability of estimates close to the value of the population parameter increases as sample size increases.

Constant-yield price trajectory A graph that illustrates the change in the price of a fixed-income bond over time assuming no change in yield-to-maturity. The trajectory shows the "pull to par" effect on the price of a bond trading at a premium or a discount to par value.

Constituent securities With respect to an index, the individual securities within an index.

Consumer surplus The difference between the value that a consumer places on units purchased and the amount of money that was required to pay for them.

Contingency provision Clause in a legal document that allows for some action if a specific event or circumstance occurs.

Contingent claims Derivatives in which the payoffs occur if a specific event occurs; generally referred to as options.

Contingent convertible bonds Bonds that automatically convert into equity if a specific event or circumstance occurs, such as the issuer's equity capital falling below the minimum requirement set by the regulators. Also called *CoCos*.

Continuation patterns A type of pattern used in technical analysis to predict the resumption of a market trend that was in place prior to the formation of a pattern.

Continuous random variable A random variable for which the range of possible outcomes is the real line (all real numbers between $-\infty$ and $+\infty$ or some subset of the real line).

Continuous time Time thought of as advancing in extremely small increments.

Continuous trading market A market in which trades can be arranged and executed any time the market is open.

Continuously compounded return The natural logarithm of 1 plus the holding period return, or equivalently, the natural logarithm of the ending price over the beginning price.

Contra account An account that offsets another account.

Contract rate See *mortgage rate*.

Contraction The period of a business cycle after the peak and before the trough; often called a *recession* or, if exceptionally severe, called a *depression*.

Contraction risk The risk that when interest rates decline, the security will have a shorter maturity than was anticipated at the time of purchase because borrowers refinance at the new, lower interest rates.

Contractionary Tending to cause the real economy to contract.

Contractionary fiscal policy A fiscal policy that has the objective to make the real economy contract.

Contracts for differences See *non-deliverable forwards*.

Contribution margin The amount available for fixed costs and profit after paying variable costs; revenue minus variable costs.

Controlling shareholders A particular shareholder or block of shareholders holding a percentage of shares that gives them significant voting power.

Convenience yield A non-monetary advantage of holding an asset.

Conventional bond See *plain vanilla bond*.

Conventional cash flow A conventional cash flow pattern is one with an initial outflow followed by a series of inflows.

Convergence The tendency for differences in output per capita across countries to diminish over time; in technical analysis, a term that describes the case when an indicator moves in the same manner as the security being analyzed.

Conversion price For a convertible bond, the price per share at which the bond can be converted into shares.

Conversion ratio For a convertible bond, the number of common shares that each bond can be converted into.

Conversion value For a convertible bond, the current share price multiplied by the conversion ratio.

Convertible bond Bond that gives the bondholder the right to exchange the bond for a specified number of common shares in the issuing company.

Convertible preference shares A type of equity security that entitles shareholders to convert their shares into a specified number of common shares.

Convexity adjustment For a bond, one half of the annual or approximate convexity statistic multiplied by the change in the yield-to-maturity squared.

Core inflation The inflation rate calculated based on a price index of goods and services except food and energy.

Corporate governance The system of internal controls and procedures by which individual companies are managed.

Correlation A number between −1 and +1 that measures the comovement (linear association) between two random variables.

Correlation coefficient A number between −1 and +1 that measures the consistency or tendency for two investments to act in a similar way. It is used to determine the effect on portfolio risk when two assets are combined.

Cost averaging The periodic investment of a fixed amount of money.

Cost of capital The rate of return that suppliers of capital require as compensation for their contribution of capital.

Cost of carry See *carry*.

Cost of debt The cost of debt financing to a company, such as when it issues a bond or takes out a bank loan.

Cost of preferred stock The cost to a company of issuing preferred stock; the dividend yield that a company must commit to pay preferred stockholders.

Cost-push Type of inflation in which rising costs, usually wages, compel businesses to raise prices generally.

Cost structure The mix of a company's variable costs and fixed costs.

Counterparty risk The risk that the other party to a contract will fail to honor the terms of the contract.

Coupon rate The interest rate promised in a contract; this is the rate used to calculate the periodic interest payments.

Cournot assumption Assumption in which each firm determines its profit-maximizing production level assuming that the other firms' output will not change.

Covariance A measure of the co-movement (linear association) between two random variables.

Covariance matrix A matrix or square array whose entries are covariances; also known as a variance–covariance matrix.

Covenants The terms and conditions of lending agreements that the issuer must comply with; they specify the actions that an issuer is obligated to perform (affirmative covenant) or prohibited from performing (negative covenant).

Covered bond Debt obligation secured by a segregated pool of assets called the cover pool. The issuer must maintain the value of the cover pool. In the event of default, bondholders have recourse against both the issuer and the cover pool.

Credit analysis The evaluation of credit risk; the evaluation of the creditworthiness of a borrower or counterparty.

Credit curve A curve showing the relationship between time to maturity and yield spread for an issuer with comparable bonds of various maturities outstanding, usually upward sloping.

Credit default swap (CDS) A type of credit derivative in which one party, the credit protection buyer who is seeking credit protection against a third party, makes a series of regularly scheduled payments to the other party, the credit protection seller. The seller makes no payments until a credit event occurs.

Credit derivatives A contract in which one party has the right to claim a payment from another party in the event that a specific credit event occurs over the life of the contract.

Credit enhancements Provisions that may be used to reduce the credit risk of a bond issue.

Credit-linked coupon bond Bond for which the coupon changes when the bond's credit rating changes.

Credit-linked note (CLN) Fixed-income security in which the holder of the security has the right to withhold payment of the full amount due at maturity if a credit event occurs.

Credit migration risk The risk that a bond issuer's creditworthiness deteriorates, or migrates lower, leading investors to believe the risk of default is higher. Also called *downgrade risk*.

Credit risk The risk of loss caused by a counterparty's or debtor's failure to make a promised payment. Also called *default risk*.

Credit scoring model A statistical model used to classify borrowers according to creditworthiness.

Credit spread option An option on the yield spread on a bond.

Credit tranching A structure used to redistribute the credit risk associated with the collateral; a set of bond classes created to allow investors a choice in the amount of credit risk that they prefer to bear.

Credit-worthiness The perceived ability of the borrower to pay what is owed on the borrowing in a timely manner; it represents the ability of a company to withstand adverse impacts on its cash flows.

Cross-default provisions Provisions whereby events of default such as non-payment of interest on one bond trigger default on all outstanding debt; implies the same default probability for all issues.

Cross-price elasticity of demand The percentage change in quantity demanded for a given percentage change in the price of another good; the responsiveness of the demand for Product A that is associated with the change in price of Product B.

Cross-sectional analysis Analysis that involves comparisons across individuals in a group over a given time period or at a given point in time.

Cross-sectional data Observations over individual units at a point in time, as opposed to time-series data.

Crossing networks Trading systems that match buyers and sellers who are willing to trade at prices obtained from other markets.

Crowding out The thesis that government borrowing may divert private sector investment from taking place.

Cryptocurrency An electronic medium of exchange that lacks physical form.

Cryptography An algorithmic process to encrypt data, making the data unusable if received by unauthorized parties.

Cumulative distribution function A function giving the probability that a random variable is less than or equal to a specified value.

Cumulative preference shares Preference shares for which any dividends that are not paid accrue and must be paid in full before dividends on common shares can be paid.

Cumulative relative frequency For data grouped into intervals, the fraction of total observations that are less than the value of the upper limit of a stated interval.

Cumulative voting A voting process whereby each shareholder can accumulate and vote all his or her shares for a single candidate in an election, as opposed to having to allocate their voting rights evenly among all candidates.

Currencies Monies issued by national monetary authorities.

Currency option bonds Bonds that give the bondholder the right to choose the currency in which he or she wants to receive interest payments and principal repayments.

Currency swap A swap in which each party makes interest payments to the other in different currencies.

Current account A component of the balance of payments account that measures the flow of goods and services.

Current assets Assets that are expected to be consumed or converted into cash in the near future, typically one year or less. *Also called liquid assets.*

Current cost With reference to assets, the amount of cash or cash equivalents that would have to be paid to buy the same or an equivalent asset today; with reference to liabilities, the undiscounted amount of cash or cash equivalents that would be required to settle the obligation today.

Current government spending With respect to government expenditures, spending on goods and services that are provided on a regular, recurring basis including health, education, and defense.

Current liabilities Short-term obligations, such as accounts payable, wages payable, or accrued liabilities, that are expected to be settled in the near future, typically one year or less.

Current ratio A liquidity ratio calculated as current assets divided by current liabilities.

Current yield The sum of the coupon payments received over the year divided by the flat price; also called the *income* or *interest yield* or *running yield.*

Curve duration The sensitivity of the bond price (or the market value of a financial asset or liability) with respect to a benchmark yield curve.

Customs union Extends the free trade area (FTA) by not only allowing free movement of goods and services among members, but also creating a common trade policy against nonmembers.

CVaR Conditional VaR, a tail loss measure. The weighted average of all loss outcomes in the statistical distribution that exceed the VaR loss.

Cyclical See *cyclical companies.*

Cyclical companies Companies with sales and profits that regularly expand and contract with the business cycle or state of economy.

Daily settlement See *mark to market* and *marking to market.*

Dark pools Alternative trading systems that do not display the orders that their clients send to them.

Data mining The practice of determining a model by extensive searching through a dataset for statistically significant patterns. Also called *data snooping.*

Data science An interdisciplinary field that brings computer science, statistics, and other disciplines together to analyze and produce insights from Big Data.

Data snooping See *data mining.*

Day order An order that is good for the day on which it is submitted. If it has not been filled by the close of business, the order expires unfilled.

Day's sales outstanding Estimate of the average number of days it takes to collect on credit accounts.

Days in receivables Estimate of the average number of days it takes to collect on credit accounts.

Days of inventory on hand An activity ratio equal to the number of days in the period divided by inventory turnover over the period.

Dealers A financial intermediary that acts as a principal in trades.

Dealing securities Securities held by banks or other financial intermediaries for trading purposes.

Death cross A technical analysis term that describes a situation where a short-term moving average crosses from above a longer-term moving average to below it; this movement is considered bearish.

Debentures Type of bond that can be secured or unsecured.

Debt incurrence test A financial covenant made in conjunction with existing debt that restricts a company's ability to incur additional debt at the same seniority based on one or more financial tests or conditions.

Debt-rating approach A method for estimating a company's before-tax cost of debt based upon the yield on comparably rated bonds for maturities that closely match that of the company's existing debt.

Debt-to-assets ratio A solvency ratio calculated as total debt divided by total assets.

Debt-to-capital ratio A solvency ratio calculated as total debt divided by total debt plus total shareholders' equity.

Debt-to-equity ratio A solvency ratio calculated as total debt divided by total shareholders' equity.

Declaration date The day that the corporation issues a statement declaring a specific dividend.

Decreasing returns to scale When a production process leads to increases in output that are proportionately smaller than the increase in inputs.

Deductible temporary differences Temporary differences that result in a reduction of or deduction from taxable income in a future period when the balance sheet item is recovered or settled.

Deep learning Machine learning using neural networks with many hidden layers.

Deep learning nets Machine learning using neural networks with many hidden layers.

Default probability The probability that a borrower defaults or fails to meet its obligation to make full and timely payments of principal and interest, according to the terms of the debt security. Also called *default risk.*

Default risk The probability that a borrower defaults or fails to meet its obligation to make full and timely payments of principal and interest, according to the terms of the debt security. Also called *default probability.*

Default risk premium An extra return that compensates investors for the possibility that the borrower will fail to make a promised payment at the contracted time and in the contracted amount.

Defensive companies Companies with sales and profits that have little sensitivity to the business cycle or state of the economy.

Defensive interval ratio A liquidity ratio that estimates the number of days that an entity could meet cash needs from liquid assets; calculated as (cash + short-term marketable investments + receivables) divided by daily cash expenditures.

Deferred coupon bond Bond that pays no coupons for its first few years but then pays a higher coupon than it otherwise normally would for the remainder of its life. Also called *split coupon bond.*

Deferred income A liability account for money that has been collected for goods or services that have not yet been delivered; payment received in advance of providing a good or service.

Deferred revenue A liability account for money that has been collected for goods or services that have not yet been delivered; payment received in advance of providing a good or service.

Deferred tax assets A balance sheet asset that arises when an excess amount is paid for income taxes relative to accounting profit. The taxable income is higher than accounting profit and income tax payable exceeds tax expense. The company expects to recover the difference during the course of future operations when tax expense exceeds income tax payable.

Deferred tax liabilities A balance sheet liability that arises when a deficit amount is paid for income taxes relative to accounting profit. The taxable income is less than the accounting profit and income tax payable is less than tax expense. The company expects to eliminate the liability over the course of future operations when income tax payable exceeds tax expense.

Defined benefit pension plans Plans in which the company promises to pay a certain annual amount (defined benefit) to the employee after retirement. The company bears the investment risk of the plan assets.

Defined contribution pension plans Individual accounts to which an employee and typically the employer makes contributions during their working years and expect to draw on the accumulated funds at retirement. The employee bears the investment and inflation risk of the plan assets.

Deflation Negative inflation.

Degree of confidence The probability that a confidence interval includes the unknown population parameter.

Degree of financial leverage (DFL) The ratio of the percentage change in net income to the percentage change in operating income; the sensitivity of the cash flows available to owners when operating income changes.

Degree of operating leverage (DOL) The ratio of the percentage change in operating income to the percentage change in units sold; the sensitivity of operating income to changes in units sold.

Degree of total leverage The ratio of the percentage change in net income to the percentage change in units sold; the sensitivity of the cash flows to owners to changes in the number of units produced and sold.

Degrees of freedom (df) The number of independent observations used.

Delta The sensitivity of the derivative price to a small change in the value of the underlying asset.

Demand curve Graph of the inverse demand function. A graph showing the demand relation, either the highest quantity willingly purchased at each price or the highest price willingly paid for each quantity.

Demand function A relationship that expresses the quantity demanded of a good or service as a function of own-price and possibly other variables.

Demand-pull Type of inflation in which increasing demand raises prices generally, which then are reflected in a business's costs as workers demand wage hikes to catch up with the rising cost of living.

Demand shock A typically unexpected disturbance to demand, such as an unexpected interruption in trade or transportation.

Dependent With reference to events, the property that the probability of one event occurring depends on (is related to) the occurrence of another event.

Depository bank A bank that raises funds from depositors and other investors and lends it to borrowers.

Depository institutions Commercial banks, savings and loan banks, credit unions, and similar institutions that raise funds from depositors and other investors and lend it to borrowers.

Depository receipt A security that trades like an ordinary share on a local exchange and represents an economic interest in a foreign company.

Depreciation The process of systematically allocating the cost of long-lived (tangible) assets to the periods during which the assets are expected to provide economic benefits.

Depression See *contraction.*

Derivative pricing rule A pricing rule used by crossing networks in which a price is taken (derived) from the price that is current in the asset's primary market.

Derivatives A financial instrument whose value depends on the value of some underlying asset or factor (e.g., a stock price, an interest rate, or exchange rate).

Descriptive statistics The study of how data can be summarized effectively.

Development capital Minority equity investments in more mature companies that are seeking capital to expand or restructure operations, enter new markets, or finance major acquisitions.

Diffuse prior The assumption of equal prior probabilities.

Diffusion index Reflects the proportion of the index's components that are moving in a pattern consistent with the overall index.

Diluted EPS The EPS that would result if all dilutive securities were converted into common shares.

Diluted shares The number of shares that would be outstanding if all potentially dilutive claims on common shares (e.g., convertible debt, convertible preferred stock, and employee stock options) were exercised.

Diminishing balance method An accelerated depreciation method, i.e., one that allocates a relatively large proportion of the cost of an asset to the early years of the asset's useful life.

Diminishing marginal productivity Describes a state in which each additional unit of input produces less output than previously.

Direct debit program An arrangement whereby a customer authorizes a debit to a demand account; typically used by companies to collect routine payments for services.

Direct financing leases Under US GAAP, a type of finance lease, from a lessor perspective, where the present value of the lease payments (lease receivable) equals the carrying value of the leased asset. No selling profit is recognized at lease inception. The revenues earned by the lessor are financing in nature.

Direct format With reference to the cash flow statement, a format for the presentation of the statement in which cash flow from operating activities is shown as operating cash receipts less operating cash disbursements. Also called *direct method.*

Direct method See *direct format.*

Direct taxes Taxes levied directly on income, wealth, and corporate profits.

Direct write-off method An approach to recognizing credit losses on customer receivables in which the company waits until such time as a customer has defaulted and only then recognizes the loss.

Disbursement float The amount of time between check issuance and a check's clearing back against the company's account.

Discount To reduce the value of a future payment in allowance for how far away it is in time; to calculate the present value of some future amount. Also, the amount by which an instrument is priced below its face (par) value.

Discount interest A procedure for determining the interest on a loan or bond in which the interest is deducted from the face value in advance.

Discount margin See *required margin.*

Discount rates In general, the interest rate used to calculate a present value. In the money market, however, discount rate is a specific type of quoted rate.

Discounted cash flow models Valuation models that estimate the intrinsic value of a security as the present value of the future benefits expected to be received from the security.

Discounted payback period the number of years it takes for the cumulative discounted cash flows from a project to equal the original investment.

Discouraged worker A person who has stopped looking for a job or has given up seeking employment.

Discrete random variable A random variable that can take on at most a countable number of possible values.

Discriminatory pricing rule A pricing rule used in continuous markets in which the limit price of the order or quote that first arrived determines the trade price.

Diseconomies of scale Increase in cost per unit resulting from increased production.

Dispersion The variability around the central tendency.

Display size The size of an order displayed to public view.

Distressed investing Investing in securities of companies in financial difficulty. Private equity funds that specialize in distressed investing typically buy the debt of mature companies in financial difficulty.

Distributed ledger A type of database that may be shared among entities in a network.

Distributed ledger technology Technology based on a distributed ledger.

Divergence In technical analysis, a term that describes the case when an indicator moves differently from the security being analyzed.

Diversification ratio The ratio of the standard deviation of an equally weighted portfolio to the standard deviation of a randomly selected security.

Dividend A distribution paid to shareholders based on the number of shares owned.

Dividend discount model (DDM) A present value model that estimates the intrinsic value of an equity share based on the present value of its expected future dividends.

Dividend discount model based approach An approach for estimating a country's equity risk premium. The market rate of return is estimated as the sum of the dividend yield and the growth rate in dividends for a market index. Subtracting the risk-free rate of return from the estimated market return produces an estimate for the equity risk premium.

Dividend payout ratio The ratio of cash dividends paid to earnings for a period.

Divisor A number (denominator) used to determine the value of a price return index. It is initially chosen at the inception of an index and subsequently adjusted by the index provider, as necessary, to avoid changes in the index value that are unrelated to changes in the prices of its constituent securities.

Domestic content provisions Stipulate that some percentage of the value added or components used in production should be of domestic origin.

Double bottoms In technical analysis, a reversal pattern that is formed when the price reaches a low, rebounds, and then sells off back to the first low level; used to predict a change from a downtrend to an uptrend.

Double coincidence of wants A prerequisite to barter trades, in particular that both economic agents in the transaction want what the other is selling.

Double declining balance depreciation An accelerated depreciation method that involves depreciating the asset at double the straight-line rate. This rate is multiplied by the book value of the asset at the beginning of the period (a declining balance) to calculate depreciation expense.

Double top In technical analysis, a reversal pattern that is formed when an uptrend reverses twice at roughly the same high price level; used to predict a change from an uptrend to a downtrend.

Down transition probability The probability that an asset's value moves down in a model of asset price dynamics.

Downgrade risk The risk that a bond issuer's creditworthiness deteriorates, or migrates lower, leading investors to believe the risk of default is higher. Also called *credit migration risk.*

Drag on liquidity When receipts lag, creating pressure from the decreased available funds.

Drawdown A percentage peak-to-trough reduction in net asset value.

Dual-currency bonds Bonds that make coupon payments in one currency and pay the par value at maturity in another currency.

DuPont analysis An approach to decomposing return on investment, e.g., return on equity, as the product of other financial ratios.

Duration A measure of the approximate sensitivity of a security to a change in interest rates (i.e., a measure of interest rate risk).

Duration gap A bond's Macaulay duration minus the investment horizon.

Dutch Book theorem A result in probability theory stating that inconsistent probabilities create profit opportunities.

Early repayment option See *prepayment option.*

Earnings per share The amount of income earned during a period per share of common stock.

Earnings surprise The portion of a company's earnings that is unanticipated by investors and, according to the efficient market hypothesis, merits a price adjustment.

Economic costs All the remuneration needed to keep a productive resource in its current employment or to acquire the resource for productive use; the sum of total accounting costs and implicit opportunity costs.

Economic indicator A variable that provides information on the state of the overall economy.

Economic loss The amount by which accounting profit is less than normal profit.

Economic order quantity–reorder point (EOQ–ROP) An approach to managing inventory based on expected demand and the predictability of demand; the ordering point for new inventory is determined based on the costs of ordering and carrying inventory, such that the total cost associated with inventory is minimized.

Economic profit Equal to accounting profit less the implicit opportunity costs not included in total accounting costs; the difference between total revenue (TR) and total cost (TC). Also called *abnormal profit* or *supernormal profit.*
Economic stabilization Reduction of the magnitude of economic fluctuations.
Economic union Incorporates all aspects of a common market and in addition requires common economic institutions and coordination of economic policies among members.
Economies of scale Reduction in cost per unit resulting from increased production.
Effective annual rate The amount by which a unit of currency will grow in a year with interest on interest included.
Effective convexity A *curve convexity* statistic that measures the secondary effect of a change in a benchmark yield curve on a bond's price.
Effective duration The sensitivity of a bond's price to a change in a benchmark yield curve.
Effective interest rate The borrowing rate or market rate that a company incurs at the time of issuance of a bond.
Efficient market A market in which asset prices reflect new information quickly and rationally.
Elastic Said of a good or service when the magnitude of elasticity is greater than one.
Elasticity The percentage change in one variable for a percentage change in another variable; a general measure of how sensitive one variable is to a change in the value of another variable.
Elasticity of demand A measure of the sensitivity of quantity demanded to a change in a product's own price: $\%\Delta Q^D/\%\Delta P$.
Elasticity of supply A measure of the sensitivity of quantity supplied to a change in price: $\%\Delta Q^S/\%\Delta P$.
Electronic communications networks See *alternative trading systems.*
Electronic funds transfer (EFT) The use of computer networks to conduct financial transactions electronically.
Elliott wave theory A technical analysis theory that claims that the market follows regular, repeated waves or cycles.
Embedded option Contingency provisions that provide the issuer or the bondholders the right, but not the obligation, to take action. These options are not part of the security and cannot be traded separately.
Empirical probability The probability of an event estimated as a relative frequency of occurrence.
Employed The number of people with a job.
Engagement/active ownership An ESG investment style that uses shareholder power to influence corporate behavior through direct corporate engagement (i.e., communicating with senior management and/or boards of companies), filing or co-filing shareholder proposals, and proxy voting that is directed by ESG guidelines.
Enterprise risk management An overall assessment of a company's risk position. A centralized approach to risk management sometimes called firmwide risk management.
Enterprise value A measure of a company's total market value from which the value of cash and short-term investments have been subtracted.
Equal weighting An index weighting method in which an equal weight is assigned to each constituent security at inception.
Equipment trust certificates Bonds secured by specific types of equipment or physical assets.
Equity Assets less liabilities; the residual interest in the assets after subtracting the liabilities.
Equity risk premium The expected return on equities minus the risk-free rate; the premium that investors demand for investing in equities.
Equity swap A swap transaction in which at least one cash flow is tied to the return to an equity portfolio position, often an equity index.
ESG An acronym that encompasses environmental, social and governance.
ESG integration The integration of qualitative and quantitative environmental, social, and governance factors into traditional security and industry analysis; also known as *ESG incorporation.*
ESG investing The consideration of environmental, social, and governance factors in the investment process.
Estimate The particular value calculated from sample observations using an estimator.
Estimation With reference to statistical inference, the subdivision dealing with estimating the value of a population parameter.
Estimator An estimation formula; the formula used to compute the sample mean and other sample statistics are examples of estimators.
Ethical principles Beliefs regarding what is good, acceptable, or obligatory behavior and what is bad, unacceptable, or forbidden behavior.
Ethics The study of moral principles or of making good choices. Ethics encompasses a set of moral principles and rules of conduct that provide guidance for our behavior.
Eurobonds Type of bond issued internationally, outside the jurisdiction of the country in whose currency the bond is denominated.
European option An option that can only be exercised on its expiration date.
European-style Said of an option contract that can only be exercised on the option's expiration date.
Event Any outcome or specified set of outcomes of a random variable.
Ex-dividend date The first date that a share trades without (i.e., "ex") the dividend.
Excess kurtosis Degree of kurtosis (fatness of tails) in excess of the kurtosis of the normal distribution.
Exchanges Places where traders can meet to arrange their trades.
Exclusionary screening An ESG implementation approach that excludes certain sectors or companies that deviate from an investor's accepted standards. Also called *negative screening* or *norms-based screening.*
Execution instructions Instructions that indicate how to fill an order.
Exercise The process of using an option to buy or sell the underlying.
Exercise price The fixed price at which an option holder can buy or sell the underlying. Also called *strike price, striking price,* or *strike.*
Exercise value The value obtained if an option is exercised based on current conditions. Also known as *intrinsic value.*
Exhaustive Covering or containing all possible outcomes.
Expansion The period of a business cycle after its lowest point and before its highest point.
Expansionary Tending to cause the real economy to grow.
Expansionary fiscal policy Fiscal policy aimed at achieving real economic growth.

Expected inflation The level of inflation that economic agents expect in the future.

Expected loss Default probability times Loss severity given default.

Expected value The probability-weighted average of the possible outcomes of a random variable.

Expenses Outflows of economic resources or increases in liabilities that result in decreases in equity (other than decreases because of distributions to owners); reductions in net assets associated with the creation of revenues.

Experience curve A curve that shows the direct cost per unit of good or service produced or delivered as a typically declining function of cumulative output.

Export subsidy Paid by the government to the firm when it exports a unit of a good that is being subsidized.

Exports Goods and services that an economy sells to other countries.

Extension risk The risk that when interest rates rise, fewer prepayments will occur because homeowners are reluctant to give up the benefits of a contractual interest rate that now looks low. As a result, the security becomes longer in maturity than anticipated at the time of purchase.

Externality An effect of a market transaction that is borne by parties other than those who transacted.

Extra dividend A dividend paid by a company that does not pay dividends on a regular schedule, or a dividend that supplements regular cash dividends with an extra payment.

Extreme value theory A branch of statistics that focuses primarily on extreme outcomes.

Face value The amount of cash payable by a company to the bondholders when the bonds mature; the promised payment at maturity separate from any coupon payment.

Factor A common or underlying element with which several variables are correlated.

Fair value The amount at which an asset could be exchanged, or a liability settled, between knowledgeable, willing parties in an arm's-length transaction; the price that would be received to sell an asset or paid to transfer a liability in an orderly transaction between market participants.

Fed funds rate The US interbank lending rate on overnight borrowings of reserves.

Federal funds rate The US interbank lending rate on overnight borrowings of reserves.

Fiat money Money that is not convertible into any other commodity.

Fibonacci sequence A sequence of numbers starting with 0 and 1, and then each subsequent number in the sequence is the sum of the two preceding numbers. In Elliott Wave Theory, it is believed that market waves follow patterns that are the ratios of the numbers in the Fibonacci sequence.

Fiduciary call A combination of a European call and a risk-free bond that matures on the option expiration day and has a face value equal to the exercise price of the call.

FIFO method The first in, first out, method of accounting for inventory, which matches sales against the costs of items of inventory in the order in which they were placed in inventory.

Fill or kill See *immediate or cancel order*.

Finance lease From the lessee perspective, under US GAAP, a type of lease which is more akin to the purchase of an asset by the lessee. From the lessor perspective, under IFRS, a lease which "transfers substantially all the risks and rewards incidental to ownership of an underlying asset."

Financial account A component of the balance of payments account that records investment flows.

Financial flexibility The ability to react and adapt to financial adversity and opportunities.

Financial leverage The extent to which a company can effect, through the use of debt, a proportional change in the return on common equity that is greater than a given proportional change in operating income; also, short for the financial leverage ratio.

Financial leverage ratio A measure of financial leverage calculated as average total assets divided by average total equity.

Financial risk The risk that environmental, social, or governance risk factors will result in significant costs or other losses to a company and its shareholders; the risk arising from a company's obligation to meet required payments under its financing agreements.

Financing activities Activities related to obtaining or repaying capital to be used in the business (e.g., equity and long-term debt).

Fintech Technological innovation in the design and delivery of financial services and products in the financial industry.

Firm commitment offering See *underwritten offering*.

First-degree price discrimination Where a monopolist is able to charge each customer the highest price the customer is willing to pay.

First lien debt Debt secured by a pledge of certain assets that could include buildings, but may also include property and equipment, licenses, patents, brands, etc.

First mortgage debt Debt secured by a pledge of a specific property.

Fiscal multiplier The ratio of a change in national income to a change in government spending.

Fiscal policy The use of taxes and government spending to affect the level of aggregate expenditures.

Fisher effect The thesis that the real rate of interest in an economy is stable over time so that changes in nominal interest rates are the result of changes in expected inflation.

Fisher index The geometric mean of the Laspeyres index.

Fixed charge coverage A solvency ratio measuring the number of times interest and lease payments are covered by operating income, calculated as (EBIT + lease payments) divided by (interest payments + lease payments).

Fixed costs Costs that remain at the same level regardless of a company's level of production and sales.

Fixed-for-floating interest rate swap An interest rate swap in which one party pays a fixed rate and the other pays a floating rate, with both sets of payments in the same currency. Also called *plain vanilla swap* or *vanilla swap*.

Fixed rate perpetual preferred stock Nonconvertible, noncallable preferred stock that has a fixed dividend rate and no maturity date.

Flags A technical analysis continuation pattern formed by parallel trendlines, typically over a short period.

Flat price The full price of a bond minus the accrued interest; also called the *quoted* or *clean* price.

Float In the context of customer receipts, the amount of money that is in transit between payments made by customers and the funds that are usable by the company.

Float-adjusted market-capitalization weighting An index weighting method in which the weight assigned to each constituent security is determined by adjusting its market capitalization for its market float.

Float factor An estimate of the average number of days it takes deposited checks to clear; average daily float divided by average daily deposit.

Floaters See *floating-rate notes*.

Floating-rate notes A note on which interest payments are not fixed, but instead vary from period to period depending on the current level of a reference interest rate.

Flotation cost Fees charged to companies by investment bankers and other costs associated with raising new capital.

Foreclosure Allows the lender to take possession of a mortgaged property if the borrower defaults and then sell it to recover funds.

Foreign currency reserves Holding by the central bank of non-domestic currency deposits and non-domestic bonds.

Foreign direct investment Direct investment by a firm in one country (the source country) in productive assets in a foreign country (the host country).

Foreign exchange gains (or losses) Gains (or losses) that occur when the exchange rate changes between the investor's currency and the currency that foreign securities are denominated in.

Foreign portfolio investment Shorter-term investment by individuals, firms, and institutional investors (e.g., pension funds) in foreign financial instruments such as foreign stocks and foreign government bonds.

Forward commitments Class of derivatives that provides the ability to lock in a price to transact in the future at a previously agreed-upon price.

Forward contract An agreement between two parties in which one party, the buyer, agrees to buy from the other party, the seller, an underlying asset at a later date for a price established at the start of the contract.

Forward curve A series of forward rates, each having the same timeframe.

Forward market For future delivery, beyond the usual settlement time period in the cash market.

Forward price The fixed price or rate at which the transaction scheduled to occur at the expiration of a forward contract will take place. This price is agreed on at the initiation date of the contract.

Forward rate The interest rate on a bond or money market instrument traded in a forward market. A forward rate can be interpreted as an incremental, or marginal, return for extending the time-to-maturity for an additional time period.

Forward rate agreements A forward contract calling for one party to make a fixed interest payment and the other to make an interest payment at a rate to be determined at the contract expiration.

Fractile A value at or below which a stated fraction of the data lies.

Fractional reserve banking Banking in which reserves constitute a fraction of deposits.

Free cash flow The actual cash that would be available to the company's investors after making all investments necessary to maintain the company as an ongoing enterprise (also referred to as free cash flow to the firm); the internally generated funds that can be distributed to the company's investors (e.g., shareholders and bondholders) without impairing the value of the company.

Free cash flow to equity (FCFE) The cash flow available to a company's common shareholders after all operating expenses, interest, and principal payments have been made, and necessary investments in working and fixed capital have been made.

Free-cash-flow-to-equity models Valuation models based on discounting expected future free cash flow to equity.

Free cash flow to the firm (FCFF) The cash flow available to the company's suppliers of capital after all operating expenses have been paid and necessary investments in working capital and fixed capital have been made.

Free float The number of shares that are readily and freely tradable in the secondary market.

Free trade When there are no government restrictions on a country's ability to trade.

Free trade areas One of the most prevalent forms of regional integration, in which all barriers to the flow of goods and services among members have been eliminated.

Frequency distribution A tabular display of data summarized into a relatively small number of intervals.

Frequency polygon A graph of a frequency distribution obtained by drawing straight lines joining successive points representing the class frequencies.

Full integration An ESG investment style that focuses on the explicit inclusion of ESG factors into the traditional financial analysis of individual stocks for the purpose of valuation (e.g., as inputs into cash flow forecasts and/or cost-of-capital estimates).

Full price The price of a security with accrued interest; also called the *invoice* or *dirty* price.

Fundamental analysis The examination of publicly available information and the formulation of forecasts to estimate the intrinsic value of assets.

Fundamental value The underlying or true value of an asset based on an analysis of its qualitative and quantitative characteristics. Also called *intrinsic value*.

Fundamental weighting An index weighting method in which the weight assigned to each constituent security is based on its underlying company's size. It attempts to address the disadvantages of market-capitalization weighting by using measures that are independent of the constituent security's price.

Funds of hedge funds Funds that hold a portfolio of hedge funds, more commonly shortened to *funds of funds*.

Future value (FV) The amount to which a payment or series of payments will grow by a stated future date.

Futures contract A variation of a forward contract that has essentially the same basic definition but with some additional features, such as a clearinghouse guarantee against credit losses, a daily settlement of gains and losses, and an organized electronic or floor trading facility.

Futures price The agreed-upon price of a futures contract.

FX swap The combination of a spot and a forward FX transaction.

G-spread The yield spread in basis points over an actual or interpolated government bond.

Gains Asset inflows not directly related to the ordinary activities of the business.

Game theory The set of tools decision makers use to incorporate responses by rival decision makers into their strategies.

Gamma A numerical measure of how sensitive an option's delta (the sensitivity of the derivative's price) is to a change in the value of the underlying.

GDP deflator A gauge of prices and inflation that measures the aggregate changes in prices across the overall economy.

General partner The partner that runs the business and ultimately bears unlimited liability for the business's debts and obligations.

Geometric mean A measure of central tendency computed by taking the *n*th root of the product of *n* non-negative values.

Giffen goods Goods that are consumed more as the price of the good rises because it is a very inferior good whose income effect overwhelms its substitution effect when price changes.

Gilts Bonds issued by the UK government.

Giro system An electronic payment system used widely in Europe and Japan.

Global depository receipt A depository receipt that is issued outside of the company's home country and outside of the United States.

Global minimum-variance portfolio The portfolio on the minimum-variance frontier with the smallest variance of return.

Global registered share A common share that is traded on different stock exchanges around the world in different currencies.

Gold standard With respect to a currency, if a currency is on the gold standard a given amount can be converted into a prespecified amount of gold.

Golden cross A technical analysis term that describes a situation where a short-term moving average crosses from below a longer-term moving average to above it; this movement is considered bullish.

Good-on-close An execution instruction specifying that an order can only be filled at the close of trading. Also called *market on close.*

Good-on-open An execution instruction specifying that an order can only be filled at the opening of trading.

Good-till-cancelled order An order specifying that it is valid until the entity placing the order has cancelled it (or, commonly, until some specified amount of time such as 60 days has elapsed, whichever comes sooner).

Goodwill An intangible asset that represents the excess of the purchase price of an acquired company over the value of the net assets acquired.

Government equivalent yield A yield that restates a yield-to-maturity based on 30/360 day-count to one based on actual/actual.

Green bonds A bond used in green finance whereby the proceeds are earmarked towards environmental-related products.

Green finance A type of finance that addresses environmental concerns while achieving economic growth.

Grey market The forward market for bonds about to be issued. Also called "when issued" market.

Gross domestic product The market value of all final goods and services produced within the economy in a given period of time (output definition) or, equivalently, the aggregate income earned by all households, all companies, and the government within the economy in a given period of time (income definition).

Gross margin Sales minus the cost of sales (i.e., the cost of goods sold for a manufacturing company).

Gross profit Sales minus the cost of sales (i.e., the cost of goods sold for a manufacturing company).

Gross profit margin The ratio of gross profit to revenues.

Grouping by function With reference to the presentation of expenses in an income statement, the grouping together of expenses serving the same function, e.g. all items that are costs of goods sold.

Grouping by nature With reference to the presentation of expenses in an income statement, the grouping together of expenses by similar nature, e.g., all depreciation expenses.

Growth cyclical A term sometimes used to describe companies that are growing rapidly on a long-term basis but that still experience above-average fluctuation in their revenues and profits over the course of a business cycle.

Growth investors With reference to equity investors, investors who seek to invest in high-earnings-growth companies.

Guarantee certificate A type of structured financial instrument that provides investors capital protection. It combines a zero-coupon bond and a call option on some underlying asset.

Haircut See *repo margin.*

Harmonic mean A type of weighted mean computed by averaging the reciprocals of the observations, then taking the reciprocal of that average.

Head and shoulders pattern In technical analysis, a reversal pattern that is formed in three parts: a left shoulder, head, and right shoulder; used to predict a change from an uptrend to a downtrend.

Headline inflation The inflation rate calculated based on the price index that includes all goods and services in an economy.

Hedge funds Private investment vehicles that typically use leverage, derivatives, and long and short investment strategies.

Hedge portfolio A hypothetical combination of the derivative and its underlying that eliminates risk.

Held-to-maturity Debt (fixed-income) securities that a company intends to hold to maturity; these are presented at their original cost, updated for any amortisation of discounts or premiums.

Herding Clustered trading that may or may not be based on information.

Hidden order An order that is exposed not to the public but only to the brokers or exchanges that receive it.

High-frequency trading A form of algorithmic trading that makes use of vast quantities of data to execute trades on ultra-high-speed networks in fractions of a second.

High-water mark The highest value, net of fees, that a fund has reached in history. It reflects the highest cumulative return used to calculate an incentive fee.

Histogram A bar chart of data that have been grouped into a frequency distribution.

Historical cost In reference to assets, the amount paid to purchase an asset, including any costs of acquisition and/or preparation; with reference to liabilities, the amount of proceeds received in exchange in issuing the liability.

Historical equity risk premium approach An estimate of a country's equity risk premium that is based upon the historical averages of the risk-free rate and the rate of return on the market portfolio.

Historical simulation Another term for the historical method of estimating VaR. This term is somewhat misleading in that the method involves not a *simulation* of the past but rather what *actually happened* in the past, sometimes adjusted to reflect the fact that a different portfolio may have existed in the past than is planned for the future.

Holder-of-record date The date that a shareholder listed on the corporation's books will be deemed to have ownership of the shares for purposes of receiving an upcoming dividend.

Holding period return The return that an investor earns during a specified holding period; a synonym for total return.

Homogeneity of expectations The assumption that all investors have the same economic expectations and thus have the same expectations of prices, cash flows, and other investment characteristics.

Horizon yield The internal rate of return between the total return (the sum of reinvested coupon payments and the sale price or redemption amount) and the purchase price of the bond.

Horizontal analysis Common-size analysis that involves comparing a specific financial statement with that statement in prior or future time periods; also, cross-sectional analysis of one company with another.

Horizontal demand schedule Implies that at a given price, the response in the quantity demanded is infinite.

Hostile takeover An attempt by one entity to acquire a company without the consent of the company's management.

Household A person or a group of people living in the same residence, taken as a basic unit in economic analysis.

Human capital The accumulated knowledge and skill that workers acquire from education, training, or life experience and the corresponding present value of future earnings to be generated by said skilled individual.

Hurdle rate The rate of return that must be met for a project to be accepted.

Hypothesis With reference to statistical inference, a statement about one or more populations.

Hypothesis testing With reference to statistical inference, the subdivision dealing with the testing of hypotheses about one or more populations.

I-spread The yield spread of a specific bond over the standard swap rate in that currency of the same tenor.

Iceberg order An order in which the display size is less than the order's full size.

If-converted method A method for accounting for the effect of convertible securities on earnings per share (EPS) that specifies what EPS would have been if the convertible securities had been converted at the beginning of the period, taking account of the effects of conversion on net income and the weighted average number of shares outstanding.

Immediate or cancel order An order that is valid only upon receipt by the broker or exchange. If such an order cannot be filled in part or in whole upon receipt, it cancels immediately. Also called *fill or kill*.

Impact lag The lag associated with the result of actions affecting the economy with delay.

Implicit price deflator for GDP A gauge of prices and inflation that measures the aggregate changes in prices across the overall economy.

Implied forward rates Calculated from spot rates, an implied forward rate is a break-even reinvestment rate that links the return on an investment in a shorter-term zero-coupon bond to the return on an investment in a longer-term zero-coupon bond.

Implied volatility The volatility that option traders use to price an option, implied by the price of the option and a particular option-pricing model.

Import license Specifies the quantity of a good that can be imported into a country.

Imports Goods and services that a domestic economy (i.e., house-holds, firms, and government) purchases from other countries.

In the money Options that, if exercised, would result in the value received being worth more than the payment required to exercise.

Incentive fee Fees paid to the general partner from the limited partner(s) based on realized net profits.

Income Increases in economic benefits in the form of inflows or enhancements of assets, or decreases of liabilities that result in an increase in equity (other than increases resulting from contributions by owners).

Income elasticity of demand A measure of the responsiveness of demand to changes in income, defined as the percentage change in quantity demanded divided by the percentage change in income.

Income tax paid The actual amount paid for income taxes in the period; not a provision, but the actual cash outflow.

Income tax payable The income tax owed by the company on the basis of taxable income.

Income trust A type of equity ownership vehicle established as a trust issuing ownership shares known as units.

Increasing marginal returns When the marginal product of a resource increases as additional units of that input are employed.

Increasing returns to scale When a production process leads to increases in output that are proportionately larger than the increase in inputs.

Incremental cash flow The cash flow that is realized because of a decision; the changes or increments to cash flows resulting from a decision or action.

Indenture Legal contract that describes the form of a bond, the obligations of the issuer, and the rights of the bondholders. Also called the *trust deed*.

Independent With reference to events, the property that the occurrence of one event does not affect the probability of another event occurring.

Independent projects Independent projects are projects whose cash flows are independent of each other.

Independently and identically distributed (IID) With respect to random variables, the property of random variables that are independent of each other but follow the identical probability distribution.

Index-linked bond Bond for which coupon payments and/or principal repayment are linked to a specified index.

Index of Leading Economic Indicators A composite of economic variables used by analysts to predict future economic conditions.

Indexing An investment strategy in which an investor constructs a portfolio to mirror the performance of a specified index.

Indifference curve A curve representing all the combinations of two goods or attributes such that the consumer is entirely indifferent among them.

Indirect format With reference to cash flow statements, a format for the presentation of the statement which, in the operating cash flow section, begins with net income then shows additions and subtractions to arrive at operating cash flow. Also called *indirect method*.

Indirect method See *indirect format*.

Indirect taxes Taxes such as taxes on spending, as opposed to direct taxes.

Industry A group of companies offering similar products and/or services.

Industry analysis The analysis of a specific branch of manufacturing, service, or trade.

Inelastic Said of a good or service when the magnitude of elasticity is less than one. Insensitive to price changes.

Inferior goods A good whose consumption decreases as income increases.

Inflation The percentage increase in the general price level from one period to the next; a sustained rise in the overall level of prices in an economy.

Inflation-linked bond Type of index-linked bond that offers investors protection against inflation by linking the bond's coupon payments and/or the principal repayment to an index of consumer prices. Also called *linkers*.

Inflation premium An extra return that compensates investors for expected inflation.

Inflation rate The percentage change in a price index—that is, the speed of overall price level movements.

Inflation Reports A type of economic publication put out by many central banks.

Inflation uncertainty The degree to which economic agents view future rates of inflation as difficult to forecast.

Information cascade The transmission of information from those participants who act first and whose decisions influence the decisions of others.

Information-motivated traders Traders that trade to profit from information that they believe allows them to predict future prices.

Informationally efficient market A market in which asset prices reflect new information quickly and rationally.

Initial coin offering An unregulated process whereby companies raise capital by selling crypto tokens to investors in exchange for fiat money or another agreed-upon cryptocurrency.

Initial margin The amount that must be deposited in a clearinghouse account when entering into a futures contract.

Initial margin requirement The margin requirement on the first day of a transaction as well as on any day in which additional margin funds must be deposited.

Initial public offering (IPO) The first issuance of common shares to the public by a formerly private corporation.

Input productivity The amount of output produced by workers in a given period of time—for example, output per hour worked; measures the efficiency of labor.

Intangible assets Assets lacking physical substance, such as patents and trademarks.

Interbank market The market of loans and deposits between banks for maturities ranging from overnight to one year.

Interbank money market The market of loans and deposits between banks for maturities ranging from overnight to one year.

Interest Payment for lending funds.

Interest coverage A solvency ratio calculated as EBIT divided by interest payments.

Interest-only mortgage A loan in which no scheduled principal repayment is specified for a certain number of years.

Interest rate A rate of return that reflects the relationship between differently dated cash flows; a discount rate.

Interest rate swap A swap in which the underlying is an interest rate. Can be viewed as a currency swap in which both currencies are the same and can be created as a combination of currency swaps.

Intergenerational data mining A form of data mining that applies information developed by previous researchers using a dataset to guide current research using the same or a related dataset.

Intermarket analysis A field within technical analysis that combines analysis of major categories of securities—namely, equities, bonds, currencies, and commodities—to identify market trends and possible inflections in a trend.

Internal rate of return (IRR) The discount rate that makes net present value equal 0; the discount rate that makes the present value of an investment's costs (outflows) equal to the present value of the investment's benefits (inflows).

Internet of Things A network arrangement of structures and devices whereby the objects on the network are able to interact and share information.

Interpolated spread The yield spread of a specific bond over the standard swap rate in that currency of the same tenor.

Interquartile range The difference between the third and first quartiles of a dataset.

Interval With reference to grouped data, a set of values within which an observation falls.

Interval scale A measurement scale that not only ranks data but also gives assurance that the differences between scale values are equal.

Intrinsic value See *exercise value*.

Inventory blanket lien The use of inventory as collateral for a loan. Though the lender has claim to some or all of the company's inventory, the company may still sell or use the inventory in the ordinary course of business.

Inventory investment Net change in business inventory.

Inventory turnover An activity ratio calculated as cost of goods sold divided by average inventory.

Inverse demand function A restatement of the demand function in which price is stated as a function of quantity.

Inverse floater A type of leveraged structured financial instrument. The cash flows are adjusted periodically and move in the opposite direction of changes in the reference rate.

Investing activities Activities associated with the acquisition and disposal of property, plant, and equipment; intangible assets; other long-term assets; and both long-term and short-term investments in the equity and debt (bonds and loans) issued by other companies.

Investment banks Financial intermediaries that provide advice to their mostly corporate clients and help them arrange transactions such as initial and seasoned securities offerings.

Investment opportunity schedule A graphical depiction of a company's investment opportunities ordered from highest to lowest expected return. A company's optimal capital budget is found where the investment opportunity schedule intersects with the company's marginal cost of capital.

Investment policy statement (IPS) A written planning document that describes a client's investment objectives and risk tolerance over a relevant time horizon, along with constraints that apply to the client's portfolio.

Investment property Property used to earn rental income or capital appreciation (or both).

January effect Calendar anomaly that stock market returns in January are significantly higher compared to the rest of the months of the year, with most of the abnormal returns reported during the first five trading days in January. Also called *turn-of-the-year effect*.

Joint probability The probability of the joint occurrence of stated events.

Joint probability function A function giving the probability of joint occurrences of values of stated random variables.

Just-in-time (JIT) method Method of managing inventory that minimizes in-process inventory stocks.

Key rate duration A method of measuring the interest rate sensitivities of a fixed-income instrument or portfolio to shifts in key points along the yield curve.

Keynesians Economists who believe that fiscal policy can have powerful effects on aggregate demand, output, and employment when there is substantial spare capacity in an economy.

Kondratieff wave A 54-year long economic cycle postulated by Nikolai Kondratieff.

Kurtosis The statistical measure that indicates the combined weight of the tails of a distribution relative to the rest of the distribution.

Labor force The portion of the working age population (over the age of 16) that is employed or is available for work but not working (unemployed).

Labor productivity The quantity of goods and services (real GDP) that a worker can produce in one hour of work.

Laddering strategy A form of active strategy which entails scheduling maturities on a systematic basis within the investment portfolio such that investments are spread out equally over the term of the ladder.

Lagging economic indicators Turning points that take place later than those of the overall economy; they are believed to have value in identifying the economy's past condition.

Laspeyres index A price index created by holding the composition of the consumption basket constant.

Law of demand The principle that as the price of a good rises, buyers will choose to buy less of it, and as its price falls, they will buy more.

Law of diminishing marginal returns The observation that a variable factor's marginal product must eventually fall as more of it is added to a fixed amount of the other factors.

Law of diminishing returns The smallest output that a firm can produce such that its long run average costs are minimized.

Law of one price The condition in a financial market in which two equivalent financial instruments or combinations of financial instruments can sell for only one price. Equivalent to the principle that no arbitrage opportunities are possible.

Lead underwriter The lead investment bank in a syndicate of investment banks and broker–dealers involved in a securities underwriting.

Leading economic indicators Turning points that usually precede those of the overall economy; they are believed to have value for predicting the economy's future state, usually near-term.

Legal tender Something that must be accepted when offered in exchange for goods and services.

Lender of last resort An entity willing to lend money when no other entity is ready to do so.

Leptokurtic Describes a distribution that has fatter tails than a normal distribution.

Lessee The party obtaining the use of an asset through a lease.

Lessor The owner of an asset that grants the right to use the asset to another party.

Letter of credit Form of external credit enhancement whereby a financial institution provides the issuer with a credit line to reimburse any cash flow shortfalls from the assets backing the issue.

Level of significance The probability of a Type I error in testing a hypothesis.

Leverage In the context of corporate finance, leverage refers to the use of fixed costs within a company's cost structure. Fixed costs that are operating costs (such as depreciation or rent) create operating leverage. Fixed costs that are financial costs (such as interest expense) create financial leverage.

Leveraged buyout A transaction whereby the target company's management team converts the target to a privately held company by using heavy borrowing to finance the purchase of the target company's outstanding shares.

Liabilities Present obligations of an enterprise arising from past events, the settlement of which is expected to result in an outflow of resources embodying economic benefits; creditors' claims on the resources of a company.

Life-cycle stage The stage of the life cycle: embryonic, growth, shakeout, mature, declining.

LIFO layer liquidation With respect to the application of the LIFO inventory method, the liquidation of old, relatively low-priced inventory; happens when the volume of sales rises above the volume of recent purchases so that some sales are made from relatively old, low-priced inventory. Also called *LIFO liquidation*.

LIFO method The last in, first out, method of accounting for inventory, which matches sales against the costs of items of inventory in the reverse order the items were placed in inventory (i.e., inventory produced or acquired last are assumed to be sold first).

LIFO reserve The difference between the reported LIFO inventory carrying amount and the inventory amount that would have been reported if the FIFO method had been used (in other words, the FIFO inventory value less the LIFO inventory value).

Likelihood The probability of an observation, given a particular set of conditions.

Limit down A limit move in the futures market in which the price at which a transaction would be made is at or below the lower limit.

Limit order Instructions to a broker or exchange to obtain the best price immediately available when filling an order, but in no event accept a price higher than a specified (limit) price when buying or accept a price lower than a specified (limit) price when selling.

Limit order book The book or list of limit orders to buy and sell that pertains to a security.

Limit up A limit move in the futures market in which the price at which a transaction would be made is at or above the upper limit.

Limitations on liens Meant to put limits on how much secured debt an issuer can have.

Limited partners Partners with limited liability. Limited partnerships in hedge and private equity funds are typically restricted to investors who are expected to understand and to be able to assume the risks associated with the investments.

Line chart In technical analysis, a plot of price data, typically closing prices, with a line connecting the points.

Linear interpolation The estimation of an unknown value on the basis of two known values that bracket it, using a straight line between the two known values.

Linear scale A scale in which equal distances correspond to equal absolute amounts. Also called *arithmetic scale*.

Linker See *inflation-linked bond*.

Liquid market Said of a market in which traders can buy or sell with low total transaction costs when they want to trade.

Liquidation To sell the assets of a company, division, or subsidiary piecemeal, typically because of bankruptcy; the form of bankruptcy that allows for the orderly satisfaction of creditors' claims after which the company ceases to exist.

Liquidity The ability to purchase or sell an asset quickly and easily at a price close to fair market value. The ability to meet short-term obligations using assets that are the most readily converted into cash.

Liquidity premium An extra return that compensates investors for the risk of loss relative to an investment's fair value if the investment needs to be converted to cash quickly.

Liquidity ratios Financial ratios measuring the company's ability to meet its short-term obligations.

Liquidity risk The risk that a financial instrument cannot be purchased or sold without a significant concession in price due to the size of the market.

Liquidity trap A condition in which the demand for money becomes infinitely elastic (horizontal demand curve) so that injections of money into the economy will not lower interest rates or affect real activity.

Load fund A mutual fund in which, in addition to the annual fee, a percentage fee is charged to invest in the fund and/or for redemptions from the fund.

Loan-to-value ratio The ratio of a property's purchase price to the amount of its mortgage.

Lockbox system A payment system in which customer payments are mailed to a post office box and the banking institution retrieves and deposits these payments several times a day, enabling the company to have use of the fund sooner than in a centralized system in which customer payments are sent to the company.

Locked limit A condition in the futures markets in which a transaction cannot take place because the price would be beyond the limits.

Lockup period The minimum holding period before investors are allowed to make withdrawals or redeem shares from a fund.

Logarithmic scale A scale in which equal distances represent equal proportional changes in the underlying quantity.

London interbank offered rate (Libor) Collective name for multiple rates at which a select set of banks believe they could borrow unsecured funds from other banks in the London interbank market for different currencies and different borrowing periods ranging from overnight to one year.

Long The buyer of a derivative contract. Also refers to the position of owning a derivative.

Long-lived assets Assets that are expected to provide economic benefits over a future period of time, typically greater than one year. Also called *long-term assets.*

Long position A position in an asset or contract in which one owns the asset or has an exercisable right under the contract.

Long-run average total cost The curve describing average total cost when no costs are considered fixed.

Longitudinal data Observations on characteristic(s) of the same observational unit through time.

Look-ahead bias A bias caused by using information that was unavailable on the test date.

Loss aversion The tendency of people to dislike losses more than they like comparable gains.

Loss severity Portion of a bond's value (including unpaid interest) an investor loses in the event of default.

Losses Asset outflows not directly related to the ordinary activities of the business.

Lower bound The lowest possible value of an option.

M^2 A measure of what a portfolio would have returned if it had taken on the same total risk as the market index.

M^2 alpha Difference between the risk-adjusted performance of the portfolio and the performance of the benchmark.

Macaulay duration The approximate amount of time a bond would have to be held for the market discount rate at purchase to be realized if there is a single change in interest rate. It indicates the point in time when the coupon reinvestment and price effects of a change in yield-to- maturity offset each other.

Machine learning Computer based techniques that seek to extract knowledge from large amounts of data by "learning" from known examples and then generating structure or predictions. ML algorithms aim to "find the pattern, apply the pattern."

Macroeconomics The branch of economics that deals with aggregate economic quantities, such as national output and national income.

Maintenance covenants Covenants in bank loan agreements that require the borrower to satisfy certain financial ratio tests while the loan is outstanding.

Maintenance margin The minimum amount that is required by a futures clearinghouse to maintain a margin account and to protect against default. Participants whose margin balances drop below the required maintenance margin must replenish their accounts.

Maintenance margin requirement The margin requirement on any day other than the first day of a transaction.

Management buy-ins Leveraged buyout in which the current management team is being replaced and the acquiring team will be involved in managing the company.

Management buyout A leveraged buyout event in which a group of investors consisting primarily of the company's existing management purchase at least controlling interest in its outstanding shares. At the extreme, they may purchase all shares and take the company private.

Management fee A fee based on assets under management or committed capital, as applicable, also called a *base fee.*

Manufacturing resource planning (MRP) The incorporation of production planning into inventory management. A MRP analysis provides both a materials acquisition schedule and a production schedule.

Margin The amount of money that a trader deposits in a margin account. The term is derived from the stock market practice in which an investor borrows a portion of the money required to purchase a certain amount of stock. In futures markets, there is no borrowing so the margin is more of a down payment or performance bond.

Margin bond A cash deposit required by the clearinghouse from the participants to a contract to provide a credit guarantee. Also called a *performance bond.*

Margin call A request for the short to deposit additional funds to bring their balance up to the initial margin.

Margin loan Money borrowed from a broker to purchase securities.

Marginal cost The cost of producing an additional unit of a good.

Marginal probability The probability of an event *not* conditioned on another event.

Marginal product Measures the productivity of each unit of input and is calculated by taking the difference in total product from adding another unit of input (assuming other resource quantities are held constant).

Marginal propensity to consume The proportion of an additional unit of disposable income that is consumed or spent; the change in consumption for a small change in income.

Marginal propensity to save The proportion of an additional unit of disposable income that is saved (not spent).

Marginal revenue The change in total revenue divided by the change in quantity sold; simply, the additional revenue from selling one more unit.

Marginal value curve A curve describing the highest price consumers are willing to pay for each additional unit of a good.

Mark to market The revaluation of a financial asset or liability to its current market value or fair value.

Market anomaly Change in the price or return of a security that cannot directly be linked to current relevant information known in the market or to the release of new information into the market.

Market bid–ask spread The difference between the best bid and the best offer.

Market-capitalization weighting An index weighting method in which the weight assigned to each constituent security is determined by dividing its market capitalization by the total market capitalization (sum of the market capitalization) of all securities in the index. Also called *value weighting*.

Market discount rate The rate of return required by investors given the risk of the investment in a bond; also called the *required yield* or the *required rate of return*.

Market float The number of shares that are available to the investing public.

Market liquidity risk The risk that the price at which investors can actually transact—buying or selling—may differ from the price indicated in the market.

Market model A regression equation that specifies a linear relationship between the return on a security (or portfolio) and the return on a broad market index.

Market multiple models Valuation models based on share price multiples or enterprise value multiples.

Market-on-close An execution instruction specifying that an order can only be filled at the close of trading.

Market order Instructions to a broker or exchange to obtain the best price immediately available when filling an order.

Market-oriented investors With reference to equity investors, investors whose investment disciplines cannot be clearly categorized as value or growth.

Market rate of interest The rate demanded by purchasers of bonds, given the risks associated with future cash payment obligations of the particular bond issue.

Market risk The risk that arises from movements in interest rates, stock prices, exchange rates, and commodity prices.

Market value The price at which an asset or security can currently be bought or sold in an open market.

Marketable limit order A buy limit order in which the limit price is placed above the best offer, or a sell limit order in which the limit price is placed below the best bid. Such orders generally will partially or completely fill right away.

Markowitz efficient frontier The graph of the set of portfolios offering the maximum expected return for their level of risk (standard deviation of return).

Matching principle The accounting principle that expenses should be recognized in the same period in which the associated revenue is recognized.

Matching strategy An active investment strategy that includes intentional matching of the timing of cash outflows with investment maturities.

Matrix pricing Process of estimating the market discount rate and price of a bond based on the quoted or flat prices of more frequently traded comparable bonds.

Maturity premium An extra return that compensates investors for the increased sensitivity of the market value of debt to a change in market interest rates as maturity is extended.

Maturity structure A factor explaining the differences in yields on similar bonds; also called *term structure*.

Mean absolute deviation With reference to a sample, the mean of the absolute values of deviations from the sample mean.

Mean–variance analysis An approach to portfolio analysis using expected means, variances, and covariances of asset returns.

Measure of central tendency A quantitative measure that specifies where data are centered.

Measure of value A standard for measuring value; a function of money.

Measurement scales A scheme of measuring differences. The four types of measurement scales are nominal, ordinal, interval, and ratio.

Measures of location A quantitative measure that describes the location or distribution of data; includes not only measures of central tendency but also other measures such as percentiles.

Median The value of the middle item of a set of items that has been sorted into ascending or descending order; the 50th percentile.

Medium of exchange Any asset that can be used to purchase goods and services or to repay debts; a function of money.

Medium-term note A corporate bond offered continuously to investors by an agent of the issuer, designed to fill the funding gap between commercial paper and long-term bonds.

Menu costs A cost of inflation in which businesses constantly have to incur the costs of changing the advertised prices of their goods and services.

Mesokurtic Describes a distribution with kurtosis identical to that of the normal distribution.

Mezzanine financing Debt or preferred shares with a relationship to common equity resulting from a feature such as attached warrants or conversion options. Mezzanine financing is subordinate to both senior and high-yield debt but is senior to equity. It is referred to as "mezzanine" because of its location on the balance sheet.

Microeconomics The branch of economics that deals with markets and decision making of individual economic units, including consumers and businesses.

Minimum efficient scale The smallest output that a firm can produce such that its long-run average total cost is minimized.

Minimum-variance portfolio The portfolio with the minimum variance for each given level of expected return.

Minority shareholders A particular shareholder or block of shareholders holding a small proportion of a company's outstanding shares, resulting in a limited ability to exercise control in voting activities.

Minsky moment Named for Hyman Minksy: A point in a business cycle when, after individuals become overextended in borrowing to finance speculative investments, people start realizing that something is likely to go wrong and a panic ensues leading to asset sell-offs.

Mismatching strategy An active investment strategy whereby the timing of cash outflows is not matched with investment maturities.

Modal interval With reference to grouped data, the most frequently occurring interval.

Mode The most frequently occurring value in a set of observations.

Modern portfolio theory (MPT) The analysis of rational portfolio choices based on the efficient use of risk.

Modified duration A measure of the percentage price change of a bond given a change in its yield-to-maturity.

Momentum oscillators A graphical representation of market sentiment that is constructed from price data and calculated so that it oscillates either between a high and a low or around some number.

Monetarists Economists who believe that the rate of growth of the money supply is the primary determinant of the rate of inflation.

Monetary policy Actions taken by a nation's central bank to affect aggregate output and prices through changes in bank reserves, reserve requirements, or its target interest rate.

Monetary transmission mechanism The process whereby a central bank's interest rate gets transmitted through the economy and ultimately affects the rate of increase of prices.

Monetary union An economic union in which the members adopt a common currency.

Money A generally accepted medium of exchange and unit of account.

Money convexity For a bond, the annual or approximate convexity multiplied by the full price.

Money creation The process by which changes in bank reserves translate into changes in the money supply.

Money duration A measure of the price change in units of the currency in which the bond is denominated given a change in its yield-to-maturity.

Money market The market for short-term debt instruments (one-year maturity or less).

Money market securities Fixed-income securities with maturities at issuance of one year or less.

Money market yield A yield on a basis comparable to the quoted yield on an interest-bearing money market instrument that pays interest on a 360-day basis; the annualized holding period yield, assuming a 360-day year.

Money multiplier Describes how a change in reserves is expected to affect the money supply; in its simplest form, 1 divided by the reserve requirement.

Money neutrality The thesis that an increase in the money supply leads in the long-run to an increase in the price level, while leaving real variables like output and employment unaffected.

Money-weighted return The internal rate of return on a portfolio, taking account of all cash flows.

Moneyness The relationship between the price of the underlying and an option's exercise price.

Monopolistic competition Highly competitive form of imperfect competition; the competitive characteristic is a notably large number of firms, while the monopoly aspect is the result of product differentiation.

Monopoly In pure monopoly markets, there are no substitutes for the given product or service. There is a single seller, which exercises considerable power over pricing and output decisions.

Monte Carlo simulation An approach to estimating a probability distribution of outcomes to examine what might happen if particular risks are faced. This method is widely used in the sciences as well as in business to study a variety of problems.

Moral principles Beliefs regarding what is good, acceptable, or obligatory behavior and what is bad, unacceptable, or forbidden behavior.

Mortgage-backed securities Debt obligations that represent claims to the cash flows from pools of mortgage loans, most commonly on residential property.

Mortgage loan A loan secured by the collateral of some specified real estate property that obliges the borrower to make a predetermined series of payments to the lender.

Mortgage pass-through security A security created when one or more holders of mortgages form a pool of mortgages and sell shares or participation certificates in the pool.

Mortgage rate The interest rate on a mortgage loan; also called *contract rate* or *note rate*.

Moving average The average of the closing price of a security over a specified number of periods. With each new period, the average is recalculated.

Moving-average convergence/divergence oscillator (MACD) A momentum oscillator that is constructed based on the difference between short-term and long-term moving averages of a security's price.

Multi-factor model A model that explains a variable in terms of the values of a set of factors.

Multi-market indexes Comprised of indexes from different countries, designed to represent multiple security markets.

Multi-step format With respect to the format of the income statement, a format that presents a subtotal for gross profit (revenue minus cost of goods sold).

Multilateral trading facilities See *alternative trading systems*.

Multinational corporation A company operating in more than one country or having subsidiary firms in more than one country.

Multiplication rule for probabilities The rule that the joint probability of events A and B equals the probability of A given B times the probability of B.

Multiplier models Valuation models based on share price multiples or enterprise value multiples.

Multivariate distribution A probability distribution that specifies the probabilities for a group of related random variables.

Multivariate normal distribution A probability distribution for a group of random variables that is completely defined by the means and variances of the variables plus all the correlations between pairs of the variables.

Municipal bonds A type of non-sovereign bond issued by a state or local government in the United States. It very often (but not always) offers income tax exemptions.

Munis A type of non-sovereign bond issued by a state or local government in the United States. It very often (but not always) offers income tax exemptions.

Mutual fund A comingled investment pool in which investors in the fund each have a pro-rata claim on the income and value of the fund.

Mutually exclusive projects Mutually exclusive projects compete directly with each other. For example, if Projects A and B are mutually exclusive, you can choose A or B, but you cannot choose both.

***n* Factorial** For a positive integer n, the product of the first n positive integers; 0 factorial equals 1 by definition. n factorial is written as $n!$.

Narrow money The notes and coins in circulation in an economy, plus other very highly liquid deposits.

Nash equilibrium When two or more participants in a non-coop-erative game have no incentive to deviate from their respective equilibrium strategies given their opponent's strategies.

National income The income received by all factors of production used in the generation of final output. National income equals gross domestic product (or, in some countries, gross national product) minus the capital consumption allowance and a statistical discrepancy.

Natural language processing Computer programs developed to analyze and interpret human language.

Natural rate of unemployment Effective unemployment rate, below which pressure emerges in labor markets.

Negative screening An ESG investment style that focuses on the exclusion of certain sectors, companies, or practices in a fund or portfolio on the basis of specific ESG criteria.

Neo-Keynesians A group of dynamic general equilibrium models that assume slow-to-adjust prices and wages.

Net book value The remaining (undepreciated) balance of an asset's purchase cost. For liabilities, the face value of a bond minus any unamortized discount, or plus any unamortized premium.

Net exports The difference between the value of a country's exports and the value of its imports (i.e., value of exports minus imports).

Net income The difference between revenue and expenses; what remains after subtracting all expenses (including depreciation, interest, and taxes) from revenue.

Net operating cycle An estimate of the average time that elapses between paying suppliers for materials and collecting cash from the subsequent sale of goods produced.

Net present value (NPV) The present value of an investment's cash inflows (benefits) minus the present value of its cash outflows (costs).

Net profit margin An indicator of profitability, calculated as net income divided by revenue; indicates how much of each dollar of revenues is left after all costs and expenses. Also called *profit margin* or *return on sales.*

Net realisable value Estimated selling price in the ordinary course of business less the estimated costs necessary to make the sale.

Net revenue Revenue after adjustments (e.g., for estimated returns or for amounts unlikely to be collected).

Net tax rate The tax rate net of transfer payments.

Neural networks Computer programs based on how our own brains learn and process information.

Neutral rate of interest The rate of interest that neither spurs on nor slows down the underlying economy.

New classical macroeconomics An approach to macroeconomics that seeks the macroeconomic conclusions of individuals maximizing utility on the basis of rational expectations and companies maximizing profits.

New Keynesians A group of dynamic general equilibrium models that assume slow-to-adjust prices and wages.

No-load fund A mutual fund in which there is no fee for investing in the fund or for redeeming fund shares, although there is an annual fee based on a percentage of the fund's net asset value.

Node Each value on a binomial tree from which successive moves or outcomes branch.

Nominal GDP The value of goods and services measured at current prices.

Nominal rate A rate of interest based on the security's face value.

Nominal risk-free interest rate The sum of the real risk-free interest rate and the inflation premium.

Nominal scale A measurement scale that categorizes data but does not rank them.

Non-accelerating inflation rate of unemployment Effective unemployment rate, below which pressure emerges in labor markets.

Non-agency RMBS In the United States, securities issued by private entities that are not guaranteed by a federal agency or a GSE.

Non-cumulative preference shares Preference shares for which dividends that are not paid in the current or subsequent periods are forfeited permanently (instead of being accrued and paid at a later date).

Non-current assets Assets that are expected to benefit the company over an extended period of time (usually more than one year).

Non-current liabilities Obligations that broadly represent a probable sacrifice of economic benefits in periods generally greater than one year in the future.

Non-cyclical A company whose performance is largely independent of the business cycle.

Non-deliverable forwards Cash-settled forward contracts, used predominately with respect to foreign exchange forwards. Also called *contracts for differences.*

Non-financial risks Risks that arise from sources other than changes in the external financial markets, such as changes in accounting rules, legal environment, or tax rates.

Non-participating preference shares Preference shares that do not entitle shareholders to share in the profits of the company. Instead, shareholders are only entitled to receive a fixed dividend payment and the par value of the shares in the event of liquidation.

Non-recourse loan Loan in which the lender does not have a shortfall claim against the borrower, so the lender can look only to the property to recover the outstanding mortgage balance.

Non-renewable resources Finite resources that are depleted once they are consumed, such as oil and coal.

Non-sovereign bonds A bond issued by a government below the national level, such as a province, region, state, or city.

Non-sovereign government bonds A bond issued by a government below the national level, such as a province, region, state, or city.

Nonconventional cash flow In a nonconventional cash flow pattern, the initial outflow is not followed by inflows only, but the cash flows can flip from positive (inflows) to negative (outflows) again (or even change signs several times).

Nonparametric test A test that is not concerned with a parameter, or that makes minimal assumptions about the population from which a sample comes.

Nonsystematic risk Unique risk that is local or limited to a particular asset or industry that need not affect assets outside of that asset class.

Normal distribution A continuous, symmetric probability distribution that is completely described by its mean and its variance.

Normal goods Goods that are consumed in greater quantities as income increases.

Normal profit The level of accounting profit needed to just cover the implicit opportunity costs ignored in accounting costs.

Notching Ratings adjustment methodology where specific issues from the same borrower may be assigned different credit ratings.

Note rate See *mortgage rate.*

Notice period The length of time (typically 30–90 days) in advance that investors may be required to notify a fund of their intent to redeem some or all of their investment.

Notional principal An imputed principal amount.

Number of days of inventory An activity ratio equal to the number of days in a period divided by the inventory ratio for the period; an indication of the number of days a company ties up funds in inventory.

Number of days of payables An activity ratio equal to the number of days in a period divided by the payables turnover ratio for the period; an estimate of the average number of days it takes a company to pay its suppliers.

Number of days of receivables Estimate of the average number of days it takes to collect on credit accounts.

Objective probabilities Probabilities that generally do not vary from person to person; includes a priori and objective probabilities.

Off-the-run Seasoned government bonds are off-the-run securities; they are not the most recently issued or the most actively traded.

Offer The price at which a dealer or trader is willing to sell an asset, typically qualified by a maximum quantity (ask size).

Official interest rate An interest rate that a central bank sets and announces publicly; normally the rate at which it is willing to lend money to the commercial banks. Also called *official policy rate* or *policy rate.*

Official policy rate An interest rate that a central bank sets and announces publicly; normally the rate at which it is willing to lend money to the commercial banks.

Oligopoly Market structure with a relatively small number of firms supplying the market.

On-the-run The most recently issued and most actively traded sovereign securities.

One-sided hypothesis test A test in which the null hypothesis is rejected only if the evidence indicates that the population parameter is greater than (smaller than) θ_0. The alternative hypothesis also has one side.

One-tailed hypothesis test A test in which the null hypothesis is rejected only if the evidence indicates that the population parameter is greater than (smaller than) θ_0. The alternative hypothesis also has one side.

Open economy An economy that trades with other countries.

Open-end fund A mutual fund that accepts new investment money and issues additional shares at a value equal to the net asset value of the fund at the time of investment.

Open interest The number of outstanding contracts in a clearinghouse at any given time. The open interest figure changes daily as some parties open up new positions, while other parties offset their old positions.

Open market operations The purchase or sale of bonds by the national central bank to implement monetary policy. The bonds traded are usually sovereign bonds issued by the national government.

Operating activities Activities that are part of the day-to-day business functioning of an entity, such as selling inventory and providing services.

Operating breakeven The number of units produced and sold at which the company's operating profit is zero (revenues = operating costs).

Operating cash flow The net amount of cash provided from operating activities.

Operating cycle A measure of the time needed to convert raw materials into cash from a sale; it consists of the number of days of inventory and the number of days of receivables.

Operating efficiency ratios Ratios that measure how efficiently a company performs day-to-day tasks, such as the collection of receivables and management of inventory.

Operating lease An agreement allowing a lessee to use some asset for a period of time; essentially a rental.

Operating leverage The use of fixed costs in operations.

Operating profit A company's profits on its usual business activities before deducting taxes. Also called *operating income.*

Operating profit margin A profitability ratio calculated as operating income (i.e., income before interest and taxes) divided by revenue. Also called *operating margin.*

Operating risk The risk attributed to the operating cost structure, in particular the use of fixed costs in operations; the risk arising from the mix of fixed and variable costs; the risk that a company's operations may be severely affected by environmental, social, and governance risk factors.

Operational independence A bank's ability to execute monetary policy and set interest rates in the way it thought would best meet the inflation target.

Operational risk The risk that arises from inadequate or failed people, systems, and internal policies, procedures, and processes, as well as from external events that are beyond the control of the organization but that affect its operations.

Operationally efficient Said of a market, a financial system, or an economy that has relatively low transaction costs.

Opportunity cost The value that investors forgo by choosing a particular course of action; the value of something in its best alternative use.

Option A financial instrument that gives one party the right, but not the obligation, to buy or sell an underlying asset from or to another party at a fixed price over a specific period of time. Also referred to as *contingent claim* or *option contract.*

Option-adjusted price The value of the embedded option plus the flat price of the bond.

Option-adjusted spread OAS = Z-spread – Option value (in basis points per year).

Option-adjusted yield The required market discount rate whereby the price is adjusted for the value of the embedded option.

Option contract See *option.*

Option premium The amount of money a buyer pays and seller receives to engage in an option transaction.

Order A specification of what instrument to trade, how much to trade, and whether to buy or sell.

Order-driven markets A market (generally an auction market) that uses rules to arrange trades based on the orders that traders submit; in their pure form, such markets do not make use of dealers.

Order precedence hierarchy With respect to the execution of orders to trade, a set of rules that determines which orders execute before other orders.

Ordinal scale A measurement scale that sorts data into categories that are ordered (ranked) with respect to some characteristic.

Ordinary annuity An annuity with a first cash flow that is paid one period from the present.

Ordinary shares Equity shares that are subordinate to all other types of equity (e.g., preferred equity). Also called *common stock* or *common shares*.

Organized exchange A securities marketplace where buyers and seller can meet to arrange their trades.

Other comprehensive income Items of comprehensive income that are not reported on the income statement; comprehensive income minus net income.

Out-of-sample test A test of a strategy or model using a sample outside the time period on which the strategy or model was developed.

Out of the money Options that, if exercised, would require the payment of more money than the value received and therefore would not be currently exercised.

Outcome A possible value of a random variable.

Over-the-counter (OTC) markets A decentralized market where buy and sell orders initiated from various locations are matched through a communications network.

Overbought A market condition in which market sentiment is thought to be unsustainably bullish.

Overcollateralization Form of internal credit enhancement that refers to the process of posting more collateral than needed to obtain or secure financing.

Overfitting An undesirable result from fitting a model so closely to a dataset that it does not perform well on new data.

Overlay/portfolio tilt An ESG investment style that focuses on the use of certain investment strategies or products to change specific aggregate ESG characteristics of a fund or investment portfolio to a desired level (e.g., tilting an investment portfolio toward a desired carbon footprint).

Oversold A market condition in which market sentiment is thought to be unsustainably bearish.

Own price The price of a good or service itself (as opposed to the price of something else).

Own-price elasticity of demand The percentage change in quantity demanded for a percentage change in good's own price, holding all other things constant.

Owners' equity The excess of assets over liabilities; the residual interest of shareholders in the assets of an entity after deducting the entity's liabilities. Also called *shareholders' equity* or *shareholders' funds*.

Paasche index An index formula using the current composition of a basket of products.

Paired comparisons test A statistical test for differences based on paired observations drawn from samples that are dependent on each other.

Paired observations Observations that are dependent on each other.

Pairs arbitrage trade A trade in two closely related stocks involving the short sale of one and the purchase of the other.

Panel data Observations through time on a single characteristic of multiple observational units.

Par curve A sequence of yields-to-maturity such that each bond is priced at par value. The bonds are assumed to have the same currency, credit risk, liquidity, tax status, and annual yields stated for the same periodicity.

Par value The amount of principal on a bond.

Parallel shift A parallel yield curve shift implies that all rates change by the same amount in the same direction.

Parameter A descriptive measure computed from or used to describe a population of data, conventionally represented by Greek letters.

Parametric test Any test (or procedure) concerned with parameters or whose validity depends on assumptions concerning the population generating the sample.

Pari passu On an equal footing.

Partial duration See *key rate duration.*

Participating preference shares Preference shares that entitle shareholders to receive the standard preferred dividend plus the opportunity to receive an additional dividend if the company's profits exceed a pre-specified level.

Pass-through rate The coupon rate of a mortgage pass-through security.

Passive investment A buy and hold approach in which an investor does not make portfolio changes based on short-term expectations of changing market or security performance.

Passive strategy In reference to short-term cash management, it is an investment strategy characterized by simple decision rules for making daily investments.

Payable date The day that the company actually mails out (or electronically transfers) a dividend payment.

Payback period the number of years required to recover the original investment in a project. The payback is based on cash flows.

Payment date The day that the company actually mails out (or electronically transfers) a dividend payment.

Payments system The system for the transfer of money.

Peak The highest point of a business cycle.

Peer group A group of companies engaged in similar business activities whose economics and valuation are influenced by closely related factors.

Pennants A technical analysis continuation pattern formed by trendlines that converge to form a triangle, typically over a short period.

Per capita real GDP Real GDP divided by the size of the population, often used as a measure of the average standard of living in a country.

Per unit contribution margin The amount that each unit sold contributes to covering fixed costs—that is, the difference between the price per unit and the variable cost per unit.

Percentiles Quantiles that divide a distribution into 100 equal parts.

Perfect competition A market structure in which the individual firm has virtually no impact on market price, because it is assumed to be a very small seller among a very large number of firms selling essentially identical products.

Perfectly elastic When the quantity demanded or supplied of a given good is infinitely sensitive to a change in the value of a specified variable (e.g., price).

Perfectly inelastic When the quantity demanded or supplied of a given good is completely insensitive to a change in the value of a specified variable (e.g., price).

Performance bond See *margin bond.*

Performance evaluation The measurement and assessment of the outcomes of investment management decisions.

Performance fee Fees paid to the general partner from the limited partner(s) based on realized net profits.

Period costs Costs (e.g., executives' salaries) that cannot be directly matched with the timing of revenues and which are thus expensed immediately.

Periodicity The assumed number of periods in the year, typically matches the frequency of coupon payments.

Permanent differences Differences between tax and financial reporting of revenue (expenses) that will not be reversed at some future date. These result in a difference between the company's effective tax rate and statutory tax rate and do not result in a deferred tax item.

Permissioned networks Networks that are fully open only to select participants on a DLT network.

Permissionless networks Networks that are fully open to any user on a DLT network.

Permutation An ordered listing.

Perpetual bonds Bonds with no stated maturity date.

Perpetuity A perpetual annuity, or a set of never-ending level sequential cash flows, with the first cash flow occurring one period from now. A bond that does not mature.

Personal consumption expenditures All domestic personal consumption; the basis for a price index for such consumption called the PCE price index.

Personal disposable income Equal to personal income less personal taxes.

Personal income A broad measure of household income that includes all income received by households, whether earned or unearned; measures the ability of consumers to make purchases.

Plain vanilla bond Bond that makes periodic, fixed coupon payments during the bond's life and a lump-sum payment of principal at maturity. Also called *conventional bond.*

Platykurtic Describes a distribution that has relatively less weight in the tails than the normal distribution.

Point and figure chart A technical analysis chart that is constructed with columns of X's alternating with columns of O's such that the horizontal axis represents only the number of changes in price without reference to time or volume.

Point estimate A single numerical estimate of an unknown quantity, such as a population parameter.

Point of sale (POS) Systems that capture transaction data at the physical location in which the sale is made.

Policy rate An interest rate that a central bank sets and announces publicly; normally the rate at which it is willing to lend money to the commercial banks.

Population All members of a specified group.

Population mean The arithmetic mean value of a population; the arithmetic mean of all the observations or values in the population.

Population standard deviation A measure of dispersion relating to a population in the same unit of measurement as the observations, calculated as the positive square root of the population variance.

Population variance A measure of dispersion relating to a population, calculated as the mean of the squared deviations around the population mean.

Portfolio company In private equity, the company in which the private equity fund is investing.

Portfolio demand for money The demand to hold speculative money balances based on the potential opportunities or risks that are inherent in other financial instruments.

Portfolio planning The process of creating a plan for building a portfolio that is expected to satisfy a client's investment objectives.

Position The quantity of an asset that an entity owns or owes.

Positive screening An ESG investment style that focuses on the inclusion of certain sectors, companies, or practices in a fund or portfolio on the basis of specific minimum ESG criteria.

Posterior probability An updated probability that reflects or comes after new information.

Potential GDP The level of real GDP that can be produced at full employment; measures the productive capacity of the economy.

Power of a test The probability of correctly rejecting the null—that is, rejecting the null hypothesis when it is false.

Precautionary money balances Money held to provide a buffer against unforeseen events that might require money.

Precautionary stocks A level of inventory beyond anticipated needs that provides a cushion in the event that it takes longer to replenish inventory than expected or in the case of greater than expected demand.

Preference shares A type of equity interest which ranks above common shares with respect to the payment of dividends and the distribution of the company's net assets upon liquidation. They have characteristics of both debt and equity securities. Also called *preferred stock.*

Preferred stock See *preference shares.*

Premium In the case of bonds, premium refers to the amount by which a bond is priced above its face (par) value. In the case of an option, the amount paid for the option contract.

Prepaid expense A normal operating expense that has been paid in advance of when it is due.

Prepayment option Contractual provision that entitles the borrower to prepay all or part of the outstanding mortgage principal prior to the scheduled due date when the principal must be repaid. Also called *early repayment option.*

Prepayment penalty mortgages Mortgages that stipulate a monetary penalty if a borrower prepays within a certain time period after the mortgage is originated.

Prepayment risk The uncertainty that the timing of the actual cash flows will be different from the scheduled cash flows as set forth in the loan agreement due to the borrowers' ability to alter payments, usually to take advantage of interest rate movements.

Present value (PV) The present discounted value of future cash flows: For assets, the present discounted value of the future net cash inflows that the asset is expected to generate; for liabilities, the present discounted value of the future net cash outflows that are expected to be required to settle the liabilities.

Present value models Valuation models that estimate the intrinsic value of a security as the present value of the future benefits expected to be received from the security. Also called *discounted cash flow models.*

Pretax margin A profitability ratio calculated as earnings before taxes divided by revenue.

Price elasticity of demand Measures the percentage change in the quantity demanded, given a percentage change in the price of a given product.

Price index Represents the average prices of a basket of goods and services.

Price limits Limits imposed by a futures exchange on the price change that can occur from one day to the next.

Price multiple A ratio that compares the share price with some sort of monetary flow or value to allow evaluation of the relative worth of a company's stock.

Price priority The principle that the highest priced buy orders and the lowest priced sell orders execute first.

Price relative A ratio of an ending price over a beginning price; it is equal to 1 plus the holding period return on the asset.

Price return Measures *only* the price appreciation or percentage change in price of the securities in an index or portfolio.

Price return index An index that reflects *only* the price appreciation or percentage change in price of the constituent securities. Also called *price index.*

Price stability In economics, refers to an inflation rate that is low on average and not subject to wide fluctuation.

Price takers Producers that must accept whatever price the market dictates.

Price to book value A valuation ratio calculated as price per share divided by book value per share.

Price to cash flow A valuation ratio calculated as price per share divided by cash flow per share.

Price to earnings ratio (P/E ratio or P/E) The ratio of share price to earnings per share.

Price to sales A valuation ratio calculated as price per share divided by sales per share.

Price value of a basis point A version of money duration, it is an estimate of the change in the full price of a bond given a 1 basis point change in the yield-to-maturity.

Price weighting An index weighting method in which the weight assigned to each constituent security is determined by dividing its price by the sum of all the prices of the constituent securities.

Priced risk Risk for which investors demand compensation for bearing (e.g. equity risk, company-specific factors, macroeconomic factors).

Primary bond markets Markets in which issuers first sell bonds to investors to raise capital.

Primary capital markets (primary markets) The market where securities are first sold and the issuers receive the proceeds.

Primary dealers Financial institutions that are authorized to deal in new issues of sovereign bonds and that serve primarily as trading counterparties of the office responsible for issuing sovereign bonds.

Primary market The market where securities are first sold and the issuers receive the proceeds.

Prime brokers Brokers that provide services that commonly include custody, administration, lending, short borrowing, and trading.

Principal The amount of funds originally invested in a project or instrument; the face value to be paid at maturity.

Principal–agent relationship A relationship in which a principal hires an agent to perform a particular task or service; also known as an *agency relationship.*

Principal amount Amount that an issuer agrees to repay the debt holders on the maturity date.

Principal business activity The business activity from which a company derives a majority of its revenues and/or earnings.

Principal value Amount that an issuer agrees to repay the debt holders on the maturity date.

Principle of no arbitrage See *arbitrage-free pricing.*

Prior probabilities Probabilities reflecting beliefs prior to the arrival of new information.

Priority of claims Priority of payment, with the most senior or highest ranking debt having the first claim on the cash flows and assets of the issuer.

Private equity fund A hedge fund that seeks to buy, optimize, and ultimately sell portfolio companies to generate profits. See *venture capital fund.*

Private equity securities Securities that are not listed on public exchanges and have no active secondary market. They are issued primarily to institutional investors via non-public offerings, such as private placements.

Private investment in public equity (PIPE) An investment in the equity of a publicly traded firm that is made at a discount to the market value of the firm's shares.

Private placement Typically, a non-underwritten, unregistered offering of securities that are sold only to an investor or a small group of investors. It can be accomplished directly between the issuer and the investor(s) or through an investment bank.

Probability A number between 0 and 1 describing the chance that a stated event will occur.

Probability density function A function with non-negative values such that probability can be described by areas under the curve graphing the function.

Probability distribution A distribution that specifies the probabilities of a random variable's possible outcomes.

Probability function A function that specifies the probability that the random variable takes on a specific value.

Producer price index Reflects the price changes experienced by domestic producers in a country.

Production function Provides the quantitative link between the levels of output that the economy can produce and the inputs used in the production process.

Productivity The amount of output produced by workers in a given period of time—for example, output per hour worked; measures the efficiency of labor.

Profession An occupational group that has specific education, expert knowledge, and a framework of practice and behavior that underpins community trust, respect, and recognition.

Profit The return that owners of a company receive for the use of their capital and the assumption of financial risk when making their investments.

Profit and loss (P&L) statement A financial statement that provides information about a company's profitability over a stated period of time. Also called the *income statement.*

Profit margin An indicator of profitability, calculated as net income divided by revenue; indicates how much of each dollar of revenues is left after all costs and expenses.

Profitability index (PI) For a simple project, the PI is the present value of a project's future cash flows divided by the initial investment.

Profitability ratios Ratios that measure a company's ability to generate profitable sales from its resources (assets).

Project sequencing To defer the decision to invest in a future project until the outcome of some or all of a current project is known. Projects are sequenced through time, so that investing in a project creates the option to invest in future projects.

Promissory note A written promise to pay a certain amount of money on demand.

Property, plant, and equipment Tangible assets that are expected to be used for more than one period in either the production or supply of goods or services, or for administrative purposes.

Prospectus The document that describes the terms of a new bond issue and helps investors perform their analysis on the issue.

Protective put An option strategy in which a long position in an asset is combined with a long position in a put.

Proxy contest Corporate takeover mechanism in which shareholders are persuaded to vote for a group seeking a controlling position on a company's board of directors.

Proxy voting A process that enables shareholders who are unable to attend a meeting to authorize another individual to vote on their behalf.

Pseudo-random numbers Numbers produced by random number generators.

Public offer See *public offering.*

Public offering An offering of securities in which any member of the public may buy the securities. Also called *public offer.*

Pull on liquidity When disbursements are paid too quickly or trade credit availability is limited, requiring companies to expend funds before they receive funds from sales that could cover the liability.

Pure discount bonds See *zero-coupon bonds.*

Pure-play method A method for estimating the beta for a company or project; it requires using a comparable company's beta and adjusting it for financial leverage differences.

Put An option that gives the holder the right to sell an underlying asset to another party at a fixed price over a specific period of time.

Put–call–forward parity The relationship among puts, calls, and forward contracts.

Put–call parity An equation expressing the equivalence (parity) of a portfolio of a call and a bond with a portfolio of a put and the underlying, which leads to the relationship between put and call prices.

Put/call ratio A technical analysis indicator that evaluates market sentiment based upon the volume of put options traded divided by the volume of call options traded for a particular financial instrument.

Put option An option that gives the holder the right to sell an underlying asset to another party at a fixed price over a specific period of time.

Putable bonds Bonds that give the bondholder the right to sell the bond back to the issuer at a predetermined price on specified dates.

Quantile A value at or below which a stated fraction of the data lies. Also called *fractile.*

Quantitative easing An expansionary monetary policy based on aggressive open market purchase operations.

Quantity equation of exchange An expression that over a given period, the amount of money used to purchase all goods and services in an economy, $M \times V$, is equal to monetary value of this output, $P \times Y$.

Quantity theory of money Asserts that total spending (in money terms) is proportional to the quantity of money.

Quartiles Quantiles that divide a distribution into four equal parts.

Quasi-fixed cost A cost that stays the same over a range of production but can change to another constant level when production moves outside of that range.

Quasi-government bonds A bond issued by an entity that is either owned or sponsored by a national government. Also called *agency bond.*

Quick assets Assets that can be most readily converted to cash (e.g., cash, short-term marketable investments, receivables).

Quick ratio A stringent measure of liquidity that indicates a company's ability to satisfy current liabilities with its most liquid assets, calculated as (cash + short-term marketable investments + receivables) divided by current liabilities.

Quintiles Quantiles that divide a distribution into five equal parts.

Quota rents Profits that foreign producers can earn by raising the price of their goods higher than they would without a quota.

Quotas Government policies that restrict the quantity of a good that can be imported into a country, generally for a specified period of time.

Quote-driven market A market in which dealers acting as principals facilitate trading.

Quoted interest rate A quoted interest rate that does not account for compounding within the year. Also called *stated annual interest rate.*

Quoted margin The specified yield spread over the reference rate, used to compensate an investor for the difference in the credit risk of the issuer and that implied by the reference rate.

Random number An observation drawn from a uniform distribution.

Random number generator An algorithm that produces uniformly distributed random numbers between 0 and 1.

Random variable A quantity whose future outcomes are uncertain.

Range The difference between the maximum and minimum values in a dataset.

Ratio scales A measurement scale that has all the characteristics of interval measurement scales as well as a true zero point as the origin.

Real GDP The value of goods and services produced, measured at base year prices.

Real income Income adjusted for the effect of inflation on the purchasing power of money. Also known as the *purchasing power of income.* If income remains constant and a good's price falls, real income is said to rise, even though the number of monetary units (e.g., dollars) remains unchanged.

Real interest rate Nominal interest rate minus the expected rate of inflation.

Real risk-free interest rate The single-period interest rate for a completely risk-free security if no inflation were expected.

Realizable (settlement) value With reference to assets, the amount of cash or cash equivalents that could currently be obtained by selling the asset in an orderly disposal; with reference to liabilities, the undiscounted amount of cash or cash equivalents expected to be paid to satisfy the liabilities in the normal course of business.

Rebalancing Adjusting the weights of the constituent securities in an index.

Rebalancing policy The set of rules that guide the process of restoring a portfolio's asset class weights to those specified in the strategic asset allocation.

Recession A period during which real GDP decreases (i.e., negative growth) for at least two successive quarters, or a period of significant decline in total output, income, employment, and sales usually lasting from six months to a year.

Recognition lag The lag in government response to an economic problem resulting from the delay in confirming a change in the state of the economy.

Recourse loan Loan in which the lender has a claim against the borrower for any shortfall between the outstanding mortgage balance and the proceeds received from the sale of the property.

Redemption yield See *yield to maturity.*

Redemptions Withdrawals of funds by investors, as allowed by the notice period and other terms in the partnership agreement.

Refinancing rate A type of central bank policy rate.

Registered bonds Bonds for which ownership is recorded by either name or serial number.

Relative/best-in-class screening An ESG investment style that focuses on sectors, companies, or projects selected for ESG performance relative to industry peers.

Relative dispersion The amount of dispersion relative to a reference value or benchmark.

Relative frequency With reference to an interval of grouped data, the number of observations in the interval divided by the total number of observations in the sample.

Relative price The price of a specific good or service in comparison with those of other goods and services.

Relative strength analysis A comparison of the performance of one asset with the performance of another asset or a benchmark based on changes in the ratio of the securities' respective prices over time.

Relative strength index A technical analysis momentum oscillator that compares a security's gains with its losses over a set period.

Renewable resources Resources that can be replenished, such as a forest.

Rent Payment for the use of property.

Reorganization Agreements made by a company in bankruptcy under which a company's capital structure is altered and/or alternative arrangements are made for debt repayment; US Chapter 11 bankruptcy. The company emerges from bankruptcy as a going concern.

Replication The creation of an asset or portfolio from another asset, portfolio, and/or derivative.

Repo A form of collateralized loan involving the sale of a security with a simultaneous agreement by the seller to buy the same security back from the purchaser at an agreed-on price and future date. The party who sells the security at the inception of the repurchase agreement and buys it back at maturity is borrowing money from the other party, and the security sold and subsequently repurchased represents the collateral.

Repo margin The difference between the market value of the security used as collateral and the value of the loan. Also called *haircut.*

Repo rate The interest rate on a repurchase agreement.

Repurchase agreement A form of collateralized loan involving the sale of a security with a simultaneous agreement by the seller to buy the same security back from the purchaser at an agreed-on price and future date. The party who sells the security at the inception of the repurchase agreement and buys it back at maturity is borrowing money from the other party, and the security sold and subsequently repurchased represents the collateral.

Repurchase date The date when the party who sold the security at the inception of a repurchase agreement buys the security back from the cash lending counterparty.

Repurchase price The price at which the party who sold the security at the inception of the repurchase agreement buys the security back from the cash lending counterparty.

Required margin The yield spread over, or under, the reference rate such that an FRN is priced at par value on a rate reset date.

Required rate of return See *market discount rate.*

Required yield See *market discount rate.*

Required yield spread The difference between the yield-to-maturity on a new bond and the benchmark rate; additional compensation required by investors for the difference in risk and tax status of a bond relative to a government bond. Sometimes called the *spread over the benchmark.*

Reserve accounts Form of internal credit enhancement that relies on creating accounts and depositing in these accounts cash that can be used to absorb losses. Also called *reserve funds.*

Reserve funds See *reserve accounts.*

Reserve requirement The requirement for banks to hold reserves in proportion to the size of deposits.

Resistance In technical analysis, a price range in which selling activity is sufficient to stop the rise in the price of a security.

Responsible investing The practice of identifying companies that can efficiently manage their financial, environmental, and human capital resources to generate attractive long-term profitability; often synonymous with *sustainable investing.*

Restricted payments A bond covenant meant to protect creditors by limiting how much cash can be paid out to shareholders over time.

Retracement In technical analysis, a reversal in the movement of a security's price such that it is counter to the prevailing longerterm price trend.

Return-generating model A model that can provide an estimate of the expected return of a security given certain parameters and estimates of the values of the independent variables in the model.

Return on assets (ROA) A profitability ratio calculated as net income divided by average total assets; indicates a company's net profit generated per dollar invested in total assets.

Return on equity (ROE) A profitability ratio calculated as net income divided by average shareholders' equity.

Return on sales An indicator of profitability, calculated as net income divided by revenue; indicates how much of each dollar of revenues is left after all costs and expenses. Also referred to as *net profit margin.*

Return on total capital A profitability ratio calculated as EBIT divided by the sum of short- and long-term debt and equity.

Revaluation model Under IFRS, the process of valuing long-lived assets at fair value, rather than at cost less accumulated depreciation. Any resulting profit or loss is either reported on the income statement and/or through equity under revaluation surplus.

Revenue The amount charged for the delivery of goods or services in the ordinary activities of a business over a stated period; the inflows of economic resources to a company over a stated period.

Reversal patterns A type of pattern used in technical analysis to predict the end of a trend and a change in direction of the security's price.

Reverse repo A repurchase agreement viewed from the perspective of the cash lending counterparty.

Reverse repurchase agreement A repurchase agreement viewed from the perspective of the cash lending counterparty.

Reverse stock split A reduction in the number of shares outstanding with a corresponding increase in share price, but no change to the company's underlying fundamentals.

Revolving credit agreements The strongest form of short-term bank borrowing facilities; they are in effect for multiple years (e.g., 3–5 years) and may have optional medium-term loan features.

Rho The sensitivity of the option price to the risk-free rate.

Ricardian equivalence An economic theory that implies that it makes no difference whether a government finances a deficit by increasing taxes or issuing debt.

Risk Exposure to uncertainty. The chance of a loss or adverse outcome as a result of an action, inaction, or external event.

Risk averse The assumption that an investor will choose the least risky alternative.

Risk aversion The degree of an investor's inability and unwillingness to take risk.

Risk budgeting The establishment of objectives for individuals, groups, or divisions of an organization that takes into account the allocation of an acceptable level of risk.

Risk exposure The state of being exposed or vulnerable to a risk. The extent to which an organization is sensitive to underlying risks.

Risk factor/risk premium investing An ESG investment style that focuses on the inclusion of ESG information in the analysis of systematic risks as, for example, in smart beta and factor investment strategies (similar to size, value, momentum, and growth strategies).

Risk governance The top-down process and guidance that directs risk management activities to align with and support the overall enterprise.

Risk management The process of identifying the level of risk an organization wants, measuring the level of risk the organization currently has, taking actions that bring the actual level of risk to the desired level of risk, and monitoring the new actual level of risk so that it continues to be aligned with the desired level of risk.

Risk management framework The infrastructure, process, and analytics needed to support effective risk management in an organization.

Risk-neutral pricing Sometimes said of derivatives pricing, uses the fact that arbitrage opportunities guarantee that a risk-free portfolio consisting of the underlying and the derivative must earn the risk-free rate.

Risk-neutral probabilities Weights that are used to compute a binomial option price. They are the probabilities that would apply if a risk-neutral investor valued an option.

Risk premium An extra return expected by investors for bearing some specified risk.

Risk shifting Actions to change the distribution of risk outcomes.

Risk tolerance The amount of risk an investor is willing and able to bear to achieve an investment goal.

Risk transfer Actions to pass on a risk to another party, often, but not always, in the form of an insurance policy.

Robo-adviser A machine-based analytical tool or service that provides technology-driven investment solutions through online platforms.

Robust The quality of being relatively unaffected by a violation of assumptions.

Rule of 72 The principle that the approximate number of years necessary for an investment to double is 72 divided by the stated interest rate.

Running yield See *current yield.*

Safety-first rules Rules for portfolio selection that focus on the risk that portfolio value will fall below some minimum acceptable level over some time horizon.

Safety stock A level of inventory beyond anticipated needs that provides a cushion in the event that it takes longer to replenish inventory than expected or in the case of greater than expected demand.

Sales Generally, a synonym for revenue; "sales" is generally understood to refer to the sale of goods, whereas "revenue" is understood to include the sale of goods or services.

Sales risk Uncertainty with respect to the quantity of goods and services that a company is able to sell and the price it is able to achieve; the risk related to the uncertainty of revenues.

Sales-type leases Under US GAAP, a type of finance lease, from a lessor perspective, where the present value of the lease payments (lease receivable) exceeds the carrying value of the leased asset. The revenues earned by the lessor both a selling profit at inception and financing (interest) revenues.

Sample A subset of a population.

Sample excess kurtosis A sample measure of the degree of a distribution's kurtosis in excess of the normal distribution's kurtosis.

Sample kurtosis A sample measure of the degree of a distribution's peakedness.

Sample mean The sum of the sample observations, divided by the sample size.

Sample selection bias Bias introduced by systematically excluding some members of the population according to a particular attribute—for example, the bias introduced when data availability leads to certain observations being excluded from the analysis.

Sample skewness A sample measure of degree of asymmetry of a distribution.

Sample standard deviation The positive square root of the sample variance.

Sample statistic A quantity computed from or used to describe a sample.

Sample variance A sample measure of the degree of dispersion of a distribution, calculated by dividing the sum of the squared deviations from the sample mean by the sample size minus 1.

Sampling The process of obtaining a sample.

Sampling distribution The distribution of all distinct possible values that a statistic can assume when computed from samples of the same size randomly drawn from the same population.

Sampling error The difference between the observed value of a statistic and the quantity it is intended to estimate.

Sampling plan The set of rules used to select a sample.

Say on pay A process whereby shareholders may vote on executive remuneration (compensation) matters.

Say's law Named for French economist J.B. Say: All that is produced will be sold because supply creates its own demand.

Scatter plot A two-dimensional plot of pairs of observations on two data series.

Scenario analysis Analysis that shows the changes in key financial quantities that result from given (economic) events, such as the loss of customers, the loss of a supply source, or a catastrophic event; a risk management technique involving examination of the performance of a portfolio under specified situations. Closely related to stress testing.

Screening The application of a set of criteria to reduce a set of potential investments to a smaller set having certain desired characteristics.

Seasoned offering An offering in which an issuer sells additional units of a previously issued security.

Second-degree price discrimination When the monopolist charges different per-unit prices using the quantity purchased as an indicator of how highly the customer values the product.

Second lien A secured interest in the pledged assets that ranks below first lien debt in both collateral protection and priority of payment.

Secondary bond markets Markets in which existing bonds are traded among investors.

Secondary market The market where securities are traded among investors.

Secondary precedence rules Rules that determine how to rank orders placed at the same time.

Sector A group of related industries.

Sector indexes Indexes that represent and track different economic sectors—such as consumer goods, energy, finance, health care, and technology—on either a national, regional, or global basis.

Secured bonds Bonds secured by assets or financial guarantees pledged to ensure debt repayment in case of default.

Secured debt Debt in which the debtholder has a direct claim—a pledge from the issuer—on certain assets and their associated cash flows.

Securitization A process that involves moving assets into a special legal entity, which then uses the assets as guarantees to secure a bond issue.

Securitized assets Assets that are typically used to create asset-backed bonds; for example, when a bank securitizes a pool of loans, the loans are said to be securitized.

Security characteristic line A plot of the excess return of a security on the excess return of the market.

Security market index A portfolio of securities representing a given security market, market segment, or asset class.

Security market line (SML) The graph of the capital asset pricing model.

Security selection The process of selecting individual securities; typically, security selection has the objective of generating superior risk-adjusted returns relative to a portfolio's benchmark.

Self-investment limits With respect to investment limitations applying to pension plans, restrictions on the percentage of assets that can be invested in securities issued by the pension plan sponsor.

Sell-side firm A broker/dealer that sells securities and provides independent investment research and recommendations to their clients (i.e., buy-side firms).

Semi-strong-form efficient market A market in which security prices reflect all publicly known and available information.

Semiannual bond basis yield An annual rate having a periodicity of two; also known as a *semiannual bond equivalent yield*.

Semiannual bond equivalent yield See *semiannual bond basis yield*.

Semideviation The positive square root of semivariance (sometimes called *semistandard deviation*).

Semilogarithmic Describes a scale constructed so that equal intervals on the vertical scale represent equal rates of change, and equal intervals on the horizontal scale represent equal amounts of change.

Semivariance The average squared deviation below the mean.

Seniority ranking Priority of payment of various debt obligations.

Sensitivity analysis Analysis that shows the range of possible outcomes as specific assumptions are changed.

Separately managed account (SMA) An investment portfolio managed exclusively for the benefit of an individual or institution.

Serial maturity structure Structure for a bond issue in which the maturity dates are spread out during the bond's life; a stated number of bonds mature and are paid off each year before final maturity.

Settlement The process that occurs after a trade is completed, the securities are passed to the buyer, and payment is received by the seller.

Settlement date Date when the buyer makes cash payment and the seller delivers the security.

Settlement price The official price, designated by the clearinghouse, from which daily gains and losses will be determined and marked to market.

Share repurchase A transaction in which a company buys back its own shares. Unlike stock dividends and stock splits, share repurchases use corporate cash.

Shareholder activism Strategies used by shareholders to attempt to compel a company to act in a desired manner.

Shareholder engagement The process whereby companies engage with their shareholders.

Shareholders' equity Assets less liabilities; the residual interest in the assets after subtracting the liabilities.

Sharpe ratio The average return in excess of the risk-free rate divided by the standard deviation of return; a measure of the average excess return earned per unit of standard deviation of return.

Shelf registration Type of public offering that allows the issuer to file a single, all-encompassing offering circular that covers a series of bond issues.

Short The seller of an asset or derivative contract. Also refers to the position of being short an asset or derivative contract.

Short position A position in an asset or contract in which one has sold an asset one does not own, or in which a right under a contract can be exercised against oneself.

Short-run average total cost The curve describing average total cost when some costs are considered fixed.

Short selling A transaction in which borrowed securities are sold with the intention to repurchase them at a lower price at a later date and return them to the lender.

Shortfall risk The risk that portfolio value will fall below some minimum acceptable level over some time horizon.

Shutdown point The point at which average revenue is equal to the firm's average variable cost.

Simple interest The interest earned each period on the original investment; interest calculated on the principal only.

Simple random sample A subset of a larger population created in such a way that each element of the population has an equal probability of being selected to the subset.

Simple random sampling The procedure of drawing a sample to satisfy the definition of a simple random sample.

Simple yield The sum of the coupon payments plus the straight-line amortized share of the gain or loss, divided by the flat price.

Simulation Computer-generated sensitivity or scenario analysis that is based on probability models for the factors that drive outcomes.

Simulation trial A complete pass through the steps of a simulation.

Single-step format With respect to the format of the income statement, a format that does not subtotal for gross profit (revenue minus cost of goods sold).

Sinking fund arrangement Provision that reduces the credit risk of a bond issue by requiring the issuer to retire a portion of the bond's principal outstanding each year.

Situational influences External factors, such as environmental or cultural elements, that shape our behavior.

Skewed Not symmetrical.

Skewness A quantitative measure of skew (lack of symmetry); a synonym of skew.

Small country A country that is a price taker in the world market for a product and cannot influence the world market price.

Smart beta Involves the use of simple, transparent, rules-based strategies as a basis for investment decisions.

Smart contract A computer program that is designed to self-execute on the basis of pre-specified terms and conditions agreed to by parties to a contract.

Socially responsible investing An investment approach that excludes investments in companies or industries that deviate from an organization's beliefs and sometimes includes investments with favorable environmental or social profiles.

Solvency With respect to financial statement analysis, the ability of a company to fulfill its long-term obligations.

Solvency ratios Ratios that measure a company's ability to meet its long-term obligations.

Solvency risk The risk that an organization does not survive or succeed because it runs out of cash, even though it might otherwise be solvent.

Sovereign A bond issued by a national government.

Sovereign bond A bond issued by a national government.

Sovereign yield spread An estimate of the country spread (country equity premium) for a developing nation that is based on a comparison of bonds yields in country being analyzed and a developed country. The sovereign yield spread is the difference between a government bond yield in the country being analyzed, denominated in the currency of the developed country, and the Treasury bond yield on a similar maturity bond in the developed country.

Spearman rank correlation coefficient A measure of correlation applied to ranked data.

Special dividend A dividend paid by a company that does not pay dividends on a regular schedule, or a dividend that supplements regular cash dividends with an extra payment.

Special purpose entity A non-operating entity created to carry out a specified purpose, such as leasing assets or securitizing receivables; can be a corporation, partnership, trust, limited liability, or partnership formed to facilitate a specific type of business activity. Also called *special purpose vehicle* or *variable interest entity*.

Special purpose vehicle See *special purpose entity*.

Specific identification method An inventory accounting method that identifies which specific inventory items were sold and which remained in inventory to be carried over to later periods.

Speculative demand for money The demand to hold speculative money balances based on the potential opportunities or risks that are inherent in other financial instruments. Also called *portfolio demand for money*.

Speculative money balances Monies held in anticipation that other assets will decline in value.

Split coupon bond See *deferred coupon bond*.

Sponsored A type of depository receipt in which the foreign company whose shares are held by the depository has a direct involvement in the issuance of the receipts.

Spot curve A sequence of yields-to-maturity on zero-coupon bonds. Sometimes called *zero* or *strip curve* because coupon payments are "stripped" off of the bonds.

Spot markets Markets in which assets are traded for immediate delivery.

Spot prices The price of an asset for immediately delivery.

Spot rates A sequence of market discount rates that correspond to the cash flow dates; yields-to-maturity on zero-coupon bonds maturing at the date of each cash flow.

Spread In general, the difference in yield between different fixed income securities. Often used to refer to the difference between the yield-to-maturity and the benchmark.

Spread over the benchmark See *required yield spread*.

Spread risk Bond price risk arising from changes in the yield spread on credit-risky bonds; reflects changes in the market's assessment and/or pricing of credit migration (or downgrade) risk and market liquidity risk.

Spurious correlation A correlation that misleadingly points toward associations between variables.

Stackelberg model A prominent model of strategic decision making in which firms are assumed to make their decisions sequentially.

Stagflation When a high inflation rate is combined with a high level of unemployment and a slowdown of the economy.

Staggered boards Election process whereby directors are typically divided into multiple classes that are elected separately in consecutive years—that is, one class every year.

Stakeholder management The identification, prioritization, and understanding of the interests of stakeholder groups, and managing the company's relationships with these groups.

Stakeholders Individuals or groups of individuals who may be affected either directly or indirectly by a decision and thus have an interest, or stake, in the decision.

Standard deviation The positive square root of the variance; a measure of dispersion in the same units as the original data.

Standard normal distribution The normal density with mean (μ) equal to 0 and standard deviation (σ) equal to 1.

Standardizing A transformation that involves subtracting the mean and dividing the result by the standard deviation.

Standards of conduct Behaviors required by a group; established benchmarks that clarify or enhance a group's code of ethics.

Standing limit orders A limit order at a price below market and which therefore is waiting to trade.

Stated annual interest rate A quoted interest rate that does not account for compounding within the year. Also called *quoted interest rate*.

Statement of changes in equity (statement of owners' equity) A financial statement that reconciles the beginning-of-period and end-of-period balance sheet values of shareholders' equity; provides information about all factors affecting shareholders' equity. Also called *statement of owners' equity*.

Statement of financial condition The financial statement that presents an entity's current financial position by disclosing resources the entity controls (its assets) and the claims on those resources (its liabilities and equity claims), as of a particular point in time (the date of the balance sheet).

Statement of financial position The financial statement that presents an entity's current financial position by disclosing resources the entity controls (its assets) and the claims on those resources (its liabilities and equity claims), as of a particular point in time (the date of the balance sheet).

Statement of operations A financial statement that provides information about a company's profitability over a stated period of time.

Statistic A quantity computed from or used to describe a sample of data.

Statistical inference Making forecasts, estimates, or judgments about a larger group from a smaller group actually observed; using a sample statistic to infer the value of an unknown population parameter.

Statistically significant A result indicating that the null hypothesis can be rejected; with reference to an estimated regression coefficient, frequently understood to mean a result indicating that the corresponding population regression coefficient is different from 0.

Statutory voting A common method of voting where each share represents one vote.

Step-up coupon bond Bond for which the coupon, which may be fixed or floating, increases by specified margins at specified dates.

Stock dividend A type of dividend in which a company distributes additional shares of its common stock to shareholders instead of cash.

Stock-out losses Profits lost from not having sufficient inventory on hand to satisfy demand.

Stock split An increase in the number of shares outstanding with a consequent decrease in share price, but no change to the company's underlying fundamentals.

Stop-loss order See *stop order*.

Stop order An order in which a trader has specified a stop price condition. Also called *stop-loss order*.

Store of value The quality of tending to preserve value.

Store of wealth Goods that depend on the fact that they do not perish physically over time, and on the belief that others would always value the good.

Straight-line method A depreciation method that allocates evenly the cost of a long-lived asset less its estimated residual value over the estimated useful life of the asset.

Straight voting A shareholder voting process in which shareholders receive one vote for each share owned.

Strategic analysis Analysis of the competitive environment with an emphasis on the implications of the environment for corporate strategy.

Strategic asset allocation The set of exposures to IPS-permissible asset classes that is expected to achieve the client's long-term objectives given the client's investment constraints.

Strategic groups Groups sharing distinct business models or catering to specific market segments in an industry.

Street convention Yield measure that neglects weekends and holidays; the internal rate of return on cash flows assuming payments are made on the scheduled dates, even when the scheduled date falls on a weekend or holiday.

Stress testing A specific type of scenario analysis that estimates losses in rare and extremely unfavorable combinations of events or scenarios.

Strong-form efficient market A market in which security prices reflect all public and private information.

Structural (or cyclically adjusted) budget deficit The deficit that would exist if the economy was at full employment (or full potential output).

Structural subordination Arises in a holding company structure when the debt of operating subsidiaries is serviced by the cash flow and assets of the subsidiaries before funds can be passed to the holding company to service debt at the parent level.

Structured financial instruments Financial instruments that share the common attribute of repackaging risks. Structured financial instruments include asset-backed securities, collateralized debt obligations, and other structured financial instruments such as capital protected, yield enhancement, participation and leveraged instruments.

Subjective probability A probability drawing on personal or subjective judgment.

Subordinated debt A class of unsecured debt that ranks below a firm's senior unsecured obligations.

Subordination Form of internal credit enhancement that relies on creating more than one bond tranche and ordering the claim priorities for ownership or interest in an asset between the tranches. The ordering of the claim priorities is called a senior/subordinated structure, where the tranches of highest seniority are called senior followed by subordinated or junior tranches. Also called *credit tranching*.

Substitutes Said of two goods or services such that if the price of one increases the demand for the other tends to increase, holding all other things equal (e.g., butter and margarine).

Sunk cost A cost that has already been incurred.

Supervised learning A machine learning approach that makes use of labeled training data.

Supply shock A typically unexpected disturbance to supply.

Support In technical analysis, a price range in which buying activity is sufficient to stop the decline in the price of a security.

Support tranche A class or tranche in a CMO that protects the PAC tranche from prepayment risk.

Supranational bonds A bond issued by a supranational agency such as the World Bank.

Surety bond Form of external credit enhancement whereby a rated and regulated insurance company guarantees to reimburse bondholders for any losses incurred up to a maximum amount if the issuer defaults.

Survey approach An estimate of the equity risk premium that is based upon estimates provided by a panel of finance experts.

Survivorship bias The bias resulting from a test design that fails to account for companies that have gone bankrupt, merged, or are otherwise no longer reported in a database.

Sustainable growth rate The rate of dividend (and earnings) growth that can be sustained over time for a given level of return on equity, keeping the capital structure constant and without issuing additional common stock.

Sustainable investing The practice of identifying companies that can efficiently manage their financial, environmental, and human capital resources to generate attractive long-term profitability; often synonymous with *responsible investing*.

Sustainable rate of economic growth The rate of increase in the economy's productive capacity or potential GDP.

Swap contract An agreement between two parties to exchange a series of future cash flows.

Syndicated loans Loans from a group of lenders to a single borrower.

Syndicated offering A bond issue that is underwritten by a group of investment banks.

Systematic risk Risk that affects the entire market or economy; it cannot be avoided and is inherent in the overall market. Systematic risk is also known as non-diversifiable or market risk.

Systematic sampling A procedure of selecting every *k*th member until reaching a sample of the desired size. The sample that results from this procedure should be approximately random.

***t*-Test** A hypothesis test using a statistic (*t*-statistic) that follows a *t*-distribution.

Tactical asset allocation The decision to deliberately deviate from the strategic asset allocation in an attempt to add value based on forecasts of the near-term relative performance of asset classes.

Target balance A minimum level of cash to be held available—estimated in advance and adjusted for known funds transfers, seasonality, or other factors.

Target capital structure A company's chosen proportions of debt and equity.

Target independent A bank's ability to determine the definition of inflation that they target, the rate of inflation that they target, and the horizon over which the target is to be achieved.

Target semideviation The positive square root of target semivariance.

Target semivariance The average squared deviation below a target value.

Tariffs Taxes that a government levies on imported goods.

Tax base The amount at which an asset or liability is valued for tax purposes.

Tax expense An aggregate of an entity's income tax payable (or recoverable in the case of a tax benefit) and any changes in deferred tax assets and liabilities. It is essentially the income tax payable or recoverable if these had been determined based on accounting profit rather than taxable income.

Tax loss carry forward A taxable loss in the current period that may be used to reduce future taxable income.

Taxable income The portion of an entity's income that is subject to income taxes under the tax laws of its jurisdiction.

Taxable temporary differences Temporary differences that result in a taxable amount in a future period when determining the taxable profit as the balance sheet item is recovered or settled.

Technical analysis A form of security analysis that uses price and volume data, which is often displayed graphically, in decision making.

Technology The process a company uses to transform inputs into outputs.

Tender offer Corporate takeover mechanism which involves shareholders selling their interests directly to the group seeking to gain control.

Tenor The time-to-maturity for a bond or derivative contract. Also called *term to maturity*.

Term maturity structure Structure for a bond issue in which the bond's notional principal is paid off in a lump sum at maturity.

Term structure See *maturity structure*.

Term structure of credit spreads The relationship between the spreads over the "risk-free" (or benchmark) rates and times-to-maturity.

Term structure of yield volatility The relationship between the volatility of bond yields-to-maturity and times-to-maturity.

Terminal stock value The expected value of a share at the end of the investment horizon—in effect, the expected selling price. Also called *terminal value*.

Terminal value The expected value of a share at the end of the investment horizon—in effect, the expected selling price.

Terms of trade The ratio of the price of exports to the price of imports, representing those prices by export and import price indexes, respectively.

Text analytics The use of computer programs to analyze and derive meaning from typically large, unstructured text- or voice-based datasets.

Thematic investment An ESG investing style that focuses on investing in themes or assets specifically relating to ESG factors, such as clean energy, green technology, or sustainable agriculture.

Third-degree price discrimination When the monopolist segregates customers into groups based on demographic or other characteristics and offers different pricing to each group.

Time-period bias The possibility that when we use a time-series sample, our statistical conclusion may be sensitive to the starting and ending dates of the sample.

Time-series data Observations of a variable over time.

Time tranching The creation of classes or tranches in an ABS/MBS that possess different (expected) maturities.

Time value The difference between the market price of the option and its intrinsic value.

Time value decay Said of an option when, at expiration, no time value remains and the option is worth only its exercise value.

Time value of money The principles governing equivalence relationships between cash flows with different dates.

Time-weighted rate of return The compound rate of growth of one unit of currency invested in a portfolio during a stated measurement period; a measure of investment performance that is not sensitive to the timing and amount of withdrawals or additions to the portfolio.

Tokenization The process of representing ownership rights to physical assets on a blockchain or distributed ledger.

Top-down analysis An investment selection approach that begins with consideration of macroeconomic conditions and then evaluates markets and industries based upon such conditions.

Total comprehensive income The change in equity during a period resulting from transaction and other events, other than those changes resulting from transactions with owners in their capacity as owners.

Total cost The summation of all costs, for which costs are classified as fixed or variable.

Total factor productivity A scale factor that reflects the portion of growth that is not accounted for by explicit factor inputs (e.g. capital and labor).

Total fixed cost The summation of all expenses that do not change as the level of production varies.

Total invested capital The sum of market value of common equity, book value of preferred equity, and face value of debt.

Total probability rule A rule explaining the unconditional probability of an event in terms of probabilities of the event conditional on mutually exclusive and exhaustive scenarios.

Total probability rule for expected value A rule explaining the expected value of a random variable in terms of expected values of the random variable conditional on mutually exclusive and exhaustive scenarios.

Total return Measures the price appreciation, or percentage change in price of the securities in an index or portfolio, plus any income received over the period.

Total return index An index that reflects the price appreciation or percentage change in price of the constituent securities plus any income received since inception.

Total return swap A swap in which one party agrees to pay the total return on a security. Often used as a credit derivative, in which the underlying is a bond.

Total variable cost The summation of all variable expenses.

Tracking error The standard deviation of the differences between a portfolio's returns and its benchmark's returns; a synonym of active risk.

Tracking risk The standard deviation of the differences between a portfolio's returns and its benchmarks returns. Also called *tracking error.*

Trade creation When regional integration results in the replacement of higher cost domestic production by lower cost imports from other members.

Trade credit A spontaneous form of credit in which a purchaser of the goods or service is financing its purchase by delaying the date on which payment is made.

Trade diversion When regional integration results in lower-cost imports from non-member countries being replaced with higher-cost imports from members.

Trade payables Amounts that a business owes to its vendors for goods and services that were purchased from them but which have not yet been paid.

Trade protection Government policies that impose restrictions on trade, such as tariffs and quotas.

Trade surplus (deficit) When the value of exports is greater (less) than the value of imports.

Trading securities Under US GAAP, a category of debt securities held by a company with the intent to trade them. Also called *held-for-trading securities.*

Traditional investment markets Markets for traditional investments, which include all publicly traded debts and equities and shares in pooled investment vehicles that hold publicly traded debts and/or equities.

Transactions money balances Money balances that are held to finance transactions.

Transactions motive In the context of inventory management, the need for inventory as part of the routine production–sales cycle.

Transfer payments Welfare payments made through the social security system that exist to provide a basic minimum level of income for low-income households.

Transparency Said of something (e.g., a market) in which information is fully disclosed to the public and/or regulators.

Treasury Inflation-Protected Securities A bond issued by the United States Treasury Department that is designed to protect the investor from inflation by adjusting the principal of the bond for changes in inflation.

Treasury stock method A method for accounting for the effect of options (and warrants) on earnings per share (EPS) that specifies what EPS would have been if the options and warrants had been exercised and the company had used the proceeds to repurchase common stock.

Tree diagram A diagram with branches emanating from nodes representing either mutually exclusive chance events or mutually exclusive decisions.

Trend A long-term pattern of movement in a particular direction.

Treynor ratio A measure of risk-adjusted performance that relates a portfolio's excess returns to the portfolio's beta.

Triangle patterns In technical analysis, a continuation chart pattern that forms as the range between high and low prices narrows, visually forming a triangle.

Trimmed mean A mean computed after excluding a stated small percentage of the lowest and highest observations.

TRIN A flow of funds indicator applied to a broad stock market index to measure the relative extent to which money is moving into or out of rising and declining stocks.

Triple bottoms In technical analysis, a reversal pattern that is formed when the price forms three troughs at roughly the same price level; used to predict a change from a downtrend to an uptrend.

Triple tops In technical analysis, a reversal pattern that is formed when the price forms three peaks at roughly the same price level; used to predict a change from an uptrend to a downtrend.

Trough The lowest point of a business cycle.

True yield The internal rate of return on cash flows using the actual calendar including weekends and bank holidays.

Trust deed The governing legal credit agreement, typically incorporated by reference in the prospectus. Also called *bond indenture.*

Trust receipt arrangement The use of inventory as collateral for a loan. The inventory is segregated and held in trust, and the proceeds of any sale must be remitted to the lender immediately.

Turn-of-the-year effect Calendar anomaly that stock market returns in January are significantly higher compared to the rest of the months of the year, with most of the abnormal returns reported during the first five trading days in January.

Two-fund separation theorem The theory that all investors regardless of taste, risk preferences, and initial wealth will hold a combination of two portfolios or funds: a risk-free asset and an optimal portfolio of risky assets.

Two-sided hypothesis test A test in which the null hypothesis is rejected in favor of the alternative hypothesis if the evidence indicates that the population parameter is either smaller or larger than a hypothesized value.

Two-tailed hypothesis test A test in which the null hypothesis is rejected in favor of the alternative hypothesis if the evidence indicates that the population parameter is either smaller or larger than a hypothesized value.

Two-week repo rate The interest rate on a two-week repurchase agreement; may be used as a policy rate by a central bank.

Type I error The error of rejecting a true null hypothesis.

Type II error The error of not rejecting a false null hypothesis.

Unanticipated (unexpected) inflation The component of inflation that is a surprise.

Unconditional probability The probability of an event *not* conditioned on another event.

Underemployed A person who has a job but has the qualifications to work a significantly higher-paying job.

Underlying An asset that trades in a market in which buyers and sellers meet, decide on a price, and the seller then delivers the asset to the buyer and receives payment. The underlying is the asset or other derivative on which a particular derivative is based. The market for the underlying is also referred to as the *spot market.*

Underwriter A firm, usually an investment bank, that takes the risk of buying the newly issued securities from the issuer, and then reselling them to investors or to dealers, thus guaranteeing the sale of the securities at the offering price negotiated with the issuer.

Underwritten offering A type of securities issue mechanism in which the investment bank guarantees the sale of the securities at an offering price that is negotiated with the issuer. Also known as *firm commitment offering.*

Unearned revenue A liability account for money that has been collected for goods or services that have not yet been delivered; payment received in advance of providing a good or service. Also called *deferred revenue* or *deferred income.*

Unemployed People who are actively seeking employment but are currently without a job.

Unemployment rate The ratio of unemployed to the labor force.

Unexpected inflation The component of inflation that is a surprise.

Unit elastic An elasticity with a magnitude of negative one. Also called *unitary elastic.*

Unit labor cost The average labor cost to produce one unit of output.

Unit normal distribution The normal density with mean (μ) equal to 0 and standard deviation (σ) equal to 1.

Units-of-production method A depreciation method that allocates the cost of a long-lived asset based on actual usage during the period.

Univariate distribution A distribution that specifies the probabilities for a single random variable.

Universal owners Long-term investors, such as pension funds, that have significant assets invested in globally diversified portfolios.

Unlimited funds An unlimited funds environment assumes that the company can raise the funds it wants for all profitable projects simply by paying the required rate of return.

Unsecured debt Debt which gives the debtholder only a general claim on an issuer's assets and cash flow.

Unsponsored A type of depository receipt in which the foreign company whose shares are held by the depository has no involvement in the issuance of the receipts.

Unsupervised learning A machine learning approach that does not make use of labeled training data.

Up transition probability The probability that an asset's value moves up.

Validity instructions Instructions which indicate when the order may be filled.

Valuation allowance A reserve created against deferred tax assets, based on the likelihood of realizing the deferred tax assets in future accounting periods.

Valuation ratios Ratios that measure the quantity of an asset or flow (e.g., earnings) in relation to the price associated with a specified claim (e.g., a share or ownership of the enterprise).

Value at risk (VaR) A money measure of the minimum value of losses expected during a specified time period at a given level of probability.

Value investors With reference to equity investors, investors who are focused on paying a relatively low share price in relation to earnings or assets per share.

VaR See *value at risk.*

Variable costs Costs that fluctuate with the level of production and sales.

Variance The expected value (the probability-weighted average) of squared deviations from a random variable's expected value.

Variation margin Additional margin that must be deposited in an amount sufficient to bring the balance up to the initial margin requirement.

Veblen goods Goods that increase in desirability with increasing price.

Vega A measure of the sensitivity of an option's price to changes in the underlying's volatility.

Venture capital Investments that provide "seed" or startup capital, early-stage financing, or later-stage financing (including mezzanine-stage financing) to companies that are in early development stages and require additional capital for expansion or preparation for an initial public offering.

Venture capital fund A hedge fund that seeks to buy, optimize, and ultimately sell portfolio companies to generate profits. See *private equity fund.*

Vertical analysis Common-size analysis using only one reporting period or one base financial statement; for example, an income statement in which all items are stated as percentages of sales.

Vertical demand schedule Implies that some fixed quantity is demanded, regardless of price.

Volatility As used in option pricing, the standard deviation of the continuously compounded returns on the underlying asset.

Voluntarily unemployed A person voluntarily outside the labor force, such as a jobless worker refusing an available vacancy.

Voluntary export restraint A trade barrier under which the exporting country agrees to limit its exports of the good to its trading partners to a specific number of units.

Vote by proxy A mechanism that allows a designated party—such as another shareholder, a shareholder representative, or management—to vote on the shareholder's behalf.

Warehouse receipt arrangement The use of inventory as collateral for a loan; similar to a trust receipt arrangement except there is a third party (i.e., a warehouse company) that supervises the inventory.

Warrant Attached option that gives its holder the right to buy the underlying stock of the issuing company at a fixed exercise price until the expiration date.

Weak-form efficient market hypothesis The belief that security prices fully reflect all past market data, which refers to all historical price and volume trading information.

Wealth effect An increase (decrease) in household wealth increases (decreases) consumer spending out of a given level of current income.

Weighted average cost method An inventory accounting method that averages the total cost of available inventory items over the total units available for sale.

Weighted average cost of capital A weighted average of the aftertax required rates of return on a company's common stock, preferred stock, and long-term debt, where the weights are the fraction of each source of financing in the company's target capital structure.

Weighted average coupon rate Weighting the mortgage rate of each mortgage loan in the pool by the percentage of the mortgage outstanding relative to the outstanding amount of all the mortgages in the pool.

Weighted average life A measure that gives investors an indication of how long they can expect to hold the MBS before it is paid off; the convention-based average time to receipt of all principal repayments. Also called *average life*.

Weighted average maturity Weighting the remaining number of months to maturity for each mortgage loan in the pool by the amount of the outstanding mortgage balance.

Weighted mean An average in which each observation is weighted by an index of its relative importance.

Wholesale price index Reflects the price changes experienced by domestic producers in a country.

Winsorized mean A mean computed after assigning a stated percent of the lowest values equal to one specified low value, and a stated percent of the highest values equal to one specified high value.

Working capital The difference between current assets and current liabilities.

Working capital management The management of a company's short-term assets (such as inventory) and short-term liabilities (such as money owed to suppliers).

World price The price prevailing in the world market.

Yield The actual return on a debt security if it is held to maturity.

Yield duration The sensitivity of the bond price with respect to the bond's own yield-to-maturity.

Yield to maturity Annual return that an investor earns on a bond if the investor purchases the bond today and holds it until maturity. It is the discount rate that equates the present value of the bond's expected cash flows until maturity with the bond's price. Also called *yield-to-redemption* or *redemption yield*.

Yield to redemption See *yield to maturity*.

Yield-to-worst The lowest of the sequence of yields-to-call and the yield-to-maturity.

Zero-coupon bonds Bonds that do not pay interest during the bond's life. It is issued at a discount to par value and redeemed at par. Also called *pure discount bonds*.

Zero volatility spread (Z-spread) Calculates a constant yield spread over a government (or interest rate swap) spot curve.